# Economic Analysis of Regional Trading Arrangements

# The International Library of Critical Writings in Economics

*Series Editor:* Mark Blaug

Professor Emeritus, University of London, UK
Professor Emeritus, University of Buckingham, UK
Visiting Professor, University of Amsterdam, The Netherlands
Visiting Professor, Erasmus University of Rotterdam, The Netherlands

This series is an essential reference source for students, researchers and lecturers in economics. It presents by theme a selection of the most important articles across the entire spectrum of economics. Each volume has been prepared by a leading specialist who has written an authoritative introduction to the literature included.

A full list of published and future titles in this series is printed at the end of this volume.

Wherever possible, the articles in these volumes have been reproduced as originally published using facsimile reproduction, inclusive of footnotes and pagination to facilitate ease of reference.

For a list of all Edward Elgar published titles visit our site on the World Wide Web at
http://www.e-elgar.co.uk

# Economic Analysis of Regional Trading Arrangements

*Edited by*

# Richard Pomfret

*Professor of Economics*
*University of Adelaide, Australia*

THE INTERNATIONAL LIBRARY OF CRITICAL WRITINGS IN ECONOMICS

**An Elgar Reference Collection**
Cheltenham, UK • Northampton, MA, USA

Published by
Edward Elgar Publishing Limited
Glensanda House
Montpellier Parade
Cheltenham
Glos GL50 1UA
UK

Edward Elgar Publishing, Inc.
136 West Street
Suite 202
Northampton
Massachusetts 01060
USA

A catalogue record for this book is available from the British Library.

**Library of Congress Cataloguing in Publication Data**

Economic analysis of regional trading arrangements / edited by Richard Pomfret.
     p. cm. — (The international library of critical writings in economics ; 161)
    Includes index.
    1. Trade blocs. 2. Regionalism—Economic aspects. I. Pomfret, Richard W. T. II. Series.

  HF1418.7.E26 2003
  382'.91—dc21

2003047762

ISBN   1 84376 128 9

Printed and bound in Great Britain by MPG Books Ltd, Bodmin, Cornwall

# Contents

# Acknowledgements

The editor and publishers wish to thank the authors and the following publishers who have kindly given permission for the use of copyright material.

American Economic Association for articles: Paul Wonnacott and Ronald Wonnacott (1981), 'Is Unilateral Tariff Reduction Preferable to a Customs Union? The Curious Case of the Missing Foreign Tariffs', *American Economic Review*, **71** (4), September, 704–14; John McCallum (1995), 'National Borders Matter: Canada-U.S. Regional Trade Patterns', *American Economic Review*, **85** (3), June, 615–23; Charles Engel and John H. Rogers (1996), 'How Wide is the Border?', *American Economic Review*, **86** (5), December, 1112–25; Philip I. Levy (1997), 'A Political-Economic Analysis of Free-Trade Agreements', *American Economic Review*, **87** (4), September, 506–19; Arvind Panagariya (2000), 'Preferential Trade Liberalization: The Traditional Theory and New Developments', *Journal of Economic Literature*, **XXXVIII** (2), June, 287–331; Alberto Alesina, Enrico Spolaore and Romain Wacziarg (2000), 'Economic Integration and Political Disintegration', *American Economic Review*, **90** (5), December, 1276–96; Dani Rodrik (2000), 'How Far Will International Economic Integration Go?', *Journal of Economic Perspectives*, **14** (1), Winter, 177–86.

Blackwell Publishing Ltd for articles: R.G. Lipsey (1960), 'The Theory of Customs Unions: A General Survey', *Economic Journal*, **70** (279), September, 496–513; Robert A. Mundell (1964), 'Tariff Preferences and the Terms of Trade', *Manchester School of Economic and Social Studies*, **XXXII** (1), January, 1–13; C.A. Cooper and B.F. Massell (1965), 'A New Look at Customs Union Theory', *Economic Journal*, **75** (300), December, 742–7; John F. Helliwell (1996), 'Do National Borders Matter for Quebec's Trade?', *Canadian Journal of Economics/Revue Canadienne d'Economique*, **XXIX** (3), August, 507–22.

Cambridge University Press for excerpt: L. Alan Winters (1999), 'Regionalism vs. Multilateralism', in Richard Baldwin, Daniel Cohen, Andre Sapir and Anthony Venables (eds), *Market Integration, Regionalism and the Global Economy*, Chapter 2, 7–49.

Carnegie Endowment for International Peace for excerpt: Jacob Viner (1950), 'The Economics of Customs Unions', in *The Customs Union Issue*, Chapter IV, 41–81, references.

Elsevier Science for articles: Murray C. Kemp and Henry Y. Wan, Jr. (1976), 'An Elementary Proposition Concerning the Formation of Customs Unions', *Journal of International Economics*, **6**, 95–7; Alasdair Smith and Anthony J. Venables (1988), 'Completing the Internal Market in the European Community: Some Industry Simulations', *European Economic Review*, **32** (7), September, 1501–25; Kyle Bagwell and Robert W. Staiger (1997), 'Multilateral Tariff Cooperation During the Formation of Customs Unions', *Journal of International Economics*, **42** (1/2), February, 91–123.

Federal Reserve Bank of Kansas City for excerpt: Lawrence H. Summers (1991), 'Regionalism and the World Trading System', in *Policy Implications of Trade and Currency Zones*, 295–301.

*Intereconomics: Review of European Economic Policy* for article: Detlef Lorenz (1991), 'Regionalisation versus Regionalism – Problems of Change in the World Economy', *Intereconomics*, **26** (1), January/February, 3–10.

Kiel Institute of World Economics for article: Richard Pomfret (1986), 'The Theory of Preferential Trading Arrangements', *Weltwirtschaftliches Archiv*, **CXXII** (3), 439–64.

MIT Press for excerpt: Paul R. Krugman (1991), 'Is Bilateralism Bad?', in Elhanan Helpman and Assaf Razin (eds), *International Trade and Trade Policy*, Chapter 1, 9–23.

Oxford University Press Australia (http://www.oup.com.au) for excerpt: Richard Pomfret (1996), 'Sub-regional Economic Zones', in Bijit Bora and Christopher Findlay (eds), *Regional Integration and the Asia-Pacific*, Chapter 14, 207–22.

Routledge, Taylor & Francis Books Ltd for excerpt: Anne O. Krueger (1999), 'Free Trade Agreements as Protectionist Devices: Rules of Origin', in James R. Melvin, James C. Moore and Raymond Riezman (eds), *Trade, Theory and Econometrics: Essays in Honor of John S. Chipman*, Studies in the Modern World Economy, Volume 15, 91–102.

Southern Economic Association for article: Richard Blackhurst (1972), 'General Versus Preferential Tariff Reduction for LDC Exports: An Analysis of the Welfare Effects', *Southern Economic Journal*, **XXXVIII** (3), January, 350–62.

University of Chicago Press for articles: W.M. Corden (1972), 'Economies of Scale and Customs Union Theory', *Journal of Political Economy*, **80** (3, Part 1), May–June, 465–75; Eitan Berglas (1979), 'Preferential Trading Theory: The *n* Commodity Case', *Journal of Political Economy*, **87** (2), April, 315–31; David Cox and Richard Harris (1985), 'Trade Liberalization and Industrial Organization: Some Estimates for Canada', *Journal of Political Economy*, **93** (1), February, 115–45; Richard E. Baldwin (1992), 'Measurable Dynamic Gains from Trade', *Journal of Political Economy*, **100** (1), February, 162–74; Wilfred J. Ethier (1998), 'Regionalism in a Multilateral World', *Journal of Political Economy*, **106** (6), December, 1214–45.

Every effort has been made to trace all the copyright holders but if any have been inadvertently overlooked the publishers will be pleased to make the necessary arrangement at the first opportunity.

In addition the publishers wish to thank the Marshall Library of Economics, Cambridge University, the Library of the University of Warwick, B & N Microfilm, London and the Library of Indiana University at Bloomington, USA for their assistance in obtaining these articles.

# Introduction

*Richard Pomfret*

A feature of the global economy over the last half-century has been the proliferation of regional trading arrangements and ongoing debate over the relationship between regionalism and multilateralism. The initial success of western European integration in the 1960s and then the adoption of bilateralism by the USA in the 1980s were high tides of regionalism, while the abandonment of many regional trading arrangements among developing countries in the 1970s and the completion of the Uruguay Round of trade negotiations and establishment of the World Trade Organization (WTO) in the mid-1990s marked low points for regionalism. In the early years of the 21st century the debate continues to flourish as the European Union expands eastwards, the USA looks to strengthening hemispheric relations, and East Asian countries consider regional arrangements more seriously after the 1997 regional crisis.

This volume collects together some major contributions to the economic analysis of regional trading arrangements (RTAs). It is not concerned with either the history of specific arrangements or of the extent or role of regionalism in the world economy. Nor does it deal with empirical studies, apart from where such studies have impinged upon the analytical debate. While the collection can be used as a text for a course on the economics of regional trading arrangements, it is conceived as supplementary reading to such a course or as a reference resource for people working on regional trading arrangements.[1]

## Vinerian Customs Union Theory

The economic analysis of regional trading arrangements emerged from the economics of preferential trading arrangements. In modern form this had its origin in the fourth chapter of Jacob Viner's 1950 book *The Customs Union Issue*, specifically on pages 43–4 of the original article that is Chapter 1 in this volume. Before Viner, debates were confused. Some free-traders supported preferential trading arrangements as steps towards free trade, while others opposed them for retaining restrictions upon trade with some trading partners. Some protectionists supported preferential trading arrangements for increasing the margin of preference for favoured suppliers, while others opposed such arrangements for reducing protection of domestic producers against imports from the favoured suppliers. Viner's great contribution was to show that the resource allocation effects are inevitably ambiguous because while preferential tariff reductions increase global efficiency by encouraging displacement of domestic producers by more efficient suppliers in the favoured partner (the *trade creation* effect), the preferential cuts introduce new sources of allocative inefficiency insofar as goods from favoured suppliers displace goods from the global least-cost supplier (the *trade diversion* effect). In sum, no general conclusion about whether preferential trading arrangements improve or damage global resource allocation, or the economic welfare of the discriminating importer, is possible.

Viner's insight had significance beyond the field of international trade because he had uncovered what became known as the general theory of the second best. A movement towards the global optimum (e.g. by removing barriers on some international trade) will not necessarily be welfare-improving as long as any other deviations from the global optimality conditions (e.g. the retention of barriers on some international trade) exist. This does not mean that we cannot evaluate specific examples of second-best policy changes, but it does mean that we cannot generalize to say that every regional trading arrangement will be welfare-improving or welfare-decreasing.

Initially this branch of international economics was known as customs union theory, in part because the main applications during the 1950s and 1960s appeared to be to the customs union between Belgium, France, Germany, Italy, Luxembourg and the Netherlands, and to less successful attempts to form customs unions in Latin America and in Africa. Richard Lipsey (Chapter 2) synthesized the early development of customs union theory in an influential 1960 survey article, which focused on refining the trade-creation and trade-diversion concepts. The partial equilibrium analysis was presented in several other articles dealing with such issues as how to classify any increase in demand for imports which arises from the preferential tariff cuts. Harry Johnson's 1960 article is a good example of this genre (see Chapter 3).

The literature faltered during the 1960s because it failed to explain why countries would form a customs union, when they could realize all the trade creation benefits and avoid any trade diversion costs by reducing tariffs in a non-preferential manner. Charles Cooper and Benton Massell (Chapter 4) formalized this proposition.[2] The Cooper-Massell proposition that customs union formation could never be superior to unilateral trade liberalization implied that customs unions had to be explained by some economic motive other than improving resource allocation (e.g. promoting specific activities) or on political grounds. Such alternative motivations could readily be found, as South American RTAs were justified as promoting a regional import-substituting industrialization strategy, and in western Europe proponents of the Treaty of Rome saw customs union formation as an integrating step which would forestall a reprise of the Franco-German wars of 1870–1945. The disjuncture between the reality of RTA formation and the second-best resource allocation outcome from such arrangements was, however, not a very comfortable conclusion for economists in the 1960s, before the development of the literature on the political economy of trade barriers highlighted that sectional interests could achieve policy outcomes that were not the most desirable for the population as a whole.

Outside the Vinerian mainstream, a general equilibrium approach to analysing preferential trading arrangements was pioneered by Jaroslav Vanek in his 1965 book *General Equilibrium of International Discrimination: The Case of Customs Unions* (Harvard University Press, Cambridge MA). The work of Eitan Berglas (Chapter 6) is representative of this approach.[3] The most influential contribution in this branch of the literature was a short and elegant piece by Murray Kemp and Henry Wan (Chapter 5) showing that the Cooper-Massell proposition holds in the general equilibrium as well as in the partial equilibrium setting. Also outside the mainstream was a contribution by Paul and Ronald Wonnacott (Chapter 7) arguing that the foreign tariff was a key omission from both the Cooper-Massell and the Kemp-Wan analysis, and that its inclusion could reverse their conclusion.

Both branches of the literature were weak in dealing with how prices are determined, typically reducing each country to an extreme role as price-setter or a price-taker. Robert

Mundell (Chapter 8) made the only major contribution in the 1960s to address this issue, but for many years trade theorists ignored Mundell's insights, which were set in a macroeconomic framework. Richard Blackhurst (Chapter 9) provided a partial equilibrium analysis with upward-sloping supply curves. The reintegration of the terms of trade into the analysis was the focus of a 1986 survey article by Richard Pomfret (Chapter 10).

Other potentially important extensions of the mainstream analysis were acknowledged even in Lipsey's 1960 survey, but received little attention. Max Corden (Chapter 11) showed that in the presence of scale economies, trade creation and trade diversion needed to be supplemented by cost reduction and trade suppression effects. Analysis of technical efficiency, or shifts in the production function associated with preferential tariff reductions, were mooted but not followed up; a rare exception, which could equally have been included in the section on the new regionalism, was the work of Richard Baldwin (Chapter 12) during the early 1990s. These considerations, however, assumed increased importance during the 1980s and early 1990s as justification for the new regional initiatives such as the European Union's 1992 program for deeper integration and the North American Free Trade Area (NAFTA).

## The New Regionalism

The new regionalism drew on the so-called new trade theories of the late 1970s and early 1980s, which emphasized imperfect competition. Particularly influential in transporting these ideas into the analysis of regional trading arrangements were applied general equilibrium models of the impact of North American regional integration by David Cox and Rick Harris (Chapter 13) and of European integration by Alasdair Smith and Tony Venables (Chapter 14). The empirical results from these models were indicative rather than compelling estimates, and they were often challenged or superseded, but the original articles were influential in suggesting that realization of scale economies or industrial organization considerations could be the dominant consequence of regional trading arrangements.

There was also a burgeoning literature on non-tariff elements of regionalism, emphasizing deeper integration in such areas as competition policy, regulatory and tax harmonization and so forth. Much of the literature on new regionalism appeared outside of academic journals due to its emphasis on details of agreements rather than general propositions.[4] Opponents of regionalism argued that the devil in the details was generally harmful, and that complexity was itself a source of adverse consequences of regional arrangements. Rules of origin were an important battleground in this debate, and one specific to preferential trade policies. Rules of origin act as a tax on use of inputs from outside the RTA members, and in general such a tax will be trade-diverting. The ability of pressure groups to influence the design of rules of origin, however, adds a political economy dimension that is likely to increase the potential for trade diversion or even trade suppression. Anne Krueger (Chapter 15) was an influential contributor to the analysis of rules of origin.

In wider discussions a key point of contention has been whether regional trading arrangements are building blocks towards the first-best outcome of global trade liberalization or stumbling blocks. The stumbling block case has been most forcefully argued by Jagdish Bhagwati, and in joint contributions by Bhagwati and Panagariya.[5] Alan Winters (Chapter 16) assesses the debate initiated by Bhagwati. Arvind Panagariya (Chapter 17) also reviews these arguments in his more wide-ranging recent survey of developments in preferential trade theory.

Regardless of the economic and systemic arguments, regionalism was clearly a widespread phenomenon during the 1990s, and several authors developed political economy models to explain the choice between regionalism and multilateralism and to determine whether they are substitutes or complements. Wilfred Ethier (Chapter 18) argues that in an increasingly integrated global economy, small countries seek novel ways to establish a competitive advantage, and membership in a regional trading arrangement might provide such an edge by attracting producers of intermediates to locate in a country. In Ethier's model regional arrangements are conduits into the multilateral trading system.[6] Philip Levy (Chapter 19) uses a median voter model to show that regional options reduce the incentive for multilateral cooperation. Kyle Bagwell and Robert Staiger (Chapter 20) introduce a time element, arguing that during the formation of a regional trading arrangement regionalism and multilateralism may be complementary, but in the mature operation of the RTA market power motives may undermine the incentives to play by multilateral rules.

## Systemic Analysis

Increased interest in regionalism led to analytical consideration of how far the process is likely to go. In 1991, at the high point of the new regionalism, two high-profile American economists, Paul Krugman (Chapter 21) and Larry Summers (Chapter 22), made contributions supporting bilateralism as a trade policy option. Krugman's paper, however, contains a warning that the long-run tendency is towards three trade blocs, which is the pessimum rather than an optimum. The conclusion, although derived from a simple model with strong symmetry assumptions, highlights again the second-best world of regionalism, where a little discrimination may be beneficial but with substantial discrimination (as in a world economy divided into three trade blocs) trade diversion costs dominate. Summers allows for asymmetries among trading nations, and he discusses the concept of the natural trading partners among whom an RTA may beneficially be formed.

Once the basic trade unit is allowed to be endogenous, the question of the optimum size of the unit arises. Alberto Alesina, Enrico Spolaore and Romain Wacziarg (Chapter 23) have analysed the forces leading to larger and smaller trading units, emphasizing the scale economies from larger size and political benefits of reaching generally acceptable decisions in smaller political units. Dani Rodrik (Chapter 24) has put these arguments in a dynamic setting, forecasting that as an increasing number of economic issues require supranational solutions the 21st century will see the decline of the nation state and rise of global federalism – followed by wars of secession in the 22nd century.

As the previous paragraphs suggest, the economic analysis of regionalism has increasingly come to focus on fundamental elements of international economics. Despite challenges to the use of the nation state as the basic unit in international economics, there is strong empirical evidence in favour of the traditional emphasis. Even in the highly integrated North American market, Canadian trade exhibits a surprisingly large home-country bias. This puzzle was highlighted by John McCallum (Chapter 25), and his result has been reproduced by John Helliwell (Chapter 26) and, with a different methodology, by Charles Engel and John Rogers (Chapter 27).

Detlef Lorenz (Chapter 28) stressed at an early point in the regionalism debates that we should be careful to distinguish between regionalism as a policy-induced pattern and regionalization, which might occur naturally in the global economy or within national economies. Another international aspect of this distinction is between regional arrangements among countries and the tendency of subregions of countries to form close ties with neighbouring subregions. The phenomenon of subregional zones is widespread, as in the Great Lakes industrial region, the Tijuana–San Diego area of North America or in the heartland of the European Union. Richard Pomfret (Chapter 29) reviews the phenomenon in the context of East Asian policy debates in the 1990s after the Pearl River Delta and the subregion centred on Singapore became identified as areas of rapid integrated growth.

## Conclusions

The economic analysis of RTAs evolved substantially over the second half of the 20th century. Viner's original contribution was a seminal piece, leading to a fundamental concept in modern economics, the theory of the second best. To some, this theory represents a depressing picture of agnosticism, but on a more positive view it should encourage deeper analysis of specific second-best situations because we cannot rely on simple but false generalizations such as 'all RTAs are good' or 'all RTAs are bad'.

Within the field of preferential trade policies, Viner's key insight was to highlight the possibility of trade diversion. Politically, trade diversion is often more acceptable than trade creation because the losers (domestic taxpayers and non-preferred foreign suppliers) are politically weak, whereas the costs from trade creation are born by domestic producer interests, who are typically better organized and more politically influential. That constellation of interests makes it all the more important for economic analysts to keep trade diversion in view, and not to accept producer-biased arguments in favour of preferential trade policies which are not in the wider public interest.

During the 1980s and 1990s the analysis of RTAs moved beyond the theory of tariff preferences. For one thing, 50 years of multilateral trade liberalization had reduced the potential margin for preferential treatment on all but a few traded goods, at least so far as the higher income countries were concerned. Secondly, RTAs have increasingly covered new areas beyond preferential tariffs. Although the initial impetus for the new regionalism came from new trade theories emphasizing scale economies and imperfect competition, actual RTAs broadened to include trade-related issues and other areas, rather than being narrowly restricted to trade preferences. This led on to more fundamental questions about the nature of the appropriate unit of analysis. In western Europe, for example, is it the European Union, the nation state or sub-national units such as northern Italy or Bavaria (which are economically different from other regions of Italy or Germany)?

Analysis of regional trading arrangements has always recognized the interplay of economics and politics. This collection emphasizes the economic analysis of RTAs, and strays into politics only in the restricted sense of looking for economic explanations of political developments. Yet for many RTAs the impetus has been overwhelmingly political and old results, such as the Cooper-Massell Kemp-Wan proposition, remain powerful reminders that in the long run there is little economic support for any trade policy other than non-discriminatory free trade.

Theoretical exceptions can be found, but practical exceptions are often pushed by sectional pressure groups rather than reflecting the public interest.

In practice, although policymakers have toyed with regional options, the practical outcome over the last half century has generally been to avoid going far down the path of preferential trade policies. The most salient RTAs in the current world economy (the European Union, the North American Free Trade Area, or Closer Economic Relations between Australia and New Zealand) all have liberal external trade policies, so that they could properly be called regional arrangements for matters beyond trade. Attempts to form seriously discriminating RTAs have generally foundered in Latin America and Africa, and failed to even get off the ground in Asia, largely because policymakers did not want to bear the trade diversion costs of importing from inefficient producers in partner countries. Despite fears in 1989 that formerly centrally planned economies would be tempted to form eastern European RTAs or former Soviet Union RTAs, these countries have opted for multilateralism in their trade policies.[7]

Nevertheless, while fundamental analytical truths remain valid, economists have been spurred into new areas of inquiry by the ongoing conflict between regionalism and multilateralism in the modern global economy. The theory of discriminatory trade policies is well developed, but as Lorenz stresses, developments in the global trading system may be driven not by policies aimed at regionalism but rather reflect other fundamental forces which have been leading to regionalization. The nation state itself appears to be in a more precarious condition than at any time since the rise of nationalism in the 19th century, and it is threatened both by the increasing powers being assigned to supranational organizations and by the threat of secession (or at least demands for more powers for regions within countries). The ideas represented in this collection by writers such as Krugman, Alesina *et al.*, Rodrik or McCallum are leading into exciting unchartered waters.

## Notes

1. The contents roughly follow the order of analysis in the second section of R. Pomfret, 2002, *The Economics of Regional Trading Arrangements* (updated paperback edition, Oxford University Press). That book also integrates the economic analysis with the history and empirical studies of regional trading arrangements.
2. Harry Johnson (1965) ('An Economic Theory of Protectionism, Tariff Bargaining and the Formation of Customs Unions', *Journal of Political Economy*, **73**, 256–83) made a similar point.
3. In a different approach, Sven Arndt (1969) ('Customs Unions and the Theory of Tariffs', *American Economic Review*, **59**, 108–18) extended the analysis from a three country to a five country model by introducing substitutes and complements.
4. An influential book in popularizing the term 'deeper integration' was Robert Z. Lawrence (1996), *Regionalism, Multilateralism, and Deeper Integration* (Brookings Institution, Washington DC).
5. See Jagdish Bhagwati and Arvind Panagariya (1996), *The Economics of Preferential Trade Agreements* (American Enterprise Institute Press, Washington DC).
6. Ethier (1998) (in 'the New Regionalism', *The Economic Journal*, **108**, July, 1149–61) has generalized the argument to make the case that the new regionalism is a consequence of multilateral trade liberalization and is a vehicle for bringing additional (small emerging market) economies into the liberal global economy.
7. The exceptions have been the attempts by eastern European and southeast Asian countries to adhere to existing RTAs (the EU and ASEAN). Agreements among transition countries proliferated on paper in the early 1990s, but with little practical consequence (Richard Pomfret (2001), 'Reintegration

of Formerly Centrally Planned Economies into the Global Trading System', *ASEAN Economic Bulletin*, **18**, April, 35–47). By 2001, all of the formerly centrally planned economies except Turkmenistan (and still centrally planned North Korea) had either joined the WTO or had applications in process.

# Part I
# Vinerian Customs Union Theory

# [1]

## THE ECONOMICS OF CUSTOMS UNIONS

### 1. *Customs Union as an Approach to Free Trade*

The literature on customs unions in general, whether written by economists or non-economists, by free-traders or protectionists, is almost universally favorable to them, and only here and there is a sceptical note to be encountered, usually by an economist with free-trade tendencies. It is a strange phenomenon which unites free-traders and protectionists in the field of commercial policy, and its strangeness suggests that there is something peculiar in the apparent economics of customs unions. The customs union problem is entangled in the whole free-trade–protection issue, and it has never yet been properly disentangled.

The free-trader and the protectionist, in their reasoning about foreign trade, start from different premises—which they rarely state fully—and reach different conclusions. If in the case of customs unions they agree in their conclusions, it must be because they see in customs unions different sets of facts, and not because an identical customs union can meet the requirements of both the free-trader and the protectionist. It will be argued here that customs unions differ from each other in certain vital but not obvious respects, and that the free-trade supporter of customs union expects from it consequences which if they were associated in the mind of the protectionist with customs union would lead him to oppose it. It will also be argued, although with less conviction because it involves judgments about quantities in the absence of actual or even possible measurement, that with respect to most customs union projects the protectionist is right and the free-trader is wrong in regarding the project as something, given his premises, which he can logically support.

To simplify the analysis, it will at first be confined to perfect customs unions between pairs of countries; and the "administrative" advantages of customs unions, such as the shortening of customs walls, and the "administrative" disadvantages, such as the necessity of co-

41

ordinating customs codes and of allocating revenues by agreed formula, will be tentatively disregarded. Also, to separate the problem of customs unions *per se* from the question of whether in practice customs unions would result in a higher or in a lower "average level" of duties [1] on imports into the customs union area from outside the area, it will be assumed that the average level of duties on imports from outside the customs area is precisely the same for the two countries, computed as it would be if they had not formed the customs union. It will at first be assumed that the duties are of only two types: [2] (*a*) "nominal duties," that is, duties which have no effect on imports because there would be no imports of commodities of the kind involved even in the absence of any import duties on them; [3] and (*b*) "effective protective duties," that is, duties which operate to reduce imports not only by making commodities of the specific kind involved more expensive to potential consumers and so lessening their consumption, but also, and chiefly, by diverting consumption from imported commodities to the products of corresponding domestic industries. The analysis will be directed toward finding answers to the following questions: in so far as the establishment of the customs union results in change in the national locus of production of goods purchased, is the net change one of diversion of purchases to lower or higher money-cost sources of supply, abstracting from duty-elements in money costs: (*a*) for each of the customs union countries taken separately; (*b*) for the two combined; (*c*) for the outside world; (*d*) for the world as a whole? If the customs union is a movement in the direction of free trade, it must be predominantly a movement in the direction of goods being supplied from lower money-cost sources than before. If the customs union has the effect of diverting purchases to higher money-cost sources, it is then a device for making tariff protection more effective. None of these questions

---

[1] Whether it is possible to give this concept of an "average level" of duties both some degree of precision of definition and economic significance is taken up later. See *infra*, pp. 66–68.

[2] "Revenue duties" are dealt with subsequently. See *infra*, pp. 65–66.

[3] Such duties, while they have no effect on imports, can have other effects of some economic importance, though these are not directly relevant here. In countries where an approach to perfect competition does not prevail, which means most countries, import duties may protect monopolistic or government-supported domestic price levels instead of protecting domestic production.

can be answered *a priori,* and the correct answers will depend on just how the customs union operates in practice. All that *a priori* analysis can do, is to demonstrate, within limits, how the customs union must operate if it is to have specific types of consequence.

The removal of "nominal" duties, or duties which are ineffective as barriers to trade, can be disregarded, and attention can be confined to the consequences of the removal, as the result of customs union, of duties which previously had operated effectively as a barrier, partial or complete, to import.

There will be commodities, however, which one of the members of the customs union will now newly import from the other but which it formerly did not import at all because the price of the protected domestic product was lower than the price at any foreign source plus the duty. This shift in the locus of production as between the two countries is a shift from a high-cost to a lower-cost point, a shift which the free-trader can properly approve, as at least a step in the right direction, even if universal free trade would divert production to a source with still lower costs.

There will be other commodities which one of the members of the customs union will now newly import from the other whereas before the customs union it imported them from a third country, because that was the cheapest possible source of supply even after payment of duty. The shift in the locus of production is now not as between the two member countries but as between a low-cost third country and the other, high-cost, member country. This is a shift of the type which the protectionist approves, but it is not one which the free-trader who understands the logic of his own doctrine can properly approve.[4]

[4] A third possibility should be mentioned. The import duty on a particular commodity may be so high in one of the countries that it is prohibitive of import, but domestic production may be impossible or excessively costly, so that there is no consumption. Upon formation of the customs union, the commodity in question may be imported from the other member country, where its cost of production may be high or low as compared to costs elsewhere but is assumed to be lower than outside costs plus the duty on imports from outside the customs union. The original duty thus served as a sumptuary measure rather than as a protective or revenue measure. Whether the removal of a sumptuary measure is of benefit for the country particularly concerned as potential consumer is not a type of question which the economist has any special capacity to answer. But if as the result of customs union country A removes a duty of this kind preferen-

**44**                        THE CUSTOMS UNION ISSUE

Simplified as this exposition is, it appears to cover most of the basic economic issues involved. The primary purpose of a customs union, and its major consequence for good or bad, is to shift sources of supply, and the shift can be either to lower- or to higher-cost sources, depending on circumstances. It will be noted that for the free-trader the benefit from a customs union to the customs union area as a whole derives from that portion of the new trade between the member countries which is wholly new trade, whereas each particular portion of the new trade between the member countries which is a substitute for trade with third countries he must regard as a consequence of the customs union which is injurious for the importing country, for the external world, and for the world as a whole, and is beneficial only to the supplying member country. The protectionist, on the other hand, is certain to regard the substitution of trade between the member countries for trade with third countries as the major beneficial feature of customs union from the point of view of the participating countries and to be unenthusiastic about or even to regard as a drawback—at least for the importing country—the wholly new trade which results from the customs union.

From the free-trade point of view, whether a particular customs union is a move in the right or in the wrong direction depends, therefore, so far as the argument has as yet been carried, on which of the two types of consequences ensue from that custom union.

Where the trade-creating force is predominant, one of the members at least must benefit, both may benefit, the two combined must have a net benefit, and the world at large benefits; but the outside world loses, in the short-run at least, and can gain in the long-run only as the result of the general diffusion of the increased prosperity of the customs union area. Where the trade-diverting effect is predominant, one at least of the member countries is bound to be injured, both may be injured, the two combined will suffer a net injury, and there will be injury to the outside world and to the world at large. The question as to what presumptions can reasonably be held to pre-

---

tially for imports from the other member country, B, there is a clear loss for A as compared to the removal of duty regardless of source if B is a high-cost source of supply. There is an unquestionable benefit here, however, for the supplying country, and it does not injure outside countries in any direct way.

vail with respect to the relative importance in practice of the two types of effects will be examined subsequently.

To the reasoning presented above, there is one qualification in favor of customs union which needs to be made, on which both free-traders and protectionists can with reason find some common ground, although, in the opinion of the writer, they both tend to exaggerate its importance for the customs union problem. It has here been assumed hitherto that in so far as a customs union has effects on trade these must be either trade-creating or trade-diverting effects. This would be true if as output of any industry in a particular country increases over the long-run relative to the national economy as a whole, its money costs of production per unit relative to the general level of money costs also tended to rise. Economists are generally agreed, however, that there are firms, and consequently also industries, where this rule does not hold but instead unit costs decrease as output expands. From this they conclude that where a small country by itself, because of the limited size of its domestic market (and, it should be added, the prevention by foreign tariffs of its finding a market outside), may be unable to reach a scale of production large enough to make low unit-costs of production possible, two or more such countries combined may provide a market large enough to make low unit-cost production possible. If an industry which thus expands, whether from zero or from a previous small output, is in country A, and the other member of the customs union is country B, the diversion of B's imports from a country, C, outside the customs union to country A, may be a beneficial one for B as well as for A, and, moreover, there may be suppression of trade, namely, of the imports of A from C of the commodity in question, which may also be beneficial to A. Whether such diversion—and suppression—of trade will, from the free-trade point of view, be beneficial or injurious to A will depend on several circumstances. The cost of production in A of the commodity in question is now lower than it was before. There is gain, therefore, for A as compared to the precustoms-union situation with respect to that portion of its present output which corresponds to its previous output (which may have been zero), and there is clear gain on such of its additional output as is now exported to B. On additional output beyond this, however, there is loss to A if the new cost, though lower than the previous one, is higher than the cost (before duty) at which it is obtainable from C, but there is additional gain to A if the new cost is lower than the cost (before duty) at which it is obtainable from C. For B, there is loss by the amount imported by B times the per unit amount by which A's price exceeds the price at which B's import needs could be supplied by C; there is gain to B only if A's price is now lower than C's price (before duty). There is thus a possibility—though not, as is generally taken for granted in the literature, a certainty—that if the unit-cost of production falls as the result of the enlarged protected market consequent upon customs union there will be a gain from customs union for one of the members, for both the members, and/or for the union as a whole, but there is also a possibility—and often a probability—that there will be loss in each case.

It does not seem probable that the prospects of reduction in unit-costs of production as the result of enlargement of the tariff area are ordinarily substantial, even when the individual member countries are quite small in economic size. The arguments for substantial economies from increased scale of industry presented by economists rest wholly or mostly on alleged economies of scale for *plants* or *firms*, and on the assumption that large-scale plants or firms are not practicable in small *industries* and therefore in small countries. It seems to the writer unlikely, however, that substantial efficiency-economies of scale of plant are common once the plants are of moderate size, and he is convinced that in most industries plants can attain or approach closely their optimum size for efficiency even though the industries are not large in size. Were it not for trade barriers, moreover, even small countries could have large industries.

There are few industries, even in countries where large-scale production is common, in which there are not plants of moderate size which are as efficient, or nearly as efficient, measured in unit-costs, as the giant plants; and there are few giant firms which do not maintain some of their plants, presumably at a profit, on a moderate scale. There are few manufacturing industries—and the economies of scale of plant or industry are generally conceded to be confined mainly or only to such industries—which have not been able to maintain themselves on a low-cost basis in one or more small countries, such as Switzerland, Sweden, Denmark, or Belgium. If the applicability of this argument is confined to products which nowhere are produced at a low unit-cost from plants which are quite small, either absolutely or as compared to the maximum size elsewhere, the scope of the argument is much more limited than is commonly taken for granted. It may be asked in rebuttal, how then explain the existence of giant plants and giant firms? It is at least a partial answer: (1) as to size of plants, that the survival of plants of moderate size in competition with the giant plants calls equally for explanation; and (2) as to size of firms, that there are in an imperfectly competitive world many incentives to growth in size of firm even at the cost of efficiency in production—firms of quite undistinguished records in efficiency of production have been known to grow by absorption of more efficient smaller firms and by the use of monopoly power in buying and in retention of customers, and, generally speaking, growth in size is more often the result of efficiency than contributory to efficiency.

The general rule appears to be that once an industry is large enough to make possible optimum scale—and degree of specialization of production—in plants, further expansion of the industry in a national economy of constant over-all size is bound to be under conditions of increasing unit-costs as output increases, in the absence of new inventions. To expand, the industry must draw away from other industries increased amounts of the resources it uses, and consequently must pay higher prices per unit for resources of the type which it uses more heavily than does industry at large, and must reduce the extent to which it uses them relative to other types of resources, thus bringing into operation the law of diminishing returns. It may be objected that this will not hold true in the case of a customs union, since this in effect increases the over-all size of the "national" economy. It is the supply conditions of factors of production, however, which are the relevant restrictive factor on expansion of output of an industry without increase of unit-costs, and unless customs union appreciably increases the inter-member mobility of factors of production it does not in this sense increase the "scale" of the "national" economy from the point of view of production conditions even if it does increase it from the point of view of the size of the protected market for sales.

Few free-traders have dealt with the economics of customs unions in any detail, and one must resort in some measure to inference from the implications of brief dicta to find the explanation for their general support of customs union as constituting an approach to their ideal of the territorial allocation of production in accordance with comparative costs of production. The major explanation seems to lie in an unreflecting association on their part of any removal or reduction of trade barriers with movement in the direction of free trade. Businessmen, however, and governments which have had to try simultaneously to satisfy both special interests seeking increased protection and voters hostile to protection, have long known of ways of making increased protection look like movement in a free-trade direction. They have known how, under suitable circumstances, protection against foreign competition could be increased by *reducing* duties and reduced by increasing duties. Let us suppose that there are import duties both on wool and on woolen cloth, but that no wool is produced at home despite the duty. Removing the duty on wool while leaving the duty unchanged on the woolen cloth results in increased protection for the cloth industry while having no significance for wool-raising. Or suppose that the wool is all produced at home, and sold to domestic clothmakers at the world price plus duty, but would be all produced at home even if there were no duty on wool, but would then be sold at the world price. Removal of the duty on wool again increases the protection for the woolen industry without reducing the volume of domestic production of wool.

When the customs union operates to divert trade from its previous channels rather than to create new trade, the partial removal of duties which it involves operates in analogous manner to increase the protective effect for high-cost producers of the duties which remain, not, however, by reducing imports into their own national territory but by extending the operation in their favor of the protective duty to the territory of the other partner of the customs union. It would in theory be possible that if two areas were joined in customs union, the customs union would have no trade-creating effect and only trade-diverting effect, i.e., no industry in either area would meet with new competition from the other area, while some high-cost industries, existing or potential, in each area would acquire a new set of consumers in the other area who would be placed at their mercy because the customs union tariff will now shut them off from low-cost sources of supply. A set of connected tariff walls can give more market-dominance to high-cost producers than a set of independent tariff walls, if the former set has had its internal sections knocked out.

This is well, though ingenuously, brought out in one of the leading treatises in favor of customs unions, where the author, after arguing that free-traders should like them because they eliminate trade barriers, proceeds to argue that protectionists should also like them because of the extension of the (protected) market area which they provide for producers within the territory of the customs union; "as for the internal competition, it will not be formidable if care is exercised in choosing as partners in customs unions countries which are complementary [in production] rather than competitive." [5]

Free-traders sometimes in almost the same breath disapprove of preferential reductions of tariffs but approve of customs unions, which involve 100 per cent preference, and this is the position at present of the United States Government and the doctrine of the Havana Charter.[6]   If the distinction is made to rest, as often seems to be the case, on some supposed virtue in a 100 per cent preference, which suddenly turns to maximum evil at 99 per cent, the degree of evil tapering off as the degree of preference shrinks, it is a distinction as illogical, the

---

[5] L. Bosc, *op. cit.*, p. 98.  He moves on to a perfect *non sequitur:* "Thanks to this judicious choice, *there will be established within the customs union a fecund division of labor*, while the customs frontiers thus extended further territorially will protect the internal market against the superiority of other countries." (Italics supplied.)

[6] Cf. Clair Wilcox, *A Charter for World Trade* (New York, 1949), p. 70:

"Preferences have been opposed and customs unions favored, in principle, by the United States.  This position may obviously be criticized as lacking in logical consistency.  In preferential arrangements, discrimination against the outer world is partial; in customs unions, it is complete.  But the distinction is none the less defensible.  A customs union creates a wider trading area, removes obstacles to competition, makes possible a more economic allocation of resources, and thus operates to increase production and raise planes of living.  A preferential system, on the other hand, retains internal barriers, obstructs economy in production, and restrains the growth of income and demand.  It is set up for the purpose of conferring a privilege on producers within the system and imposing a handicap on external competitors.  A customs union is conducive to the expansion of trade on a basis of multilateralism and non-discrimination; a preferential system is not."

There would seem to be little or nothing in what is said here about the *evils* of preference which is not potentially true also for customs unions; and equally little in what is said here about the *benefits* of customs unions which is acceptable further than as being potentially true if circumstances are right, and which, where true at all, is not also potentially true, if circumstances are right, of preferences.

50        THE CUSTOMS UNION ISSUE

writer believes, as this way of putting it makes it sound.[7]  On the
legal side, the discussion of the bearing of the *degree* of preference on
its compatibility with most-favored-nation obligations has sometimes
led to the opposite conclusion, namely, that, on the principle *a majori
ad minus,* if a customs union with its 100 per cent preferences is compatible with the most-favored-nation principle, still more must fractional preferences be compatible.[8]  This seems plausible enough until
it is realized that acceptance of this reasoning would have the practical
consequence that 100 per cent preferences would be legal if incident
to customs union and lesser preferences would be legal because
greater ones were, so that *all* preferences would be legal.  The moral
is that on both the economic and legal side the problem is too complex
to be settled by simple maxims.[9]  A 50 per cent preference is economically either less desirable or more desirable than a 100 per cent preference according only as preference at all is under the circumstances
desirable or undesirable.[10]

There is one ground only on which, aside from administrative considerations, it can consistently be held that preferences are economically bad and are increasingly bad as they approach 100 per cent, but
that customs union is an economic blessing.  Customs union, if it is
complete, involves a cross-the-board removal of the duties between
the members of the union; since the removal is non-selective by its
very nature, the beneficial preferences are established along with the

[7] One is reminded of Dryden's "My wound is great because it is so small,"
and Saint-Evremond's rejoinder, "Then 'twould be greater, were it none at all."
   [8] Sandor von Matlekovits, *Die Zollpolitik der österreichisch-ungarischen Monarchie und des Deutschen Reiches seit 1868 und deren nächste Zukunft* (Leipzig, 1891).
   [9] The following illustration of the ambiguous working in practice of the *a
majori ad minus* principle is not, it is hoped, wholly without relevance:
   "It being made felony by an act of parliament to steal *horses,* it was doubted
whether stealing *one horse only* was within the statute: in construction of penal
law, the less number may not be included under the greater, but the reverse can
never follow.   Cf. the King of Prussia's error when he comments that, an
English law prohibiting bigamy, a man accused of having five wives was ac-
quitted, as not coming under the law."  Daines Barrington, *Observations on the
More Ancient Statutes,* 4th ed. (London, 1755), p. 547.  (Italics in the original.)
   [10] It is to be remembered that administrative economies are here disregarded.
If they were to be taken into account, a 100 per cent preference could be held
more desirable than say a 99 per cent one on the ground that it made the economic wastes of customs formalities unnecessary—if it did—even though otherwise the smaller the preference the less objectionable it would be.

injurious ones, the trade-creating ones along with the trade-diverting ones.  Preferential arrangements, on the other hand, can be, and usually are, selective, and it is possible, and in practice probable, that the preferences selected will be predominantly of the trade-diverting or injurious kind.  But aside from possible administrative economies, cross-the-board 100 per cent preferences without customs union are economically as good—or as bad—as customs union.

From the free-trade point of view, that is, the point of view that movement in the direction of international specialization in production in accordance with comparative costs is economically desirable, there can be formulated in accordance with the preceding analysis a series of propositions as to the conditions which need to be met to justify the presumption that the establishment of a particular customs union will represent a movement toward free trade rather than away from it.

A customs union is more likely to operate in the free-trade direction, whether appraisal is in terms of its consequence for the customs union area alone or for the world as a whole:

(1) the larger the economic area of the customs union and therefore the greater the potential scope for internal division of labor;

(2) the lower the "average" tariff level on imports from outside the customs union area as compared to what that level would be in the absence of customs union;

(3) the greater the correspondence in kind of products of the range of high-cost industries as between the different parts of the customs union which were protected by tariffs in both of the member countries before customs union was established, i.e., the *less* the degree of complementarity—or the *greater* the degree of rivalry—of the member countries with respect to *protected* industries, prior to customs union; [11]

(4) the greater the differences in unit-costs for protected industries of the same kind as between the different parts of the customs union, and therefore the greater the economies to be derived from free trade with respect to these industries within the customs union area;

---

[11] In the literature on customs union, it is almost invariably taken for granted that rivalry is a disadvantage and complementarity is an advantage in the formation of customs unions.  See *infra*, pp. 73 ff., with reference to the Benelux and Franco-Italian projects.

(5) the higher the tariff levels in potential export markets outside the customs union area with respect to commodities in whose production the member countries of the customs union would have a comparative advantage under free trade, and therefore the less the injury resulting from reducing the degree of specialization in production as between the customs union area and the outside world;

(6) the greater the range of protected industries for which an enlargement of the market would result in unit-costs lower than those at which the commodities concerned could be imported from outside the customs union area;

(7) the smaller the range of protected industries for which an enlargement of the market would not result in unit-costs lower than those at which the commodities concerned could be imported from outside the customs union area but which would nevertheless expand under customs union.

Confident judgment as to what the over-all balance between these conflicting considerations would be, it should be obvious, cannot be made for customs unions in general and in the abstract, but must be confined to particular projects and be based on economic surveys thorough enough to justify reasonably reliable estimates as to the weights to be given in the particular circumstances to the respective elements in the problem. Customs unions are, from the free-trade point of view, neither necessarily good nor necessarily bad; the circumstances discussed above are the determining factors. As has been pointed out earlier, it would be easy to set up a hypothetical model where customs union would mean nothing economically except an intensification of uneconomic protection, an increase in the effectiveness of trade barriers as interferences with international division of labor. A universal customs union, on the other hand, would be the equivalent of universal free trade. Actual customs unions must fall somewhere between these two extremes.

The non-technical reader is again warned that this analysis not only takes for granted the validity—at least when only purely economic considerations are taken into account—of the argument for free trade from a cosmopolitan point of view, but that its results are much less favorable to customs union in general than the position taken by most free-trade economists who have discussed the issue.[12] One of the few exceptions is Lionel Robbins, whose formulation of the issue as here quoted is, in the opinion of the writer, excellent:

[12] For conclusions, by economists sympathetic to free trade, more favorable to customs union, see especially: Gottfried von Haberler, *The Theory of International Trade* (London, 1936), pp. 383–91 and *idem*, "The Political Economy of Regional or Continental Blocs," in Seymour E. Harris, *ed., Postwar Economic Problems* (New York, 1943), especially pp. 330–34, and other writings of Haberler; John de Beers, "Tariff Aspects of a Federal Union," *Quarterly Journal of Economics* (1941), 49–92; and *Customs Unions, 1947*, pp. 75 ff., which follows Haberler's treatment closely and uncritically.

The more favorable conclusions with respect to customs unions reached by these writers are the consequence, mainly: (1) of failure to give consideration, or to give adequate consideration, to the effect of customs union in extending the area over which preexisting import duties exercise a protective effect; (2) of confusing the problem of the effect on location of production of customs union with the different, and for present purposes inconsequential, problem of the "incidence of import duties," or the location of impact of burden of payment of import duties actually collected; and (3) of applying the standard techniques of partial equilibrium analysis, traditionally applied to the analysis of the determination of prices of particular commodities taken one at a time, to foreign trade as a whole and to the tariff problem where its findings are either totally without significance or of totally indeterminable significance.

The present writer's own questioning in print of the usual arguments for customs union began in 1931: see "The Most-Favoured-Nation Clause," *Index*, VI (1931), p. 11. Haberler and de Beers have in the writings cited above found fault with the present writer's treatment as unduly critical of customs union, in part on the basis of reasoning of the type commented on in the preceding paragraph, and in part on the ground that the possibility of increased division of labor within the area of the customs union was denied or overlooked. In the few sentences devoted to the problem in the above-mentioned *Index* article, the writer asserted only the *possibility* that preferential duties would mean a greater diversion of trade from its free-trade pattern than uniform protection. He did not discuss the possibilities more favorable to customs union. Nor can he find in that article anything corresponding to the proposition attributed to him by de Beers, that an increase of imports must come from the same sources as under free trade, if there is to be gain. De Beers, however, cites a statement made by the present writer in 1933: ". . . if a regional agreement, preferential as between the countries within that region, is beneficial to both those countries, it must necessarily follow that had it been extended to the entire world no substantial change would have resulted in the effect of the agreement." This *is* a faulty statement. It is taken from a non-verbatim report of an extemporaneous discussion which the writer had no opportunity to edit— and, may add, did not know until some years later to have been put into print. (See International Studies Conference, *The State and Economic Life* [Paris, 1934], p. 50). He makes no claim, however, to have been misreported, and is not now in a position to deny that it correctly represented the state of his thinking at that time.

. . . The purpose of international division of labour is not merely to make possible the import of things which cannot be produced on the spot; it is rather to permit the resources on the spot to be devoted wholly to the production of the things they are best fitted to produce, the remainder being procured from elsewhere. . . .

It follows, therefore, that the gain from regional regrouping or wider units of any kind is not a gain of greater self-sufficiency, but a gain of the abolition of so much self-sufficiency on the part of the areas which are thus amalgamated. . . .[13]

. . . From the international point of view, the tariff union is not an advantage in itself. It is an advantage only in so far as, on balance, it conduces to more extensive division of labour. It is to be justified only by arguments which would justify still more its extension to all areas capable of entering into trade relationships. . . . No doubt if we could coax the rest of the world into free trade by a high tariff union against the produce of the Eskimos that would be, on balance, an international gain. But it would be inferior to an arrangement whereby the Eskimos were included. The only completely innocuous tariff union would be directed against the inaccessible produce of the moon.[14]

Another exception, however, seems to go further than is justified. R. G. Hawtrey writes as follows:

The most-favoured-nation clause has been criticised in that it prevented a relaxation of tariffs between adjacent countries, by which at any rate a beginning might have been made in the removal of obstacles to trade. A reduction of import duties by Belgium and Holland in favour of one another's products would have involved discrimination against other countries, such as Great Britain. . . .

But to suppose that agreements of that kind would be a move towards free trade is a delusion. The preferential treatment that would have been given by Belgium and Holland to one another would have made their existing protective tariffs more exclusive against other countries. In fact the wider the extent of economic activity encircled by a tariff barrier of given height, the greater is its effect in excluding the goods of foreign producers. The break-up of the Austro-Hungarian Empire resulted in the creation of new frontiers, and the new tariff barriers obstructed trade between one succession State and another. But if the import duties had remained at the same level as before, the markets which the succession

---

[13] Under customs union, there would be a decrease in the degree of self-sufficiency of each member area, but an increase in the degree of self-sufficiency of the customs union area as a whole.

[14] Lionel Robbins, *Economic Planning and International Order* (London, 1937), pp. 120–22.

States lost in one another would have been more accessible than before to outside producers.[15]

Reduction of the extent of division of labor between the customs union area and the outside world is the major objective and would be a major consequence of most projected customs unions, and would be a consequence in some degree of *any* customs union with protective duties, unless the duties on imports from outside the customs union were drastically cut upon establishment of the union. But Hawtrey should not leave out of consideration the increase in the extent to which division of labor *within* the customs union area prevails as the result of customs union.

## 2. *Customs Union and the "Terms of Trade"*

There is a possibility, so far not mentioned, of economic benefit from a tariff to the tariff-levying country which countries may be able to exploit more effectively combined in customs union than if they operated as separate tariff areas. This benefit to the customs area, however, carries with it a corresponding injury to the outside world. A tariff does not merely divert consumption from imported to domestically produced commodities—this is, from the free-trade point of view, the economic disadvantage of a tariff for the tariff-levying country and one of its disadvantages for the rest of the world—but it also alters in favor of the tariff-levying country the rate at which its exports exchange for the imports which survive the tariff, or its "terms of trade," and within limits—which may be narrow and which can never be determined accurately—an improvement in the national "terms of trade" carries with it an increase in the national total benefit from trade. The greater the economic area of the tariff-levying unit, the greater is likely to be, other things being equal, the improvement in its terms of trade with the outside world resulting from its tariff.[16] A customs union, by increasing the extent of the territory which operates

---

[15] R. G. Hawtrey, *Economic Destiny* (London [1944]), pp. 135–36.
[16] The greater the economic area of the tariff unit, other things equal, the greater is likely to be the elasticity of its "reciprocal demand" for outside products and the less is likely to be the elasticity of the "reciprocal demand" of the outside world for its products, and consequently the greater the possibility of improvement in its terms of trade through unilateral manipulation of its tariff.

under a single tariff, thus tends to increase the efficacy of the tariff in improving the terms of trade of that area vis-à-vis the rest of the world.

The terms of trade of a customs area with the outside world can be influenced not only by its own tariff but by the tariffs of other countries. The higher the tariffs of other countries on its export products, the less favorable, other things equal, will be the terms of trade of a customs area with the outside world. But the level of foreign tariffs can be affected in some degree through tariff-bargaining, and the larger the bargaining unit the more effective its bargaining can be. The Balkans, for instance, could have secured better terms from Nazi Germany during the 1930's if they had bargained collectively with Germany rather than singly. This consideration has been an important element in fostering aspirations on the part of small countries for customs union. An abundance of historical evidence is available to show how significant has been its role in the movement for tariff unification, whether in the customs union form or in other forms, although not as a rule expounded in the sophisticated language of the "terms of trade" argument. A few historical instances will be cited.

The argument that under the Articles of Confederation, which left each state with its separate tariff, the United States was at a serious disadvantage in dealing with the commercial policy of Europe, and especially of Britain, was current among the founding fathers of the Republic and helped to create readiness on the part of the public to accept a closer federal union with tariff policy centrally controlled.[17]

In 1819–1820, France imposed heavy import duties on cattle. Baden, Württemberg, and some of the Swiss cantons which were hard hit by these duties thereupon negotiated an agreement whereby they were to engage jointly in retaliatory measures against France. The

[17] Cf. the reports of the Committee on Commercial Policy, September 29, 1783, October 9, 1783, U. S. Continental Congress, *Journals of the Continental Congress 1774–1789*, W. C. Ford and Gaillard Hunt, *eds.* (Washington, 1904–37), XXV, 628–30, 661–64; message to President Washington by John Adams, Benjamin Franklin, and John Jay, from Paris, September 10, 1783, in *The Revolutionary Diplomatic Correspondence of the United States*, Francis Wharton, *ed.* (Washington, 1889), VI, 691; President Washington, August 22, 1785, as cited in O. L. Elliott, *The Tariff Controversy in the United States, 1789–1833* (Palo Alto, 1892), p. 46; the *Federalist* [1777–1778], No. XI; Joseph Story, *Commentaries on the Constitution*, Sections 1056–1073.

agreement was operative from 1822 to 1824, when it lapsed because of the refusal of some of the Swiss cantons to give their adherence to the agreement and its consequent conflict with the customs provisions of the Swiss constitution, which prohibited separate action on the part of the cantons but provided no procedures for assuring concerted action. This demonstration that without more centralization of Swiss tariff authority no effective tariff-bargaining policy could be carried out helped in preparing the way for the Swiss Constitution of 1848, which put commercial policy under Federal Government control.[18]

The movement which sprang up in Europe toward the end of the nineteenth century for a "United States of Europe" arose in large part from the widespread belief that only through some form of European economic union could the "American menace" be satisfactorily dealt with. Often invoked in support of the movement was the doctrine, expounded especially by the German historical school of economists, that small countries are at a serious disadvantage in commercial competition with large countries. But the movement focused more particularly on the unfavorable impact of American competition and American tariff policy on disunited Europe. Many aspects of American-European commercial relations were pointed to as calling for concerted defensive action: effective American competition, first with European agriculture as overseas freight costs fell and the American West was opened up, next with European manufacturing industries as large-scale exports by the United States of manufactured products made their appearance; the high and ever-rising American tariff; the refusal of the United States to participate in the network of commercial treaties by which European tariffs were being lowered or at least their rise checked; the adherence by the United States to the conditional interpretation of the most-favored-nation clause, whereby it was able to withhold from third countries what tariff concessions it did make to particular countries in "reciprocity" agreements, while claiming successfully the extension to imports from the United States of the concessions which European countries were

[18] Cf. Joseph Litschi, "Das Retorsions-Konkordat vom Jahre 1822," *Zeitschrift für schweizerische Statistik*, XXVIII (1892), 1–22; Werner Bleuler, *Studien über Aussenhandel und Handelspolitik der Schweiz* (Zurich, 1929), pp. 35–36; *Mémoires et souvenirs de Augustin–Pyramus de Candolle* (Geneva, 1862), p. 313.

making to each other; [19] the emergence of talk of customs union between the United States and Latin America; the export methods of
the new but lusty American "trusts"; and so forth.[20]

Since until the advent of the Roosevelt Administration there was
no improvement from the European point of view in American commercial policy, and the severity of American competition in world
trade was, if anything, more pronounced than ever before, the interwar phase of the movement for European union still retained, if less
pronouncedly and less frankly than before, a distinctly anti-American
orientation.[21]

### 3. *Administrative Economies of Customs Union*

#### (a) *The Removal of Internal Tariff Walls.*

The burdens on trade of a customs tariff, and its hindrances to
trade, arise not only from the actual levy of duties—which for all the

[19] For an explanation of how this was achieved, see Jacob Viner, "The Most-
Favored-Nation Clause in American Commercial Treaties," *loc. cit.*, pp. 119–20.

[20] No systematic study has apparently ever been made of the anti-American
orientation of the movement for European union, 1880 and earlier to 1914. For
comment by an American scholar, see George M. Fisk, "Continental Opinion
regarding a Proposed Middle European Tariff Union," *Johns Hopkins University Studies in Historical and Political Science*, XX (1902), Nos. 11–12. The
European source material is voluminous; the following items are representative:
Henri Richelot, *L'Association douanière allemande* (Paris, 1845), p. 22; Michel
Chevalier, "La guerre et la crise européenne," *Revue des deux mondes*, XXXVI[2]
(1866), 758–85; Alexander Peez (an Austrian and a leader in the movement),
*Die amerikanische Konkurrenz* (Leipzig, 1881), and "A propos de la situation
douanière en Europe," *Revue d'économie politique*, V (1891), especially p. 138;
Auguste Oncken, "L'Article onze du Traité de Paix de Francfort," *ibid.*, p. 602;
Edmond Théry, *Europe et Etats-Unis d'Amérique* (Paris, 1899), the preface
by Marcel Dubois; Ernst von Halle, "Das Interesse Deutschlands an der
amerikanischer Präsidentenwahl des Jahres 1896," *Jahrbuch für Gesetzgebung,
Verwaltung und Volkswirtschaft* ("Schmoller's *Jahrbuch*"), New Series,
XX (1896), 263–96; Gaston Domerque, "Le péril américain," *La réforme économique*, May 26, 1901, February 2, 1902, June 15, 1902, etc.; Richard Calwer,
*Die Meistbegünstigung der Vereinigten Staaten von Nordamerika* (Berlin,
1902); Rudolf Kobatsch, *La politique économique internationale* (Paris, 1913),
pp. 375–89. Cf. also L. Bosc, *op. cit.*, pp. 428–86.

[21] See, e.g., the report of a speech in Vienna in 1926 by Reichstag President
Loebe in M. Margaret Ball, *Post-War German-Austrian Relations; The Anschluss Movement, 1918–1936* (Stanford University, 1937), p. 72, and the comment of *Izvestia*, as reported in Kathryn W. Davis, *The Soviets at Geneva*
(Geneva, 1934), p. 227, note, on Briand's plan for European union, as primarily
a European defense against "American capitalist aggression on the one hand
and Bolshevist revolutionary aggressiveness on the other."

countries concerned taken in the aggregate are, of course, exactly off-set, in monetary terms at least, by the revenues accruing to the levying government—but also from the costs involved, for exporter and importer, in meeting the customs regulations, and the costs involved, for the tariff-levying government, in administering the customs machinery. These costs are often, in fact, more important than the duties themselves as hindrances to trade,[22] so that if the duties were lowered to a nominal level but the customs administrative code remained as before, the tariff could still constitute an important restriction on trade. But the United States is an outstanding offender in this respect. In the case of most other tariffs, their removal would not involve comparable administrative economies.

If a customs union were "complete" or "perfect," so that the tariff wall were completely removed between its members, this would constitute therefore an important relaxation of trade barriers between members of the union aside from the removal of the duties themselves as well as a reduction of administrative expense to the governments of the member countries, since the frontier—or frontiers—between them would no longer have to be watched for customs purposes.[23] The more important economically, and the longer or more difficult to watch, the removed tariff frontier was, the more important per unit volume of trade would be the administrative economies resulting from its removal. Given the economic area of the customs union, the larger also the number of tariff frontiers eliminated as a result of the formation of the union, the greater, other things equal, would be the administrative economies resulting therefrom per unit volume of trade. Customs union, however, even if complete, results in the full elimination for administrative purposes of tariff frontiers only if and to the extent that the territories of the members of the union are contiguous territories. Even if no third country intervenes between

---

[22] Cf. *Monthly Review, The Bank of Nova Scotia*, New Series, No. 26, Toronto, July, 1948: "Nor are the barriers against imports into the United States a matter of tariff rates alone. Canadian exporters have long maintained that the difficulties connected with U. S. customs procedures, the complexity of the regulations, and the delays and uncertainties arising out of their administration are in some cases an even greater hindrance to trade than the tariff rates themselves." See also R. Elberton Smith, *Customs Valuation in the United States* (Chicago, 1948).

[23] This assumes that import duties are the only deliberate trade barriers, or that quantitative restrictions, etc., are also removed.

two members of a customs union, the existence between them of "high seas" is sufficient to cut down, perhaps drastically, the administrative economies of customs union. "The sea, it is said, unites and does not separate, which is true in a sense, but is not true for the purpose of a Zollverein." [24] Customs unions, actual or projected, however, appear invariably to include only contiguous territory.[25]

It would be a mistake, however, to assume that the administrative changes consequent upon customs union all involve economies. Where the administration of the customs union is not entrusted wholly to one of the members of the union, there are additional burdens of negotiation, of coordination of codes, and of mutual supervision which may substantially reduce the net economies as well as give rise to political frictions. The necessity of coordination and of mutual supervision may force a standardization and simplification of duties which on other grounds may be undesirable. It has been suggested, for instance, that the number of countries which had a right to participate in the administration of the German Zollverein made it necessary to confine the Zollverein tariff mainly to specific duties, since the administrative task of assuring that ad valorem duties would be uniformly interpreted and applied at all the frontiers of the Zollverein would have been an almost insuperable one.[26]

Where excise taxes are important and customs union does not carry with it standardization of excise taxes throughout the territory of the union, the "tariff wall" between the members of the union, moreover, cannot wholly be removed, since otherwise the excise tax systems would be undermined by the flow of commodities affected from the untaxed, or low tax, areas to the tax, or higher tax, areas. In the earlier days of customs unions, this was a major problem in the negotiation and administration of such unions, since excise taxes were then relatively more important than they are today as sources of government revenue, and the texts of earlier customs union treaties

[24] Sir Robert Giffen, *Economic Inquiries and Studies* (London, 1904), II, 393.

[25] If the relations of metropolitan France with those of its colonies which are "assimilated" to France for tariff purposes, and the relations of the United States with Puerto Rico may be taken to constitute "customs union," they provide illustrative instances of the administrative economies of customs union being only partially available because of the existence of high seas between the members of the union.

[26] W. O. Henderson, *op. cit.*, p. 278.

show how much attention had to be given to this problem, and how complex were the administrative measures required to deal with it. The complexity of the problem may, in fact, have been a significant factor in preventing customs union agreements from being reached.[27] Even today, moreover, especially given the revival of resort on a large scale to indirect taxation as a source of government revenue, a good deal of the possible administrative economy of customs union would be likely to be lost if the establishment of uniformity of excise taxes did not accompany the formation of the customs union.

It may be objected that American experience demonstrates that this is not an important problem, since the absence of tariff walls between the States has proved to be consistent with the levy by the States of non-uniform excise taxes. But state excise taxes in the United States, though growing in range and severity, are still levied as a rule only on a very limited range of commodities and at very moderate rates. They have not been unassociated, moreover, with the development of troublesome and irritating equivalents of state tariff walls, which have rightly become a matter of growing concern.[28]

Furthermore, the growth under "central planning" of disguised inflation, non-equilibrium exchange rates, price controls, subsidies, and so forth, makes it impossible today completely to remove trade barriers unless economic union is carried far beyond the customs union stage. But this applies, probably with greater force, to general as well as to preferential removals of trade barriers.[29]

[27] Cf. G. de Molinari, "Union douanière de l'Europe," *Journal des économistes,* 4th Series, 2d year, V (1879), pp. 314-15: "The most serious difficulty, and we can even say the sole genuinely serious difficulty which the formation of an international *Zollverein* will face, rests in the standardization of excise régimes. This difficulty has not yet been entirely overcome in Germany, where there has not been achieved a uniform tax on beer and spirits, which has made necessary the maintenance of a frontier (*ligne*) for the protection of the excises between the North and the South."

[28] Cf. Frederick E. Melder, *State and Local Barriers to Interstate Commerce in the United States* (Orono, Maine, 1937), and U. S. Department of Commerce, Bureau of Foreign and Domestic Commerce, *Bibliography of Barriers to Trade between States* (Washington, 1942).

[29] Cf. Etienne Mantoux, *The Carthaginian Peace* (New York, 1946), p. 189: "whatever increases the economic significance of the State will inevitably increase the economic significance of frontiers. How, in the present trend of economic policy, it is possible to make insignificant frontiers coexist with all-pervading states is utterly beyond the present writer's powers of imagination."

(b) *The Elimination of Taxes on Goods in Transit.*

One type of economy associated with customs union, namely, the elimination of transit duties, and of ordinary import duties on goods in transit, for members of the union, which was once of great importance, is now of little or no significance.   In the early part of the nineteenth century, when transportation costs were high and the importance of using the lowest-cost route therefore great, heavy transit duties were common.   Countries in a favorable geographical position exploited to the full the opportunity to levy toll on commerce crossing their territories.   The exemption from transit duties on commerce crossing Prussian territory was a major inducement which Prussia could offer other German states to enter into customs union with her, since Prussian territory lay astride all the major routes for commerce between and through the German states to the north and the southern German states.[30]

Collection of duties on imported goods in transit to a third state, in conjunction with discriminatory railway rates, played an especially important role in the history of the movement toward customs union in South Africa.   The Transvaal and the Orange Free State—later the Orange River Colony—were shut off from direct access to the sea to the south by Cape Colony and Natal and elsewhere by absence of railroads or even roads.   The coastal colonies exploited their geographical position to the fullest extent which their rivalry with each

[30] A petition for customs union submitted in 1818 by a German group under the chairmanship of Friedrich List contains the following passage:

"To make a commercial shipment from Hamburg to Austria and from Berlin to Switzerland, one must cross ten states, study ten sets of customs regulations, pay six different transit duties.   He who has the misfortune to reside at a frontier where three or four states touch each other, passes his entire life bickering with customs officials; he has not got a fatherland."   Cited in J. Pentmann, *Die Zollunionsidee und ihre Wandlungen* (1917), p. 9.

Cf. also the dispatch to the Foreign Office from the British envoy to the German Diet, December, 1834, cited in Herbert C. F. Bell, *Lord Palmerston* (London, 1936), I, 159, from the British Foreign Office archives: ". . . hemmed in by a line of Custom Houses all round the Gates of the Town, its [Frankfort's] commercial intercourse with the interior of Germany was greatly harassed and restricted.   . . . its commerce and trade had already fallen off considerably, and . . . great apprehensions were entertained that its Fairs would be irretrievably injured unless the Union with Prussia was speedily effected; . . . the British Houses . . . finding their old customers deterred from frequenting the Fairs and their buyers diminish, had themselves become the advocates of the Union with Prussia. . . ."

THE ECONOMICS OF CUSTOMS UNIONS     63

other permitted by levying their full import duties on imports from outside Africa passing to the interior republics through their territory and also by charging heavier rates for transportation on their railways of commodities coming from overseas than for competing commodities of their own production.[31] At one time the Transvaal, under Oom Paul Kruger, sought escape from these exactions by building a railroad to Delagoa Bay in Portuguese East Africa and, to force traffic from overseas to take the Delagoa Bay route, imposed heavy freight rates on the portion of the Cape-to-Johannesburg railroad which lay within Transvaal territory. The Orange Free State did not have even this alternative available, and its only defense was in its ability to thwart the railway-building plans of the coastal colonies by excluding their lines from its territory. "But much as he [President Brand of the Free State] wanted the money, he wanted the railways more. The colonies knew it and continued to rob the republic." [32]

It might be supposed that these were just the types of evil in commercial relations for which customs union would provide an effective remedy. But when the South African Customs Union Conventions of 1903 and 1906 were negotiated, the former Boer republics, defeated in war, had not yet been given responsible government, and were represented at the negotiations by British officials. It was not until the establishment of political union between the four colonies in 1910 that the allocation of customs revenues and the structure of railway

[31] The treatment of sugar by Natal was a notorious example. Cf. Transvaal, *Report of the Customs & Industries Commission* (Pretoria, 1908), p. 5: "Natal sugar is carried at a very much lower rate than sugar imported from oversea, the result being that the further inland the sugar travels the higher the protection afforded against the oversea traffic. In consequence of this and of the fact that the production of sugar in Natal is far below the consumption of the Union, the bulk of the sugar produced is sent inland to the Transvaal, Orange River and Cape Colonies, while Natal very largely imports sugar from oversea for its own consumption; on these importations the Natal Government collects and retains duties amounting to a considerable sum, to a large proportion of which the Transvaal Government is fairly entitled." Cf. also the Memorandum prepared by the Earl of Selborne, January, 1907, in A. P. Newton, *ed.*, *Select Documents relating to the Unification of South Africa* (London, 1924), II, 418. This was *after* customs union was established, and was possible because the customs union agreement left to each territory, with some exceptions, the customs duties collected within that territory.

[32] Jean Van der Poel, *Railway and Customs Policies in South Africa 1885–1910* (London, 1933), pp. 11–12.

rates ceased to be patently unfair to the Transvaal and the Orange Free State.[33]

For European countries, the revolution in transportation which occurred in the nineteenth century resulted in shippers as a rule not being confined to single practicable routes and therefore deprived countries of the power of exacting as monopolists high tolls on transit trade, and, instead, caused them to eliminate transit duties and to compete for transit traffic by improving traffic facilities, lowering freight rates on railroads, and reducing administrative obstructions to economical transportation. By the end of the century transit duties had almost wholly disappeared in Europe. They were outlawed for signatory countries by the Covenant of the League of Nations, and by the Barcelona Conference on Communications and Transit of 1921. Article 33 of the Havana Charter reproduces and strengthens the provisions for freedom of transit of the Barcelona Conference.

The elimination of transit duties is, indeed, the only significant nineteenth-century reform in the field of commercial policy which is surviving unimpaired in the twentieth century; to economic developments which make almost any country's departure from freedom of transit patently unprofitable to it, rather than to international diplomacy, the progress of economic enlightenment, or the will to international economic cooperation, belongs the credit. The improvement of transportation facilities which, by opening up the possibility of competition between alternative routes for the transit business, led to the

---

[33] In addition to the references given above, A. J. Bruwer, *Protection in South Africa* (Stellenbosch, 1923), a University of Pennsylvania doctoral dissertation, can be profitably consulted. There is an extensive bibliography in Bruwer of literature published up to 1921.

The fear that the United States would resume the collection of customs duties on traffic from Europe to the Province of Canada (i.e., Ontario and Quebec) was an important contributory factor to the formation of the Canadian Confederation. An Act of Congress of 1845 provided for drawbacks of customs duties on through traffic to Canada across American territory and other legislation granted such traffic the privilege of transit in bond without payment of duties. It was feared in Canada that, with the Southern states for the time being deprived of a voice in Congress and the North aggressive because of anti-British animosity and annexationist ambitions, these privileges would be withdrawn. Canadian Confederation would make possible construction of a railway route to the Atlantic wholly in Canadian territory. Cf. Donald C. Masters, *The Reciprocity Treaty of 1854* (London, 1937), p. 229, and R. G. Trotter, *Canadian Federation* (Toronto, 1924), pp. 126 ff. In this case, the duties on transit trade levied by one state operated to foster unification of *other* states.

elimination of transit duties, by intensifying competition between countries also led to a general raising of tariffs.[34]  For the customs union question the significance of this development is that the formation of customs unions no longer has a major contribution to make to the freeing of transit trade from artificial burdens.

## 4. *Revenue Duties*

In the discussion so far, the question of revenue duties has not been dealt with.  If the revenue yield of the tariff as a whole is substantial for one or more of the countries entering into customs union, this will complicate the problem of negotiation of the union.  If the revenue yield of the customs union tariff is substantial, there will be the problem of how to allocate these revenues between the members.  These problems will be considered in a subsequent section.

In so far as the effect of the formation of customs unions on international specialization in production is concerned, the existence of revenue duties raises no new question of principle.  It is not easy sharply to distinguish between revenue duties and protective duties. For present purposes, revenue duties may be regarded as those duties productive of revenue which do not act as effective stimulus to the domestic production of commodities *similar* to those paying the duties. Even such duties, however, if they are not offset by general excises on commodities of domestic production, operate to increase the proportion of aggregate domestic consumption which is directed toward domestically produced commodities.  The only differences, then, between revenue duties and protective duties which are significant for present purposes is that revenue duties have only a generalized protective effect, whereas protective duties have both this generalized effect and a specific effect in stimulating the domestic production of commodities similar to those subject to the protective duty, with the consequence that protective duties tend to be more effective than

---

[34] Cf. G. de Molinari, "Union douanière le l'Europe centrale," *loc. cit.*, p. 318: "Is it not absurd to pay at the same time engineers to facilitate the transport of persons and merchandise, and customs officers to make it more difficult?"

In a memorandum of 1815 to the Government of the Canton of Geneva, Sismondi argued that the widened range of transportation routes which had become available made it impracticable for Geneva to levy transit duties. See Jean-R. De Salis, *Sismondi 1775–1842; Lettres et documents inédits* (Paris, 1932), p. 23.

revenue duties as restraints on importation. Revenue duties can be regarded therefore as the equivalent of protective duties of slight effectiveness, or a high revenue duty may be regarded as the equivalent of a moderate protective duty, for present purposes.

The existence of revenue duties, therefore, does not make it necessary to change in any respect the conclusions as to the effect of customs union on international specialization reached on the basis of the assumption that there were no revenue duties. If a customs union should be established, however, between two countries which before had only revenue duties and if all the duties levied by the customs union continue to operate as "pure" revenue duties, the appraisal of the customs union would turn chiefly on its administrative economies or inconveniences, or on political aspects, and the foregoing analysis would be largely irrelevant for it. Some of the intercolonial customs unions are wholly or substantially in this category.[35]

## 5. *The "Level" of the Customs Union Tariff*

Whatever tendency the formation of a customs union may have to lessen the extent of international specialization, the lower the rates of duty in the customs union tariff, the less effect of this kind, other things equal, will it have.

Resolutions in favor of customs union often have a proviso that the customs union tariff should not be "higher" than the tariffs of the member countries prior to the formation of the union. The Havana Charter (Article 44, paragraph 2) sanctions the formation of customs union without the requirement of prior approval by the International Trade Organization provided the duties (and other restrictions) on imports into the union are "not on the whole . . . higher or more restrictive than the general incidence" of the duties (and other restrictions) on imports of the member countries prior to the formation of such union. What meaning can be given to such provisos?

There is no way in which the "height" of a tariff as an index of its restrictive effect can be even approximately measured, or, for that

---

[35] The fear that customs union would result in loss of revenues has sometimes operated for both the prospective members as a factor against proceeding with customs union negotiations. It is of course a probable result where the prospective members have a large volume of dutiable trade with each other before customs union, and also where customs union will divert a large amount of import trade from outside countries to member countries.

matter, even defined with any degree of *significant* precision.[36]   It is possible to say that some proposed methods of measurement are less illogical than others.   It may be possible to say, after careful examination and in the light of extensive background information, that one tariff is clearly higher than another.   But it is scarcely possible to find a way of measuring the relative height in quantitative terms of two tariffs.   An identical tariff might be high for one country or at one time and low for another country or at another time.

In the case of a customs union, if its tariff is made up of the highest rates on each class of imports previously levied by either (or any) of the member countries—and still more if the customs union rates are set even higher than this—the new tariff is clearly "more restrictive" of imports from outside the union than were the previous tariffs. But even if the new tariff is made up of the *lowest* rates previously levied by either (or any) of the member countries on each class of imports dutiable in both, it may still be "more restrictive" in fact, whether or not in the intent of the Havana Charter provision, than the previous tariffs, because customs union operates to convert revenue duties to protective duties.[37]   Some part of an old higher rate may

[36] Cf. Jacob Viner, "The Measurement of the 'Height' of Tariff Levels," Joint Committee, Carnegie Endowment–International Chamber of Commerce, *The Improvement of Commercial Relations between Nations* (Paris, 1936), pp. 58–68.

[37] There is little likelihood that the Havana Charter provision will be given so exacting an interpretation.   In the Benelux customs union, the new level of duties is commonly said to be about half-way between the (lower) rates of the previous Netherlands tariff and the (higher) rates of the previous Belgium-Luxemburg tariff, although this is true only in a limited sense.   The Dutch tariff of 1934 comprised only 160 dutiable classes of items, and all unenumerated articles were exempt from duty.   The Belgian tariff listed many more dutiable articles, and moreover made subject to duty all items not expressly exempted.   In the Benelux tariff it is only on items which were common to the two tariffs that the new rates are half-way between the previous Netherlands and the previous Belgium-Luxemburg tariff rates, and all items not expressly exempted are made dutiable.   The new tariff is therefore much closer to the previous higher Belgian tariff than to the previous Netherlands tariff.   The relations between the old and the new tariffs are in fact more complicated than this indicates, because of changes in classification, the substitution of ad valorem for specific duties, and other factors.   Examination of the old and the new tariffs by an American expert has resulted in the conclusion that "it may be stated generally that the Benelux Tariff is more protectionist than the Netherlands tariff, and that it apparently is not less protectionist than the Belgo-Luxembourg tariff." W. Buchdahl, "The New 'Benelux' Union—Western Europe Tariff Pattern?"

have been ineffective for the country levying it because even a lower rate would have been completely prohibitive of imports, while the lower rate of the other country may previously have been low enough to permit imports from third countries, whereas now, because of preferential treatment of imports from the other member country, it operates to exclude imports from third countries completely, or at least more completely than before. Thus a customs union tariff which, in the interpretations commonly given to "level of tariff," is lower than the average level of the previous tariffs of the member countries, and even one which is lower than either (or any) of these tariffs, may still be "more restrictive" of imports into the customs union territory from outside that territory than were the previous tariffs of the member countries. But customs union tariffs have not typically been "low" even in these senses of the term.

## 6. *Increased Tariff Protection as the Major Economic Objective of Customs Unions*

The tariff unification movement, in the nineteenth century and since, in so far as it culminated in actual arrangements or at least reached the stage of serious negotiations on an official basis, was primarily a movement to make high protection feasible and effective for limited areas going beyond the frontiers of single states, and to promote self-sufficiency for these larger areas because self-sufficiency for single states was clearly impracticable or too costly; it was not a movement to promote the international division of labor. It would be exceedingly difficult to demonstrate this, partly because clear definition and statement of objectives is often not essential for nor even helpful to effective negotiation, partly because there were obvious and weighty reasons why it would have been inexpedient to attract attention to

---

U. S. Department of Commerce, *Foreign Commerce Weekly,* October 11, 1947, pp. 3–5, 32. Since the increase in protection is not overt and unambiguous, however, there has been no suggestion from any quarter that this involves any conflict with the Havana Charter. An American Congressional Subcommittee has commented: "This procedure of establishing new common tariffs at, roughly, the average of the old tariffs is in accordance with the draft charter of the International Trade Organization." U. S. Congress, House Select Committee on Foreign Aid, Subcommittee on France and the Low Countries, Preliminary Report Twenty-Four, *The Belgian-Luxemburg-Netherlands Customs and Economic Union* (1948), p. 2.

this phase of the movement.    There is nevertheless no lack of circumstantial evidence to support this interpretation.    This objective becomes explicit here and there in the literature of advocacy of customs unions,[38] and underlies all of the nineteenth century literature favoring European Economic Union as a means of coping with American competition.    It reveals itself in the special provisions in customs union agreements intended to check the intensification of competition between the member areas which would otherwise result from the arrangement.[39]    The aversion to opening their markets to the competition from each other's industries has been the chief factor economic in character which was responsible for so few customs unions actually being consummated when so many projects were launched.

Where of two potential members of a customs union one is predominantly free-trade or low-tariff in interest and sentiment while the other is protectionist and provides only a negligible market for the staple exports of the first, the low-tariff territory will not voluntarily enter into the union except as part of a political union and for predominantly political reasons, and even after it has entered it is likely to find the union economically irksome because the chief economic consequence of the union is to make its territory an additional field of operation for the tariff protection of its partner's industries.    Such has been largely the case for the Transvaal and the Orange River Colony vis-à-vis the South African Customs Union, for the Prairie Provinces of Canada vis-à-vis Canadian Confederation, for Western Australia in relation to the Australian Commonwealth.    Such was also the case for

[38] Cf. especially Henry Masson, "Les unions douanières," an extract from the Report of the Congrès International d'Expansion Economique Mondiale, held at Mons, Belgium, 1905.

[39] The role of the "Zwischenzoll" in the history of the Austro-Hungarian Customs Union is especially pertinent here.    The major difficulty in keeping the customs union intact arose out of the insistence of the members, and especially of Hungary, that the customs union should not remove the barriers to competition between the members.    Cf. Rudolf Sieghart, *Zolltrennung und Zolleinheit: Die Geschichte der österreichisch ungarischen Zwischenzoll-linie* (Vienna, 1915) ; Ivor L. Evans, "Economic Aspects of Dualism in Austria-Hungary," *The Slavonic Review,* VI (1927–28), 529–42; Louis Eisenmann, *Le compromis austro-hongrois de 1867; étude sur le dualisme* (Paris, 1904) ; Joseph Grunzel, *Handelspolitik und Ausgleich in Österreich-Ungarn* (Vienna, 1912), especially pp. 115, 224, 237. For the manipulation of railway rates within Austria-Hungary, as a substitute for internal import duties, see Ivor Evans, *op. cit.,* p. 539.

the Southern States in relation to the American Federal Union prior
to the industrialization of the South.   Such was for a time at least the
case with respect to the Swiss Federal Union.[40]   It was largely true
also in the history of the German Zollverein, although Prussia for a
variety of reasons—partial conversion to free-trade views, willingness
to make economic concessions in order to establish a base for eventual
political unification, readiness to keep the Zollverein tariff low in order
to lessen Austrian determination to obtain entrance to it—for a time
supported a low-tariff policy for the Zollverein.

The Tanganyika-Kenya Customs Union provides a striking instance where a territory was brought into a customs union by external
authority in order to provide an expanded field for the tariff protection
of the industries of another territory.[41]   Tanganyika, captured by the
British from the Germans in World War I, is a mandate territory.
The British first introduced a new tariff in Tanganyika in 1921, higher
than the German one, and then in 1923 changed the tariff again, making it identical with the still higher tariff of the Kenya-Uganda customs union, while abolishing the customs barriers between the three
territories, all in preparation for full customs union.   In 1927 full
customs union was established, despite questioning from the British
Governor of Tanganyika as to its suitability to the mandate's economic
interests.   The customs union operated to create a protected market
in Tanganyika for the produce of the small colony of British planters

[40] Cf. Werner Bleuler, *Studien über Aussenhandel und Handelspolitik der
Schweiz* (Zurich, 1929), p. 37, with reference to the situation in Switzerland in
the 1830's:
"These free-trade traditions, in conjunction with the hereditary federalist
views were an obstacle to the tariff unification of the land; for the economic
controversy, Free Trade versus Protection, stood in the then prevailing opinion
and circumstances in close connection with the political issue Federalism versus
Centralization.   The attitude was widespread that a unified Swiss tariff policy
would at the same time be a protectionist one.   People said to themselves, a
unification of the customs would work in two ways: first it would reduce the
political autonomy of the Cantons and would make openings for centralizing
activities in other spheres, and second it would have the consequence that they
would be gradually drawn into the channel of protectionist politics.   Thus both
the convinced Free traders and the extreme Federalists were opposed to the
unification movement."
[41] The relation of the Transvaal and the Orange River Colony to the South
African Customs Union provides an analogous earlier instance.   See *supra*, pp.
62 ff.

in Kenya, for whose welfare the British Government has shown a constant and marked solicitude. To reinforce the tariff in providing a preferential market for Kenya produce in Tanganyika, a system of preferential rates on the railways, under which commodities of external origin paid higher rates than customs-union produce, also was introduced. After an investigation of the operation of the customs union on behalf of the British Colonial Office, Sir Sydney Armitage-Smith, an economist of repute and an objective civil servant, reached the conclusion that "Tanganyika should take steps forthwith to levy customs import duty at the same rates on foodstuffs imported from Kenya and Uganda as those chargeable on foodstuffs imported from foreign parts, and should cease to deplete her revenue and impoverish her citizens by protecting the products of her neighbours." [42]

The progressive contraction in range of application and decline in efficacy of the most-favored-nation clause have increased the range of special commercial arrangements which permit concerted action to restrict imports from countries outside the arrangement without involving either the removal of the barriers to competition between the members or sharp conflict with most-favored-nation obligations to third countries. A significant illustration is provided by the Argentine-Brazil commercial treaty of November, 1941, and the Argentine-Chile trade agreement of August, 1943, both designated as providing a base for eventual customs union, and both clearly and frankly designed to extend the effective area of protection from external competition of the industries of the participant countries without increasing the competition between the industries of the two countries. The crucial provisions in the Argentine-Brazil treaty are the following:

ARTICLE I.—I. The High Contracting Parties undertake to promote, stimulate and facilitate the installation in their respective countries of industrial and agricultural and livestock activities as yet not in existence in either of the two, mutually undertaking:

[42] "Report by Sir Sydney Armitage-Smith, on a Financial Mission to Tanganyika, 26th September, 1932. Presented by the Secretary of State for the Colonies to Parliament, October, 1932." British Parliamentary Papers, Cmd. 4182, 1932, p. 25. See also Charlotte Leubuscher, *Tanganyika Territory; A Study of Economic Policy under Mandate* (London, 1944), pp. 101–20, for an excellent treatment of this problem. Miss Leubuscher criticizes the League of Nations Mandates Commission for not giving sufficient attention to the economic effects of the customs union.

(*a*) Not to collect import duties during a period of ten years from the date of the entry into force of this Treaty on the products of such new activities;

.     .     .     .     .

(*c*) To arrive at protective measures with respect to competition by similar products from other sources when these can be classed as "dumping."

2. For the purposes of this Treaty industrial and agricultural and livestock activities described as non-existent are those not installed in either of the two countries at the date of the signature of this Treaty.

3. In order to enjoy the advantages provided for herein, the articles not included in the list referred to in Article IV will be considered not produced in either of the two countries.

ARTICLE II.  With respect to the articles produced in one of the two countries or which are of little economic importance in one of them the High Contracting Parties undertake not to apply, during a period of ten years from the date of entry into force of this Treaty, duties of a protectionist nature on imports, but rather, on the contrary, to grant them special preference, not to be extended to other suppliers.

.     .     .     .     .

ARTICLE III.  The High Contracting Powers mutually agree to extend the benefits of the preceding Article to those products of economic importance customs tariffs on which may be gradually reduced or eliminated without affecting present production or national economy.

ARTICLE IV.  In order to put into effect the preceding provisions, the High Contracting Parties undertake to draw up, within a term of six months from the date of the signature of this Treaty, a list of all the articles already produced in each country, indicating the economic importance of such production, that is to say: the number of factories, capital invested, value and volume of present production, maximum capacity of production, total consumption of such products in the country, and other facts of interest for the study of the form in which free trade may be established between the two countries without affecting existing production and national economy.

ARTICLE VIII.  The High Contracting Parties will appoint, once the lists referred to in Article IV have been exchanged, the organisms in charge of putting into practice the provisions of the present Treaty.[48]

The Argentine-Chile treaty was similar in character.  The essential feature of both treaties was that they provided for removal or relaxation of trade barriers on a preferential basis only for such commodities

[48] *Customs Unions, 1947,* pp. 92–93.  The Spanish text corresponding to the words "special preference" in Article II reads: *"favores especiales de países limítrofes." Informaciones argentinas,* December 15, 1941, p. 3.

THE ECONOMICS OF CUSTOMS UNIONS **73**

as involved little or no competition between themselves, and to effectuate this, provided for the non-competitive development of new industries. Later, apparently, Chile closed with Brazil an agreement by which Brazil undertook not to establish a domestic nitrate industry, and with the Argentine an agreement by which the Argentine obligated itself for a minimum period of ten years to use only Chilean nitrates [44]—developments in the same direction.

The development of quantitative restrictions on imports has facilitated the removal of tariff barriers between pairs of countries without involving the opening of each other's territory to full competition from the industries of the other. The Benelux Customs Union Agreement, signed at London September 5, 1944, which as revised by the Hague Protocol of March 14, 1947, came into operation on January 1, 1948, provided for removal of tariff duties between the members and a common tariff against imports from the outside world, but left intact, except as subsequently to be altered by mutual agreement, the whole machinery of import quotas, import licenses, special license dues and administrative fees, and subsidies, both with respect to imports from outside the Union and with respect to the intra-Union trade. These devices can, in principle, be so operated as to make an economic union confined to ordinary tariffs operate in such a way as to involve no over-all relaxation in the effective barriers to competition between the industries of the member countries.

In the planning for further economic unification now in process, distinction is being made between "complementary," "parallel," and potentially or actually "rival" industries, and it seems clear from press reports that it is intended on both sides to provide, at least for a lengthy transition period, obstacles to free competition within the customs union area of rival industries.

For an important list of industries,[45] the governments must consult in the Council of the Economic Union before they sanction expansion. Likewise, there is a Committee for Industrial Development in which representatives of the three governments sit with delegates of trade

---

[44] *New York Times,* April 24, 1943, dispatch from Santiago.
[45] Window glass, carbonic acid, copper sulphate, explosives, coal and coke, sodium carbonate, steel, ball-bearings, steel balls, chains, plywood, furniture, strawboard, cement, rubber manufactures, sugar manufactures, rice-hulling, vegetable oils, flour-milling, beer, nitrogen.

organizations to deal with the same problem.   There will also be, on a third level, reliance on government-sanctioned cartel agreements to restrain competition within the customs-union area between rival national industries.[46]

The negotiations for a Franco-Italian Customs Union now in progress are following similar lines.   The First Joint Commission, acting in accordance with instructions received in September, 1947, in its Report of December 22, 1947, stated in unexceptional if vague terms the function of a customs union:

> The purpose of a customs union is essentially to permit, by virtue of the establishment of a more extensive economic territory, a division of labor more developed, better adapted to the existing natural and economic conditions, and consequently a more abundant and lower-cost production destined for a greater market.[47]

As the Report proceeds to examine particular products, however, it finds difficulties everywhere except where the economies of the two countries are "complementary" (that is, where customs union would operate to extend the area of effective protection against competition from outside) ; and where industries are parallel or are rival, it emphasizes the need for regulation and understandings for coordinated export of their products and for coordinated import of their raw materials, to avoid competition in trade with the outside world.   To avoid "dangerous competition" *within* the Union, allocation of capital and raw materials, industrial agreements, and other unspecified measures are suggested, but the general drift of the discussion of this problem, though vague at crucial points, indicates that full economic unification of the area, with competition between the areas as free—or as restricted—as within each area, is the long-run goal.[48]

The Second Joint Commission, set up in June, 1948, has recently submitted its report, and negotiations are proceeding toward an even-

[46] See "Benelux . . . An Example of Unity in a Divided World," *Rotterdamsche Bank Quarterly Review*, 1947, No. 4, pp. 5–42, and "Benelux and Industrial Development," *Amsterdamsche Bank Quarterly Review*, No. 80, April, 1948, p. 15.

[47] Commission Mixte Franco-Italienne pour l'Etude d'une Union Douanière entre la France et l'Italie, *Rapport final* (Paris: Imprimerie Nationale, 1948), p. 6.

[48] *Ibid.*, pp. 48–49.

tual customs union on the basis of the procedures recommended by this report. Here also the problem of "rival" industries receives emphasis. An interim period is contemplated when competition between the industries of the two countries will be restricted by compensatory taxes in the country of lower costs, by cartel agreements, and by regulated specialization in types of products. For the long run, however, the issue of rival industries is more frankly faced and competition between them within the Union accepted as unavoidable:

Certainly the Customs Union between France and Italy will derive its chief interest from the competition which this Union will establish between the two economies, which are only, as is known, very partially complementary. It is to be expected that there will result from this competition a more developed specialization, either because each country extends its production of those commodities for which it is better situated naturally, or because within the same category of products the two countries agree to specialize on specified types.[49]

### 7. Cartels in Relation to Customs Unions

There has long been an association of sorts between the tariff union idea and the international cartel idea as remedies through international cooperation for the problems arising in European countries from "excessive competition" in their markets from other countries, usually the United States.[50] This association has perhaps most often taken the form of rivalry, but frequently enough the two ideas became combined to constitute joint elements in a single plan for lessening the severity of international competition. Beginning with the preparatory work for the Geneva Economic Conference of 1927, proposals came from many sources for sponsorship of international cartelization, both as a method of international economic cooperation which would lessen the need for attempts to lower tariff barriers by multilateral agreement and as a method of making tariff reduction safe for high-cost domestic industries. The French were most prominent in furthering these ideas, but they received more or less qualified support

[49] *Compte Rendu de la Commission Mixte Franco-Italienne d'Union Douanière, Paris, le 22 janvier 1949* (Paris: Imprimerie Nationale, 1949), p. 96.
[50] See Harry D. Gideonse, "Economic Foundations of Pan-Europeanism," *Annals of the American Academy of Political and Social Science*, CXLIX (1930), for the early association of these ideas.

from the International Chamber of Commerce and from League of Nations committees and conferences. M. Louis Loucheur, French Minister of Commerce, who was the original sponsor and one of the main participants in the Geneva Economic Conference, was an enthusiastic protagonist of international cartels and of international tariff agreements to facilitate their operation as means of lessening international competition, and the documentation and proceedings of the conference show that his ideas received substantial support. But for the most part the discussion remained on an abstract level.[51]

With the coming of the depression, the search for means of alleviating its impact on Europe through international collaboration led to a revival of the discussion, under League of Nations auspices, of cartels in relation to European "economic union." Various committees and conferences of the League of Nations gave support simultaneously to international cartelization and to multilateral agreements to lower trade barriers, but there was apparently only one definite proposal to link the two together as related parts of a single project.

This proposal was made by the French Government to a meeting of the League Commission of Enquiry for European Union in May, 1931. A strengthening and extension of international cartel agreements was to be sponsored. Since strong cartels reserve the national markets for the domestic producers of the respective acceding countries and limit imports to agreed quotas and prices, tariffs become unnecessary to protect national industries. The lowering of tariffs, therefore, becomes possible without adversely affecting the national economies. However, "the producers in countries which were not

---

[51] Some of the references to the idea that the multiplication of international cartels would facilitate the reduction of tariffs by reducing the need for them made in the course of the Geneva Economic Conference apparently were related to expositions of the idea which M. Loucheur had made outside the conference. After a series of eulogies of international cartels had been presented in the meetings of the Industry Committee of the conference, a Soviet delegate, Mr. Sokolnikoff, made the following pertinent comment:

"Industrial and commercial ententes would not lead to social and economic peace. The danger of a rise in prices was only too real. This was shown by the fact that it was being proposed to replace Customs Tariffs, the object of which was to maintain prices at a high level, by cartellisation, which enabled the same result to be attained by more modern methods." League of Nations, *Report and Proceedings of the World Economic Conference*, Geneva, 1927 (Document C.356.M.129.1927.II), II, 152.

disposed to take part in international agreements would not be allowed to benefit from Customs exemptions." Moreover, the tariff reductions would amount to a bounty to all who voluntarily accepted the discipline of the cartel.[52] The French proposed that the League and the governments take the cartel agreements under their sponsorship and stimulate the private efforts in this direction. These agreements would be less difficult to negotiate than a simultaneous multilateral reduction of tariffs, and would be better than a customs union. Tariffs would be retained, since they would be needed to forestall dumping, but the duties collected could be refunded with respect to all products carrying a cartel certificate.[53]

Nothing came immediately from the French proposal of 1931, but the idea it expounded did not die.[54] In the negotiations for the further development of Benelux, and in the negotiations for the formation of a Franco-Italian customs union, it is clear that much reliance is being placed on cartel agreements, sanctioned and probably also participated in by the member governments, both to eliminate competition in the import and export trade with non-members and to keep within bounds the rivalry for the customs union market between the industries of the respective member countries.[55]

There seems likelihood, therefore, that in the framing of future customs unions and in the development of existing ones, cartel agreements or their equivalent will be used as supplement or substitute for other means of assuring that the removal of the tariff wall between the members of the customs union shall not result in more increase of

[52] It is not clear to the present writer how a bounty would result for cartel members in non-exporting countries.

[53] League of Nations, Commission of Enquiry for European Union, *Minutes of the Third Session of the Commission*, May 15–21, 1931 (Document C.395. M.158.1931.VII), pp. 16–24; 79–88.

[54] In a 1937 Report, the Economic Committee of the League of Nations drew attention to the possibility of using cartel agreements as a substitute for prohibitive tariffs in dealing with competition from low-cost producers. "It may be pointed out that this difficulty could be met if arrangements could be reached between the industries concerned which would give an assurance against such excessive competition. Quotas applied solely as guarantees for these arrangements are not open to criticism." League of Nations, Economic Committee, *Remarks on the Present Phase of International Economic Relations*, September, 1937 (Document C.358.M.242.1937.II.B), pp. 14–15.

[55] See *supra*, pp. 73–75.

competition between the industries of the respective member countries than is desired.   It is also likely, on the basis of the past record, that a minimum of increase in such competition will be desired.   This is a reasonable forecast, I think, despite the fact that the Havana Charter contains the statement (Article 44, paragraph 1) that the members "recognize that the purpose of a customs union or free-trade area should be to facilitate trade between the parties and not to raise barriers to the trade of other Member countries with such parties."

## 8. *The Allocation of Customs Revenues*

Whenever customs revenues are important, the method of their allocation as between members of a customs union is almost certain to become a major issue,[56] which has a close counterpart in the controversies which have always arisen in federal unions over the distribution of revenues, or the allocation of taxation rights, as between the central and the regional political authorities.   The greater the disparity in economic levels between the members, and the greater the differences as between the members in the customary consumption of imported commodities, the greater is likely to be the difficulty in finding a formula for allocation of customs receipts which will be mutually acceptable.

In the German Zollverein the simplest possible formula of allocation, namely, according to population, was found generally practicable, but modification was necessary in at least two instances for members with relatively high per capita income levels and with specially important trade relations outside the Zollverein; the City of Frankfort was allotted a share in the Zollverein customs receipts approximately four and a half times what it would have been entitled to on a population basis, while the rural districts of Frankfort received a lesser supplement; Hanover also was allowed a supplement.   The problem of allocation of revenues as between Germany and Austria arising out of the different economic levels of the two regions was stated by Bismarck in 1864 to constitute an insurmountable obstacle to customs union with Austria:

---

[56] For details as to methods of allocating customs revenues in customs unions, see T. E. Gregory, *Tariffs: A Study in Method* (London, 1921), pp. 16–18, and *Customs Unions*, *1947*, pp. 17–19.

I regarded a customs union as an impracticable Utopia on account of the differences in the economic and administrative conditions of both parties. The commodities which formed the financial basis of the customs union in the north do not come into use at all in the greater part of Austro-Hungarian territory. The difficulties which the differences in habits of life and in consumption between North and South Germany brought about even now within the Zollverein, would be insurmountable, if both districts were to be included in the same customs boundary with the eastern provinces of Austria-Hungary. A fairer scale of distribution, or one more corresponding with the existing consumption of dutiable goods, could not be arrived at; every scale would be either unfair to the Zollverein, or unacceptable to public opinion in Austria-Hungary. There is no common measure of taxation for the Slovack or Galician with his few wants on the one side, and on the other for the inhabitant of the Rhenish provinces and of Lower Saxony.[57]

In the customs unions in which British Crown Colonies participated, as well as in some other customs unions, allocation was in general according to place of consumption. This formula would be difficult to apply either where imported raw materials were processed in one member territory for sale in another, or where wholesale distribution was concentrated in one territory. Two instances can be cited where the application of this formula gave rise either to difficulties of administration or to complaints of inequitable division of revenues.

When the Australian Commonwealth was established, the States were for a five-year period allotted shares in the customs revenue collections of the Commonwealth in proportion to consumption within the States of the imported commodities. Application of this formula involved elaborate bookkeeping, extremely burdensome administrative red tape, and extensive controversy.[58]

In the case of the customs union between Ruanda-Urundi, a territory under League of Nations mandate to Belgium, and the Belgian-Congo, duties collected on imports are credited to the territory of destination, which in application is taken to be the territory of last wholesale transaction. A member of the Mandates Commission, Mr. Merlin, in 1926 objected that the wholesale destination was often the

[57] *Bismarck the Man and the Statesman; Being the Reflections and Reminiscences of Otto Prince von Bismarck,* translated from the German under the supervision of A. J. Butler (London, 1898), I, 377–78.

[58] See Stephen Mills, *Taxation in Australia* (London, 1925), pp. 200–1.

80                    THE CUSTOMS UNION ISSUE

Belgian Congo when the ultimate consumption was in Ruanda-Urundi. To this the Belgian representative before the Commission replied "that the situation explained by M. Merlin was the inevitable result of the Customs union the establishment of which was permitted by the mandate, and the consequences of which it was necessary to accept." [59]

In the various South African customs unions where allocation was according to consumption, the territory in which the import duties were actually collected was allowed a fraction of the receipts as compensation for administrative expense.  In the Poland-Danzig Customs Union, which was established under League of Nations auspices in accordance with provisions in the Treaty of Peace with Germany following World War I, the allocation of customs revenues was to be by agreement between Poland and Danzig, but with consumption to be taken into account.  Agreement was reached that division of total revenues was to be presumptively in accordance with per capita consumption, but that it was to be assumed that average consumption per head in Danzig was six times that in Poland; this arrangement was to be reconsidered at three-year intervals.[60]

In other customs unions receipts were divided according to agreed percentages (e.g., Austria-Modena, 1852; Austria-Liechtenstein, 1852), or a lump sum per annum allocation was made to a small member (e.g., Prussia-Schwarzburg, 1819; Italy-Albania, 1939), or special modifications were made in the allocation-by-consumption or allocation-by-collections formulas.  In the Austro-Hungarian Customs Union, as in other cases where customs union was associated with political union, no provision was made for division of customs revenue.  In the Austro-Hungarian case, not only did all the customs revenue go into the Dual Kingdom's treasury, but in addition "quotas" were assigned to the constituent states to meet the remainder of the needs of the central government.

[59] League of Nations, Permanent Mandate Commission, *Minutes of the Ninth Session,* Geneva, 1926, pp. 98–101.
[60] For the Danzig-Poland negotiations, and for general discussion of the problems arising out of the allocation of customs union revenues, see Martin Jos. Funk, *Die danzig-polnische Zollunion: Der bisherige und der künftige Zollverteilungschlüssel* (Jena, 1926).

THE ECONOMICS OF CUSTOMS UNIONS                81

An unusual provision was contained in the customs union agreements of 1930 of the Union of South Africa with Northern Rhodesia and with Southern Rhodesia.  These agreements were really partial abrogations of the preexisting customs unions.  As part of the movement toward tariff autonomy of the Rhodesias, it was provided in these agreements that each of the members of the respective unions was to pay the other specified percentages of the value of its manufactures exported to the other.  These provisions seem to be instances where revenues lost as a result of effective protection of the industries of one member in the territory of the other had to be made up by the member profiting by the tariff protection, a type of provision which the Canadian Prairie Provinces, or Western Australia, would no doubt be happy to have applied to their relationships to the Dominion, or the Commonwealth, tariffs.

In the Report of the Second Joint Committee on Franco-Italian Customs Union there is no systematic discussion of the question of the mode of allocation of customs receipts, and the only comment suggests that allocation of receipts by ultimate destination of the imports is planned, and that the technical difficulties associated with this procedure are being seriously underestimated.  When a common tariff is in operation—

the question of transfer of customs receipts will arise only in the case where an importer enters for customs in a territory of the union other than the territory of destination goods which will subsequently be sent on to this latter territory; it would seem that this question can be dealt with in a satisfactory manner, if each of the customs administrations sets up a special statistical service; the two governments could, to this effect, negotiate a special protocol.

# References

Ball, M. Margaret. Post-War German-Austrian Relations; The Anschluss Movement, 1918–1936. Stanford University, California: Stanford University Press, 1937.

Barrington, Daines. Observations on the More Ancient Statutes. 4th edition. London, 1775.

Beers, John S. de. "Tariff Aspects of a Federal Union," Quarterly Journal of Economics (Boston, Harvard University), Vol. 56 (1941), pp. 49–92.

Bell, Herbert C. F. Lord Palmerston. London: Longmans, Green & Company, 1936.

"Benelux, An Example of Unity in a Divided World," Rotterdamsche Bank, Quarterly Review, 1947, No. 4, pp. 5–42.

"Benelux and Industrial Development," Amsterdamsche Bank, Quarterly Review, No. 80, April, 1948, p. 15.

Bismarck, Otto von. Correspondence diplomatique de M. de Bismarck (1851–1859), pub. d'après l'édition allemande de M. de Poschinger. Traduction de M. L. Schmitt. Paris: E. Plon et Cie, 1883. II, 307 ff.; 423 ff.

Bleuler, Werner. Studien über Aussenhandel und Handelspolitik der Schweiz. Zurich: Schulthess & Co., 1929.

Bosc, L. Unions douanières et projets d'unions douanières. Paris: A. Rousseau, 1904.

Calwer, Richard. Die Meistbegünstigung der Vereinigten Staaten von Nord-amerika. Berlin-Bern: Akademischer Verlag für social Wissenschaften, 1902.

Chevalier, Michel. "La guerre et la crise européenne," Revue des deux mondes (Paris), XXXVI[2] (1866), 758–85.

Davis, Kathryn W. The Soviets at Geneva; The U.S.S.R. and the League of Nations, 1919–1933. Geneva: Librairie Kundig, 1934.

Domerque, Gaston. "Le péril américain," La réforme économique (May 26, 1901, February 2, 1902, June 15, 1902, etc.).

Eisenmann, Louis. Le compromis austro-hongrois de 1867; Etude sur le dualisme. Paris: Bellais, 1904.

Elliott, O. L. The Tariff Controversy in the United States, 1789–1833. Palo Alto, California: Stanford University, 1892.

Evans, Ivor L. "Economic Aspects of Dualism in Austria-Hungary," Slavonic Review (London), VI (1927–28), 529–42.

Fisk, George M. "Continental Opinion regarding a Proposed Middle European Tariff Union," Johns Hopkins University Studies in Historical and Political Science, Series XX, Nos. 11–12 (November–December, 1902). Baltimore: Johns Hopkins Press, 1902.

Funk, Martin Jos. Die danzig-polnische Zollunion: Der bisherige und der künftige Zollverteilungs-schlüssel. Jena: Gustav Fischer, 1926.

Gideonse, Harry D. "Economic Foundations of Pan-Europeanism," Annals of the American Academy of Political and Social Science, CXLIX (1930).

Giffen, Sir Robert. "The Dream of a British Zollverein," Nineteenth Century (London), May, 1902; reprinted in Giffen, Economic Inquiries and Studies (London, 1904), Vol. II, pp. 394–95.

Gregory, T. E. Tariffs; A Study in Method. London: Griffin, 1921.

Grunzel, Josef. Handelspolitik und Ausgleich in Österreich-Ungarn. Wien und Leipzig: Alfred Hölder, 1912.

Haberler, Gottfried von. The Theory of International Trade with its Applications to Commercial Policy. London: Macmillan & Co., Ltd., 1936.

Halle, Ernst von. "Das Interesse Deutschlands an der amerikanischer Präsidentenwahl des Jahres 1896," Jahrbuch für Gesetzgebung, Verwaltung, und Volkswirtschaft ("Schmollers Jahrbuch"), New Series, XX (1896), 263–96.

Hawtrey, R. G. Economic Destiny. London: Longmans, Green & Company, 1944.

Henderson, William Otto. The Zollverein. Cambridge: University Press, 1939.

International Studies Conference. 6th, London, 1933. The State and Economic Life. Paris: International Institute of Intellectual Cooperation, 1934.

Kobatsch, Rudolph. La politique économique internationale. Paris, 1913.

League of Nations. Remarks on the Present Phase of International Economic Relations, September 1937. Document C.358.M.242.1937.II.B. Pp. 14–15.

———. Permanent Mandates Commission. Minutes of the Ninth Session. Geneva, 1926. Pp. 98–101.

Leubuscher, Charlotte. Tanganyika Territory; A Study of Economic Policy under Mandate. London: Oxford University Press, 1944.

Litschi, Joseph. "Das Retorsions-Konkordat vom Jahre 1822," Zeitschrift für schweizerische Statistik (Bern), XXVIII (1892), 1–22.

Mantoux, Etienne. The Carthaginian Peace; or The Economic Consequences of Mr. Keynes. New York: Oxford University Press, 1946.

Masson, Henry. "Les unions douanières." (Extract from Report of the Congrès International d'Expansion Economique Mondiale, held at Mons, Belgium, 1905.)

Masters, Donald C. The Reciprocity Treaty of 1854; Its History, its Relation to British Colonial and Foreign Policy and to the Development of Canadian Fiscal Autonomy. London: Longmans, Green & Company, 1937.

Matlekovits, Sandor von. Die Zollpolitik der österreichisch-ungarischen Monarchie und des Deutschen Reiches seit 1868 und deren nächste Zukunft. Leiipzig: Duncker und Humbolt, 1891.

Melder, Frederick E. State and Local Barriers to Interstate Commerce in the United States. Orono, Maine, 1937.

Mills, Stephen. Taxation in Australia. London: Macmillan and Co., Limited, 1925.

Molinari, G. de. "Union douanière de l'Europe central," Journal des économistes. Vol. 5, Series 4, February 1879, pp. 309–18.

Newton, A. P., *ed.* Select Documents relating to the Unification of South Africa. London: Longmans, Green and Co., 1924.

Peez, Alexander von. "A propos de la situation douanière en Europe," Revue d'économie politique (Paris), V (1891).

———. Die Amerikanische Konkurrenz. Leipzig, 1881.

Pentmann, J. Die Zollunionsidee und ihre Wandlungen im Rahmen der wirtschaftspolitischen Ideen und der Wirtschaftspolitik des 19. Jahrhunderts bis zur Gegenwart. Jena: Gustav Fischer, 1917.

Poel, Jean van der. Railway and Customs Policies in South Africa, 1885–1910. London: Longmans, Green & Company, 1933.

Richelot, Henri. L'Association douanière allemande. Paris, 1845.

Robbins, Lionel C. Economic Planning and International Order. London: Macmillan and Co., Ltd., 1937.

Salis, Jean R. de. Sismondi, 1773–1842; Letttres et documents inédits. Paris: H. Champion, 1932.

Sieghart, Rudolf. Zolltrennung und Zolleinheit; Die Geschichte der österreichisch-ungarischen Zwischenzoll-linie. Wien: Manz, 1915.

Smith, R. Elberton. Customs Valuation in the United States; A Study in Tariff Administration. Chicago: University of Chicago Press, 1948.

Story, Joseph. Commentaries on the Constitution. Sections 1056–1073.

Théry, Edmond. Europe et Etats-Unis d'Amérique. Paris: E. Flammarion, 1899.

Transvaal. Report of the Customs and Industries Commission. Presented to both houses of Parliament by command of His Excellency the Governor. Pretoria: Government Printing and Stationery Office, 1908.

Viner, Jacob. "The Measurement of the 'Height' of Tariff Levels," Joint Committee, Carnegie Endowment-International Chamber of Commerce, The Improvement of Commercial Relations between Nations (Paris, 1936), pp. 58–68.

———. "The Most-Favored-Nation Clause," Index (Svenska Handelsbanken, Stockholm), VI (1931), p. 11.

Wilcox, Clair. A Charter for World Trade. New York: The Macmillan Company, 1949.

"Customs Union Will Not Go Beyond Regional Pacts," The Observer (London), August 17, 1947, p. 5.

# [2]

## THE THEORY OF CUSTOMS UNIONS:
## A GENERAL SURVEY[1]

THIS paper is devoted mainly to a survey of the development of customs-union theory from Viner to date; since, however, the theory must be meant at least as an aid in interpreting real-world data, some space is devoted to a summary of empirical evidence relating to the gains from European Economic Union. It is necessary first to define customs-union theory. In general, the tariff system of any country may discriminate between commodities and/or between countries. Commodity discrimination occurs when different rates of duty are levied on different commodities, while country discrimination occurs when the same commodity is subject to different rates of duty, the rate varying according to the country of origin. The theory of customs unions may be defined as that branch of tariff theory which deals with the effects of geographically discriminatory changes in trade barriers.

Next we must turn our attention to the scope of the existing theory. The theory has been confined mainly to a study of the effects of customs unions on welfare rather than, for example, on the level of economic activity, the balance of payments or the rate of inflation. These welfare gains and losses, which are the subject of the theory, may arise from a number of different sources: (1) the specialisation of production according to comparative advantage which is the basis of the classical case for the gains from trade; (2) economies of scale;[2] (3) changes in the terms of trade; (4) forced changes in efficiency due to increased foreign competition; and (5) a change in the rate of economic growth. The theory of customs unions has been almost completely confined to an investigation of (1) above, with some slight attention to (2) and (3), (5) not being dealt with at all, while (4) is ruled out of traditional theory by the assumption (often contradicted by the facts) that production is carried out by processes which are technically efficient.

Throughout the development of the theory of customs unions we will find an oscillation between the belief that it is possible to produce a general conclusion of the sort: " Customs unions will always, or nearly always, raise welfare," and the belief that, depending on the particular circumstances present, a customs union may have any imaginable effect on welfare. The

[1] An earlier version of this paper was read before the Conference of the Association of University Teachers of Economics at Southampton, January 1959. I am indebted for comments and suggestions to G. C. Archibald, K. Klappholz and Professor L. Robbins.
[2] Points (1) and (2) are clearly related, for the existence of (1) is a *necessary* condition for (2), but they are more conveniently treated as separate points, since (1) is not a *sufficient* condition for the existence of (2).

earliest customs-union theory was largely embodied in the oral tradition, for it hardly seemed worthwhile to state it explicitly, and was an example of an attempt to produce the former sort of conclusion. It may be summarised quite briefly. Free trade maximises world welfare; a customs union reduces tariffs and is therefore a movement towards free trade; a customs union will, therefore, *increase* world welfare even if it does not lead to a world-welfare *maximum*.

Viner showed this argument to be incorrect. He introduced the now familiar concepts of trade creation and trade diversion [1] which are probably best recalled in terms of an example. Consider the figures in the following Table:

TABLE I

*Money Prices (at Existing Exchange Rates) of a Single
Commodity (X) in Three Countries*

| Country | A | B | C |
|---|---|---|---|
| Price | 35s. | 26s. | 20s. |

A tariff of 100% levied by country A [2] will be sufficient to protect A's domestic industry producing commodity X. If A forms a customs union with either country B or country C she will be better off; if the union is with B she will get a unit of commodity X at an opportunity cost of 26 shillingsworth of exports instead of at the cost of 35 shillingsworth of other goods entailed by domestic production. [3] This is an example of trade creation. If A had been levying a somewhat lower tariff, a 50% tariff, for example, she would already have been buying X from abroad before the formation of any customs union. If A is buying a commodity from abroad, and if her tariff is non-discriminatory, then she will be buying it from the lowest-cost source—in this case country C. Now consider a customs union with country B. B's X, now exempt from the tariff, sells for 26s., while C's X, which must still pay the 50% tariff, must be sold for 30s. A will now buy X from B at a price, in terms of the value of exports, of 26s., whereas she was formerly buying it from C at a price of only 20s. This is a case of Viner's trade diversion, and since it entails a movement from lower to higher real cost sources of supply, it represents a movement from a more to a less efficient allocation of resources.

[1] Jacob Viner, *The Customs Union Issue* (New York: Carnegie Endowment for International Peace, 1950). See the whole of Chapter 4, especially pp. 43–4.

[2] In everything that follows the "home country" will be labelled A, the "union partner" B and the rest of the world C.

[3] This argument presumes that relative prices in each country reflect real rates of transformation. It follows that the resources used to produce a unit of X in country A could produce any other good to the value of 35s. and, since a unit of X can be had from B by exporting goods to the value of only 26s., there will be a surplus of goods valued at 9s. accruing to A from the transfer of resources out of X when trade is opened with country B.

This analysis is an example of what Mr. Lancaster and I have called
" The General Theory of Second Best ": [1] if it is impossible to satisfy *all* the
optimum conditions (in this case to make all relative prices equal to all rates
of transformation in production), then a change which brings about the
satisfaction of *some* of the optimum conditions (in this case making some
relative prices equal to some rates of transformation in production) may
make things better or worse.[2]

Viner's analysis leads to the following classification of the possibilities
that arise from a customs union between two countries, A and B:

> 1. Neither A nor B may be producing a given commodity.  In
> this case they will both be importing this commodity from some third
> country, and the removal of tariffs on trade between A and B can cause
> no change in the pattern of trade in this commodity;  both countries
> will continue to import it from the cheapest possible source outside of
> the union.
>
> 2. One of the two countries may be producing the commodity
> inefficiently under tariff protection while the second country is a non-
> producer.  If country A is producing commodity X under tariff pro-
> tection this means that her tariff is sufficient to eliminate competition
> from the cheapest possible source.  Thus if A's tariff on X is adopted
> by the union the tariff will be high enough to secure B's market for A's
> inefficient industry.
>
> 3. Both countries may be producing the commodity inefficiently
> under tariff protection.  In this case the customs union removes tariffs
> between country A and B and ensures that the least inefficient of the
> two will capture the union market.[3]

In case 2 above any change must be a trade-diverting one, while in case 3
any change must be a trade-creating one.  If one wishes to predict the
welfare effects of a customs union it is necessary to predict the relative
strengths of the forces causing trade creation and trade diversion.

This analysis leads to the conclusion that customs unions are likely to
cause losses when the countries involved are complementary *in the range of
commodities that are protected by tariffs*.  Consider the class of commodities
produced under tariff protection in each of the two countries.  If these
classes overlap to a large extent, then the most efficient of the two countries
will capture the union market and there will be a re-allocation of resources
in a more efficient direction.  If these two classes do not overlap to any

---

[1] R. G. Lipsey and K. J. Lancaster, " The General Theory of Second Best," *Review of Economic Studies*, Vol. XXIV (1), No. 63, 1956–57.

[2] The point may be made slightly more formally as follows: the conditions necessary for the maximising of *any* function do not, in general, provide conditions sufficient for an increase in the value of the function when the maximum value is not to be obtained by the change.

[3] One of the two countries might be an efficient producer of this commodity needing no tariff protection, in which case, *a fortiori*, there is gain.

great extent, then the protected industry in one country is likely to capture the whole of the union market when the union is formed, and there is likely to be a re-allocation of resources in a less-efficient direction. This point of Viner's has often been misunderstood and read to say that, in some general sense, the economies of the two countries should be competitive and not complementary. A precise way of making the point is to say that the customs union is more likely to bring gain, the greater is the degree of overlapping between the class of commodities produced under tariff protection in the two countries.

A subsequent analysis of the conditions affecting the gains from union through trade creation and trade diversion was made by Drs. Makower and Morton.[1] They pointed out that, *given that trade creation was going to occur*, the gains would be larger the more dissimilar were the cost ratios in the two countries. (Clearly if two countries have almost identical cost ratios the gains from trade will be small.) They then defined competitive economies to be ones with similar cost ratios and complementary economies to be ones with dissimilar ratios, and were able to conclude that unions between complementary economies would, if they brought gain at all, bring large gains. The conclusions of Viner and Makower and Morton are in no sense contradictory. Stated in the simplest possible language, Viner showed that gains will arise from unions if both countries are producing the same commodity; Makower and Morton showed that these gains will be larger the larger is the difference between the costs at which the same commodity is produced in the two countries.[2]

We now come to the second major development in customs-union theory —the analysis of the welfare effects of *the substitution between commodities* resulting from the changes in relative prices which necessarily accompany a customs union. Viner's analysis implicitly assumed that commodities are consumed in some fixed proportion which is independent of the structure of relative prices. Having ruled out substitution between commodities, he was left to analyse only bodily shifts of trade from one country to another. The way in which Viner's conclusion that trade diversion necessarily lowers welfare depends on his implicit demand assumption is illustrated in Fig. 1. Consider the case of a small country, A, specialised in the production of a single commodity, Y, and importing one commodity, X, at terms of trade independent of any taxes or tariffs levied in A. The fixed proportion in

[1] H. Makower and G. Morton, "A Contribution Towards a Theory of Customs Unions," ECONOMIC JOURNAL, Vol. LXII, No. 249, March 1953, pp. 33–49.

[2] Care must be taken to distinguish between complementarity and competitiveness in costs and in tastes, both being possible. In the Makower–Morton model these relations exist only on the cost side. An example of the confusion which may arise when this distinction is not made can be seen in F. V. Meyer's article, "Complementarity and the Lowering of Tariffs," *The American Economic Review*, Vol. XLVI, No. 3, June 1956. Meyer's definitions, if they are to mean anything, must refer to the demand side. Hence he is not entitled to contrast his results with those of Makower and Morton, or of Viner, all of whom were concerned with cost complementarity and competitiveness.

which commodities are consumed is shown by the slope of the line $OZ$, which is the income- and price-consumption line for all (finite) prices and incomes.    $OA$ indicates country A's total production of commodity Y, and the slope of the line $AC$ shows the terms of trade offered by country C, the lowest cost producer of X.   Under conditions of free trade, country A's equilibrium will be at $e$, the point of intersection between $OZ$ and $AC$.   A will consume $Og$ of Y, exporting $Ag$ in return for $ge$ of X.   Now a tariff which does not affect A's terms of trade and is not high enough to protect a domestic industry producing Y will leave her equilibrium position un- changed at $e$.[1]   The tariff changes relative prices, but consumers' purchases

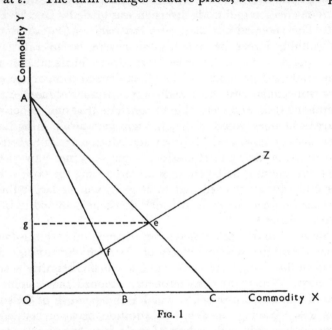

FIG. 1

are completely insensitive to this change and, if foreign trade continues at terms indicated by the slope of the line $AC$, the community must remain in equilibrium at $e$.   Now consider a case where country A forms a trade- diverting customs union with country B.   This means that A must buy her imports of X at a price in terms of Y higher than she was paying before the union was formed.   An example of this is shown in Fig. 1 by the line $AB$. A's equilibrium is now at $f$, the point of intersection between $AB$ and $OZ$; less of both commodities are consumed, and A's welfare has unambiguously diminished.   We conclude therefore that, under the assumed demand conditions, trade diversion (which necessarily entails a deterioration in A's terms of trade) *necessarily* lowers A's welfare.

[1] It is assumed throughout all the subsequent analysis that the tariff revenue collected by the Government is either returned to individuals by means of lump-sum subsidies or spent by the Government on the same bundle of goods that consumers would have purchased.

Viner's implicit assumption that commodities are consumed in fixed proportions independent of the structure of relative prices is indeed a very special one. A customs union necessarily changes relative prices and, in general, we should expect this to lead to some substitution between commodities, there being a tendency to change the volume of already existing trade with more of the now cheaper goods being bought and less of the now more expensive. This would tend to increase the volume of imports from a country's union partner and to diminish both the volume of imports obtained from the outside world and the consumption of home-produced commodities. The importance of this substitution effect in consumption seems to have been discovered independently by at least three people, Professor Meade,[1] Professor Gehrels [2] and myself.[3]

In order to show the importance of the effects of substitutions in consumption we merely drop the assumption that commodities are consumed in fixed proportions. I shall take Mr. Gehrels' presentation of this analysis because it illustrates a number of important factors. In Fig. 2 *OA* is again country A's total production of Y, and the slope of the line *AC* indicates the terms of trade between X and Y when A is trading with country C. The free-trade equilibrium position is again at *e*, where an indifference curve is tangent to *AC*. In this case, however, the imposition of a tariff on imports of X, even if it does not shift the source of country A's imports, will cause a reduction in the quantity of these imports and an increase in the consumption of the domestic commodity Y. A tariff which changes the relative price in A's domestic market to, say, that indicated by the slope of the line *A'C'* will move A's equilibrium position to point *h*. At this point an indifference curve cuts *AC* with a slope equal to the line *A'C'*; consumers are thus adjusting their purchases to the market rate of transformation and the tariff has had the effect of reducing imports of X and increasing consumption of the home good Y. In these circumstances it is clearly possible for country A to form a trade-diverting customs union and yet gain an increase in its welfare. To show this, construct a line through *A* tangent to the indifference curve *I″* to cut the *X* axis at some point *B*. If A forms a trade-diverting customs union with country B and buys her imports of X from B at terms of trade indicated by the slope of the line *AB*, her welfare will be unchanged. If, therefore, the terms of trade with B are worse than those given by C but better than those indicated by the slope of the line *AB*, A's welfare will be increased by the trade-diverting customs union. A's

---

[1] J. E. Meade, *The Theory of Customs Unions* (Amsterdam: North Holland Publishing Company, 1956).

[2] F. Gehrels, "Customs Unions from a Single Country Viewpoint," *Review of Economic Studies*, Vol. XXIV (1), No. 63, 1956–57.

[3] R. G. Lipsey, "The Theory of Customs Unions: Trade Diversion and Welfare," *Economica*, Vol. XXIV, No. 93, February 1957. My own paper was first written in 1954 as a criticism of the assumption of fixed ratios in consumption made by Dr. Ozga in his thesis (S. A. Ozga, *The Theory of Tariff Systems*, University of London Ph.D. thesis, unpublished).

welfare will be diminished by this trade-diverting union with B only if B's terms of trade are worse than those indicated by the slope of *AB*.

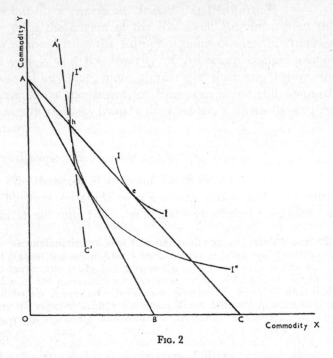

FIG. 2

The common-sense reason for this conclusion may be stated as follows:

"The possibility stems from the fact that whenever imports are subject to a tariff, the position of equilibrium must be one where an indifference curve [surface or hyper-surface as the case may be] cuts (*not* is tangent to) the international price line. From this it follows that there will exist an area where indifference curves higher than the one achieved at equilibrium lie below the international price line. In Fig. 2 this is the area above *I"* but below *AC*. As long as the final equilibrium position lies within this area, trade carried on in the absence of tariffs, at terms of trade worse than those indicated by *AC*, will increase welfare. In a verbal statement this possibility may be explained by referring to the two opposing effects of a trade-diverting customs union. First, A shifts her purchases from a lower to a higher cost source of supply. It now becomes necessary to export a larger quantity of goods in order to obtain any given quantity of imports. Secondly, the divergence between domestic and international prices is eliminated when the union is formed. The removal of the tariff has the effect of allowing . . . consumer[s] in A to adjust . . . purchases to a domestic price ratio which now is equal to the rate at which . . . [Y] can be transformed into . . . [X] by means of international trade. The final welfare effect of the trade-diverting customs union must be the net effect of these two opposing tendencies; the first working to lower welfare and the second to raise it." [1]

On this much there is general agreement.  Professor Gehrels, however, concluded that his analysis established a general presumption in favour of gains from union rather than losses.  He argued that " to examine customs unions in the light only of *production* effects, as Viner does, will give a biased judgment of their effect on countries joining them," [2] and he went on to say that the analysis given above established a general presumption in favour of gains from union.  Now we seemed to be back in the pre-Viner world, where economic analysis established a general case in favour of customs unions.  In my article " Mr. Gehrels on Customs Union " [3] I attempted to point out the mistake involved.  The key is that Gehrels' model contains only two commodities: one domestic good and one import.  There is thus only one optimum condition for consumption: that the relative price between X and Y equals the real rate of transformation (in domestic production or international trade, whichever is relevant) between these two commodities.  The general problems raised by customs unions must, however, be analysed in a model containing a minimum of three types of commodities: domestic commodities (A), imports from the union partner (B) and imports from the outside world (C).  When this change is made Gehrels' general presumption for gain from union disappears.  Table II

### TABLE II

| Free trade (col. 1) | Uniform *ad valorem* tariff on all imports (col. 2) | Customs union with country B (col. 3) |
|---|---|---|
| $\dfrac{P_{Ad}}{P_{Bd}} = \dfrac{P_{Ai}}{P_{Bi}}$ | $\dfrac{P_{Ad}}{P_{Bd}} < \dfrac{P_{Ai}}{P_{Bi}}$ | $\dfrac{P_{Ad}}{P_{Bd}} = \dfrac{P_{Ai}}{P_{Bi}}$ |
| $\dfrac{P_{Ad}}{P_{Cd}} = \dfrac{P_{Ai}}{P_{Ci}}$ | $\dfrac{P_{Ad}}{P_{Cd}} < \dfrac{P_{Ai}}{P_{Ci}}$ | $\dfrac{P_{Ad}}{P_{Cd}} < \dfrac{P_{Ai}}{P_{Ci}}$ |
| $\dfrac{P_{Bd}}{P_{Cd}} = \dfrac{P_{Bi}}{P_{Ci}}$ | $\dfrac{P_{Bd}}{P_{Cd}} = \dfrac{P_{Bi}}{P_{Ci}}$ | $\dfrac{P_{Bd}}{P_{Cd}} < \dfrac{P_{Bi}}{P_{Ci}}$ |

Subscripts $A$, $B$ and $C$ refer to countries of origin, $d$ to prices in A's domestic market, and $i$ to prices in the international market.

shows the three optimum conditions that domestic prices and international prices should bear the same relationship to each other for the three groups of commodities, A, B and C.[4]  In free trade all three optimum conditions

[1] R. G. Lipsey, " Trade Diversion and Welfare," *op. cit.*, pp. 43–4.  The changes made in the quotation are minor ones necessary to make the notation in the example comparable to the one used in the present text.

[2] Gehrels, *op. cit.*, p. 61.

[3] R. G. Lipsey, " Mr. Gehrels on Customs Unions," *Review of Economic Studies*, Vol. XXIV (3), No. 65, 1956–57, pp. 211–14.

[4] If we assume that consumers adjust their purchases to the relative prices ruling in their domestic markets, then the optimum conditions that rates of substitution in consumption should equal rates of transformation in trade can be stated in terms of equality between relative prices ruling in the domestic markets and those ruling in the international market.

will be fulfilled. If a uniform tariff is placed on both imports, then the relations shown in column 2 will obtain, for the price of goods from both B and C will be higher in A's domestic market than in the international market. When a customs union is formed, however, the prices of imports from the union partner, B, are reduced so that the first optimum condition is fulfilled, but the tariff remains on imports from abroad (C) so that the third optimum condition is no longer satisfied. The customs union thus moves country A from one non-optimal position to another, and in general it is impossible to say whether welfare will increase or diminish as a result. We are thus back to a position where the theory tells us that welfare may rise or fall, and a much more detailed study is necessary in order to establish the conditions under which one or the other result might obtain.

The above analysis has lead both Mr. Gehrels and myself [1] to distinguish between *production effects* and *consumption effects* of customs unions. The reason for attempting this is not hard to find. Viner's analysis rules out substitution in consumption and looks to shifts in the location of production as the cause of welfare changes in customs unions. The analysis just completed emphasises the effects of substitution in consumption. The distinction on this basis, however, is not fully satisfactory, for consumption effects will themselves cause changes in production. A more satisfactory distinction would seem to be one between *inter-country substitution* and *inter-commodity substitution*. Inter-country substitution would be Viner's trade creation and trade diversion, when one country is substituted for another as the source of supply for some commodity. Inter-commodity substitution occurs when one commodity is substituted, at least at the margin, for some other commodity as a result of a relative price shift. This is the type of substitution we have just been analysing. In general, either of these changes will cause shifts in both consumption and production.

Now we come to Professor Meade's analysis. His approach is taxonomic in that he attempts to classify a large number of possible cases, showing the factors which would tend to cause welfare to increase when a union is formed and to isolate these from the factors which would tend to cause welfare to diminish.[2] Fig. 3 (i) shows a demand and a supply curve for any imported commodity. Meade observes that a tariff, like any tax, shifts the supply curve to the left (to $S'S'$ in Fig. 3) and raises the price of the imported commodity. At the new equilibrium the demand price differs from the supply price by the amount of the tariff. If the supply price indicates the utility of the commodity to the suppliers and the demand price its utility to the purchasers, it follows that the utility of the taxed import is higher to purchasers than to suppliers, and the money value of this difference in utility is

---

[1] Gehrels, *op. cit.*, p. 61, and Lipsey, " Trade Diversion and Welfare," *op. cit.*, pp. 40–1.

[2] The point of his taxonomy or of any taxonomy of this sort, it seems to me, must be merely to illustrate how the model works. Once one has mastered the analysis it is possible to work through any particular case that may arise, and there would seem to be no need to work out all possible cases beforehand.

the value of the tariff. Now assume that the marginal utility of money is the same for buyers and for sellers. It follows that, if one more *unit of expenditure* were devoted to the purchase of this commodity, there would be a net gain to society equal to the proportion of the selling price of the commodity composed of the tariff. In Fig. 3 the rate of tariff is $\frac{cb}{ab}$%, the supply price is $ab$ and the demand price is $ac$, so that the money value of the " gain " (" loss ") to society resulting from a marginal increase (decrease) in expenditure on this commodity is $bc$.

Now assume that the same *ad valorem* rate of tariff is imposed on all imports so that the tariff will be the same proportion of the market price of

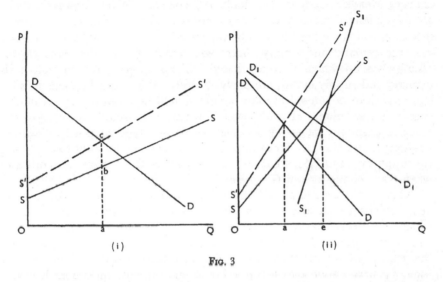

Fɪɢ. 3

each import. Then the gain to society from a marginal increase in expenditure (say one more " dollar " is spent) on any import is the same for all imports, and this gain is equal to the loss resulting from a marginal reduction in expenditure (one less " dollar " spent) on any import. Now consider *a marginal reduction* in the tariff on one commodity. This will cause a readjustment of expenditure, in the various possible ways analysed by Meade, so that in general more of some imports and less of others will be purchased. Since, *at the margin*, the gain from devoting one more unit of expenditure to the purchase of any import is equal to the loss from devoting one less unit of expenditure to the purchase of any import, the welfare consequences of this discriminatory tariff reduction may be calculated by comparing the increase in the volume of imports (trade expansion) with the decrease in the volume of other imports (trade contraction). If there is a net increase in the volume of trade the customs union will have raised economic welfare. A study of the welfare consequences of customs unions can, therefore, be devoted to the factors which will increase or decrease the volume of international trade. If the influences which tend to cause trade expansion are found to predominate it may be predicted that a customs union will raise welfare. The main body of Meade's analysis is in fact devoted to a study of those factors which would tend to increase, and to those which would tend to decrease, the volume of trade. Complications can, of course, be introduced, but they do not affect the main drift of the argument.[1]

Meade's analysis, which makes use of demand and supply curves, suffers from one very serious, possibly crippling, limitation. It will be noted that we were careful to consider only *marginal reductions* in tariffs. For such changes Meade's analysis is undoubtedly correct. When, however, there are *large* changes in many tariffs, as there will be with most of the customs unions in which we are likely to be interested, it can no longer be assumed that the demand and supply curves will remain fixed; the *ceteris paribus* assumptions on which they are based will no longer hold, so that both demand and supply curves are likely to shift. When this happens it is no longer obvious how much welfare weight should be given to any particular change in the volume of trade (even if we are prepared to make all of the other assumptions necessary for the use of this type of classical welfare analysis). In Fig. 3 (ii), for example, if the demand curve shifts to $D_1D_1$ and the supply curve to $S_1S_1$, what are we to say about the welfare gains or losses when trade changes from $Oa$ to $Oe$?

There is not time to go through a great deal of Professor Meade's or my own analysis which attempts to discover the particular circumstances in which it is likely that a geographically discriminatory reduction in tariffs will raise welfare. I shall, therefore, take two of the general conclusions that emerge from various analyses and present these in order to illustrate the type of generalisation that it is possible to make in customs-union theory.

The first generalisation is one that emerges from Professor Meade's analysis and from my own. I choose it, first, because there seems to be general agreement on it and, second, although Professor Meade does not make this point, because it is an absolutely general proposition in the theory of second best; it applies to all sub-optimal positions, and customs-union theory only provides a particular example of its application. Stated in terms of customs unions, this generalisation runs as follows: when only some

---

[1] For example, the same rate of tariff might not be charged on all imports. In this case it is only necessary to weight each dollar's increase or decrease in trade by the proportion of this value that is made up by tariff—the greater is the rate of tariff the greater is the gain or loss. It is also possible, if one wishes to make inter-country comparisons, to weight a dollar's trade in one direction by a different amount than a dollar's trade in some other direction. These complications, however, do not affect the essence of Meade's analysis, which is to make a *small change* in some tariffs and then to observe that the welfare consequences depend on the net change in the volume of trade and to continue the study in order to discover in what circumstances an increase or a decrease in the net volume of trade is likely.

tariffs are to be changed, welfare is more likely to be raised if these tariffs are merely *reduced* than if they are completely *removed*. Proofs of this theorem can be found in both Meade [1] and Lipsey and Lancaster,[2] and we shall content ourselves here with an intuitive argument for the theorem in its most general context. Assume that there exist many taxes, subsidies, monopolies, etc., which prevent the satisfaction of optimum conditions. Further assume that all but one of these, say one tax, are fixed, and inquire into the second-best level for the tax that is allowed to vary. Finally, assume that there exists a unique second-best level for this tax.[3] Now a change in this one tax will either move the economy towards or away from a second-best optimum position. If it moves the economy away from a second-best position, then, no matter how large is the change in the tax, welfare will be lowered. If it moves the economy in the direction of the second-best optimum it may move it part of the way, all of the way or past it. If the economy is moved sufficiently far past the second-best optimum welfare will be lowered by the change. From this it follows that, if there is a unique second-best level for the tax being varied, a small variation is more likely to raise welfare than is a large variation.[4]

The next generalisation concerns the size of expenditure on the three classes of goods—those purchased domestically, from the union partner, and from the outside world—and is related to the gains from inter-commodity substitution. This generalisation follows from the analysis in my own thesis [5] and does not seem to have been stated in any of the existing customs-union literature. Consider what happens to the optimum conditions, which we discussed earlier, when the customs union is formed (see Table II). On the one hand, the tariff is taken off imports from the country's union partner, and the relative price between these imports and domestic goods is brought into conformity with the real rates of transformation. This, by itself, tends to increase welfare. On the other hand, the relative price between imports from the union partner and imports from the outside world are moved away from equality with real rates of transformation. This by itself tends to reduce welfare. Now consider both of these changes. As far as the prices of the goods from a country's union partner are concerned, they are brought

[1] *Op. cit.*, pp. 50–1.

[2] *Op. cit.*, Section V.

[3] A unique second-best level (*i.e.*, the level which maximises welfare subject to the existence and invariability of all the other taxes, tariffs, etc.) for any one variable factor can be shown to exist in a large number of cases (see, for example, Lipsey and Lancaster, *op. cit.*, Sections V and VI), but cannot be proved to exist in general (*ibid.*, Section VIII).

[4] This may be given a more formal statement. Consider the direction of the change—towards or away from the second-best optimum position—caused by the change in the tax. Moving away from the second-best optimum is a *sufficient*, but not a necessary, condition for a reduction in welfare. Moving towards the second-best optimum is a *necessary*, but not a sufficient, condition for an increase in welfare.

[5] R. G. Lipsey, *The Theory of Customs Unions: A General Equilibrium Analysis*, University of London Ph.D. thesis, unpublished, pp. 97–9, and Mathematical Appendix to Chapter VI.

into equality with rates of transformation *vis à vis* domestic goods, but they are moved away from equality with rates of transformation *vis à vis* imports from the outside world. These imports from the union partner are thus involved in both a gain and a loss and their size is *per se* unimportant; what matters is the relation between imports from the outside world and expenditure on domestic commodities: the larger are purchases of domestic commodities and the smaller are purchases from the outside world, the more likely is it that the union will bring gain. Consider a simple example in which a country purchases from its union partner only eggs while it purchases from the outside world only shoes, all other commodities being produced and consumed at home. Now when the union is formed the " correct " price ratio (*i.e.*, the one which conforms with the real rate of transformation) between eggs and shoes will be disturbed, but, on the other hand, eggs will be brought into the " correct " price relationship with all other commodities —bacon, butter, cheese, meat, etc., and in these circumstances a customs union is very likely to bring gain, for the loss in distorting the price ratio between eggs and shoes will be small relative to the gain in establishing the correct price ratio between eggs and all other commodities. Now, however, let us reverse the position of domestic trade and imports from the outside world, making shoes the only commodity produced and consumed at home, eggs still being imported from the union partner, while everything else is now bought from the outside world. In these circumstances the customs union is most likely to bring a loss; the gains in establishing the correct price ratio between eggs and shoes are indeed likely to be very small compared with the losses of distorting the price ratio between eggs and all other commodities. If, to take a third example, eggs are produced at home, shoes imported from the outside world, while everything else is obtained from the union partner, the union may bring neither gain nor loss; for the union disturbs the " correct " ratio between shoes and everything else except eggs, and establishes the " correct " one between eggs and everything else except shoes. This example serves to show that the size of trade with a union partner is not the important variable; it is the relation between imports from the outside world and purchases of domestic goods that matters.

This argument gives rise to two general conclusions, one of them appealing immediately to common sense, one of them slightly surprising. The first is that, *given a country's volume of international trade*, a customs union is more likely to raise welfare the higher is the proportion of trade with the country's union partner and the lower the proportion with the outside world. The second is that a customs union is more likely to raise welfare the lower is the total volume of foreign trade, for the lower is foreign trade, the lower must be purchases from the outside world relative to purchases of domestic commodities. This means that the sort of countries who ought to form customs unions are those doing a high proportion of their foreign trade with their union partner, and making a high proportion of their total expenditure on domestic trade. Countries which are likely to lose from a customs union, on the other hand, are those countries in which a low proportion of total trade is domestic, especially if the customs union does not include a high proportion of their foreign trade.

We may now pass to a very brief consideration of some of the empirical work. Undoubtedly a serious attempt to predict and measure the possible effects of a customs union is a very difficult task. Making all allowances for this, however, a surprisingly large proportion of the voluminous literature on the subject is devoted to guess and suspicion, and a very small proportion to serious attempts to measure. Let us consider what empirical work has been done on the European Common Market and the Free Trade Area, looking first at attempts to measure possible gains from specialisation. The theoretical analysis underlying these measurements is of the sort developed by Professor Meade and outlined previously.

The first study which we will mention is that made by the Dutch economist Verdoorn, subsequently quoted and used by Scitovsky.[1] The analysis assumes an elasticity of substitution between domestic goods and imports of minus one-half, and an elasticity of substitution between different imports of minus two. These estimates are based on some empirical measurements of an aggregate sort and the extremely radical assumption is made that the same elasticities apply to all commodities. The general assumption, then, is that one import is fairly easily substituted for another, while imports and domestic commodities are not particularly good substitutes for each other.[2]

Using this assumption, an estimate was made of the changes in trade when tariffs are reduced between the six Common Market countries, the United Kingdom and Scandinavia. The estimate is that intra-European trade will increase by approximately 17%, and, when this increase is weighted by the proportion of the purchase price of each commodity that is made up of tariff and estimates for the reduction in trade in other directions are also made, the final figure for the gains from trade to the European countries is equal to about one-twentieth of one per cent of their annual incomes. In considering this figure, the crude estimate of elasticities of substitution must cause some concern. The estimate of an increase in European trade of 17% is possibly rather small in the face of the known fact that Benelux trade increased by approximately 50% after the formation of that customs union. A possible check on the accuracy of the Verdoorn method would have been to apply it to the pre-customs union situation in the Benelux countries, to use the method to predict what would happen to

---

[1] T. de Scitovsky, *Economic Theory and Western European Integration* (Allen and Unwin, 1958), pp. 64–78.

[2] Note also that everything is assumed to be a substitute for everything else; there are no relations of complementarity.

Benelux trade and then to compare the prediction with what we actually know to have happened. Whatever allowances are made, however, Scitovsky's conclusion is not likely to be seriously challenged:

> " The most surprising feature of these estimates is their smallness. . . . As estimates of the total increase in intra-European trade contingent upon economic union, Verdoorn's figures are probably underestimates; but if, by way of correction, we should raise them five- or even twenty-five-fold, that would still leave unchanged our basic conclusion that the gain from increased intra-European specialisation is likely to be insignificant." [1]

A second empirical investigation into the possible gains from trade, this time relating only to the United Kingdom, has been made by Professor Johnson.[2] Johnson bases his study on the estimates made by *The Economist* Intelligence Unit of the increases in the value of British trade which would result by 1970, first, if there were only the Common Market and, second, if there were the Common Market and the Free Trade Area. Professor Johnson then asks what will be the size of the possible gains to Britain of participation in the Free Trade Area? His theory is slightly different from that of Professor Meade, but since it arrives at the same answer, namely that the gain is equal to the increased quantity of trade times the proportion of the purchase price made up of tariff, we do not need to consider the details. From these estimates Johnson arrives at the answer that the possible gain to Britain from joining the Free Trade Area would be, *as an absolute maximum*, 1% of the national income of the United Kingdom.

Most people seem to be surprised at the size of these estimates, finding them smaller than expected. This leads us to ask: might there not be some inherent bias in this sort of estimate? and, might not a totally different approach yield quite different answers? One possible approach is to consider the proportion of British factors of production engaged in foreign trade. This can be taken to be roughly the percentage contribution made by trade to the value of the national product, which can be estimated to be roughly the value of total trade as a proportion of G.N.P., first subtracting the import content from the G.N.P. This produces a rough estimate of 18% of Britain's total resources engaged in foreign trade. The next step would be to ask how much increase in efficiency of utilisation for these resources could we expect: (1) as a result of their re-allocation in the direction of their comparative advantage, and (2) as a result of a re-allocation among possible consumers of the commodities produced by these resources. Here is an outline for a possible study, but, in the absence of such a study, what would we guess? Would a 10% increase in efficiency not be a rather conservative

[1] Scitovsky, *op. cit.*, p. 67.
[2] H. G. Johnson, " The Gains from Free Trade with Europe: An Estimate," *Manchester School*, Vol. XXVI, September 1958.

estimate?    Such a gain in efficiency would give a net increase in the national income of 1·8%.    If the resources had a 20% increase in efficiency, then an increase in the national income of 3·6% would be possible.    At this stage these figures can give nothing more than a common-sense check on the more detailed estimates of economists such as Verdoorn and Johnson.    Until further detailed work has been done, it must be accepted that the best present estimates give figures of the net gain from trade amounting to something less than 1% of the national income (although we may not, of course, have a very high degree of confidence in these estimates).

When we move on from the possible gains from new trade to the question of the economic benefits arising from other causes, such as economies of scale or enforced efficiency, we leave behind even such halting attempts at measurement as we have just considered.    Some economists see considerable economies of scale emerging from European union.    Others are sceptical. In what what follows, I will confine my attention mainly to the arguments advanced by Professor H. G. Johnson.[1]    His first argument runs as follows:

> " It is extremely difficult to believe that British industry offers substantial potential savings in cost which cannot be exploited in a densely-populated market of 51 million people with a G.N.P. of £18 billion, especially when account is taken of the much larger markets abroad in which British industry, in spite of restrictions of various kinds, has been able to sell its products.[2]

Let us make only two points about Professor Johnson's observation. First, many markets will be very much less than the total population.    What, for example, can we say about a product sold mainly to upper middle-class males living more than 20 miles away from an urban centre?    Might there not be economies of scale remaining in the production of a commodity for such a market?    Secondly, in the absence of some theory that tells us the statement is true for 51 and, say, 31, but not 21, million people, the argument must remain nothing more than an unsupported personal opinion.    As another argument, Professor Johnson asks, " Why are these economies of scale, if they do exist, not already being exploited? "[3]    It is, of course, well known that unexhausted economies of scale are incompatible with the existence of perfect competition, but it is equally well known that unexhausted economies of scale are compatible with the existence of imperfect competition as long as long-run marginal cost is declining faster than

---

[1] In singling out Professor Johnson, I do not wish to imply that he is alone in practising the sort of economics which I am criticising.    On the contrary, he is typical of a very large number of economists who have attempted to obtain quantitative conclusions from qualitative arguments.

[2] H. G. Johnson, " The Criteria of Economic Advantage," *Bulletin of the Oxford University Institute of Statistics*, Vol. 19, February 1957, p. 35.    See also "The Economic Gains from Free Trade with Europe," *Three Banks Review*, September 1958, for a similar argument.

[3] Johnson, " Economic Gains," *op. cit.*, p. 10, and " Economic Advantage," *op. cit.*, p 35.

marginal revenue. Here it is worthwhile making a distinction, mentioned by Scitovsky,[1] between the long-run marginal cost of producing more goods, to which the economist is usually referring when he speaks of scale effects, and the marginal cost of making and selling more goods (which must include selling costs). This leads to a distinction between increasing sales when the whole market is expanding and increasing sales when the market is static, and thus increasing them at the expense of one's competitors. The former is undoubtedly very much easier than the latter. It is quite possible for the marginal costs of *production* to be declining while the marginal costs of *selling* in a static market are rising steeply. This would mean that production economies would not be exploited by the firms competing in the market, but that if the market were to expand so that *all* firms in a given industry could grow, then these economies would be realised.

Let us also consider an argument put forward in favour of economies of scale. Writing in 1955, Gehrels and Johnson argue that very large gains from economies of scale can be expected.[2] In evidence of this they quote the following facts: American productivity (*i.e.*, output per man) is higher than United Kingdom productivity for most commodities; the differential is, how-ever, greatest in those industries which use mass-production methods. From this they conclude that there are unexploited economies of mass production in the United Kingdom. Now this may well be so, but, before accepting the conclusion, we should be careful in interpreting this meagre piece of evidence. What else might it mean? Might it not mean, for example, that the ratios of capital to labour differed in the two countries so that, if we calculate the productivity of a factor by dividing total production by the quantity of one factor employed, we will necessarily find these differences? Secondly, would we not be very surprised if we did not find such differences in com-parative costs between the two countries? Are we surprised when we find America's comparative advantage centred in the mass-producing industries, and, if this is the case, must we conclude that vast economies of mass pro-duction exist for Europe?

Finally, we come to the possible gains through forced efficiency. Busi-ness firms may not be adopting methods known to be technically more efficient than those now in use due to inertia, a dislike of risk-taking, a willing-ness to be content with moderate profits, or a whole host of other reasons. If these firms are thrown into competition with a number of firms in other countries who are not adopting this conservative policy, then the efficiency of the use of resources may increase because technically more efficient produc-tion methods are forced on the business-man now facing fierce foreign com-petition. Here no evidence has as yet been gathered, and, rather than report the opinions of others, I will close by recording the personal guess that this

---

[1] Scitovsky, *op. cit.*, pp. 42 ff.

[2] Gehrels and Johnson, " The Economic Gains from European Integration," *Journal of Political Economy*, August 1955.

is a very large potential source of gain, that an increase in competition with foreign countries who are prepared to adopt new methods might have a most salutary effect on the efficiency of a very large number of British and European manufacturing concerns.[1]

R. G. LIPSEY

*London School of Economics.*

---

[1] Milton Friedman's argument that survival of the fittest proves profit maximisation notwithstanding (see *Essays in Positive Economics*, Chicago: University of Chicago Press, 1953). What seems to me to be a conclusive refutation of the Friedman argument is to be found in G. C. Archibald, " The State of Economic Science," *British Journal of the Philosophy of Science*, June 1959.

# [3]
# The Economic Theory of Customs Union[1]

*Harry G. Johnson*

The economic theory of customs union is of great practical relevance. It has an obvious immediate bearing on the formation of regional blocs of countries, such as the European Common Market, the Free Trade Area, and the India-Pakistan-Ceylon customs union which has sometimes been suggested; this is especially so because, quite irrationally, international convention condemns preferential systems except when the degree of preference is 100 per cent, as it is within national boundaries or in customs unions. It also has a direct bearing on the internal affairs and politics of countries containing economically distinct regions, particularly if these regions correspond with political or other cultural distinctions; in such countries, the question of regional gains or losses from participation in the national economy may be an important, and chronic, source of political discord – witness the problem of the maritime provinces in Canada, the Scottish and Welsh nationalist movements in the United Kingdom, and the position of East Pakistan in Pakistan.

The economic theory of customs union is also, unfortunately, complicated. The reason, as Viner pointed out in his pioneer analysis of the problem,[2] is that it combines elements of freer trade with elements of greater protection. While it provides freedom of trade between the participating countries, it also provides more protection for producers [14] inside the customs union area against competition from outside the area, since the protected market available to these producers is enlarged by the creation of a protected position in the markets of other countries partner to the union in addition to their protected position in their domestic market. This is the main reason for much of the confusion of popular thought on the subject of customs union: a particular customs union may be advocated by both free traders and protectionists, and conversely may be condemned by both, for opposite reasons.

The fact that a customs union is a mixture of freer trade and more protection means that it cannot be analysed by established welfare economics theory, which is concerned with the conditions for maximum welfare – the optimum conditions. Instead, the analysis of customs union requires the development of a theory capable of dealing with the conditions for improving welfare, for making things better rather than achieving the best possible, for maximizing welfare subject to arbitrary constraints which preclude the technically possible maximum-sub-optimum conditions or, to coin a phrase, melior conditions. The elements of such a theory were originated by Viner, with specific reference to the customs union problem.[3] More recently

Meade,[4] drawing on a seminal article by Marcus Fleming,[5] has developed the general theory of such problems, 'the theory of second-best' which still more recently has been restated and further generalized by Lipsey and Lancaster.[6] 'The general theorem of second-best' at which these authors arrive may be stated simply as follows: if an economy is prevented from attaining *all* the conditions for maximum welfare simultaneously, the fulfilment of one of these conditions will not necessarily make the country better off than would its non-fulfilment. The achievement of the maximum *attainable* welfare will generally require violation of the conditions for maximum welfare; and the effect on welfare of a [15] movement towards fulfilment of one of the optimum conditions will depend on the precise circumstances of the case.

Before proceeding to the customs union problem, let me illustrate the difference between traditional optimum theory and second-best theory by reference to the familiar proposition that a tax on a specific commodity imposes an excess burden. In so doing I assume (what is not always so) that money prices and costs represent real social values and costs; and I employ Marshallian consumers' surplus analysis, even though in its crude form this entails certain well-known difficulties associated with changes in the marginal utility of income. For simplicity, I also assume constant costs in production.

The traditional argument is illustrated in Figure 1, where DD is the demand curve, PQR the constant-cost supply curve, and P'Q' the supply curve including the tax. The tax shifts the equilibrium point from R to Q', imposing a loss of consumers' surplus P'Q'RP, of which P'Q'QP is balanced by tax revenue accruing to the government, leaving Q'QR as the net loss of consumers' surplus due to the taxation commodity, or the 'excess burden' of the tax; so that if the tax were removed and replaced by, for example, a lump sum tax, there would be a gain Q'QR of consumers' surplus.

This analysis rests on the assumption that value to consumers is equal to production cost at the margin elsewhere in the economy. But value may exceed cost for other commodities, either because of imperfections in the markets for these commodities or, as I shall assume, because they also bear taxes. The analysis of the effects on welfare of replacing the specific tax on the original commodity by a lump sum tax in this case can be carried out on two alternative lines, depending on whether the government is assumed to maintain tax rates unchanged, or to adjust the amount of lump sum taxation so as to maintain an unchanged total revenue.[7]

On the first assumption in order to expand consumption from OT to OS consumers must reduce expenditure on other goods by QTSR. To the extent that other goods are taxed, reduction of expenditure on them releases resources which were not required to [16] produce consumer satisfaction but instead were being used by the government for its own purposes; the corresponding reduction in the amount of government tax revenue and activity must be counted as a loss, against the gain in consumers' surplus on the commodity freed from taxation. This loss is illustrated in Figure 2, where AB is the constant-cost supply curve of other commodities (treated as an aggregate for convenience) A'B''B' is the supply curve including taxes, dd is the demand curve when the original commodity is taxed, and d'd' the demand curve when the tax on the original commodity is replaced by a lump sum tax.[8] The replacement of the tax on the original commodity reduces expenditure on other commodities by B'DD'B'' (equal to QTSR in Figure 1); but of this amount, only CDD'C' was required to produce the initial quantity of other commodities consumed, B'CC'B'' going to the government as tax revenue financing governmental services. In diverting expenditure from other commodities to the commodity on which the tax is replaced, the community must sacrifice not only the consumption of other

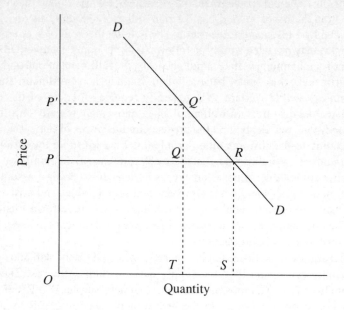

*Figure 1*

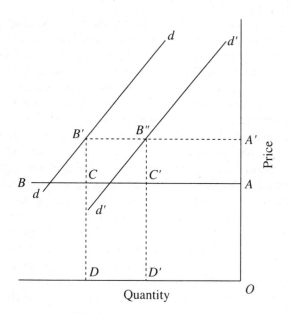

*Figure 2*

commodities but also the consumption of the governmental services previously financed by taxes levied on the sacrificed consumption. There is a net gain only if this latter sacrifice is less than the gain in consumers' surplus on the increased consumption of the tax-freed commodity, that is, if Q'QR in Figure 1 exceeds B'CC'B" in Figure 2.

On the second assumption, for production of the tax-freed commodity to increase from OT to OS resources to the value QTSR must shift out of other lines of production. To the extent that other lines of production bear taxes, expenditure on other goods must fall by more than the value of the resources required to expand production of the tax-freed commodity, the excess corresponding to the additional lump sum taxes required to compensate the government for the loss of tax revenue due to reduced consumption of these other goods; the corresponding reduction in total consumer expenditure on commodities is a loss which must be counted against the gain in consumers' surplus on the commodity freed from taxation. This loss can also be illustrated by Figure 2, if the definitions of its construction are slightly modified so as to equate CDD'C', the reduction in the quantity of resources employed in other industries due to the tax replacement, with QTSR in Figure 1. The diversion of resources to production of [17] the tax-freed commodity entails a reduction of expenditure on other commodities of B'DD'B", and a net reduction of expenditure of B'CC'B" which corresponds to the increase in lump sum taxes required to compensate the government for the loss of tax revenue B'CC'B". There will be a net gain only if the reduction of consumer expenditure is less than the gain in consumers' surplus on the tax-freed commodity, that is, if QQ'R in Figure 1 exceeds B'CC'B" in Figure 2.

The two alternative lines of analysis I have just expounded correspond to two ways of looking at the excess of value to consumers over cost in production of the other commodities than the one freed of tax. The first emphasizes the fact that it costs less to produce a given amount of (marginal) satisfaction in the taxed than in the untaxed industry, so that to maintain satisfaction unchanged while switching consumption to the latter industry it is necessary to obtain additional resources by reducing government activity. The second emphasizes the fact that a given amount of resources produces more (marginal) satisfaction in the taxed than in the untaxed industry, so that a re-allocation of production towards the untaxed industry must reduce the total of consumers' satisfaction obtained.

There is a further, important complication to the analysis. The foregoing argument assumes that other commodities than the tax-freed good can be treated as an aggregate, subject to a common rate of taxation, expenditure on which is simply diverted to the commodity on which the tax is replaced. In fact, some of these commodities will be substitutional, and others complementary, with the good on which the tax is replaced; and they will bear taxes at different rates. The effect of the replacement of the tax on a particular commodity by a lump sum tax will be to divert expenditure from the substitutes for that commodity to its complements, as well as to the commodity itself; insofar as the complements are subject to higher taxes than the substitutes, this diversion will involve a gain (which may be reckoned in either of the two ways discussed previously) additional to the increase in consumers' surplus on the tax-freed good and conversely, insofar as complements are subject to lower taxes than substitutes, there will be an additional loss. There will be a net gain or loss to the economy from the replacement of the tax by a lump sum subsidy, according as the net reduction in the amount of taxes collected on other commodities is less or greater than the increase in consumers' surplus on the commodity on which the tax is replaced. [18]

Let us now turn to the application of this kind of analysis to the problem of tariffs and commercial policy. To avoid the problem of welfare changes associated with the re-shuffling of internal production between goods bearing different tax rates, let us assume that there are no taxes on domestically produced goods;[9] and to avoid the complications arising from the fact that in practice the rate of tariff on an imported good often depends on the particular country from which it comes, let us assume that the tariff does not discriminate between imports of the same commodity according to their country of origin.

The effect of tariffs is to foster production of domestic goods which meet the consumers' demands at a higher real cost than would imports from abroad. This is because the consumer chooses between domestic and imported goods on the basis of their price inside the country: in the case of a domestically-produced good this price is equal to cost at the margin, whereas in the case of an import this price is above cost by the amount of the tariff collected on the good. The higher cost of want-satisfaction brought about by tariffs has two aspects: on the one hand, it takes the form of higher-cost domestic production of goods identical with those that would otherwise be imported; on the other hand, it takes the form of domestic production of other goods which meet the same need as imports would, but which cost more to produce. In both ways, the tariff promotes the choice of more expensive domestic as compared with cheaper foreign means of satisfying demand. But as between alternative sources of foreign goods, the tariff does not interfere with the choice of the cheaper source: because the tariff rate on imports is (by assumption) the same whatever their source, the import from the cheapest source will have the lowest price after the tariff has been paid and the commodity landed in the importing country.

A customs union involves eliminating the tariff on imports from some foreign sources ('the partner country', for short) but not from others ('the foreign country', for short). One effect of this is to promote a shift from consumption of higher-cost domestic products to consumption of lower-cost foreign products originating in the partner country. This shift has two aspects, parallelling the two aspects of the effects of tariffs just discussed: domestic production of [19] goods identical with those produced abroad is reduced or eliminated, the good now being imported from the partner country; and there is increased consumption of partner-country substitutes for domestic goods which formerly satisfied the need at a higher cost. In short, the demand for imports increases for two reasons: the replacement of domestic by partner production of the same goods – 'the production effect' – and increased consumption of partner substitutes for domestic goods – 'the consumption effect'; the production effect and the consumption effect together constitute 'the trade creation effect' of the customs union. Corresponding to its two components, trade creation entails an economic gain of two sorts: the saving on the real cost of goods previously produced domestically and now imported from the partner country; and the gain in consumers' surplus from the substitution of lower-cost for higher-cost means of satisfying wants. The gain from trade creation is illustrated diagrammatically in Figure 3. In the figure, DD is the domestic demand curve for a commodity, SS its domestic supply curve, PQR the partner supply curve (assumed contant cost) and P′Q′R′ the partner supply curve with the tariff added to the partner price. With the tariff, the country consumes OS′, of which OT′ is supplied by domestic production and T′S′ imported. When the tariff is eliminated, domestic production falls to OT and consumption rises to OS. The saving of cost on domestic production replaced by imports is QQ′M, and the gain in consumers' surplus from substitution of imports for other goods previously domestically produced is R′NR, so that the total gain from trade creation is the sum of these two areas, approximately equal to half the product of the change in the quantity of imports (TT′ plus S′S) and the money amount of the tariff per unit of imports (PP′). (The area P′PQQ′ represents a transfer of producers' surplus to consumers, and the area Q′MNR′ a transfer of tax proceeds to consumers' surplus, both of which cancel for the country as a whole.)

In addition to the trade creation effect, however, the elimination of the tariff on imports from partner but not from foreign sources has the effect of promoting shifts in the source of imports from lower-cost foreign to higher-cost partner sources. As before, such shifts have two aspects: an increase in the cost of identical goods owing to the shift from foreign to partner sources; and substitution of higher-cost partner goods for lower-cost foreign goods of a different description but suitable for satisfying the same needs. Such shifts constitute [20] 'the trade diversion effect' of customs union. The loss to the country from this source is measured by the difference in cost between the two sources of imports multiplied by the amount of trade diverted.

The loss from trade diversion is illustrated diagrammatically in Figure 4. DD is the demand curve, PT and $\pi$R the foreign and partner supply curves (assumed constant cost) and P′Q′ and $\pi$Q″ these curves after the tariff. These supply curves can be thought of either as relating to physically identical products, or as relating to the quantities of different products required to produce the same consumer satisfaction. With the tariff applied to both sources of imports, the country imports OS′ from the foreign country at a total cost of OPTS′. When the tariff on partner imports is eliminated, the country shifts to importing OS from the partner country; for its previous consumption OS′ it now pays a total cost O$\pi$RS′, representing an increase in cost (a loss) of $\pi$RTP. This loss must be weighed against the gain from trade creation (increased total consumption) of Q′RQ.

The foregoing argument assumes perfect foreign and partner elasticity of supply of importable goods. If supplies are not perfectly elastic, the trade diversion effect has two further consequences. In the first place, as trade is diverted from foreign to partner sources the foreign supply price falls. In consequence, the country enjoys a terms-of-trade gain on any trade with the foreign country which survives the formation of the customs union. In addition, any such survival reduces the amount of, and loss from, trade diversion. This has an important implication: the greater the exploitation of the foreigner through a favourable movement of the terms of trade, the less the loss from trade diversion. This implication is to be contrasted with the argument often put forward in favour of customs union by protectionists, that a customs union is a means of favouring the partner country at the expense of the foreigner (rather than of domestic industry) – to the extent that imports from the partner expand at the expense of the foreigner, it is the domestic consumer who loses. The second consequence of imperfectly elastic supplies is that the partner supply price rises as trade is diverted. This means that the loss to the country per unit of trade diverted is greater than it would have been with constant costs: on the other hand it implies that part of this loss is not a net loss to the domestic and partner economies taken together, but simply a transfer from domestic consumers' surplus to partner producers' surplus. [21]

In addition to the consequences of customs union previously analysed, there may also be various secondary repercussions. For example, if some particular foreign goods are complementary to imports from partner country sources, the trade creation effect of elimination of tariffs on partner imports will also create trade with the foreign country, thereby resulting in

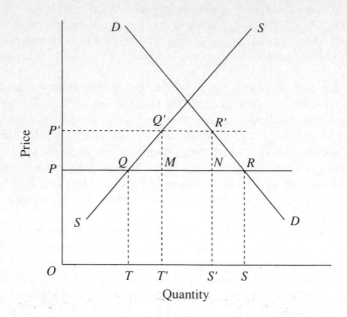

*Figure 3*

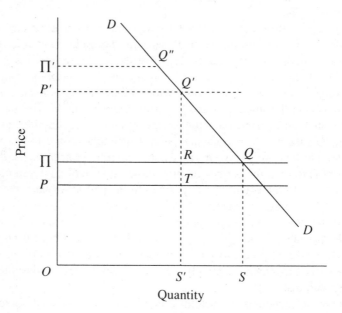

*Figure 4*

additional gains. Similarly, if the country's exports to the partner country which are stimulated by customs union are substitutes in domestic consumption for foreign goods, the country may increase its imports from the foreign country and so enjoy again from increased imports from the foreign country. Conversely, complementarity-substitutionary relations between goods might accentuate the country's loss from trade diversion.

Similar gains and losses to those discussed above would result from the elimination of partner duties on the country's exports resulting from customs union. Most of these would accrue to the partner country; but insofar as domestic supply of exports was inelastic, the country would enjoy a terms of trade gain with the partner country from elimination of its import duties.

A full analysis of the factors which determine the gains and losses from the formation of a customs union accruing to the individual members would require more space than is available. The foregoing analysis does indicate certain general principles relevant to this question. In the first place, a country is more likely to gain from the creation of trade resulting from a customs union the higher the initial level of its tariffs, and the more elastic the domestic demand for and supply of goods which the partner country is capable of producing. In the second place, a country is less likely to lose from trade diversion the smaller are the initial differences in cost between the partner and the foreign sources of supply for goods which both can produce, the more elastic is the partner supply of such goods, and the less elastic is the foreign supply of them; also, the less the degree of substitutability in consumption between goods from partner and from foreign sources. Thirdly, the country is more likely to gain on its terms of trade with the foreign country the more inelastic is the foreign supply of imports to it, and the more inelastic the foreign demand for its exports. Further, since a customs union usually involves some change in the level of the tariff on imports from foreign sources, the loss from trade diversion will tend to be less, and the possibility of gains on the terms of trade with foreign sources also less, the lower [22] the tariff on foreign sources after the formation of the customs union as compared with the level of that tariff before the formation of the union.

These general principles can be summarized, very roughly, in the form of a statement about the relation between the natures of the countries embarking on a customs union and the probable gains from such a union. Statements of this kind, however, must be recognized as dangerous, since a general description of the nature of a country is not an adequate substitute for detailed analysis of the probabilities of trade creation, trade diversion, and terms of trade effects. With that qualification, it can be said that a country is more likely to reap a gain from entering on a customs union, the more it and its partner country (countries) are initially similar in the products they produce but different in the patron of relative prices at which they produce them. This is especially true if the products both produce are things which are consumed in rapidly increasing quantities as the standard of living rises, since in this case the income-raising effect of trade creation is self-reinforcing. Further, members are more likely to gain the more different they are from the rest of the world, since this implies that the possibility of losses from trade diversion is less; and the more dependent the rest of the world is on member countries for the import of products in inelastic supply in the rest of the world or the export of products in inelastic demand in the rest of the world, since these imply the possibility of gains on the terms of trade with the rest of the world. (There is some conflict between these last two criteria, since exploitation of the foreigner through a favourable movement of the terms of trade change requires the possibility of some diversion of imports or exports away from the foreigner towards members of the union.)

This general statement implies that a customs union between heavily protected manufacturing countries, such as the European Common Market, is likely to lead to considerable gain, especially if each uses some of the income derived from its manufacturing skill to protect its agriculture from foreign competition. Similarly, agricultural areas of a similar kind each bent on industrialization are likely to gain from entering a customs union.

To reverse the statement, a country is less likely to gain from entering a customs union, the more different it is from its partners, the more the partners produce close substitutes for goods produced in [23] foreign countries, and the greater the difference in real costs between foreign and partner supplies of such products; also the more elastic is the foreign supply of such products, and the more the country concerned is a producer for the world market rather than for the market of one or more of the partner countries. An example of a country unlikely to gain from participation in a customs union is an economy with strong advantages in agricultural production uniting with a manufacturing region. The usual objection to such a union is that an agricultural region is unlikely to industrialize without substantial protective tariffs on manufactures. This argument is not particularly cogent, because the comparative advantage of the economy may well lie in agricultural production and the effect of tariffs be to reduce its real income; the fundamental objection in this case is that the customs union renders it subject to exploitation by the inefficient manufacturing partner country, so that it loses its comparative advantages without compensation. This may have been the case, for example, with the maritime and western provinces of Canada, in the past, when both could compete on a world market for their products but through their participation in Confederation were forced to buy manufactures from central Canadian manufacturing industry.

The argument so far has been concerned with possible gains and losses from the effects of customs union on the efficiency of specialization and division of labour within the customs union and between it and the outside world. There are other economic aspects of customs union which may also be important. In particular, the enlargement of the internal market brought about by customs union may bring economic advantages besides those of more efficient allocation of production and consumption between countries on the basis of costs of production of commodities before the formation of customs union. For one thing, formation of a customs union may bring about more widespread and effective competition between firms and industries, with a consequent elimination of monopolistic distortions of the economy. In the argument presented so far, it has been assumed that competition prevailed within national markets, so that prices conformed to real costs; if this is untrue, increased competition brought about by customs union may have significant effects in increasing the efficiency of production, apart from specializing production on producers with lowest real production costs. Second, and possibly of greatest long run importance, formation of a customs union may [24] increase the average rate of growth of the member economies, since the larger size of the internal market available to individual industries may both make it safer for the individual firm to invest resources and effort in the introduction of innovations and the deliberate pursuit of expansion, and put increased competitive pressure on individual firms to exploit whatever opportunities they have for expanding their share of the market and their absolute level of sales. Third, formation of a customs union may permit individual firms and also industries, to exploit the possibilities of economies of scale in production. The possibility of exploiting economies of scale does not, however, necessarily mean that each partner, or all members together, will be better off with the customs union than without; for even though such economies reduce cost of production, inside the union that cost may still be higher than the cost of supplies formerly imported from outside the union.

This point is illustrated in Figure 5. In the figure, $S_h S_h$ is the supply curve of domestic output in the home country, and $D_h D_h$ the home demand curve; $S_f S_f$ is the foreign supply curve, and $S'_f S'_f$ that supply curve with the tariff initially levied by the home and partner countries; $D_h + D_p \, D_h + D_p$ is the demand curve of the home and partner countries together. Before union, the home country consumes $OT'$ of domestically-produced output at a total cost of $OT'QS'_f$; while the partner country consumes $T'S'$ of imports, at a cost of $T'S'ST$.[10] With the formation of the customs union, partner consumption is diverted to home-country supply, which expands and in so doing lowers cost, the final equilibrium entailing production and consumption in the market as a whole of $OQ''$ at a cost of $OQ''Q'M$. The two countries together enjoy a gain of consumers' surplus from expanded consumption of $RVQ'$; on its previous level of consumption the home country enjoys a reduction of real cost in the amount $MNQS'_f$; the partner country, however, suffers an increase in the real cost of its previous consumption in the amount $TSVN$, which may outweigh its gain of consumers' surplus from expanded consumption $RV'Q'$ and may be large enough to outweigh the home country's gains from lower real cost and expanded consumption as well – as [25] shown by the magnitudes in the diagram. This case, it should be noted, requires that the partner country previously met its wants by imports: if both previously met their wants from protected domestic production, concentration of production in one country where it was subject to economies of scale would necessarily be beneficial to both.

The three possible favourable effects of the enlargement of the market brought about by customs union just discussed all assume that the enlargement of the market will be of the right type to promote such favourable effects. Whether this will be so or not depends on the nature of the existing markets in the member countries and the effects of enlargement through customs union on the nature of the resulting market. If the separate markets of the various members are divided by serious geographical barriers which require high transport costs to overcome them, the enlargement of the market may be more apparent than real; similarly, cultural differences may preserve the separation of member markets despite the removal of tariffs. Again, the Canadian case, at least in its early stages, offers an example of the limitations of removal of taxation barriers in the presence of important physical and cultural barriers to a mass market. This problem is obviously even more acute in the case of Pakistan.

Let me conclude this paper by turning from the economic theory of customs union to some of the problems which arise in the negotiation of them. In discussing these, I shall draw in a general way on the recent experience of the Common Market and Free Trade Area negotiations. The motivation towards the formation of a customs union is often political rather than economic; the economic urge may spring either from a desire for more effective protection, or from a desire for the advantages of greater freedom of trade. In the latter case, the formation of a customs union appears to offer a way around the difficulties of bargaining for mutual tariff reductions within the framework of the most-favoured-nation clause, a framework which impedes progress after a certain point because much of the benefit of a tariff concession goes to third countries, and even more because commodity-by-commodity bargaining accentuates the influence of vested interests in protection in the bargaining countries. The vested interests in protection, however, keep re-asserting themselves in the negotiations. The central problem of establishing a customs union is to determine the height and the pattern of the common tariff. Both offer scope for conflict between the protectionist interests of various countries, as well as

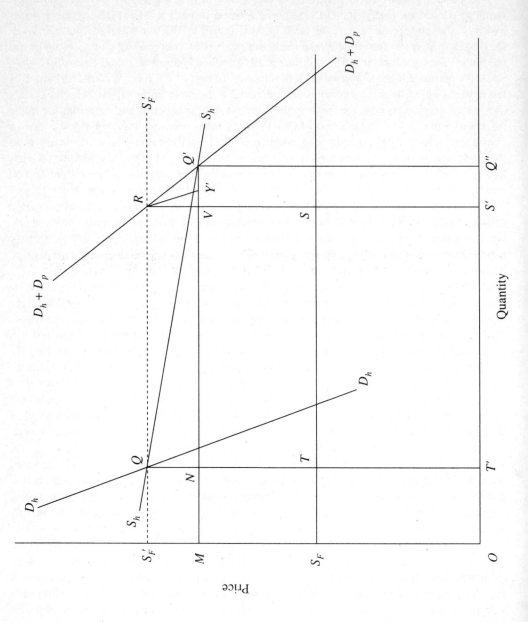

*Figure 5*

between protectionists [26] and free traders. One problem which has been important in the Common Market negotiations concerns the treatment of components and materials, where there is a conflict between countries which rely on imports and find their comparative advantage in the processing and advanced stages of production, and those which protect domestic production of such things from imported substitutes: The fixing of the common tariff level determines the distribution of loss between the materials-using industries of the former group and the materials-producing industries of the latter group. Needless to say, the straight averaging of rates which is sometimes resorted to solve such problems, and is also often taken as a standard ensuring that the degree of protection against outside countries is not increased, has no simple economic rationale – as can be readily inferred from the foregoing analysis of welfare effects.

Two problems which may be of considerable practical importance, particularly for customs unions among underdeveloped countries, are the division of the revenue from the common tariff – especially difficult if certain ports carry on entrepot activity – and the replacement of lost tariff revenue by other taxes, which may easily have equivalent protective effects. Again, the practical rules of thumb which tend to suggest themselves are often difficult to rationalize in terms of the theory of the welfare effects of customs union and of taxation.

Finally, since freedom of trade between countries both increases the risks of competitive enterprise and reduces the autonomy of domestic economic policy, negotiations for establishment of a customs union (or a free trade area, for that matter) tend to encounter demands for the co-ordination of national economic policies and in particular for the 'harmonization' of laws, regulations and other practices affecting the competitive position in the common market area of producers in different countries. Such demands, particularly those for 'harmonization', can generally be shown to rest on fallacious arguments stemming from ignorance of the principle of comparative cost, or from an implicit assumption that domestic wage-price levels and the exchange rate are both absolutely rigid; but they may nevertheless cause misunderstanding and bedevil negotiations. [27]

## Notes

1.  This paper is based on the notes of a lecture delivered in the University of Dacca, in August 1958. A customs union is defined as an agreement between members of a group of countries to remove tariffs levied by each on imports from the others, while establishing a tariff at common rates on imports into the member countries from non-member countries. It is to be distinguished from a free trade area, which allows members to fix their own separate tariff rates on imports from non-members, though they remove tariffs on trade among themselves. Both are narrower than an economic union, which may involve agreement on many other matters of international economic relations, including particularly freedom of factor movements between members. The economic theory of all three has much in common, and the analysis of the present paper is generally applicable to a free trade area as well as a customs union.
2.  Jacob Viner, *The Customs Union Issue*, (New York, Carnegie Endowment for International Peace, 1950).
3.  op. cit.
4.  J.E. Meade, *The Theory of International Economic Policy: Volume II, Trade and Welfare*, (London, Oxford University Press, 1955); also ibid, *The Theory of Customs Unions* (Amsterdam, North Holland Publishing Company, 1956).

5. J.M. Fleming, 'On Making the Best of Balance of Payments Restrictions on Imports', *Economic Journal*, 1951.
6. R.G. Lipsey and Kelvin Lancaster, 'The General Theory of Second Best', *Review of Economic Studies*, 1956–57.
7. It is assumed that the location of DD is not affected by the difference between the two assumptions. This, as well as the implicit assumption of the ensuing analysis that changes in government revenue can be cancelled against consumers' surplus, implies that the level of government expenditure is optimal and that changes in it can be treated as small.
8. Movement from d d to d'd' involves no loss of consumers' surplus; all changes in consumers' surplus are already taken into account in Figure 1.
9  We also abstract from divergences between price and marginal cost due to imperfect competition.
10. For diagrammatic simplicity it is assumed that the home tariff rate is just sufficient to protect domestic output from foreign competition, i.e. the difference between the cost at which domestic demand can be satisfied and the foreign cost is just equal to the tariff rate.

# [4]

## A NEW LOOK AT CUSTOMS UNION THEORY [1]

CUSTOMS union theory can be said to date from the publication in 1950 of Viner's pioneering work.[2]   Viner showed that a customs union can result in either trade creation or trade diversion: the former involves a shift from high-cost domestic production to lower-cost production in a partner country; the latter a shift from the lowest-cost external producer to a higher-cost partner.   Viner pointed out that trade creation raises the home country's welfare, and trade division lowers it.   This distinction has formed the basis of most subsequent analysis of the welfare implications of customs unions.

Viner's analysis has been extended and modified by Lipsey, Meade, Gehrels and others [3] to take account of intercommodity substitution, or " consumption effects."   Lipsey, for example, argues that " when consumption effects are allowed for, the simple conclusions that trade creation is ' good ' and trade diversion ' bad ' are no longer valid." [4]   Although he does not try to establish that trade creation can lower welfare, he does show that trade diversion can raise welfare.[5]   When a tariff is imposed it introduces a divergence between relative prices facing consumers and real opportunity costs of goods to the economy.   It is, in this respect, identical to an excise tax, and constrains consumers to a non-optimal consumption equilibrium.   When a customs union is formed, some dutiable goods formerly imported from outside sources will be replaced by the same goods imported from a partner country, duty-free but at a higher real cost.   The shift to a higher-cost source of supply tends to lower the country's real income, and consequently consumer welfare; but the removal of the constraint on consumption may raise welfare.   If the second effect is favourable, and outweighs the first effect, there is a net rise in welfare.

This paper is concerned with the " pure theory " of customs unions—as surveyed in Lipsey's classic article [5]—and rules out gains from changes in the terms of trade, economies of scale and other considerations not forming part of the pure theory.

[1] Any views expressed in this paper are those of the authors.   They should not be interpreted as reflecting the view of the Rand Corporation or of the Centre for Economic Research.

The authors are indebted to Professors Richard N. Cooper and Harry G. Johnson for helpful comments.

[2] Jacob Viner, *The Customs Union Issue* (New York: Carnegie Endowment for International Peace, 1950).

[3] See, for example, R. G. Lipsey, " Trade Diversion and Welfare," *Economica*, Vol. XXIV, February 1957, pp. 40–6; R. G. Lipsey, " The Theory of Customs Unions: A General Survey," ECONOMIC JOURNAL, September 1960, pp. 496–513; J. E. Meade, *The Theory of Customs Unions* (Amsterdam: North Holland Publishing Co., 1956); F. Gehrels, " Customs Unions from a Single Country Viewpoint," *Review of Economic Studies*, Vol. XXIV (1), No. 63, 1956–7.

[4] R. G. Lipsey, " Trade Diversion and Welfare," *op. cit.*, p. 41.

[5] R. G. Lipsey, " The Theory of Customs Unions: A General Survey," *op. cit.*, pp. 506–9.

We shall argue the following:

(1) Analytically the welfare effect of a customs union—whether trade creating, trade diverting or both—can be split into two components: (*a*) a tariff reduction component, and (*b*) a pure trade diversion component.

(2) Using the standards of traditional customs union analysis, the tariff reduction component is the sole source of any gain in consumers' welfare that might result from a customs union. It accounts for both trade creation and the consumption effect.

(3) Using as a point of reference an *appropriate* policy of non-preferential protection, a customs union necessarily results in pure trade-diversion, and is consequently " bad " in the traditional welfare sense.

(4) The " free trade point of view " underlying the Vinerian analysis fails to explain why a customs union would ever be preferred to a non-preferential tariff policy.

(5) Recognition of the purposes served by tariffs permits an explanation of the existence of customs unions, and the extension of customs-union analysis to a greater variety of issues than has hitherto been the case.

## Customs Unions and Consumer Welfare

Fig. 1 shows the home market for any individual product affected by the customs union.[1] In the Fig. $D$ is the home demand curve; $S_h$ is the supply curve of domestic producers; $S_{h+p}$, the supply curve of the home-plus-partner countries, assuming that the partner's goods are admitted duty free; and $S_w$, the world supply curve.[2] For greater generality, we have assumed rising costs in the home and partner countries.[3] But to rule out terms-of-trade effects, the home country is assumed not to account for a substantial proportion of total world imports of the item; consequently the world supply curve, $S_w$, will appear horizontal in this market, even if there are rising costs.[4]

First, consider that the country initially has a non-preferential tariff equal to $RQ$, so that the relevant supply curve is $RBT$. Then quantity $ON$ will be consumed at price $OQ$. Of this amount, $OL$ will be produced domestically and the remainder, $LN$, imported from the lowest-cost (world) supplier.

Second, consider an initial non-preferential tariff below $RQ$. The price is then below $OQ$, consumption in excess of $ON$ and local production less

---

[1] The diagram is similar to that used by Harry G. Johnson in *Money, Trade, and Economic Growth* (Cambridge: Harvard University Press, 1962), p. 65.

[2] For clarity of exposition, it is assumed that the partner country cannot sell in the home-country market in the absence of a tariff preference. This assumption is not essential to the analysis.

[3] Constant costs in either country can be treated as a limiting case of the following analysis without materially affecting the results.

[4] In other words, with respect to imports, the country is a price-taker rather than a price-maker.

than $OL$, with imports supplying that part of consumption that is not locally supplied.

In either of these two cases forming a customs union leaves the price, quantity consumed and level of local production unchanged.[1]   However,

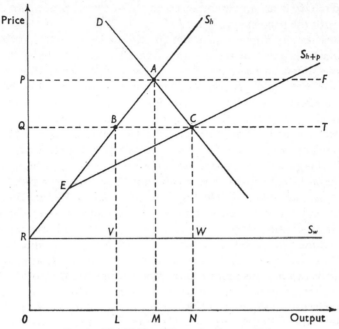

FIG. 1.—The Welfare Effects of a Customs Union.

the higher-cost partner country displaces the lowest-cost world supplier,[2] raising the real cost of the item to the economy, and reducing the customs revenue.[3]   We shall term this *pure* trade diversion.

Third, consider a tariff in excess of $RP$.   The effective world supply curve (including the tariff) then lies above $PF$, and the entire local demand is supplied out of local production.   Quantity $OM$ is sold at price $OP$.   In this case forming a customs union results in trade creation; the partner displaces (in part) local production.   The price falls to $OQ$, consumption increase to $ON$, local production declines to $OL$ and the partner supplies $LN$.

---

[1] We are making the traditional assumption that the pre-union tariff remains effective with respect to imports from countries other than the partner.

[2] The partner will displace at least some imports if the tariff is high enough for the customs union to be effective, *i.e.*, if the tariff shifts $S_w$ enough to intersect $S_h$ above point $E$.   The partner will *entirely* displace imports if the tariff is equal to $RQ$.

[3] From the home country's point of view the increase in real cost will equal the loss in customs revenue.   If the tariff equals $RQ$ this will be shown by the area of the rectangle $BCWV$; if the tariff is less than $RQ$ the increase in cost will be less.

Fourth, if the tariff is between $RQ$ and $RP$ the price is between $OQ$ and $OP$. Local demand is then supplied jointly by local production and imports. The quantity consumed is between $OM$ and $ON$; local production between $OL$ and $OM$; and imports make up the difference. A customs union then results in both trade creation and trade diversion. The price is again reduced to $OQ$, consumption increases to $ON$ and local production is reduced to $OL$, with the partner supplying $LN$.

Present theory argues that trade creation is beneficial, that trade diversion is harmful and that the consumption effect may be either.[1] Whether a customs union on balance raises or lowers consumer welfare depends on whether or not trade creation plus (or minus, as the case may be) the consumption effect outweigh trade diversion.

According to present theory, then, our first two examples (pure trade diversion) are bad. The third and fourth examples cannot be evaluated without reference to what is happening elsewhere in the economy. The type of analysis regarded as appropriate is the theory of second-best.

We establish our first two points by noting that in examples 3 and 4 the country has the option of selecting a tariff equal to $RQ$, making $RBT$ the effective supply curve. Consumption will be equal to $ON$; the price $OQ$; domestic production $OL$; and imports $LN$. Thus, this lower tariff will provide the same price, level of consumption and domestic production obtained in the customs union. But with the lower non-preferential tariff (as compared with the customs union), imports from the outside world (the lowest-cost supplier) entirely displace imports from the partner, providing a net gain to the country equal to the difference in the total cost of supply from the two alternative sources: the area of rectangle $BCWV$. Moreover, customs revenue will be greater by the same amount.

It is then convenient to split the effect of a customs union into two components: (1) a non-preferential tariff reduction to $RQ$, and (2) a move from this position to a customs union with the initial tariff.[2] This analytical distinction shows clearly that any rise in consumer welfare as a consequence of forming a customs union, whether as a result of trade creation or a favourable consumption effect, is due entirely to the tariff reduction component of the move. Moving to a customs union from the position obtainable as a result of the non-preferential tariff reduction is simply pure trade diversion—a substitution of the high-cost partner's goods for goods from the lowest-cost world supplier—which lowers welfare. Whether a customs union is on balance beneficial (compared with the initial non-preferential tariff) will depend on whether the tariff-reduction effect outweighs the pure trade diversion effect.

But this result implies that a customs union is necessarily inferior to an

---

[1] In the diagram the consumption effect is necessarily beneficial; but it may be more than offset by harmful effects possibly arising from a reduction in the consumption of other items.

[2] If the initial tariff is no greater than $RQ$, then there is no tariff reduction.

*appropriate* policy of non-preferential protection. Even without the option of forming a customs union, the home country already has the option of lowering its initial tariff and thereby reaping the beneficial effects that a customs unions would provide without the offsetting costs. Moreover, because a customs union is always purely trade-diverting compared with the best non-preferential tariff, then the theory of second-best is not helpful in evaluating the welfare effects of the customs union *per se*; second-best theory is relevant only for evaluating the welfare effect of the tariff reduction component.

The difficulty posed for customs union analysis by the intermingling of tariff reduction and pure trade diversion effects shows up clearly in Lipsey's classic article.[1] In order to analyse the consumption effect of a customs union, Lipsey must first neutralise the impact of the implicit tariff reduction. He does this by assuming " that the tariff revenue collected by the government is either returned to individuals by means of lump-sum subsidies or spent by the government on the same bundle of goods that consumers would have purchased." [2] Without this assumption, which eliminates the revenue effect of tariffs, it would be necessary to consider the economic consequences of replacing the revenue lost in forming a customs union. Since forming a customs union does not, *per se*, generate new sources of revenue, the Government must employ an alternative that existed before. As this source of revenue was previously by-passed, there is a presumption that the Government regarded it as inferior to the tariff actually chosen. If not, the Government could shift to this alternative source of revenue even without forming a customs union. But this means that a customs union cannot be judged " good " or " bad " without taking into account the harmful effects of raising the revenue previously generated by the pre-union tariff. Moreover, this difficulty is not confined to the issue of replacing revenue. Whatever the purpose of pre-union tariffs—whether as revenue-raising, protective or balance-of-payments devices—the cost of replacing them in a customs union must be considered.

Viner was explicit that trade creation is good and trade diversion bad *from a free trade point of view*. As he also regarded tariffs as an inefficient means of raising revenue, it followed that any pre-union tariff has to be ill-advised. It is then certainly possible for a customs union to bring about a gain—even though an even larger gain could be achieved through a simple reduction in the non-preferential tariff.

We certainly do not question the logic of Viner's analysis. What we do question is the usefulness of this type of analysis as a basis for the evaluation of customs unions. It fails to show why a customs union may be acceptable when a tariff reduction is not, and it fails to analyse how a customs union may more efficiently serve the ends previously served by non-preferential

[1] R. G. Lipsey, *op. cit.*
[2] *Ibid.*, p. 500.

protection.   We would argue that the answer to the latter is the key to the former.   It may be that policy-makers are sufficiently obtuse not to notice that a " good " customs union has moved them towards free trade and away from protection, but this assumption of political myopia does not appear to be well founded.   And without this assumption, by failing to explain why countries have tariffs, customs-union theory fails to explain also why customs unions are formed.

By making explicit the economic ends served by tariffs, the stage is set for an extension of customs-union analysis.   Much of the recent controversy surrounding customs unions has, in fact, been carried on from this point of view.   The possible gains from a customs union resulting from improvements in the terms of trade, economies of scale and reductions in disguised un-employment have received considerable attention.   These gains, of course, do not show up as the simple trade-creation gains considered in the Vinerian model.   Little, if any, attention has been given, however, to the comparison of the relative efficiency of preferential and non-preferential tariff systems as protective devices.   By permitting customs-union participants to draw on one another's markets, a customs union may make it possible for its members to maintain a protected domestic market at less sacrifice in income than is possible through non-preferential protection.   To analyse the prospective gains from such " market-swapping " requires a different analytical frame-work from that provided by traditional customs-union theory.[1]   By depart-ing from the traditional framework, economists will have more to say about issues hitherto left for the policy-makers to grapple with.

C. A. COOPER
B. F. MASSELL

*The Rand Corporation,*
    *Santa Monica, California.*
*The Centre for Economic Research,*
    *Nairobi, Kenya.*

[1] For our own attempt to provide an analytical discussion of market-swapping, see C. A. Cooper and B. F. Massell, " Toward a General Theory of Customs Unions for Developing Countries," *The Journal of Political Economy*, forthcoming.

# Part II
# Outside the Mainstream

# [5]

Journal of International Economics 6 (1976) 95–97. © North-Holland Publishing Company

## AN ELEMENTARY PROPOSITION CONCERNING THE FORMATION OF CUSTOMS UNIONS

Murray C. KEMP*

*University of New South Wales, Sydney, Australia*

Henry Y. WAN, Jr.

*Cornell University, Ithaca, NY 14853, U.S.A.*

## 1. Introduction

In the welter of inconclusive debate concerning the implications of customs unions, the following elementary yet basic proposition seems to have been almost lost to sight.[1]

*Proposition.  Consider any competitive world trading equilibrium, with any number of countries and commodities, and with no restrictions whatever on the tariffs and other commodity taxes of individual countries, and with costs of transport fully recognized. Now let any subset of the countries form a customs union. Then there exists a common tariff vector and a system of lump-sum compensatory payments, involving only members of the union, such that there is an associated tariff-ridden competitive equilibrium in which each individual, whether a member of the union or not, is not worse off than before the formation of the union.*[2]

A detailed list of assumptions, and a relatively formal proof, may be found in section 2. Here we merely note that there exists a common tariff vector which is consistent with pre-union world prices and, therefore, with pre-union trade patterns and pre-union levels of welfare for nonmembers.

The proposition is interesting in that it contains no qualifications whatever

---

*We acknowledge with gratitude the useful comments of Jagdish Bhagwati, John Chipman and two referees.

[1]A crude version of the proposition, together with an indication of the lines along which a proof may be constructed, can be found in Kemp (1964, p. 176). A geometric proof for the canonical three-countries, two-commodities case has been furnished by Vanek (1965, pp. 160–179). Negishi (1972, p. 187) has provided an algebraic treatment of the same canonical case.

[2]With the same common tariff vector and system of lump-sum payments there may be associated other competitive equilibria which are not Pareto-comparable to the pre-union equilibrium. For this reason, the assertion is worded with care.

concerning the size or number of the countries which are contemplating union, their pre- or post-union trading relationships, their relative states of development or levels of average income, and their propinquities in terms of geography or costs of transportation.

The proposition is interesting also because it implies that an incentive to form and enlarge customs unions persists until the world is one big customs union, that is, until world free trade prevails. More precisely, given any initial trading equilibrium, there exist finite sequences of steps, at each step new customs unions being created or old unions enlarged, such that at each step no individual is made worse off and such that after the last step the world is free-trading. (In general, at each step some individual actually benefits.) Indeed, on the basis of these observations one might attempt to rehabilitate the vague pre-Vinerian view that to form a customs union is to move in the direction of free trade.

Evidently the incentive is latent and insufficiently strong; tariffs and other artificial obstacles to trade persist. That the world is not free-trading must be explained in terms of:

(1) the game-theoretic problems of choosing partners, dividing the spoils and enforcing agreements;

(2) the noneconomic objectives of nations; and

(3) the possibility that the 'right' common tariff vector and system of compensatory payments might be associated with the 'wrong' post-union equilibrium, that is, an equilibrium in which some members are worse off than before the union.[3]

A role may be found also for:

(4) inertia and ignorance concerning the implications of possible unions (in particular, concerning the long list of lump-sum compensatory payments required) and, in the short run, for

(5) the restraint exercised by international agreements to limit tariffs and other restrictions on trade.

However (5) can form no part of an explanation of the persistence of trading blocks in the long run.

Topics (1)–(4) form a possible agenda for the further study of customs unions. For a preliminary analysis of (1) the reader may consult Caves (1971); and for suggestive work on (2) he is referred to Cooper and Massell (1965), Johnson (1965) and Bhagwati (1968).

## 2. Proof of the proposition

Suppose that (ia) the consumption set of each individual is closed, convex and bounded below, (ib) the preferences of each individual are convex and

---

[3]See footnote 2.

representable by a continuous ordinal utility function, (ic) each individual can survive with a consumption bundle each component of which is somewhat less than his pre-union consumption bundle, (ii) the production set of each economy is closed, convex, contains the origin and is such that positive output requires at least one positive input (impossibility of free production).

Consider a fictitious economy composed of the member economies but with a net endowment equal to the sum of the member endowments plus the equilibrium pre-union net excess supply of the rest of the world. In view of (i) and (ii), the economy possesses an optimum and any optimum can be supported by at least one internal price vector (Debreu (1959, pp. 92–93, 95–96)). Either the pre-union equilibrium of the member countries is a Pareto-optimal equilibrium of the fictitious economy (that is, corresponds to a maximal point of the utility possibility set), or it is not; in the latter case, a preferred Pareto-optimal equilibrium can be attained by means of lump-sum transfers among individuals in the fictitious economy. That essentially completes the proof. It only remains to note that the required vector of common tariffs may be computed as the difference between the vector of pre-union world prices and the vector of internal union prices.

Commodities can be indexed by location. Hence the resource-using activity of moving commodities from one country to another is accommodated in the several production sets; no special treatment of cost of transportation is needed.

## References

Debreu, G., 1959, Theory of value (John Wiley, New York).

Kemp, M.C., 1964, The pure theory of international trade (Prentice-Hall, Englewood Cliffs, NJ).

Cooper, C.A. and B.F. Massell, 1965, Towards a general theory of customs unions for developing countries, Journal of Political Economy 73, 461–476.

Johnson, H.G., 1965, An economic theory of protectionism, tariff bargaining, and the formation of customs unions, Journal of Political Economy 73, 256–283.

Vanek, J., 1965, General equilibrium of international discrimination: The case of customs unions (Harvard University Press, Cambridge, MA).

Bhagwati, J., 1968, Trade liberalization among LDCs, trade theory, and GATT rules, in: J.N. Wolfe, ed., Value, capital, and growth: Papers in honour of Sir John Hicks (Edinburgh University Press, Edinburgh) 21–43.

Caves, R.E., 1971, The economics of reciprocity: Theory and evidence on bilateral trading arrangements, Harvard Institute of Economic Research, Discussion Paper No. 166 (Harvard University, Cambridge, MA).

Negishi, T., 1972, General equilibrium theory and international trade (North-Holland, Amsterdam).

# [6]

## Preferential Trading Theory: The *n* Commodity Case

Eitan Berglas

*Tel-Aviv University*

This is a general equilibrium analysis of preferential trading. A method was developed which allows the analysis of the many-good case and which suggests the tools for empirical studies. It is shown that increasing the number of commodities beyond two introduces new considerations. It is, however, always possible to identify welfare-increasing tariff changes. The study analyzes the inter-relationship between preferential trading and a unilateral movement to free trade. The effect of a customs union on income distribution among union members is emphasized.

### Introduction

Any analysis of customs unions must start with a reference to Viner's *The Customs Union Issue* (1950). Viner clearly recognizes that the evaluation of benefits from customs unions is a problem of second best; in fact, his book is one of the earliest contributions to the literature of second best. Furthermore, he coined the terms "trade creation" and "trade diversion," which are still widely used (although sometimes misused).

Viner's is a partial equilibrium analysis. If country $A$ imports cloth from country $B$, and they form a customs union, the elimination of the tariff will cause producer and consumer prices in $A$ to fall, thus increasing consumption and reducing production of cloth in $A$. This is the trade creation which results in an increase in welfare. Trade

This paper relies heavily on my discussion paper (1976*b*) written during my stay at the University of Rochester. I am indebted to Ronald W. Jones for both constructive criticism and helpful suggestions. Partial financial support from the Foerder Institute of Economic Research is gratefully acknowledged.

[*Journal of Political Economy*, 1979, vol. 87, no. 2]

diversion occurs if, as a result of the reduction of the tariff on imports from $B$, $A$ starts to import machinery from $B$ which was formerly imported from a more efficient producer, $C$. This, of course, is an undesirable change in resource allocation. The Viner approach had the advantage of being a relatively simple method for estimating gains and losses from the formation of customs unions.[1]

For reasons that will become clear as we proceed, it was recognized that the partial equilibrium approach frequently may be misleading; the problem of customs unions should be analyzed within the framework of general equilibrium models. The modern formulations of this approach are by Vanek (1965) and Kemp (1969). Given the complexity of general equilibrium analysis, the number of commodities is severely reduced in these studies. Their analysis, which depends heavily on offer curves, is most complete for the two-commodity case. Some extensions are made by Vanek for the three-good case, at the cost of considerable simplification of the underlying production structure. Furthermore, it is very difficult to use the results of their approach for empirical studies.

This paper uses the second-best approach developed in trade and public finance theory. An early use of these instruments for the customs-union problem can be found in Meade (1955); the present paper can be regarded as a reformulation and extension of Meade's contribution. Satisfactory answers are provided to some of the objections to this approach raised by Lipsey (1960) and Vanek (1965). The main body of the paper analyzes the three-commodity case. This is done for purposes of exhibition, but the method can be used for any number of commodities. An outline for the extension to the $n$ commodity case appears in the Appendix.

Some qualifications are important. We ignore the important effects of economies of scale and specialization arising from larger markets. Given larger markets, foreign firms can find it profitable to invest in the customs union countries, thus effectively avoiding external tariff walls. In some cases (e.g., the European Common Market), a customs union increases factor mobility within the union. Increased mobility requires some harmonization of the economic policies of member states and thus considerably restricts their governments' freedom to make policy. This has important economic consequences.[2] Similar qualifications apply to other studies in this field.

---

[1] For a modern textbook presentation of Viner's analysis, see Caves and Jones (1973, chap. 15).

[2] In our analysis, we do not presuppose that governments maximize welfare. Therefore, restricting the set of policy choices may improve welfare. For the analysis of these aspects with regard to free-trade areas, see Johnson (1971, chap. 16). If we consider the case of a customs union with free-factor mobility, we are facing a situation which is similar to the interaction between local governments. I have demonstrated elsewhere (1976a) that this may stimulate efficiency in government operation.

It may be important to note here, however, that Kemp deals exhaustively with the case of capital mobility for the two-commodity case. Since it is easy to analyze the case of many commodities with our method, it is relatively easy to extend the analysis to the case of capital mobility. However, for reasons of space and complexity, we have decided against doing so at this stage.

## A Three-Good Model

In this section we introduce a three-good model. From the following analysis, it will be obvious that the existence of a third commodity introduces very important considerations which are absent in the two-commodity model. The extension from three commodities to $n$ commodities is made in the Appendix, since it does not significantly affect the results. It seems worthwhile to spend some time on developing the basic concepts in the three-commodity model in order to simplify the demonstration.

The flow of trade in the three-commodity model is presented in the following arrow diagram; $A$, $B$, and $C$ denote the three countries in the world, and 1, 2, and 3 denote the three commodities (fig. 1). We shall discuss preferential trade agreements between $A$ and $B$. Without loss of generality, $C$ can be regarded as the rest of the world, which can represent many countries provided the tariff structure of these countries is unchanged throughout the analysis.

The flow diagram introduces a basic asymmetry between countries $A$ and $B$. The trade between $A$ and $B$ is restricted to commodities 1 and 2, where $A$ imports commodity 1 from $B$ and exports commodity 2 to $B$. No trade in commodities 1 and 2 exists between $B$ and $C$. At the same time, $A$ trades in commodities 1 and 2 with both countries $B$ and $C$. This asymmetry exists whenever we exclude the possibility that a country will export and import the same commodity. When we increase the number of commodities, we shall allow for some commodities to be exported from $B$ to both $A$ and $C$ and other commodities to be exported from $A$ to both $B$ and $C$. In many cases,

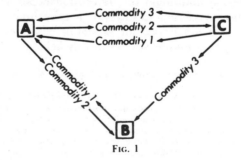

Fig. 1

however, such as a customs union between, say, the United States and Canada or the EEC and Israel, $B$ may be a small country that enters into an agreement with a large country $A$, and the asymmetry represents the difference in the size of the two countries.

Observe that no trade in commodity 3 exists between $A$ and $B$, and both $A$ and $B$ are net importers of 3. This creates the possibility that when tariffs between $A$ and $B$ are eliminated, commodity 3 will be imported only by the country with the lower tariff and transshipped to the other, thus avoiding the higher tariff walls. We rule out this possibility. The restriction can be given the following alternative interpretations: (a) $t_3$, the tariff on commodity 3, is the same in $A$ and $B$; (b) the tariff difference is smaller than the transport cost of commodity 3 between $A$ and $B$; or (c) the tariff agreement does not include commodity 3.

In most of the following analysis, we assume that the terms of trade are fixed and are determined by the large country, $C$.[3] However, as will be demonstrated later, this analysis is also the convenient first step to the discussion of the case of variable terms of trade.

This study starts from the same framework used by Vanek (1965) and Kemp (1969). It departs from these two studies by adding a third commodity (commodity 3 in the flow diagram). In order to be able to discuss three (or more) commodities simultaneously, it was necessary to discard the offer-curve analysis used by Vanek and Kemp and substitute instead a simple algebraic analysis. However, our study is more restrictive than Kemp's in two respects: First, we shall not discuss the possibility of international flow of investment; second, we shall not discuss the possibility that the trade agreements may reverse the flow of trade. More specifically, we assume that the trade before and after the agreements can be presented by the same flow diagram. We refrain from discussing these important cases in order to simplify the analysis, although they can be incorporated in the following analysis.

There are several general equilibrium studies of customs unions in which the number of commodities exceeds two; among them are Meade (1955), Lipsey (1960), Vanek (1965), and Corden (1976). In order to be able to derive conclusions, all of these studies adopt very restrictive assumptions about supply or demand elasticities. Thus, their results hold for very special cases. In the following analysis, no special restrictions on these elasticities are necessary.

We introduce the following notation: $P_i^j (j = A, B, C,$ and $i = 1, 2, 3)$ denotes the price of commodity $i$ in country $j$, and $100\, t_i^j$ denotes the tariff rate on commodity $i$ in country $j$ as a percentage of the world

[3] Only small alterations in the analysis are necessary if we assume instead that country $A$ is the large country.

PREFERENTIAL TRADING THEORY                                            319

price of this commodity. In order to allow differential tariffs, we
denote the tariff rate on $A$'s imports of commodity 1 from country $B$
by $\tau_1$, and from $C$ by $t_1^A$. Before the trade agreement, we assume
uniform tariffs in $A$; thus, $t_1^A = \tau_1$. A preferential trade agreement
implies $\tau_1 < t_1^A$, and a customs union implies $\tau_1 = 0$. Given this
notation, table 1 summarizes the internal prices in each country. Now,
consider a preferential trade agreement between $A$ and $B$ by which
tariffs on trade between these two countries are reduced (or even
completely eliminated) while tariffs on trade with $C$ remain unchanged. In terms of our notation, both $\tau_1$ and $t_2^B$ are reduced (or
equated to zero). Observe that this agreement will have no effect on
prices in $A$; in $B$, $P_1^B$ will rise, $P_2^B$ will fall, and $P_3^B$ will remain unchanged. It is important to note that although the price of commodity
1 to the consumer in $A$ does not change, the price paid for the imports
of commodity 1 from $B$ rises by the amount of the reduction in $\tau_1$. The
difference in the behavior of prices in the two union countries is a
result of the asymmetry mentioned above.

The traditional approach of customs-union theory is to investigate
the effect of trade agreements on welfare. We shall analyze the welfare effect in $A$ and $B$ separately, then suggest a method of exact
compensation so that we can talk about the effect on the joint welfare
of the two countries. We ignore the welfare effect on country $C$. If we
assume that no tariffs (and no other disturbances to a competitive
market) exist in $C$, then the assumption that prices are not affected in
$C$ implies that welfare in $C$ is not affected. If this is not the case, then
the welfare measure developed below can be applied to $C$ as well.

The measure of welfare for small changes is

$$dW^j = \sum_i P_i^j dD_i^j, \qquad j = A,B \text{ and } i = 1,2,3, \tag{1}$$

where $P_i$ are consumer prices and $dD$ are small changes in consumption.[4]

In order to use this welfare criterion, we first define the resource
constraint in the two countries:

$$\sum_{i=1}^{3} D_i^A P_i^A = \sum_{i=1}^{3} X_i^A P_i^A + t_1^A P_1 (E_1^A + E_1^B) - \tau_1 P_1 E_1^B + t_3^A P_3 E_3^A \tag{2}$$

[4] This measure is widely applied to trade analysis by Caves and Jones (1973). Assuming that the preferences of each country can be represented by a well-behaved utility
function $u = u(D_1, D_2, \ldots, D_n)$, then, differentiating, we get $du = \Sigma(\partial u/\partial D_i)dD_i$. Define
$dW = du/(\partial u/\partial D_1)$; then $dW = dD_1 + \Sigma_{i=2}^{n} (\partial u/\partial D_i)/(\partial u/\partial D_1)dD_i$. For the utility maximizing consumer, $(\partial u/\partial D_i)/(\partial u/\partial D_1) = P_i/P_1$. Thereby, $dW = P_i dD_i$ where $P_1 = 1$. Later,
we shall allow for changes in world prices; however, we shall keep $P_1 = 1$, a restriction
which has no effect on the analysis. This expression is also the basic measure used in
cost-benefit studies. For an alternative set of assumptions that lead to this welfare
criterion and are used in cost-benefit studies, see Harberger (1971).

TABLE 1

LOCAL PRICES (Including Tariffs)

|              | $P_i^A$              | $P_i^B$                      | $P_i^{c}$ |
|--------------|---------------------|------------------------------|-----------|
| Commodity 1  | $P_1(1 + t_1^A)$    | $P_1(1 + t_1^A - \tau_1)$    | $P_1$     |
| Commodity 2  | $P_2$               | $P_2(1 + t_2^B)$             | $P_2$     |
| Commodity 3  | $P_3(1 + t_3^A)$    | $P_3(1 + t_3^B)$             | $P_3$     |

and

$$\sum_{i=1}^{3} D_i^B P_i^B = \sum_{i=1}^{3} X_i^B P_i^B + t_2^B P_2 E_2^B + t_3^B P_3 E_3^B, \tag{3}$$

where $X_i^j$ is the production of commodity $i$ in country $j$, and $E_i^j = D_i^j - X_i^j$. The two resource constraints mean that in each country the value of consumption is equal to the value of production plus the tariff revenue, where both consumption and production are evaluated in local prices. We assume that tariff revenues are redistributed to consumers as a lump-sum subsidy. The expression for tariff revenues in $A$ is somewhat more complicated in order to allow for the possibility that a different tariff rate will be applied to the import of commodity 1 according to the country of origin. Observe that when $\tau_1 = t_1^A$, equations (2) and (3) are completely symmetric.

In order to check the effect of a preferential trade agreement, we consider the case where both $\tau_1$ and $t_2^B$ are slightly reduced. Taking the differentials of equations (2) and (3), using (a) the definitions of local prices in table 1, (b) the welfare definition of equation (1), and (c) taking the fact that (assuming competition) profit maximization requires $\sum_{i=1}^{3} P_i^j dX_i^j = 0$, we get

$$dW^A = t_1^A P_1 dE_1^A + (t_1^A - \tau_1)P_1 dE_1^B - P_1 E_1^B d\tau_1 + t_3^A P_3 dE_3^A \tag{4}$$

and

$$dW^B = P_1 E_1^B d\tau_1 + t_2^B P_2 dE_2^B + t_3^B P_3 dE_3^B. \tag{5}$$

The interpretation of equation (4) is straightforward. Since internal prices in $A$ did not change, the change in welfare in $A$ is equal to the change in tariff revenue. The expression $(t_1^A - \tau_1)P_1 dE_1^B - P_1 E_1^B d\tau_1$ is the loss in tariff revenue due to the reduction in tariff rate on imports from $B$ and is necessarily negative ($E_1^B$, $dE_1^B$, and $d\tau_1 < 0$). Since internal prices did not change, $dE_1^A = dD_1^A$ and $dE_3^A = dD_3^A$; demand changes due to the loss in tariff revenue. It is sufficient that the two commodities are normal for $dE_1^A$ and $dE_3^A$ to be negative and, thus, $dW^A < 0$.[5]

[5] Observe that even if commodities 1 and 3 are inferior, $dW^A$ may be (or even is likely to be) negative.

Turning to equation (5), the change in welfare in $B$ is composed of three expressions. The first is the gain due to the reduction in tariff on its export of commodity 1. Since $E_1^B < 0$ and $d\tau_1 < 0$, $P_1 E_1^B d\tau_1 > 0$. The sign of the second expression depends on the change in excess demand for commodity 2. Since the price of commodity 2 falls while the price of commodity 1 rises and that of commodity 3 is unchanged, due to the substitution effect it is likely that $dE_2^B > 0$. The sign of $dE_2^B$ is, however, also affected by changes in income. In a two-commodity world ("strong inferiority aside"),[6] $dE_2^B > 0$; thus, the welfare of $B$ must rise. However, once we add a third commodity, this result does not necessarily hold.

With regard to the third expression, observe that $dP_1^B > dP_3^B = 0 > dP_2^B$. Thus, the sign of $dE_3^B$ is not a priori defined, and $dW^B$ may be negative. It should be emphasized that the ambiguous sign of $dW^B$ is due to the fact that we have discussed the effect of a simultaneous reduction of $\tau_1$ and $t_2^B$. Had we analyzed the effect of a reduction of $\tau_1$ alone, then gross substitution would be sufficient to guarantee $dW^B > 0$.

By our analysis, $dW^A < 0$ and the sign of $dW^B$ is ambiguous. But even in the case where $dW^B$ is positive, the joint welfare of the two countries may decline. It is useful to define a criterion for joint welfare. It turns out that in this model an exact compensation measure is straightforward. Recalling that internal prices in $A$ are unchanged, it follows that when $A$ is compensated for its loss of tariff on commodity 1, then its pattern of consumption and production will remain unchanged, or $dW^A = 0$. Let $B$ pay the exact compensation, $(t_1^A - \tau_1) P_1 dE_1^B - P_1 E_1^B d\tau_1$. We can define the change in welfare in $B$, holding $A$'s welfare constant,[7] as

$$dW^B \Big|_{dW^A = 0} = t_2^B P_2 dE_2^B + t_3^B P_3 dE_3^B + (t_1^A - \tau_1) P_1 dE_1^B. \qquad (6)$$

In the case where $dW^B \Big|_{dW^A = 0} > 0$, there exists some reduction in the tariffs on bilateral trade $(d\tau_1, dt_2^B < 0)$ that will allow $B$ to raise its welfare while $A$'s welfare is unchanged.

This result is different from that obtained in the two-commodity model; a comparison will facilitate our understanding. Rewriting equation (6) for the two-commodity case, we get

$$dW^B \Big|_{dW^A = 0} = t_2^B P_2 dE_2^B + (t_1^A - \tau_1) P_1 dE_1^B. \qquad (6')$$

---

[6] This terminology is from Kemp (1969).

[7] Observe that although prices differ in the two countries, the size of the compensation is not ambiguous. Since I have defined the price of commodity 1 in $C$ as the "numeraire," $P_1^C = 1$, then the compensation is in units of commodity 1.

starting from an initial stage of uniform tariffs $t_1^A = \tau_1$. The compensated change in welfare is thus equal to $t_2^B P_2 dE_2^B$, which (strong inferiority aside) is positive. Thus, equation (6') and equation (5), where commodity 3 is eliminated, provide an alternative proof for Kemp's result: "Strong inferiority aside, the creation of the preferential trading club operates to the advantage of whichever member trades only with the other member, and operates to the disadvantage of the latter. [Furthermore, for small changes starting from $\tau_1 = t_1^A$], B could over-compensate A for its loss and yet remain better off than in the initial equilibrium."[8]

Our analysis, therefore, yields exactly the same results as Kemp's analysis in the two-commodity case. The introduction of a third commodity and (even more important) the introduction of tariffs on imports to B from the rest of the world make it impossible to derive welfare implications by a priori considerations. This result should not be surprising. Once we introduce $t_3^B \neq 0$ by well-known second-best considerations, the movement of $P_1^B$ and $P_2^B$ toward world prices need not improve welfare. Since, in the empirical analysis of customs unions, it is always the case that tariffs with respect to the rest of the world exist and are not eliminated by the trade agreement, one should be very careful in applying propositions derived from the two-commodity model to the evaluation of actual agreements.

In the analysis of actual agreements, we cannot restrict the analysis to the case of small changes. Preferential trade agreements always involve noninfinitesimal reductions in tariffs; customs-union agreements usually result in the setting of $\tau_1 = t_2^B = 0$. The welfare effect of large changes in tariffs can be derived from equations (4), (5), and (6) by appropriate integration.[9] The effect of large changes in tariffs need not be in the same direction as the effect of small changes. This can be illustrated by a close inspection of equation (6'). We have demonstrated there that a small reduction in the tariff rate starting from $t_1^A = \tau_1$ will result in welfare improvement. But as we go on and reduce $\tau_1$, then $t_1^A - \tau_1$ becomes positive, since $dE_1^B < 0$, the second

---

[8] Kemp 1969, p. 31.

[9] An empirical estimate of the joint gain (loss) of welfare due to the elimination of tariffs on trade between A and B is given by

$$dW^B \Big|_{dW^A = 0} = \int_{t_2^B}^0 [t_2^B P_2 \, \partial E_2^B / \partial t_2^B + t_3^B P_3 \, \partial E_3^B / \partial t_2^B] \, dt_2^B \Big|_{t_1^A = \tau_1}$$

$$+ \int_{t_1^A}^0 [t_3^B P_3 \, \partial E_3^B / \partial t_1^A + (t_1^A - \tau_1) P_1 \, \partial E_1^B / \partial \tau_1] \, d\tau_1 \Big|_{t_2^B = 0}.$$

This is, admittedly, an inexact measure. However, it is the measure used in cost-benefit studies. See Harberger (1971) for a strong defense of this approach. A more exact measure, using compensated demand functions, is presented by Diamond and McFadden (1974).

expression in equation (6'), is negative, thus causing a reduction in welfare. It can be shown that the reduction of $t_2^B$ and $\tau_1$ beyond a certain level reduces joint welfare.[10] Thus, the complete elimination of tariffs may result in the reduction of joint welfare.

Returning to our more general (three-commodity) model, it is possible to make the following observations: If $B$ actually has to compensate $A$ for all of its losses, then $A$ will produce and consume exactly the same quantities as it did before the trade agreement. Thus, whatever advantages $B$ can get from the agreement, it can gain by an independent policy. Furthermore, the policy that can maximize $B$'s welfare (assuming that world terms of trade are fixed) is the elimination of all tariffs. This result can also be derived from equation (6). A necessary condition for welfare maximization is that $dW^B\big|_{dW^A = 0} = 0$. Observe that if $t_2^B = t_3^B = t_1^A - \tau_1$ then

$$dW^B\big|_{dW^A = 0} = t_2^B \sum_{i=1}^{3} p_i dE_i^B = 0,$$

since the sum of excess demands in foreign prices must equal zero. But $t_2^B = t_3^B = t_1^A - \tau_1$ means that relative local prices in $B$ are equal to world terms of trade. A customs union that eliminates tariffs on bilateral trade ($t_2^B = \tau_1 = 0$) while maintaining positive tariffs ($t_3^B$, $t_1^A > 0$) on trade with the rest of the world is prevented from reaching this optimal solution.[11]

## Welfare-improving Tariff Changes

Once it is recognized that the bilateral elimination of tariffs between $A$ and $B$ results in a distorted allocation, it is interesting to find out which part of the change in tariff from the initial distorted allocation is welfare improving and which part is welfare decreasing. To answer this question, we first derive several propositions for welfare-improving changes in tariffs in a single country and then apply these results to customs-union theory.[12] It is useful to start with the follow-

[10] See Berglas (1976b) for a detailed analysis.

[11] The departure of national governments from a free-trade policy can be explained by the assumption that governments do not try to maximize welfare in the traditional sense but have additional objectives. For an analysis along these lines, see Johnson (1971, chap. 10) and Krauss (1972). If this is the case, the analysis of this paper may still be useful by suggesting a method for the measurement of the welfare cost of these objectives.

[12] There is fast-growing literature on piecemeal, welfare-improving policies. See, e.g., Foster and Sonnenschein (1970), Bruno (1972), Dixit (1975), Hatta (1977), and Kawamata (1977). All the propositions that we derive have appeared before. In our derivation, we use gross substitution (GS) as a sufficient condition. Other writers have assumed other (weaker) sets of sufficient conditions. It is important to note that eq. (6) and other expressions for $dW$ that we develop do not depend on GS; thus, a general test for any piecemeal, welfare-improving policy is $dW > 0$.

ing problem: Given world terms of trade and an arbitrary distortion such as $t_3^B > 0$ (say, the preunion tariff rate), what is the optimal tariff on commodity ($\overline{t}_2^B$)? This is a typical case of second-best optimal taxation; it can be analyzed by taking the derivatives of equation (3) with respect to $t_2^B$ and then setting $dW^B = 0$:

$$\partial W^B/\partial t_2^B = t_2^B P_2\, \partial E_2^B/\partial t_2^B + t_3^B P_3\, \partial E_3^B/\partial t_2^B = 0 \tag{7}$$

and

$$\overline{t}_2^B = -\, t_3^B P_3(\partial E_3^B/\partial t_2^B)/[P_2(\partial E_2^B/\partial t_2^B)]. \tag{8}$$

From this result, we get sign $\overline{t}_2^B$ = sign $t_3^B\, \partial E_3^B/\partial t_2^B$, or $\overline{t}_2^B$ is positive if commodity 3 is a gross substitute for 2 and the distortion is positive.[13] Thus, we have established that the optimal tax on commodity 2 is not zero. Furthermore, if all commodities are gross substitutes, $P_3\, \partial E_3^B/\partial t_2^B < (-P_2\, \partial E_2^B/\partial t_2^B)$, which means that $0 < \overline{t}_2^B < t_3^B$. This result is represented in figure 2.

The contours in figure 2 are equal welfare curves.[14] Welfare is maximized at point $F$ where $t_3^B = t_2^B = 0$. Given $1 + t_3^B$, we can find $1 + \overline{t}_2^B$ by the tangency to the highest equal welfare curve. Given universal gross substitution, $1 + \overline{t}_2^B$ must be below the 45° line. If initially $t_2^B \neq \overline{t}_2^B$, there exists a change in the tariff rate on bilateral trade that will improve welfare in the two countries.

We now turn to other possible variations in tariff rates which we shall show later to be important for customs-unions analysis. Consider a proportional reduction in taxes, $dt_3^B/(1 + t_3^B) = dt_2^B/(1 + t_2^B)$. This is equivalent to the welfare effect of an export subsidy for commodity 1, which is given by

$$dW^B = \sum_{i=1}^{3} t_i^B P_i\, \partial E_i^B/\partial t_1^B, \tag{9}$$

where $t_1^B$ is the rate of subsidy on the export of commodity 1. It follows from the resource constraint ($\Sigma P_i dE_i^B = 0$) and GS that an increase in the subsidy rate $t_1^B$ results in an increase in welfare ($dW^B > 0$) as long as $t_1^B < t_2^B, t_3^B$.

Another welfare-improving policy is the reduction of the largest tariff, holding other rates constant. This result is easy to prove. Let $t_1^B = 0$ and $t_3^B > t_2^B$; then, the effect of the reduction of the largest tariff is given by

$$dW^B = t_2^B P_2\, \partial E_2^B/\partial t_3^B + t_3^B P_3\, \partial E_3^B/\partial t_3^B. \tag{10}$$

---

[13] The advantage of the approach suggested in this paper can be seen by comparing eq. (8) to the expression for optimal tax derived by Vanek (1965, p. 194, eq. A.11), which he is unable to interpret. Furthermore, his result is derived under the more restrictive assumption that each country produces only one product.

[14] The equal welfare curves can be derived by choosing a pair of $t_2\, t_3$ and taking small changes in the two tariff rates that will maintain $dW = t_2^B P_2 dE_2^B + t_3^B P_3 dE_3^B = 0$.

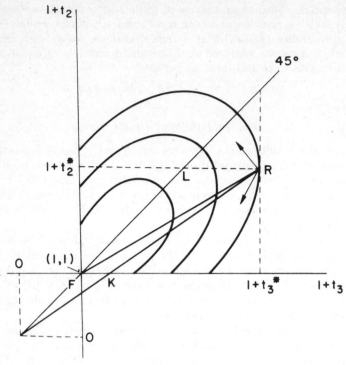

FIG. 2

From GS and the resource constraint, it follows that a reduction in $t_3^B$ results in $dW^B > 0$.

These two results hold for large changes, the effect of which can be regarded as the cumulative effect of repeated small changes. In terms of figure 2, these results imply that tariff changes along *RKF* or *RLF* continuously improve welfare. Furthermore, since movements along *RF* can be decomposed into proportional reductions in $1 + t_i$ and a reduction in the largest tariff, it follows that movement along *RF* (which is a policy of equiproportionate reduction in all tariffs) continuously improves welfare. It is now obvious that it is possible to design many other welfare-improving policies, some of which hold only for small changes. The arrows in figure 1 provide examples of such policies.

The implications of these propositions to the theory of preferential trading are straightforward. Suppose we start from a situation where $t_1^A, t_2^B, t_3^B > 0$ and consider a small reduction of tariffs in bilateral trade ($d\tau_1, dt_2^B < 0$). It follows from the analysis of piecemeal policy that a reduction in $t_2^B$ improves welfare if, initially, $t_2^B > \bar{t}_2^B$. The effect of a reduction in $\tau_1$, if $B$ is to compensate $A$, is exactly equal to a subsidy in $B$ on the export of commodity 1 (technically, cf. eqq. [6] and [9]); it is welfare improving when we start from an initial position of $t_1^A = \tau_1$. Thus, we may conclude that, depending on initial conditions such as $t_2^B > \bar{t}_2^B$, mutual small reductions in tariff rates on bilateral trade may be welfare improving.

But the more interesting question concerns large changes. We distinguish three cases, depending on preagreement tariff rates.

Case 1: Initially, $0 < t_1^A = \tau_1 < t_2^B, t_3^B$. In this case, the elimination of $\tau_1$ is welfare improving (equivalent to a move along $RK$ in fig. 2). The joint welfare of $A$ and $B$ may be improved even further by a reduction in $t_2^B$. But the optimal $\bar{t}_2^B$ is positive, and $t_1^A < \bar{t}_2^B < t_3^B$. Any further reduction of $t_2^B$ below its optimal level is welfare decreasing.

Case 2: Initially, $t_1^A = \tau_1, t_2^B > t_3^B$. In this case, a reduction in both $\tau_1$ and $t_2^B$ such that $t_1^A - \tau_1 = t_2^B = t_3^B$ maximizes joint welfare. Observe that internal prices after this reduction in $B$ are equal to world prices. Any further reduction in either $\tau_1$ or $t_2^B$ is welfare decreasing.

Case 3: Initially, $t_1^A = \tau_1 > t_3^B > t_2^B$. In this case, a reduction in $\tau_1$ such that $t_1^A - \tau_1 = t_3^B$ is welfare improving. Furthermore, for the given initial $t_2^B$, $t_3^B$, it is possible to derive an optimal $\bar{\tau}_1$ that maximizes welfare.[15] It can be shown that $t_3^B > t_1^A - \bar{\tau}_1 > t_2^B$. Once we set $\tau_1$ at $\bar{\tau}_1$, any further reduction in $\tau_1$ or $t_2^B$ is welfare decreasing. Observe that joint welfare can be further increased by increasing $t_2^B$ and appropriately changing $\tau_1$.

In all three cases (and it is easy to similarly analyze other cases), it is possible to decompose the elimination of tariffs on bilateral trade into two parts: one which increases welfare, and one which decreases welfare. Aggregate effect depends on the relative magnitude of the two components.[16] It seems that the decomposition into welfare-improving and welfare-decreasing tariff changes is more meaningful in this context than the traditional division into trade creation and trade diversion, which in the case of many commodities is difficult (or impossible) to identify.

The three-commodity model is rich enough to consider the effect of tariff changes with respect to the rest of the world. In customs-union theory, this usually appears as tariff-rate unification with respect to imports by member countries from the rest of the world. In terms of our model, we assume that a customs union exists in the sense that $t_2^B = \tau_1 = 0$, and we analyze the welfare effect of changes in $t_3^A$ and $t_3^B$. We start with the case where $B$ does not compensate $A$; then

[15] The derivation is completely equivalent to the derivation of $\bar{t}_2^B$ above.
[16] For the empirical estimates of the total welfare effect, the reader is reminded of n. 9 above.

it is optimal for $B$ to set $t_3^B = 0$. This is the best situation for $B$, since its inhabitants pay world prices for their import goods 2 and 3 while its exports are subsidized by $A$. The reduction of $t_3^B$ will decrease the welfare of $A$, since it will increase the exports of commodity 1 from $B$ to $A$. Internal prices in $A$ are $P_1(1 + t_1^A)$, $P_2$, and $P_3(1 + t_3^A)$. Given $t_1^A >$ 0, there exists $\bar{t}_3^A$ (to be derived by exactly the same procedure as $\bar{t}_2^B$ above) such that $0 < \bar{t}_3^A < t_1^A$, which will maximize welfare in $A$. The changes in $t_3^A$ do not affect the welfare of $B$.

These results apply directly to the question of tariff unification. Suppose that initially $t_3^A < t_3^B$ and the lower tariff rate is adopted as the common rate. The effect is an improvement of the welfare in $B$ and a deterioration in $A$. For another example, if $t_3^A > t_3^B > t_1^A$ and $t_3^B$ is adopted as the common rate, the effect of the tariff unification is to increase the welfare of $A$ without affecting $B$. Suppose now that $t_1^A > t_3^A$ $= \bar{t}_3^A > t_3^B$. Adopting $t_3^B$ as the union rate will reduce welfare in $A$ without affecting $B$. Thus, we can conclude that tariff reductions on commodities imported by the two members from the rest of the world will not necessarily improve welfare.[17]

It is easy to derive propositions for joint welfare or for the case where $B$ always fully compensates $A$. If $B$ is to compensate $A$, it is no longer true that any reduction in $t_3^B$ is welfare improving. This can be easily derived from equation (6), setting $t_2 = \tau_1 = 0$. It follows directly from the resource constraint and GS that any reduction in $t_3^B$ is welfare improving as long as $t_3^B > t_1^A$. Furthermore, it can be shown that given these assumptions, the optimal tax on commodity 3 ($\bar{t}_3^B$) should be $0 < \bar{t}_3^B < t_1^A$. As before, changes in $t_3^A$ do not affect welfare in $B$ and thus should be chosen to maximize welfare in $A$. The optimal rate $\bar{t}_3^A$, by the same consideration, should be in the interval $0 < \bar{t}_3^A <$ $t_1^A$; however, $\bar{t}_3^B$ and $\bar{t}_3^A$ that maximize joint welfare generally will not be equal.

We may thus conclude that for a customs union that eliminates tariffs on bilateral trade among member countries, unification of tariffs with respect to trade with the rest of the world is not necessary for welfare maximization. Furthermore, the reduction of tariffs on commodities that are imported by all the member countries is not necessarily welfare improving.

## Variable Terms of Trade

Thus far, we have assumed that the formation of a customs union does not affect the world terms of trade. We now briefly analyze the

[17] In the two-good case with fixed terms of trade, a reduction in tariff with respect to the rest of the world will improve welfare (see Kemp [1969] for an analysis of this case).

case in which the terms of trade are variable. The first observation is that it is impossible to determine a priori which way the terms of trade will change. To illustrate this, consider an agreement between $A$ and $B$ to eliminate $t_2^B$ and $\tau_1$. At the old terms of trade, excess demand for commodity 2 in $A$ ($B$) will fall (rise) as a result of a fall (increase) in real income; furthermore, the effect of the change in relative prices in $B$ will increase excess demand. Thus, it is not known whether aggregate excess demand rises or falls, so it is impossible to predict whether the international price $P_2$ will rise or fall.[18]

The second observation is that a change in the terms of trade affects the welfare of member countries differently. If $P_2$ does rise, this is likely to affect the welfare of $A$ ($B$) which exports (imports) commodity 2 favorably (unfavorably). The result is much more complicated when we talk of simultaneous changes in several prices.

The third observation is from Kemp and Wan (1976). Let any two countries form a customs union by eliminating tariffs on bilateral trade and simultaneously change tariffs on external trade such that the trade with the rest of the world is at the level and composition that existed before the agreement. It is easy to prove that with an appropriate scheme of compensation welfare in the two union countries improves while that of the rest of the world is unaffected. Observe that although the terms of trade are potentially variable they would not change, since the pattern of trade with the rest of the world is unaltered. Given this observation, it is easy to see that by adding members to the union its members' welfare always increases until the whole world is included in the customs union (i.e., free trade).[19] The importance of this observation is the identification that a welfare-increasing customs union is always possible, but its weakness is that the compensation scheme is too complicated to be adopted in reality.

## Summary and Conclusions

The study of customs unions is a study in the theory of second best. It is in the nature of second-best problems that there exists a multiplicity of cases. We have chosen to concentrate on only a few of the more

[18] It is interesting to note that in the two-commodity case, when compensation is actually paid, there is a presumption of a favorable change in the terms of trade of the union versus the rest of the world (see Berglas 1976*b*). But this result does not hold when the number of commodities exceeds two.

[19] Observe, however, that the set of tariffs suggested by Kemp and Wan (1976) does not maximize welfare of union countries. Once tariffs within the union are eliminated, the welfare-maximizing tariff is the "optimal tariff." It follows that with an appropriate compensation, it always pays to add members to a customs union that adopts optimal tariffs with respect to the rest of the world. This is true as more countries join the union until the whole world is included in the union.

interesting ones. We deliberately ignored the possibility that the formation of a customs union would extinguish or reverse the flow of trade and did not discuss special cases that arise from extreme inferiority.[20] The method suggested in this paper can easily be applied to these problems. Although we have restricted the analysis to a few cases, the results are too numerous to be repeated here; we shall summarize only the main results.

In a three-good model, two small countries facing fixed terms of trade can benefit from the formation of a trade agreement by partially reducing tariffs on bilateral trade. However, joint welfare maximization may require a reduction in the tariffs of only one of the two countries. Complete elimination of tariffs on trade between member countries results in the substitution of one distorted equilibrium for another, and it is impossible to decide by a priori considerations which of the two equilibria is preferable. This paper suggests an empirical method by which it is possible to compare the welfare of the two countries separately and jointly in the two situations.

Even if the union is not beneficial to both countries and no compensation is paid, one country is likely to gain. It is important to note that if a trade agreement does not affect the terms of trade, then it does not allow for any mutually beneficial policy opportunities which are not open to each of the member countries separately.

When tariffs between members are zero, it is possible that even in high-tariff countries a reduction of tariffs on commodities that are imported by all the member countries will not be beneficial. However, allowing for simultaneous changes in all tariffs, rules for mutually beneficial policies can be derived.

Allowing for variable terms of trade, trade agreements increase the set of available policies. Mutually beneficial agreements are possible. The best policy for member countries, assuming no retaliation from the rest of the world, is a complete elimination of tariffs between members and a "single country" optimal tariff with respect to the rest of the world. The analogue in the case of fixed terms of trade is the elimination of all tariffs (i.e., free trade).

Given these results, it seems that the traditional approach to the analysis of customs unions (and this paper is no exception) essentially ignores several of the main effects of these unions. It is doubtful that existing customs unions can be characterized as agreements among groups of countries to apply optimal tariffs with respect to the (passive) rest of the world. Furthermore full compensation schemes are rarely adopted, implying that, by our analysis, some countries are likely to lose. What induces these countries to join a union? Even an

---

[20] These cases are analyzed by Vanek (1965) and Kemp (1969).

outside follower of debates surrounding the EEC is impressed that other considerations play an important role. Several of these considerations were mentioned in the Introduction as qualifications to this paper. It seems likely that the systematic study of these considerations will extend our understanding of customs unions.

## Appendix

It is useful to extend our results to the many-good case. Suppose that $B$ exports to $A$ commodities $1, 2, \ldots, n$; $B$ imports from $A$ commodities $n+1$, $n+2, \ldots, m$; and $B$ imports from $C$ commodities $m+1, \ldots, k$. Then, for given terms of trade and small changes in tariffs in $A$ and $B$,

$$dW^B\Big|_{dW^A = 0} = \sum_{i=n+1}^{k} t_i^B P_i dE_i^B + \sum_{i=1}^{n} (t_i^A - \tau_i^A) dE_i^B. \tag{11}$$

Optimal tariff $\bar{t}_i^B$, given other tariffs, is given by

$$\bar{t}_i^B = \sum_{j \neq i} t_j^B P_j (\partial E_j^B / \partial P_i) / [P_i(\partial E_i^B / \partial P_i)]. \tag{12}$$

Furthermore, if $t_i^B = \bar{t}_i^B$ for $i = n+1, n+2, \ldots, m$, then a reduction in the tariffs on commodities $n+1, \ldots, m$ is not beneficial.

However, this generalization is not complete, as can be seen from equation (11), which measures changes in the welfare of $B$ while holding $W^A$ constant and which includes only variables of country $B$. The reason for this asymmetry is that we have assumed throughout that there are no commodities that $A$ imports only from $B$. Thus, the internal terms of trade in $A$ are not affected when $A$ changes its tariffs or imports from $B$. This was a natural assumption when we dealt with three commodities, but it may be less appropriate when we have many commodities. If this is not the case, we can add a group of commodities that are exported by $B$ to both $A$ and $C$ ($A$ imports these commodities only from $B$). Equations (11) and (12) still apply if those commodities are a partial group of commodities $m+1, \ldots, k$ and their tariff is not changed. In order to analyze the effect of changes of tariffs on those commodities, we can form an expression for

$$dW^A\Big|_{dW^B = 0}$$

which is completely symmetrical to equation (11).

Finally, we can also add nontradeable goods, denoted by $k+1, \ldots, r$. If these commodities are not taxed, equation (11) is unaffected. If they are subject to commodity taxes, let their producer prices be denoted by $P_i$ and consumer prices by $P_i(1 + t_i^B)$. Then, the expression for

$$dW^B\Big|_{dW^A = 0}$$

(eq. [11]) should be augmented by

$$\sum_{i=k+1}^{r} (t_i^B P_i dD_i^B - t_i^B D_i^B dP_i).$$

## References

Berglas, E. "Distribution of Tastes and Skills and the Provision of Local Public Goods." *J. Public Econ.* 6, no. 4 (November 1976): 409–23. (*a*)

———. "On the Theory and Measurement of Gains from Preferential Trading." Discussion Paper no. 767, Univ. Rochester, April 1976. (*b*)

Bruno, Michael. "Market Distortions and Gradual Reform." *Rev. Econ. Studies* 39, no. 3 (July 1972): 373–83.

Caves, Richard E., and Jones, Ronald W. *World Trade and Payments: An Introduction.* Boston: Little, Brown, 1973.

Corden, W. M. "Customs Union Theory and the Nonuniformity of Tariffs." *J. Internat. Econ.* 6 (February 1976): 99–108.

Diamond, P. A., and McFadden, D. L. "Some Uses of the Expenditure Function in Public Finance." *J. Public Econ.* 3, no. 1 (February 1974): 3–21.

Dixit, A. "Welfare Effects of Tax and Price Changes." *J. Public Econ.* 4 (February 1975): 103–23.

Foster, Edward, and Sonnenschein, Hugo. "Price Distortion and Economic Welfare." *Econometrica* 38, no. 2 (March 1970): 281–97.

Harberger, Arnold C. "Three Basic Postulates for Applied Welfare Economics: An Interpretive Essay." *J. Econ. Literature* 9 (September 1971): 785–97.

Hatta, Tatsuo. "A Theory of Piecemeal Policy Recommendation." *Rev. Econ. Studies* 44, no. 1 (February 1977): 1–21.

Johnson, Harry G. *Aspects of the Theory of Tariffs.* London: Allen & Unwin, 1971.

Kawamata, Kunio. "Price Distortion and the Second Best Optimum." *Rev. Econ. Studies* 44, no. 1 (February 1977): 23–29.

Kemp, Murray C. *A Contribution to the General Equilibrium Theory of Preferential Trading.* Amsterdam: North-Holland, 1969.

Kemp, Murray C., and Wan, Henry Y., Jr. "An Elementary Proposition concerning the Formation of Customs Unions." *J. Internat. Econ.* 6 (February 1976): 95–97.

Krauss, Melvyn B. "Recent Developments in Customs Union Theory: An Interpretive Survey." *J. Econ. Literature* 10 (June 1972): 413–36.

Lipsey, Richard G. "The Theory of Customs Union: A General Survey." *Econ. J.* 70 (September 1960): 496–513.

Meade, James E. *The Theory of Customs Unions.* Amsterdam: North-Holland, 1955.

Vanek, Jaroslav. *General Equilibrium of International Discrimination: The Case of Customs Unions.* Cambridge, Mass.: Harvard Univ. Press, 1965.

Viner, Jacob. *The Customs Union Issue.* New York: Carnegie Endowment Internat. Peace, 1950.

# [7]

# Is Unilateral Tariff Reduction Preferable to a Customs Union? The Curious Case of the Missing Foreign Tariffs

*By* Paul Wonnacott and Ronald Wonnacott*

During the past decade and a half, an important part of the literature on customs unions has dealt with the question of whether a country might obtain the gains it would achieve from a customs union (*CU*) in an alternative way, by a unilateral tariff reduction (*UTR*). (*UTR* may involve a partial reduction in tariffs, or a reduction all the way to zero.) A widely accepted conclusion (see Eitan Berglas, p. 329; C. A. Cooper and B. F. Massell, 1965b, pp. 745–47; Roma Dauphin, ch. 2; Harry Johnson, p. 280; Melvyn Krauss, pp. 417–19; and Peter Robson)[1] is that *UTR* does indeed hold out the prospect for all the gains from a *CU*—without the disadvantages—if two important simplifying assumptions are made; namely, that we ignore economies of scale and the effects of a customs union on the terms of trade.[2] In the words of Berglas: "It is important to note that if a [preferential] trade agreement does not affect the terms of trade, then it does not allow for any mutually beneficial policy opportunities which are not open to each of the member countries separately [through *UTR*]" (p. 329).

If this conclusion is correct, it is very important, in that it undercuts the earlier literature on customs unions. The question asked by Jacob Viner in his pioneering work —whether a *CU* represents a net gain or a net loss in economic efficiency—becomes unimportant, except insofar as a customs

union is based on terms-of-trade effects[3] or economies of scale,[4] since a *CU* can be summarily rejected in favor of *UTR*. The *UTR* case would mean that, for economists, the puzzle is not to identify the efficiency gains (or losses) from a *CU*, but rather to explain why countries form customs unions in the first place (Berglas, p. 329; Cooper and Massell, 1965b, p. 247; and Johnson, p. 270). Indeed, in his survey of *CU* theory, Krauss identifies the problem raised by Cooper and Massell—of *why* countries form customs unions—as "...the theoretical issue of the past decade [the 1960's] just as in the prior one the major issue, as explicitly defined by Jacob Viner (1950), was whether a customs union represented a movement towards freer trade or greater protection" (p. 413). The typical reply to the Cooper-Massell question is: Countries tend to form a *CU* for noneconomic reasons (Berglas, pp. 329–30).[5]

---

*University of Maryland and University of Western Ontario, respectively. We thank Christopher Clague, Mel Krauss, Clark Leith, Richard Lipsey, Arvind Panagariya, and John Williamson.

[1] The three primary articles are Berglas; Cooper and Massell, 1965b; and Johnson. The other works are surveys or elaborations of the primary articles.

[2] Johnson (pp. 274–82) discusses a third source of mutual benefit from a *CU*; namely, the existence of externalities in manufacturing.

[3] On terms of trade and customs unions, see Sven Arndt (1968, 1969); and Krauss (pp. 421–24).

[4] There has been a tendency in the *CU* literature, tracing back to Viner (p. 47), to dismiss economies of scale as unimportant (for example, see Krauss, p. 420). In our empirical work on North American free trade (1967), we concluded that economies of scale were much more important than the triangular welfare gains identified by traditional theory. In many cases, we question how enlightening it is to study a *CU* without considering economies of scale. Nevertheless, in this paper, we will stay within the traditional framework and ignore economies of scale, since we are studying a specific theoretical issue which has arisen in the literature. (On economies of scale and customs unions, see also W. M. Corden and John Williamson.)

[5] Johnson (pp. 258, 270, 279–81) explained why customs unions may be formed for a partly political reason. Specifically, he assumed that countries have a "...collective preference for industrial production..." (p. 258). Cooper and Massell (1965a) offer a similar rationale for the formation of customs unions among developing countries. Another argument for preferring a *CU* to *UTR* is that each member provides the other(s) with protection against third-country imports; this may

In this paper, our contention is that the *UTR* literature is not correct. (We believe that the earlier question raised by Viner—of the effects of a *CU* on efficiency—is the most important one, although the answers suggested by Viner were not completely satisfactory, as has been pointed out by such writers as Franz Gehrels; Richard Lipsey, 1957; and James Meade.) The *UTR* literature is fundamentally wrong, not in the sense of having made logical errors, but wrong in having begun from a series of assumptions—some explicit and some implicit—which in effect rule out the principal advantages of a *CU*. Suppose that we were to ask the average politician or business executive the $64 question raised by the *UTR* literature: "What economic advantage can there possibly be in forming a customs union?" The probable reply would be: "To get down the tariffs of our partners in the proposed customs union, and thus gain better access to their markets." It is therefore surprising that, in arguing the case for *UTR*, Cooper and Massell (1965b, p. 747) make only a concluding reference to market swapping, but conduct no analysis of the elimination of tariffs by the *CU* partner.[6] While this oversight is corrected elsewhere in the literature—most notably by Berglas— Berglas makes strong assumptions about Country *C* which mean that Country *A* cannot possibly gain from its newly acquired access to *B*'s markets. These include the implicit assumptions that Country *C* has no tariffs, and there are no transportation costs.[7] (We follow the standard terminology of two prospective *CU* partners, *A* and *B*, and an

outside Country *C*. The establishment of a *CU* involves the elimination of tariffs on trade between *A* and *B*, and the adoption by *A* and *B* of a common tariff on imports from *C*.)

Our major contention is that, in a world in which tariffs and other obstacles to trade exist, it is meaningless to analyze the effects of freeing trade between *CU* members if we assume that there are no impediments to trade with outsider *C*. It is misleading to analyze a *CU*, and in particular to compare a *CU* and *UTR*, unless all countries are recognized to have tariffs to begin with. Anything else is Hamlet without the prince. In more detail, we argue that:

1) In making the case for *UTR*, its proponents make either or both of the following assumptions (explicitly or implicitly): (a) That partner *B*'s tariffs can be ignored. (b) That outsider *C* has no tariffs, and there are no transportation costs in trade with *C*.

2) If we depart from both of these assumptions, a country can achieve gains from a customs union which are not possible with *UTR*.

3) This conclusion, that the dominance of *UTR* over a *CU* collapses if we reject assumptions 1a and 1b, holds even if we make the standard assumption that there are no gains in the terms of trade with outside Country *C*. Furthermore, it collapses even if we assume that the terms of trade among the members of the *CU* remain unchanged as a result of the formation of the *CU*. (In practice, there is very little chance that the terms of trade will remain constant. However, we shall examine this case because it occurs in parts of the literature,[8] and also because there is some confusion over intraunion terms of trade.)[9]

---

sustain the demand for labor and reduce short-run unemployment and other dislocation costs associated with a change in commercial policy.

[6] Cooper and Massell's conclusion is based on demand and supply curves for a single good, the import of Country *A*. No analysis is made of *A*'s exports to *B*.

[7] These implicit assumptions may be found in Figure 1 and Table 1 of the Berglas article. In his Figure 1, Berglas has outside Country *C* importing only one good (commodity 2). The price of that good in Country *C* is shown in his Table 1 to be identical to its price $P_2$ in exporting Country *A*. This can be so only if no tariffs or transportation costs are added to the price of commodity 2 as it goes from *A* to *C*. (More generally, his Table 1 involves the assumption that there are no transportation costs on any trade.)

[8] For example, Berglas makes such an assumption; or, more precisely, he assumes that a country is committed to compensate a partner for any adverse change in its bilateral terms of trade.

[9] Most notably, Krauss in his survey (p. 417) states that Cooper and Massell assume that the home Country *A* is unable to affect its terms of trade because the partner *B* and third Country *C* are large. This conclusion is incorrect; a *CU* is *especially* likely to lead to an improvement in the terms of trade if the partner is a big country. See our point 4 which will be explained later

4) When a *CU* is being established, the terms of trade is a slippery concept; we should be careful to state propositions about terms of trade precisely. For example, the assumption that *A* is very small, and is faced by a large *B* and a large *C*, does not mean that terms of trade can be ignored, since *B*'s agreement to cut tariffs will affect *A*'s terms of trade. Indeed, an important reason for *A* to want to get rid of *B*'s tariffs is to be able, for the first time, to trade at *B*'s domestic terms of trade.

5) The standard assumption, that *A* is very small compared to *C*, is not so reasonable as it seems at first glance; in particular, it is not nearly so reasonable in a many-good world as it seems in the common two- and three-good models of trade theory. In fact, no outside country or group of outside countries is likely to be predominant in the pricing of all goods.

One further preliminary point should be clarified. In attacking the case that *UTR* offers all the gains of a *CU* (except for terms of trade and economies of scale), we are not arguing that *UTR* never dominates a *CU*. That would obviously be going too far. (For example, many countries with high tariffs could improve efficiency by *UTR*; and for such a country it would be easy to imagine a heavily diverting potential *CU* that would reduce efficiency. Therefore, we should be able without difficulty to find examples of potential customs unions which are dominated by *UTR*.) What we do dispute is that a *general* case has been made that "...a more efficient allocation of resources could not be the reason why customs unions are formed..." (Krauss, p. 417).

### I. A Preliminary Puzzle

Before we turn to our five main points, let us look at an example—quite different in its details and assumptions from the literature we criticize—which shows the implausibility of the argument that *UTR* will provide all the gains from a *CU*, provided economies of

scale and terms-of-trade effects are ignored. Consider a *CU* that would involve all the countries of the world except Nepal. Assume the special case where the *CU* would leave the terms of trade among members unchanged. For any member, such a *CU* would be essentially indistinguishable from worldwide free trade in the benefits it would provide. And any terms-of-trade effect with the third country (Nepal) would be trivial for the members of the *CU*. The *UTR* literature would have us believe that such a *CU* is no better than *UTR*. But surely there is something wrong here. For any member, this *CU* would offer essentially the same benefits as worldwide free trade, which in turn offers something that *UTR* doesn't: namely, the abolition of foreign tariffs. And the abolition of foreign tariffs is a clear and unambiguous advantage.[10] Somehow, somewhere, in coming to the wrong conclusion the *UTR* literature has made assumptions whose critical importance has gone unrecognized. Our task will be to explain the importance of these assumptions.

### II. Reciprocal Gains from a Customs Union, with Terms of Trade Unchanged

In our example, with Nepal as outside Country *C*, we have eliminated the importance of terms-of-trade changes in a manner quite different from the *UTR* literature cited earlier. In order to bring our argument back toward the main body of *UTR* literature, we now make the more standard assumption: The *CU* partners live in a world in which outsider *C* is not small. Indeed, *C* is so large that its demand and supply functions appear

---

with Figure 4. (Actually, only Krauss, and not Cooper and Massell, made this error. Cooper and Massell assumed only that the third country is large, the partner is not.)

[10] Curiously, the comparison of *UTR* and *CU* led Johnson to argue that *multilateral* tariff reduction is no better than *UTR*. This argument of Johnson is considered in the final section of this paper. (On the face of it, Johnson's focus on the burden of the home tariff to the exclusion of foreign tariffs is puzzling. As Abba Lerner demonstrated, a 10 percent across-the-board import tariff is equivalent in equilibrium to an across-the-board export levy of the same height. But this in turn is equivalent to an across-the-board foreign levy on our exports, with one notable exception: the foreign government rather than the home government gets the revenue. Thus, there is a presumption that foreign tariffs create a greater burden than home tariffs of the same height.)

*Economic Analysis of Regional Trading Arrangements*

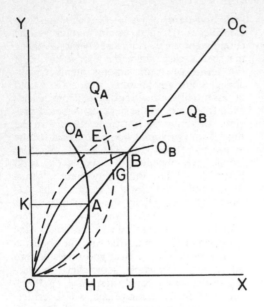

FIGURE 1. LARGE COUNTRY HAS NO TARIFFS
OR TRANSPORTATION COSTS

perfectly horizontal to *CU* members *A* and *B*. In a two-commodity general equilibrium framework, *C*'s offer curve is a perfectly straight line.

In Figure 1, we derive the principal conclusion in the *UTR* literature (namely, that a *CU* offers nothing—apart from terms-of-trade improvements and economies of scale—that cannot be obtained through *UTR*).[11] We begin with the situation where *C* has no tariffs (although *A* and *B* do), and transportation costs between *C* and *CU* members are ignored. Not surprisingly, the offer curve of Country *C*, $O_C$ has a dominant effect on international prices; *A* and *B* can trade any amount they like with *C* without affecting

the relative prices given by the slope of *C*'s offer curve. Prior to the establishment of the *CU*, the offer curves of *A* and *B* are $O_A$ and $O_B$, respectively. Country *A* trades at point *A*, exporting *OH* of good *X* in exchange for *OK* of *Y*, and Country *B* trades at *B*, exporting *OL* of good *Y* in exchange for *OJ* of *X*.

Now suppose that a *CU* is formed between *A* and *B*, with a prohibitive common tariff on imports from *C*. Their offer curves, as seen by the *CU* partner, will move to the dashed curves $Q_A$ and $Q_B$. With the prohibitive external tariff, no trade will take place with Country *C*, and equilibrium between *A* and *B* will occur at point *E*.

From the point of view of Country *A*, its move from *A* to *E* represents an improvement. Moreover, *E* is better than Country *A* can do by unilaterally eliminating its tariff and thus moving to *G*. But *B* could do better by a simple unilateral elimination of its tariffs, moving to point *F*. While Country *A* is better off at *E* (with a *CU*) than at *G* (with unilateral free trade), it has the problem (noted by Berglas) of persuading *B* to join the *CU*. If, in order to induce *B* to join, *A* has to compensate *B* for the amount by which *E* is inferior to *F*, then Country *A* would be better off to move unilaterally to reduce tariffs. (With standard assumptions, it can be shown that Country *B*'s loss at *E* compared to *F* is greater than the amount by which Country *A* prefers *E* over *G*.) *UTR* dominates a *CU*. Indeed, within this framework, each partner should move all the way to unilateral free trade.[12]

(The country against which the terms of trade shift as a result of *CU*—Country *B* in our illustration—may be better or worse off as a result of a *CU* (at *E*) as compared to original point *B*, depending on the shapes and positions of the offer curves. But, in either case, it will be better off with a unilateral elimination of tariffs and a move to *F* than it would be with a customs union at *E*. Furthermore, in no case will Country *A* be able to "bribe" *B* to join a *CU* without itself ending at a position inferior to that obtainable through *UTR*.)

[11] In this paper, we use offer curves to explain our case. In the *UTR* literature, the standard analytic tool has been single product demand and supply functions, with welfare triangles being the center of attention. Thus, there is some danger that, in using a different theoretical framework, we are writing at cross purposes to the other authors. To make clear how our points fit into the theoretical framework of the earlier articles, we elsewhere (1980) review the literature, explain in more detail how the authors fall into the traps we allege, and repeat our arguments with single product diagrams.

[12] Thus, this offer-curve framework, like Cooper and Massell's single product analysis (1965b, p. 747), leaves the puzzle of why countries have tariffs in the first place.

The main feature of this *UTR* argument is that *C* is freezing the world terms of trade at the slope of $O_C$: *C* will buy or sell unlimited quantities of *X* or *Y* at the relative price shown by its offer curve. Consequently, *A* and *B* have nothing to gain collectively by trading with each other rather than with *C*. Prior to the *CU*, it is a matter of indifference to Country *B* whether it conducts *OA* amount of trade with Country *A* and the remaining *AB* with Country *C*, or whether its total trade of *OB* is with Country *C*. And a *CU* is not collectively beneficial for *A* and *B*, compared to nondiscriminatory tariff removal and trade with *C*; while one country (*A*) will prefer a *CU*, the other (*B*) will even more strongly prefer trade with *C*. (In the special case where *E* falls on $O_C$, there is no difference between the outcome with a *CU* and that with unilateral moves to free trade by Countries *A* and *B*.)

The question is: In the real world, do prospective members of a *CU* have anything to offer one another that is not readily available from the outside world? The answer is yes. But what? Consider the United Kingdom and Germany. What can they gain from trade with one another that they can't gain from trade with the United States? A partial answer: they may *each* be in a position to offer the other a better price than the other could get by trading with the United States. How can that be? Because, in trading (for example) steel for coal with one another, they don't have to pay the costs of transportation to and from the United States, nor do they have to pay U.S. tariffs. In other words, by trading with each other, they can both benefit by sharing their net saving on transportation costs and U.S. tariffs.[13] A major problem, therefore, with the *UTR* literature is that it is based on the assumption that outsider *C* is not only large but it has no transportation costs nor tariffs. As a consequence, this literature has missed the important way in which a *CU* can provide mutual benefit to its members.

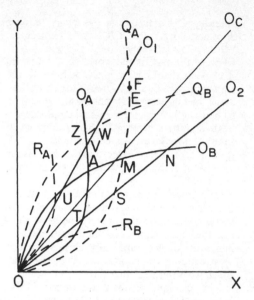

FIGURE 2. LARGE COUNTRY HAS TARIFFS AND TRANSPORTATION COSTS

The case where *C* has transportation costs and tariffs is shown in Figure 2. With this figure, we illustrate the point at issue; that is, the possibility that a *CU* can provide gains not possible through *UTR*. With the introduction of *C*'s transportation costs and tariffs, Country *C* now presents not one, but rather two, offer curves. While the relative prices within *C* remain at the slope of $O_C$, the offer curve of *C* as seen by *A* and *B* will be either $O_1$ (if *A* or *B* purchase *X* by exporting *Y*) or $O_2$ (if *A* or *B* purchase *Y* by exporting *X*).

Thus, *C*'s transportation costs and tariffs drive a wedge between *C*'s offer curves (just as they drive a gap between the domestic and world prices in a simple demand/supply model). If this wedge—defined by the angle between $O_1$ and $O_2$—is wide enough, so that *A* and *B* trade within it both before (at *A*) and after the *CU* (at *E*),[14] it is as though

---

[13] *Net* saving on transportation costs; that is, the saving from transportation costs to the extent that they are lower between the U.K. and Germany than they are between Europe and America.

[14] The question may arise as to why, prior to the *CU*, Country *A* would be satisfied with point *A*, and not try to pick preferred point *V* by trading with Country *C*. The answer is that point *V* is not an option open to Country *A*. Point *V* is on the offer curve $O_1$ where

Country $C$ did not exist. Its overwhelming dominance over $A$ and $B$'s trade disappears. With $C$ "out of the picture," the question of whether the rest of the world (i.e., countries $A$ and $B$) should form a $CU$ reduces to the standard two-country free-trade question. Thus, in this case a $CU$ can easily be shown to be beneficial under standard assumptions; both countries have a higher welfare at $E$ than $A$. Moreover, for each country, a $CU$ dominates unilateral free trade: $A$ has higher welfare at $E$ than $M$, while $B$ is better off at $E$ than $W$.[15]

(We ignore transportation costs between Countries $A$ and $B$. Adding them unnecessarily complicates the analysis without altering the conclusions—so long as the $CU$ is made up of geographically close members, with internal transportation costs less than those with third countries.)

This example resolves two puzzles. First, how can the contention of $UTR$ writers—that $UTR$ is always at least as good as a $CU$—be correct if $C$ has prohibitive tariffs, so that trade with $C$ is not even an option for $A$ and $B$? The answer is that the $UTR$ contention is incorrect; $C$'s prohibitive tariffs open up a sufficiently wide wedge between $O_1$ and $O_2$ to drive $C$ out of the picture, as in Figure 2, thus leaving a $CU$ as the preferred policy. The second is the Nepal paradox. Nepal is so small that its offer curves are indistinguishable from the origin; curves $O_1$ and $O_2$ in such a diagram don't appear. Once again, in choosing between $A$ and $E$, the two $CU$

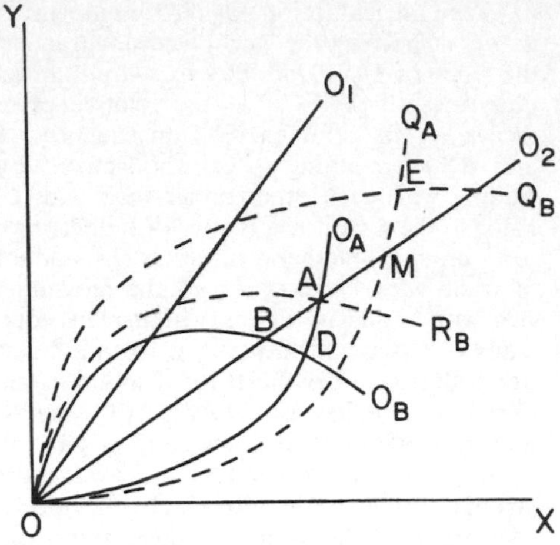

FIGURE 3. GAINS IN SPITE OF TRADE DIVERSION

members face the standard free-trade question.

### A. Gains with Trade Diversion

Figure 2 presents an example of trade creation, where $CU$ benefits are relatively easy to show. (An even simpler example would be the case where preunion tariffs of Countries $A$ and $B$ were high enough to completely prevent trade in these products, as shown by offer curves $R_A$ and $R_B$.) However, our main point—that a $CU$ may provide gains not possible through $UTR$—is valid also in the more complicated case of trade diversion (where diversion is defined simply as the shifting of the source of supply from outside Country $C$ to partner $B$). This is shown with Figure 3.

Consider first the situation prior to a $CU$. Country $A$ is such a large supplier of $X$ that, if there were only bilateral trade with $B$, trade would take place at $D$. However, this price is lower than Country $A$ can get from $C$; $A$ therefore carries on some trade with $C$, at the after-transportation, after-tariff relative prices shown by the slope of $O_2$. Continuing our simplifying assumption that there are no transportation costs between countries $A$ and $B$, we note that Country $B$ chooses to trade with $A$ at the relative set of

---

Country $C$ exports $X$ and imports $Y$. But Country $A$ wants to export $X$ and import $Y$. Because of tariffs and transportation costs, Country $C$ is willing to import $X$ and export $Y$ only at a relatively high price for $Y$; that is, only at the relative prices given by offer curve $O_2$. Thus, in trading with $C$, Country $A$ would end up at $T$, not $V$, and point $A$ is clearly better for it than point $T$. Similarly, if Country $B$ trades with $C$, it will end up at $U$, not $N$; and $A$ is clearly preferred to $U$. Thus, Countries $A$ and $B$ choose trade with each other at point $A$, rather than trade with Country $C$ at points $T$ and $U$, respectively.

[15] If Country $A$ unilaterally eliminates its tariffs, it still trades with Country $B$; its equilibrium with $B$ (which still has tariffs) is at point $M$, and this is preferable to the point ($S$) that it could pick in trade with Country $C$. However, if Country $B$ unilaterally removes tariffs, it will trade with $C$, since point $W$ dominates $Z$.

prices which $A$ offers in its trade with $C$; that is, the slope of $O_2$. Thus, prior to the $CU$, quantity $OB$ of trade takes place between countries $A$ and $B$, while $BA$ takes place between countries $A$ and $C$.

After the $CU$ is established, trade takes place at point $E$. Countries $A$ and $B$ now trade only with one another; diversion of $BA$ of trade has taken place.

The question is, how does each country compare the $CU$ outcome with $UTR$? Consider first $A$'s options. Unilaterally, $A$ can improve its situation by eliminating tariffs, moving to point $M$. (The case here is the same as for unilateral free trade in Figure 1.) Clearly, for Country $A$, point $E$ is better than $UTR$ point $M$; a $CU$ dominates $UTR$.

For Country $B$, unilateral gains are possible by a partial tariff cut which rotates its offer curve to $R_B$ and increases its trade by $BA$.[16] Through negotiation of a $CU$ and thereby reciprocal tariff elimination with Country $A$, Country $B$ can achieve a further move from point $A$ to $E$. We cannot be certain that $E$ is superior to $UTR$ point $A$ from Country $B$'s viewpoint: $M$ is better than $A$, but $E$ may be either superior or inferior to $M$, depending on the elasticity of $Q_A$. But our principal point holds: for Country $B$, point $E$ *may* be superior to $A$ (if $Q_A$ is highly elastic and/or distance $AM$ is large). Thus, for all members, a trade-diverting $CU$ may represent a gain compared both to the original equilibrium, and to the options open under $UTR$.

Following the literature cited in our first paragraph, we have focused here on changes in welfare of the members of the $CU$. For these two countries, it does not matter whether the wedge between $O_1$ and $O_2$ is caused by tariffs or transportation costs. (More precisely, it does not matter provided that $C$'s tariffs are fixed, and not open to negotiation.) However, if we consider world

welfare, it does matter. A wedge caused by transportation costs involves the use of productive resources, and in this case a $CU$ which improves the welfare of the member countries also improves world welfare. But insofar as the wedge reflects $C$'s tariffs, a $CU$ may mean a less efficient allocation of world resources, even though Countries $A$ and $B$ both gain. Specifically, the diversion of trade $BA$ away from Country $C$ in Figure 3 involves the loss of tariff revenues by $C$. In any worldwide welfare calculation, this loss must be weighed against the gains of the member countries.

Several loose ends remain to be tied up: the complications raised by the existence of more than one outside Country $C$; the existence of more than two goods; and ambiguities and confusions regarding the terms of trade.

### III. Many Outside Countries

If $A$ and $B$ are trading with $C$, and $C$ is a single large country, its tariffs are borne by $A$ and $B$; the prices at which $A$ or $B$ can sell to $C$ are reduced by the full amount of $C$'s tariffs, and the full amount of $C$'s tariffs (together with transportation costs) shows up in the gaps between $O_C$ and $O_1$ and between $O_C$ and $O_2$. In a more realistic case, where there are many outside countries, the situation is more complex, with the tariffs of outside countries falling partly on domestic consumers and partly on trading partners. In this case only part of an outside country's tariffs show up in the wedge in Figure 2. Indeed, it is conceivable that, if there are many outside countries operating in a highly competitive international marketplace, the tariffs of each of these countries will fall completely on their own consumers, and will have no effect on international prices at all. (This seems to be the implicit assumption of much of the literature.) But even in this case, there is a wedge because of transportation costs to and from outside countries; or, more precisely, because of higher transportation costs with outside countries than between members of the $CU$.

Our analysis of this wedge illustrates the obvious (but frequently ignored) reason why

---

[16]As we noted earlier in fn. 14, Country $B$ can export good $Y$ to Country $C$ in exchange for $X$ only at terms of trade $O_1$ because of $C$'s tariffs and transportation costs. $B$ can exchange at terms of trade $O_2$ only in trade with Country $A$. And, in the absence of reciprocal tariff cuts by Country $A$, the quantity of trade at such relative prices is limited to $OA$.

a *CU* usually includes geographically close countries, and excludes distant ones. Distance opens up the terms-of-trade wedge with outside countries, thus allowing mutually beneficial trade to take place between the members. Thus, this analysis raises doubts about the desirability from an efficiency viewpoint of geographically dispersed preferential systems such as the old British Commonwealth, where intermember transportation costs were generally no lower than transportation costs with third countries. (Of course, transportation costs are not the only thing to be considered when evaluating such an arrangement.)

## IV. Many Goods

While offer curves provide a great advantage in drawing attention to general-equilibrium issues, they suffer from the severe limitation that only two goods can be considered. Logically, the offer curve analysis might be seen as involving *N* commodities in an *N*-dimensional space. But the problem is that a two-dimensional diagram like Figure 2 cannot be used to describe just two of the goods ($X, Y$) in an *N*-good world. In a two-good world, the exports of $X$ will equal the imports of $Y$ in equilibrium, but there is no presumption in an *N*-good world that the exports of any particular good, $X$, will equal any particular import, $Y$.

Faced with this problem, we depart from the formal model to offer some impressionistic conclusions regarding the plausibility, in a many-good world, of the common assumption that the terms of trade with the large third country are unaffected by $A$ and $B$'s tariffs. In a many-good world, even a huge country may not produce large amounts of every product. After all, even moderately sized single countries at present have substantial influence over the market of particular goods (Saudi Arabia in oil, Brazil in coffee, Canada in wheat). Thus, it seems implausible to see outside Country $C$ as predominant in all commodities, and we must therefore question the rigid *UTR* assumption that $C$ freezes the world terms of trade. For example, it is difficult to argue that the rest of the world could offer fixed terms of trade

to a South American *CU*. However, in order to directly address the *UTR* case on its own grounds, we have assumed in Figure 1 that $C$'s offer curves do reflect fixed terms of trade, and we continue to make that assumption (together with the companion assumption that there are no economies of scale).

## V. Further Terms of Trade Issues

We now consider how a *CU* may affect the terms of trade between members $A$ and $B$. First, observe that we have drawn Figure 2 so that the terms of trade between the two members are the same at $E$ as at point $A$. This illustrates our main contention: Each country ($A$ and $B$) can obtain gains from a *CU* which it cannot achieve unilaterally, even if the *CU* does not change the terms of trade between members within the union, or between the union and outside Country $C$. Of course, as we noted earlier, there is little chance that the terms of trade between $A$ and $B$ will in fact remain exactly the same. But even where there is some deterioration in the terms of trade of one of the partners, that partner may achieve gains from a *CU* which are not available through *UTR*. This was just shown with Figure 3, in the comparison of points $E$ and $A$ from Country $B$'s viewpoint. And it shows up even more strongly in Figure 2, if $Q_B$ is redrawn to intersect $Q_A$ at point $F$. Although the *CU* results in a deterioration in $B$'s terms of trade as the equilibrium moves from $A$ to $F$, it provides benefits not possible through unilateral free trade (for the same reason that $E$ dominates $W$).

The second point is that, even if we assume that $B$ is a large country, presenting Country $A$ with an infinitely elastic offer curve, $A$ can still have a terms of trade change and a gain from a *CU*. Indeed, $A$'s gain will come precisely because its terms of trade improve as a result of $B$'s tariff elimination, as illustrated in Figure 4.[17] The elimination of tariffs by $B$ will cause its offer curve to rotate counterclockwise from $O_B$ to $Q_B$, giving $A$ better terms of trade and higher

---

[17] For more detail, see Lipsey (1970, pp. 88–89).

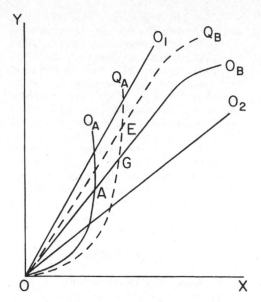

FIGURE 4. COUNTRY *B* MUCH LARGER THAN
COUNTRY *A*

terms of trade gain for *A* when *B* also agrees to eliminate tariffs[18]—causing a move from *M* to *E*—will, in this special case, exactly offset the terms of trade loss from *A*'s initial move (and will leave each *CU* partner with a higher welfare than at initial point *A*).

The need for care in dealing with terms of trade issues becomes apparent if we consider a passage in which Johnson referred to the terms of trade in evaluating the relative merits of *UTR* and tariff bargaining:[19]

> ...the form and logic of bargaining for reciprocal tariff reductions [are] phenomena which are incomprehensible to the classical approach to tariff theory, according to which the source of gain is the replacement of domestic production by lower-cost imports, whereas *increased exports yield no gain (improved terms of trade apart)* to the exporting country, but a gain to the foreigner through the same replacement of domestic production by lower-cost im-

real income at *CU* point *E* than at original point *A*. This equilibrium *E*—which represents a Pareto optimum (provided that Country *C*'s policy is taken as a given not subject to change)—is not achievable through unilateral tariff moves, since Country *B* has nothing to gain by removing its tariffs unilaterally. (They are borne by foreign rather than domestic consumers.) But it will be in the collective interest of countries *A* and *B* to get to point *E* by forming a *CU*; Country *A* will be able to compensate *B* for the establishment of a *CU* if *B* makes this a condition for agreement. Thus, optimum point *E* may be achievable through bilateral (customs union) bargaining.

Finally, we should be careful in fitting the terms of trade issue into the overall case for a *CU*. Returning to Figure 2, we note that, while the terms of trade do not change between the preunion point *A* and postunion point *E*, the terms of trade are not rigid; they can be changed by national action. For example, if, instead of forming a *CU*, Country *A* unilaterally eliminates its tariff, this will result in a deterioration in its terms of trade with the movement to point *M*. The

[18]Recognition of how a partner's tariff elimination may improve the terms of trade is important in disposing of another long-held belief—that when Country *A* diverts trade from outsider *C* to partner *B*, it necessarily incurs a terms-of-trade loss because it is no longer buying from the cheapest source *C*. (Lipsey and others have correctly pointed out that it will get a production and consumption gain, and the discussion has focused on how these two gains compare with the terms-of-trade loss.) However, there may not be a terms-of-trade loss at all; there may be a gain. Partner *B* may all along have been the cheapest free-trade source. But if this was the case, why wouldn't *A* have bought from *B* in the first place, before the *CU*? The answer is: *B*'s tariff may have prevented such trade. To illustrate, consider the following extreme case: Suppose *B* is the lowest-cost free-trade source, but *B* has imposed a prohibitive tariff that has precluded trade with all countries. Accordingly, *A* has been driven to trade with a less protectionist country, *C*. But if *A* and *B* form a *CU*, *A* will now trade with *B*, its lowest-cost free-trade source. (In less extreme cases, this same result may occur if *B*'s initial tariff is higher than *C*'s and sufficiently so to have choked off *A*'s natural initial trade with *B* and replaced it with trade with *C*.) In such circumstances, a failure to see beyond its own tariff could lead *A* erroneously to presume that *C* is its lowest-cost source. In this case, a *CU* is *A*'s means of diverting imports from a higher-cost source (outsider *C*) to its reciprocally cheapest source, *B*.

[19]Johnson applied this argument both to customs union bargaining and to multilateral, most-favored-nation bargaining.

ports. Since these gains are attainable by unilateral action, the classical approach provides no explanation of the necessity and nature of the bargaining process.   [p. 270, emphasis added]

A problem in interpreting this argument is an ambiguity in the passage we have italicized. If it is interpreted to mean that there can be no gain unless terms of trade change, then Johnson was wrong, as we have seen from our comparison of points *A* and *E* in Figure 2.

But there is a second possible interpretation of the italicized passage. Johnson may have been comparing points *M* and *E* in Figure 2 from Country *A*'s viewpoint.[20] That is, he may have been saying that there is no gain to *A* from a reduction in *B*'s tariff, if we ignore any change in the terms of trade associated with that reduction. But this interpretation makes Johnson's statement vacuous. *The* economic objective of *A* in negotiating foreign tariff cuts is to increase the demand for its exports. This involves a rotation in *B*'s offer curve, and an improvement in *A*'s terms of trade.[21] Johnson's argument that there is nothing, improved terms of trade apart, to be gained from foreign tariff cuts amounts to the proposition that there is nothing to be gained if the foreign offer curve is unaffected. But this means that the foreigners had no tariff to begin with. This is not a very enlightening line of argument. In brief, our plea for care in stating terms-of-trade issues is related to our plea that foreign tariffs not be implicitly assumed away in comparing *UTR* with a *CU*.

---

[20] This second interpretation is apparently what Johnson had in mind. See the later passage in Johnson where he argued that the case for a *CU* rather than *UTR* "...must rest on the possible terms-of-trade loss from unilateral tariff reduction and on the possible terms-of-trade gain for the union as a whole from discrimination against the outside world" (p. 280).

[21] There are two possible exceptions to the proposition that the rotation of *B*'s offer curve will improve *A*'s terms of trade: a) If there is a dominant third country, as explained with Figure 1. b) If Country *A* itself has a perfectly elastic offer curve. (In this instance, the *UTR* case is undercut, since *A*'s tariffs fall on foreigners, not on domestic consumers.) The context of Johnson's passage makes it clear that he was not depending on either of these exceptions.

This paper demonstrates that *UTR* need not dominate a *CU* from an economic viewpoint. The proposition that *UTR* is dominant was based on an overemphasis on the cost-reducing effects of a country's own tariff reductions, and an underemphasis on the advantages in terms of the better access to foreign markets which follows the partner's tariff reductions. Once foreign tariffs are taken into account, there is no further reason for subscribing to the idea that *CU*s tend to be formed exclusively for noneconomic reasons. Such reasons may be present, and may be very important. But economists need not dismiss economic motives; in our view, the economic consequences of customs unions is a promising field for research.

## REFERENCES

S. W. Arndt, "On Discriminatory vs. Non-preferential Tariff Policies," *Econ. J.*, Dec. 1968, *78*, 971–79.

———, "Customs Union and the Theory of Tariffs," *Amer. Econ. Rev.*, Mar. 1969, *59*, 108–18.

E. Berglas, "Preferential Trading Theory: The *n* Commodity Case," *J. Polit. Econ.*, Apr. 1979, *87*, 315–31.

C. A. Cooper and B. F. Massell, (1965a) "Towards a General Theory of Customs Unions for Developing Countries," *J. Polit. Econ.*, Oct. 1965, *73*, 461–76.

——— and ———, (1965b) "A New Look at Customs Union Theory," *Econ. J.*, Dec. 1965, *75*, 742–47.

W. M. Corden, "Economies of Scale and Customs Union Theory," *J. Polit. Econ.*, May 1972, *80*, 465–75.

Roma Dauphin, *The Impact of Free Trade in Canada*, Ottawa 1978.

F. Gehrels, "Customs Union from a Single-Country Viewpoint," *Rev. Econ. Stud.*, No. 1, 1956, *24*, 61–64.

H. G. Johnson, "An Economic Theory of Protectionism, Tariff Bargaining and the Formation of Customs Unions," *J. Polit. Econ.*, June 1965, *73*, 256–83.

M. B. Krauss, "Recent Developments in Customs Union Theory: An Interpretive Survey," *J. Econ. Lit.*, June 1972, *10*, 413–36.

A. P. Lerner, "The Symmetry between Import

and Export Taxes," *Economica*, Aug. 1936, 3, 306–13.

Richard G. Lipsey, "The Theory of Customs Unions: Trade Diversion and Welfare," *Economica*, Feb. 1957, 24, 40–46.

_____, *The Theory of Customs Unions: A General Equilibrium Analysis*, London 1970.

James E. Meade, *The Theory of Customs Unions*, Amsterdam 1955.

Peter Robson, *The Economics of International Integration*, London 1980.

Jacob Viner, *The Customs Union Issue*, New York 1950.

John Williamson, "Trade and Economic Growth," in J. Pinder, ed., *The Economics of Europe*, London 1971.

Ronald J. Wonnacott and Paul Wonnacott, *Free Trade between the United States and Canada: The Potential Economic Effects*, Cambridge, Mass. 1967.

_____ and _____, "Is Unilateral Tariff Reduction Preferable to a Customs Union? The Curious Case of the Missing Foreign Tariffs; or, Beware of the Large Country Assumption," work. paper 80-37, Dept. of Econ. and Bur. Bus. Econ. Res., Univ. Maryland 1980.

# Part III
# Extensions

# A
# Terms of Trade

# [8]

# Tariff Preferences and the Terms of Trade

The impact of tariff preferences on resource allocation and welfare has been the subject of notable theoretical advances in the past decade,[1] but there is a gap in the literature on the closely-related question of their effect on the terms of trade, changes in which might significantly affect the distribution of the gains or losses among members, and between the preference area as a whole and the rest of the world. The purpose of this note is to fill part of this gap by establishing what appear to be the main propositions valid for an arbitrary number of countries, and to contrast the results with those which derive from the traditional theory of non-discriminatory tariffs.

## I

I make three simplifying assumptions : (1) initial tariffs are low ; (2) the contemplated tariff reductions are small ; and (3) all exports are gross substitutes in world consumption in the sense that a rise in the price of any country's exports, all other prices remaining constant, creates an excess demand for the exports of every other country.[2] The significance of these assumptions will be dealt with later.

Consider a three-country system in which $A$ and $B$ denote the prospective member countries and $C$, the rest of the world.

[1] Three main works on the theory of customs unions are : Jacob Viner, *The Customs Union Issue* (Carnegie Endowment for International Peace : New York, 1950) ; James E. Meade, *The Theory of Customs Unions* (North Holland : Amsterdam 1956) ; and Tibor Scitowsky, *Economic Theory and Western European Integration* (Stanford University Press : Stanford 1958) ; but mention should also be made of H. Makower and G. Morton, "A Contribution Towards a Theory of Customs Unions", *Economic Journal*, Vol. LXIII No. 249 (March 1953) ; R. G. Lipsey, "The Theory of Customs Unions : Trade Diversion and Welfare," *Economica*, Vol. XXIV No. 93 (February 1957) ; H. G. Johnson, "Discriminatory Tariff Reduction : A Marshallian Analysis," *Indian Journal of Economics*, Vol. XXXVIII No. 148 (July 1957) ; and R. G. Lipsey, "The Theory of Customs Union : A General Survey", *Economic Journal*, Vol. LXX No. 279 (September 1960), 496-513.

[2] In "The Pure Theory of International Trade," *American Economic Review*, Vol. L No. 1 (March 1960) I compared the traditional two-country model of international trade with a multiple-country system, and found (for tariffs, income transfers, productivity changes, consumption and production taxes) that the two models yield practically identical qualitative results provided that all exports are gross substitutes.

1

2                                        *The Manchester School*

The problem is to deduce the changes in the world (relative) prices of the three countries when the tariff concessions are initiated. The simplest approach to the solution is to investigate, for each tariff reduction in isolation, the changes in the balances of trade on the tentative supposition that international prices remain constant.

Let us examine first the reduction in $A$'s tariff on $B$'s exports. At constant international prices the price of $B$'s goods in $A$ falls by the amount of the tariff reduction. This *price* effect, assuming for now that all goods are substitutes in $A$'s consumption,[1] shifts demand in $A$ away from home goods and $C$'s goods onto $B$'s goods, occasioning an improvement in $B$'s balance and a worsening of $C$'s balance. It can also be shown, however, that $A$'s balance worsens since the difference between the improvement in $B$'s balance and the worsening of $C$'s balance must equal the change in $A$'s balance (by Cournot's law that the sum of all balances is identically zero), and because the improvement in $B$'s balance must exceed the worsening of $C$'s balance by the reduced spending in $A$ on home goods (by Walras's law that all excess demands sum to zero within any country).[2] The price effect thus induces an

[1] Some goods might be complements in a nation's consumption without interfering with the assumption that all goods are gross substitutes in world markets. I assume here that all goods are *net* and *gross* substitutes in $A$'s consumption, but the implications of relaxing this assumption will be discussed later.

[2] Let $A$, $B$, and $C$ be the balances of the three countries, and $dt$ the change in $A$'s tariff. With units chosen to make each price initially unity, the change in $B$'s balance at constant terms of trade, as a proportion of the tariff change, is

$$\left(\frac{\delta B}{\delta t}\right)' = \left(\frac{\delta I_{ba}}{\delta t}\frac{1}{I_{ba}}\right)I_{ba} = -\eta_{ba \cdot b}I_{ba}$$

where $I_{ba}$ is the level of imports from $B$ to $A$ and $\eta_{ba \cdot b}$ is the negative (own) elasticity of demand for $B$'s goods in $A$ due to a change in the price of $B$'s goods ; and the change in $C$'s balance can be written

$$\left(\frac{\delta C}{\delta t}\right)' = \left(\frac{\delta I_{ca}}{\delta t}\frac{1}{I_{ca}}\right)I_{ca} = -\eta_{ca \cdot b}I_{ca}$$

where $\eta_{ca \cdot b}$ is the positive (cross) elasticity of demand for $C$'s goods in $A$ due to the change in price of $B$'s goods. Now by Cournot's law we have

$$\left(\frac{\delta A}{\delta t}\right)' + \left(\frac{\delta B}{\delta t}\right)' + \left(\frac{\delta C}{\delta t}\right)' = 0$$

so

$$\left(\frac{\delta A}{\delta t}\right)' = (\eta_{ba \cdot b}I_{ba} + \eta_{ca \cdot b}I_{ca}).$$

On the other hand, from Walras' law, we have

$$\eta_{aa \cdot b}I_{aa} + \eta_{ba \cdot b}I_{ba} + \eta_{ca \cdot b}I_{ca} = 0$$

where $\eta_{aa \cdot b}$ is the positive (cross) elasticity of $A$'s demand for home goods due to a change in $B$'s price, and $I_{aa}$ is home consumption. It follows that

$$\left(\frac{\delta A}{\delta t}\right)' = -\eta_{aa \cdot b}I_{aa} < 0$$

improvement in $B$'s balance and deteriorations in $A$'s and $C$'s balances.

The price effect, however, is partly offset by the *budgetary effect*—$A$'s government experiences a budget deficit equal to the reduced tariff proceeds, and this deficit must be corrected by decreased government spending or increased taxes. The final result therefore depends on whether or not the change in spending due to the method by which the government restores balance in its budget is sufficient to offset the initial price effect. In principle either result is possible depending on which taxes are increased or how the government reduces spending, but there is a strong presumption that the initial price effect will dominate. For example, if income taxes are raised the reduced level of disposable income of the community means that consumers in $A$ will spend less on all goods (in the absence of inferior commodities), but this budgetary effect is exactly equal, for small tariff changes, to the income effect implicit within the initial price effect,[1] leaving only

[1]The price effects treated in the preceding note can be split into pure substitution elasticities and income propensities as follows :

$$-\eta_{ba \cdot b} I_{ba} = -n_{ba \cdot b}{}' I_{ba} + m_{ba} I_{ba}$$

and

$$-\eta_{ca \cdot b} I_{ca} = -\eta_{ca \cdot b}{}' I_{ca} + m_{ca} I_{ba}$$

where $m_{ba}$ and $m_{ca}$ are the marginal propensities to spend in $A$ on imports from $B$ and $C$, and the primes denote that the elasticities have no income effects.

The increased income taxes reduce disposable income in $A$ by $I_{ba} dt$ so that the budgetary effects alter $B$'s and $C$'s balances as a proportion of the tariff change, according to the equations

$$\left(\frac{\delta B}{\delta t}\right)'' = -m_{ba} I_{ba}$$

and

$$\left(\frac{\delta C}{\delta t}\right)'' = -m_{ca} I_{ba}.$$

The combined impact of the price and budgetary effects, before world prices change, is therefore

$$\frac{\delta B}{\delta t} = \left(\frac{\delta B}{\delta t}\right)' + \left(\frac{\delta B}{\delta t}\right)'' = -\eta'_{ba \cdot b} I_{ba} > 0$$

and

$$\frac{dC}{\delta t} = \left(\frac{\delta C}{\delta t}\right)' + \left(\frac{\delta C}{\delta t}\right)'' = -\eta_{ca \cdot b} I_{ca} < 0.$$

In "The Pure Theory of International Trade : Comment, "*American Economic Review*, Vol. L No. 4 (September 1960), 721-2, Professor H. G. Johnson corrected a conclusion of my earlier paper (Mundell, *op. cit.*, n. 30) where the income effect implicit within the tariff reduction was wrongly weighted ; his *Comment* has helped to clarify my present analysis of income effects.

pure substitution terms which work in the same direction as the original price effect. Only in exceptional cases where reduction in government spending is the method used to balance the budget and where it is heavily biased against one of the goods, can the budgetary effect dominate. In what follows I ignore these exceptional cases.

The tariff reduction, then, tends to improve $B$'s balance and worsen $A$'s and $C$'s balances at constant international prices. The latter must therefore move, if equilibrium is to be restored, in a direction which worsens $B$'s balance and improves the balances of $A$ and $C$. Figure I provides a method of determining this direction.

The lines $AA'$, $BB'$ and $CC'$ trace the loci of the world prices of $A$ and $B$, relative to the world prices of $C$, which permit equilibrium (before the tariff changes) in the balances of $A, B$ and $C$ respectively. The following characteristics of these curves are implied by the assumption that all goods are substitutes in world markets :

(1) $AA'$ and $BB'$ have positive slopes.[1] This follows because a rise in $A$'s price (relative to $C$'s price) must be associated with a rise in $B$'s price (relative to $C$'s price) along any iso-balance line, since a *c.p.* rise in $A$'s price worsens $A$'s and improves $B$'s balance, while a *c.p.* rise in $B$'s price worsens $B$'s and improves $A$'s balance. Similarly, $CC'$ has a negative slope because a rise in $A$'s price (relative to $C$'s price) would improve $C$'s balance and must therefore be associated, along $C$'s iso-balance schedule, with a fall in $B$'s price which would worsen $C$'s balance (the assymmetrical position of $C$'s curve derives from the (unimportant) assumption that $C$'s goods serve as *numeraire*).

(2) The slope of $AA'$ must exceed, and the slope of $BB'$ must fall short of the slope of a line from $O$ to $Q$. This follows because a movement along this line is a proportionate movement of $B$'s and $A$'s prices, and is therefore the same (in a "homogeneous" price system) as a *c.p.* movement of $C$'s price. Any point on $OQ$ must therefore be a point of balance-of-payments surplus for $A$ and $B$ and balance-of-payments deficit for $C$, while any point

[1]The three schedules are drawn as straight lines to emphasize that the analysis is exact for small changes only.

*Tariff Preferences and the Terms of Trade*                    5

along *OQ extended* must be a point of surplus for *C* and deficit for *A* and *B*.

(3)  When the system is not in equilibrium at the point *Q* the situations of deficit or surplus in the balances of the three countries must be those indicated by the inequalities in the six sectors.

The diagram can now be used to establish the direction of change in the terms of trade.  From the initial equilibrium *Q* the tariff reduction in *A* causes the three schedules to shift.  At constant international prices, i.e., at the point *Q*, the tariff reduction causes *B*'s balance to be in surplus and *A*'s and *C*'s balances to be in deficit, so world prices must move in a direction which worsens *B*'s balance and improves those of *A* and *C*.  In other words, the new point of equilibrium must lie in Quadrant I where, from the point of view of the situation before the tariff change, *A*'s and *C*'s balances are in surplus and *B*'s is in deficit.  The characteristics of Quadrant I therefore outline the changes in relative prices which must take place as a result of the tariff reduction ; in this quadrant *B*'s price has risen relative to the prices of *A* and *C*. This establishes the most important proposition about discriminatory tariff reductions : *a tariff reduction in a member country unambiguously improves the terms of trade of the partner country*.

Notice that it cannot be determined, *a priori*, whether the terms of trade of the tariff-reducing country (*A*) rise or fall relative to the foreign country ; an equilibrium in Quadrant I is consistent with either result.  But given the elasticities of demand in *A* for the goods of *B* and *C* (these elasticities determine the change in the balances at constant international prices), there exists a line which determines the new equilibria for successively larger tariff reductions in *A*.  Thus, if the point *a* represents the new equilibrium as a result of a small tariff reduction in *A*, then the point *a'* would indicate that for a slightly larger tariff reduction.  The line *Qaa'* I shall call *A*'s "tariff-reduction line".  Its slope as drawn is negative but in fact all that can be definitely established is that it must lie between the slopes of *QC* and *QA'*.

Now let us consider the effect of reduction in *B*'s tariff on *A*'s goods and the combined effect of both *A*'s and *B*'s tariff reductions.  *B*'s tariff reduction creates a surplus in *A*'s balance and deficits in the balances of *B* and *C*, necessitating an improvement in *A*'s terms of trade relative to both other countries.  In the diagram the new equilibrium, as a result of $B$'s tariff reduction alone, must be in Quadrant III following the same line of reasoning as in the analysis of $A$'s tariff reduction. $B$'s tariff-reduction line is described by $Qbb'$, with any slope between that of $QB'$ and $QC'$.

The final effect of any given set of mutual discriminatory tariff reductions can be determined by adding the results. If $A$'s tariff reduction results in a new equilibrium at, say, $a$, and $B$'s tariff reduction results in a new equilibrium at, say, $b$, the combined effect is determined by completing the parallelogram formed by the two tariff-reduction lines $Qa$ and $Qb$, establishing the point $T_1$ as the new equilibrium. Similarly, the points $T_2$, $T_3$ and $T_4$ are the new equilibria for the respective sets of points on the tariff-reduction lines, $(a', b')$, $(a, b')$ and $(a', b)$.

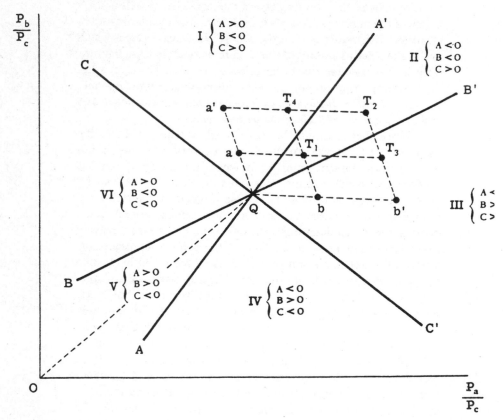

## II

All the attainable points lie northeast of $CC'$ but they might lie in any of the three Quadrants, I, II and III. The characteristics of these quadrants indicate the general conclusions which follow from discriminatory tariff reductions : in Quadrant I, $B$'s terms of trade have unambiguously improved ; in Quadrant III, $A$'s terms of trade have unambiguously improved ; and in Quadrant II, $C$'s terms of trade have unambiguously worsened (the indicated change in the terms of trade is unambiguous in the sense that the improvement or deterioration is with respect to both the other countries). In all three quadrants the terms of trade of the rest of the world worsens with respect to at least one and perhaps both of the member countries.

The entire area northeast of $CC$, however, is not attainable by given tariff reductions ; given the elasticities of demand in the two member countries, only the area east of $A$'s and north of $B$'s tariff-reduction line encloses the point of final equilibrium, and this area is necessarily smaller than the area northeast of $CC$. But the attainable area must nevertheless enclose all of Quadrant II, yielding another important conclusion : *some sets of tariff reductions necessarily improve the terms of trade of both member countries with respect to the rest of the world* (this might not include the specific tariff reductions implied by a free-trade area, however) A special case is where the members lower tariffs in a ratio which preserves the original intra-union terms of trade resulting in a new equilibrium along $OQ$ extended ; in this case it is obvious that the terms of trade of the outside world unambiguously fall since the balance of payments of each individual country in the union improves while that of the outside world worsens, as a result of the tariff reductions at constant world prices. But this special case is only one of many instances in which the terms of trade of the outside world fall with respect to both members ; indeed, there is a general presumption that this is the normal case since the balance of payments of the union as a whole necessarily improves (at constant prices) while that of each country in the rest of the world worsens.

Finally, one can consider the possibility of independence or complementarity in national (but not in world) consumptions. The smaller are the cross elasticities of demand in member countries between the exports of the partner country and the exports of third countries, the greater is the likelihood that the terms of trade of one of the member countries will deteriorate with respect to foreign countries. At the limit—where $A$'s tariff reduction does not reduce imports into $A$ from foreign countries, and where $B$'s tariff reduction does not reduce imports into $B$ from foreign countries—the terms of trade of one of the member countries is likely to improve, while that of the other member country is likely to fall, since the tariff reductions cause a deficit in one member and a surplus in the other member, whereas the balance of the rest of the world is unaltered (there is an exception if the tariffs are reduced in a way which preserves the intra-union balance ; in that case world prices remain unchanged). As we pass the limit—as some complementarity appears in the consumptions of member countries—there arises the possibility that the terms of trade of the rest of the world improve with respect to both member countries. Thus, if $B$'s and $C$'s goods were complementary and, similarly, if $A$'s and $C$'s goods were complementary in $B$'s consumption, $B$'s tariff reduction alone would prompt a fall in $B$'s terms of trade. Then the combined tariff reductions would stimulate, at constant world prices, a surplus in foreign countries and a deficit in the union as a whole, occasioning an improvement in the terms of trade of the outside world relative to the union.

III

The following generalizations now emerge from this study of tariff preferences :

(1)  A discriminatory tariff reduction by a member country improves the terms of trade of the partner country with respect to both the tariff-reducing country and the rest of the world, but the terms of trade of the tariff-reducing country might rise or fall with respect to third countries.

(2)  The degree of improvement in the terms of trade of the partner country is likely to be larger the greater is the member's tariff reduction ; this establishes the presumption that a member's gain from a free-trade area will be larger the higher are the initial tariffs of partner countries.

(3)  It cannot be established, *a priori*, that arbitrary sets of discriminatory tariff reductions by member countries must

improve the terms of trade of both member countries ; it is possible that the terms of trade of one of the members deteriorate relative to third countries.

(4)  Nevertheless, there exists a presumption that the terms of trade of both member countries improve relative to the outside world.  This presumption is established by the fact that the balance of trade of the preference area as a whole must improve, while that of each country in the rest of the world must deteriorate.  It follows immediately that the terms of trade of one of the members improve relative to third countries ; if, for example, the balance of trade of a member country deteriorates as a result of the tariff reduction (at constant world prices) the terms of trade of the partner country must improve.

(5)  Moreover, there are numerous sets of tariff reductions that must improve the terms of trade of both member countries. A special case is where tariffs are reduced so as to leave the intra-union terms of trade unaltered.

(6)  The above propositions hold where all goods are substitutes in national consumptions.  If complementarity is present between the goods of partner countries and the outside world there arises the possibility that the terms of trade of the latter improve relative to both member countries.

## IV

It remains now to indicate briefly the significance of the three assumptions made at the beginning, and to contrast the results with those which derive from traditional tariff theory. The assumption that initial tariffs are low ensures that the tariff reductions reduce the value of tariff proceeds and create deficits in the government budgets ; our conclusions would not hold if, for example, initial tariffs were prohibitive.  The assumption that the tariff changes are small is necessary for similar reasons, because large tariff changes would be likely to change the composition of imports and exports ; and because the proposition relating to the equality of the budgetary effect (when income taxes are raised) and the income effect implicit within the price change would not be exact.  The assumption of substitution in world markets, however, is one which requires more intensive examination.

If complementarity is present in the world economy the conclusions reached in this paper might be fundamentally changed ; in general terms (even if the requirement that the system is dynamically stable be imposed) almost any result can occur. Analysis of complementarity would therefore deteriorate into a difficult exercise in taxonomy, and one which is probably unrewarding unless actual statistics can be introduced. The assumption of substitution seems to be necessary in order to get definite results, and to establish a useful "normal" case with which more complicated examples can be compared.

It must not be thought, however, that the restrictive assumption of universal substitution is any less necessary in analysis of the traditional theory of tariffs or, indeed, in any of the other branches of international trade theory. The certain results which appear to derive from traditional theory are equally based on the assumption of substitution, but the assumption is hidden by the usual two-country model employed in that branch of analysis ; whereas an analysis of discriminatory tariffs logically requires at least a three-country model of the world economy and thus explicit recognition of the problem of complementarity. Only if complementarity is assumed to be slight or absent does the proposition of traditional tariff theory, that an (undiscriminatory) tariff reduction worsens the terms of trade of the tariff-reducing country, hold, just as this assumption is necessary to establish that an undiscriminatory tariff reduction improves the terms of trade of the partner country.

*Tariff Preferences and the Terms of Trade*                                11

## APPENDIX

The propositions now established for three countries hold also for an arbitrary number of countries. Suppose that there are $n + 1$ countries, numbered 0, 1, 2, . . ., $n$, and that the exports of country 0 are *numeraire*. Let $B_i$ be the balance of trade (or payments) of the $i$-th country, expressed in terms of the *numeraire*, and let $p_j$ denote the price of the exports of the $j$-th country, with $p_j$ initially equal to unity (by appropriate choice of units). The system can be written as follows :

$$B_i(p_1, \ldots, p_n; t) = 0 \qquad (1)$$

where $t$ is a parameter representing the combined tariff reductions. By differentiation we obtain

$$\sum_{j=1}^{n} \frac{\delta B_i}{\delta p_j} \frac{dp_j}{dt} = -\frac{\delta B_i}{\delta t} \quad (i = 1, 2, \ldots, n). \qquad (2)$$

The solution for $\dfrac{dp_i}{dt}$ is

$$\frac{dp_i}{dt} = -\sum_{j=1}^{n} \frac{\delta B_j}{\delta t} \frac{\triangle_{ji}}{\triangle} \qquad (3)$$

where $\triangle$ is the Jacobian $\dfrac{\delta (B_1, \ldots, B_n)}{\delta (p_1, \ldots, p_n)}$ and $\triangle_{ji}$ is the co-factor of its $j$-th row and $i$-th column. The assumption of gross substitution in world markets implies that $\triangle_{ji}$ and $\triangle$ are of opposite sign, so that the ratio of the two is negative.[1]

Suppose that countries 0 and 1 are the member countries. Then it follows immediately that a tariff reduction in *one* of the

[1]By Mosak's theorem that : if the off-diagonal elements of $\triangle$ are positive (implied by the assumption of gross substitution) and *if* the matrix of $\triangle$ is Hicksian, then *all* the elements of $\triangle^{-1}$ are negative ; and by the stability theorems of Arrow and Hurwicz, Hahn, Negishi and Uzawa that : if all the off-diagonal elements of $\triangle$ are positive and the row- or column-sums are negative, the matrix of $\triangle$ *is* Hicksian. References are given in my article previously cited.

member countries, say country $1$,[1] improves the terms of trade of the partner country since, in that case, $\dfrac{\delta B_j}{\delta t} < 0$ for *every* $j = 1$, $2, \ldots, n$ ; the expression on the right of (3) is negative.

Taking the tariff changes in both countries into account, it is not definite that a member country's terms of trade rise. This can be seen by separating the first term in (3) from the other to get

$$\frac{dp_i}{dt} = -\frac{\delta B_l}{\delta t}\frac{\triangle_{li}}{\triangle} - \sum_{j=2}^{n}\frac{\delta B_j}{\delta t}\frac{\triangle_{ji}}{\triangle} \tag{4}$$

The first term might be positive or negative depending on the elasticities of demand in the two member countries and on the size of the relative tariff reductions. But if a member's balance worsens as a result of the tariff reductions, it follows that partner's terms of trade must improve ; the uncertainty as to sign only appears to apply if the balances of both members improve.

It is readily shown, however, that the terms of trade of both members cannot deteriorate. To see this, consider the intra-union terms of trade, and note that this might change in any direction. But if the intra-union terms of trade of one of the members improve, then the terms of trade of that member must improve relative to third countries. Suppose, for instance, that the intra-union terms of trade of country 0 improve so that

$$\frac{dp_l}{dt} = -\frac{\delta B_l}{\delta t}\frac{\triangle_{ll}}{\triangle} - \sum_{j=2}^{n}\frac{\delta B_j}{\delta t}\frac{\triangle_{jl}}{\triangle} < 0. \tag{5}$$

It follows, from (5) that

$$\frac{\delta B_l}{\delta t} = -\zeta - \sum_{j=2}^{n}\frac{\delta B}{\delta t}\frac{\triangle_{jl}}{\triangle_{ll}} \tag{6}$$

---

[1] The proof that : if a country $o$ lowers its tariff, the terms of trade of country $l$ improve, is slightly more difficult, and requires the introduction of a theorem developed by Metzler for the Keynesian case (Lloyd Metzler, "A Multiple-Country Theory of Income Transfers," *Journal of Political Economy*, Vol. LIX, No. 1 (February 1951), p. 21 and applied to the classical case in my article (no. 29) ; but the reader's intuition should persuade him that the analysis in the text is sufficient since the choice of numeraire cannot affect *relative* prices.

*Tariff Preferences and the Terms of Trade*     13

where $\zeta$ is a positive number. Substituting (6) in (4) we get

$$\frac{dp_i}{dt} = \left[ \zeta + \sum_{j=2}^{n} \frac{\delta B_j}{\delta t} \frac{\Delta_{ji}}{\Delta_{ll}} \right] \frac{\Delta_{li}}{\Delta} - \sum_{j=2}^{n} \frac{\delta B_j}{\delta t} \frac{\Delta_{ji}}{\Delta}$$

$$= \zeta \frac{\Delta_{li}}{\Delta} + \sum_{j=2}^{n} \frac{\delta B_j}{\delta t} \frac{\Delta_{jl} \Delta_{li} - \Delta_{ji} \Delta_{ll}}{\Delta \Delta_{ll}} \qquad (7)$$

Now the first term is obviously negative. The second term will be negative provided the numerator and the denominator of the term containing determinants are of the same sign ; this is readily shown to be the case, making use of Mosak's theorem and another theorem about determinants.[1] This is sufficient to prove that one of the member country's terms of trade must improve.

There are a number of special cases in which the terms of trade of both members improve, relative to outside countries. The case considered in the text is where the intra-union terms of trade are unchanged ; the proof in the general case follows readily by setting the expression in (5) equal to zero, and substituting in (4) to get the same results as in (7) without the first term.

*McGill University.*     ROBERT A. MUNDELL.

---

[1]The following identity is true for any determinant :
$$\Delta \, \Delta_{ll, \, ji} = \Delta_{ll} \, \Delta_{ji} - \Delta_{ji} \, \Delta_{li} ;$$
but from Mosak's theorem, and the stability theorems, it follows that the two terms on the left have the same sign, so that the difference on the right is positive. This means that the ratio of the determinants in the second equation is negative.

See Metzler (*op. cit.*, p. 26) for a previous application to the generalized Keynesian system.

# [9]

## GENERAL VERSUS PREFERENTIAL TARIFF REDUCTION FOR LDC EXPORTS: AN ANALYSIS OF THE WELFARE EFFECTS

RICHARD BLACKHURST*

*The Johns Hopkins University*
*Bologna Center*

The purpose of this paper is to develop a theoretical model for evaluating the relative welfare effects of two alternative methods of stimulating the exports of the less developed countries (LDCs)—in particular their exports to the developed countries. The more traditional of the two involves the general (non-discriminatory) reduction of developed country tariffs on commodities of interest to the LDCs. The other approach assumes that the developed countries reduce their tariffs on a discriminatory basis so as to give LDC exports preferential access to their domestic markets.[1]

The basic model is developed in the first part of the paper. Part II explores the application of the model to a multi-product world.

### I. THE BASIC MODEL

The model utilizes excess demand and supply curves (that is, demand curves net of domestic supply, and supply curves net of

domestic demand) in combination with the standard *ceteris paribus* assumptions; the welfare effects of the alternative tariff reduction strategies are evaluated on the basis of changes in consumers' and producers' surplus.[2] The world is assumed to consist of three countries: $A$, representing a single developed country; $B$, representing an aggregate of all other non-LDC countries; and $C$, representing the LDC aggregate. It is assumed, in addition, that (i) originally tariffs are the only restrictions on international trade, (ii) there are no transportation costs, and (iii) domestic supply curves reflect social costs.[3, 4]

---

[2] The analysis, which draws on a model developed by Johnson [5, 46-74], is in terms of what happens when one developed country follows a particular tariff reduction strategy for one commodity. To analyze the actual situation envisaged by the proponents of the two strategies—one which involves several developed countries and several commodities—the methods must be applied successively to each commodity and country, with the tariff-cutting country always identified as $A$, and the results aggregated to yield the net change. In this context it should be kept in mind that the results, since they flow from a partial equilibrium model, cannot be aggregated directly.

The straightforward use of excess demand and supply curves requires the assumption that each commodity is perfectly homogeneous in the sense that buyers do not discriminate on the basis of country of origin or brand name. For a brief discussion of why this assumption may not be as restrictive as it generally is assumed to be see [2, Appendix, Part I].

[3] With respect to the latter assumption it should be noted that a potentially important source of discrepancy between private and social costs arises if the model is expanded to include international trade in intermediate goods—that is, if the theory of tariff structures is introduced into the analysis. See [6].

[4] Throughout the analysis $A$'s domestic supply curve, and $B$'s and $C$'s export supply curves, are assumed to be imperfectly elastic. (The model is

---

*I would like to thank Harry Johnson and Arnold Harberger for their comments and suggestions on an earlier draft. The paper has also benefitted from suggestions made by the Journal's referee.

[1] Although the latter is not a new concept—the Commonwealth preference system and the United States/Philippine preference system have long histories, while the system of reciprocal preferences between the EEC and certain African countries is a more recent example—interest in its implications increased considerably when the granting of tariff preferences emerged as one of the five basic recommendations of the 1964 United Nations Conference on Trade and Development. Subsequent to the Conference, tariff preferences were granted to the LDCs by the Soviet Union (1965), Australia (1966), Hungary (1968), the EEC (1971), and Japan (1971). The Nixon Administration indicated in the spring of 1971 that it would seek Congressional approval to grant such preferences. See [4] for a general introduction to the tariff preference proposal.

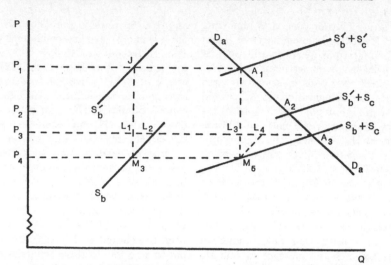

FIGURE 1. S.I when both $B$ and $C$ are exporting prior to tariff elimination.

The following abbreviations will be used throughout the paper to refer to the alternative tariff reduction strategies:

S.I  *Strategy I (general elimination)*: developed countries eliminate tariffs on a selected group of products, the concessions being extended to all countries.

S.II  *Strategy II (preferential elimination)*: developed countries eliminate tariffs on imports of selected products from the LDCs while maintaining existing tariffs on imports of these products from non-LDC countries.

Discussions of the tariff perference proposal frequently assume that the amount of a commodity which would be allowed entry under the preference would be limited by a quota. To cover this possibility a third strategy will be considered after the two basic strategies have been analyzed:

S.II.Q  *Strategy II—Quotas:* same as S.II except the developed countries are assumed to apply quotas on imports from the LDCs of commodi-

easily extended to handle any other combination of assumptions about the supply elasticities.)

Finally, it is assumed that exchange rates remain constant—that is, that they are not affected by the tariff changes.

ties subject to preferential treatment.

The remainder of this section is divided into four parts: in the first three the model is applied to situations in which (i) $A$ is importing from $B$ and $C$ prior to tariff elimination, (ii) $A$ imports only from $B$ prior to tariff elimination, and (iii) a quota is imposed on commodities granted preferential entry. Part four summarizes the impact of the three tariff reduction strategies on each of the three areas taken individually and as an aggregate.

### Both $B$ and $C$ Assumed to be Exporting to $A$ Prior to Tariff Elimination

Figure 1 refers to the situation in which $B$ and $C$ are both exporting to $A$ prior to the implementation of either tariff elimination strategy. Country $A$'s excess demand curve is $D_a$, $S_b$ and $S_c$ are $B$'s and $C$'s excess supply curves exclusive of the tariff, and $S'_b$ and $S'_c$ are their excess supply curves inclusive of the tariff. $B$'s and $C$'s individual supply curves (the latter is not shown separately in the figure) have been summed to obtain the joint supply curves which confront $A$'s consumers under varying assumptions about $A$'s tariff policy.

352                          RICHARD BLACKHURST

Prior to tariff elimination $A$ is importing $P_1J (= P_4M_3)$ of the commodity from $B$ and $JA_1 (= M_3M_5)$ from $C$, the world price is $P_4$, the price in $A$'s domestic market is $P_1$, and $A$'s tariff revenue is measured by area $P_1A_1M_5P_4$. Implementation of S.I would shift the equilibrium point from $A_1$ to $A_3$; if S.II were introduced, the new equilibrium would be at $A_2$. To keep the figures uncluttered, a separate figure will be used to analyze the latter strategy.

With reference to Figure 1, introduction of S.I shifts the equilibrium to $A_3$. At the new price $P_3$ domestic consumption is larger and domestic production is smaller. The sum of the consumption and production effects is equal to the increase in imports $(L_3A_3)$ resulting from the trade creation effect of S.I.[5] $B$'s exports have increased by $L_1L_2$, while $C$'s have increased by $L_4A_3$ (the latter is obtained by locating $L_4$ so that $L_3L_4 = L_1L_2$).

As a result of introducing S.I, $A$ has undergone two types of changes; first, there has been a transfer from producers' surplus (not shown) and from tariff revenue $(P_1A_1L_3P_3)$ into consumers' surplus; second, it is likely that $A$'s aggregate welfare has changed. The latter change may be divided into: (1) a gain equal to $A_1A_3L_3$ (received in the form of an increase in consumers' surplus) following from the increase in consumption and from the substitution of imports for a part of domestic production; (2) a loss due to the adverse effect of S.I on $A$'s terms of trade with $B$ that has increased the cost of the original volume of imports by $P_3L_1M_3P_4$; and (3) a similar loss vis-à-vis $C$ that has increased the cost of the original volume of imports from $C$ by $L_1L_3M_5M_3$. Determination of the net effect of S.I on $A$'s welfare thus involves comparing the first item with the second two.

$B$'s total gain of $P_3L_2M_3P_4$ is composed of (1) an increase in the value of the original volume of exports equal to $P_3L_1M_3P_4$ (this corresponds to $A$'s loss on item two in the previous paragraph), and (2) an increase of $L_1L_2M_3$ in producers' surplus resulting from the additional production for export. Similarly, $C$'s gain can be broken down into (1) an increase equal to $L_1L_3M_5M_3$ in the value of the original volume of exports (corresponding to $A$'s loss listed as item three above), and (2) an increase of $L_4A_3M_5$ in producers' surplus due to expanded production for export.[6]

The world as a whole clearly has gained from S.I. All of $A$'s loss $(P_3L_3M_5P_4)$ has been transferred to $B$ and $C$ and thus nets out to zero for the three countries taken together. Meanwhile, $A$ has gained area $A_1A_3L_3$ and $B$ and $C$ have gained from increases in producers' surplus of $L_3L_4M_5$ $(= L_1L_2M_3)$ and $L_4A_3M_5$ respectively. On net, world welfare has increased by area $A_1A_3M_5$.

Figure 2, incorporating the relevant parts of Figure 1, refers to the analysis of S.II. Elimination of the tariff on imports from $C$ while maintaining it on imports from $B$ shifts the equilibrium from $A_1$ to $A_2$. At price $P_2$ $A$'s consumption is larger and domestic production is smaller. The sum of the production and consumption effects is equal to the net increase in imports $(K_4A_2)$ and measures the trade creation effect of S.II. The trade diversion effect of S.II is measured by the decline of $K_1K_2$ in $B$'s production for export (down to $P_2K_1$ from $P_1J$).

$C$'s exports have increased from $JA_1$ to $K_1A_2$, an amount equal to $K_3A_2$ (line $A_1M_4$ is parallel to $S'_b$; therefore $K_1K_3 = JA_1$). Since $K_3K_4$ is equal to $K_1K_2$, it is clear that the increase in $C$'s exports is equal to the sum of the trade creation and trade diversion effects of S.II; more specifically, the increase in $C$'s exports is the result of (1) an

---

[5] This definition, which follows Johnson, is in contrast to the practice of treating changes in consumption separately from trade creation (and trade diversion). See [5, 53fn].

[6] Since triangles $L_1L_2M_3$ and $L_2L_4M_5$ are equal, $C$'s total gain may be measured either by the sum of areas $L_1L_3M_5M_3$ and $L_4A_3M_5$, or by area $L_2A_3M_5M_3$.

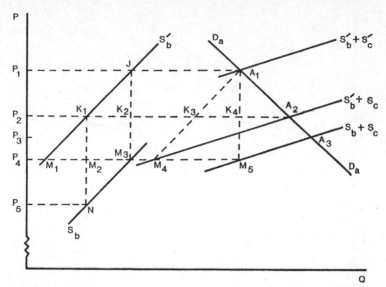

FIGURE 2. S.II when both $B$ and $C$ are exporting prior to tariff elimination.

increase in $A$'s consumption, (2) a decline in $A$'s production, and (3) a decline in $B$'s exports of the commodity to $A$.

As before, the effect of the tariff elimination on $A$ has been to (a) redistribute part of $A$'s producers' surplus and part of the tariff revenue into consumers' surplus, and (b) possibly alter $A$'s welfare. The latter may be divided into four parts: (1) a gain, measured by area $A_1A_2K_4$, due to the increase in consumption and to the decline in domestic production; (2) a gain from the effect of the trade diversion on $A$'s terms of trade with $B$ ($A$ now buys the surviving volume of imports from $B$ at a saving of $P_4M_2NP_5$ over the old cost); (3) a loss due to the fact that the reduction in $B$'s exports was replaced by $C$'s exports at a higher total cost equal to $K_1K_2M_3M_2$; and (4) a loss from the deterioration of $A$'s terms of trade with $C$ which has raised the total cost of the original volume of imports from that country by $K_2K_4M_5M_3$. $A$ can either gain or lose from S.II, depending on the importance of the first two items relative to the last two.

On the other hand $B$ has definitely suf-

fered a loss, equal to $P_4M_3NP_5$. This can be broken down into (1) the loss resulting from the effect on the surviving volume of exports of the worsening of its terms of trade (measured by $P_4M_2NP_5$, corresponding to $A$'s second source of gain), and (2) the loss of producers' surplus resulting from the decline in production for export (measured by $M_2M_3N$).

Conversely, $C$ clearly has gained. As with $A$ and $B$, $C$'s gain ($K_1A_2M_4M_1$) can be subdivided into (1) the increase in value of the original volume of exports due to a terms of trade gain (the increase is equal to $K_1K_3M_4M_1 = K_2K_4M_5M_3$; this is the same as $A$'s loss on item four), and (2) the increase in producers' surplus ($K_3A_2M_4$) due to the increase in production for export.

To determine the net effect of S.II on the world as a whole the effects on $A$, $B$ and $C$ are summed. After allowing for changes that cancel out, there remain two sources of gain ($A_1A_2K_4 + K_3A_2M_4$) and two sources of loss ($K_1K_2M_3M_2 + M_2M_3N$). Whether the gain outweighs the loss can be shown to depend on the relation between the amount of trade creation and the amount of trade

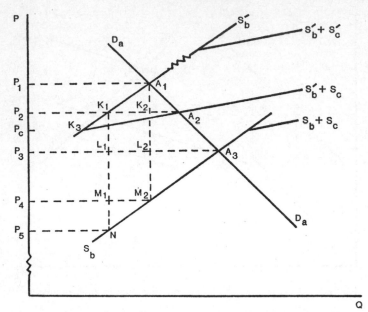

FIGURE 3. Tariff elimination when $C$ can compete only under S.II.

diversion.[7] More specifically, if less than half of $C$'s increase in exports is the result of trade diversion, the world gains; if more than half of the increase can be traced to trade diversion, the world as a whole loses.

### C Assumed Not to Be Exporting To A Prior to Tariff Elimination

The main thrust behind the proposal for preferences is the desire to make it possible for the LDCs to complete in markets in which currently they have difficulty competing—that is, in the markets for semimanufactured and manufactured products. This suggests that the analysis should include the

[7] If $A_1K_4K_3$ is added to the gains and $JK_2K_1$ ($= A_1K_4K_3$) to the losses, the two areas are now respectively $A_1A_3M_4$ and $JM_2NK_1$. On the assumption that the demand and supply curves are straight lines and that the tariff is a specific duty (both explicit in all of the figures), the gain area is equal to ½($K_3A_3$) ($P_1P_4$) and the loss area is equal to ($K_1K_2$) ($P_1P_4$). Cancelling the $P_1P_4$ terms, multiplying each side by two, and substracting $K_1K_2$ ($= K_3K_4$) from each side, leaves $K_4A_3$ and $K_1K_3$ respectively. Thus, the gain will exceed the loss if trade creation exceeds trade diversion and vice versa.

situation in which $C$ currently is not selling the commodity in $A$'s market.

There are three variants of the situation in which $C$ is not exporting the commodity to $A$ prior to the implementation of S.I or S.II. First, there is the situation in which $C$ could not compete, even with preferential entry; for this to be true $C$'s minimum supply price exclusive of the tariff must be greater than the existing tariff-inclusive price in $A$'s market. The other two variants are more interesting from the viewpoint of the preference issue. Under each variant, $C$ is able to compete with the aid of S.II; the distinction lies in whether or not $C$ also can compete under S.I.

The situation in which $C$ can compete only with the aid of S.II is depicted in Figure 3. The pre-tariff-elimination equilibrium is at $A_1$, with $P_1$ the price in $A$'s market. This price exceeds $C$'s minimum supply price ($P_c$) but the tariff is large enough to price $C$ out of $A$'s market, and all of $A$'s imports ($P_1A_1$) come from $B$.

Implementation of S.I causes the price to

fall to $P_3$ and the new equilibrium is at $A_3$. $P_3$ is below $C$'s minimum supply price and thus S.I has no effect on $C$—that is, it remains uncompetitive in $A$'s market. However, $B$'s exports have increased from $P_1A_1$ to $P_3A_3$ as a result of the effect of the price reduction on $A$'s consumption (an increase) and production (a decline)—the two together representing, as before, the trade creation effect of S.I. $A$ has suffered a terms of trade loss vis-à-vis $B$ which has increased the cost of the original volume of imports by $P_3L_2M_2P_4$, while at the same time gaining an amount equal to area $A_1A_3L_2$ as a result of the trade creation. $B$ gains from the increased value of the original volume of exports (area $P_3L_2M_2P_4$; this is the same as $A$'s loss), and from the increase in producers' surplus consequent upon the increase in production for export. World welfare has benefited from a net increase measured by area $A_1A_3M_2$.

If S.II is implemented instead of S.I, the new equilibrium is at $A_2$. With S.II, $C$ finds that it can compete in $A$'s market, and its exports of the commodity increase from zero to $K_1A_2$. The increase is due to the simultaneous increase in consumption and decline in production in $A$ (the two together totaling $K_2A_2$), and to the decline in $B$'s exports from $P_1A_1$ to $P_2K_1$ (a reduction of $K_1K_2$). The former two represent the trade creation effect of S.II, while the latter measures the trade diversion effect.

$C$ has gained via an increase of $K_1A_2K_3$ in producers' surplus. The loss suffered by $B$ divides into a decline of $P_4M_1NP_5$ in the value of its surviving exports due to a worsening of its terms of trade with $A$, and a loss of producers' surplus equal to $M_1M_2N$ as a result of the decline in production for export. The effect of S.II on $A$ is as follows: a gain of $P_4M_1NP_5$ representing the effect of the reduction in the price of the remaining imports from $B$ (this is equal to $B$'s terms of trade loss), a gain equal to $A_1A_2K_2$ due to the increased consumption and to the replacement of part of domestic production

by additional imports, and a loss measured by $K_1K_2M_2M_1$ representing the increase in the cost of the imports previously purchased from $B$.

After allowing for changes that cancel out, there remain two sources of gain (areas $A_1A_2K_2$ and $K_1A_2K_3$) and two sources of loss (areas $K_1K_2M_2M_1$ and $M_1M_2N$). The net effect of S.II on world welfare thus turns on the size of the first two areas relative to the second two.

If $A_1K_2K_1$ is added to the gain area and to the loss area, the two become $A_1A_2K_3$ and $A_1M_2NK_1$ respectively. The first is equal to $\frac{1}{2}(K_1A_2)$ $(P_1P_c)$, the second to $(K_1K_2)$ $(P_1P_4)$. Let trade diversion $(K_1K_2)$ account for one half of the total increase in $C$'s exports $(K_1A_2)$; then $\frac{1}{2}(K_1A_2) = K_1K_2$. As $P_1P_c$ always is smaller than $P_1P_4$, the loss will exceed the gain when trade diversion and trade creation are equal. To find conceptually the point where the two areas are equal, $\frac{1}{2}(K_1A_2)$, $P_1P_c$, and $P_1P_4$ can be taken as given, and $K_1K_2$ reduced until it is small enough relative to $\frac{1}{2}(K_1A_2)$ to offset the fact that $P_1P_c$ is smaller than $P_1P_4$. At the point where the gain just balances the loss, the amount of trade diversion will account for less than one half of the total increase in $C$'s trade; that is, at the break-even point trade creation must exceed trade diversion. This is in contrast to the results of the situation in which $C$ is assumed to be exporting the commodity to $A$ prior to S.II—in that situation the break-even point from the world viewpoint is when trade creation and diversion are equal.

The second of the two interesting situations in which initially $C$ is not exporting the product to $A$ occurs when $P_c$ lies below $P_3$. That is, the distinction between the two cases lies in the relation of $C$'s minimum supply price to the free trade price. In the previous example $P_c$ was above the free trade price, making it impossible for $C$ to compete under S.I. Here, in contrast, the free trade price exceeds $P_c$, and it is clear that $C$

356                                    RICHARD BLACKHURST

would be able to compete under either tariff elimination strategy.

Analysis of the changes in each country's welfare brought about by S.I or S.II parallels exactly that of the previous example, except that S.I will give $C$ an increase in producers' surplus. Once again it can be shown that for the world to break even under S.II the amount of trade creation must exceed the amount of trade diversion. (However, with reference to the previous example, the break-even point for the world in this case occurs at a point where the amount of trade creation is more nearly equal to the amount of trade diversion.)[8]

### The Effect of Putting Quotas on Imports of Products Accorded Preferential Treatment

The analysis so far has not considered the consequences of placing import quotas on those products granted preferential entry to developed country markets. Since limitations of this kind are likely to be included in any arrangement involving the granting of trade preferences their implications warrant exploration.

On the plausible assumption that the quota would be larger than the current volume of imports from the LDCs, one obvious effect of S.II.Q—to the extent that the quota limit became effective—would be to reduce the amounts of trade creation and diversion, as well as the extent of the improvement in $A$'s terms of trade on the surviving imports from $B$, that would have been produced by S.II. There are, in addition, other important but somewhat less obvious issues involved in the proposal to include quotas in the preference plan.

The situation in which preference-receiving imports from $C$ are subject to quotas may be analyzed with the aid of Figure 4. To simplify the figure only $C$'s supply curve is shown.[9] The pre-preference equilibrium is at $A_1$, with a tariff-inclusive price in $A$'s market of $P_1$; in response to a world price of $P_4$, $C$ is exporting $P_4K$ ($= P_1A_1$) units of the commodity to $A$. Implementation of S.II would shift the equilibrium to $A_2$ and $C$'s exports would increase by an amount measured by $JA_2$. $C$ would gain from an improvement in its terms of trade with $A$ which would increase the value of the original volume of exports by an amount measured by the sum of areas (4) and (7), and from an increase in producers' surplus measured by the sum of areas (5), (6) and (8).

To specify the way in which the outcome is changed by the introduction of S.II.Q rather than S.II it is necessary to determine (i) whether the quota limits the physical volume or the total value of the commodity that may enter at the preferential rate of duty, and (ii) whether it is a global LDC quota (imports enter on a first come, first served basis) or an arrangement involving permits (permits to import if given to residents; permits to export if given to the LDCs).[10]

If the quota restricts duty free imports from $C$ to $OY$ units per period, the excess supply curve will be distorted in the manner indicated by the broken line and the post-preference equilibrium will be at $A_q$. The interesting feature of S.II.Q is now apparent—the price in $A$'s market is $P_q$, but $C$ would be willing to supply $OY$ units at a

---

[8] In each case the amount of trade diversion must be sufficiently smaller than one half $C$'s increase in trade to offset the difference between $P_1P_e$ and $P_1P_4$. Since $P_1P_e$ is more nearly equal to $P_1P_4$ in the latter case, there is "less to offset," and thus the extent to which the amount of trade diversion must be smaller than the amount of trade creation is reduced. More formally, in each example the world will gain if

$$\frac{\text{trade creation}}{\text{trade diversion}} > \frac{2P_1P_4}{P_1P_e} - 1.$$

[9] The figure thus refers either to a situation in which $B$ is not exporting to $A$, or $D_e$ represents the excess demand curve facing $C$ after both $A$'s and $B$'s supply curves (the latter inclusive of $A$'s tariff) have been "subtracted" from $A$'s domestic demand curve.

[10] The discussion in this section draws on the work of James Meade [8, 276–88]. It is assumed that either the quota is absolute, or, if it is a tariff-rate quota—as Figure 4 implies—that no imports enter at the penalty rate.

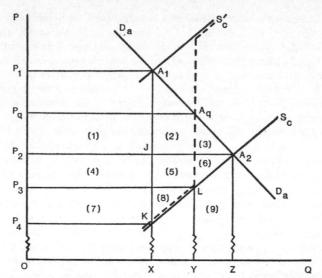

FIGURE 4. The effect of placing a quota on imports of the commodity granted preferential entry.

price per unit of $P_3$. This raises the issue of who receives the margin between the buying and selling prices (worth, in terms of revenue, an amount measured by the sum of areas (1), (2), (4) and (5)); the answer to this question is crucial for if $C$ receives the spread between the two prices, it is possible that $C$ would benefit more from S.II.Q than from S.II.

More specifically, under S.II, $C$ gained an amount equal to the sum of areas (4), (5), (6), (7) and (8); under S.II.Q, $C$ is certain of receiving only areas (7) and (8). However, in the latter case $C$ may be able to capture the margin between the buying and selling prices; if so, and if the sum of areas (1) and (2) exceeds area (6), then the increase in $C$'s welfare will be larger under S.II.Q than under S.II. And, if the sum of areas (1) and (2) exceeds the sum of areas (6) and (9), the increase in foreign exchange earnings also will be larger under S.II.Q.

The effect of S.II.Q (relative to S.II) on $A$ is, to a degree, the reciprocal of its effect on $C$. For example, if $A$ is able to capture the margin, a switch from S.II to S.II.Q

would cause $A$ to lose area (3), but in return $A$ would gain areas (4) and (5). Alternatively, if $C$ is in a position to capture the margin, a switch to S.II.Q would lead to a loss of areas (1), (2), and (3), and $A$ clearly would be worse off relative to the position under S.II.

To determine the net effect on $A$ of switching from S.II to S.II.Q when $B$ is exporting to $A$ it would be necessary to combine the calculations in the preceding paragraph with an estimate of S.II.Q's effect on the amounts of trade diversion and creation, as well as its effect on the change in $A$'s terms of trade with $B$.

In the absence of price control in $A$ the "quota profit" will go to one of three parties: (i) $A$'s government—for example, if they auction permits; (ii) $A$'s importers; or (iii) $C$'s exporters. The first alternative may be ruled out if it is assumed that the developed countries would not couple the granting of preferences with a measure designed to capture the quota profit. To determine which of the two remaining alternatives holds it is necessary to specify whether the quota is a global quota or a system involving permits.

With a global LDC quota it is impossible to determine ahead of time who will receive the quota profit.[11] Conversely, if a system of free permits is used it is clear that the traders who receive the permits will capture the quota profit; depending on their nationality, the extra benefit will accrue to $A$ or to $C$.[12]

The preceding analysis applies to quotas expressed in physical units. An alternative approach is to have a quota which limits the total value of imports of a particular commodity from the LDCs which may enter at the preferential rate.[13]

If $A$'s importers are in a position to capture the quota profit the analysis is essentially the same. For example, with a quota equal to area $P_3LYO$ the implementation of S.II.Q will cause $C$'s exports to increase until the quota becomes effective at $OY$ units.

When $C$'s exporters are able to capture the extra benefit the analysis is only slightly more involved. If the sum of the tariff revenue and the revenue $C$ was receiving prior to S.II.Q happens to just equal the quota, imports from $C$ will remain at $OX$ units and $C$ will receive $A$'s market price of $P_1$—provided $D_a$ to the right of $A_1$ is elastic; if the quota exceeds (is less than) the sum, imports from $C$ will increase (decrease) until the quota limit is reached. Once the new

equilibrium is determined the analysis of whether $C$ is better off under S.II.Q than under S.II parallels exactly the analysis of the previous case in which the quota limited the physical volume of imports.

In summary, an important aspect of quotas is the possibility that the welfare gain to the LDCs would be larger with quotas than without. As long as the quota becomes effective, the physical volume of LDC exports will always be less with a quota, and this means a smaller increase in producers' surplus (due to additional production). However, an effective quota also means that there is a margin between the buying and selling prices, and if the LDCs are able to capture the margin their terms of trade will be more favorable under S.II.Q. Clearly, under certain circumstances the terms of trade gain will outweigh the fact that the increase in producers' surplus (on the additional production) is smaller.

The larger are $C$'s exports of the product prior to implementation of either strategy, the greater the probability that S.II.Q could lead to a larger welfare gain for $C$ than S.II (because the terms of trade gain would cover a larger physical volume of exports). If $C$ is exporting a significant amount of the product prior to tariff elimination the chance that it will be granted preferential entry is smaller; on the other hand, if the developed countries agree to include some already competitive products in the group granted preferential entry, such products are more probable candidates for quotas than are products which the LDCs are not currently exporting.

---

[11] "Since anyone is free to import the commodity until the quota has been filled, there will be a rush to the frontier with the goods. Some dealers will be lucky and will reach the frontier before others. Those who are lucky will enjoy the abnormal profit; but there is no *a priori* reason to believe that they will be the exporters of [C] rather than the importers of [A] or vice versa" [8, 282].

[12] Both this statement and the preceding one are subject to qualification if $A$'s import market and/or $C$'s export market is (are) not competitive. Some of the implications of non-competitive import and/or export markets are considered in [8, 53–67; 1].

[13] Note that the broken line in Figure 4 is not relevant when the quota restricts total revenue rather than the total number of units.

### Summary of the Effects of the Three Tariff Reduction Strategies

*The LDC Aggregate: C.* If $C$ is exporting some of the commodity to $A$ before either of the tariff elimination strategies is implemented, S.I will lead to a terms of trade gain on the original volume of exports, and to a gain in producers' surplus on the additional production for export. Under S.II the nature of the gains to $C$ are the same, but the amounts are larger. The increase in the value of the original volume of exports will be greater than under S.I since the new price in $A$'s domestic market must be higher under S.II. And, the increase in $C$'s exports (and thus in producers' surplus) will be greater under S.II.

When $C$ is not initially exporting to $A$, the effect of S.I or S.II will depend on $C$'s minimum supply price. If it exceeds the tariff-inclusive price in $A$'s market, obviously neither strategy will make $C$ competitive. A minimum supply price below the original market price in $A$ but above the free trade price means that $C$ can compete under S.II but not under S.I; if it is below the free trade price, $C$ will begin exporting to $A$ under either strategy. In the latter two cases, $C$'s increase (from zero) in exports to $A$ will always be larger under S.II, and therefore the gain in producers' surplus will always be larger with the preferential strategy.

The placing of an effective quota on the amount of the product permitted preferential entry will, in certain circumstances, lead to a larger gain for $C$ than would have occurred under S.II. A necessary condition is that $C$ receive the margin between the buying and selling prices. If this condition is fulfilled, the answer turns on the importance of the better terms of trade under S.II.Q relative to the larger gain in producers' surplus under S.II.

*The Aggregate of Non-LDC Countries (Except A):* $B$. If initially $C$ is exporting some of the commodity to $A$, $B$ will gain from S.I and lose from S.II. Under either strategy the net gain (loss) is composed of a gain (loss) on its terms of trade with $A$, and a gain (loss) of producers' surplus. If $C$ is not competitive prior to tariff elimination, $B$ again will always gain from S.I; $B$ will lose under S.II if $C$'s minimum supply price exclusive of the tariff is below $B$'s supply price inclusive of the tariff. In short, $B$ will always lose from the implementation of S.II,

except when $C$ cannot compete even with the aid of preferential entry.

Because the amount of trade diversion will be smaller under S.II.Q than under S.II (provided the quota is effective), $B$'s losses will be less if the preference-receiving products are subject to import quotas.

*The Country Whose Tariff is Eliminated:* $A$. The introduction of S.I will cause the price in $A$'s domestic market to decline, and this will in turn produce two welfare-increasing changes—an increase in consumption, and the substitution of imports for a part of the high-cost domestic production. However, $A$ will suffer a terms of trade loss vis-à-vis $B$ (and $C$, if initially $A$ was importing some of the commodity from $C$), and as a result the cost of the original volume of imports will increase. The larger the amount of trade creation, the greater the probability that the gain will offset the terms of trade loss.

The effect of S.II on $A$ will differ slightly according to whether or not $C$ is assumed to be exporting some of the commodity to $A$ initially. Under either assumption $A$ gains from the effect of the price decline on domestic production and consumption (the amount of trade creation is smaller under S.II because there is less of a price reduction in $A$'s domestic market), and from an improvement in its terms of trade on the surviving imports from $B$. Offsetting the gains—to a greater or lesser degree—is the loss associated with the increased cost of the trade diverted from $B$ to $C$. In addition, if originally $A$ was importing some of the commodity from $C$, there is a loss from the worsening of its terms of trade on the original volume of imports.

It is impossible to determine, *a priori*, which strategy will leave $A$ better off. Under S.II there is a greater terms of trade loss vis-à-vis $C$, a loss on the trade diverted from $B$ to $C$, and the gain from trade creation is smaller; on the other hand, instead of suffering a terms of trade loss vis-à-vis $B$ (as under S.I), there is a terms of trade gain on

360                              RICHARD BLACKHURST

the surviving imports from $B$, and under certain circumstances this gain will more than offset the negative aspects of S.II.

If $A$ places an effective quota on the amount of imports eligible for preferential entry, the way in which the outcome will differ from what would have happened under S.II depends on which country receives the margin between the buying and selling prices. Should $A$'s own importers be in a position to appropriate the extra profit, $A$ could be better off under S.II.Q; if $C$ receives the extra profit, $A$ must be worse off under S.II.Q.

*The World: $A + B + C$.* Tariff elimination alters the welfare of each country involved through changes in the terms of trade, and through trade creation and trade diversion. Since terms of trade changes net out to zero from the world viewpoint, only trade creation and trade diversion need to be considered when analyzing the effects of the various tariff elimination strategies on world welfare.

Non-discriminatory tariff elimination can produce only trade creation and therefore S.I must lead to an increase in world welfare. S.II, on the other hand, produces both trade creation and trade diversion. In such cases, if $C$ were exporting to $A$ prior to S.II, the world would gain if the amount of trade creation exceeds the amount of trade diversion; if initially $C$ were not exporting to $A$, the requirement for the world to gain is more strict in the sense that the welfare break-even point occurs where the amount of trade diversion is less than the amount of trade creation, rather than when the two are equal.

Since S.I produces only trade creation, while S.II produces both trade creation (less, however, than S.I in any given situation) and trade diversion, it follows that within the context of this model non-discriminatory tariff elimination must benefit world welfare more than preferential elimination.

The effect on world welfare of switching from S.II to S.II.Q is one of diminishing whatever change S.II would have produced. That is, if S.II would have led to an increase (decrease) in world welfare, the increase (decrease) will be smaller if an effective quota is placed on imports of products granted preferential entry.

## II. WELFARE EFFECTS IN A MULTI-PRODUCT WORLD

In [7] James Meade developed a method of estimating the net effect on world welfare of small (marginal) changes in tariffs. He begins by noting that a tariff creates a difference between the price paid by consumers and the price received by producers. This leads to a situation in which the value of a unit of the commodity to consumers exceeds its value to suppliers by the amount of the tariff. Therefore, if because of a small change in some exogenous variable there are changes in the levels of expenditures on commodities subject to tariffs, world welfare generally will be altered. A simplified version of the relationship may be expressed as follows:

$$dW = \sum_i dx_i(p_i - c_i) \qquad (1)$$

where $W$ represents world welfare, $dx_i$ is the change in the amount bought and sold of the $i$th commodity, and $p_i$ and $c_i$ represent the per unit price and cost of the $i$th commodity.[14]

This approach may be adapted as follows to the analysis of the problem at hand.[15] Assume that $A$ is importing two commodities from $B$ and $C$ ($x_1$ and $x_2$), that imports from both countries are subject to tariffs ($t_1$ and $t_2$), and that $A$ has granted $C$ a "small" margin of preference by lowering the tariffs on imports from $C$. Adding a second subscript to each variable to indicate the country from which the imports originate and the

---

[14] See [7, 120–21] for the complete derivation of the equation. Note that because the change is differential, the effect of the change on the tariff itself is not taken into account.

[15] The following analysis draws on an article by Arnold Harberger [3].

tariff applicable to those imports, it is possible to rewrite equation (1) as follows:

$$dW = \left[ t_{c1} \frac{\partial X_{c1}}{\partial t_{c1}} + t_{b1} \frac{\partial X_{b1}}{\partial t_{c1}} + t_{c2} \frac{\partial X_{c2}}{\partial t_{c1}} \right.$$

$$\left. + t_{b2} \frac{\partial X_{b2}}{\partial t_{c1}} \right] dt_{c1} + \left[ t_{c1} \frac{\partial X_{c1}}{\partial t_{c2}} \right. \quad (2)$$

$$\left. + t_{b1} \frac{\partial X_{b1}}{\partial t_{c2}} + t_{c2} \frac{\partial X_{c2}}{\partial t_{c2}} + t_{b2} \frac{\partial X_{b2}}{\partial t_{c2}} \right] dt_{c2}.$$

To apply this expression to a situation in which S.II is introduced (that is, in which the changes in the tariffs are finite), it is necessary to integrate the small changes over the range of the tariff on each commodity. On the assumption that the relevant structural relations are linear (that is, that the partial derivatives in the second equation remain constant over the range of integration), the following expression is obtained,[16]

$$\Delta W = \tfrac{1}{2} t_{c1}(\Delta X_{c1}) + t_{b1}(\Delta X_{b1})$$

$$+ \tfrac{1}{2} t_{c2}(\Delta X_{c2}) + t_{b2}(\Delta X_{b2}). \quad (3)$$

Trade diversion ($D_1$ and $D_2$) is equal to $-\Delta X_{b1}$ and $-\Delta X_{b2}$, while trade creation ($K_1$ and $K_2$) is equal to $\Delta X_{c1} + \Delta X_{b1}$ and $\Delta X_{c2} + \Delta X_{b2}$. Making the assumption that imports from $B$ and $C$ pay the same tariffs, it follows that

$$\Delta W = \tfrac{1}{2} t_1(K_1 - D_1)$$

$$+ \tfrac{1}{2} t_2(K_2 - D_2). \quad (4)$$

In a situation in which $m$ developed countries grant trade preferences on $n$ commodities, equation (4) becomes

$$\Delta W = \tfrac{1}{2} \sum_{i=1}^{m} \sum_{j=1}^{n} (K_{ij} - D_{ij}) t_{ij}. \quad (5)$$

This expression, which agrees with the condition derived geometrically in Part I, will hold as long as (a) $C$ is exporting each commodity initially, and (b) the only distortions are tariffs on the commodities involved in the preference agreement.[17]

[16] See the mathematical note at the end of the paper for the derivation of equation (3).

[17] The values of $\Delta X_{cij}$ and $\Delta X_{bij}$ will not be simple functions of the own-price elasticities of

In a similar way the following expression for the change in world welfare under S.I. may be derived from equation (1):

$$\Delta W = \tfrac{1}{2} \sum_{i=1}^{m} \sum_{j=1}^{n} K_{ij} t_{ij}. \quad (6)$$

To apply the formulas to commodities which $C$ is not initially exporting to $A$, the tariffs on imports from $C$ must be replaced by the difference between the original tariff-inclusive price in $A$ ($p_{a1}$ and $p_{a2}$ in the two commodity world), and $C$'s minimum supply price ($p_{c1}$ and $p_{c2}$). In this case the expression which corresponds to equation (3) is

$$\Delta W = \tfrac{1}{2}(p_{a1} - p_{c1})(\Delta X_{c1}) + t_1(\Delta X_{b1})$$

$$+ \tfrac{1}{2}(p_{a2} - p_{c2})(\Delta X_{c2}) + t_2(\Delta X_{b2}). \quad (7)$$

Noting that $p_{a1} - p_{c1} = t_1 - (p_{c1} - p_{w1})$, where $p_{w1}$ is the pretariff-elimination world price received by $B$, it is possible to write the first two terms of equation (7) as

$$\Delta W_1 = \tfrac{1}{2} t_1(\Delta X_{c1}) - \tfrac{1}{2}(p_{c1} - p_{w1}) \Delta X_{c1}$$

$$+ t_1(\Delta X_{b1})$$

or

$$\Delta W_1 = \tfrac{1}{2} t_1(K_1 - D_1) \quad (8)$$

$$- \tfrac{1}{2}(p_{c1} - p_{w1}) \Delta X_{c1}.$$

In a multi-country, multi-product world equation (8) becomes

$$\Delta W = \tfrac{1}{2} \sum_{i=1}^{m} \sum_{j=1}^{n} (K_{ij} - D_{ij}) t_{ij}$$

$$- (p_{cij} - p_{wij}) \Delta X_{cij}. \quad (9)$$

As was noted above, the preceding analysis is based on the assumption that the only distortions are the tariffs on those commodities included in the tariff elimination agree-

supply and demand in the various countries but will be instead the change in the equilibrium values of the exports produced by the composite change in tariffs on several commodities by several countries (for example, if $X_{c11}$ is beef and $X_{c12}$ is mutton, then $\Delta X_{c11}$ will be greater when there is a preference on beef alone than when mutton is included in the preference plan).

362                           RICHARD BLACKHURST

ment. If this assumption were relaxed it
would be necessary to allow for the influence
of changes in the equilibrium values of those
commodities outside the tariff elimination
group which are subject to distortions. The
treatment of such interrelations would
parallel essentially the approach exemplified
in equation (2).

*Note on the Derivation of Equation (3)*

Beginning with the first element in the
first half of equation (2), the integral is

$$\int_0^{t_{c1}^{\bullet}} t_{c1} \frac{\partial X_{c1}}{\partial t_{c1}} dt_{c1} = \frac{1}{2} t_{c1}^* \frac{\partial X_{c1}}{\partial t_{c1}} t_{c1}^* . \quad (1')$$

The change following from the effect of the
elimination of $t_{c1}$ on $X_{c2}$ is

$$\int_0^{t_{c1}^{\bullet}} t_{c2} \frac{\partial X_{c2}}{\partial t_{c1}} dt_{c1} = t_{c2}^* \frac{\partial X_{c2}}{\partial t_{c1}} t_{c1}^* . \quad (2')$$

When $t_{c2}$ is subsequently eliminated, the
change produced via its effect on $X_{c2}$ is,

$$\int_0^{t_{c2}^{\bullet}} t_{c2} \frac{\partial X_{c2}}{\partial t_{c2}} dt_{c2} = \frac{1}{2} t_{c2}^* \frac{\partial X_{c2}}{\partial t_{c2}} t_{c2}^* . \quad (3')$$

The effect of the elimination of $t_{c2}$ on $X_{c1}$ is
ignored because $t_{c1}$ is now zero.

Provided the integrability condition
$\partial X_{c1}/\partial t_{c2} = \partial X_{c2}/\partial t_{c1}$ holds, equation (2')
may be split into

$$\frac{1}{2} t_{c2} \frac{\partial X_{c2}}{\partial t_{c1}} t_{c1} \quad (4a')$$

and

$$\frac{1}{2} t_{c1} \frac{\partial X_{c1}}{\partial t_{c2}} t_{c2} . \quad (4b')$$

To obtain the total effect on $C$'s exports
of eliminating $t_{c1}$ and $t_{c2}$, expressions (4b')
and (1') are summed, as are expressions
(4a') and (3'); this yields

$$\tfrac{1}{2} t_{c1}(\Delta X_{c1}) \quad \text{and} \quad \tfrac{1}{2} t_{c2}(\Delta X_{c2}).$$

The effect of tariff elimination on $B$'s
exports may be found in a similar way. If
the second element in each term of the right
hand side of equation (2) is integrated and
the integrals summed, $t_{b1}(\Delta X_{b1})$ is obtained.
Similarly, $t_{b2}(\Delta X_{b2})$ is found from the fourth
elements of each term of the equation.

REFERENCES

1. Bhagwati, J., "On the Equivalence of Tariffs
   and Quotas" in R. Baldwin et al. *Trade,
   Growth and the Balance of Payments.* Chicago: Rand McNally and Co., 1965.
2. Blackhurst, R., "A Model for Estimating the
   Impact of Tariff Manipulation on the Volume of Imports," *Staff Research Studies.*
   Washington: United States Tariff Commission, forthcoming.
3. Harberger, A., "The Measurement of Waste,"
   *American Economic Review,* May 1964, 58–76.
4. Johnson, H. G. *Economic Policies Toward the
   Less Developed Countries.* Washington: The
   Brookings Institution, 1966.
5. ——. *Money, Trade and Economic Growth.*
   Cambridge, Mass.: Harvard University Press,
   1962.
6. ——, "The Theory of Effective Protection
   and Preferences," *Economica,* May 1969,
   119–38.
7. Meade, J. *The Theory of Customs Union.* Amsterdam: North-Holland Publishing Co., 1956.
8. ——. *The Theory of International Economic
   Policy, Vol. I, The Balance of Payments.*
   London: Oxford University Press, 1951.

# [10]

## The Theory of Preferential Trading Arrangements

By

### Richard Pomfret

———

Contents: I. Introduction. – II. Some Pre-Vinerian Contributions. – III. Mainstream Customs Union Theory. – IV. The Vanek-Kemp Branch. – V. The Search for the Missing Prince. – VI. Why Do Preferential Arrangements Exist? – VII. Conclusions.

## I. Introduction

I n view of the proliferation of preferential trading arrangements since the war, one might expect the analysis of discriminatory trade policies to occupy a central position in international trade theory[1]. In fact it was a backwater during the late 1960s and the 1970s. The accepted theory had limited applicability, there was little consensus on the reliability of existing measures of the welfare effects even of the most important preferential arrangements (such as the European Community), and the conventional explanation of the establishment of such arrangements rested on "non-economic" arguments. Recent theoretical developments have improved the situation by incorporating new elements into the theoretical framework, which provide the basis for more convincing explanations of why discriminatory trade policies exist. In conjunction with growing disrespect by policymakers for the nondiscrimination principle which is the cornerstone of the GATT, these developments indicate the need for an up-to-date survey of the theory of preferential trading arrangements.

There are some good reasons for the deficiencies of this branch of international trade theory. The theory of trade preferences belongs to the

*Remark:* I am grateful to Dermot McAleese, Jim Riedel, Ed Tower and Alan Winters for helpful and encouraging comments on earlier drafts, even if not all of their advice was acted upon.

[1] The terms preferences, discrimination and preferential trading arrangements are here used interchangeably to refer to different treatment for different trading partners; nondiscrimination and MFN treatment are used for the opposite situation. The list of postwar preferential arrangements is too lengthy to reproduce, but by the 1980s the majority of international trade was being conducted on a preferential basis [Pomfret, 1985]. For the European Community, half of members' imports were intra-EC trade and over half of the remainder was covered by the EFTA agreement, the Lomé Convention, Mediterranean agreements, the Generalized System of Preferences (GSP), the Multi-fibre Arrangement (MFA), and trade with Comecon – "most-favored-nation" treatment applied to a residual seven countries. For the United States, the main proponent of nondiscrimination, ten percent of imports are covered by the MFA, the Autopact with Canada, GSP and Comecon trade, while many non-tariff barriers are discriminatory and there is current pressure in Congress for reciprocity in commercial policy (i.e. discriminatory measures against countries not granting "fair" treatment to U.S. exports). On other major preferential schemes see El-Agraa [1982].

440                              Richard Pomfret

world of second-best, and generalizations are hard to make[2]. The 2 x 2 x 2 model is not applicable, since at least three countries must be involved[3]. Even granted these obstacles of outcome and method, however, the literature has made disappointing progress, primarily because inappropriate assumptions have been overused in order to surmount the methodological problem; these have enabled some strong conclusions to be reached, but they are divorced from many practical cases. In particular, international price changes have often been ruled out by assumption, which in turn ensures that analytical attention is focused on the preference donor rather than the recipient and biases the analysis against finding welfare gains from preferences. To the extent that the literature looks beyond the donor, it is to analyze the global welfare effects of preferences, obviously a useful goal, but in avoiding the distribution of welfare gains and losses, it sheds little light on the political economy of preferences.

The aim of this paper is, by surveying the literature on preferential trading, to identify the reason for this lackluster performance. Section II resurrects three earlier contributions which remain relevant. The third and fourth sections survey the literature of the 1950s and 1960s in order to trace the genesis of the situation described above. During the 1970s and early 1980s there were signs of dissatisfaction and attempts to incorporate some missing piece which would make the theoretical framework more satisfying; four types of pieces are examined in Section V. After relaxing the assumption of constant costs and giving price changes a larger role, discrimination in international trade may be rational from a national perspective; Section VI sketches the economic motives for preferences and applies them to the major postwar preferential trading arrangements. The main conclusions are summarized in the final section.

## II. Some Pre-Vinerian Contributions

The theory of preferences (or customs union theory) is frequently interpreted as beginning de novo with Viner's 1950 book. This is clearly a simplification; most tariff regimes before 1950 had been discriminatory, proposals for customs unions had been frequent and some important ones had been implemented, and there had been informed discussion of all this. Yet there had been no resolution of the fundamental dilemma posed to advocates both of free trade and of protection: are preferential tariff reductions better than no tariff reductions or, alternatively expressed, is protection against some foreign suppliers better than no protection? Neither from a national nor a

---

[2] Thus a movement towards one condition for Pareto optimality by reducing tariffs on imports from some sources may not be welfare-improving when other conditions are not fulfilled (which they necessarily are not when tariffs remain on non-preferred imports) [Lipsey, Lancaster, 1956/57].

[3] There is some debate over the minimum number of commodities (see Section V.1 below).

global welfare perspective could this be categorically answered. Viner's great contribution was to prove indeterminacy, and, by introducing the concepts of trade creation and trade diversion, to provide tools for identifying conditions under which preferential arrangements are welfare improving[4]. Nevertheless, there had been important insights before 1950, three of which will now be described.

The controversy which Viner resolved had focused on a preferential tariff's impact on the donor. Some consideration had been given to global considerations, but most contributors took a nationalist viewpoint. Little attention was paid to the impact on the preference recipient, perhaps because it appeared obvious and had been spelled out long ago: "When a nation binds itself by treaty . . . to exempt the goods of one country from duties to which it subjects those of all others, the country, or at least the merchants and manufacturers of the country, whose commerce is so favoured, must necessarily derive great advantage from the treaty" [Smith, 1776, Book IV, Ch. 6]. By emphasizing the gain to the preference recipient Smith makes an important point about the distribution of gains (both among and within affected countries); the point aroused little controversy, but by the 1960s it appeared to be largely forgotten, or assumed away.

The most controversial word in the above quotation is "great". The direction of change seems incontrovertible, but its magnitude is not. In an article foreshadowing Viner, Taussig [1892] showed that the incidence of the costs and benefits from preferences depends upon the market share of the recipient. He illustrated this with two examples. Preferences given by the USA to Hawaiian sugar in 1876 scarcely affected American prices (because the Hawaiian market share remained small) but yielded a windfall gain to the Hawaiian producer, i. e. the welfare effect was a transfer from U.S. government revenue to Hawaiian producer surplus. Taussig [1892, p. 28] concluded that ". . . any remission of duty which does not apply to the total importations, but leaves a considerable amount still coming in under the duty, puts so much money into the pockets of the foreign producer". His second example concerned the other extreme where the preferred partner provides almost all imports, illustrated by the U.S. granting preferential treatment to imports of wool from Australia. In this case, if the price elasticity of import supply is high, the primary beneficiaries are domestic consumers. Taussig's examples

---

[4] O'Brien [1976] has argued that the concept of trade diversion was discussed by classical economists from Hume and Smith on, and especially by McCulloch in the nineteenth century. In the first half of the twentieth century it is less prominent, and many writers only emphasized the trade creation aspects of preferences. To me, O'Brien's limited concession to Viner's originality in focusing attention on trade creation and trade diversion, in contrast to previous references which were "short discussions in the context of rather wider issues" [*ibid.*, p. 560], underrates the key insight that it is the possibility of either outcome which is the source of ambiguity of welfare effects; previous writers tended instead to argue for or against preferential arrangements, stating only one side of the argument.

442                          Richard Pomfret

indicate that the distribution of the preferences' welfare effects depends upon
what happens to prices, i.e. upon whether the exporter is "large" or "small".
Taussig's paper is a precursor of Viner's work insofar as it identifies the
ambiguous impact of preferences on the donor (in his examples the USA),
although in less general terms than Viner's[5].

Along a different track, Torrens [1844] developed an argument for
preferences based on the nationally optimum tariff in the presence or absence
of other countries' reactions. He opposed unilateral tariff abolition on the
grounds of negative terms of trade effects and increased vulnerability to other
countries' manipulation of the terms of trade, and advocated bilateral
negotiation of commercial treaties on a reciprocity basis. Torrens rejected
charges that he was opposed to free trade in general; free trade was the
ultimate objective but it could only be imposed upon political dependencies,
while independent (large) countries could gain by levying their nationally
optimum tariff unless this was made costly by retaliatory tariffs[6]. Torrens'
analytical contribution is valuable because he recognized the argument that a
country could maximize national welfare by operating as a discriminating
monopolist even though the global optimum was free trade, and because he
related preferences to changes in the terms of trade, which occupied
center-stage in his policy discussion; a position which they vacated, with
unhappy consequences, in later work.

### III. Mainstream Customs Union Theory

Viner's distinction between trade creation and trade diversion as effects of
a preferential tariff reduction was seminal. The distinction is important
because the resource misallocation associated with trade diversion is the
fundamental cost of discriminatory trading arrangements which has to be
weighed against the benefits of a lower tariff on some imports. Unfortunately,
however, the branch of economics opened up by Viner proved disappointing,
partly because of its focus on trade diversion and trade creation. The most
powerful apparatus for illustrating these concepts involved assumptions
which ruled out many interesting aspects of discrimination and which
focused exclusively on the situation of the preference donor. After classifying
and clarifying the trade diversion / trade creation aspects of discrimination,
the literature centered around the proposition that customs unions were
irrational in the standard economic sense.

---

[5] For other precursors see O'Brien [1976].

[6] "It is by the enforcement of retaliatory duties throughout the ports of the British empire that
free trade is to be conquered" [Torrens, 1844, p. 67]. On page 102 he calls for "a British commercial
league – a colonial Zollverein" to counter foreign rivals' hostile tariffs. His analysis of commercial
policy is contained particularly in letters II, III and the postscript to letter IX; the clearest statement
of policy recommendations is on pages 47–48. For a modern commentary on Torrens' work see
Robbins [1958, Ch. 7].

Jacob Viner's seminal contribution is contained in the fourth chapter of *The Customs Union Issue*[7]. Despite the book's title, Viner emphasizes that the customs union is but one of possible preferential trading arrangements whose economic differences are slight [Viner, 1950, p. 4]. The key passage concerns his explanation of the trade creating and trade diverting effects of a customs union on p. 43: "There will be commodities, however, which one of the members of the customs union will now newly import from the other but which it formerly did not import at all because the price of the protected domestic product was lower than the price at any foreign source plus the duty. This shift in the locus of production as between the two countries is a shift from a high-cost to a lower-cost point ... There will be other commodities which one of the members of the customs union will now newly import from the other whereas before the customs union it imported them from a third country, because that was the cheapest possible source of supply even after payment of duty. The shift in the locus of production is now not as between the two member countries but as between a low-cost third country and the other, high-cost, member country" and his initial evaluation on p. 44: "From the free-trade point of view, whether a particular customs union is a move in the right or in the wrong direction depends, therefore, so far as the argument has yet been carried, on which of the two types of consequences ensue from that customs union. Where the trade-creating force is predominant, one of the members at least must benefit, both may benefit, the two combined must have a net benefit, and the world at large benefits; but the outside world loses, in the short-run at least .... Where the trade-diverting effect is predominant, one at least of the member countries is bound to be injured, both may be injured, the two combined will suffer a net injury, and there will be injury to the outside world and to the world at large".

Viner goes on to discuss two other sources of benefits from customs union, scale economies [pp. 45–47] and terms of trade changes [pp. 55–56], but he downplays the former as unlikely to be substantial and the latter as a welfare transfer involving "corresponding injury to the outside world". His prime interest in chapter 4 is in assessing the net impact of a customs union compared to the pre-union situation and he concludes that confident judgment "cannot be made for customs unions in general and in the abstract, but must be confined to particular projects" [p. 52]. He does not explicitly compare customs unions with unilateral commercial policies, although he does advocate the preferability of multilateral nondiscriminatory tariff reductions [p. 135].

---

[7] The possibility of trade diversion had been briefly raised in an earlier article [Viner, 1931, p. 11], but Viner acknowledges in his book [1950, p. 53] that his mind was still unclear on the issue in the early 1930s.

444                          Richard Pomfret

During the decade following Viner's book emphasis was largely on clarifying the concepts of trade creation and trade diversion and identifying situations under which each would be more likely. The major theoretical development was to identify a possible welfare-increasing aspect of trade diversion; the lower price in the preference-donor would encourage additional consumption of the imported good, involving increased consumer surplus whether or not the additional imports were from the least-cost supplier[8]. Meade referred to this as "trade expansion", and later commentators found the amendment largely semantic (because trade creation could be extended to include all post-preference imports which were not previously imported) without altering Viner's basic evaluation[9]. Meade's 1955 lectures contained the fullest tracing out of preferences' effects through the primary impact of trade flows in the preferred goods, the secondary impact on substitutes and complements, and the tertiary impact via any need for balance-of-payments adjustment, although his verbal reasoning did not make a lasting impression. Other writers, notably Scitovsky [1956; 1958], focused on the realization of scale economies and increased efficiency due to greater competition in domestic markets as the major sources of welfare gain from customs unions. The domination of trade creation and trade diversion is, however, reflected in Lipsey's influential 1960 survey of the field, which mentions the scale economy, technical efficiency, terms of trade and growth aspects, but whose analytical core is related to the resource allocation aspects of customs unions.

The year 1960 represented a watershed in customs union theory (as the theory of preferences had come to be known) in that it saw the popularization of the diagram which dominated future textbook presentations of the theory. One problem with Vinerian theory was the lack of rigor of the original exposition, almost all the relevant parts of which have been quoted above. As Meade [1955, p. 36] pointed out, Viner's analysis is most suitable where demand elasticities are zero and supply elasticities are infinite. Whether Viner made these assumptions is doubtful and Meade certainly saw any analysis based on them as incomplete, but it became the practice to base customs union theory on infinite supply elasticities of all foreign suppliers[10].

---

[8] The point was made at more or less the same time by Meade [1955], Gehrels [1956/57] and Lipsey [1957].

[9] This definition was proposed by Johnson [1960a] and endorsed by Corden [1965]. The issue returned in a fruitless debate over welfare improvements from trade diversion [e.g. Bhagwati, 1971; 1973; Kirman, 1973], which had to be settled by Johnson [1974]. In terms of Figure 1 Johnson defines both CB and GH (and not just the former) as trade creation; this is the definition adopted in the remainder of the present paper.

[10] Arguments over "What Viner really said" still continued a quarter of a century later. Viner [1965] denied making either assumption, although Michaely [1976] shows that Viner neglected demand changes and was inconsistent and ambiguous about whether costs were constant or increasing. See also the Bhagwati [1971; 1973] and Kirman [1973] debate.

Given this assumption, Figure 1 illustrates trade creation, trade diversion and the primary consumption effect in the simplest manner, with the standard conclusion that the net welfare effect (ABC + FGH – BEJG) may be positive or negative[11]. Although the diagram is a splendid heuristic device, it is ironic that its method runs counter to that of Viner and Meade, its putative fathers. In a long footnote Viner [1950, p. 53] criticized previous analyses of customs unions for, among other things, "applying the standard techniques of partial equilibrium analysis... to the tariff problem where its findings are either totally without significance or of totally indeterminable significance". Meade [1955]; by his emphasis on the secondary and tertiary impacts, also saw preferences as requiring a general equilibrium framework of analysis. Even within the partial equilibrium framework Humphrey and Ferguson, for example, recognized the restrictiveness of assuming horizontal supply curves from the preference recipient and the rest of the world, but their Model II incorporating increasing costs did not provide any real insights and was largely forgotten[12]

Figure 1 – *Partial Equilibrium Analysis of Discrimination with Perfectly Elastic Supply of Imports*

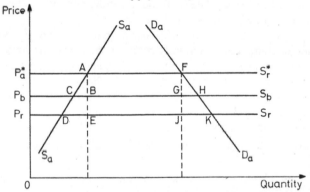

*Note:* $S_a$ and $D_a$ are domestic supply and demand curves in A. $S_b$ is the supply of Imports from the preferred source, B, which is perfectly elastic at a price $P_b$. $S_r$ is the supply of imports from the rest of the world, and $P_r$ is the world price; $S_r^*$ is the tariff-inclusive supply curve, and $P_a^*$ is the pre-preference domestic price in A.

---

[11] The use of producer and consumer surplus (and the welfare triangles) had already been described by Meade [1955, pp. 35–43], but he had not drawn the diagram. Figure 1 appears in Johnson [1960a] and Humphrey, Ferguson [1960]. Whether either article was the source of its popularity is impossible to say, as Lipsey's survey (which used a constant cost example to explain Viner's argument) and Johnson's influential costs of protection article (which applied the same technique to nondiscriminatory trade barriers) appeared in the same year, and it is a short step from them to Figure 1.

[12] A similar approach had been used by Johnson [1957; 1958] in articles which also remained neglected. See Section V.3. (below) for further developments.

Both the mainstream theoretical and empirical literature of the next dozen years could be placed within the framework of Figure 1. The net welfare effect of the preferential tariff reduction in Figure 1 can be no better (and will normally be worse) than that of unilaterally eliminating the tariff on a nonpreferential basis, i.e. ADE + FJK. The implication is that preferential trading arrangements are economically irrational and can only be explained by noneconomic motives [Johnson, 1965; Cooper, Massell, 1965]. The disappointingly small estimates of the welfare triangles (ABC + FGH) for such a major customs union as the European Community led more empirically oriented authors to conclude that scale, technical efficiency, or other considerations were the key ones, but little progress was made in quantifying these so-called dynamic effects[13].

## IV. The Vanek-Kemp Branch

Figure 1 and its progeny (specifically the Cooper-Massell-Johnson proposition about the noneconomic motivation for preferential trading) dominated preferential trading theory through the 1960s and 1970s, and became the textbook presentation of the subject. There was, however, a substream which developed along its own lines more or less independently of the mainstream literature; its primary source was Vanek's 1965 book.

Vanek uses the neoclassical 2 x 2 general equilibrium model with production possibility frontiers and community indifference curves, extended to include a third country. The advantage of this approach is to bring prices back to center-stage, a point emphasized by Vanek [1965, p. 26]: "... perhaps the most important ... [economic variables] ... are the terms of trade prevailing within the union, and in world markets after integration". The drawback of Vanek's approach is that in a two-commodity world pre-union trade patterns can only take two possible forms (see below); either A and B trade with one

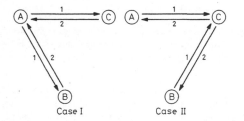

Case I         Case II

*Legend:*
1 and 2 are
the two *goods;*
A, B and C the
three *countries*

[13] The distinction between static and dynamic effects was popularized by Balassa [1961]. Kreinin [1964] tried to pin down the dynamic effects (although why, say, scale economies are dynamic remains a mystery) and pointed out the possibility of negative dynamic effects on the rest of the world; Kreinin's empirical work is brought together in his 1974 book. Balassa [1975] is a useful collection of empirical studies. Pelkmans, Gremmen [1983] provide a critique of work on the static effects.

another or they do not: The second case is almost trivial (unless trade reversal occurs and B starts to export good 2 to A)[14], while the first case will likely have strongly asymmetrical effects.

These effects are explored by Vanek, Negishi [1969] and Kemp [1969]. The propositions which emerge are typically second-best: "The only general conclusion as to the welfare effects of customs unions is that they can be either beneficial or detrimental to the world as a whole. Any more specific statement must contain further qualifications" [Vanek, 1965, p. 6]. Kemp [1969, p. 31] derives a stronger conclusion about the impact on A and B individually: "Strong inferiority aside, the creation of the preferential trading club operates to the advantage of whichever member trades only with the other member, and operates to the disadvantage of the latter". But this only holds if trade with C does not fall sufficiently for A's terms of trade to improve enough for A to gain and B to lose. He also shows that A and B together will normally gain vis-à-vis the pre-union situation, in the sense that the loser can be compensated and the gainer retain a net benefit, but even this is not necessarily true if capital flows exist and B is a net creditor [*ibid.*, p. 49].

The strongest conclusion arises when not only the disadvantaged partner is compensated, but also the rest of the world is compensated by setting the union's common external tariff so that external terms of trade are unchanged. Under these conditions the post-union utility-possibility function is consistently superior to the pre-union utility-possibility function; i.e. if the welfare of B and C is held constant then A will be better off after forming a customs union than before it [Vanek, 1965, Ch. 7]. This elementary proposition was restated in a more general form by Kemp, Wan [1976], who went on to ask why we do not observe continuous customs union formation culminating in free trade. They mention difficulties of partner selection, noneconomic objectives, and international restrictions on preferential arrangements, but the central point seems to be what they refer to as ignorance and inertia, especially with respect to "the long list of lump-sum compensatory payments required". Thus the Vanek-Kemp-Wan proposition, which is potentially interesting as an economic justification for preferential trading arrangements, has an esoteric air as an explanation of preferences in the real world[15]. A further practical problem is that the compensating common external tariff is not necessarily the welfare-maximizing tariff from the union members'

---

[14] One feature of case II is that A and B in unison can impose an optimum tariff on good 2. This is analyzed in Section V.3. below.

[15] Grinols [1981] has proposed a feasible compensation scheme and applied it to British accession to the European Community [Grinols, 1984], which to some extent could overcome Kemp and Wan's complexity and ignorance point but which does not resolve the problems caused by lack of respect for other countries' interests.

perspective; so, if there is the global consensus for other countries' interests to be respected, why not agree to move directly to universal free trade?

It is easy to see why the Figure 1 literature with its simple exposition and strong (but limited) conclusions remained popular while, at the same time, articles kept emerging in the Vanek-Kemp tradition since this was the only general equilibrium branch of the literature. The two branches of the literature were brought together by Berglas [1979], who used a variant of Vanek's case I to show that anything A and B could gain by preferential trading could be gained by unilateral tariff reduction. Berglas' conclusion is based on the assumption that world prices do not change; in his model A or C is a large country and the others small, so that the only domestic prices to change are those of B, whose export good's price goes up by the amount of A's tariff and whose import good's price falls by the amount of her own tariff. After A and B form a customs union A will lose tariff revenue, while there is a presumption that B gains both A's foregone tariff revenue and from her own tariff reduction (depending on unknown income effects). Berglas demonstrates that, if B compensates A for the latter's loss, then all remaining gains to B could be achieved by unilateral nonpreferential tariff reduction. Constant terms of trade thus yield the Johnson-Cooper-Massell unilateral tariff reduction (UTR) proposition either in a Figure 1 framework or in a Vanek framework.

## V. The Search for the Missing Prince

In contrast to the landmark contributions between 1950 and 1965 by Viner, Meade, Lipsey, Johnson, Mundell, Vanek and Cooper and Massell, the next fifteen years saw a marked lack of advances in preferential trading theory. Kemp and Berglas developed Vanek's model, the Wonnacotts and Corden cast further light on the relevance of scale economies, and Krauss' 1972 survey attracted some attention (but less than Lipsey's 1960 survey had)[16]. In the late 1960s Caves and Johnson [1968, p. viii] could still refer to the "large and fast-growing literature" on customs union theory, but during the 1970s disillusionment with this branch of economic theory grew. The cause was not a lack of preferential trading arrangements[17], but rather the twin conclusions of customs union theory that (a) a preferential tariff reduction could be either better or worse than no tariff cut from the home

---

[16] Krauss also attracted criticism for non sequitur [Michaely, 1976] and for missing the point of one paper and other "interpretative lapses" [Bhagwati, 1973, p. 897].

[17] Existing arrangements were extended, e.g. the enlargement of the European Community, the Lomé Convention and the Multifibre Arrangement, and the Generalized System of Preferences for developing countries (GSP) was implemented. The major studies on GSP were concerned with how restricted the actual schemes were [Murray, 1977], how inferior they were to MFN tariff reductions [Baldwin, Murray, 1977], and how the developing countries would do better to participate in

country's and the world's perspective, and (b) a nondiscriminatory tariff reduction will never be inferior to the preferential reduction from these perspectives. Thus, the only generalization that seemed to emerge was that in the absence of domestic distortions a preferential trading arrangement was inexplicable for a welfare-maximizing importing country.

This unhappy state of the art engendered a belief that something must have been omitted from the analysis; customs union theory was "Hamlet without the prince", in the words of Wonnacott, Wonnacott [1981, p. 705]. Their own candidate for the prince's role is tariffs in the rest of the world, but there were other candidates too. Lipsey [1960] had already suggested possible terms-of-trade effects, scale economies, improved technical efficiency and higher growth rates, and although the latter two have not attracted much interest among economists (in contrast to among policymakers) the first two have received some attention[18]. Another direction in the search for a missing component was to increase the dimensionality of models.

## 1. Higher Dimensionality

The theory of preferential trading must diverge from the two country / two commodity ($2 \times 2$) trade theory model by introducing a third country, but there is little agreement as to whether more commodities (or countries) are desirable. An analytical framework with more commodities permits complements as well as substitutes, whose significance Meade [1955] described in his secondary effects, which in turn suggests a need for at least two outside countries to capture the different impact on producers of complements and substitutes [Arndt, 1969]. Nevertheless, the *essential* elements of preferential trading could possibly be dealt with in a $3 \times 2$ model, as Vanek [1965, p. 13] and Kemp [1969, p. 21] believed. A series of authors during the 1970s challenged this belief by gaining new insights through $3 \times 3$ models, but the

---

multilateral GATT bargaining than to seek preferential treatment [Balassa, 1980]. There was little attempt to analyze (or measure) the welfare effects of GSP or to explain why GSP was introduced; Blackhurst [1972] took the welfare analysis some steps further (see below), and McCulloch, Pinera [1976] tackled the motivation issue, but despite an economic apparatus their main conclusions relied on noneconomic factors.

[18] Technical inefficiency is not readily explained within standard microeconomic models unless markets are not competitive. Several writers have referred to the gains from reducing domestic monopoly power as a possible side-benefit from freer access to preferred imports, as they are with any tariff reduction, but this argument has not been formally developed. Growth effects independent of the resource allocation effects are also difficult to formalize within standard models. The main practical case is when preferences stimulate a relocation of investment from outside to within the preferred area (as seems to have happened in the EC and with other preferential trade agreements [e.g. Pomfret, 1982]); this will increase GDP and growth within the preferred area but with an offsetting cost to the rest of the world if it is capital diversion – indeed the global effect may be negative if the productivity of the investment was higher in a nonpreferred location [Kreinin, 1964, p. 195].

overall record was clouded by the startling differences in conclusions reached by different authors.

There are four new elements which three-ness permits. Firstly, it can avoid the asymmetry of most two-good models (as in Vanek–Kemp dissimilar economies), although not all 3 x 3 models are symmetrical. The possibility of symmetry was recognized by Vanek [1965, p. 13], emphasized by Collier [1979], and used by Riezman [1979], but ruled out by assumption by Berglas [1979]. Secondly, if a country can have more than one import, then changes in import structures are a possible source of welfare change [Corden, 1976; Collier, 1979]. Thirdly, complementarity relationships can be analyzed, as emphasized by Meade and taken up by Berglas [1979]; McMillan, McCann [1981]; and Ethier, Horn [1984, pp. 213–217], in whose models the degree of substitutability between countries' products becomes a determinant of the welfare changes. Fourthly, the introduction of more than one relative price introduces further second-best possibilities due to divergences between the ratio of marginal rates of substitution in consumption and marginal rates of transformation [Lipsey, 1970]. Lloyd [1982, p. 62] concludes that "3 x 3 are the minimum dimensions for models of customs unions". Yet the outcome so far has been disappointing because the operation of the last three elements just described depends upon the assumed trade patterns, so that each model (because based on different assumptions) can generate different conclusions; "every 3 x 3 model is a very special case" [Lloyd, 1982, p. 62]. Thus, despite the advantages of higher dimensionality, such models have had limited influence[19].

## 2. Tariffs in the Rest of the World

Wonnacott, Wonnacott [1981] provide a trenchant criticism of the proposition that, if a preferential trade agreement does not affect the terms of trade, then it does not allow for any mutually beneficial policy opportunities which are not open to each of the member countries separately by unilateral tariff reduction[20]. Their main argument is based on the existence of a tariff in (or net transport costs to) C which opens up a wedge between the price which A receives from her export to C and the price which B pays to import the same good from C. By forming a customs union to divert trade to one another A and B can trade within the wedge, gaining out of C's foregone tariff revenue.

---

[19] This summary treatment is not to deny the potential of these models nor the value of existing explorations; rather it reflects that this branch of the literature has already been the subject of an excellent survey [Lloyd, 1982], to which there is nothing to add in the present paper's context. Lloyd also points out that further benefits could come from introducing intermediate inputs (or service payments on imported capital), which would allow shifts in the transformation surface.

[20] This is Berglas' [1979, p. 329] formulation, which subsumes the earlier Johnson-Cooper-Massell proposition. Domestic distortions (including scale economies) are assumed absent.

In a two-good world the wedge is formed by B and A facing different tariff-inclusive offer curves from C, and the mutual gain from preferential trading is easily demonstrated. The main caveat to this argument is that in practice the rest of the world (C) is not a single country and part of the burden of tariffs will be borne by domestic consumers in the rest of the world. In such a case Wonnacott, Wonnacott argue that differences in net transport costs will still create a wedge, which explains why geographical neighbors tend to form customs unions. This is not completely satisfactory insofar as the narrower the wedge becomes, the smaller the welfare gains from trading within it, and because geographically dispersed countries have formed preferential trading arrangements (e.g. the British Commonwealth, the Lomé Convention, Comecon), suggesting that there is something else involved.

The Wonnacotts' analysis is hampered by the self-imposed limitation in their terms of reference. To refute the proposition on its own grounds, they exclude any changes in the terms of trade. Yet this, in combination with the existence of tariffs in the rest of the world, provides a more potent argument for preferential treatment; the point being to reduce the welfare gains to the rest of the world from levying a tariff which improves its terms of trade (as Torrens had argued much earlier). If there are other barriers to equal multilateral trade (e.g. some currencies are not convertible), then there is also a benefit from discrimination[21]. Indeed, it would be surprising if the move toward Pareto optimality by nonpreferential tariff reductions were necessarily welfare improving in a tariff-ridden world, since the foreign tariffs exclude the first-best outcome. In sum, the Wonnacotts' wedge is sufficient to refute the UTR proposition, but alone it is an unconvincing reason for widespread discrimination.

### 3. The Terms of Trade

Building higher-dimensioned models and introducing foreign tariffs into the analysis indicate dissatisfaction with existing theory, but do not get to the heart of the matter. One reason for the lacunae in preferential trading theory is the analytical apparatus of Figure 1, which highlights the trade diversion / trade creation concept by making assumptions which rule out other effects of preferences. The horizontal import supply curves exclude price effects or any welfare implications of change in exports. This is not just a result of the partial equilibrium framework, but rather concerns assumptions about costs and about how prices are set. In the general equilibrium framework of Figure 2 a

---

[21] This was generally recognized by postwar policymakers as a source of conflict with the IMF's position in favor of nondiscrimination. If country A had insufficient hard currency to pay for imports from the United States, but could pay for the same imports from a soft currency country (B) by exports to B, then A, B and the world would be made better off by A discriminating in favor of imports from B [Patterson, 1966, Ch. 2].

452                                    Richard Pomfret

customs union between two small countries (A and B), with prohibitive
external tariff, would bring A and B to point S, where B is better off than with
nonpreferential tariff elimination (point L) but A is worse off (than at point
M); B cannot compensate A sufficiently, so the welfare optimum is L and M,
i.e. the situation after nonpreferential removal of tariffs by A and B.


Figure 2 – *General Equilibrium (Offer Curve) Analysis of a Customs Union
Involving Two Small Countries*

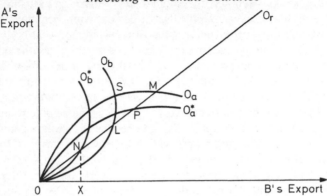

*Note:* $O_a^*$ and $O_b^*$ are the initial tariff-inclusive offer curves of A and B. $O_a$ and $O_b$ are their
tariff-exclusive offer curves. $O_r$ is the rest of the world's offer curve. Initially A trades at point P and B
at point N. Their welfare-maximizing positions, given the world price ratio, are M and L.


    In the recent debate over the UTR proposition between the Wonnacotts
[1981] and Berglas [1983] both sides agree to assume no changes in the terms
of trade, and this represents the central tradition of the postwar literature.
This is, however, an implausible assumption for general analysis of preferential trading arrangements[22]. One symptom of the implausibility of Figures 1
and 2 is the stories they tell about the sources of imports (which is after all
what discrimination is all about); in Figure 1 all of A's imports come from the
rest of the world when there is no discrimination and they all come from B
with preferential treatment, while in Figure 2 the source of A's imports and
destination of B's exports up to quantity OX is indeterminate before the
customs union. The all or nothing import share stories are tied to the simple
treatment of prices[23].

---

    [22] The assumption may, of course, be justified and useful in specific cases. Berglas [1979] appears
to have in mind an arrangement such as the EC-Israel free trade area, where terms-of-trade effects
may well be minimal [Pomfret, 1978], but this is not a general case.

    [23] Vanek [1965, p. 30] allowed the terms of trade to change, although the direction of change can
go either way. As mentioned above, however, this branch of the literature failed to reach firm
conclusions, until Berglas [1979] introduced assumptions which ruled out international price
changes.

The introduction of increasing costs is sufficient to create the possibility of both B and the rest of the world exporting to A. This can be analyzed within a partial equilibrium framework (Figure 3)[24]. With a uniform tariff A imports CE from B and $P_1C$ from the rest of the world. If B is granted duty-free access, her exports to A increase to FK, while the rest of the world continues to export $P_2F$. The welfare gain to B arises from a better price on her previous exports (GJYW) plus the producer surplus on her additional exports (HKX). The welfare effect for A consists of the triangles (CGF + EJK) minus the higher expenditure on goods previously imported and now bought from B (FJYV) plus the lower expenditure on remaining imports from the rest of the world ($P_4VZP_5$), whose net sign is indeterminate. The rest of the world unambiguously loses from the preferential tariff cut (by $P_4VZP_5 + VWZ$), and the global welfare effect may be positive or negative. Thus Viner's central insight remains, although in slightly different terms, since it is no longer possible to identify high and low cost foreign suppliers. The terms of trade

Figure 3 – *Partial Equilibrium Analysis of Discrimination with Upward Sloping Supply Curves*

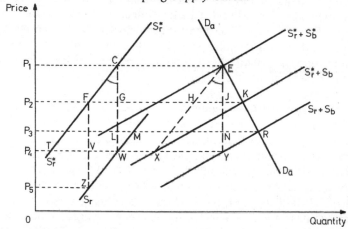

*Note:* $D_a$ is A's import demand. $S_b$ is the supply of imports from preferred sources and $S_r$ is the supply of imports from the rest of the world; $S_b^*$ and $S_r^*$ are the same including A's tariff. Assuming no nontariff barriers or transport costs and no exchange rate changes, E, K and R represent demand/supply equilibria with A's tariff, with free access for B's goods and without A's tariff, and $P_1$, $P_2$ and $P_3$ are the corresponding domestic prices. $P_4$ is the price received by exporters to A when A's tariff is in place, and $P_5$ is the price received by nonpreferred exporters to A when B receives preferential access.

---

[24] Variations of Figure 3 have appeared in the literature several times, apparently independently, without displacing Figure 1 as the norm; e.g. Johnson [1957; 1958]; Humphrey and Ferguson's Model II [1960, pp. 205–210]; and Blackhurst [1972]. One indication of how little impact the analysis has made is that a recent article in a major refereed journal could call B's producer surplus on increased exports an effect "neglected by previous contributors" [Collier, 1979, p. 92].

454                              Richard Pomfret

effects, however, which from a global perspective must net out, introduce
distributional effects on B and in third countries, while B also benefits from
the producer-surplus on new exports[25].

Blackhurst [1972] uses the Figure 3 to compare the welfare effects of
preferential and nonpreferential tariff cuts by A. From a global perspective
the latter effect is positive and must be at least as big as the welfare effect of a
preferential tariff reduction. But from A's perspective this is not necessarily
the case because one positive aspect of a discriminatory tariff cut is lost if the
cut is nonpreferential, viz. the improvement in A's terms of trade with third
countries. The partner, B, is, of course, better off with the preferential·
reduction. Thus, the introduction of increasing costs, and hence changes in
the terms of trade, qualifies the UTR proposition, since A (and B) may gain
more from a preferential than from a nonpreferential reduction in A's tariff.

The preceding analysis is partial equilibrium, but it can readily be turned
into general equilibrium on the assumptions of low initial tariffs, a small tariff
change and all exports are gross substitutes in world consumption. Now B's
terms of trade improve, and the rest of the world's deteriorate. The sum of
these changes is equal to the initial change in A's terms of trade, although the
final outcome also depends on a budget effect, i.e. how A reacts to her
reduced tariff revenues. The terms of trade between A and the rest of the
world may end up going either way, but this does not affect "the most
important proposition about discriminatory tariff reductions: a tariff reduction in a member country unambiguously improves the terms of trade of the
partner country" [Mundell, 1964, p. 5].

Mutual preferential tariff reductions between A and B can change the
partners' terms of trade with the rest of the world in either direction. This is in
contrast to a popular view that formation of a customs union will improve the
members' terms of trade with the rest of the world, although they can be
reconciled under certain conditions[26]. With Mundell's assumptions some sets
of reductions necessarily improve both members' terms of trade with the rest
of the world [Mundell, 1964, p. 7]. These sets congregate around the case
where the terms of trade between A and B are unchanged, which may be a
plausible outcome from a preferential trade arrangement based on roughly
reciprocal "concessions". Even if A and B do not both improve their terms of

---

[25] The unambiguous gain to B, the clearest message from Figure 3, recalls the passage from
Adam Smith quoted in Section II. If the rest of the world consists of several countries then some of
these clearly may gain, viz. those importing the same good as A [Arndt, 1969].

[26] The popular view is usually a variant of the argument by Viner [1950, p. 55] that formation of a
customs union would, *ceteris paribus*, increase the improvement in members' terms of trade resulting
from their tariff, because a larger economic unit faces a less elastic offer curve. Riezman [1979] sets up
a 3 x 3 model where the terms of trade of A and B improve vis-à-vis C but not necessarily vis-à-vis one
another; in this case mutually profitable customs unions are most likely among countries which trade
mainly with nonmembers (e.g. LAFTA).

trade, mutual preferential tariff reductions will always improve the terms of trade of one of the two countries.

So far I have considered the terms of trade changes likely to result from preferences, but it may be that the terms of trade are themselves the objective. Two variations of the optimum tariff argument are relevant to preferential trading. Melvin [1969] has argued that the terms-of-trade effect will usually reduce A's welfare gain from a preferential tariff reduction because her MFN tariff may be optimal (from a national welfare perspective) and any change will be welfare-reducing. This is not necessarily so. Even if A's tariff is optimal, like any wielder of monopoly power A could improve her welfare by market segmentation if different partners have different offer curves: the less elastic the partner's offer curve, the higher A's optimum tariff on imports from that source[27]. A second optimum tariff argument is that A and B in combination can wield greater market power than either can alone. Thus, if A imposes a tariff on goods which her suppliers can also sell to B, then the impact will be to change trade patterns, restricting the improvement in A's terms of trade; but if the two similar economies A and B form a union then they can set a union-welfare-maximizing common external tariff; in this situation "what country A really desires from country B is an appropriate protective policy against the outside world" [Arndt, 1968, p. 976][28].

## 4. Economies of Scale

A final missing player in preferential trading theory is scale economies. The earlier literature on European integration gave it a large role [e.g. Scitovsky, 1956; 1958; Balassa, 1961], but most writers have left it out or kept it in the background[29]. To some extent this reflects a wider problem: Scale economies can be a source of gains from trade, but lead to indeterminacy – a problem usually evaded in international trade theory by assuming that the closed economy conditions for Pareto optimality are met (including perfectly competitive markets). The same assumption could be made in analyzing preferences, but, given policymakers' emphasis on scale economies as a

---

[27] Caves [1974] analyzes within a Vanek-Kemp framework the gains from market segmentation. See also Michaely [1977, pp. 214–215]. McCulloch, Pinera [1977] suggest this as a possible motive for GSP schemes (assuming a high elasticity of supply of exports from developing countries).

[28] Similar arguments are made by Viner [1950], and by Spraos [1964]. Although these are part of the customs union literature [see also Michaely, 1977, pp. 215–216; Riezman, 1985], cartel behavior by countries with common interests does not require preferential treatment; OPEC members, for example, try to agree on a common price and to minimize the free-rider problem without forming any economic union or necessarily discriminating among oil purchasers.

[29] One example is Massell [1968] who after discussing noneconomic and terms-of-trade arguments devotes one sentence to scale economies as a third reason for customs unions, saying that these may be the most important! In Lipsey's 1960 survey they are listed as one of the five sources of welfare gain or loss but only appear in the (inconclusive) next-to-last paragraph.

456                                    Richard Pomfret

reason for, say, joining a customs union, reference is often made to the importance of scale economies (without analysis). The two major analytical contributions are those of Corden and the Wonnacotts, although future developments within the framework of Chamberlinian monopolistic competition trade models seem likely [e.g. Ethier, Horn, 1984, pp. 217–225].

Corden [1972] introduced scale economies into basic theory of preferences and found that trade creation and trade diversion remained relevant concepts but should be supplemented by two other effects. If preferred imports from B replace A's domestic production, then the cost-reduction effect of realizing scale economies yields additional gains. If B's exports are replacing goods previously imported by A from a third country (C), there may be trade-suppression if B's lower costs and C's higher costs lead to further reductions in C's exports to A and B (even though C may remain the lowest-cost producer). Corden's cost-reduction and trade suppression effects leave intact Viner's fundamental insight about the sign of the welfare effect, although they accentuate the gains from trade creation and losses from trade diversion[30].

Figure 4 – *An Industry with Decreasing Costs Facing Trade Barriers*

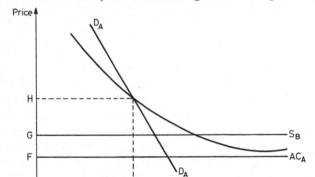

*Note:* $D_A$ is domestic demand in country A and $AC_A$ is the decreasing average cost curve of the producer in A. Producers in B operate under constant cost conditions with a supply curve $S_B$ at a price of OG. FG is B's tariff. Assuming average cost pricing, barriers to imports and no opportunity to segment markets, A's firm will produce OK and sell at a price OH. Removal of B's tariff permits A's producer to increase output, selling at a price between OF and OG in B's market.

Wonnacott, Wonnacott [1967] provide empirical support for the common presumption that countries gain from joining a free trade area or customs union via access to a wider market. From their studies the Wonnacotts find

---

[30] Viner [1950, pp. 45–47] had recognized the former point and Meade [1955, pp. 93–94] described the magnification of trade creation and trade diversion with two examples, although neither treated the matter as thoroughly as Corden.

most Canadian industries to have cost curves such as that in Figure 4. Removal of the United States' tariff would permit expansion of Canadian output on the basis of exports, leading with a fixed exchange rate to higher wages in Canada (or with a flexible exchange rate to improved terms of trade). The Wonnacotts estimate the gain to Canada from a North American free trade area at 10.5 percent of GNP of which around 4 percent comes from Canadian tariff cuts and the remainder from the effect just described, i.e. the realization of scale economies is the main source of Canadian gain. This analysis is, however, distinct from all the literature so far discussed insofar as the effects of scale economies do not arise from the home country's preferential trade reduction. What the analysis does do, is to emphasize the gains from freer access to other countries' markets (in Figure 4 this does not have to be preferential access). The only sense in which the Wonnacotts' study provides a case for preferential treatment is if reduction in one's own tariff is a critical bargaining counter in convincing other countries to reduce their trade barriers.

## VI. Why Do Preferential Trading Arrangements Exist?

Three sets of motives explain the existence of most preferential trading arrangements. Firstly, arguments for nondiscriminatory trade barriers can be adapted to preferences. Secondly, preferential treatment can be used as a bargaining tool. Thirdly, the terms of trade changes and gains to exporters described in the previous section yield benefits from preferential arrangements which are not to be gained from unilateral policies. Each of these will be considered in turn, and then the role of noneconomic motives will be assessed.

The optimum tariff argument's extension to discriminatory monopsonistic behavior has already been mentioned. There may also be a case for forming a customs union to realize administrative economies and increase net revenue. In practice, however, the main motivation for postwar trade barriers has been the protection of import-competing sectors, especially when they have well-organized and effective lobbies. For institutional reasons new trade barriers have frequently taken the form of orderly marketing arrangements or voluntary export quotas, negotiated on a bilateral basis and hence discriminatory. Whether such measures are effective in providing protection depends upon the size of the cross-price elasticities among trading partners. If these elasticities are large, then the barrier must be extended to all significant suppliers (in the limit becoming nondiscriminatory) or it will provide little protection[31]. If substitution possibilities are small, then a discriminatory

---

[31] A perfect example of proliferation is the history of textiles and clothing protection from the first Japanese voluntary export quotas to the USA in the 1950s through the cotton textile arrangements of the 1960s to the MFA in the 1970s [Keesing, Wolf, 1980]. Similar tendencies were

458                              Richard Pomfret

barrier will provide protection, but its impact differs little from a nonpreferential measure[32]. In sum, the protection argument is not a strong one for discrimination *per se*, although apparently discriminatory measures may be adopted or actually discriminatory measures taken as the first steps towards general barriers.

The bargaining motive for preferential treatment of trading partners has a long history[33] and follows naturally from policymakers' view of trade barrier reductions as concessions. Economic rationale for this motive is provided by Torrens' emphasis on the incentives for countries to levy nationally optimal tariffs if these are not contingent on tariff levels abroad and by the Wonnacotts' emphasis on the importance of gaining market access for exports. Presumably, however, the argument is about means rather than ends – Torrens, for example, continually proclaimed his belief in free trade as the *optimum optimorum*. Whether the goal can be better achieved by bilateral confrontation or via multilateral GATT negotiations is not self-evident, nor is it readily analyzed by economists' tools[34]. My impression is that economists tend to favor the GATT approach, but the "reciprocity" proposals in Congress suggest that American policymakers are tilting towards the bilateral threat approach[35].

The clearest economic arguments for discrimination arise from the gain to the preference recipient as exporter. If the preferences are reciprocal then all partners will be the favored exporter of some products, and in nonconstant

---

observed during the 1977–1981 footwear OMAs imposed by the USA on Taiwan and South Korea [Pearson, 1983], and seem to be happening in the wake U.S. restrictions on steel imports from Europe.

[32] Quotas on Japanese autos to the United States seem to have had this effect during the 1980s (although it may be that short-run and long-run cross-price elasticities differ in the auto industry and given time Korean or Brazilian autos would replace barred Japanese autos).

[33] It lay behind French and Spanish opposition to unconditional MFN treatment during the interwar years (they argued that high tariff countries, such as the USA, should lower their tariffs, before they could expect equal access to low tariff countries' markets) and behind American use of conditional MFN clauses before 1919.

[34] Cline [1982] draws up a taxonomy of outcomes, but the key issue is the probability of each outcome. In a two-country model there must be a negotiated agreement which dominates the Nash equilibrium outcome of a tariff war [Mayer, 1981], which is consistent with Whalley's [1985, Ch. 14] high estimates of post-tariff-war U.S. and EC tariffs and the associated welfare loss relative to free trade. Generalization of these results to threatened discriminatory tariff increases is difficult because in a multi-country world the scope for imposing costs on other countries by own-welfare-increasing tariff hikes is negatively related to the number of substitute markets.

[35] The stated arguments emphasize that GATT negotiations have been biased against U.S. interests (by omitting, for example, trade in services and foreign investment) and that other countries have circumvented GATT concessions by nontariff barriers [Hay, Sulzenco, 1982]. This may be a result of distorted vision [Cline, 1982] or a route to disguised protectionism, but even if the arguments are valid it is unclear whether reciprocity measures would produce the desired effect on other countries.

cost industries will enjoy gains from increased exports. From a macroeconomic perspective, as long as internal terms of trade are unchanged all partners in the preferential trading area enjoy improved terms of trade with the rest of the world. This may be a sufficient explanation of economic benefits from the European Common Market which could not be realized by unilateral policies[36]. The potential importance of these effects is also illustrated by the application of computable general equilibrium models. Hamilton and Whalley [1983] found that bilateral free trade areas among the major trading nations may or may not raise global welfare, but in all cases one of the FTA members (and usually both) gains, while outsiders usually suffer welfare losses[37].

The major new preferential agreements of the 1970s (GSP and Lomé) involved nonreciprocal preferential treatment of developing countries' exports. Here the gain to exporters explains the recipients' lobbying for the GSP and acceptance of the Lomé Convention. There is, however, little economic gain to the preference donor; indeed in the case of a large country giving preferential treatment to a small supplying country, all the gains go to the latter, while the large country loses tariff revenue on preferred imports. Thus this type of arrangement has a noneconomic motivation on one side. The history of the GSP negotiations is one of political accommodation by the industrialized countries to one aspect of the demands for New International Economic Order; in view of the small size of the foregone tariff revenue due to actual GSP schemes, the economic cost of political accommodation has not been large. The Lomé Convention (and also the bilateral agreements with Mediterranean countries) reflects political motivation on the European Community's part, as it uses one of its limited arsenal of policy tools to create spheres of influence[38]; again the cost from the donor's perspective is not

---

[36] Petith [1977] applies Mundell's model to the EC case and finds terms of trade gains to be substantially larger than the welfare triangles from trade creation.

[37] This paper and Whalley's 1985 book point to the importance of the participating countries' initial levels of protection and relative size, while they downplay the Vinerian trade creation/trade diversion effects of preferential trade agreements. Such conclusions may reflect the simplicity of their model and are sensitive to key parameter values (in this context particularly the elasticity of substitution between imports from alternative sources), but the Whalley model exhibits some robustness and yields plausible results in other contexts. There is also a problem in identifying the Vinerian effects in a computable general equilibrium model, as Meade's identification of tertiary effects due to macroeconomic adjustment implies.

[38] The Mediterranean agreements are discussed in Pomfret [1986]. The argument in this paragraph was also made by Viner [1950, pp. 91–92]: "Of the more serious movements which involved a great power and a small country or a number of small countries, it appears to have been the case without exception for the great power that political objectives were the important ones", while for the small countries in such arrangements "only the economic consequences as a rule were regarded as attractive, while the political aspects were thought of as involving risks which might have to be accepted for the sake of the economic benefits with which they were unfortunately associated".

large, while the gain from increased export earnings is economically riskless and may be substantial compared to economic magnitudes in the preference recipient.

What role is there here for the Johnson-Cooper-Massell argument? Starting from the UTR proposition this argument relates the motivation for preferences to internal divergences of prices from social opportunity costs, e.g. because of a desire for industrialization. Such a desire could be fulfilled by subsidizing production, but if the home market is limited then GATT restrictions on export subsidies deter this strategy. Customs union provides a solution to the dilemma because preferential market access is equivalent to an export subsidy in this context, and customs unions are permitted under GATT. The argument can be generalized insofar as in the presence of a domestic distortion a discriminatory tariff charge may or may not be superior to a nondiscriminatory tariff change. It's dominance of the field is, however, surprising given its second-best nature even from a national perspective; especially as it seems difficult to explain in these terms customs unions and free trade areas among developed countries or one-way preferences such as the GSP and Lomé Convention. Given the three sets of motivation described above it also appears unnecessary to invoke purely noneconomic motives for preferential trading arrangements.

## VII. Conlusions

The theory of preferential trading has been one of the more disappointing branches of postwar economics. That is despite Viner's great insight about the ambiguity of welfare effects, which led to the theory of second best. Indeed, ironically, it was the codification of Viner's concepts in the form of Figure 1 which may explain the subsequent stultification. By assuming constant costs the terms of trade effects were limited and the possibility of gains from increased exports eliminated. Yet these should be two key features of the theory of preferences. Terms of trade changes, while not altering the global evaluation, have distributional effects such that costs are imposed on third countries while the participants in a preferential arrangement may enjoy gains not available from nondiscriminatory policies. Either increasing or decreasing costs open up the prospect of welfare gains to a preference recipient from increased exports, and the export expansion will be at least as great as from nonpreferential tariff reduction by the donor. Once these two features are permitted it becomes easier to explain why preferential trading arrangements exist (and are increasing) in terms of the economic gains to the principal parties. These modifications do not, however, improve the global assessment of discriminatory practices – rather by pointing out conflicts between national and global interest they reinforce the case for a framework such as the GATT to set and arbiter the rules.

# References

**Arndt, Sven W.,** "On Discriminatory versus Non-Preferential Tariff Policies". *The Economic Journal,* Vol. 78, 1968, pp. 971–979.

–, "Customs Union and the Theory of Tariffs". *The American Economic Review,* Vol. 59, 1969, pp. 108–118.

**Balassa, Bela A.,** *The Theory of Economic Integration.* Homewood, Ill., 1961.

– **(Ed.),** *European Economic Integration.* Amsterdam 1975.

–, "The Tokyo Round and the Developing Countries". *Journal of World Trade Law,* Vol. 14, 1980, pp. 93–118.

**Baldwin, Robert E., Tracy Murray,** "MFN Tariff Reductions and Developing Country Trade Benefits under the GSP". *The Economic Journal,* Vol. 87, 1977, pp. 30–46.

**Berglas, Eitan,** "Preferential Trading Theory; The n Commodity Case". *Journal of Political Economy,* Vol. 87, 1979, pp. 315–331.

–, "The Case for Unilateral Tariff Reductions: Foreign Tariffs Rediscovered". *The American Economic Review,* Vol. 73, 1983, pp. 1141–1142.

**Bhagwati, Jagdish N.,** "Trade-Diverting Customs Unions and Welfare Improvement: A Clarification". *The Economic Journal,* Vol. 81, 1971, pp. 580–587.

–, "A Reply to Professor Kirman". *The Economic Journal,* Vol. 83, 1973, pp. 895–897.

**Blackhurst, Richard,** "General versus Preferential Tariff Reduction for LDC Exports: An Analysis of the Welfare Effects". *Southern Economic Journal,* Vol. 38, 1972, pp. 350–362.

**Caves, Richard E.,** "The Economics of Reciprocity: Theory and Evidence on Bilateral Trading Arrangements". In: Willy Sellekaerts (Ed.), *International Trade and Finance. Essays in Honour of Jan Tinbergen.* London 1974, pp. 17–54.

–, **Harry G. Johnson (Eds.),** *Readings in International Economics.* Homewood, Ill., 1968.

**Cline, William R.,** *"Reciprocity": A New Approach to World Trade Policy?* Washington 1982.

**Collier, Paul,** "The Welfare Effects of Customs Unions: An Anatomy". *The Economic Journal,* Vol. 89, 1979, pp. 84–95.

**Cooper, Charles A., Benton F. Massell,** "A New Look at Customs Unions Theory". *The Economic Journal,* Vol. 75, 1965, pp. 742–747.

**Corden, W. Max,** *Recent Developments in the Theory of International Trade.* Special Papers in International Economics, 7. Princeton 1965.

–, "Economies of Scale and Customs Union Theory". *Journal of Political Economy,* Vol. 80, 1972, pp. 456–475.

–, "Customs Union Theory and the Nonuniformity of Tariffs". *Journal of International Economics,* Vol. 6, 1976, pp. 99–106.

**El-Agraa, Ali M. (Ed.),** *International Economic Integration.* New York 1982.

**Ethier, Wilfred J., Henrik Horn,** "A New Look at Economic Integration". In: Henryk Kierzkowski (Ed.), *Monopolistic Competition and International Trade.* Oxford 1984, pp. 207–229.

**Gehrels, Franz,** "Customs Unions from a Single Country's Viewpoint". *Review of Economic Studies,* Vol. 24, 1956/57, No. 63, pp. 61–64.

462 Richard Pomfret

Grinols, Earl L., "An Extension of the Kemp-Wan Theorem on the Formation of Customs Unions". *Journal of International Economics*, Vol. 11, 1981, pp. 259–266.

–, "A Thorn in the Lion's Paw. Has Britain Paid too much for Common Market Membership?" *Journal of International Economics*, Vol. 14, 1984, pp. 271–293.

Hamilton, Bob, John Whalley, *Geographically Discriminatory Trade Arrangements.* University of Western Ontario Centre for the Study of International Economic Relations Working Paper, No. 8321C. London, November 1983.

Hay, Keith A. J., Andrei B. Sulzenco, "US Trade Policy and 'Reciprocity' ". *Journal of World Trade Law*, Vol. 16, 1982, pp. 471–479.

Humphrey, Don D., Charles E. Ferguson, "The Domestic and World Benefits of a Customs Union". *Economia Internazionale*, Vol. 13, 1960, pp. 197–216.

Johnson, Harry G., "Discriminatory Tariff Reduction: A Marshallian Analysis". *Indian Journal of Economics*, Vol. 38, 1957, No. 148, pp. 39–47.

–, "Marshallian Analysis of Discriminatory Tariff Reductions: An Extension". *Indian Journal of Economics*, Vol. 39, 1958, No. 59, pp. 177–181 (reprinted in Johnson, 1962).

– [1960 a], "The Cost of Protection and the Scientific Tariff". *Journal of Political Economy*, Vol. 68, 1960, pp. 327–345.

– [1960 b], "The Economic Theory of Customs Union". *Pakistan Economic Journal*, Vol. 10, 1960, pp. 14–32 (reprinted in Johnson, 1962).

–, *Money, Trade and Economic Growth.* London 1962.

–, "An Economic Theory of Protectionism, Tariff Bargaining and the Formation of Customs Unions". *Journal of Political Economy*, Vol. 73, 1965, pp. 256–283.

–, "Trade Diverting Customs Unions: A Comment". *The Economic Journal*, Vol. 84, 1974, pp. 618–621.

Keesing, Donald B., Martin Wolf, *Textile Quotas against Developing Countries.* Thames Essays, No. 23. London 1980.

Kemp, Murray C., *A Contribution to the General Equilibrium Theory of Preferential Trading.* Amsterdam 1969.

–, Henry Y. Wan, Jr., "An Elementary Proposition Concerning the Formation of Customs Unions". *Journal of International Economics*, Vol. 6, 1976, pp. 95–97.

Kirman, Alan P., "Trade Diverting Customs Unions and Welfare Improvement: A Comment". *The Economic Journal*, Vol. 83, 1973, pp. 890–894.

Krauss, Melvyn B., "Recent Developments in Customs Union Theory: An Interpretative Survey". *Journal of Economic Literature*, Vol. 10, 1972, pp. 413–436.

Kreinin, Mordechai E., "On the Dynamic Effects of a Customs Union". *Journal of Political Economy*, Vol. 72, 1964, pp. 193–195.

–, *Trade Relations of the EEC: An Empirical Investigation.* New York 1974.

Lipsey, Richard G., "Mr. Gehrels on Customs Unions". *Review of Economic Studies*, Vol. 24, 1956/57, No. 65, pp. 211–214.

–, "The Theory of Customs Unions: Trade Diversion and Welfare". *Economica*, Vol. 24, 1957, pp. 40–46.

–, "The Theory of Customs Unions: A General Survey". *The Economic Journal*, Vol. 70, 1960, pp. 496–513.

–, *The Theory of Customs Unions: A General Equilibrium Analysis.* London 1970.

**Lipsey, Richard G., Kelvin Lancaster,** "The General Theory of 'Second Best' ". *Review of Economic Studies,* Vol. 24, 1956/57, No. 63, pp. 11–32.

**Lloyd, Peter J.,** "3 × 3 Theory of Customs Unions". *Journal of International Economics,* Vol. 12, 1982, pp. 41–63.

**McCulloch, Rachel, José Pinera,** "Trade as Aid: The Political Economy of Tariff Preferences for Developing Countries". *The American Economic Review,* Vol. 67, 1977, pp. 959–967.

**McMillan, John, Ewen McCann,** "Welfare Effects in Customs Unions". *The Economic Journal,* Vol. 91, 1981, pp. 697–703.

**Mayer, Wolfgang,** "Theoretical Considerations on Negotiated Tariff Adjustments". *Oxford Economic Papers,* Vol. 33, 1981, pp. 135–153.

**Meade, James E.,** *The Theory of Customs Unions.* Amsterdam 1955.

**Melvin, James R.,** "Comments on the Theory of Customs Unions". *Manchester School of Economic and Social Studies,* Vol. 37, 1969, No. 2, pp. 161–168.

**Michaely, Michael,** "The Assumptions of Jacob Viner's Theory of Customs Unions". *Journal of International Economics,* Vol. 6, 1976, pp. 75–93.

–, *Theory of Commercial Policy, Trade and Protection.* Chicago 1977.

**Mundell, Robert A.,** "Tariff Preferences and the Terms of Trade". *Manchester School of Economic and Social Studies,* Vol. 32, 1964, pp. 1–13.

**Murray, Tracy W.,** *Trade Preferences for Developing Countries.* London 1977.

**Negishi, Takashi,** "The Customs Union and the Theory of Second Best". *International Economic Review,* Vol. 10, 1969, pp. 391–398.

**O'Brien, Denis,** "Customs Unions: Trade Creation and Trade Diversion in Historical Perspective". *History of Political Economy,* Vol. 8, 1976, pp. 540–563.

**Patterson, Gardner,** *Discrimination in International Trade: The Policy Issues 1945–1965.* Princeton 1966.

**Pearson, Charles S.,** *Emergency Protection in the Footwear Industry.* Thames Essay, No. 36. London 1983.

**Pelkmanns, Jacques, Hans Gremmen,** "The Empirical Measurement of Static Customs Unions Effects". *Rivista Internazionale di Scienze Economiche e Commerciali,* Vol. 30, 1983, pp. 612–622.

**Petith, Howard C.,** "European Integration and the Terms of Trade". *The Economic Journal,* Vol. 87, 1977, pp. 246–272.

**Pomfret, Richard W.,** "The Economic Consequences for Israel of Free Trade in Manufactured Goods with the EEC". *Weltwirtschaftliches Archiv,* Vol. 114, 1978, pp. 526–539.

–, "Trade Preferences and Foreign Investment in Malta". *Journal of World Trade Law,* Vol. 16, 1982, pp. 236–250.

–, "Discrimination in International Trade: Extent, Motivation, and Implications". *Economia Internazionale,* Vol. 38, 1985, pp. 49–65.

–, *Mediterranean Policy of the European Community: A Study of Discrimination in Trade.* London 1986.

**Riezman, Raymond G.,** "A 3 x 3 Modell of Customs Unions". *Journal of International Economics,* Vol. 9, 1979, pp. 341–354.

–, "Customs Unions and the Core". *Journal of International Economics,* Vol. 19, 1985, pp. 355–365.

464                               Richard Pomfret

**Robbins, Lionel C.,** *Robert Torrens and the Evolution of Classical Economics.* London 1958.

**de Scitovsky, Tibor,** "Economies of Scale, Competition, and European Integration". *The American Economic Review,* Vol. 46, 1956, pp. 71–91.

–, *Economic Theory and Western European Integration.* Stanford 1958.

**Smith, Adam,** *An Inquiry into the Nature and Causes of the Wealth of Nations.* London 1776.

**Spraos, John,** "The Condition for a Trade-Creation Customs Union". *The Economic Journal,* Vol. 74, 1964, pp. 101–108.

**Taussig, Frank W.,** "Reciprocity". *Quarterly Journal of Economics,* Vol. 7, 1892, pp. 26–39.

**Torrens, Robert,** *The Budget: On Commercial and Colonial Policy.* London 1844.

**Vanek, Jaroslav,** *General Equilibrium of International Discrimination: The Case of Customs Unions.* Cambridge 1965.

**Viner, Jacob,** "The Most-Favoured-Nation Clause". *Index VI,* 1931, No. 61, pp. 2–17.

–, *The Customs Union Issue.* New York 1950.

–, "Letter to W.M. Corden of 13 March 1965". *Journal of International Economics,* Vol. 6, 1976, pp. 107–108.

**Whalley, John,** *Trade Liberalization among Major World Trading Areas.* Cambridge, Mass., 1985.

**Wonnacott, G. Paul, Ronald J. Wonnacott,** "Is Unilateral Tariff Reduction Preferable to a Customs Union? The Curious Case of the Missing Foreign Tariffs". *The American Economic Review,* Vol. 71, 1981, pp. 704–714.

**Wonnacott, Ronald, J., G. Paul Wonnacott,** *Free Trade between the United States and Canada: The Potential Economic Effects.* Cambridge, Mass., 1967.

*       *       *

# B
# Scale Economies

# [11]

# Economies of Scale and Customs Union Theory

## W. M. Corden

*Nuffield College, Oxford*

Internal economies of scale are incorporated systematically into customs union theory. The familiar concepts of trade creation and trade diversion remain relevant, but two new concepts are added, the *cost-reduction effect* and the *trade-suppression effect*. Each has a production and a consumption component. Two union countries facing given world prices from outside are assumed. The main analysis is partial equilibrium and verbal. Three cases are considered: initial production of the importable in both union countries, in one only, and in neither. Some account is taken of oligopoly, product differentiation, and general equilibrium in a multigood model.

Orthodox customs union theory assumes constant or increasing costs for each industry and is frequently criticized for failing to allow for economies of scale. The aim of this article is to incorporate economies of scale systematically in customs union theory. In particular, we want to see whether the familiar concepts of *trade creation* and *trade diversion* are still relevant.[1]

The approach will initially be partial equilibrium and static, this being also the way in which the principal propositions of established customs union theory were originally expounded. The economies of scale will be assumed to be *internal* to firms, so that the traditional assumption of perfect competition cannot be maintained. A crucial simplification will be the assumption that the countries forming the union face given prices from the outside world, economy-of-scale effects in the outside world as a result of the formation of the union being insignificant. We shall assume

---

[1] Viner (1950, pp. 45–46) has a substantial discussion of economies of scale, but this has not been followed up in the literature. Some of his conclusions differ from those in the present paper, possibly because his (unspecified) assumptions differ. See also Johnson (1962, pp. 60–61).

three countries, countries $A$ and $B$, which form the union, and country $C$, representing the rest of the world.

## I.  Simple Model: Two New Effects Introduced

We begin with a single homogeneous product which is produced in country $C$ and is at least capable of being produced in the two union countries. There is a single actual or potential producer in each of the union countries. He has a declining average cost curve which indicates private and social average costs. He is assumed to pay constant prices for his factors of production whatever the scale of output, so that there are no factor rents. The average cost curve is assumed to include normal profits. Each union country faces a given c.i.f. import and f.o.b. export price set by country $C$; because of transport costs and $C$'s tariff, the export price is below the import price. It is convenient, though not essential, to assume that the two countries face the same import and export prices for the product. The average cost curve in each country is assumed to reach its minimum at a level above the export price, so that exporting the product to country $C$ is ruled out. We also assume that, because of their tariffs and their relatively high costs, neither country initially exports to the other.[2]

We must now introduce tariffs. We have a choice of two simple assumptions. (1) We could assume that the two countries have the same tariff rate on the product before the union is formed. This is not a very realistic assumption, but it is implicit in much of orthodox customs union theory and means that one can focus on the effects of the freeing of trade within the union and need not be concerned with the establishment of a common external tariff, since such a tariff already exists. Since we want to define precisely what has to be added to orthodox theory when economies of scale are introduced, we should explore this case. (2) Alternatively, we could assume that tariff rates are "made to measure" at levels designed to make the tariff-inclusive import price just equal to average costs, including normal profits, hence avoiding any excess profits. If there is no domestic production, there will be no tariff. This may be a more realistic assumption, and we consider it in the next section. But we begin with assumption 1.

Subject to a qualification to be considered below, in each country the domestic price is determined by the cost of imports from $C$ plus the given tariff on imports from $C$. At this price there is a given quantity of domestic demand, and at this quantity there will be an average cost of

---

[2] The requirements for this condition emerge precisely from the diagram in the Appendix.

actual or potential production. If this average cost is less than the domestic price, there will be domestic production and no imports; and if the average cost of the potential domestic producer exceeds the domestic price at that quantity, there will be imports and no domestic production.[3] The qualification is that the price of imports from $C$, including tariff, sets only an upper limit to the price a domestic producer can charge. It might pay a profit-maximizing producer to charge less. But we assume at this stage that he maximizes profits by charging right up to the "import-preventing" price. The same analysis applies once the customs union is formed, provided we assume no transport costs within the union. Either the union demand will be supplied wholly by imports from $C$, or there will be a single domestic producer within the union. In the latter case he might price below the price set by imports from $C$, but we shall assume at this stage that he prices up to the limit price. This has the important implication that the prices facing consumers are not affected by the establishment of the union: hence ($a$) the total market for the product in each country remains unchanged and ($b$) there are no welfare effects on consumers. This assumption will be removed in the next section.

Now we come to the main analysis, which can be very brief. Initially there may be production of the product in both countries, in one only, or in neither. We consider each of these three cases briefly.

## 1. Initial Production in Both Countries

When the union is formed, one of the two producers, say country $A$'s, will capture the whole union market, the other going out of business. Hence the average costs of country $A$'s producer fall. Total costs of producing the product in the union thus decline because of specialization. This effect can be decomposed into two parts. ($a$) Country $B$'s expensive domestic production is replaced by imports from $A$ which are cheaper to produce; hence there has, in a sense, been a movement to a cheaper source of supply through the opening up of trade between $A$ and $B$, and hence an orthodox *trade-creation effect*. But it must be remembered that the domestic price in $B$ is assumed to be given at this stage. So none of the gain will go to $B$; it will all go to excess profits in $A$, and indeed $B$ may lose, since its expelled producer may have earned excess profits. ($b$) Country $A$ obtains its domestic supplies at lower cost of production. This can be called the *cost-reduction effect*. While it is a consequence of the creation of trade with $B$, it is not an orthodox trade-creation effect, since it is the result not of a movement to a cheaper source of supply

---

[3] See Corden (1967). The present article is essentially an extension of the analysis of this earlier paper to customs union theory.

but rather of the cheapening of an existing source of supply. Country $A$'s consumers will gain nothing (because they face the same price as before), and the whole gain will go in profits to the producer.

## 2. Initial Production in Country A Only

There are two possibilities now. The most likely is that country $A$'s producer captures the whole union market.[4] The effects can again be decomposed: (*a*) Country $B$ replaces imports from $C$ with imports from $A$. The latter are dearer than imports from $C$, since otherwise $A$ would not have needed the formation of the union to break into $B$'s market. Hence $B$ loses from *trade diversion,* a dearer source of imports replacing a cheaper source of imports. The trade diversion loss to $B$ will be equal to the loss of tariff revenue on imports from $C$. For the union as a whole the trade diversion loss may be less, since $A$'s producer may earn some excess profits on imports to $B$. (*b*) As in our earlier example, $A$ obtains its own product at lower cost now, so that there is a *cost-reduction effect* equal to the extra profits earned on sales at home.

The other possibility—*production reversal*—seems less likely. When the union is formed, production in $B$ may start, and $B$'s producer may drive $A$'s producer out of business and capture the whole union market. His costs will be less than $A$'s were before the union was formed, so that this time there is a trade-creation gain through $A$ obtaining its needs from a cheaper source (though this gain will go wholly to $B$), while $B$ loses through the replacement of cheap imports from $C$ with somewhat dearer domestic production. The costs of its newly established producer when he is supplying the whole union market must be greater than the cost of imports from $C$, for otherwise he could have become established even before the union was formed. When imports from $C$ are replaced by domestic production, there is a *trade-suppression effect.*[5] It is akin to the trade-diversion effect, since a dearer source replaces a cheaper source, but this time the dearer source is a newly established domestic producer, not the partner country.

## 3. Initial Production in Neither Country

When the union is established, production in, say, country $A$ may begin for the first time, since its average costs may now fall below the given domestic price. They will still be above the costs of imports from $C$, excluding duty, for otherwise $A$ could have broken into $B$'s market even

---

[4] See the Appendix for a geometric exposition of this case. This case is also expounded geometrically in Johnson (1962, p. 59) and is described in Viner (1950, pp. 45–46).

[5] The term comes from Viner (1950, p. 45).

without the union and so obtained the benefits of the combined market. In this case there is a *trade-suppression effect* for *A* (more expensive domestic production replaces cheaper imports from *C*) and a *trade-diversion effect* for *B* (more expensive imports from the partner replace cheaper imports from *C*). In both countries the whole loss is reflected in the loss of tariff revenue; this revenue loss will exceed the combined real income loss if the new producer earns excess profits.

*Our conclusion is that the trade-creation and trade-diversion concepts are still relevant but that they must be supplemented by two other concepts, the "cost-reduction effect" and the "trade-suppression effect." This is the main conclusion of this paper and remains even when some of the awkward or limiting assumptions are removed.* Our examples suggest that the *cost-reduction effect* is likely to be the more important of the two.

## II. Made-to-Measure Tariff Making: Consumption Effects Introduced

The assumption that the tariffs in country *A* and country *B* are the same initially, so that a common external tariff already exists, and that domestic producers always price up to the tariff-inclusive price, has conveniently eliminated any consumption effects but has led to the peculiar result in our first example that the trade creation gain through *B* getting its product from a cheaper source goes wholly to country *A*. It seems more sensible to assume that the purpose of tariffs is protection, not revenue, and that either a tariff will be high enough to bring domestic production into being (with imports wholly excluded) or it will not be imposed at all. Furthermore, we can now assume, as an interesting limiting case, that if a tariff is provided, it is just high enough to allow the domestic producer to cover his costs plus normal profits. These are the two components of what can be called *made-to-measure tariff making*.[6] Thus there are now no tariff revenues and no excess profits. All gains and losses will be borne by consumers. With this revised approach let us look at two of our cases.

### 1. Initial Production in Both Countries

The average costs of country *A*'s producer when he supplies the whole union will be less than his costs when he supplied only his home market, and less than the costs of the former producer in *B* when he was supplying *his* own market. Thus the union domestic price can be less than the

---

[6] The term comes from Australia; the complicated structure of the Australian tariff system can be explained partly by an attempt to apply (not entirely consciously) the made-to-measure principle.

domestic price ruling initially in either country. Given made-to-measure tariff making, the common external tariff will thus be less than the two initial tariffs and consumers in both countries will gain from the establishment of the union. (*a*) In country *B* there is a familiar trade-creation gain having two components: the production effect results from the replacement of dearer domestic production by cheaper imports from *A*, and the consumption effect results from the increased consumption induced by the lower domestic price. (*b*) In country *A* there is a cost-reduction gain going to its consumers; this has also a production and a consumption component. The production effect is that the original amount of production sold domestically is now obtained at a lower price, while the consumption effect is that at the lower price an extra amount is purchased on which consumer's surplus is obtained.

The fact that the made-to-measure policy requires the common external tariff to be less than both initial tariffs suggests that made-to-measure tariff making may not be a wholly realistic assumption. In practice the result may be intermediate to that of this model and the previous one: the tariff may fall in at least one country, the gain going mainly or wholly to consumers there, while in the other country the gain goes in excess profits to the union producer (who may not belong to that country).

## 2. Initial Production in Country A Only

The made-to-measure model is applied quite easily to this case. Only one point need be noted here. If country *B* initially did not have domestic production, then its tariff will have been zero. If country *A* is to capture *B*'s market—which *A* is assumed not to have captured before—this will result not from the freeing of trade within the union but from country *B* imposing a tariff—that is, from the establishment of the common external tariff at a positive level. The price to domestic consumers in *B* will then rise, and their losses can be divided into production- and consumption-effect components: the new, lower, amount consumed is now obtained at a higher cost than before, this being a shift to a dearer source of supply—the familiar trade-diversion effect—and in addition there is a loss in consumer's surplus on the reduced amount of consumption induced by the higher price. This latter consumption effect of trade diversion does not emerge in orthodox partial-equilibrium customs union theory.

*We can conclude that our four effects—trade creation, trade diversion, cost reduction, and trade suppression—each have a production and a consumption component. In a limiting case (the model of Section I) the consumption components disappear. In another limiting case (the present section) all the gains and losses (whether from production or consumption effects) are borne by consumers.* One can conceive of intermediate cases where there are some consumption effects and where some of the gains go in excess profits and some of the losses are borne by the government through loss of customs revenue. The extent of consumption effects and of excess profits depends on the extent to which the tariff system permits monopolists to exploit their position and whether they choose to do so. The distribution of gains and losses among government, producers, and consumers is crucial, since it affects the distribution of the gains and losses between the partner countries.

## III. Oligopoly and Product Differentiation

We now depart from the assumption of a single producer in each country and in the union and allow for oligopoly and product differentiation.

### 1. Initial Production in Both Countries

Suppose that there are initially *two* producers in each country. It can no longer be assumed that the increased size of the market must lead to scale economies; if the two firms in each country did not amalgamate originally, or one of them did not attempt to out-compete the other, there is no strong reason to assume that amalgamation or competition would operate in the larger area. Of course, in the world of oligopoly anything is possible, but it is conceivable that the four producers all stay in business, dividing up the market of the union among them. They may do this by differentiating their products, and since there can now be four versions of each product available to each consumer instead of two, there will be a welfare gain; this is essentially a trade-creation effect. There need be no cost-reduction effect, since the increased trade in differentiated products need not necessarily be associated with increased output by any firm.

There may initially have been more than one firm in each country because the potentially dominant producer was reluctant to swallow up the weaker firms for fear of public hostility to monopoly, leading possibly to public intervention. When the customs union is established, it becomes possible to preserve the semblance of competition while eliminating all but one producer in each country; indeed, a government may urge the national firms to amalgamate so as to strengthen the competitive power of domestic production. The two remaining firms—one in each country— may not combine either because of fear of antimonopoly action or because of the difficulty of arranging amalgamations of firms across countries, combined with hostility to, or legislation against, takeovers by foreign firms. The reduction in the number of producers will then lead to a cost-reduction gain. In addition, trade across the borders may increase, or start for the first time, as a result of product differentiation. This may or may not represent a trade-creation gain. On the one hand, the number of firms the consumer can choose to purchase from is the same as before, so he may have no more choice in variety of product; but, on the other hand, he can now choose between products made in different countries.

### 2. Initial Production in Country A Only'

There may be several producers in country $A$; when the union is formed, they all enter $B$'s market, and there is the usual cost-reduction gain for $A$ and trade-diversion loss for $B$. Two complications can be noted. (*a*) If the expansion of output by the various producers has brought them all closer to scales of output where average costs are at the minimum, the joint loss that they incur by failing to amalgamate is reduced; hence it becomes likelier that the oligopolistic situation will persist. (*b*) Some of the cost-reduction gains may be lost because producers in $B$ may enter the field for the first time, since they now have a larger potential market available.

## IV. General Equilibrium

A really satisfactory general-equilibrium customs union model with economies of scale is difficult to produce. Some of the propositions of orthodox customs union theory have been expounded in terms of the two-good model, and this has led to results similar to those that emerge from the partial-equilibrium exposition. Models with more goods become rather complicated and tend to be expounded in a piecemeal way. There seems little point in developing the economies-of-scale argument in terms of a two-good model; it generally leads to the result that a country produces only one product, though no doubt many of the results produced so far in partial-equilibrium terms could be obtained. Here an alternative approach will be sketched out. It should be borne in mind that the aim is to isolate economy-of-scale effects.

There are many import-competing products; each product is produced, or potentially produced, in each country by only one firm. For each product the average cost curve is downward sloping up to a point, the curve turning upward eventually, so as to rule out exports of the product to country $C$. In addition, there is an export product with constant costs. There is a single mobile factor of production—labor—and its money wage is given. The cost curves for each product are thus independent of each other, since they depend only on the given money wage and the relevant production functions. In the initial situation each country has a made-to-measure tariff structure, leading to domestic production of some products and imports of others. Our partial-equilibrium analysis can now be applied directly. When the union is formed, production of some products will expand as the partner's market is taken over (cost reduction), production of others will cease as the domestic market is vacated for the partner (trade creation), and imports from *C* may cease because they are replaced either by imports from the partner (trade diversion) or by domestic production (trade suppression). All our four effects will happen at the same time.

Are there any general equilibrium complications? First, the demand curves for different products may shift because real income as a whole and income distribution may change, and because there are cross-elasticities. A fall in the price of one product would shift the demand curve for another product to the left. For any particular product the level of demand is crucial in determining either the tariff rate required to sustain a domestic industry or, alternatively, whether a domestic industry can be sustained with a given tariff rate. Furthermore, it determines the actual volume of output. Because of these demand relationships one cannot look at each product separately as if the general-equilibrium story were just made up of a set of separable partial-equilibrium stories. But it remains true that there are our four effects.

A second general-equilibrium complication is the need to maintain balance-of-payments equilibrium, which (with constant money wages) would be brought about through exchange-rate adjustment. In the first instance, with a given exchange rate, many of country *A*'s industries might expand into *B*'s market, while many of *B*'s industries close down. Such a situation will then provoke appreciation of *A*'s and depreciation of *B*'s currency, and hence declines in the prices facing *A*'s producers and increases in the prices facing *B*'s producers (each in terms of their own currencies). This will then cause some of *A*'s industries to go out of business and some of *B*'s industries to revive again. In considering our effects in a general-equilibrium model, we should compare the initial preunion situation with the situation after the union is formed, each situation having its own equilibrium exchange rate.


## V.  Dynamic Considerations

There is nothing essentially "dynamic" about economies of scale. The whole of the analysis so far has been comparative static. But it is true that in a comparative-static model when there are economies of scale it is not possible to describe precisely the equilibrium that will be reached

474　　　　　　　　　　　　　　JOURNAL OF POLITICAL ECONOMY

in a customs union. If initially our product is produced in both partner countries, we can say that when the union is formed one country might take over the whole market. But we cannot say which country it will be: that depends on dynamic considerations—on the nature of oligopolistic competition, the relative rates of gross investment in the two countries, and so on.[7] In the comparative-static model it is clear that, if only one firm survives, there will be trade-creation and cost-reduction effects, both of which represent gains to someone, but one cannot say which country will obtain the trade-creation and which the cost-reduction effect.

More generally, customs union theory may not tell us much about the reallocation of existing resources, owing to their immobility, but it can tell us something about the allocation and productivity of new investment. In the short run capital is immobile and industries do not just "take over" the whole market in another country or "close down" as neatly as a comparative-static model might suggest. Assuming a "putty-clay" model, the more gross investment there is in proportion to existing output, the more outputs will respond over a given period to price changes. Hence the effects described in this paper will take time, how much depending on the rate of gross investment.

## Appendix

In figure 1. $DD'$ is country $A$'s demand curve for the product. and $LL'$ is the horizontal sum of country $A$'s and country $B$'s demand curve. The c.i.f. import price (when importing from $C$) is $OP_m$. and the f.o.b. export price (to $C$) is $P_x$. These prices are identical for countries $A$ and $B$. We illustrate the argument of Section I of the paper here. The given tariff is $P_mT$. Before the union is formed $B$ has to pay this tariff on imports from $A$ as well as from $C$. so that the combined demand curve facing $A$'s producer is $TQRVZP_x'$. Once the union is formed, the demand curve facing him is $TWZP_x'$.

Curve $AA'$ is country $A$'s average-cost curve. If it cuts $DD'$ below $Q$ (as drawn) then there is domestic production in $A$ before the union is formed: if it cuts $DD'$ above $Q$, the whole amount of domestic consumption $TQ$ will be imported (unless there are exports to $B$). If $AA'$ cuts $LL'$ above $V$ (as drawn), there will be no exports to $B$ in the absence of the union (unless there are exports to $C$) because $B$ will find imports from $C$ cheaper, while with the union production will depend on a positive common external tariff. If $AA'$ cuts $LL'$ below $V$ there will be exports to $B$ even in the absence of the union, and with the union production will not depend on a positive common tariff; furthermore. there will be production in $A$ even if $AA'$ happens to cut $DD'$ above $Q$. If

---

[7] One might envisage a process of cutthroat competition to decide which of the two firms will survive. The firm that would have the relatively lower average costs if it supplied the union market on its own will have an advantage; this may depend on relative factor intensities, and so on. If "learning by doing" counts for anything, and provided it is related to output, one might expect (other things being equal) the firm that initially enjoyed the larger home market to have the lower costs after the union is formed, and so to survive. Relative financial resources to bear temporary losses are also relevant. During the process of "sorting out," the union price may fall substantially, so that there may be a temporary income redistribution from producers to consumers.

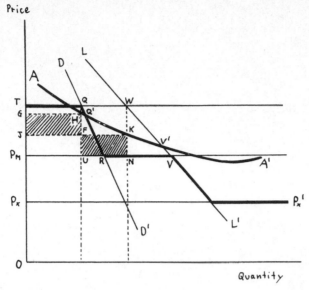

FIG. 1

$AA'$ cuts $LL'$ above $W$ (which it can do only if there is no production initially, $AA'$ also cutting $DD'$ above $Q$), then there will be no production even with the union. Provided the minimum-cost point on $AA'$ is above $P_x P_x'$ (as drawn), there will be no exports to $C$.

The diagram assumes ($a$) that even though $B$ may have produced initially, it vacates production once the union is formed, and ($b$) that there are no transport costs within the union.

If (1) the producer prices right up to the import-preventing price $OT$ and (2) $B$ imported from $C$ before the union, then the cost-reduction effect is $GHFJ$ and the trade-diversion effect for the union as a whole is $FKNU$ (both shaded). The loss of customs revenue to $B$, and hence the total loss to $B$, is $UQWN$, of which the trade-diversion effect $FKNU$ is a net loss to the union countries combined and $FQWK$ is a redistribution toward $A$'s producer, who gains $FQWK$ plus the cost-reduction effect. From the point of view of $B$ alone, one would describe the customs revenue loss $UQWN$ as the "trade-diversion effect."

If the made-to-measure system operated, the price to $A$'s consumers before the union is formed would be given by the point $Q'$, and the price to $A$'s and $B$'s consumers after the union is formed, by $V'$. Bearing this in mind, the diagram could be used to illustrate the various arguments of Section II.

### References

Corden, W. M. "Monopoly, Tariffs and Subsidies." *Economica* 34 (February 1967): 50–58.

Johnson, H. G. *Money, Trade and Economic Growth*. London: Allen & Unwin, 1962.

Viner, J. *The Customs Union Issue.* London: Carnegie Endowment Internat. Peace, 1950.

# C
# Technical Efficiency

# [12]

## Measurable Dynamic Gains from Trade

Richard E. Baldwin

*Columbia University*

Productive factors, such as human and physical capital, accumulate, and trade policy can affect their steady-state levels. Consequently, in addition to the usual static effects, trade liberalization has dynamic effects on output and welfare as the economy moves to its new steady state. The output impact of this dynamic effect is measurable and appears to be quite large. The welfare impact of this dynamic effect is also measurable. The size of this dynamic gain from trade depends on the wedge between social and private returns to capital. Rough numerical estimates of the output and welfare effects are provided.

Empirical researchers consistently find that trade liberalizations raise aggregate income by an amount that is negligible (0.1 percent [Deardorff and Stern 1986]) or small (8.6 percent [Harris and Cox 1984]). The oral tradition in international trade counters this "Harberger triangle problem" with the assertion that the most important gains from trade are dynamic, not static. Empirical studies of trade liberalizations ignore such factors since dynamic trade effects are poorly understood and supposedly impossible to measure. This paper exposits and measures one type of dynamic effect of trade liberalization. The results confirm the oral tradition by showing that dynamic output effects are large. The source of this particular dynamic effect is simple. If a liberalization raises the return to capital, it will induce

I gratefully acknowledge the comments and suggestions of Elhanan Helpman, Peter Svedberg, Victor Norman, Jim Markusen, and Torsten Persson. Avinash Dixit suggested the use of Laplace transforms in gauging welfare effects. I thank the Institute for International Economic Studies in Stockholm for providing a fertile environment for this work and the Centre for Economic Policy Research for financial support.

[*Journal of Political Economy*, 1992, vol. 100, no. 1]

capital formation and thereby raise output more than static effects alone would predict. Since capital accumulation takes time, the effect shows up as a medium-term rise in the growth rate. The welfare gain from this effect is also measurable and depends on the divergence between the social and private returns to capital.

Ricardo (1815) first emphasized the link between trade and steady-state factor supplies. In his model the steady-state growth rate is zero because of diminishing returns; however, trade postponed the arrival date of the steady state since "England's agriculture is stationary, but Manchester and Birmingham make her the workshop of the world which pays in food and primary products for the expanding output of the workshop" (Findlay 1984, p. 190). Stiglitz (1970), Findlay (1978), Srinivasan and Bhagwati (1980), Findlay and Kierzkowski (1983), Galor (1989), Manning and Markusen (1989), and others have explored the link more formally. Findlay (1984) and Smith (1984) survey the literature. None of these papers quantifies the output or welfare impact of induced capital formation, and most assume a constant savings rate. This effect is quite distinct from the Grossman-Helpman models of trade and growth.[1] Those models link long-run growth rates to trade policy. The current paper looks at the link between liberalization and the steady-state level of factors. Baldwin (1989) studies the impact of liberalization on growth but does not present a formal model and does not consider welfare implications.

Section I presents the basic model and a comparative steady-state analysis of liberalization. Section II examines the welfare consequences. Section III quantifies the output and welfare effects for an explicit model. Section IV presents concluding remarks.

## I. Induced Capital Formation

By the Stolper-Samuelson theorem, trade liberalization may raise or lower the return to capital. Consequently, liberalization has effects similar to a subsidy (tax) on the steady-state capital stock. The resulting capital accumulation (decumulation) amplifies (mitigates) the standard output effects of the liberalization. Section III presents an explicit model that permits quantification; however, to emphasize their generality, the results are first derived in an implicit model. Assume that the world's real output, $y$, is well approximated by $f[k, \tau]$, where $k$ is the world capital stock (other factors are suppressed for convenience), $\tau$ is an index of global trade barriers, $f_k > 0$, and $f_\tau < 0$ (subscripts denote partial derivatives). The real return on forgone

---

[1] The seminal papers are Grossman and Helpman (1990, 1991). Also see Krugman (1988) and Murphy, Shleifer, and Vishny (1988).

consumption, $r$, is assumed to be well approximated by $r[k, \tau]$, where $r_k < 0$ and $r_\tau$ may be positive or negative (according to the Stolper-Samuelson theorem). Furthermore, assume that investment is forgone consumption. If one ignores depreciation,

$$\dot{k} = y - c, \tag{1}$$

where $c$ is real consumption. The representative, infinitely lived consumer maximizes

$$U = \frac{1}{1 - (1/\sigma)} \int_0^\infty e^{-\rho t} c(t)^{1 - (1/\sigma)} dt \tag{2}$$

subject to a lifetime budget constraint. Here $\rho$ and $\sigma$ are the constant discount rate and the intertemporal elasticity of substitution. The necessary conditions imply

$$\frac{\dot{c}}{c} = \sigma[r(t) - \rho]. \tag{3}$$

Denoting steady-state levels of $c$ and $k$ with a bar, we get

$$\bar{c} = f[\bar{k}, \tau], \quad r[\bar{k}, \tau] = \rho. \tag{4}$$

The eigenvalues of the Jacobian evaluated at $\bar{c}$ and $\bar{k}$ are $f_k \pm [(f_k^2 - 4\sigma r_k)^{1/2}/2]$. Since $r_k < 0$ and $f_k > 0$, the system is saddle path stable.

Liberalization has two effects on income in this model:

$$\frac{dy/y}{d\tau/\tau} = \left(\frac{\partial f/y}{\partial k/k}\right)\left(-\frac{\partial r/r}{\partial \tau/\tau} \bigg/ \frac{\partial r/r}{\partial k/k}\right) + \frac{\partial f/y}{\partial \tau/\tau}. \tag{5}$$

The second term captures the usual static efficiency effects. The first term reflects the induced capital formation effect. If liberalization raises (lowers) $r$, it induces capital accumulation (decumulation), thereby amplifying (mitigating) the output impact of the static effect. The welfare interpretation of this add-on effect is not as straightforward as the output effect. To the infinitely lived consumer, the rise in consumption due to induced capital accumulation is largely, or entirely, offset by the necessary forgone consumption.

## II. Welfare: Dynamic Gains from Trade

The direct way to measure the welfare effects would be to solve for the adjustment path of $c$ and evaluate it with the utility function. Since the system is nonlinear, this is not possible. Another approach would be to linearize the system around the steady state and work with the resulting linear system. Since my aim is to show that dynamic effects are large, an approach that is correct only for very small changes in $c$ and $y$ is unsatisfactory. Judd (1985, 1987) shows that welfare effects can be obtained without an analytic solution for the consumption path. To see this, note that the optimal consumption path is a function of time and $\tau$. If we differentiate (2) (evaluated at $\bar{c}$) with respect to $\tau$, $dU/d\tau$ is $\bar{c}^{-1/\sigma} \int_0^\infty e^{-\rho t} c_\tau(t)\, dt$. In other words, the welfare impact depends on the Laplace transform of the induced change in the consumption path. This comment is germane since Judd (1985) showed that it is easier to deal with the Laplace transforms of state variables' paths than with the paths themselves.

Consider a general perturbation of the time path of $\tau$. Inserting $\tau[1 + \epsilon h(t)]$ in (1) and (3) in place of $\tau$, where $h(t)$ is an arbitrary time path, differentiating with respect to $\epsilon$, and evaluating the result at $\epsilon = 0$ yield

$$\begin{pmatrix} \dot{c}_\epsilon \\ \dot{k}_\epsilon \end{pmatrix} = \mathbf{J} \begin{pmatrix} c_\epsilon \\ k_\epsilon \end{pmatrix} + \begin{pmatrix} \tau \bar{c} \sigma h(t)\, r_\tau \\ \tau h(t) f_\tau \end{pmatrix}, \tag{6}$$

where

$$\mathbf{J} = \begin{pmatrix} 0 & \bar{c}\sigma r_k \\ -1 & f_k \end{pmatrix},$$

and the Jacobian is evaluated at $\bar{c}$ and $\bar{k}$. Next, multiply by $e^{-\omega t}$, integrate over time, and then integrate the left-hand side by parts to get

$$\begin{pmatrix} C_\epsilon(\omega) \\ K_\epsilon(\omega) \end{pmatrix} = (\omega \mathbf{I} - \mathbf{J})^{-1} \begin{pmatrix} \tau \bar{c} \sigma H(\omega)\, r_\tau + c_\epsilon(0) \\ \tau H(\omega) f_\tau \end{pmatrix}, \tag{7}$$

where $C_\epsilon(\omega)$, $K_\epsilon(\omega)$, and $H_\epsilon(\omega)$ are the Laplace transforms of $c_\epsilon$, $k_\epsilon$, and $h_\epsilon$; for example, $C_\epsilon(\omega)$ is defined as $\int_0^\infty e^{-\omega t} c_\epsilon(t)\, dt$. Notice that integration by parts turns the differential equations into an algebraic system in Laplace transforms. Since capital does not jump, the only unknown in (7) is the size of the consumption jump at time 0, $c_\epsilon(0)$.

By the transversality condition, $K_\epsilon(\omega)$ must remain finite for all values of $\omega$. Consider $\omega$ equal to the positive eigenvalue of $\mathbf{J}$ (call this $\mu$). Since $\mu \mathbf{I} - \mathbf{J}$ is singular, it must be true that (see Judd [1985] for details)

$$\tau \bar{c} \sigma H(\mu)\, r_\tau + c_\epsilon(0) - \mu \tau H(\mu) f_\tau = 0. \tag{8}$$

This fact pins down $c_\epsilon(0)$, so the welfare impact is

$$\frac{dU/d\epsilon}{\bar{c}^{-1/\sigma}} = \tau \left( \left( \frac{\rho - f_k}{\Delta} \right) \{ \bar{c} \sigma r_\tau [H(\rho) - H(\mu)] + H(\mu) f_\tau \mu \} \right.$$

$$\left. + \left( \frac{\bar{c} \sigma r_k}{\Delta} \right) [f_\tau H(\rho)] \right), \tag{9}$$

where $\Delta$ is the determinant of $\rho I - J$, and all partials are evaluated at $\bar{c}$ and $\bar{k}$. For many policy changes, $h(t)$, it is possible to obtain a closed-form solution for $H(\omega)$. For such $h(t)$, it is a straightforward exercise to evaluate (9). For example, in the case of a one-off change in $\tau$,

$$
\frac{dU/\bar{U}}{d\tau/\tau} \bigg/ \frac{dU/\bar{U}}{dc/c} = \left[ \left(\frac{1}{\rho}\right) \left(\frac{\partial y/\bar{y}}{\partial \tau/\tau}\right) \right]
$$

$$
+ \left[ \left(\frac{\rho - f_k}{\bar{c}\sigma r_k + \rho^2 - \rho f_k}\right) \sigma\rho \left(\frac{1}{\rho} - \frac{1}{\mu}\right) \left(\frac{\partial r/\bar{r}}{\partial \tau/\tau}\right) \right]. \quad (10)
$$

This expression is easy to interpret. The first term is equal to the present discounted value of the static gain. The second term captures the welfare effect of the induced capital formation. If there are no external economies of scale in the employment of capital, then $r[\bar{k}, \tau] = f_k[\bar{k}, \tau] = \rho$, so the dynamic gain from trade is zero. Although induced capital formation amplifies the output effect, it does not contribute to welfare (as predicted by the envelope theorem). The consumer is optimizing (taking $\tau$ as a parameter) between consumption today and savings that will yield consumption in the future. For small changes in $\tau$, the change in the objective function is the same with and without reoptimizing on $k$.

If there are external economies of scale or other distortions such as taxes, the social return to capital may exceed the private rate, so there will be dynamic gains from trade due to induced capital formation. To see this, note that with external economies $r[\bar{k}, \tau]$ need not equal the social marginal product of capital, $f_k[\bar{k}, \tau]$. Consequently, $\rho$ can be less than $f_k[\bar{k}, \tau]$. The determinant of $\rho I - J$ is negative and the positive eigenvalue of $J$ is greater than $r[\bar{k}, \tau]$, so the second term in (10) has the same sign as $r_\tau[\bar{k}, \tau]$. Proposition 1 summarizes this discussion.

PROPOSITION 1. *Necessary condition for dynamic gains from trade.*—If the social and private returns to capital are identical, induced capital formation has no effect on welfare on the margin. If the social rate exceeds the private rate, then induced capital formation has a positive welfare effect on the margin *only if* the liberalization raises the return to capital. If the liberalization lowers the return to capital, the dynamic welfare effects tend to offset the static gains from trade.

The result that induced capital formation may lower welfare should be interpreted in the light of the theory of the second best. External economies drive a wedge between the private and social rates of return. In all such cases, many types of intervention may improve welfare. The best policy (if one ignores the efficiency cost of government revenue) is to subsidize capital formation directly *and* liberalize trade. Evaluating the exact impact of a large policy change would require the solution of nonlinear differential equations. Nevertheless, extension of the envelope theorem implies that even when the social and private returns to capital coincide, a large liberalization leads to dynamic gains from trade.

## III.  An Explicit Model

This section adopts an explicit model that enables quantification of the positive and welfare effects. As we shall see, the derived functional forms imply that $r$ is everywhere decreasing in $\tau$. Of course, one can construct models in which liberalization has the opposite effect on $r$.

Consider a two-country world in which each country produces $N$ distinct goods. Preferences of the infinitely lived, representative consumer in each country are given by (2) taking $c$ to be

$$2N \prod_{i=1}^{2N} c_i(t)^{1/2N},$$

where $c_i$ is consumption of good $i$. Investment is forgone consumption; depreciation is ignored. Countries are endowed with $\overline{L}$ units of labor. Technology is identical for all goods, requiring each firm to incur a fixed cost of $\kappa$ units of labor each period, after which capital, $k_i$, and labor, $l_i$, produce output according to $Ak_i^\alpha l_i^{1-\alpha}$ ($A$ is total factor productivity). There are $m$ firms producing each good and playing Cournot in the home and foreign markets, which are assumed segmented. Trade is subject to nontariff barriers that have the effect of "melting" $\tau$ percent of exports without giving rise to revenue.[2] The typical firm maximizes $p_i x_i + [p_i^* x_i^*/(1 + \tau)] - wl_i - rk_i - w\kappa$, subject to $x_i + x_i^* = Ak_i^\alpha l_i^{1-\alpha}$. In equilibrium, $p_i^* = p_i(1 + \tau)$, and the quantity of resources devoted to making good $i$ for domestic and foreign consumption is unaffected by $\tau$.

It can be shown that firms' first-order conditions for capital and labor together with the aggregate demand function imply

$$\left(\frac{\alpha}{K}\right) A\beta K^\alpha L^{1-\alpha} \left(1 - \frac{1}{m}\right) = \frac{r}{P(t)} \tag{11}$$

---

[2] Most trade barriers in the industrialized world do not give rise to revenue. For instance, the average tariff receipts are only 2.43 percent of imports for OECD countries (OECD 1985, p. 27). This prevalence of nonrevenue barriers is also evident in the fact that the vast majority of liberalization effects in the Uruguay Round talks do not involve revenue-producing trade barriers.

and

$$\left(\frac{1 - \alpha}{L}\right) A\beta K^\alpha L^{1-\alpha}\left(1 - \frac{1}{m}\right) = \frac{w}{P(t)}, \tag{12}$$

where $\beta$ is $(1 + \tau)^{-1/2}$, $L = \bar{L} - mN\kappa$, $K$ is the national capital stock, and $P = \Pi_{i=1}^{2N} (p_i)^{1/2N}$. Likewise, it can be shown that nominal gross domestic product is given exactly by the function

$$PY = PA\beta K^\alpha L^{1-\alpha}. \tag{13}$$

The true determinants of total factor productivity are not well understood. The neoclassical growth model assumes that it is driven by exogenous technological progress, whereas the new growth theory (see Romer 1983, 1986, 1987$a$, 1987$b$; Lucas 1988) endogenizes the advancement of primary factor productivity. The dynamic effect demonstrated here does not depend on the exact source of productivity growth, so rather than tie the model to a specific school of thought, assume that $A = e^{\eta t} K^\theta L^\varphi$, where $\eta$ is the exogenous rate of technological progress and $\theta$ captures the external economies in the usage of capital. There are several possible interpretations of $\theta$ and $\varphi$. The most straightforward is standard external economies of scale. That is, the typical production function is $Y^\psi k_i^\alpha l_i^{1-\alpha}$, where $\psi$ measures external scale economies. In this case, $\alpha + \theta = \alpha/(1 - \psi)$ and $1 - \alpha + \varphi = (1 - \alpha)/(1 - \psi)$. Alternatively, Romer (1987$a$) argues that external economies are entirely captured by $K^{\alpha+\theta}$, and $\eta$ and $\varphi$ are zero. In the Solow model, $\theta$ is zero and $\varphi = 1 - \alpha$. For convenience, take $L$ equal to unity and $\eta$ equal to zero. Allowing for exogenous technological progress is a straightforward exercise.

With these additional assumptions, the proportional rise in $Y$ due to a liberalization is

$$\hat{Y} = \left(\frac{1}{\alpha + \theta} - 1\right)^{-1} \hat{\beta} + \hat{\beta}, \tag{14}$$

where a circumflex indicates percentage change and $\hat{\beta}$ is the static output effect of the liberalization considered (the increase in gross national product with no change in the capital stock). Measurement of the size of this output effect requires only two readily available estimates: the capital-output elasticity of the GNP function $(\alpha + \theta)$ and an estimate of the size of the static gain $(\hat{\beta})$. To illustrate the measurability of this effect, let us take the European Community's 1992 program as an example.

The size of $\alpha + \theta$ is an unsettled empirical question. Prior to the new growth literature, it was widely assumed that $\alpha + \theta$ equaled capital's share of income (or one minus labor's share of income).

TABLE 1

ESTIMATES OF AGGREGATE CAPITAL-OUTPUT ELASTICITY ($\alpha + \theta$)

| Source | France | Germany | Netherlands | United Kingdom | Belgium |
|---|---|---|---|---|---|
| Denison (1967) and Denison and Chung (1976) | .23 | .263 | .26 | .222 | |
| Maddison (1987) | .305 | .3 | .296 | .255 | |
| Kendrick (1981) | .382 | .349 | | .348 | |
| Christensen, Cummings, and Jorgenson (1980) | .403 | .386 | .446 | .385 | |
| Caballero and Lyons (1989a) | .366 | .477 | | .339 | .426 |
| Minus one standard error | .288 | .39 | | .195 | .276 |
| Plus one standard error | .444 | .564 | | .483 | .576 |

SOURCE.—First four rows from Maddison (1987), table 8. Fifth row from Caballero and Lyons (1989a), taking .3 as capital's share of income. The first four rows of figures come from the growth accounting calibration procedure and thus have no standard errors.

Table 1 reproduces a number of such estimates for France, Germany, the Netherlands, and the United Kingdom. The numbers range from .446 to .222. A recent survey (Maddison 1987) takes .3 as the consensus figure. Econometric estimation of the GNP function is problematic because of simultaneity between optimal factor choice and random productivity shocks. Hall (1988a) and Caballero and Lyons (1989a, 1989b) have pioneered new techniques to skirt this problem. Using these, Caballero and Lyons (1989a) estimate the sum of capital and labor output elasticities for France, Germany, Belgium, and the United Kingdom. To recover $\alpha + \theta$ from the Caballero-Lyons numbers, we must multiply their aggregate number by capital's cost share. Since the authors use panel data on capital's cost share, it is not possible to recover the exact $\alpha + \theta$. We get a rough approximation by multiplying the Caballero-Lyons aggregate numbers by Maddison's .3. To test the results for sensitivity to the estimates, the same calculation must be done for their point estimates plus and minus one standard error. Table 1 lists the resulting numbers.

Equation (14) shows that the induced capital formation effect can be thought of as a multiplier on the static effect. The size of this multiplier can by itself tell us how important the induced capital formation effect is. For instance, the low estimate of $\alpha + \theta$ for France yields a multiplier of 30 percent. In other words, when the endogeneity of capital is ignored, empirical estimates of the static effect alone underestimate the total output effect by at least 30 percent. Table 2 presents the multipliers that correspond to the high and low values of $\alpha + \theta$ from table 1 for each country. They range from 24 to 136 percent.

TABLE 2

UNDERESTIMATE OF GDP RISE BY IGNORING INDUCED CAPITAL FORMATION (%)

|        | France | Germany | Netherlands | United Kingdom | Belgium |
|--------|--------|---------|-------------|----------------|---------|
| Low    | 30     | 36      | 35          | 24             | 38      |
| High   | 80     | 129     | 124         | 93             | 136     |

NOTE.—Figures were calculated by the author. The percentage underestimate is 100 times $(\alpha + \theta)/(1 - \alpha - \theta)$.

To get estimates of this dynamic effect of the 1992 program, multiply the various estimates of the multiplier by an estimate of the static output impact of 1992. Here we employ the Cecchini, Catinat, and Jacquemin (1988) estimate that 1992 will lead to a one-off increase in the European Community GDP of between 2.5 and 6.5 percent. Take the high and low estimates of the multiplier for each country from table 2 and multiply these by the high and low estimates of the static effect from Cecchini et al. The results are listed in table 3. The first and second rows in table 3 present 1992's effect on the European Community GDP (in percentage points) due solely to the indirect effect. Of course there would be no indirect effect without the static gain, so the total effect (the static range of 2.5–6.5 plus the high and low ranges from the first row) of 1992 on the European Community GDP is presented in the third and fourth rows of table 3. The most robust conclusion from table 3 is that the indirect effect is considerable in all cases. At the very least, it means that the endogenous rise in capital will boost the European Community GDP by an extra 0.6 percent.

TABLE 3

EVENTUAL INCREASE IN GDP DUE TO 1992

|        | France | Germany | Netherlands | United Kingdom | Belgium |
|--------|--------|---------|-------------|----------------|---------|
| Indirect Effect on GDP Due to Rise in Steady-State Capital Stock* | | | | | |
| Low    | .8–2     | .9–2.3   | .9–2.3   | .6–1.6   | 1–2.5    |
| High   | 2–5.2    | 3.2–8.4  | 3.1–8.1  | 2.3–6    | 3.4–8.9  |
| Total Effect (Static Plus Dynamic)[†] | | | | | |
| Low    | 3.3–8.5  | 3.4–8.8  | 3.4–8.8  | 3.1–8.1  | 3.5–9    |
| High   | 4.5–11.7 | 5.7–14.9 | 5.6–14.2 | 5.8–12.5 | 5.9–15.4 |

NOTE.—Based on table 2 and the estimate of the static effect in Cecchini et al. (1988).
* Percentage points are to be added to the static range.
† The percentage rise in GDP due to 1992.

For our explicit model, the proportional changes of $r$ and $Y$ with respect to $\tau$ are identical, so

$$\frac{dU/\overline{U}}{d\epsilon} \bigg/ \frac{dU/\overline{U}}{dC/C} = \frac{1}{\rho}\frac{\partial Y/\overline{Y}}{\partial \tau/\tau} + \phi\frac{\partial Y/\overline{Y}}{\partial \tau/\tau}, \tag{15}$$

where

$$\phi \equiv \left[\frac{\theta}{1 - \alpha - \theta + (\theta/\sigma)}\right]\left(\frac{1}{\rho} - \frac{1}{\mu}\right),$$

and the positive eigenvalue of $\mathbf{J}$, $\mu$, equals

$$\left(\frac{\rho}{2\alpha}\right)\{\alpha + \theta + [(\alpha + \theta)^2 + 4\alpha\sigma(1 - \alpha - \theta)]^{1/2}\}.$$

The term $(\partial Y/\overline{Y})/(\partial \tau/\tau)$ is what empirical studies of trade liberalizations measure. Consequently, it may be useful to think of $\phi$ as a welfare multiplier. That is, in addition to the well-known static gains from trade, the induced capital formation effect leads to a further welfare gain that is proportional to the static gain. Let us now turn to approximating its size.

Estimates of all the parameters in the multiplier are readily available in the literature. Table 4 presents the calculated values of the welfare multiplier for the Caballero-Lyons capital-output elasticities and these estimates plus one standard error. In all cases, the discount rate is equal to .05, the intertemporal elasticity of substitution is .1 (this is the average figure from Hall [1988*b*]), and $\alpha$ is equal to Maddison's .3.

The main point to emerge from table 4 is that this dynamic gain from trade is significant. For France, Germany, the United Kingdom,

TABLE 4

SIZE OF THE WELFARE MULTIPLIER

|  | France | Germany | United Kingdom | Belgium |
|---|---|---|---|---|
|  | Caballero-Lyons Estimates of $\alpha + \theta$ | | | |
| Multiplier | .29 | .64 | .17 | .50 |
| $\alpha + \theta$ | .37 | .48 | .34 | .43 |
|  | Caballero-Lyons Estimates Plus One Standard Error | | | |
| Multiplier | .53 | .83 | .64 | .87 |
| $\alpha + \theta$ | .44 | .56 | .48 | .58 |

NOTE.—Figures were calculated by the author on the basis of rows 5 and 6 of table 1. The welfare multiplier is due to the dynamic effect. Numbers are to be multiplied by the static effect on GDP.

and Belgium the multiplier ranges from .17 to .87. That is, the induced capital formation effect accounts for an extra rise in welfare that is somewhere between 15 and 90 percent of the static output effect of the liberalization. However, the dynamic gain from trade is small relative to the static gain from trade. The welfare impact of the static effect is the percentage rise in output (with $k$ held constant) multiplied by something like 20 (for $\rho = .05$). The welfare impact of the dynamic effect is the output effect multiplied by a number that is less than unity. Intuitively, this reflects the fact that the static gain is "for free" whereas the dynamic gain is largely offset by the forgone consumption necessary to build the capital stock.

## IV.  Conclusions

Productive factors such as human and physical capital are accumulated. Since the steady-state levels of such factors are determined endogenously, trade policy can affect these levels. A trade liberalization therefore has a dynamic effect on output and welfare as the economy moves to its new steady state. This paper shows that both the positive and normative impacts of this dynamic effect are measurable. The extra output change due to this dynamic effect appears to be quite large. The size of the welfare impact depends on the divergence between the social and private returns to capital. This dynamic effect is not dependent on the new growth models; it is present even in the Solow growth model.

## References

Baldwin, Richard. "The Growth Effects of 1992." *Econ. Policy* 4, no. 9 (October 1989): 247–83.

Caballero, Ricardo J., and Lyons, Richard K. "Increasing Returns and Imperfect Competition in European Industry." Working paper. New York: Columbia Univ., 1989. (*a*)

———. "The Role of External Economies in U.S. Manufacturing." Working Paper no. 3033. Cambridge, Mass.: NBER, 1989. (*b*)

Cecchini, Paolo; Catinat, Michel; and Jacquemin, Alexis. *The European Challenge, 1992.* Brookfield, Vt.: Gower, 1988.

Christensen, Laurits R.; Cummings, Diane; and Jorgenson, Dale W. "Economic Growth, 1947–73: An International Comparison." In *New Developments in Productivity Measurement and Analysis,* edited by John W. Kendrick and Beatrice N. Vaccara. Chicago: Univ. Chicago Press (for NBER), 1980.

Deardorff, Alan V., and Stern, Robert M. *The Michigan Model of World Production and Trade: Theory and Applications.* Cambridge, Mass.: MIT Press, 1986.

Denison, Edward F. *Why Growth Rates Differ: Postwar Experience in Nine Western Countries.* Washington: Brookings Inst., 1967.

Denison, Edward F., and Chung, William K. *How Japan's Economy Grew So Fast: The Sources of Postwar Expansion.* Washington: Brookings Inst., 1976.

Findlay, Ronald W. "An 'Austrian' Model of International Trade and Interest Rate Equalization." *J.P.E.* 86 (December 1978): 989–1007.

———. "Growth and Development in Trade Models." In *Handbook of International Economics*, vol. 1, edited by Ronald W. Jones and Peter Kenen. New York: Elsevier, 1984.

Findlay, Ronald, and Kierzkowski, Henryk. "International Trade and Human Capital: A Simple General Equilibrium Model." *J.P.E.* 91 (December 1983): 957–78.

Galor, Oded. "Tariff, Income Redistribution and Welfare in a Small Overlapping-Generations Economy." Working paper. Providence, R.I.: Brown Univ., 1989.

Grossman, Gene M., and Helpman, Elhanan. "Comparative Advantage and Long-Run Growth." *A.E.R.* 80 (September 1990): 796–815.

———. "Endogenous Product Cycles." *Econ. J.* 101 (1991), in press.

Hall, Robert E. "Increasing Returns: Theory and Measurement with Industry Data." Working paper. Stanford, Calif.: Stanford Univ., 1988. (*a*)

———. "Intertemporal Substitution in Consumption." *J.P.E.* 96 (April 1988): 339–57. (*b*)

Harris, Richard G., and Cox, David. *Trade, Industrial Policy and Canadian Manufacturing*. Toronto: Ontario Econ. Council, 1984.

Judd, Kenneth L. "Short-Run Analysis of Fiscal Policy in a Simple Perfect Foresight Model." *J.P.E.* 93 (April 1985): 298–319.

———. "The Welfare Cost of Factor Taxation in a Perfect-Foresight Model." *J.P.E.* 95 (August 1987): 675–709.

Kendrick, John W. "International Comparisons of Recent Productivity Trends." In *Essays in Contemporary Economic Problems: Demand, Productivity, and Population*, edited by William Fellner. Washington: American Enterprise Inst., 1981.

Krugman, Paul R. "Endogenous Innovation, International Trade, and Growth." Paper presented at the conference on the Problem of Development, State Univ. New York, Buffalo, May 1988.

Lucas, Robert E., Jr. "On the Mechanics of Economic Development." *J. Monetary Econ.* 22 (July 1988): 3–42.

Maddison, Angus. "Growth and Slowdown in Advanced Capitalist Economies: Techniques of Quantitative Assessment." *J. Econ. Literature* 25 (June 1987): 649–98.

Manning, R., and Markusen, James. "National Product Functions in Comparative Steady-State Analysis." Working Paper no. 8808C. London: Univ. Western Ontario, 1989.

Murphy, Kevin M.; Shleifer, Andre; and Vishny, Robert W. "Income Distribution, Market Size and Industrialization." Working paper. Chicago: Univ. Chicago, 1988.

OECD. *Costs and Benefits of Protection*. Paris: OECD Publications, 1985.

Ricardo, David. "Essay on the Influence of a Low Price of Corn on the Profits of Stocks." 1815. Reprinted in *The Works and Correspondence of David Ricardo*, vol. 4, *Pamphlets and Papers, 1815–1823*, edited by Piero Sraffa. Cambridge: Cambridge Univ. Press (for Royal Econ. Soc.), 1951.

Romer, Paul M. "Dynamic Competitive Equilibria with Externalities, Increasing Returns and Unbounded Growth." Ph.D. dissertation, Univ. Chicago, 1983.

———. "Increasing Returns and Long-Run Growth." *J.P.E* 94 (October 1986): 1002–37.

————. "Crazy Explanations for the Productivity Slowdown." In *NBER Macroeconomics Annual*, vol. 2, edited by Stanley Fischer. Cambridge, Mass.: MIT Press (for NBER), 1987. (*a*)

————. "Growth Based on Increasing Returns Due to Specialization." *A.E.R. Papers and Proc.* 77 (May 1987): 56–62. (*b*)

Smith, Alasdair. "Capital Theory and Trade Theory." In *Handbook of International Economics*, vol. 1, edited by Ronald W. Jones and Peter Kenen. New York: Elsevier, 1984.

Srinivasan, T. N., and Bhagwati, Jagdish N. "Trade and Welfare in a Steady State." In *Flexible Exchange Rates and the Balance of Payments: Essays in Memory of Egon Sohmen*, edited by John S. Chipman and Charles P. Kindleberger. Amsterdam: North-Holland, 1980.

Stiglitz, Joseph E. "Factor Price Equalization in a Dynamic Economy." *J.P.E.* 78 (May/June 1970): 456–88.

# Part IV
# The New Regionalism

# [13]

## Trade Liberalization and Industrial Organization: Some Estimates for Canada

David Cox

*University of Western Ontario*

Richard Harris

*Queen's University*

This paper provides estimates of the cost of protection to the Canadian economy for the mid-1970s. The estimates are based on an applied general equilibrium model incorporating scale economies, imperfect competition, and capital mobility. Both unilateral and multilateral tariff reductions are considered. The results of these experiments suggest that the cost of protection to the Canadian economy is considerably greater than that suggested by conventional general equilibrium analysis. Welfare gains from trade liberalization are found to be on the order of 8–10 percent of GNP. Accompanying both trade policies is a rationalization of industries with a lengthening of production runs, lowering of price-cost markups, and increases in factor productivity. Experiments investigating the sensitivity of these results to the underlying parameters of the model are also reported.

This paper reports on some trade liberalization experiments undertaken with a recently constructed general equilibrium model of the

This paper is a summary and extension of some results obtained in a larger study undertaken for the Ontario Economic Council using the general equilibrium simulation model, GET. The support of the OEC is gratefully acknowledged. The comments of seminar participants at the University of British Columbia, Ontario Economic Council, University of Alberta, University of Calgary, Queen's University, University of Western Ontario, and the World Bank are gratefully acknowledged. We also wish to thank two referees for helpful comments and suggestions. Any remaining shortcomings are the responsibility of the authors.

[*Journal of Political Economy*, 1985, vol. 93, no. 1]

Canadian economy (Harris 1984*a*, 1984*b*). The model incorporates features of industrial organization thought to be important in considering the effects of international trade on small open economies. Of these, the most significant are the inclusion of economies of scale and imperfectly competitive market structures. Both of these features are thought to be important in assessing the costs of protection in small open economies. Some economists argue that the presence of foreign and domestic tariffs, by restricting domestic industry to produce for the small domestic market, leads to highly concentrated industries in which firms do not exhaust economies of scale. The result in the manufacturing sector is industries characterized by high costs and low productivity. This view suggests that the cost of tariff protection is quite high. Freer trade, by subjecting domestic industry to increased foreign competition and allowing access to the larger world market, results in lower price-cost margins and in firms' achieving longer production runs with lower average costs of production.

This view is outside the traditional theoretical framework of neoclassical trade theory. Economists emphasizing scale economies and imperfect competition as important variables in estimating the impact of trade liberalization include Dales (1966), Balassa (1967), Eastman and Stykolt (1967), Wonnacott and Wonnacott (1967), and Corden (1972).

Although the theoretical literature integrating industrial organization and international trade is growing quite rapidly (see, e.g., Krugman 1979, 1980; Lancaster 1979; Brander 1981; Helpman 1981), to date the industrial organization (IO) approach has had little impact on empirical studies of the costs of protection.[1] In most empirical work, variants of the basic neoclassical trade model have been employed. Examples of recent studies adopting this framework are Magee (1972), Boadway and Treddenick (1978), Cline et al. (1978), Williams (1978), Brown and Whalley (1980), and Deardorff and Stern (1981). The early partial equilibrium studies are summarized in Corden (1975). These studies have found that the benefits of trade liberalization are typically quite small, often on the order of 0.0–1.0 percent of GNP. As these studies use models maintaining the assumptions of constant returns to scale and perfect competition, the results have been viewed with some skepticism, particularly in the case of

---

[1] Most of these theoretical papers emphasize product differentiation, a feature not emphasized in the results reported here. Harris (1984*b*) reports on the effect of incorporating product differentiation explicitly in the model and its quantitative impact. A recent paper by Pearson and Ingram (1980) incorporates scale economies looking at the empirical estimates of the benefits to economic integration between Ghana and the Ivory Coast.

small open economies. The purpose of the present paper is to report the impact on cost of protection estimates of the presence of economies of scale and imperfect competition in an applied general equilibrium (GE) model. The basic issue is whether or not the benefits of trade liberalization suggested by an IO approach, consistent with the data and an economic model, are significantly greater than conventional static estimates.

The results, implementing the model on a 1976 Canadian data set, suggest that the gains are considerably greater than suggested by conventional GE analysis. The benefits to two trade liberalization policies are considered: a unilateral removal of domestic tariffs, and a multilateral removal of both domestic tariffs and foreign tariffs against domestic exports. The multilateral tariff cuts yield the largest benefits, with a gain in welfare equivalent to approximately 8.5 percent of national income. This number is substantially larger than those found with the neoclassical trade models cited above and is comparable to the figure reported by Wonnacott and Wonnacott (1967) for Canada in the mid-1960s. The mechanism by which the welfare gains are achieved is also in broad agreement with that suggested by the IO view. Accompanying both trade policies is a rationalization of industries with a lengthening of production runs, a lowering of price-cost markups, and increases in factor productivity. The results indicate that rationalization effects play an important role in the adjustment of the economy to trade liberalization. The equilibrium outcome of industry rationalization is both interindustry and *intraindustry* adjustment. The results confirm the relative importance of intraindustry adjustment and suggest that for small open economies, neoclassical models may be seriously misspecified. We would caution the reader, however, that the results obtained from one data set are suggestive but not conclusive. If these results can be confirmed for other small open economies, with heavily protected manufacturing sectors, the proponents of free trade will be free of the "tyranny of triangles"—the low-welfare-cost estimates of protection.

The paper is organized as follows. An overview of the model is given in the first section. (The equations of the model are presented in the Appendix.) The discussion in this paper is limited to a brief verbal description.[2] In Section II the methodology used to calibrate the model is set out. In the third section the results of the trade liberalization experiments are presented; summary statistics are presented and discussed at both the aggregate and the industry level. In order to examine the robustness of the results reported, sensitivity

---

[2] For further discussion of the mathematical model see Harris (1984a, 1984b).

analysis is conducted with respect to a number of key parameters of the model. The conclusions of the study are summarized in the final section of the paper.

## I. Overview of the Model

The general equilibrium (GE) model consists of 29 domestic industries. Of these, 20 industries are characterized by economies of scale in production and imperfectly competitive market structures. The noncompetitive industries correspond to the Canadian manufacturing industries identified at the two-digit level of the SIC code. The remaining nine industries are perfectly competitive constant-cost industries. Among these industries are the natural resource and service sectors of the Canadian economy. In the model, commodities are distinguished not only by their physical attributes but also by their location of production: domestic or foreign. Within each of the 29 commodity categories, two commodities are therefore distinguished: the domestically produced good and its imported counterpart. Following Armington (1969), for each commodity category a commodity aggregate is formed in which the domestic and imported goods are treated as close but imperfect substitutes by all demand categories. Thus intraindustry trade or "cross-hauling" is a characteristic of trade, and one given considerable emphasis by Balassa (1967) and Grubel and Lloyd (1975). In addition, another commodity category, noncompeting imports, exists in the model. This category consists of an imported good for which there is no (observed) domestically produced substitute.

In international markets, the Canadian economy is modeled as an "almost" small open economy. In the market for imports, domestic producers and consumers are assumed to take the price of each imported good as given and in perfectly elastic supply at the world price. In export markets domestic producers are assumed to be price makers; that is, they face less than perfectly elastic demand curves for their products.[3] The elasticity of export demand facing producers will vary across industries.

There are two primary factors of production in the model: capital and labor. Each factor is assumed to be homogeneous and mobile across industries and firms. Capital is internationally mobile and in perfectly elastic supply at the world rental rate; labor is internationally immobile. The domestic wage is determined in a perfectly com-

---

[3] For empirical support, in the Canadian case, of the "almost" small open economy hypothesis, see Appelbaum and Kohli (1979).

petitive labor market. The economy's resource endowment consists of a fixed supply of labor and ownership of domestic capital.

The model takes account of a number of tax and tariff distortions in the Canadian economy. All tax, tariff, and subsidy rates are expressed in ad valorem form. Among the domestic taxes incorporated into the model are sales taxes on final domestic consumption, taxation of the use of intermediate goods by different sectors at different rates, producer subsidies, and export taxes. Tariff rates, both domestic and rest of world, are inclusive of ad valorem equivalents of nontariff barriers.

The technology of each competitive industry is represented by a unit cost function. The costs of each industry include not only labor and capital costs but also expenditures on the output of other industries, both domestically produced and imported. The unit cost function, assumed independent of industry output, is specified as a Cobb-Douglas functional form, defined over the input prices of the primary factors and price indices for each of the 30 commodity categories. The price index of each commodity aggregate is assumed to be a Cobb-Douglas subaggregator defined over the price of the corresponding domestically produced and imported commodities. With this specification of technology, substitution in production is not only possible between primary factors and intermediate commodity aggregates but, within each commodity aggregate, is also feasible between domestic and imported goods.

The assumption of constant per unit costs, together with a zero profit condition, requires, in equilibrium, that price in each competitive industry be equal to unit cost.

Each of the 20 noncompetitive industries consists of an endogenously determined number of firms. Within an industry all firms are assumed identical with respect to their technology and economic behavior. Thus it is meaningful to speak of a representative firm within each industry. Freedom of entry and exit exists in all industries, so that firms will enter and exit industries in response to the presence of economic profits or losses. In this manner, in the long run, the number of firms is determined endogenously.

The cost function of each representative firm consists of both variable and fixed costs. The use of primary factors—capital and labor—enters into both the variable and fixed costs of the firm. Variable per unit costs are assumed to be independent of the level of output produced by the firm. The functional form of the firm's unit variable cost function is identical to that of the industry unit cost function in the competitive industries. This is a Cobb-Douglas function specified over the input prices of primary factors and price indices of all commodity aggregates, where each price index is a Cobb-Douglas subaggregator.

So, at the level of the firm in each noncompetitive industry, substitution possibilities exist between intermediate goods (both domestically produced and imported) and primary factors. The fixed costs of the firm consist only of capital and labor costs. The presence of fixed costs in the firm's cost structure is explained by an indivisibility; a fixed amount of capital and labor is required to set up a plant. The specification of constant per unit variable cost plus a fixed cost component leads, at given input prices, to declining average costs that asymptotically approach unit variable cost. In these circumstances, the minimum efficient scale (MES) of the firm is defined as that level of output at which average costs are within 1 percent of unit cost. A measure of the steepness of the average cost curve is given by the cost disadvantage ratio (CDR), which measures the percentage by which average cost at an output level one-half of MES exceeds average cost at MES.

Product specialization or horizontal product diversity within the plant, as distinct from scale economies due to the plant size, has been emphasized by Balassa (1967) and Eastman and Stykolt (1967), among others. Specialization within the plant may be an important source of productivity gains were the plant to rationalize because of a cut in protection. In the model used in this paper no formal allowance is made for production specialization although the empirical scale economies estimates incorporate these costs implicitly.

In each noncompetitive industry, firms are viewed as price makers. Two hypotheses regarding how prices are chosen by firms are considered. The first hypothesis is based on the Negishi (1961) perceived-demand-curve approach. Each representative firm is assumed to perceive a constant-elasticity demand curve for its product. On the basis of this perceived demand curve, the firm chooses a markup of price over unit cost that maximizes profits. The optimal markup chosen in this manner satisfies the familiar Lerner Rule. The elasticity the firm uses in its perceived demand curve corresponds to a "true" elasticity from the underlying general equilibrium model. Price setting in this manner will be referred to as the monopolistic competitive pricing hypothesis (MCPH). The other pricing hypothesis considered will be referred to as the Eastman-Stykolt (1967) hypothesis (ESH). Under the ESH the firm sets its price equal to the price of the import-competing good, inclusive of the domestic tariff. The ESH represents a collusive form of price setting in which the price of the import-competing good acts as a "focal point" for domestic producers. In the policy simulations of the model the actual price selected by the firm is taken to be a weighted average of the prices set according to the MCPH and ESH.

Domestic final demand for each commodity is assumed to be

generated by a single consumer maximizing an aggregate utility function. The utility function takes the form of a Cobb-Douglas function defined over the 30 commodity aggregates. With the exception of the commodity noncompeting imports, each commodity aggregate takes the form of a constant elasticity of substitution (CES) aggregator defined over the domestic and imported goods within each commodity category. Use of the CES subaggregator embodies the Armington assumption that the imported and domestic goods within each commodity category are viewed as imperfect substitutes by the consumer. Given prices for all commodities and the disposable income of the consumer, the demand for each commodity is derived from the utility maximization hypothesis.

The disposable income of the consumer is derived from three sources: ownership of the domestic resource endowment—labor and domestically owned capital, possible economic profits accruing to domestically owned firms in noncompetitive industries, and government transfers. Government revenue is raised through the system of taxes, tariffs, and subsidies in place. All government revenue raised in this manner is returned to the consumer in the form of a lump-sum transfer. Demand for goods and services by government is not modeled separately but assumed to be incorporated as part of the consumer's demand.

Demand for the exports of the domestic country is assumed to be generated by an aggregate rest-of-world consumer with exogenous income. For each commodity category, the exports of domestic country and rest of world (ROW) are viewed as imperfect substitutes as represented by a CES aggregator. Cost minimization results in an export demand equation for each domestic good that is a function of the domestic commodity price, the price of ROW exports, and the foreign tariff on domestic exports. Using this specification of ROW behavior, a distinction is admitted within the export demand equation between the domestic price elasticity and the foreign tariff elasticity.

A distinction is made in the model between the short run and the long run. The short run corresponds to a period of time during which the industrial structure in each of the noncompetitive industries is assumed fixed. By industry structure is meant the markup on unit variable cost set by each firm and the number of firms existing in each industry. A short-run equilibrium of the model is defined as a set of product prices, one for each domestically produced good, and a wage rate such that all product markets and the factor market clear. Walras's Law implies that the balance of payments is in equilibrium. Balance of payments equilibrium refers to current account balance, or requires that the trade surplus be equal to the sum of rental payments on foreign-owned capital and economic profits accruing to foreign ownership of domestic industry. Consistent with a short-run equilibrium is the possibility that, in some industries, firms will be earning pure profits or losses.

The long run of the model corresponds to a time horizon long enough to allow firms to enter or exit all industries in response to the presence of pure profits or losses. A long-run equilibrium is defined as a short-run equilibrium with the additional requirements that in each industry (approximately) zero profits be earned and that the elasticity of the perceived demand curve under MCPH be equal to the elasticity of the firm's true demand curve.

The model has much in common with the traditional Heckscher-Ohlin trade model, in which comparative advantage plays the key role. The comparative advantage effects are present in the model, but in addition there is scope for intraindustry rationalization. The interaction among scale economies, pricing by firms, and free entry provides mechanisms by which intraindustry adjustment occurs. Consider, for example, a cut in the domestic tariff on one industry. If this tariff cut forces domestic firms within the industry to cut price, the existing firms will make losses. Either all firms must expand output, realizing lower costs, or some must exit, leaving remaining firms a larger output. In either case there is a cost efficiency gain as the industry produces at lower average cost. Subsequent interindustry shifts in resources will depend not only on relative factor intensities but also on relative scale economies between industries. It is generally difficult, if not impossible, to get theoretical predictions from a multi-industry model of this sort.

## II.  Calibration of the Model

The model contains a large number of parameters that must be assigned numerical values. The general approach used to parameterize the model is typical of that followed in applied GE work. The parameters of the model are chosen by reference to existing econometric studies and so as to be consistent with a given historical data set—referred to as a benchmark data set. Once the model is parameterized, the benchmark data set is reproduced as an equilibrium of the model. For the present model a benchmark data set was constructed for the Canadian economy for the year 1976. This data set is presumed to represent a short-run equilibrium of the model in which the industrial structure of the noncompetitive industries is held constant. Thus, because of the presence of plant-specific labor and capital, which are taken as fixed in the short run, firms in different industries may be making economic profits or losses. In the long run both of these factors are assumed to be variable; firms will enter and exit industries so as to bring about a situation of zero economic profit across industries. The calibration procedure is to select values for all of the parameters in the model, taking as given the observed markups and number of firms in each industry, to be consistent with the 1976 benchmark data set. The industrial structure variables are then determined endogenously by computing the long-run equilibrium of the model. It is with reference to this long-run equilibrium, referred to as the reference equilibrium, from which the counterfactual policy experiments are undertaken.

On the demand side, the exponents of the consumer's Cobb-Douglas utility function defined over the 30 commodity aggregates are given by the observed expenditure shares in the benchmark data set. Within each commodity aggregate it is not possible, from a single observation, to infer the elasticity of substitution between the imported and domestic goods. In the absence of econometric estimates, the procedure used to select the elasticities of substitution utilizes estimated price elasticities of import demand. Values of the elasticities of substitution are selected so that the own-price elasticities of the import demand functions, evaluated at the benchmark equilibrium, are consistent with the estimated demand elasticities. The selection of the import demand elasticities is based on those reported by Hazledine (1981). The actual best-guess values of the demand elasticities used in the calibration procedure are somewhat larger than those reported by Hazledine. The reason for this is twofold. First, it is known that standard econometric estimates of these elasticities are biased downward in absolute value. Second, they are available at a level of aggregation above that used in the model. Disaggregation will cause the elasticity to rise because of substitution between the various commodities within any given aggregate (see Rousslang and Parker 1981). In the reference equilibrium the import elasticities range from $-1.0$ to $-3.0$.

The export demand functions require the specification of two elasticities: an elasticity of demand for each commodity aggregate and, within each commodity aggregate, an elasticity of substitution between domestic and rest-of-world exports. Within the commodity aggregate, the elasticity of substitution is assigned the same value as the elasticity of substitution between domestic and imported goods. That is, it is assumed the degree to which Canadian and rest-of-world exports are viewed as substitutes in the world market is the same as the degree to which domestic and imported goods are viewed as substitutes by domestic residents. Estimates of export price elasticities are based on those presented in the bibliography of trade elasticities compiled by Stern, Francis, and Schumacher (SFS) (1976). For reasons advanced in the selection of import elasticities the best-guess values of the export elasticities used in the model are somewhat higher than the SFS estimates. The export elasticities in the reference equilibrium range from a low of $-0.9$ to a high of $-3.1$.

In noncompetitive industries the cost functions to be parameterized include both variable and fixed costs. The fixed labor and capital requirements of the firm are selected such that the imputed fixed costs, together with variable costs, lead to a minimum efficient scale (MES) and cost disadvantage ratio (CDR) of operating at a scale less than MES that are consistent with observed estimates. Estimates of MES and CDR for each of the two-digit Canadian manufacturing industries are constructed from the econometric estimates presented, at the three- and four-digit SIC industry levels, in Fuss and Gupta (1979). It is generally believed that econometric estimates of MES and CDR are biased downward, particularly in small economies such as Canada's. Engineering estimates are thought to be more reliable but are difficult to obtain on any comprehensive basis. To account for the downward bias in the econometric estimates, the best-guess estimates of MES and CDR used in the model were uniformly scaled up to a position approximately midway between the econometric estimates and the average engineering estimates.[4]

Once all of the parameters of the model, excluding the industrial structure variables, have been assigned numerical values, the long-run equilibrium is computed. The algorithm used to compute the equilibrium mimics the Marshallian process of adding firms to industries making economic profits and withdrawing firms from industries making economic losses. In qualitative terms the values of the economic aggregates—such as national income, the wage, and government revenues—are, in the long-run equilibrium, close to their short-run values. Finally, there is no assurance that the long-run equilibrium of the model is unique. This is a standard problem general equilibrium models encounter. In practice, however, this problem has not arisen. A number of ad hoc tests, such as beginning the algorithm at different starting points, have been undertaken and in no cases have multiple equilibria been found.

## III. Results of the Trade Liberalization Experiments

In this section the results of the trade liberalization experiments undertaken with the model will be presented. Two trade liberalization

[4] The source of the average engineering estimates is Gorecki (1978). The MES estimates used do not control for horizontal product diversity within the plant. Consequently, "scale economies" implicitly include higher fixed costs associated with a more highly diversified plant. If tariff reduction leads to reduced product diversity these fixed costs would fall. The model does not allow this to happen, which implies that the estimates of welfare gain to tariff removal are, if anything, biased downward.

policies are considered: (1) removal of all domestic tariffs or unilateral free trade (UFT), and (2) removal of all foreign tariffs on domestic exports and domestic tariffs or multilateral free trade (MFT). These policy exercises take the form of counterfactual experiments. In each case tariffs are removed and the new equilibrium of the model is computed and compared with the reference equilibrium. Comparison of the two equilibria yields a prediction of the quantitative change in the values of all of the endogenous variables due to the policy change. Each of the experiments reported considers a comparison of the long-run, zero-profit equilibria of the model.

Within the model the "multilateral free trade" experiment is to be interpreted in a very narrow sense. Strictly speaking the simulation results refer to a case in which all other countries reduce their tariff barriers on Canadian exports but leave in place tariff barriers against all other countries' exports. This would rationalize the assumptions of constant world prices and exogenous export demand functions in the multilateral simulation. For the analysis of true world free trade, one would need a world general equilibrium model in which all prices and incomes are endogenous. The "multilateral cut" simulation, as conducted in this paper, is of interest since it isolates the effect that foreign tariffs have on the Canadian economy. We shall later argue that the quantitative results on multilateral free trade are lower bound estimates for the Canadian gains from world free trade.

The foreign and domestic tariffs used in the trade experiments were derived from a variety of sources and include ad valorem equivalents of some of the relevant nontariff barriers.[5] Domestic tariffs range from a high of 33 percent on textiles and knitting mills to 0 percent in some industries, such as mining. The unweighted average tariff for the manufacturing industries is 11 percent. Foreign tariffs range from a high of 53 percent on textiles to 0 percent on a number of nonmanufacturing products, with an unweighted average on manufactured industries products of 16 percent.

In the model there are four important sets of parameters: import elasticities, export elasticities, MES and CDR estimates, and a parameter that governs, in the noncompetitive industries, the degree to which prices are set according to the two hypotheses—monopolistic competitive pricing (MCPH) and Eastman-Stykolt (1967) (ESH). The first three sets of parameters are based on empirical estimates known

[5] Domestic ad valorem tariff rates were calculated using data on total tariff payments by commodity provided by the Structural Division of Statistics Canada. Sources for the ad valorem equivalents of domestic nontariff barriers (NTB) were Hazledine (1981, table 2) and Economic Council of Canada (1975, table 2-6). Foreign ad valorem tariff rates and ad valorem NTB equivalents were constructed from the rates given by Whalley (1980, table 3) for the United States, the European Common Market (ECC), and Japan.

to be rather unreliable. The fourth parameter can be interpreted as a behavioral hypothesis. The results of the trade experiments are reported initially with the values of each of these parameters set at their best-guess values. Given the nature of all of these parameters, further sensitivity analysis is conducted to examine how the outcomes of the experiments vary as the values of the parameters are altered. The results are reported at two levels. First, results are presented for economywide aggregates such as the wage rate and GNP. Second, results are given at the industry level. Since a large number of industry variables are presented it is not possible to examine in detail each of the industries—such a task is left to the interested reader. However, some discussion will be focused on why particular industries do well and others very poorly under the policy changes.

*Unilateral Free Trade (UFT)*

Aggregate Results

A number of summary statistics that document the impact of UFT on the domestic economy are reported in table 1. With the removal of domestic tariffs, table 1 shows that the domestic economy experiences a welfare gain, measured by the Hicks equivalent variation as a percentage of GNP in the reference equilibrium, of the order of 4 percent.[6] Accompanying this gain in real income is an increase in the domestic wage of 10 percent.[7] An increase in real GNP of about 3.5 percent is also obtained. A large portion of the gain in welfare can be attributed to the rationalization of the manufacturing industries. Removing the domestic tariff has the effect, on average, of increasing the length of production runs in the manufacturing industries by close to 40 percent. Through the rationalization of these industries, the lengthening of production runs of individual firms results in a decline of average fixed costs of just under 20 percent.

The increase in cost efficiency in the manufacturing industries has quite an impact on factor productivity. In particular, there is an increase in aggregate labor productivity of 20 percent. The intersectoral allocation of resources that accompanies UFT is quite interesting. In terms of employment, the manufacturing sector gains at the expense of the rest of the economy. This result is contrary to what one would expect on the basis of traditional comparative advantage,

_____

[6] The Hicks Equivalent Variation is defined as the amount of income that would have to be taken away from the consumer, after the tariff removal, such that the consumer is just as well off as he was in the initial situation, facing the prices prevailing in the initial situation.

[7] The domestic wage is expressed in real terms. It is measured in terms of a bundle of foreign goods imported at constant prices.

TABLE 1

SUMMARY AGGREGATE STATISTICS (% Changes)

| Variable | Unilateral Free Trade | Multilateral Free Trade |
|---|---|---|
| Wage | 9.98 | 25.21 |
| GNE | 3.52 | 12.58 |
| GNP (real) | 3.49 | 7.02 |
| Welfare gain | 4.13 | 8.59 |
| Length of production runs | 41.40 | 66.84 |
| Average fixed costs | − 18.93 | − 29.94 |
| Labor productivity | 19.57 | 32.62 |
| Total factor productivity | 8.58 | 9.50 |
| Trade volume | 53.14 | 88.61 |
| Labor reallocation index | 3.93 | 6.15 |
| Intraindustry trade index | − .70 | − 1.71 |

NOTE.—All relative changes are with respect to the reference (all tariffs in place) equilibrium. (1) GNE and GNP refer to gross national expenditure and product, respectively. (2) The welfare gain is measured as the Hicks Equivalent Variation as a percentage of initial GNE. (3) The length of production run index is the weighted average of output per firm in each manufacturing industry, where the weights are the industries' shares of total manufacturing output. (4) The index of average fixed costs is the weighted average of average fixed costs per firm in each manufacturing industry, where the weights are the industries' shares of total manufacturing output. (5) Labor productivity is defined as output per unit of labor. The labor productivity index is defined as the weighted average of labor productivity in each industry, where the weights are the industries' shares of the total output of all industries. (6) Total factor productivity is measured by a geometric quantity index of all inputs. The aggregate index of total factor productivity is the weighted average of total factor productivity in each industry, where the weights are the industries' shares of the total output of all industries. (7) Total trade volume is the sum of the value of exports and imports across all industries, including noncompeting imports. (8) The intraindustry trade index is the weighted average of the Balassa-Grubel-Lloyd (BGL) intraindustry trade index in each industry, where the weights are the industries' shares of total trade volume. The BGL index is defined as

$$1 - \frac{|E_i - M_i|}{E_i + M_i},$$

where $E_i$ and $M_i$ represent the value of industry $i$'s exports and imports, respectively. (9) The labor reallocation index measures the percentage of the total labor that must reallocate between industries.

which would argue, in the case of Canada, that trade liberalization would lead to an expansion of the primary sector at the expense of manufacturing. That this did not happen suggests that the increase in absolute productive efficiency in the manufacturing sector, brought about through rationalization effects, was sufficient to shift comparative advantage in favor of manufacturing.

These results suggest that there are significant benefits to be obtained from a policy of UFT, and furthermore that most of these benefits are achieved through rationalization of the manufacturing sector.

## Industry Results

Statistics summarizing the impact of UFT on individual industries are presented in table 2. First, in terms of gross output and value added, UFT leads to an expansion in all of the nonmanufacturing industries. In the manufacturing sector, gross output increases in 75 percent of

TABLE 2

INDUSTRY STATISTICS: UNILATERAL FREE TRADE (% Changes)

| Industry | Output | Value Added | Net Exports | Labor Productivity | Scale Elasticity | Markups |
|---|---|---|---|---|---|---|
| 1. Food and beverage | 12.61 | -12.40 | -481.03 | 22.33 | 6.64 | -35.10 |
| 2. Tobacco | 28.31 | -16.80 | 72.90 | 36.80 | 12.22 | -53.78 |
| 3. Rubber and plastic | 32.06 | 16.63 | -267.42 | 15.01 | 5.15 | -27.78 |
| 4. Leather | -13.94 | -26.82 | -248.46 | 21.52 | 7.66 | -56.65 |
| 5. Textiles | 15.17 | -3.60 | -260.43 | 18.48 | 6.61 | -54.62 |
| 6. Knitting mills | -24.05 | -43.63 | -283.76 | 32.45 | 12.68 | -95.06 |
| 7. Clothing | -22.77 | -43.89 | -374.93 | 43.93 | 12.68 | -62.69 |
| 8. Wood | 10.20 | -.47 | 3.36 | 12.02 | 5.23 | -24.41 |
| 9. Furniture and fixtures | -9.07 | -21.85 | -308.93 | 20.67 | 7.85 | -46.54 |
| 10. Paper and allied products | 18.47 | 6.86 | 16.47 | 11.22 | 5.54 | -39.05 |
| 11. Printing and publishing | 5.89 | .33 | -237.63 | 10.88 | 4.47 | -20.76 |
| 12. Primary metals | 42.85 | 30.24 | 42.59 | 11.24 | 3.09 | -18.92 |
| 13. Metal fabricating | 20.94 | 9.95 | -252.43 | 14.11 | 5.08 | -29.94 |

| | | | | | | |
|---|---|---|---|---|---|---|
| 14. Machinery | 5.41 | -.44 | -221.02 | 12.25 | 3.27 | -21.81 |
| 15. Transportation equipment | 105.53 | 88.98 | 229.04 | 13.98 | 1.26 | -5.99 |
| 16. Electrical products | 5.80 | -4.46 | -244.07 | 15.23 | 5.90 | -38.50 |
| 17. Nonmetallic mineral production | 19.47 | 8.32 | 83.42 | 11.03 | 5.10 | -19.79 |
| 18. Petroleum and coal | 11.82 | 11.00 | 29.34 | 12.75 | .40 | -4.10 |
| 19. Chemical products | 13.66 | 4.38 | -231.74 | 10.90 | 3.60 | -23.38 |
| 20. Misc. manufacturing | -.44 | -9.94 | -241.45 | 15.73 | 5.19 | -40.53 |
| 21. Agriculture | 4.79 | 5.61 | -18.22 | 9.13 | | |
| 22. Forestry | 9.55 | 15.65 | -675.28 | 4.18 | | |
| 23. Fishing | 3.74 | 6.83 | -20.20 | 6.81 | | |
| 24. Mining | 5.07 | 8.02 | -51.68 | 6.98 | | |
| 25. Construction | 1.38 | 4.27 | -225.93 | 6.93 | | |
| 26. Transportation | .88 | 5.65 | -21.32 | 5.02 | | |
| 27. Communication | .85 | 6.36 | -831.36 | 4.28 | | |
| 28. Electric, power, and gas | 7.16 | 9.35 | -5.16 | 7.77 | | |
| 29. Others | 2.96 | 7.01 | -60.56 | 5.83 | | |

NOTE.—All relative changes are with respect to the reference (all tariffs in place) equilibrium. (1) Net exports are defined as the difference between exports and imports. The relative change is measured with respect to the absolute value of net exports. (2) Labor productivity is defined as output per unit of labor. (3) The scale elasticity or local measure of scale economies is measured as the ratio of marginal to average cost. (4) The markup is defined as the ratio of price to unit variable cost.

the industries, while value added increases in only eight of the 20 industries. An interesting feature of the manufacturing sector is the magnitude with which changes in output occur. Within the manufacturing sector 12 industries expand their output by greater than 10 percent, while in the nonmanufacturing sector all relative output changes are less than 10 percent. Similar results are apparent with respect to changes in value added.

The change in the pattern of trade is also quite revealing. In all industries both exports and imports rise. Thus, significant import substitution occurs, but at the same time all manufacturing industries increase their exports. Table 2 reveals that on balance, in 13 of the manufacturing industries, the increase in imports exceeds that of exports. In the case of the nonmanufacturing sector all industries experience an increase in imports relative to exports. In the reference equilibrium the net surplus of the nonmanufacturing sector, excluding noncompeting imports, is approximately $6.25 billion. In the manufacturing sector plus noncompeting imports there is a deficit of $4.11 billion. Under UFT the surplus in the nonmanufacturing sector falls to $3.18 billion, but the manufacturing sector moves into a surplus position of approximately $3.02 billion. Thus, under UFT, the trade surplus as a whole increases, offset by increases in capital imports, and both manufacturing and nonmanufacturing sectors move into approximately equal positions in terms of their net surplus position.

Under UFT, labor productivity increases in all industries. In the manufacturing sector the increases are particularly large, with labor productivity increasing by at least 10 percent in all industries. In fact, in six industries labor productivity increases by over 20 percent, with the largest increase by clothing at 44 percent. The gains in labor productivity in the manufacturing sector are apparent from the increase in the values of the scale elasticities. In all industries economies of scale have been achieved by longer production runs. The reason for the increases in the length of production runs is apparent from examining what has happened to markups in each industry. In all industries the markups have fallen and in 11 industries the fall has been quite dramatic—over 30 percent. Recall that under the ESH firms set their prices equal to the border price of the import-competing good, inclusive of the domestic tariff. The removal of the domestic tariff will thus cause firms to lower their prices. In the presence of declining average costs, the lower markup means that firms must increase their output if they are to remain profitable. In equilibrium this larger output per firm must translate into fewer firms or larger industry output. As is evident from table 2, both results have occurred in many manufacturing industries.

An examination of the changes in output and employment in the manufacturing sector indicates that while some industries prosper other industries decline as a result of UFT. In order to understand better why some industries do well and others poorly, it is instructive to examine in detail an industry in each category. On the basis of employment, transportation equipment is the overwhelming winner, with an 80 percent increase in employment. The reasons why transportation equipment does well are quite apparent. In the reference equilibrium, the ratio of fixed costs to variable costs in this industry is among the highest in the manufacturing sector. Economies of scale are far from being exhausted. Under these circumstances the possibility of substantial rationalization exists. With UFT a high degree of rationalization does in fact occur. Markups fall by 6 percent, and this is accompanied by increases in production runs of 14 percent. Given the unexploited economies of scale that exist in the reference equilibrium, the larger output leads to significant decreases in average costs. The fall in the industry price, given the very elastic export demand curve this industry faces, allows the industry to do quite well in export markets. A significant portion of the extra output is exported, as is reflected from the increase of net exports by over 200 percent.

In contrast, consider a losing industry under UFT. The biggest loser is clothing, with a 46 percent fall in employment and a 45 percent fall in value added. This industry has virtually the worst of all possible characteristics from the point of view of surviving import competition. In the reference equilibrium the domestic tariff is quite high at 32 percent. There are some unexploited scale economies but these are very moderate. The industry is very labor intensive, which means that increases in the wage rate significantly affect its costs. Nevertheless, rationalization effects do occur, with the length of production runs more than doubling, accompanied by a great deal of exit from the industry. However, this is not sufficient to prevent the industry from declining. With the removal of the tariff and the large fall in the price imports the industry faces strong foreign competition. Import substitution on the part of domestic consumers and firms leads to a large increase in the volume of imports.

*Multilateral Free Trade (MFT)*

Aggregate Results

The aggregate results of the MFT experiment are presented in table 1. In comparison with UFT it is seen that all of the aggregate variables experience larger relative changes. Under MFT the real income gain to Canadians, measured by the Hicks Equivalent Variation, is about

$13.2 billion or 8.6 percent of reference GNE. This welfare gain is more than double that achieved under UFT. The increase in the wage is also quite striking, an increase of 25 percent. Gross national expenditure increases by about $20 billion in the new equilibrium—a relative change of 12.5 percent. The primary source of these gains of real income is again the rationalization effects within industries and the resulting intersectoral reallocation of resources from a comparative advantage point of view. Evidence of rationalization within industries is apparent from examining what happens to the length of production runs and average fixed costs. The length of production runs increases by 67 percent while the index of average fixed costs falls by 30 percent. The results these rationalization effects have on productivity are quite dramatic. Labor productivity rises by 33 percent, total factor productivity by a more modest 10 percent.

The magnitude of the intersectoral resource shifts induced by MFT is not large. Six percent of the labor force is reallocated intersectorally. What is interesting is that the pattern of intersectoral shifts is, as in the case of UFT, quite the opposite of what one would expect from a traditional comparative advantage point of view. In terms of employment, the manufacturing sector gains at the expense of the rest of the economy. Total employment in manufacturing increases by 12 percent.

A dramatic increase in trade volume accompanies the move to MFT. Trade volume increases from $84 billion in the reference equilibrium to about $160 billion in the new equilibrium, a gain of 89 percent. As in the UFT case, under MFT the manufacturing sector moves from an initial deficit position in the trade account to a surplus position. The resulting change in intraindustry trade is negligible, suggesting that the increase in trade volume is accounted for, roughly, by an equal increase in intraindustry and interindustry trade.

How do the multilateral cut results relate to the results one might obtain for world free trade? Since we do not have a world model, we can only offer an educated guess. There are two effects to consider, both of which are likely to increase the Canadian gains to free trade. First, world free trade, as it is likely to be income creating, should not result in adverse shifts in Canadian export demand equations on average. Second is the question of terms-of-trade shifts. One probable scenario is that real world wages would, on average, tend to rise more than the real rental rate on capital services. As Canada, in 1976, was a net capital service importer and net commodities exporter, this terms-of-trade effect should in general raise Canadian real income. We therefore tentatively suggest that the welfare results of the multilateral tariff cuts underestimate the true 1976 gain to Canada from world free trade.

## Industry Results

In table 3 the industry results from the MFT experiments are presented. In terms of gross output almost all industries expand their production. Indeed, 15 expand their output by over 25 percent. The four industries that contract under MFT are within the manufacturing sector. The results in terms of value added are similar, though less pronounced. Twenty industries increase their production of value added, and of these 19 increase by over 10 percent. Although most industries expand their production, measured by either gross output or value added, the impact on employment is not as uniform. Only 13 industries actually increase their employment under MFT. In the manufacturing sector the results are particularly diverse, with only nine industries increasing their employment.

In examining the productivity and cost efficiency statistics the impact of rationalization effects is quite apparent. In the manufacturing sector, all industries increase the length of their production runs. In the case of 17 industries, the increase is greater than 50 percent. The lengthening of production runs is accompanied by a fall in both scale elasticities and markups in all industries. Clearly an important impact of MFT is the realization of unexploited scale economies, gains larger than those achieved under UFT.

In terms of winners and losers, the industry that does best on the basis of employment and value added is transportation equipment. The reasons why transportation equipment does so well are the same as those discussed under UFT. This industry does better under MFT than UFT, of course, because its competitive position in world markets improves with the removal of foreign tariffs. The industries that do poorly under MFT—leather, knitting mills, clothing, and furniture—share in common the characteristic of a very labor intensive technology. Clearly, the 25 percent increase in the real wage puts these industries in a very poor position relative to imports. Indeed in one case, that of knitting mills, import competition is so great that the industry is virtually wiped out.

## IV. Sensitivity Results

In tables 4 and 5 the results of some sensitivity tests with respect to the key parameters in the model are presented. Four sets of sensitivity experiments were conducted. First, the import elasticities are varied

TABLE 3

INDUSTRY STATISTICS: MULTILATERAL FREE TRADE (% Changes)

| Industry | Output | Value Added | Net Exports | Labor Productivity | Scale Elasticity | Markups |
|---|---|---|---|---|---|---|
| 1. Food and beverage | 29.07 | -4.63 | 9.63 | 36.41 | 43.06 | -46.47 |
| 2. Tobacco | 31.78 | -18.18 | 12.09 | 52.61 | 14.69 | -63.25 |
| 3. Rubber and plastic | 42.76 | 23.75 | -288.13 | 26.68 | 8.06 | -42.28 |
| 4. Leather | -13.14 | -26.85 | -277.82 | 35.74 | 11.03 | -79.11 |
| 5. Textiles | 94.17 | 62.55 | -242.05 | 30.10 | 8.77 | -70.98 |
| 6. Knitting mills | 6.74 | -21.32 | -321.94 | 41.96 | 12.82 | -114.75 |
| 7. Clothing | 68.42 | 21.86 | -127.58 | 62.18 | 14.78 | -74.55 |
| 8. Wood | 11.89 | -3.02 | -16.08 | 23.39 | 9.40 | -42.14 |
| 9. Furniture and fixtures | -18.37 | -30.15 | -385.10 | 34.11 | 11.29 | -64.87 |
| 10. Paper and allied products | 95.78 | 78.49 | 204.94 | 20.24 | 7.81 | -53.89 |
| 11. Printing and publishing | 34.23 | 27.82 | 8.84 | 20.50 | 8.36 | -37.42 |
| 12. Primary metals | 37.53 | 20.69 | -44.37 | 21.92 | 5.77 | -34.51 |
| 13. Metal fabricating | 22.61 | 10.51 | -295.93 | 25.93 | 8.23 | -47.06 |

| | | | | | | |
|---|---|---|---|---|---|---|
| 14. Machinery | −7.03 | −13.03 | −245.82 | 24.55 | 6.37 | −41.30 |
| 15. Transportation equipment | 121.84 | 98.19 | 255.68 | 25.85 | 2.56 | −11.94 |
| 16. Electrical products | 1.90 | −8.16 | −274.28 | 27.23 | 9.13 | −57.85 |
| 17. Nonmetallic mineral production | 25.21 | 11.28 | 152.22 | 20.28 | 8.66 | −32.42 |
| 18. Petroleum and coal | 25.96 | 15.75 | −19.41 | 26.94 | .91 | 9.48 |
| 19. Chemical products | 28.85 | 15.90 | −274.17 | 21.30 | 6.26 | −39.69 |
| 20. Misc. manufacturing | −10.46 | −19.93 | −284.96 | 28.79 | 8.54 | −64.60 |
| 21. Agriculture | 60.63 | 67.60 | 245.40 | 20.01 | | |
| 22. Forestry | 31.23 | 50.73 | 297.11 | 9.02 | | |
| 23. Fishing | 32.14 | 44.50 | 173.70 | 14.50 | | |
| 24. Mining | 28.46 | 38.38 | 47.21 | 16.24 | | |
| 25. Construction | 4.04 | 14.40 | −300.21 | 13.97 | | |
| 26. Transportation | 1.52 | 14.67 | −47.25 | 10.85 | | |
| 27. Communication | 2.37 | 16.73 | −1,471.70 | 9.81 | | |
| 28. Electric, power, and gas | 17.28 | 24.82 | −15.12 | 17.65 | | |
| 29. Others | 6.23 | 18.02 | −153.45 | 12.70 | | |

NOTE.—All relative changes are with respect to the reference (all tariffs in place) equilibrium. All variables are defined as in table 2.

TABLE 4

SENSITIVITY ANALYSIS: UNILATERAL FREE TRADE

| | Elasticity of Imports Scaling Parameter MSCAL | | | | |
|---|---|---|---|---|---|
| MSCAL | .33 | .66 | 1.0 | 1.33 | 1.66 |
| Welfare gain | 1.65 | 2.76 | 4.18 | 5.96 | 8.27 |
| Wage | .24 | 4.69 | 9.98 | 16.36 | 23.42 |
| Trade volume | 12.20 | 29.40 | 53.14 | 82.05 | 110.75 |
| Labor productivity | 5.62 | 11.37 | 19.57 | 30.06 | 41.20 |
| | Elasticity of Exports Scaling Parameter XSCAL | | | | |
| XSCAL | .17 | .33 | .66 | 1.0 | 2.0 |
| Welfare gain | 4.28 | 4.25 | 4.19 | 4.18 | 3.97 |
| Wage | 10.47 | 10.36 | 10.16 | 9.98 | 9.48 |
| Trade volume | 53.69 | 53.58 | 53.36 | 53.14 | 52.61 |
| Labor productivity | 19.59 | 19.58 | 19.57 | 19.57 | 19.56 |
| | Minimum Efficient Scale Scaling Parameter NSCAL | | | | |
| NSCAL | .33 | .66 | 1.0 | 1.33 | |
| Welfare gain | 2.51 | 3.23 | 4.13 | 5.40 | |
| Wage | 4.31 | 6.85 | 9.98 | 14.05 | |
| Trade volume | 33.21 | 40.97 | 53.14 | 67.65 | |
| Labor productivity | 7.04 | 11.32 | 19.57 | 31.88 | |
| | Pricing Hypothesis Parameter PSCAL | | | | |
| PSCAL | .2 | .4 | .5 | .6 | .7 |
| Welfare gain | 1.91 | 3.29 | 4.13 | 5.14 | 7.85 |
| Wage | 5.56 | 8.25 | 9.98 | 12.20 | 18.96 |
| Trade volume | 49.27 | 52.02 | 53.14 | 54.41 | 59.38 |
| Labor productivity | 16.19 | 18.26 | 19.57 | 21.38 | 27.55 |

NOTE.—The percentage changes reported in each column are relative to the all-tariffs-in-place equilibrium. In each case the values of all scaling parameters are at their base values, except for the parameter under consideration.

by uniformly scaling them up and down by a factor of proportionality referred to as MSCAL. The higher the import elasticity, the more prone domestic industries are to import competition. Furthermore, the import elasticity determines the extent to which foreign and domestic goods are viewed as substitutes. If these goods are highly substitutable, then it will have the effect of raising the price elasticity of export demand but not the foreign tariff elasticity. The second sensitivity study is on export elasticities; these are all scaled up and down by a parameter called XSCAL. An increase in the export elasticity will increase the price and foreign tariff elasticity of domestic export demand. The third sensitivity experiment is on the economies of scale estimates; the adjustment parameter is referred to as NSCAL. The final sensitivity experiment is with respect to the pricing hypothesis of firms in noncompetitive industries. Recall that the price set by firms is a weighted average of the prices determined by the monopolistically

TABLE 5

SENSITIVITY ANALYSIS: MULTILATERAL FREE TRADE

| | Elasticity of Imports Scaling Parameter MSCAL | | | | |
|---|---|---|---|---|---|
| MSCAL | .33 | .66 | 1.0 | 1.33 | 1.66 |
| Welfare gain | 8.96 | 7.96 | 8.59 | 10.07 | 12.19 |
| Wage | 22.88 | 22.85 | 25.21 | 29.51 | 34.77 |
| Trade volume | 55.09 | 68.13 | 88.60 | 114.18 | 140.00 |
| Labor productivity | 23.77 | 26.47 | 32.62 | 41.60 | 51.54 |
| | Elasticity of Exports Scaling Parameter XSCAL | | | | |
| XSCAL | .17 | .33 | .66 | 1.0 | 2.0 |
| Welfare gain | 4.89 | 5.50 | 6.90 | 8.59 | 16.70 |
| Wage | 12.53 | 14.60 | 19.46 | 25.21 | 53.24 |
| Trade volume | 58.75 | 63.96 | 75.38 | 88.60 | 146.45 |
| Labor productivity | 21.46 | 23.42 | 27.74 | 32.62 | 52.27 |
| | Minimum Efficient Scale Scaling Parameter NSCAL | | | | |
| NSCAL | .33 | .66 | 1.0 | 1.33 | |
| Welfare gain | 6.11 | 7.14 | 8.59 | 10.83 | |
| Wage | 18.07 | 20.90 | 25.21 | 31.42 | |
| Trade volume | 67.60 | 74.42 | 88.60 | 108.23 | |
| Labor productivity | 18.52 | 22.88 | 32.62 | 48.03 | |
| | Pricing Hypothesis Parameter PSCAL | | | | |
| PSCAL | .2 | .4 | .5 | .6 | .8 |
| Welfare gain | 4.31 | 6.87 | 8.59 | 10.75 | 16.32 |
| Wage | 14.73 | 20.95 | 25.21 | 30.85 | 50.84 |
| Trade volume | 70.92 | 82.07 | 88.60 | 96.55 | 122.81 |
| Labor productivity | 22.26 | 28.44 | 32.62 | 37.99 | 56.98 |

NOTE.—See table 4 n.

competitive price $p_{MCPH}$ and the Eastman-Stykolt price $p_{ESH}$. The formula is:

$$p = (1 - PSCAL) \cdot p_{MCPH} + PSCAL \cdot p_{ESH} \quad 0 \leqslant PSCAL \leqslant 1.$$

Various values of the parameter PSCAL are considered, with increases in PSCAL leading to a higher weight being attached to the more collusive ESH price.

The values of the parameters MSCAL, XSCAL, and NSCAL are all set equal to one in the reference equilibrium, while the parameter PSCAL is set equal to 0.5. First, consider the impact of altering the value of MSCAL. Letting MSCAL vary from 0.33 to 1.33 results in the real income gains of UFT varying from a low of 1.6 to a high of 8 percent—quite significant changes. Under MFT the range in which the measured real income gains vary is smaller: from 7.9 to 12 percent. In this case the welfare gain actually falls and then rises. The lower gains to MFT occur for values of MSCAL close to the base values. As one might expect the volume of trade is quite sensitive to changes in the import elasticity, for both UFT and MFT. Labor productivity is also quite sensitive to altering the import elasticities. In the case of UFT the variation in labor productivity is quite large, varying from a value of 5.6 to 41 percent. The explanation of this is straightforward: import competition will lead to more industry rationalization the greater the extent to which foreign goods actually compete with domestically produced goods. The results from this experiment indicate that the gains to UFT are quite sensitive to the actual values of the import elasticities, more so than the MFT results. For all values of the import elasticities the gains in real income under MFT are equal to or greater than 8 percent.

In the export elasticity experiment, the value of XSCAL varies from a low of one-third to a high of twice the base value. Under UFT the measured gain in welfare is very insensitive to variations in XSCAL. The welfare gain varies slightly, from a low of 4 percent to a high of 4.3 percent—quite insignificant. However, this is not true under MFT. In this case the gain in welfare varies considerably, from a low of 4.9 percent to a high of 17 percent. Particularly in the upper range of the export elasticities the welfare gains get quite large. The industry results are not reported, but for the higher values of the export elasticities, a number of domestic industries shut down. The rationalization effects become quite strong and the economy moves to a more specialized pattern of production. With regard to trade volume and labor productivity the results parallel those of the welfare measure. Under UFT, both indexes show little variation while under MFT the indexes are quite sensitive, both increasing substantially with increases in XSCAL. Trade volume increases from a low of 58 percent to a high of over 140 percent; labor productivity increases from 21 percent to 52 percent. Overall this experiment suggests that values of the export elasticities are quite significant to determining the benefits to MFT but insignificant in the case UFT.

The results of the economies-of-scale experiments are of considerable interest. Recall that the cost functions of the noncompetitive firms are scaled so as to reproduce observed MES and CDR estimates. The extent of economies of scale will thus vary directly with the magnitude of these estimates. The base estimates lie midway between the econometric and average engineering estimates. Since there is a great deal of controversy surrounding the reliability of these estimates, the parameter NSCAL was varied from a low of one-third the base value to 1.33 times the base value. Not surprisingly, both the UFT and MFT results are sensitive to these variations. Increasing NSCAL results in substantial increases in the volume of trade and labor productivity for both trade policies. Indeed, under MFT, labor productivity increases by 48 percent when NSCAL reaches 1.33. The estimated welfare gains are also quite sensitive. For UFT, the welfare gain varies from a low of 2.5 percent to a high of 5.4 percent. Under MFT, the gain varies from a low of 6.1 percent to a high of 10.8 percent. For values not reported, as NSCAL increases beyond 1.33 a number of industries cease to operate, under both UFT and MFT. As in the case of high values of the export elasticities, a movement to freer trade involves increased specialization within the manufacturing sector of the economy. It is the labor-intensive, low-economies-of-scale manufacturing industries that shut down. In summary, the benefits of both UFT and MFT are sensitive to assumptions about the degree of scale economies, although in both cases they are positive and significantly so. Even extremely conservative estimates of scale economies yield welfare gains to MFT of 6 percent.

The last set of experiments conducted report the findings of varying the pricing hypothesis parameter PSCAL. The nature of the parameter PSCAL is different from that of the others in that it influences the actual pricing behavior of domestic firms. The value of PSCAL ranges from a low of 0.2 to a high of 0.8, low values weighting greater than the MCPH hypothesis and high values the ESH. The results of the model turn out to be quite sensitive to changes in PSCAL. The gain in welfare varies considerably. Under UFT the range is from 2 percent to a high of 7.8 percent. For MFT the variation is even larger and increases from a low of 4 percent to a high of 16.3 percent. The results for trade volume and labor productivity follow a similar pattern, with high values obtaining with increases in PSCAL. At the industry level a number of industries begin to shut down as the ESH in pure form is more closely approximated; this holds true for both UFT and MFT. Again the first industries to close down are the labor-intensive ones as the economy begins to specialize. The results of this experiment indicate that the impact of UFT and MFT is sensitive to the underlying behavioral hypothesis in the noncompetitive industries. Larger benefits to freer trade are achieved the greater the degree to which domestic industry responds to foreign price competition.

## V. Conclusions

This paper has investigated the potential impact of two trade liberalization policies on the Canadian economy. Important features of the general equilibrium model used to examine these questions include the presence of economies of scale and imperfect competition within the manufacturing sector. Using a 1976 data set, we performed counterfactual policy experiments with the model. The findings of the experiments indicate that trade liberalization would provide large benefits to the Canadian economy. For a wide range of parameter values, the welfare gains from a unilateral free trade policy were found to be in a range of 2–5 percent of GNP, while the benefits to multilateral free trade were found to lie in the range of 8–10 percent of GNP—numbers much larger than conventional estimates. The mechanism through which many of these benefits are achieved is intraindustry rationalization. Indeed, the intersectoral reallocation of labor was found to be reasonably small under both trade policies, suggesting that the adjustment costs of adopting a free trade policy may not be large.

The incorporation of economies of scale and imperfect competition within a general equilibrium model provides an additional channel through which resource allocation is determined, a possibility that does not exist in conventional trade models. The results of the experiments reported here indicate that for the Canadian economy intraindustry rationalization is an important channel through which benefits from trade liberalization are achieved. The message seems to be that economic models that ignore the industrial organization aspects of the economy, at least small open economies, may seriously underestimate the benefits to trade liberalization. If one accepts economies of scale and imperfect competition as relevant to small open economies with a significant industrial sector, the policy implications are clear: the costs of protection are very high and efforts to promote free trade are well founded on grounds of gains in economic efficiency. The results were shown to be sensitive to the trade elasticities and scale economy parameters. Because of the great importance of these parameters, it is of some importance to get reliable estimates. The overall significance of the methodological framework used in this paper will be fully known only when similar studies are carried out for other small open economies.

## Appendix

This Appendix outlines the equations of the model. For the sake of brevity the model will be detailed without taxes, tariffs, or subsidies. In the empirical implementation of the model most of the relevant tax and tariff distortions are present; see Harris (1984$b$) for more details.

1. *Notation*

| | |
|---|---|
| $N$: | index set for noncompetitive industries |
| $C$: | index set for competitive industries |
| $B$: | index set for noncompeting imports |

$$M = N \cup C, \quad G = M \cup B$$

| | |
|---|---|
| $(p_i)_{i \in M}$ | domestic commodity prices |
| $(p_i^*)_{i \in M}$ | foreign commodity prices |
| $(q_i)_{i \in B}$ | foreign prices on noncompeting imports |
| $w$: | domestic wage |
| $r$: | world rental rate on capital |
| $P = (p, p^*, q, r, w)$: | price system. |

## 2. Technology

All firms have a variable unit cost function $V^i(P)$, assumed independent of the level of output, of the form

$$\log V^i(P) = \alpha_{0i} + \Sigma_{j \in M}\alpha_{ij} \log w_j^i + \Sigma_{K \in B} \log q_{ik} + \alpha_{iw} \log w + \alpha_{ir} \log r. \tag{A1}$$

$w_j^i$ is the price index of a composite input used by industry $i$, a composite of both foreign and domestic inputs from commodity $j$. $w_j^i$ is assumed to have the form

$$\log w_j^i = \beta_{ij} \log p_j + (1 - \beta_{ij}) \log p_j^*. \tag{A2}$$

If price-taking behavior in input markets is assumed, the input-output matrices for the economy are derived from the unit cost functions by applying Shepard's lemma. The domestic Leontief matrix $A(P) \equiv [a_{ij}(P)]$ is defined by

$$a_{ij}(P) = \frac{\alpha_{ij}\beta_{ij}V^i(P)}{p_j}, \tag{A3}$$

where $a_{ij}$ is the demand for domestic good $j$, per unit output of domestic good $i$. The Leontief matrix for foreign imports $A^*(P)$ is defined as

$$a_{ij}^*(P) = \frac{a_{ij}(1 - \beta_{ij})V^i(P)}{p_j^*}. \tag{A4}$$

The fixed costs of each representative firm in each noncompetitive industry, $i \in N$, are given by the function

$$F_i(r, w) = rf_K^i + wf_L^i, \tag{A5}$$

where $f_K^i$ and $f_L^i$ are the minimum amounts of capital and labor, respectively, needed to set up a plant.

## 3. Exports

We assume there is a world demand for a composite export good $Q$, which is an aggregate of all relevant countries' exports. The composite export good is defined by

$$Q = [\beta X^{-\lambda} + (1 - \beta)X^{*-\lambda}]^{-(1/\lambda)}, \tag{A6}$$

where $X$ is domestic exports and $X^*$ is all other countries' exports; $\sigma^* = 1/(1 + \lambda)$ is the elasticity of substitution between domestic and other exports in world demand. Letting $p$ and $p^*$ be the prices paid by world consumers of domestic and other exports, the dual price index for the export composite is

$$P = [\beta^{\sigma^*}p^{(1 - \sigma^*)} + (1 - \beta)^{\sigma^*}p^{*(1 - \sigma^*)}]^{1/(1 - \sigma^*)}. \tag{A7}$$

For a given $Q$, cost minimization yields the demand for domestic exports

$$X = \beta^{\sigma^*}\left(\frac{P}{p}\right)^{\sigma^*}Q. \tag{A8}$$

Assuming a constant elasticity demand for world exports of the form

$$Q = \alpha P^{-\epsilon} \tag{A9}$$

yields, on substitution into (A8), the demand for domestic exports given by

$$X = \frac{\alpha \beta^{\sigma^*} [\beta^{\sigma^*} p^{(1-\sigma^*)} + (1 - \beta)^{\sigma^*} p^{*(1-\sigma^*)}]^{(\sigma^* - \epsilon)/(1-\sigma^*)}}{p^{\sigma^*}}. \tag{A10}$$

### 4. Domestic Final Demand

The consumer's utility function over commodity aggregates is given by the log-linear form

$$\log U = a_0 + \Sigma_{i \in G} a_i \log C_i. \tag{A11}$$

For noncompeting imports, $i \in B$, $C_i$ represents the amount of the import good. For all other industries, $i \in M$, $C_i$ is the CES aggregator over foreign and domestic goods:

$$C_i = [\delta_i x_i^{\rho_i} + (1 - \delta_i) X_i^{*\rho_i}]^{1/\rho_i}. \tag{A12}$$

Given disposable income $Y$ and prices $P$, the demand for domestic good $X_i$ is given by

$$X_i = \frac{a_i Y \delta_i^{\sigma_i} p_i^{\sigma_i}}{\delta_i^{\sigma_i} p_i^{1-\sigma_i} + (1 - \delta_i)^{\sigma_i} p_i^{*1-\sigma_i}}. \tag{A13}$$

### 5. Short-Run Equilibrium

The industry structure variables held constant in the short run are markups on unit costs by firms, $i \in N$, $(m_i) = m$; number of firms in each industry, $i \in N$, $(Fm_i) = Fm$. Let $S = (m, Fm)$ be the vector of structural variables. Aggregate consumer income is given by

$$Y = wL + rK_D + \Psi \Sigma_{i \in N} \pi_i, \tag{A14}$$

where $L$ is the aggregate labor endowment, $K_D$ the domestic capital endowment, $\pi_i$ the short-run profits or losses in industry $i \in N$, and $\Psi$ the share of domestic ownership in industry.

Equilibrium commodity prices are determined by the equations

$$p_i = m_i V^i(P), \quad i \in N$$
$$p_i = V^i(P), \quad i \in C. \tag{A15}$$

Letting $X(P, Y, S)$ and $E(P)$ denote final demand vectors, commodity market clearing implies the vector of total outputs, $\mathbf{Z}$, must satisfy

$$\mathbf{Z} = [I - A(P)^T]^{-1} [X(P, Y, S) + E(P)]. \tag{A16}$$

Given the vector of domestic outputs, labor market equilibrium requires

$$L = \Sigma_{i \in M} a_{iw}(P) Z_i + \Sigma_{i \in N} Fm_i \cdot f_L^i, \tag{A17}$$

where $a_{iw}$ is the labor requirements coefficient in industry $i$. Industry profits $\pi_i$ are

$$\pi_i = Fm_i \left[ (p_i - V^i) \left( \frac{Z_i}{Fm_i} \right) - F_i(r, w) \right]. \tag{A18}$$

TRADE LIBERALIZATION                                           143

A short-run equilibrium for a given $S$ is a wage $w(S)$, domestic commodity price vector $p(S)$, income $Y(S)$, and vector of outputs $Z(S)$ satisfying (A15)–(A18). Walras's Law implies a balance of payments equilibrium of the form

$$\Sigma_{i \in M}\, p_i E_i - \Sigma_{i \in G}\, p_i^* M_i = r(K - K_D) + (1 - \Psi)\Sigma_{i \in N}\, \pi_i, \quad (A19)$$

where $K$ is the total domestic demand for capital services.

## 6. *Firm Behavior*

Under the monopolistically competitive pricing hypothesis, each firm in industry $i \in N$ perceives an industry demand curve of the constant elasticity form

$$Z_i = \Psi_i p_i^{-\epsilon_i}. \quad (A20)$$

Under the assumption that industry demand is shared equally among firms, the optimal pricing rule is given by

$$\frac{p_i - V^i}{p_i} = \frac{1}{Fm_i\epsilon_i}. \quad (A21)$$

In the long run the perceived elasticity is equated to the elasticity of the true demand curve, which is given by

$$\epsilon_i = \frac{(X_i)}{(Z_i)}\, \eta_x^i + \frac{(E_i)}{(Z_i)}\, \eta_\epsilon^i$$

$$+ \Sigma_{j \in M}\, \frac{(I_j^i)}{(Z_i)}\, \eta_I^i, \quad (A22)$$

where $\eta_x^i$ is the elasticity of final demand, $\eta_\epsilon^i$ is the elasticity of exports, $\eta_I^i$ is the elasticity of intermediate demand, and $I_j^i = a_{ji}Z_j$, intermediate use of commodity $i$ by industry $j$.

Under the Eastman-Stykolt pricing hypothesis,

$$p_i = q_i^*(1 + t_i), \quad (A23)$$

where $t_i$ is the domestic tariff.

## References

Appelbaum, Elie, and Kohli, Ulrich R. "Canada–United States Trade: Tests for the Small-Open-Economy Hypothesis." *Canadian J. Econ.* 12 (February 1979): 1–14.

Armington, Paul S. "A Theory of Demand for Products Distinguished by Place of Production." *Internat. Monetary Fund Staff Papers* 16 (March 1969): 159–78.

Balassa, Bela A. *Trade Liberalization among Industrial Countries: Objectives and Alternatives.* New York: McGraw-Hill (for Council on Foreign Relations), 1967.

Boadway, Robin W., and Treddenick, John M. "A General Equilibrium Computation of the Effects of the Canadian Tariff Structure." *Canadian J. Econ.* 11 (August 1978): 424–46.

Brander, James A. "Intra-Industry Trade in Identical Commodities." *J. Internat. Econ.* 11 (February 1981): 1–14.

Brown, Fred, and Whalley, John. "General Equilibrium Evaluations of Tariff Cutting Proposals in the Tokyo Round and Comparisons with More Extensive Liberalisation of World Trade." *Econ. J.* 90 (December 1980): 838–66.

Cline, William R.; Kawanabe, Noboru; Kronsjö, T. O. M.; and Williams, Thomas. *Trade Negotiations in the Tokyo Round: A Quantitative Assessment.* Washington: Brookings Inst., 1978.

Corden, W. M. "Economies of Scale and Customs Union Theory." *J.P.E.* 80, no. 3, pt. 1 (May/June 1972): 465–75.

———. "The Costs and Consequences of Protection: A Survey of Empirical Work." In *International Trade and Finance: Frontiers for Research,* edited by Peter B. Kenen. London: Cambridge Univ. Press, 1975.

Dales, John H. *The Protective Tariff in Canada's Economic Development.* Toronto: Univ. Toronto Press, 1966.

Deardorff, Alan V., and Stern, Robert M. "A Disaggregated Model of World Production and Trade: An Estimate of the Impact of the Tokyo Round." *J. Policy Modeling* 3 (May 1981): 127–52.

Eastman, Harry C., and Stykolt, Stefan. *The Tariff and Competition in Canada.* Toronto: Macmillan, 1967.

Economic Council of Canada. *Looking Outward: A New Trade Strategy for Canada.* Ottawa: Information Canada, 1975.

Fuss, Melvyn A., and Gupta, Vinod K. "Returns to Scale and Suboptimal Capacity in Canadian Manufacturing: A Cost Function Approach." Working Paper no. 7904. Toronto: Univ. Toronto, Inst. Policy Analysis, 1979.

Gorecki, Paul K. *Economies of Scale and Efficient Plant Size in Canadian Manufacturing Industries.* Ottawa: Bur. Competition Policy, Consumer and Corporate Affairs, 1978.

Grubel, Herbert G., and Lloyd, Peter J. *Intra-Industry Trade: The Theory and Measurement of International Trade in Differentiated Products.* New York: Wiley, 1975.

Harris, Richard G. "Applied General Equilibrium Analysis of Small Open Economies with Scale Economies and Imperfect Competition." *A.E.R.* (1984), in press. (*a*)

———. *Trade, Industrial Policy and Canadian Manufacturing.* Toronto: Ontario Econ. Council, 1984. (*b*)

Hazledine, Tim. "Protection and Prices, Profits and Productivity in Thirty-three Canadian Manufacturing Industries." Discussion Paper no. 110. Ottawa: Econ. Council of Canada, 1981.

Helpman, Elhanan. "International Trade in the Presence of Product Differentiation, Economies of Scale and Monopolistic Competition: A Chamberlin-Heckscher-Ohlin Approach." *J. Internat. Econ.* 11 (August 1981): 305–40.

Krugman, Paul R. "Increasing Returns, Monopolistic Competition, and International Trade." *J. Internat. Econ.* 9 (November 1979): 469–80.

———. "Scale Economies, Product Differentiation, and the Pattern of Trade." *A.E.R.* 70 (September 1980): 950–59.

Lancaster, Kelvin. *Variety, Equity, and Efficiency: Product Variety in an Industrial Society.* New York: Columbia Univ. Press, 1979.

Magee, Stephen P. "The Welfare Effects of Restrictions on U.S. Trade." *Brookings Papers Econ. Activity,* no. 3 (1972), pp. 647–701.

Negishi, Takashi. "Monopolistic Competition and General Equilibrium." *Rev. Econ. Studies* 28 (June 1961): 196–201.

Pearson, Scott R., and Ingram, William D. "Economies of Scale, Domestic

Divergences, and Potential Gains from Economic Integration in Ghana and the Ivory Coast." *J.P.E.* 88 (October 1980): 994–1008.

Rousslang, Donald, and Parker, Stephen. "The Effects of Aggregation on Estimated Import Price Elasticities: The Role of Intermediate Inputs." *Rev. Econ. and Statis.* 63 (August 1981): 436–39.

Stern, Robert M.; Francis, Jonathan; and Schumacher, Bruce. *Price Elasticities in International Trade: An Annotated Bibliography.* Toronto: Macmillan (for Trade Policy Res. Centre), 1976.

Whalley, John. "General Equilibrium Analysis of U.S.-E.E.C.-Japanese Trade and Trade Distorting Policies: A Model and Some Initial Findings." *Econ. Appl.* 33, no. 1 (1980): 191–230.

Williams, James R. *The Canadian–United States Tariff and Canadian Industry: A Multisectoral Analysis.* Toronto: Univ. Toronto Press, 1978.

Wonnacott, Ronald J., and Wonnacott, Paul. *Free Trade between the United States and Canada: The Potential Economic Effects.* Cambridge, Mass.: Harvard Univ. Press, 1967.

# [14]

European Economic Review 32 (1988) 1501–1525. North-Holland

## COMPLETING THE INTERNAL MARKET IN THE EUROPEAN COMMUNITY*

### Some Industry Simulations

Alasdair SMITH

*University of Sussex, Brighton BN1 9QN, UK*

Anthony J. VENABLES

*University of Southampton, Southampton SO9 5NH, UK*

This paper studies the effects of changes in the internal market of the European Community in a partial equilibrium model of imperfect competition with economies of scale. The model is numerically calibrated to data on ten industries and the effects of two policy changes are simulated. The first is a reduction in intra-EC trade barriers; the second is the elimination of firms' ability to price discriminate between different national markets. The simple reduction in intra-EC trade barriers generates modest welfare gains, but much more substantial gains are associated with integration of national markets into a single European market.

## 1. Introduction

The achievement of the European Commission's objective of removing all artificial barriers to trade in goods within the European Community by 1992 should have two principal effects on economic welfare. There could be an increased degree of competition, possibly affecting the range of products offered to consumers, as well as prices; while changes in the size of firms could lead to fuller exploitation of economies of scale. These two effects seem likely to raise economic welfare within the EC.

The aim of this paper is to investigate the size of these effects for a number of industries by undertaking simulations in a formal model. In order to capture the relevant effects we employ a model of trade under imperfect competition, in the tradition of Krugman (1979). That is, firms operate under increasing returns to scale and produce goods that may be differentiated, and the ensuing industry equilibrium involves intra-industry trade. We generalise

*This research has been supported by the European Commission and is part of a project supported by the U.K. Economic and Social Research Council under grant no. B00232149. We have benefited greatly from discussions with Caroline Digby, and from the comments of Avinash Dixit, Fabienne Ilzkovitz, Alexis Jacquemin, Paul Krugman, and Victor Norman.

the Krugman model in the specification of technology, in the description of firms' behaviour, and with respect to the market structure within which firms operate. The model is one of partial equilibrium, and is calibrated to 10 separate industries in a world economy consisting of 6 countries (France, the Federal Republic of Germany, Italy, the United Kingdom, the rest of the EC, and the rest of the world). Details of the model and its calibration are given in sections 2 and 3 respectively.

We use the model to evaluate two different policy experiments. The first is a reduction in trade barriers between member states of the EC. This policy increases the volume of intra-EC trade, and is pro-competitive, as it increases import penetration in each national market. It results in increased firm scale, lower average cost, and welfare gains in each of our industries. The magnitude of these gains depends on returns to scale, the importance of trade and the degree of concentration in each industry, but the gains are generally modest.

The second experiment is more dramatic. We consider the effect of firms acting on an integrated EC-wide basis, rather than on a segmented national market basis. This removes the monopoly power that firms have in a particular market (e.g., their domestic market) and replaces it by an EC average degree of monopoly power. This is a strongly pro-competitive policy, and for some industries the gains are substantial. This second experiment seems to be much closer to the spirit of what is meant by 'completing the internal market' than is a mere reduction in trade barriers. It is, however, questionable to what extent it is a policy experiment in a meaningful sense. Existing national trade restrictions imposed by individual EC members, together with the accompanying 'article 115' controls on intra-EC trade[1] do undoubtedly play a role in maintaining national price differences by preventing arbitrage [see Pelkmans and Winters (1988)], and their removal would tend to reduce such price differences. Yet it seems unlikely that full market integration could be imposed merely by removal of these restrictions.

We conduct these experiments in a number of different variants of our model. For all experiments we derive results both when the number of firms is fixed, and when entry and exit of firms is possible. We also compare results for cases when each firm's product range is fixed with cases where firms can change the number of product varieties that they produce, thereby achieving economies of scope. In addition, we know from the theoretical literature that results may be sensitive to whether competition is Cournot or Bertrand [Eaton and Grossman (1986)]. For all experiments we report both Cournot and Bertrand cases, although we regard Cournot competition as the more satisfactory, and treat it as our central case.

---

[1]Article 115 of the Treaty of Rome permits countries to suspend the free circulation within the EC of extra-EC imports, in order to support national import restrictions.

## 2. The model

In this section we describe our general model. Calibration of the model to particular industries is discussed in section 3, and policy experiments in the remainder of the paper. The model is one of partial equilibrium, operating at the level of a single industry. Subscripts on variables denote countries, and run from 1 to $I$, where $I$ is the number of countries. The numbers of firms active in an industry in country $i$ is denoted $n_i$, and all firms in country $i$ are assumed to be symmetric. Product differentiation is permitted, and the number of product types produced by a single one of the country $i$ firms is denoted $m_i$. These products are tradeable, and $x_{ij}$ denotes the quantity of a single product type produced by a firm in country $i$ and sold in country $j$, at price $p_{ij}$. In addition to the industries under study, the economy contains a perfectly competitive sector producing a tradeable output under constant returns to scale; this will be taken as the numeraire.

Demands in each country are derived from an aggregate welfare function. It is assumed that each country's welfare function is separable between the numeraire commodity and the differentiated products, so that we may construct a sub-utility function over differentiated products. The sub-utility function for country $j$ will be denoted $y_j$, and will be assumed to be CES, as in Dixit and Stiglitz (1972).[2] Consumers in country $j$ may consume products which are produced in each country, so the number of product types available for consumption is $\sum_{i=1}^{I} n_i m_i$, and the sub-utility function is then,

$$y_j = \left[ \sum_i a_{ij}^{1/\varepsilon} n_i m_i x_{ij}^{(\varepsilon-1)/\varepsilon} \right]^{\varepsilon/(\varepsilon-1)}, \qquad \varepsilon > 1, \; j = 1, \ldots, I, \tag{1}$$

where the $a_{ij}$ are parameters describing the preferences of a consumer in country $j$ for products produced in country $i$. The sub-utility function $y_j$ may be interpreted as a quantity index, dual to which is a price index, $q_j$ taking the form,

$$q_j = \left[ \sum_i a_{ij} n_i m_i p_{ij}^{1-\varepsilon} \right]^{1/(1-\varepsilon)}, \qquad j = 1, \ldots, I. \tag{2}$$

With preferences of this form consumer demands may be derived from a two-stage budgeting procedure. We assume that the marginal utility of income is constant and normalised at unity, so that the welfare obtained in country $j$ from consumption of differentiated products may be written as a function of $q_j$ alone. This indirect utility function will be assumed to be iso-elastic, and take the form,

---

[2]These preferences may be used for intermediate as well as for final goods, see Ethier [1982].

$$V_j = b_j q_j^{1-\mu}/(\mu - 1), \qquad j = 1, \ldots, I, \tag{3}$$

where $b_j$ is a parameter measuring the size of the market in country $j$. Demand for the quantity index of differentiated products may then be derived using Roy's identity to give,

$$y_j = b_j q_j^{-\mu}, \qquad j = 1, \ldots, I. \tag{4}$$

Given total expenditure on differentiated products, $q_j y_j$, demand for individual product types depends on prices $p_{ij}$. We obtain demand functions,

$$x_{ij} = p_{ij}^{-\varepsilon} a_{ij} q_j^\varepsilon y_j = p_{ij}^{-\varepsilon} a_{ij} b_j q_j^{\varepsilon - \mu}, \qquad i, j = 1, \ldots, I. \tag{5}$$

Each type of differentiated product is supplied by a single firm, and all firms in a particular country are assumed to be symmetric. The profits of a single firm in country $i$ may be expressed as,

$$\pi_i = m_i \sum_j x_{ij} [p_{ij}(1 - T_{ij}) - t_{ij}] - C_i(x_i, m_i), \qquad i = 1, \ldots, I, \tag{6}$$

where $T_{ij}$ and $t_{ij}$ are ad valorem and specific costs associated with selling in market $j$; they may be interpreted either as taxes, or as transport costs. $C_i$ is the firm's production cost function; it is increasing in both output per model, $x_i = \sum_j x_{ij}$, and in the number of model varieties produced, $m_i$.

In our base case we assume that markets are internationally segmented, so firms may choose sales in each national market separately. Profit maximisation with respect to $x_{ij}$ gives first order conditions of the form,

$$p_{ij}(1 - T_{ij})(1 - 1/e_{ij}) - t_{ij} = (1/m_i)\, \delta C_i/\delta x_i, \qquad i, j = 1, \ldots, I. \tag{7}$$

The perceived elasticity of demand, $e_{ij}$, depends on both the elasticity of demand for a single differentiated product, and the perceived effect of the firm's action on industry aggregate supply. The latter effect depends on the anticipated response of other firms in the industry: if it is anticipated that other firms will change prices by $v_i\%$ in response to a 1% own price change, then we have (see appendix),

$$e_{ij}(B) = \varepsilon - (\varepsilon - \mu)(v_i + (1 - v_i)s_{ij}), \qquad i, j = 1, \ldots, I, \tag{8}$$

where $s_{ij}$ is the share of a single representative firm from country $i$ in market $j$. $v_i = 0$ corresponds to Bertrand behaviour. If the anticipated response is that firms will change sales by $v_i\%$ in response to a 1% change in sales, then the elasticity is given by,

$$1/e_{ij}(C) = 1/\varepsilon - (1/\varepsilon - 1/\mu)(v_i + (1 - v_i)s_{ij}), \qquad i, j = 1, \ldots, I, \tag{9}$$

where $v_i = 0$ corresponds to Cournot behaviour.

In addition to choosing sales of each model, each firm may choose the number of models it produces. If a firm introduces a model, then that model will be sold in all countries; the first order condition for profit maximisation with respect to the number of models is then

$$\sum_j x_{ij}[p_{ij}(1 - T_{ij})(1 - \Theta_{ij}) - t_{ij}] = \delta C_i/\delta m_i, \qquad i = 1, \ldots, I. \tag{10}$$

The form of $\Theta_{ij}$ depends on two factors. The first is the perceived reactions of other firms. We permit each firm to hold non-zero conjectures about the response of other firms to a change in the number of models produced; that is, if a firm in country $i$ increases the number of models it produces by 1%, then it conjectures that other firms will increase the number of models they produce by $w_i$%. Second, adding an extra model moves the demand curves for existing models; the value of this depends on whether this shift in demand affects price or quantity of existing models. If the output game is Bertrand, then we assume that price is held constant and quantity changes as new models enter. $\Theta_{ij}$ is then given by,

$$\Theta_{ij}(B) = \{(1 - w_i)s_{ij} + w_i\}(\varepsilon - \mu)/\{e_{ij}(B)(\varepsilon - 1)\}, \qquad i, j = 1, \ldots, I. \tag{11}$$

If the output game is Cournot, then we assume that quantities are held constant and price changes as new models enter, and $\Theta_{ij}$ takes the form,

$$\Theta_{ij}(C) = \{(1 - w_i)s_{ij} + w_i\}(\varepsilon - \mu)/\{\mu(\varepsilon - 1)\}, \qquad i, j = 1, \ldots, I. \tag{12}$$

This completes the characterization of equilibrium for cases in which the numbers of firms in each country are exogenously determined and markets are segmented. If there is free entry and exit of firms in each country then we have the additional industry equilibrium conditions that profits (eqs. (6)) are equal to zero.

We also consider a case in which a subset of markets are integrated. In this case firms set a single producer price, although international differences in consumer prices may remain, because of trade costs. This removes the ability of firms to price discriminate between different markets, and means that each firm has only one degree of freedom in its pricing. If $p_i$ denotes the price charged by a firm from country $i$ in its home market, then export prices, $p_{ij}$ must satisfy

$$p_i(1 - T_{ii}) = p_{ij}(1 - T_{ij}), \qquad i = 1, \ldots, I, \; j = 1, \ldots, K, \tag{13}$$

where the first $K$ markets are integrated, and, for simplicity, we assume that $t_{ij} = 0$. (For a detailed comparison of segmented and integrated markets see Markusen and Venables (1988)).

With this restriction each firm has a single first order condition for its choice of sales in the $K$ integrated markets. Eqs. (7) are replaced by equations of the form,

$$ p_i(1 - T_{ii})(1 - 1/E_i) = (1/m_i)\delta C_i/\delta x_i, \qquad i = 1, \dots, I. \tag{14} $$

If behaviour is Bertrand then firms set price $p_i$ given the price of other firms, and the perceived elasticity $E_i(B)$ is the weighted average,

$$ E_i(B) = \sum_{j=1}^{K} x_{ij} e_{ij}(B) \bigg/ \left( \sum_{j=1}^{K} x_{ij} \right), \qquad i = 1, \dots, I. \tag{15} $$

If behaviour is Cournot then each firm chooses its total sales to the $K$ integrated markets given the total sales of the other firms. Each firm's output is divided between markets to meet demand, given the price relativities, (13). It is possible that a change in one firm's sales, given the total sales of other firms, may lead to changes in firms' sales in each separate market. Derivation of the Cournot elasticity $E_i(C)$ is complex, and is given in the appendix.

## 3. Calibration

The model is calibrated to the 3 digit industries listed in table 3. In order to illustrate the calibration and working of the model we concentrate on one particularly industry, electrical household appliances (NACE 346), and merely summarise results for other industries. Full details of data, calibration and simulation for these industries are available on request from the authors.

The calibration procedure is as follows. First, values of parameters of the model are obtained from secondary sources, where these are available. Second, base year values of endogenous variables of the model are obtained. Third, values of the remaining parameters (and other endogenous variables) are calculated such that the base year observations are an equilibrium of the model.

(i) *Parameters.* The first set of parameters that we draw from secondary sources are those describing returns to scale. Our main source is the survey by Pratten (1987). On the basis of this information we characterise economies of scale in the electrical household appliance industry as having the following two features: a firm of minimum efficient scale which halved the number of products in its range would experience an increase of 5% in the average cost of production; while if it halved the output of each of its products, its average cost would rise by 10%. The minimum efficient scale is assumed to be 200 mECU (which is somewhat larger than the representative firm size assumed in the model as described below).

The literature does not offer clear guidance on the appropriate functional form for the cost function. There are two natural candidates. The first is a linear form (i.e., fixed cost plus constant marginal cost) in which case returns to scale become exhausted as firms become large. The second is log-linear, in which case successive increases in output are associated with continued reductions in average and marginal cost. We employ a weighted average of these functional forms so that costs are given by

$$C_i(x_i, m_i) = c_i[z\{c_0 + m_i c_m + m_i x_i\} + (1 - z)\{m_i x_i^\alpha\}^\beta]. \tag{16}$$

Parameters $c_0$, $c_m$ and $\alpha$, $\beta$ are selected such that, for both the linear and the log-linear components, halving output (around mes) causes the average cost changes described above. The weights, $z$, are set such that 50% of marginal cost comes from each component of the cost curve. We assume that firms in all countries have the same cost functions.[3]

The second set of parameters that we obtain from secondary sources are the industry elasticities of demand, $\mu$. For these we used the surveys contained in Piggott and Whalley (1985), and econometric work of Deaton (1975) and Houthakker (1965) and Houthakker and Taylor (1970). For electrical household appliances we take a representative value of $\mu$ of 1.75.

(*ii*)   The base year endogenous variables required for calibration are the number of firms in each country, and the matrix of international trade and domestic sales (i.e., the matrix with representative element $n_i m_i p_{ij} x_{ij}$, giving sales in country $i$ of goods produced in country $j$). Data on international trade flows between the 'countries' was obtained from the Eurostat NACE-CLIO trade tables for 1982. Domestic production statistics for the EC countries were obtained from the Eurostat Annual Industrial Survey. In fact production statistics for the rest of the EC seem quite unreliable, and no production statistics for the rest of the world were available. In both cases a value of production was assumed that made the ratio of their production to their exports (for the rest of the EC, all exports; for the rest of the world, exports to the EC) the same as this ratio in the total of the four individual EC countries. Similarly, firm size in the rest of the world was assumed to be the same as the EC average. These numbers are needed to complete the numerical specification of the model; the fact that they have been created means that considerable caution should be exercised in interpreting the model's description of the rest of the EC and the rest of the world.

---

[3]We make no distinction between capital and other components of cost. This is equivalent to assuming perfect markets for used capital goods.

Even with these adjustments, there were some inconsistencies in the data, and three further adjustments were made to production estimates in order to deal with cases where the apparent consumption of domestic output was negative (U.K. output of office machinery (NACE 330), Italian output of footwear (NACE 451) and carpets (NACE 438)). Further details of data sources and adjustments are available on request.

Our estimate of the number of firms in each country is derived from the Eurostat *Structure and Activity of Production* data on the size distribution of firms. From this data we estimate the number of 'representative' size firms in each country on the basis of the Herfindahl index of concentration. The electrical household appliances industry covers a number of quite distinct products, and it is central to the model that we capture competitive interaction between firms at a disaggregate product level. We therefore divide the industry into a number of symmetric sub-industries; the model of section 2 operates at the level of one of these sub-industries, and the total industry is simply the sum of the sub-industries. We take the number of sub-industries to be 5; this number is chosen so that each sub-industry is of similar scale to the two largest narrowly defined product groups in the industry – washing machines and refrigerators. Table 1 reports the number of 'representative' firms, and also the Herfindahl index of concentration for each of the sub-industries, for each market (including sales by foreign firms). The index provides a useful measure of competitiveness: its reciprocal is a measure of the number of equal sized firms which are 'equivalent' to the actual distribution of firms. As a single summary measure of competition in each industry we refer below to the EC average of these indices; for electrical household appliances, this average is 0.11.

(*iii*) Given the information above, remaining parameters are calibrated so that the model supports the observations as an equilibrium. Industry equilibrium requires that firms set marginal revenue equal to marginal cost (eq. (7)), and that industry profits are equal to zero. With increasing returns to scale marginal costs are less than average cost, so, for these two conditions to hold simultaneously, price must be above marginal cost, i.e., firms must have a significant degree of monopoly power. This power may be derived from two sources. The first is that firms may anticipate that an increase in their output will increase industry aggregate supply and hence reduce price; the second is that each firm has monopoly power over its own varieties of differentiated product (see eqs. (7)–(9)).

If we assume that there is no product differentiation, then price-cost margins must be supported by non-zero conjectures, that is by non-zero values of $v_i$ in either eq. (8) or (9). This is the calibration technique followed by Dixit (1987), Krugman (1987) and Laussel et al. (1987), but we regard it as inappropriate for two reasons. First, firm level product differentiation does

Table 1

Calibration.

*346 Domestic electrical appliances*

*Production/Consumption matrix, 1982 mECU*

|       | Fr      | G       | It      | U.K.    | RoEC    | RoW     |
|-------|---------|---------|---------|---------|---------|---------|
| Fr    | 2660.24 | 93.24   | 67.19   | 92.58   | 94.27   | 226.09  |
| G     | 286.74  | 2491.38 | 93.42   | 139.34  | 372.72  | 594.19  |
| It    | 260.22  | 214.14  | 1539.39 | 253.44  | 186.59  | 429.62  |
| U.K.  | 24.03   | 23.38   | 8.72    | 1405.86 | 77.00   | 126.91  |
| RoEC  | 77.06   | 111.64  | 8.16    | 85.64   | 1635.48 | 215.76  |
| RoW   | 187.55  | 192.49  | 41.26   | 200.89  | 175.59  | 3290.17 |

*Number of firms*

| 22 | 34 | 27 | 36 | 22 | 42 |
|----|----|----|----|----|----|

*Number of sub-industries*   5

*Herfindahl index of concentration*

| 0.134 | 0.095 | 0.143 | 0.163 | 0.101 |
|-------|-------|-------|-------|-------|

*Returns to scale*

   % increase in average cost at 1/2 output per model; 10%
   % increase in average cost at 1/2 number of models; 5%
   Linear/loglinear weights; 0.5, 0.5

*Elasticity* $\mu$   1.75

*Cournot calibration*
   *Elasticity* $\varepsilon_C$   10.77

   *Tariff equivalents,* %

|       | Fr | G  | It | U.K. | RoEC |
|-------|----|----|----|------|------|
| Fr    | 0  | 31 | 34 | 34   | 34   |
| G     | 27 | 0  | 33 | 33   | 24   |
| It    | 25 | 23 | 0  | 25   | 27   |
| U.K.  | 36 | 33 | 40 | 0    | 28   |
| RoEC  | 32 | 25 | 44 | 31   | 0    |

   *Model conjectures* (%)

| w | 6.5 | 6.3 | 6.4 | 6.3 | 6.4 |
|---|-----|-----|-----|-----|-----|

*Bertrand calibration*
   *Elasticity* $\varepsilon_B$   7.78

   *Model conjectures* (%)

| w | 62.6 | 62.0 | 62.1 | 61.7 | 62.3 |
|---|------|------|------|------|------|

seem to be a characteristic of our industries (because of transport costs, if not innate product characteristics). Second, conjectural variations are widely recognized to be an unsatisfactory way of capturing interaction between firms; this applies particularly if we require that the conjectures remain unchanged as policy experiments are conducted. We therefore proceed by permitting the possibility that firms produce differentiated products. The question is then how much of firms' market power is due to differentiation, and how much to firms' perceived ability to change industry aggregates. We do not have a good measure of the extent of product differentiation in each industry, so we proceed by looking at two cases. The first is to impose Cournot behaviour on the output game, and calibrate for a value of $\varepsilon$ consistent with EC average price-cost margins. Using eqs. (9) with $v_i = 0$ we obtain $\varepsilon = 10.77$. The second is to impose Bertrand behaviour on the output game, and calibrate for $\varepsilon$. Using eqs. (8) with $v_i = 0$ we obtain $\varepsilon = 7.78$. The lower elasticity in the Bertrand case is due to the fact that Bertrand behaviour is inherently more competitive, so leaves more of the required price–marginal cost margin to be attributed to product differentiation. Notice that, in each of these cases we calibrate a single elasticity rather than country specific conjectures, $v_i$. Profits in each country may therefore differ from zero, although we impose that total profits in the EC are zero; and the range of these variations in calibrated profits is from a loss equal to $-6.51\%$ of sales in the U.K. to profits of $3.4\%$ of sales in France.

Firms in different countries differ in size, and may produce different numbers of models. For the base case we assume that all firms have the same output per model, and let the observed variations in firm size be attributed to different numbers of models produced. In some of our simulations we hold the number of models per firm constant; differences in the number of models per firm may then be interpreted simply as a device to account for variations in firm size.[4] However, we also consider cases in which the number of models per firm, $m_i$, may change; choice of $m_i$ must then be consistent with profit maximisation. We achieve this by resorting to non-zero conjectures, $w_i$, which are calibrated to ensure that the first order conditions for profit maximisation with respect to $m_i$ hold. In the Cournot variant of the model firms anticipate that adding an extra model will cause price changes at given volume. The conjectures $w_i$ are solved from eqs. (10) and (12), and the values of the conjectures so derived are small (see table 1). In the Bertrand variant firms anticipate changes in the volume of sales of existing models, at given prices. We then use eqs. (10) and (11), and obtain positive and quite large values of $w_i$ (table 1).

Calibration also requires that we find parameters to support differences in firms' shares in different national markets. Firms located in each country have smaller shares of their export markets than they do of their domestic market. This may be due to differences in consumer preferences, or distribution networks, to transport costs or to trade barriers. It is convenient to aggregate all these into a single ad valorem 'tariff equivalent' form, whose values are given (for the Cournot variant of the electrical household

---

[4]This minimises the extent to which differences in firms' output levels cause differences in the slope of their cost functions (evaluated at base output). This is desirable, given the quality of our estimates of firm size.

appliance industry) in table 1. Calibration proceeds by assuming ad valorem transport costs of 10%, and attributing the remainder of the 'tariff equivalent' to the demand parameters, $a_{ij}$. Finally, demand parameters, $b_j$, are calibrated to equate total sales in each market with their observed values.

## 4. Reduced trade barriers

In this section we model a move towards 'completion of the internal market' as a reduction in the cost of intra-EC trade. We assume that this trade liberalisation takes the form of an equiproportionate reduction in intra-EC tariff equivalent trade barriers. The size of these reductions is chosen so that the direct cost saving achieved by the policy is equal to 2.5% of the value of base level intra-EC trade. [Pelkmans and Winters (1988, ch. 2)] suggests that the removal of border measures affecting intra-EC trade should generate direct savings of between 1% and 3% of gross trade. He also, however, identifies other restrictions on free trade, such as public procurement policies, subsidies, and national standards; these are difficult to quantify, but it is possible that our figure of a 2.5% reduction in trade costs is too low. Our results may be scaled up to provide estimates (i.e., first order approximations) of the effects of larger reductions in trade costs.

For the electrical household appliance industry this experiment involves reducing the tariff equivalents from an average of 31%, to an average value of 28.5%. Table 2 reports the effect of the experiment on this industry. We assume Cournot behaviour and a constant model range; the consequences of removing these assumptions are examined in section 5. Consider first the case in which the number of firms is held constant. The first effect of the policy change is to increase the volume of intra-EC trade by 22.1%. This increased import penetration raises competitiveness in each market, as measured by the reductions in the Herfindahl concentration indices. The increased competition reduces prices, so expanding sales, raising consumer surplus, but reducing profits (except where the output expansion is sufficiently large). The national distribution of the increased production is broadly a projection of existing trade patterns, with Italy expanding the most, and the U.K. contracting. The expanded production reduces average costs, the EC average cost reduction being a modest 0.32%. Welfare, defined as the sum of profits and consumer surplus, rises by an amount equal to 0.64% of base consumption, of which 0.49% is the direct cost saving due to the reduction in trade barriers and 0.15% arises indirectly from adjustment in the industry. A useful indicator of the gains from the policy is provided by the ratio of the welfare change to the change in the value of trade: table 2 reports that 14.8% of the trade creation is pure welfare gain.

If the number of firms is permitted to vary, then exit occurs to restore

Table 2

Reduction in trade barriers; 346 Electrical household appliances (Cournot; models per firm constant).

Production and welfare change by country

| | Fixed no. of firms | | | | Variable no. of firms | | | |
|---|---|---|---|---|---|---|---|---|
| | Δ output % | Δ consumers' surplus, mECU | Δ profit mECU | Δ Herfindahl index % | Δ output % | Δ consumers' surplus, mECU | Δ number of firms | Δ Herfindahl index % |
| France | 0.75 | 33.2 | −16.9 | −8.02 | −1.77 | 16.8 | −1 | −6.34 |
| Germany | 4.32 | 24.4 | −0.4 | −5.15 | 7.11 | 30.4 | 1 | −5.15 |
| Italy | 6.40 | 18.6 | 0.5 | −5.96 | 9.70 | 24.0 | 0 | −6.52 |
| U.K. | −4.93 | 20.3 | −11.2 | −12.3 | −9.14 | 6.8 | −4 | −7.81 |
| R of EC | −0.59 | 29.2 | −13.5 | −10.4 | −5.40 | 13.4 | −2 | −8.61 |
| EC | 2.09 | 125.8 | −41.6 | — | 1.80 | 91.4 | −6 | — |

EC aggregates

| | Δ EC output % | Δ intra-EC trade % | Δ extra-EC exports % | Δ extra EC imports % | Δ average cost % | Δ welfare % consumption | Δ welfare% Δ int-EC trade |
|---|---|---|---|---|---|---|---|
| Fixed no. of firms | 2.09 | 22.1 | 1.1 | −7.6 | −0.32 | 0.64 | 14.8 |
| Variable no. of firms | 1.80 | 26.0 | 0.9 | −5.0 | −0.76 | 0.70 | 13.7 |

profits to their base level.[5] The effect of this is to increase firm scale, so giving a reduction in average costs of 0.76%. However, exit also goes part way to restoring concentration to its base level; prices rise and consumers' gains, while still positive, are reduced. Combining consumer and producer surplus, we see that the welfare gain from the policy now rises to 0.70% of base consumption, and the ratio of welfare gain to increased trade is 13.7%.

Table 2 also reports the effect of the trade liberalisation on the external trade of the EC. Imports fall as a result of the policy, and there is a small rise in exports. There are two reasons for these changes. First, the direct effect of the policy is to reduce the prices of intra-EC imports, so switching expenditure away from extra-EC imports. Second, the expanded EC output reduces firms' marginal costs, so reducing EC producers' prices both inside and outside the EC and leading to the rise in exports.

Table 3 reports a summary of the results of this experiment for all 10 industries, and additionally gives some key characteristics of each industry. For each industry, the table reports the increase in average costs at half MES (denoted RS), the share of intra-EC trade in EC consumption (denoted TS), the EC average Herfindahl concentration index (H), and the direct cost saving of the policy, expressed as a percentage of base consumption (DC). The calibrated value of $\varepsilon$ is also reported: it ranges from high values of 35 and 53 in cement (242) and footwear (451),[6] to lows of 5.8 and 7.3 in pharmaceuticals (257) and electric motors (342). The implication that different firms' products are very close substitutes in the first two industries while product differentiation is much more significant in the latter two seems in accordance with casual empiricism.

A number of remarks may be made about the results presented in table 3. First, the ratio of welfare change to trade creation is highly correlated with the degree of returns to scale in the industry. This ratio exceeds 15% in the free entry case in three industries, pharmaceuticals (257), electric motors (342) and motor vehicles (350); and these (together with cement) are the industries in our sample with the greatest returns to scale. The ratio is lowest, dropping to under 2% for footwear (451), the industry with the least returns to scale. (A negative welfare gain is recorded for the cement industry when the number of firms is fixed, reflecting the very high transport costs in this industry; the theoretical possibility of losses from trade when there are high transport costs having been demonstrated by Brander and Krugman (1983).)

Second, the change in average costs and the change in welfare expressed as

---

[5]Throughout, we shall assume that profits are restored exactly to zero, even if this involves fractional firms. We believe that this gives a more accurate picture of expected changes caused by the policy. In addition, it avoids non-uniqueness problems associated with an integer entry and exit procedure.

[6]Footwear also has very low tariff equivalents – some elements of the matrix being less than 2.5%. Because of this we model trade liberalisation in this industry as a reduction in tariff equivalents bringing a cost saving of 1% of base trade.

1514                    A. Smith and A.J. Venables, Completing the internal market

Table 3

Reduction in trade barriers; All industries (Cournot, models per firm constant).

| | Δ output % | Δ average cost % | Δ welfare % consumption | Δ welfare % Δ int-EC trade |
|---|---|---|---|---|
| 242 Cement, lime and plaster: $\varepsilon = 35.5$, RS = 20%, TS = 1.6%, H = 0.066, DC = 0.04% | | | | |
| Fixed no. of firms | 0.24 | −0.03 | −0.1 | −5.0 |
| Variable no. of firms | −0.05 | −0.10 | 0.02 | 0.8 |
| 257 Pharmaceutical products: $\varepsilon = 5.8$, RS = 22%, TS = 10.0%, H = 0.050, DC = 0.25% | | | | |
| Fixed no. of firms | 0.37 | −0.08 | 0.29 | 21.8 |
| Variable no. of firms | 0.29 | −0.13 | 0.29 | 21.6 |
| 260 Artificial and synthetic fibres: $\varepsilon = 21.5$, RS = 10%, TS = 36.4%, H = 0.050, DC = 0.91% | | | | |
| Fixed no. of firms | 4.9 | −0.51 | 0.99 | 13.0 |
| Variable no. of firms | 6.52 | −2.82 | 1.17 | 5.8 |
| 322 Machine tools: $\varepsilon = 13.6$, RS = 7%, TS = 22.4%, H = 0.004, DC = 0.56% | | | | |
| Fixed no. of firms | 1.67 | −0.12 | 0.84 | 13.8 |
| Variable no. of firms | 2.64 | −0.05 | 0.82 | 11.5 |
| 330 Office Machinery: $\varepsilon = 32.8$, RS = 10%, TS = 23.6%, H = 0.120, DC = 0.59% | | | | |
| Fixed no. of firms | 10.4 | −0.98 | 0.88 | 8.0 |
| Variable no. of firms | 15.5 | −4.27 | 1.31 | 6.4 |
| 342 Electric motors, generators etc: $\varepsilon = 7.35$, RS = 15%, TS = 8.8%, H = 0.022, DC = 0.22% | | | | |
| Fixed no. of firms | 0.37 | −0.05 | 0.29 | 19.0 |
| Variable no. of firms | 0.31 | 0.09 | 0.29 | 18.4 |
| 346 Electrical household appliances: $\varepsilon = 10.77$, RS = 10%, TS = 19.6%, H = 0.110, DC = 0.49% | | | | |
| Fixed no. of firms | 2.09 | −0.32 | 0.64 | 14.8 |
| Variable no. of firms | 1.80 | −0.76 | 0.70 | 13.7 |
| 350 Motor vehicles: $\varepsilon = 13.32$, RS = 16%, TS = 24.8%, H = 0.199, DC = 0.62% | | | | |
| Fixed no. of firms | 3.36 | −0.56 | 0.83 | 17.9 |
| Variable no. of firms | 3.16 | −1.40 | 0.95 | 15.1 |
| 438 Carpets, linoleum etc: $\varepsilon = 21.4$, RS = 6%, TS = 18.8%, H = 0.031, DC = 0.47% | | | | |
| Fixed no. of firms | 2.51 | −0.17 | 0.67 | 8.0 |
| Variable no. of firms | 2.68 | −0.45 | 0.74 | 7.1 |
| 451 Footwear: $\varepsilon = 53.3$, RS = 2%, TS = 27.0%, H = 0.010, DC = 0.27% | | | | |
| Fixed no. of firms | 3.21 | −0.03 | 0.35 | 3.1 |
| Variable no. of firms | 3.16 | −0.00 | 0.37 | 1.4 |

a proportion of base consumption are largest in artificial fibres (260), office equipment (330), and motor vehicles (350). This is explained by the fact that each of these industries has significant returns to scale together with a high proportion of their output traded within the EC (TS exceeds 20% for each of these industries). The effect of the reduction in trade barriers is therefore relatively large in these industries.

Third, the cost reduction and welfare change is (in all cases except two) larger when free entry and exit is permitted. It is only with free entry that we observe welfare gains greater than 1% of base consumption (in artificial fibres (260), office machinery (330), and associated reductions in average costs ranging up to 4%. The reason for this is that increased competition reduces profits, causing exit of firms and hence raising the scale of remaining firms. This pro-competitive effect is smaller, the more competitive is the industry originally. Thus, in machine tools (322), electric motors (342) and footwear (451), the three industries with Herfindahl indices below 0.025, we see very small, or negative, further gains from free entry.

We have quoted results on the ratio of welfare gain to trade created because this is a ratio which can easily be used to compare our results with those of other studies. Owen (1983) reports welfare gains of the order of 50% (pp. 144–147) of the value of trade created, in contrast with the numbers in our tables 3 and 4 which are mostly in the range of 8% to 22%.[7] Our results are much closer to those generated by the modelling exercise of Harris and Cox (1984, p. 114), who estimate a welfare gain of 17.5% of trade created by multilateral liberalisation of Canadian trade.

## 5. Sensitivity

The preceding section assumed Cournot behaviour and a fixed number of models per firm. While we regard this as our central case, in this section we report the effects of replacing Cournot behaviour by Bertrand, and of removing the assumption that the number of models is fixed.

The difference between Cournot and Bertrand behaviour is that the latter is more competitive in the sense that each firm's actions have less impact on the industry price indices. As noted in section 3 this implies that the calibrated elasticities are lower in the Bertrand case than in the Cournot case, these being reported in table 4 as $\varepsilon_B$ and $\varepsilon_C$. Notice that for industries in which the Herfindahl index is very small (for example 322) the two elasticities are similar. Where the Herfindahl index is large the elasticities may be very different. Thus in the cement industry (242) the Cournot elasticity is 35.5, and the Bertrand 8. It seems likely that Bertrand behaviour overestimates the level of competition in this industry, and consequently attaches more weight to product differentiation than is plausible.

What difference does Bertrand behaviour make for the effects of the reduction in trade barriers? The policy works by increasing import penetration, and hence reducing firms' shares in their domestic markets, and so increasing competitiveness. With Bertrand behaviour these changes in market share have less effect on price (as price–cost margins are largely accounted for by product differentiation); the policy therefore leads to smaller price

---

[7]There seems to be three principal sources of the difference between Owen's results and ours: Owen assumes considerably greater economies of scale than we do; he treats entry and exit asymmetrically, letting industries expand through expansion of existing firms but contract through exit; and he confines attention to uni-directional trade creation, ignoring the possibility that trade increases will involve intra-industry trade.

Table 4

Sensitivity analysis.

| | Cournot | | | | Bertrand | | | |
|---|---|---|---|---|---|---|---|---|
| | Models constant | | Models variable | | Models constant | | Models variable | |
| | Fixed no. of firms | Var. no. of firms | Fixed no. of firms | Var. no. of firms | Fixed no. of firms | Var. no. of firms | Fixed no. of firms | Var. no. of firms |
| **242 Cement, lime and plaster:** $\varepsilon_C=35.5$, $\varepsilon_B=8.0$, RS=20%, TS=1.6%, H=0.066 | | | | | | | | |
| Δ EC output % | 0.24 | −0.05 | — | — | 0.00 | 0.10 | — | — |
| Δ average costs % | −0.03 | −0.10 | — | — | −0.00 | −0.01 | — | — |
| Δ welfare % consumption | −0.1 | 0.02 | — | — | 0.04 | 0.04 | — | — |
| Δ welfare % Δ int-EC trade | −5.0 | 0.8 | — | — | 11.1 | 11.1 | — | — |
| **257 Pharmaceutical products:** $\varepsilon_C=5.8$, $\varepsilon_B=4.7$, RS=22%, TS=10.0%, H=0.05 | | | | | | | | |
| Δ EC output % | 0.37 | 0.29 | 0.45 | 0.34 | 0.22 | 0.25 | 0.27 | 0.27 |
| Δ average costs % | −0.08 | −0.13 | −0.02 | −0.12 | −0.05 | −0.03 | −0.02 | −0.03 |
| Δ welfare % consumption | 0.29 | 0.29 | 0.31 | 0.35 | 0.33 | 0.34 | 0.36 | 0.37 |
| Δ welfare % Δ int-EC trade | 21.8 | 21.6 | 23.1 | 25.2 | 29.2 | 30.1 | 31.8 | 32.7 |
| **260 Artificial and synthetic fibres:** $\varepsilon_C=21.5$, $\varepsilon_B=8.7$, RS=10%, TS=36.4%, H=0.050 | | | | | | | | |
| Δ EC output % | 4.19 | 6.52 | — | — | 1.39 | 2.74 | — | — |
| Δ average costs % | −0.51 | −2.82 | — | — | −0.17 | −0.14 | — | — |
| Δ welfare % consumption | 0.99 | 1.17 | — | — | 1.21 | 0.97 | — | — |
| Δ welfare % Δ int-EC trade | 13.0 | 5.8 | — | — | 21.4 | 9.3 | — | — |
| **322 Machine tools:** $\varepsilon_C=13.55$, $\varepsilon_B=13.24$, RS=7%, TS=22.4%, H=0.004 | | | | | | | | |
| Δ EC output % | 1.67 | 2.64 | 2.87 | 2.79 | 1.60 | 2.65 | 2.92 | 2.66 |
| Δ average costs % | −0.12 | −0.05 | −0.05 | −0.04 | −0.12 | −0.02 | −0.06 | −0.01 |
| Δ welfare % consumption | 0.84 | 0.82 | 0.86 | 0.86 | 0.85 | 0.83 | 0.86 | 0.84 |
| Δ welfare % Δ int-EC trade | 13.8 | 11.4 | 11.7 | 12.1 | 14.2 | 11.7 | 11.0 | 11.9 |

continued overleaf

*330 Office machinery:* $\varepsilon_C = 32.8$, $\varepsilon_B = 10.9$, RS = 10%, TS = 23.6%, H = 0.12

|  | | | | | | | |
|---|---|---|---|---|---|---|---|
| Δ EC output % | 10.4 | 15.5 | 13.3 | 15.0 | 2.64 | 3.80 | 4.70 | 4.06 |
| Δ average costs % | -0.98 | -4.27 | -0.49 | -4.01 | -0.10 | -0.24 | -0.16 | |
| Δ welfare % consumption | 0.88 | 1.31 | 0.62 | 1.31 | 0.92 | 0.98 | 1.14 | 1.09 |
| Δ welfare % Δ int-EC | | | | | | | | |
| trade | 8.0 | 6.4 | 5.4 | 5.9 | 17.1 | 16.2 | 15.1 | 18.2 |

*342 Electric motors, generators, etc:* $\varepsilon_C = 7.35$, $\varepsilon_B = 6.77$, RS = 15%, TS = 8.8%, H = 0.022

|  | | | | | | | |
|---|---|---|---|---|---|---|---|
| Δ EC output % | 0.37 | 0.31 | 0.41 | 0.46 | 0.29 | 0.28 | 0.30 | 0.31 |
| Δ average costs % | -0.05 | -0.09 | -0.02 | -0.09 | -0.05 | -0.01 | -0.02 | |
| Δ welfare % consumption | 0.29 | 0.29 | 0.31 | 0.39 | 0.31 | 0.31 | 0.33 | 0.33 |
| Δ welfare % Δ int-EC | | | | | | | | |
| trade | 19.0 | 18.4 | 20.0 | 24.9 | 21.7 | 21.1 | 22.3 | 22.5 |

*346 Electrical household appliances:* $\varepsilon_C = 10.7$, $\varepsilon_B = 7.8$, RS = 10%, TS = 19.6%, H = 0.11

|  | | | | | | | |
|---|---|---|---|---|---|---|---|
| Δ EC output % | 2.09 | 1.80 | 2.52 | 2.44 | 1.29 | 1.30 | 1.61 | 1.55 |
| Δ average costs % | -0.32 | -0.76 | -0.32 | -0.69 | -0.20 | -0.22 | -0.26 | -0.21 |
| Δ welfare % consumption | 0.64 | 0.70 | 0.69 | 1.08 | 0.72 | 0.71 | 0.79 | 0.88 |
| Δ welfare % Δ int-EC | | | | | | | | |
| trade | 14.8 | 13.7 | 12.2 | 18.1 | 20.6 | 17.7 | 13.9 | 21.7 |

*350 Motor Vehicles:* $\varepsilon_C = 13.3$, $\varepsilon_B = 7.2$, RS = 16%, TS = 24.8%, H = 0.199

|  | | | | | | | |
|---|---|---|---|---|---|---|---|
| Δ EC output % | 3.36 | 3.16 | 3.70 | 3.30 | 1.71 | 1.90 | 3.25 | 242 |
| Δ average costs % | -0.56 | -1.40 | -0.28 | -1.16 | -0.29 | -0.41 | -0.50 | -0.41 |
| Δ welfare % consumption | 0.83 | 0.95 | 0.76 | 1.01 | 0.91 | 0.89 | 0.82 | 1.29 |
| Δ welfare % Δ int-EC | | | | | | | | |
| trade | 17.9 | 15.1 | 15.5 | 13.8 | 25.7 | 21.7 | 13.3 | 32.1 |

*438 Carpets, linoleum, etc:* $\varepsilon_C = 21.4$, $\varepsilon_B = 17.6$, RS = 6%, TS = 18.8%, H = 0.031

|  | | | | | | | |
|---|---|---|---|---|---|---|---|
| Δ EC output % | 2.51 | 2.68 | — | — | 1.74 | 2.21 | — | — |
| Δ average costs % | -0.17 | -0.45 | — | — | -0.12 | -0.06 | — | — |
| Δ welfare % consumption | 0.67 | 0.74 | — | — | 0.71 | 0.74 | — | — |
| Δ welfare % Δ int-EC | | | | | | | | |
| trade | 8.0 | 7.1 | — | — | 9.5 | 8.5 | — | — |

*451 Footwear:* $\varepsilon_C = 53.3$, $\varepsilon_B = 42.4$, RS = 2%, TS = 27%, H = 0.01

|  | | | | | | | |
|---|---|---|---|---|---|---|---|
| Δ EC output % | 3.21 | 3.16 | — | — | 1.93 | 2.53 | — | — |
| Δ average costs % | -0.03 | -0.00 | — | — | 0.0 | 0.22 | — | — |
| Δ welfare % consumption | 0.35 | 0.37 | — | — | 0.41 | 0.38 | — | — |
| Δ welfare % Δ int-EC | | | | | | | | |
| trade | 3.1 | 1.4 | — | — | 4.0 | 2.0 | — | — |

reductions. The smaller magnitude of price reductions means that demand and output increase by less than in the Cournot case, this being accentuated by lower price elasticities. Smaller output changes lead to smaller reductions in average costs (table 4). However, despite the smaller savings in production cost, we see that, when the number of firms is fixed, the welfare gains from the policy are greater in the Bertrand case then in the Cournot case. This is because the increase in trade (which incurs transport costs) is less in this case, and because lower values of $\varepsilon$ imply greater consumer gains from the reduction in import prices.

A second consequence of the smaller price reduction in the Bertrand case is that the policy reduces profits by less. When the number of firms is variable there is therefore less exit from the industry (and there may be entry as total industry output rises), so leading to smaller reductions in average cost. The welfare gains are now also smaller, on average, although this difference is ambiguous due to lower trade costs and increased product variety, with more firms remaining in the Bertrand case.

The second dimension of sensitivity analysis explored in table 4 is to let the number of product varieties produced by each firm change. This experiment is meaningful only if there is a significant degree of differentiation in consumer demand between product varieties, or there are significant economies of scope. Table 4 therefore does not report results for the 'models variable' case for the four industries (242, 260, 438, and 451) where a high value of $\varepsilon$ indicates little product differentiation, and our information on economies of scale implies that there is little cost reduction obtained by expanding the number of models produced at given output per model. For the six industries in which this is a meaningful experiment, table 4 shows that the results of the policy are affected in three ways. First, changes in output are now generally (but not invariably) larger, due to the fact that firms have an additional instrument with which to respond to the policy change. Second, the fall in average costs is now generally (but not invariably) smaller. Firms shorten their production runs as they expand their model range. There are economies of scope, but these are smaller than returns to scale in production of a particular model. Third, the welfare gains from the policy are now generally (but not invariably) larger, as the smaller average cost reductions are compensated for by the benefits of increased product variety.

Overall, we regard the variation in results across different variants of the model as surprisingly small. From the theoretical literature we know that it is possible to construct examples where assumptions on market structure reverse the effects of policy. A sign change of this type is observed in the cement industry (242), but this is readily explicable in terms of the high transport costs in this industry. Apart from this, not only the sign, but also the order of magnitude of the welfare gains, and the ranking of industries by welfare gain are fairly stable across industries.

Table 5

Integrated markets; 346 Electrical household appliances (Cournot; models per firm constant).

Production and welfare change by country

| | Fixed no. of firms | | | | Variable no. of firms | | | |
|---|---|---|---|---|---|---|---|---|
| | Δ output % | Δ consumers' surplus, mECU | Δ profit mECU | Δ Herfindahl index % | Δ output % | Δ consumers' surplus, mECU | Δ number of firms | Δ Herfindahl index % |
| France | 13.6 | 145.1 | −63.3 | −72.6 | 12.0 | 96.2 | −3 | −67.9 |
| Germany | 1.5 | 81.9 | −52.4 | −61.4 | 1.5 | 48.6 | −5 | −54.8 |
| Italy | −0.8 | 89.7 | −62.6 | −74.3 | −6.0 | 51.4 | −6 | −69.8 |
| U.K. | 13.6 | 52.6 | −22.3 | −41.5 | 15.0 | 31.1 | −5 | −31.4 |
| R of EC | 20.2 | 100.5 | −34.4 | −63.7 | 19.6 | 71.5 | −3 | −57.4 |
| EC | 8.1 | 469.9 | −234.9 | – | 6.7 | 298.8 | −23 | – |

EC aggregates

| | Δ EC output % | Δ intra-EC trade % | Δ extra-EC exports % | Δ extra-EC imports % | Δ average cost % | Δ welfare % consumption | Δ welfare % int-EC trade |
|---|---|---|---|---|---|---|---|
| Fixed no. of firms | 8.1 | −23.0 | 2.4 | −24.4 | −1.15 | 1.79 | – |
| Variable no. of firms | | | | | | | – |

Table 6

Integrated markets. All industries (Models per firm constant).

| | Cournot | | | | Bertrand | | | |
|---|---|---|---|---|---|---|---|---|
| | Segmented | | Integrated | | Segmented | | Integrated | |
| | Fixed no. of firms | Var. no. of firms | Fixed no. of firms | Var. no. of firms | Fixed no. of firms | Var. no. of firms | Fixed no. of firms | Var. no. of firms |
| 242 Cement, lime and plaster: $\varepsilon_C=35.5$, $\varepsilon_B=8.0$, RS=20%, TS=1.60%, H=0.066 | | | | | | | | |
| Δ EC output % | 0.24 | -0.05 | 1.32 | 0.71 | 0.00 | 0.10 | 0.01 | 0.02 |
| Δ average costs % | -0.03 | -0.10 | -0.12 | -0.90 | -0.0 | -0.01 | -0.0 | -0.02 |
| Δ welfare % consumption | -0.01 | 0.02 | 0.22 | 1.08 | 0.04 | 0.04 | 0.04 | 0.04 |
| Δ int-EC trade % | 128 | 164 | -78 | -75.4 | 22.5 | 22.5 | 16.8 | 16.8 |
| 257 Pharmaceutical products: $\varepsilon_C=5.8$, $\varepsilon_B=4.7$, RS=22%, TS=10.0%, H=0.05 | | | | | | | | |
| Δ EC output % | 0.37 | 0.29 | 3.32 | 1.71 | 0.22 | 0.25 | 0.24 | 0.28 |
| Δ average costs % | -0.08 | -0.13 | -0.73 | -2.17 | -0.05 | -0.03 | -0.05 | -0.02 |
| Δ welfare % consumption | 0.29 | 0.29 | 1.11 | 1.15 | 0.33 | 0.34 | 0.33 | 0.34 |
| Δ int-EC trade % | 13.3 | 13.4 | -16.1 | -16.5 | 11.3 | 11.3 | 6.7 | 6.7 |
| 260 Artificial and synthetic fibres: $\varepsilon_C=21.0$, $\varepsilon_B=8.0$, RS=10%, TS=36.4%, H=0.050 | | | | | | | | |
| Δ EC output % | 4.19 | 6.52 | 9.59 | 10.69 | 1.39 | 2.74 | 1.43 | 2.76 |
| Δ average costs % | -0.51 | -2.82 | -1.77 | -4.25 | -0.17 | -0.14 | -0.18 | -0.14 |
| Δ welfare % consumption | 0.99 | 1.17 | 4.14 | 5.57 | 1.21 | 0.97 | 1.21 | 0.97 |
| Δ int-EC trade % | 20.4 | 55.3 | -56.5 | -55.6 | 15.5 | 28.8 | 13.7 | 27.2 |
| 322 Machine tools: $\varepsilon_C=13.6$, $\varepsilon_B=13.2$, RS=7%, TS=22.4%, H=0.004 | | | | | | | | |
| Δ EC output % | 1.67 | 2.64 | 2.05 | 2.82 | 1.60 | 2.65 | 1.60 | 2.65 |
| Δ average costs % | -0.12 | -0.05 | -0.16 | -0.12 | -0.12 | -0.02 | -0.12 | -0.01 |
| Δ welfare % consumption | 0.84 | 0.82 | 0.86 | 0.83 | 0.85 | 0.83 | 0.85 | 0.83 |
| Δ int-EC trade % | 27.1 | 32.0 | 24.6 | 29.5 | 26.8 | 31.6 | 26.6 | 31.3 |

*A. Smith and A.J. Venables, Completing the internal market*          1521

**330 Office machinery:** $\varepsilon_C = 32.8$, $\varepsilon_B = 10.9$, RS = 10%, TS = 23.6%, H = 0.12

| | | | | | | | | |
|---|---|---|---|---|---|---|---|---|
| Δ EC output % | 10.4 | 15.5 | 27.3 | 27.0 | 2.64 | 3.80 | 2.67 | 3.96 |
| Δ average costs % | -0.98 | -4.27 | -2.71 | -3.19 | -0.25 | -0.10 | -0.26 | -0.08 |
| Δ welfare % consumption | 0.88 | 1.31 | 3.88 | 4.10 | 0.92 | 0.98 | 0.91 | 0.98 |
| Δ int-EC trade % | 44.5 | 86.6 | -64.0 | -64.3 | 22.8 | 25.7 | 17.5 | 21.0 |

**342 Electric motors, generators, etc:** $\varepsilon_C = 7.35$, $\varepsilon_B = 6.77$, RS = 15%, TS = 8.8%, H = 0.022

| | | | | | | | | |
|---|---|---|---|---|---|---|---|---|
| Δ EC output % | 0.37 | 0.31 | 1.72 | 0.92 | 0.29 | 0.28 | 0.30 | 0.30 |
| Δ average costs % | -0.05 | -0.09 | -0.26 | -0.94 | -0.05 | -0.01 | -0.05 | -0.01 |
| Δ welfare % consumption | 0.29 | 0.29 | 0.52 | 0.40 | 0.31 | 0.31 | 0.31 | 0.31 |
| Δ int-EC trade % | 17.3 | 17.9 | 2.5 | 4.0 | 16.2 | 16.7 | 14.1 | 14.6 |

**346 Electrical household appliances:** $\varepsilon_C = 10.7$, $\varepsilon_B = 7.8$, RS = 10%, TS = 19.6%, H = 0.11

| | | | | | | | | |
|---|---|---|---|---|---|---|---|---|
| Δ EC output % | 2.09 | 1.80 | 8.08 | 6.70 | 1.29 | 1.30 | 1.33 | 1.38 |
| Δ average costs % | -0.32 | -0.76 | -1.15 | -3.35 | -0.20 | -0.22 | -0.19 | -0.16 |
| Δ welfare % consumption | 0.64 | 0.70 | 1.79 | 2.28 | 0.72 | 0.71 | 0.72 | 0.72 |
| Δ int-EC trade % | 22.1 | 26.0 | -23.0 | -25.8 | 17.8 | 20.5 | 9.5 | 10.9 |

**350 Motor vehicles:** $\varepsilon_C = 13.3$, $\varepsilon_B = 7.2$, RS = 16%, TS = 24.8%, H = 0.199

| | | | | | | | | |
|---|---|---|---|---|---|---|---|---|
| Δ EC output % | 3.36 | 3.16 | 10.5 | 9.68 | 1.71 | 1.90 | 1.67 | 1.95 |
| Δ average costs % | -0.56 | -1.40 | -1.72 | -2.67 | -0.29 | -0.41 | -0.27 | -0.13 |
| Δ welfare % consumption | 0.83 | 0.95 | 4.09 | 4.50 | 0.91 | 0.89 | 0.92 | 0.9 |
| Δ int-EC trade % | 18.7 | 25.3 | -61.4 | -62.4 | 14.3 | 16.5 | 0.8 | 2.7 |

**438: Carpets, linoleum, etc:** $\varepsilon_C = 21.4$, $\varepsilon_B = 17.6$, RS = 6%, TS = 18.8%, H = 0.031

| | | | | | | | | |
|---|---|---|---|---|---|---|---|---|
| Δ EC output % | 2.51 | 2.68 | 4.46 | 3.80 | 1.74 | 2.21 | 1.75 | 2.22 |
| Δ average costs % | -0.17 | -0.45 | -0.30 | -0.22 | -0.12 | -0.06 | -0.13 | -0.06 |
| Δ welfare % consumption | 0.67 | 0.74 | 0.75 | 0.75 | 0.71 | 0.74 | 0.71 | 0.74 |
| Δ int-EC trade % | 45.0 | 55.3 | 26.7 | 33.2 | 39.6 | 46.5 | 39.1 | 45.9 |

**451 Footwear:** $\varepsilon_C = 53.3$, $\varepsilon_B = 42.4$, RS = 2%, TS = 27.0%, H = 0.009

| | | | | | | | | |
|---|---|---|---|---|---|---|---|---|
| Δ EC output % | 3.21 | 3.16 | 5.53 | 5.58 | 1.93 | 2.53 | 1.93 | 2.53 |
| Δ average costs % | 0.03 | -0.00 | -0.26 | -0.42 | 0.0 | 0.22 | 0.0 | 0.22 |
| Δ welfare % consumption | 0.35 | 0.37 | 0.46 | 0.50 | 0.41 | 0.38 | 0.41 | 0.38 |
| Δ int-EC trade % | 41.4 | 99.8 | 0.0 | 8.7 | 37.7 | 70.6 | 37.6 | 70.4 |

## 6. Integrated markets

The second policy experiment we undertake is one in which, in addition to the reduction in tariff equivalents, we require that price differences between markets are equal to trade costs, so forcing firms to act on an integrated rather than segmented market basis. In order to understand the effects of this change, note that firms generally have a larger share of their domestic market than they do of foreign markets (see, e.g., table 1). This is reflected in firms setting price–cost margins higher in domestic markets than they do in foreign markets in order to exploit this market power, and in relatively high values of Herfindahl concentration indices. When markets are integrated price–cost margins (cost inclusive of trade costs) must be the same in all markets, and the relevant measure of concentration is the Herfindahl index for the EC as a whole. This causes a reduction in firms' domestic market prices, and in the degree of concentration. Essentially, firms lose the ability to price high in their relatively captive domestic markets.

These changes have two effects. First, the reduction in domestic prices causes demand to switch towards domestic producers, and so tends to reduce the value of intra-EC trade. This is illustrated for the electrical household appliances industry in table 5, where we see that (with a fixed number of models and Cournot behaviour), intra-EC trade falls by 23%. As trade is reduced, so production increases in net importing countries (notably the U.K. and the rest of the EC), while it falls in Italy. Second, the loss of domestic market power and the associated price fall cause large changes in welfare. When the number of firms is held constant, consumers' surplus rises by 3.6% of base consumption, and profits fall by 1.8% (table 5). The net welfare gain of 1.79% of base consumption is nearly three times larger than the gain from reduced tariff barriers with segmented markets.

When entry and exit is permitted, then the reduction in profits leads to significant exit – over 16% of European firms cease production. Coupling this with the increase in overall sales caused by the price reductions, remaining firms increase in scale, and average costs fall by 3%. Welfare is then raised by 2.3% of base consumption, over three times the gain recorded when markets remained segmented.

Table 6 reports the effect of this experiment across all ten industries, and for Bertrand as well as Cournot behaviour; segmented market results are also reported for purposes of comparison. As would be expected, the integration of markets only has dramatic effects when, in the base case, firms have significant market power in their domestic economy (associated with high Herfindahl indices), and when this market power is exploited (behaviour is Cournot rather than Bertrand). In the Bertrand case the welfare effects of market integration are negligible, as is the case with Cournot behaviour in the most competitive industries in the sample (e.g., 322, machine tools).

However, in other industries welfare gains from integration are very significant, exceeding 4% of base consumption in three industries.

## 7. Conclusions

It is appropriate to sound a note of caution in conclusion. The industries
that we have studied clearly have features which can be captured only in a
model of imperfect competition. The models which we have used in this
analysis do capture some important aspects of imperfectly competitive
behaviour in an intuitively appealing way but they are nevertheless at best a
crude approximation to the complexity of real-world competitive interaction.

We have examined two routes towards the completion of the internal EC
market. The first treated the policy as a quantitative change, involving small
reductions in barriers to trade. This change resulted in increased import
penetration in each country, so increasing competition and raising welfare –
although by modest amounts. The second policy change involved a qualitative change in firms' behaviour: forcing firms to act on a European-wide
'integrated market' basis, so removing firms' ability to exploit their domestic
markets. This policy yields large welfare gains. It also causes large reductions
in profit (and in the long run, exit of firms), and it is not obvious that there
exist feasible changes in EC trade policy and competition policy that could
impose such a change. In practice policy may be expected to be some
combination of our two experiments. As barriers are cut, so firms' ability to
act in a segmented market manner may be reduced. However, presenting the
two policy experiments separately is instructive. It highlights the fact that,
while some gains can be derived from moving the EC closer to being a full
customs union, more significant welfare gains may be obtained from the
creation of a genuinely unified European market.

## Appendix

*(1) Perceived elasticities.* The elasticities $e_{ij}(B)$ and $\Theta_{ij}(B)$ are obtained by
differentiating demand functions (5) with respect to $p_{ij}$ and $m_i$, respectively,
and incorporating changes through the price index, $q_j$, eq. (2).

The elasticities $e_{ij}(C)$ and $\Theta_{ij}(C)$ are obtained by differentiating the inverse
demand functions,

$$p_{ij} = x_{ij}^{-1/\varepsilon} a_{ij}^{1/\varepsilon} b_j^{1/\varepsilon} y_j^{(1/\varepsilon - 1/\mu)},$$

and incorporating changes in the sub-utility function, $y_j$, eq. (1).

*(2) Integrated markets.* Let a single firm (denoted *) in country $k$ change its
sales in the integrated markets by proportion $d \ln[\sum_{j=1}^{K} x_{kj}^*]$. Its prices are
constrained by eq. (13), but may move equiproportionately by amounts $\hat{p}_k^*$ ( ^

denotes a logarithmic derivative). Let $X$ be the matrix $x_{ij}/\sum_{j=1}^{K} x_{ij}$, $i=1,\ldots,I$, $j=1,\ldots,K$, $\hat{q}$ be the vector of log derivatives of the vector with elements $q_j$, and $\delta_k$ be a vector with 1 in the $k$th row, and zeros elsewhere. Differentiating the demand functions and adding gives,

$$\mathrm{d}\ln\left[\sum_{j=1}^{K} x_{kj}^{*}\right] = -\varepsilon\hat{p}_k^{*} + (\varepsilon-\mu)\,\delta_k^T X\hat{q}. \tag{A.1}$$

For firms that do not change their total sales we have,

$$0 = -\varepsilon\hat{p}_k^{*} + (\varepsilon-\mu)X\hat{q}, \tag{A.2}$$

where $\hat{p}$ is the log derivative of the vector with elements $p_i$. From the definition of the price indices, (2),

$$\hat{q} = S^T[\mathrm{diag}(n-\delta_k)\hat{p} + \delta_k\hat{p}_k^{*}], \tag{A.3}$$

where diag($\cdot$) denotes the diagonal matrix formed from the vector, and $S$ is the matrix.

$$S = (m_i p_{ij} x_{ij})\Big/ \sum_{j=1}^{I} n_i m_i p_{ij} x_{ij}.$$

Using (A.2) and (A.3) in (A.1) gives,

$$-E_k(C) = \mathrm{d}\ln\left[\sum_{j=1}^{K} x_{kj}^{*}\right]\Big/\hat{p}_k^{*}$$

$$= -\varepsilon + \delta_k^T[[X^T S]^{-1}/(\varepsilon-\mu) - \mathrm{diag}(n-\delta_k)/\varepsilon]^{-1}\delta_k.$$

## References

Baldwin, R. and P.R. Krugman, 1986, Market access and international competition; A simulation study of 16K random access memories, Unpublished manuscript.

Brander, J.A., 1981, Intra-industry trade in identical commodities, Journal of International Economics 11, 1–14.

Brander, J.A. and P.R. Krugman, 1983, A reciprocal dumping model of international trade, Journal of International Economics 15, 313–321.

Brander, J.A. and B.J. Spencer, 1984, Tariff protection and imperfect competition, in: H. Kierzkowski, ed., Monopolistic competition and international trade (Oxford University Press, Oxford).

Brander, J.A. and B.J. Spencer, 1985, Export subsidies and international market share rivalry, Journal of International Economics 18, 83–100.

Cox, D. and R. Harris, 1985, Trade liberalization and industrial organisation; Some estimates for Canada, Journal of Political Economy 93, 115–145.

Deaton, A.S., 1975, The measurement of income and price elasticities, European Economic Review 6, 261–273.

Dixit, A.K., 1984, International trade policy for oligopolistic industries, Economic Journal, Suppl., 1–16.

Dixit, A.K., 1987, Tariffs and subsidies under oligopoly; The case of the US automobile industry, in: H. Kierzkowski, ed., Protection and competition in international trade (Blackwell, Oxford).

Dixit, A.K. and J.E. Stiglitz, 1977, Monopolistic competition and optimum product diversity, American Economic Review 67, 297–308.

Eaton, J. and G. Grossman, 1986, Optimal trade and industrial policy under oligopoly, Quarterly Journal of Economics 101, 383–406.

Ethier, W., 1982, National and international returns to scale in the modern theory of international trade, American Economic Review 72, 389–405.

Harris, R., 1984, Applied general equilibrium analysis of small open economies with imperfect competition, American Economic Review 74, 1016–1033.

Harris, R. with D. Cox, 1984, Trade, industrial policy and Canadian manufacturing, Ontario Economic Council, Toronto.

Helpman, E. and P.R. Krugman, 1985, Increasing returns, imperfect competition, and international trade, MIT Press, Cambridge, MA.

Horstmann, I. and J.R. Markusen, 1986, Up the average cost curve; inefficient entry and the new protectionism, Journal of International Economics 20, 225–247.

Houthakker, H.S., 1965, New evidence on demand elasticities, Econometrica 33, 277–288.

Houthakker, H.S. and L.D. Taylor, 1970, Consumer demand in the United States; Analysis and projections (Harvard University Press, Cambridge, MA).

Kierzkowski, H. (ed.) 1984, Monopolistic competition and international trade (Oxford University Press, Oxford).

Kierzkowski, H. (ed.) 1987, Protection and competition in international trade (Blackwell, Oxford).

Krugman, P.R., 1979, Increasing returns, monopolistic competition and international trade, Journal of International Economics 9, 469–479.

Krugman, P.R., 1980, Scale economies, product differentiation, and the pattern of trade, American Economic Review 70, 950–959.

Krugman, P.R., 1981, Intra-industry specialization and the gains from trade, Journal of Political Economy 89, 959–973.

Krugman, P.R., 1984, Import protection as export promotion; International competition in the presence of oligopoly and economies of scale, in: H. Kierzkowski, ed., Monopolistic competition and international trade (Oxford University Press, Oxford).

Krugman, P.R., 1987, Market access and competition in high technology industries; A simulation exercise, in: H. Kierzkowski, ed., Protection and competition in international trade (Blackwell, Oxford).

Laussel, D., C. Montet and A. Peguin-Feissolle, 1988, Optimal trade policy under oligopoly; A calibrated model of the Europe–Japan rivalry in the EEC car market, European Economic Review, this issue.

Markusen, J.R. and A.J. Venables, 1988, Trade policy with increasing returns and imperfect competition; Contradictory results from competing assumptions, Journal of International Economics, forthcoming.

Owen, N., 1983, Economies of scale, competitivess, and trade patterns within the European Community (Oxford University Press, Oxford).

Pelkmans, J. and L.A. Winters, 1988, Europe's domestic market, Chatham House, London.

Piggott, J.R. and J. Whalley, 1985, U.K. tax policy and applied general equilibrium analysis (Cambridge University Press, Cambridge).

Pratten, C.F., 1987, A survey of economies of scale, Unpublished manuscript, DAE, Cambridge.

Venables, A.J., 1985, Trade and trade policy with imperfect competition; the case of identical products and free entry, Journal of International Economics 19, 1–19.

Venables, A.J., 1987, Trade and trade policy with differentiated products; A Chamberlinian–Ricardian model, Economic Journal 97, 700–718.

Venables, A.J. and A. Smith, 1986, Trade and industrial policy under imperfect competition, Economic Policy 1, 622–672.

# [15]

## FREE TRADE AGREEMENTS AS PROTECTIONIST DEVICES: RULES OF ORIGIN[1]

*Anne O. Krueger*

Until recently, little attention was paid to free trade agreements (FTAs), and most theory regarding preferential trading arrangements focused on customs unions (CUs). With the recent negotiation of the NAFTA treaty, however, attention is turning to FTAs. Most analysts have regarded FTAs as being little different in their trade effects from CUs, and the NAFTA has mostly been analyzed in the traditional CU framework. For example, it has been argued that the US–Mexican FTA is probably "natural" and hence likely to be trade creating, increasing economic efficiency[2] and thus enhancing welfare.[3]

It is the purpose of this chapter to argue that there is an important protectionist bias inherent in FTAs which is not present in CUs. To make the case, it is first necessary to sketch the traditional analysis of the welfare effects of the CUs and FTAs. Thereafter, attention turns to the fact that external tariffs differ among countries in FTAs, and that rules of origin (ROOs) can therefore automatically extend the protection of one trading partner to another FTA member. A straightforward model of incentives under an FTA is then presented, along with an arithmetic example of "exported protection" via an FTA.

Conventional wisdom has been that a country can avoid the potential trade-diversion losses of an FTA if it has very low, or no, trade barriers when it enters into an FTA. Examination of the implications of ROOs, however, suggests that not only must a country's trade barriers be low, but so also must its partner's, to insure that these costs are avoided. A final section then considers some aspects of the political economy of FTAs and of protection via ROOs.

91

A . K R U E G E R

## Traditional CU–FTA theory

It has long been recognized that the net welfare effects of customs unions and free trade areas are ambiguous. To analyze the problem of the welfare effects of CU, theorists have abstracted from the question of changes in the effects of average protection relative to excluded countries by assuming that a CU is formed among countries which then set a common external tariff equal, in some sense, to the average tariff in place in the individual countries pre-union.

Under these assumptions, a CU could be trade creating or trade diverting. Trade creation would take place when producers in member countries reduced the output of their industries previously protected against imports from CU partners and the rest of the world, and instead imported from lower-cost member countries. Trade diversion would occur when countries replaced imports from low-cost non-member countries with higher-cost production from member countries.[4]

When trade creation predominates sufficiently, there is a strong presumption that welfare of the member country or countries for which trade is "created" will improve. This is because the "created" trade shifts production from the higher-cost home country to the lower-cost partner country.[5] When trade diversion dominates for a given country, there is a presumption of welfare loss for the country in question, as the country shifts from low-cost sources of imports in the rest of the world to sourcing its imports from its partner country, whose production is protected by the external tariff. Unless consumption gains from the arrangement are large enough (because of lower prices to consumers) to offset the trade diversion effects, trade diversion leads to a welfare loss to the importing country.

To be sure, trade diversion could represent a welfare loss for one CU/FTA country and a welfare gain for another. An assessment of overall welfare effects for individual members of the CU could require a weighting of trade diversion, trade creation, and consumption effects, as well as the effects of any terms of trade gain achieved by the trading partners vis-à-vis the rest of the world.[6]

The general view has been that CUs and FTAs are equivalent in these effects: that while CUs differ from FTAs in having a common external tariff, the trade diversion and trade creation effects can be analyzed in similar fashion. Because countries retain their pre-existing external tariffs in the case of FTAs, however, it was not thought necessary to assume that the average tariff remained the same after CU as before: since no tariff was changed, it was *assumed* that that happened. Moreover, that implied that a country that itself practiced free trade could only benefit from forming an FTA with another country: it would gain access to the other country's markets and pay no costs, since its zero tariffs would lead producers to choose the low-cost source.

FREE TRADE AGREEMENTS AND RULES OF ORIGIN

## Rules of origin and the average height of tariffs[7]

In any CU or FTA negotiation, one of the critical issues concerns "rules of origin" (ROOs). The ROOs specify a criterion, or criteria, under which commodities imported by one CU or FTA partner will be deemed to have originated from within the CU or FTA and thus be eligible for duty-free treatment.

For a CU, ROOs determine eligibility for duty-free entry from the partner; the tariff is common to members.[8] In an FTA, however, ROOs have an important additional function. Without a ROO, each imported commodity would enter through the country with the lowest tariff on each commodity. If the rule were simply that some value should have been added in the country of origin, anything — the addition of a label, the final assembly or even the painting of a product — would qualify an item for duty-free entry to the other country.

The criteria adopted in ROOs can take a variety of forms. One simple and frequently-used ROO is that, in order to qualify as originating in the partner country, the item must change tariff classifications. Another is that a specified percentage of the commodity's sales price must consist of value added in the partner country. A fourth ROO specifies a percentage of purchased parts and components that must be purchased from CU or FTA members.

The criterion for the duty-free treatment is important in determining the economic effects of the ROO. The incentives provided to producers hoping to export to their trading partners obviously vary with the ROO as well as with the structure of tariffs: if materials, but not labor, are counted in establishing origin, there is an incentive to substitute materials. If domestic labor, but not capital, is included in the calculation, the incentive to substitute labor for capital is evidently present.

Even in these relatively simple cases, further elaboration of the ROO is needed. When the ROO is stated in terms of fraction of parts and components, for example, the question then is shifted back one step to determining how much domestic value added there must be in a given part or component for it to count as domestic.[9] When domestic value added is the criterion, the precise criterion for attributing capital costs must be specified.[10] Even accounting practices for allocating joint costs must be agreed upon.

Until negotiation of the NAFTA agreement, the United States used the percentage of domestic value added as its criterion for duty-exempt eligibility under the US–Canada FTA, but counted only labor costs, and not any imputed capital costs.[11]

ROOs agreed upon in forming an FTA in fact extend the protection accorded by each country to producers in other FTA member countries. As such, ROOs can constitute a source of bias toward economic inefficiency in

## A. KRUEGER

FTAs in a way they cannot do with customs union.[12] Moreover, a country with a zero-tariff level pre-FTA could find its producers post-FTA diverting their imports from low-cost third-country sources to the partner country in order to be eligible for FTA treatment of their exports to the partner country. ROOs governing treatment of Mexico's exports to the United States, for example, can induce efficient Mexican producers to shift their imports from low-cost third country suppliers to higher-cost United States sources, EVEN IF THERE ARE NO MEXICAN TARIFFS ON THE IMPORTS OF THOSE COMMODITIES.[13]

The United States can, at least in theory, therefore use an FTA agreement to gain protection for its industries in Mexican markets! Rather than inducing Mexican firms to switch to US tariff-free sources because they are then cheaper than low-cost but tariff ridden world sources – the traditional trade diversion case – an FTA could induce Mexican producers to shift their purchases of intermediate inputs knowingly from a low-cost world supplier to a higher cost US supplier in order to qualify for duty-free importation of the final product into the US market. Additional Mexican imports to the US might be incorrectly regarded as trade-creating when in fact they would result from the protection in US tariffs being extended to Mexican products entering the US. An FTA can also induce the development of production facilities in an FTA partner, even when the partner's own external tariff would make such facilities uneconomic.

ROOs can thus provide protection to one country's higher-cost producers in another country's markets even when the latter's tariff structure, when taken by itself, results in imports from the rest of the world being lower cost.

## Profit-maximizing behavior under ROOs

Customs unions have rules of origin[14] but when there is an FTA, the issue is especially important because, by definition, external tariffs differ between partner countries. A ROO may make it profitable to establish production facilities in Mexico, even though at pre-existing Mexican tariff rates such facilities are uneconomic. Alternatively, it may benefit Mexican producers to pay more for some or all of their intermediate goods from higher-priced US sources than to pay less to lower-cost world sources. The choice will clearly depend on relative costs in Mexico and the US and analysis is straightforward.

The interesting case is when the US has a significant cost advantage relative to Mexico but a cost disadvantage vis-à-vis the rest of the world in an intermediate commodity, and is able implicitly to extend its tariffs (or other protective devices) to the Mexican market through a ROO. The exact specification of the ROO was one of the last sticking points of the NAFTA agreement.[15] In those negotiations, the United States was supporting a more stringent ROO while Canada and Mexico were in favor of a lower percentage and a broader definition. It therefore seems evident that the

FREE TRADE AGREEMENTS AND RULES OF ORIGIN

United States was indeed attempting to provide protection to some US producers in the Mexican market, thus "exporting" American protection despite low Mexican tariff rates.

This can readily be seen. Profit-maximizing producers of cloth in Mexico choose $f$, the fraction of textiles purchased from the US, to maximize:

$$\pi_m = P_{us}^c - P_{us}^x fy - P_w^x(1 - f)y, \tag{1}$$

where:

$p$ is price
$t$ is the tariff rate (or tariff equivalent)
$w$ and $us$ subscripts denote the world and the US
$c$, $x$ superscripts denote clothing and textiles
$f$ = fraction of textiles purchased from US sources
$y$ = international value of textiles purchased per dollar of clothing at international prices ($y < 1$)
$r$ = rule of origin stated as a proportion of sale price of clothing
$P_{us}^x = (1 + t_{us}^x)P_w^x$
$P_{us}^c = 1$ if $P_{us}^c - P_w^x(1 - f)y < r$
$P_{us}^c = 1 + t_{us}^c$ if $P_{us}^c - P_w^x(1 - f)y \geq r$.

The world price of textiles, $P_w^x$, can be used as a numéraire and set equal to one. Then, it is evident that producers in the FTA partner country will choose to satisfy the rule of origin whenever

$$1 + t_{us}^c - (1 + t_{us}^x)fy > 1 - fy. \tag{2}$$

But the left-hand side of equation (2) is nothing other than the protection to domestic value added in the United States; while the right-hand side is value added per unit of cloth output at international prices. Dividing through by the right-hand side yields:

$$\frac{1 + t_{us}^c - (1 + t_{us}^x)fy}{1 - y} > 0 \tag{3}$$

which is the criterion for positive effective protection in the United States.

The higher the effective rate of protection in the United States for a given commodity, the more it will pay Mexican producers to buy intermediate goods from US sources despite lower foreign (Mexican tariff-inclusive) prices. To be sure, as Mexican producers increase their sales in the US, the price of their export in the US will fall while the marginal cost of production in Mexico will rise. An equilibrium eventually will be reached in which the ex ante profits are eliminated, but it may well be an equilibrium in which Mexican producers continue to buy from US sources to enable them to sell at tariff-inclusive prices.

This result can be illustrated with an arithmetic example. It is assumed

## A. KRUEGER

that the United States is exporting its protection on intermediate goods to Mexico, although a similar example could readily be constructed for Mexico to be doing the same thing: indeed, it is possible that rules of origin in an FTA could export protection in some markets in each country to the other country. Table 6.1 gives some hypothetical numbers for Mexican and US tariffs and inputs of intermediates before and after an FTA comes into effect.

The assumptions are all listed at the top of Table 6.1. It is assumed that the ROO is set in terms of a percentage of purchased parts and components.

*Table 6.1* Hypothetical rule-of-origin induced shift to higher-cost US suppliers

*Assume*: Motors, brakes, tires, and batteries are used in fixed proportions in making automobiles.

*World prices of these items are*:

| | |
|---|---|
| auto | $1,000 |
| motor | 250 |
| brakes | 200 |
| tires | 100 |
| battery | 50 |

Hence, international value added in assembling an auto is $400. Assume that Mexico has zero tariffs on autos and on each component, and assembles autos, importing all components pre-FTA.

*Let US nominal tariffs be as follows*:

| | |
|---|---|
| auto | 50% |
| motor | 40 |
| brakes | 40 |
| tires | 50 |
| battery | 50 |

Note that the effective rate of protection for auto producers in the US is 125 percent. Let the ROO be that 80 percent of components, valued at purchasers' prices, must be produced within NAFTA. Then Mexican producers will be confronted with the following choices:

| | Import parts | Buy parts in US to meet 80 percent ROO | |
|---|---|---|---|
| Selling price of auto in US | 1,000 | 1,500 | |
| Cost of components | 600 | motor | 350 (from US) |
| | | brakes | 280 (from US) |
| | | tires | 100 (imported) |
| | | battery | 50 (imported) |
| | | Total components $780 | |
| Return to domestic labor and capital | 400 | 720 | |

Note that a 90 percent ROO would protect American tire manufacturers. But even with a 100 percent ROO, it clearly pays Mexican producers to purchase parts from higher-cost US sources than to import duty-free from non-NAFTA members, unless it is cheaper to produce those parts in Mexico than to buy them in the US.

FREE TRADE AGREEMENTS AND RULES OF ORIGIN

To assume a value added criterion would complicate the example needlessly, but the principle would remain unaltered.

It is assumed that, pre-FTA, Mexico imports all components duty-free from the rest of the world (ROW) at international prices, and assembles autos, using $600 of components (valued at either world or domestic prices) to make an auto. In the United States, automobiles are subject to a 50 percent tariff, while brakes and motors are subject to 40 percent nominal tariff and tires and batteries 50 percent. This gives rise to a 61.25 percent effective rate of protection for American automobile manufacturers: they must pay $855 for their components, or 42.5 percent more than the world price but they receive 1.5 times the world price for their output.

After the formation of an FTA, Mexican producers have two choices. On the one hand, they can continue to buy all their inputs in the world market; if they do so, they do not meet the ROO. Hence their product is subject to a 50 percent duty on entry into the US, and they receive $1,000 per auto exported. On the other hand, they can shift from purchasing components from the ROW to purchasing enough of them in the US to meet the ROO.

The right-hand side of Table 6.1 shows ex ante profits from shifting components purchased from the ROW to the US in response to a ROO of 80 percent. At that ROO, Mexican auto assemblers could sell in the US market at $1,500 buying motors and brakes from the US at prices 40 percent above that of their foreign suppliers. That would meet the ROO, even though batteries and tires (with a 50 percent duty) were still purchases abroad. At a 90 percent ROO, tires purchases would be shifted toward FTA-member origin. And, at 100 percent ROO, it would pay Mexican producers to purchase all components in the US in order to be eligible for duty-exemption on auto exports to the US.

To see how a higher rule of origin is more protective, note that an 80 percent ROO extends the 40 percent nominal rate of protection to the Mexican market, but leaves batteries and tires unprotected. With a 90 percent ROO, tires are subject to 50 percent nominal protection in Mexico as well as in the US. Clearly also, a higher rate of protection on intermediate goods, or a lower nominal rate of protection on the final commodity in the US market would be consistent with inducing Mexican producers to shift from world sources to higher-cost (to them, as well as to the country) US sources.

Rules of origin can have similar effects even if there is positive effective protection in Mexico prior to the FTA, provided that the Mexican price of the final good is below the US price pre-FTA.

If one ex ante attempted to assess the trade creation and trade diversion aspects of the FTA with respect to textiles and clothing, from a US perspective, there would appear to have been trade creation as Mexican exports of clothing to the US increased. From a Mexican perspective, there might appear to have been trade creation if total imports of textiles

97

A. KRUEGER

increased (because the volume of clothing production increased as exports to the US expanded) or trade diversion (despite the absence of an external tariff).

More generally, producers of a final good in an FTA would find it advantageous to purchase higher-cost (protected) inputs from other FTA members than to purchase from lower cost ROW sources whenever: (1) the effective rate of protection in the partner country was greater than in the home country; and (2) the rule of origin would not be satisfied without such purchases.

## How protectionist is the NAFTA?

It has often been argued that such a high fraction of Mexico's trade is with the United States that Mexico is bound to gain by an FTA. That judgment may well be correct. But there are some indications that American intent was to secure as much advantage for US producers in the Mexican market as possible. One piece of evidence is the report that American negotiators evidently tried to insist that Mexico should not lower its tariff structure any further from its present average of about 9 percent.[16] The higher are Mexican tariffs, the more advantage US firms have relative to foreign competitors in the Mexican market, and the more trade diversion is likely to occur.

But ROOs were also a major issue in the negotiations. The full text of the NAFTA agreement has not yet been made public, but enough details are known to be suggestive. In at least two key sectors, ROOs are clearly important and were a major point of contention until the final hours of negotiations. First, for automobiles and parts, the ROO was set at 62.5 percent, a number which will be reached gradually over eight years starting at 50 percent (the number in the US–Canada Agreement[17]) when the pact goes into effect.[18] Both Mexico and Canada had attempted to bargain for lower numbers.[19] Expectations evidently are that Volkswagen will locate more operations in Mexico in order to comply with the requirement, while Japanese firms will have greater difficulty in meeting it, and potential new Mexican producers will be greatly discouraged from entry.[20] It is noteworthy that Canada agreed to the higher ROO only after the United States accepted a revision of the way in which FTA value added is calculated: the US agreed to include interest and other capital costs, as well as labor costs.[21]

In textiles and clothing, as well, ROOs were an important issue. There, the agreement calls for duty-free treatment of Mexican garments only if the yarn is made, the cloth woven, and all cutting and sewing is done in North America.[22]

To be sure, there are other sectors of the American economy that will be opened, at least to some degree, as a result of the NAFTA agreement. US restrictions on Mexican fruit and vegetables appear to have been relaxed

### FREE TRADE AGREEMENTS AND RULES OF ORIGIN

considerably, and that will almost certainly result in trade creation. Financial liberalization, tariff reductions, and other measures will also move in that direction.

Overall, however, it is clear that there are some fairly strong measures designed to provide protection to US producers in the NAFTA agreement. Despite Mexico's position as a "natural" trading partner, one must question the extent to which the NAFTA is truly a step toward a more open, multilateral trading system, or whether it is a step toward greater US protectionism encompassing not only the United States but all of North America.

## What is the political economy of rules of origin?

There remains a political economy puzzle. That is, conventional wisdom is that tariffs are escalated, with higher nominal rates of protection of final commodities than of intermediate goods, and higher nominal rates on intermediate goods than on raw materials. Yet, at first sight it would appear that the chief gainers in the United States from ROOs would be US producers of intermediate goods. Why should US producers of final products, such as automobiles, be "gleeful"[23] at higher ROOs for eligibility for entry into the US market? For that matter, why was it widely believed that a higher ROO would exclude Japanese automobile producers, such as Nissan, from the US market?

The answer must lie, at least in part, in production relations, and the ways in which parts and components must be "designed in" to final products. To the extent that Nissan, for example, is designed with specifications of Japanese parts and components, an attempt to shift to a Mexican, Canadian, or US supplier would involve the start-up of a new production facility. Such a facility may not be able to produce at the same costs as are incurred in Japan; moreover, if there is monopolistic competition, and fixed costs to be covered in the production of parts and components, the North American market for Nissan autos may not be large enough to permit averaging fixed costs and still be profitable. If any of these speculations are correct, the ROO does protect producers of the final product in avoiding competition from those with access to cheaper intermediate goods. The price to the final producers of receiving that protection, however, is that they must share part of it with producers of intermediate goods in the FTA.[24]

As producers of final commodities avoid some competition and receive protection, they are presumably willing to pay higher prices for purchased inputs to continue to enjoy that protection. Once that is recognized, a rule of origin may be a device through which producers of final goods and those of intermediate goods can be induced to support an FTA. If so, then the

A . K R U E G E R

political economy of FTAs suggests that they are as likely to be protectionist as they are to be trade creating.

## Notes

1  I am indebted to Martin Bronfenbrenner, Peter Dohlman, Omer Gokcekus, Bernard Hoekman, Kala Krishna, Richard Snape and members of the International Economics Workshop at Duke for helpful comments on an early version of this chapter.

2  Throughout, economic efficiency will be used to describe the relationship between marginal rates in domestic production in trade in value added terms. A situation will be regarded as economically more efficient when resources are combined in ways that produce greater value added evaluated at international prices. It is well known that IVA is maximized, and hence the economy economically most efficient, when the international marginal rates of transformation (IMRTs) (which equal international price ratios in the absence of monopoly power in trade) among commodities equal the domestic marginal rates of transformation (DMRTs). However, welfare also increases when consumers are enabled to attain larger consumption bundles. It is well known that one might have a customs union where the divergence between the IMRT and DMRT increased, but consumer welfare improved because of the lower post-FTA prices. For that reason, it is important to distinguish between economic efficiency and economic welfare. If economic efficiency increases, welfare must increase. If efficiency decreases, welfare could either increase or decrease.

3  See Summers (1991) for an application of this analysis to the proposed Western Hemisphere Free Trade Agreement (WHFTA).

4  The classic analysis is by Lipsey (1960). There is considerable evidence emerging in developing countries that increased competition subsequent to trade liberalization may result in increases in X-efficiency. That can surely happen as well subsequent to the formation of CUs and FTAs, but if ROOs do increase protection to some industries, there is no increase in competition in those cases, and the issue is therefore not pertinent to the analysis in this chapter.

5  If the partner's costs are none the less above costs in the rest of the world, the gain to the home country would be even greater if it liberalized multilaterally.

6  Kemp and Wan (1976) have shown that it is always possible for a pattern of tariffs to be established post-union which would insure at least the same level of imports and exports from the CU with the rest of the world; in that case, the CU would clearly be trade-creating.

7  The considerations discussed here are relevant for Canada, the US and Mexico. However, the argument that much support for the FTA with Mexico is protectionist in intent is based on the Mexican case. Hence, to simplify discussion, only the ramifications of US–Mexican trading relations are considered here.

8  The European Community, for example, has protected its semiconductor industry by determining that origin is assigned to the country where "a product has been wholly obtained or where it has undergone its last substantial working or processing". It then defined the "last substantial processing" to have taken place with diffusion. Diffusion, however, is such an early stage that it is not technically feasible to initiate fabrication in any place other than where diffusion is performed. The net impact was that non-EC producers had to invest in fabrication facilities within the EC to avoid border duties. See *Official Journal of the European Community*, vol. 32, February 1989, p. 23.

FREE TRADE AGREEMENTS AND RULES OF ORIGIN

9  This was the issue in the now-famous Honda case where the US challenged the eligibility of Canadian-produced Hondas to qualify for duty-free treatment in the American market.

10  Under NAFTA, it has evidently been agreed that a part or component that is more than 50 percent domestic value added will be counted as domestic value added, and interest costs on machinery used in production will also constitute domestic value added.

11  How rules of origin are actually administered may also affect their protective content. If, for example, the US authorities take the average value added within the FTA over all a firm's output of a product in question, there could even be a reduction in earlier Mexican exports to third countries as it was no longer profitable to export when purchasing intermediate goods from the US. It is reported that EFTA producers appear willing to pay duties averaging at least 6 percent of price in order to avoid the paperwork needed to establish origin. See Hoekman and Leidy (1992b: p. 19).

12  Rules of origin are also present in customs union and can, of course, bias production decisions. But since external tariffs are similar across countries, they cannot generate the sort of bias discussed here. They then become equivalent to domestic content requirement. See Grossman (1981) for an analysis.

13  This could not happen in the case of a customs union because the external tariff would be common.

14  However, the phenomenon noted here, i.e. the ability of a rule of origin to make it profitable to switch from a lower-cost source to a higher-cost source, could not happen under a customs union because the external tariff rates would be common to both countries. While a Mexican producer might therefore find himself with higher input costs after a customs union than before, any shift to a US source would be the normal trade diversion variety. Under an FTA, it is the difference in tariff rates, combined with the rule of origin, that gives rise to the possibility of a profitable shift to a source which is higher-cost to the buyer.

15  The chapter on ROOs of the NAFTA was 193 pages long in the draft of September 6, 1992.

16  *Financial Times*, June 9, 1992, p. 14.

17  To see how important administration can be, the United States is reported to have achieved the 62.5 percent rule, but to have conceded on how it is calculated. The full cost of processing materials, and interest costs on machinery and equipment had not been counted as part of domestic value added under the earlier US–Canada interpretation and would be under the new ruling. This, in effect, would mean that Honda had met the 50 percent FTA origin rule and would not be liable for duties, as it would have been had the old US formula continued to prevail. *New York Times*, August 15, 1992, p. 26.

18  *New York Times*, August 13, 1992, p. C3. The ROO for new contracts is somewhat more restrictive. See Hufbauer and Schott (1992) for a discussion.

19  See *Financial Times*, July 24, 1992, p. 4.

20  *Financial Times*, June 18, 1992, p. 6.

21. The Honda dispute with Canada was over interpretation of rules of origin. The US Customs Department "found that the engine blocks, produced in Marysville, Ohio, and exported to Canada for re-export to the US, did not contain sufficient North American content." It was further reported that

A. KRUEGER

Canadian and American authorities were still in disagreement over what constituted domestic content. See *Financial Times*, March 3, 1992.

22  *New York Times*, August 13, 1992, p. C3. Canada evidently won a partial exemption from this "bottoms up" rule for clothing.

23  *Financial Times*, August 18, 1992, p. 4.

24  See Hoekman and Leidy (1992a) for an alternative interpretation, focusing upon sharing rents between producers at various stages of production.

## Bibliography

Grossman, Gene (1981) "The Theory of Domestic Content Protection and Content Preference," *Quarterly Journal of Economics* 96: 583–603.

Hoekman, Bernard M. and Leidy, Michael P. (1992a) "Cascading Contingent Protection," *European Economic Review* 36: 883–892.

—— and —— (1992b) "Holes and Loopholes in Alternative Trade Agreements; History and Prospects," *Aussenwirtschaft* 47.

Hufbauer, Gary C. and Schott, Jeffrey (1992) *North American Free Trade: Issues and Recommendations*. Washington, DC: Institute for International Economics.

Kemp, Murray C. and Wan, Henry Jr (1976) "An Elementary Proposition Concerning the Formation of Customs Unions," *Journal of International Economics* 6: 95–97.

Lipsey, Richard G. (1960) "The Theory of Customs Unions: A General Survey," *Economic Journal* 70: 496–513.

Summers, Lawrence H. (1991) "Regionalism and the World Trading System," in Federal Reserve Bank of Kansas City, *Policy Implications of Trade and Currency Zones*, March, pp. 295–302.

# [16]
# Regionalism vs. multilateralism

L. ALAN WINTERS

## 1    Introduction

The literature on 'regionalism vs. multilateralism' is burgeoning as economists and a few political scientists grapple with the question of whether regional integration arrangements (RIAs) are good or bad for the multilateral system as a whole. Are RIAs 'building blocks or stumbling blocks', in Bhagwati's (1991) memorable phrase, or stepping stones towards multilateralism? As we worry about the ability of the WTO to maintain the GATT's unsteady yet distinct momentum towards liberalism, and as we contemplate the emergence of world-scale RIAs – the European Union, NAFTA, FTAA, APEC and, possibly, TAFTA – this question has never been more pressing.

'Regionalism vs. multilateralism' switches the focus of research from the immediate consequences of regionalism for the economic welfare of the integrating partners to the question of whether it sets up forces which encourage or discourage evolution towards globally freer trade. The answer is 'we don't know yet'. One can build models that suggest either conclusion, but to date these are sufficiently abstract that they should be viewed as parables rather than sources of testable predictions.

Moreover, even if we had testable predictions we have very little evidence. Arguably the European Union is the only RIA that is both big enough to affect the multilateral system and long-enough lived to have currently observable consequences. The European Union allows one convincingly to reject the hypothesis that one act of regionalism necessarily leads to the collapse of the multilateral system. But it is difficult to go further: the *anti-monde* to EU creation is unknown and one does not know to what extent the European Union is special. Thus any discussion of the evidence is necessarily judgemental. The majority view is, I think, that the advent of the European Union aided multilateralism. While I should like to believe this – especially now that US commitment

7

8   **L. Alan Winters**

to multilateralism is diluted by other 'lateralisms' (Summers, 1991) –
more needs to be done before it can be considered proven beyond
reasonable doubt.

This chapter has three substantive sections. Section 2 tries to define
some terms, which turns out to be much more complicated than I
expected: any reader who can define multilateralism simply can skip
section 2.1 and let me know his or her definition. It also proposes an
organisational classification for models of 'regionalism vs. multilateralism'. Section 3 discusses these models under five headings and Section 4
discusses some evidence. Section 5 offers some conclusions.

Survey articles are sometimes used to resolve issues of intellectual
precedence. I have not sought to do this and would caution against using
the dates of the papers included here as a means of doing so. In a field
barely five years old, publication delays completely distort the time
picture.

## 2    Definitions and classifications

### 2.1   Definitions

'Regionalism vs. multilateralism' is a much-discussed topic among trade
economists, but one which is surprisingly short on precise measures. I
shall define 'regionalism' loosely as any policy designed to reduce trade
barriers between a subset of countries, regardless of whether those
countries are actually contiguous or even close to each other. I shall not
define 'multilateralism' precisely, however, because – to my surprise and
regret – I find that I cannot easily do so.

Although multilateralism is a characteristic of the world economy or
world economic system, it must ultimately reside in the behaviour of
individual countries – the extent to which they behave in a multilateral
fashion. For any one country, I shall treat the latter as a positive function
of

(1) the degree to which discrimination is absent – perhaps the proportion
    of trade partners that receives identical treatment; and
(2) the extent to which the country's trading regime approximates free
    trade.

Strictly speaking criterion (1) would seem to be a sufficient definition of
multilateralism. However, it is neither very interesting in the current
context (any preferential trade arrangement with relatively few members
will worsen multilateralism) nor, I infer from their writings, what most
commentators have in mind when they debate the effects of regionalism

on multilateralism. Criterion (2) attempts to add back the missing dimension.

The weights and functional form with which the two criteria enter the index of individual multilateralism are left vague. If, starting from a universal (MFN) tariff, a country abolished tariffs on one (small) partner, that would seem to decrease its multilateralism, but if it abolished them on all but one (small) partner that would seem to increase it.[1] Similarly, I cannot pin down precisely how to combine countries into a single global index of multilateralism. Thus we need to be cautious in comparing different views of 'regionalism vs. multilateralism' – maybe their bottom lines differ.

In assessing regionalism we need also to recognise another complication. Shifting one partner into a free trade area (FTA) has a direct impact on our measure of multilateralism but, far more importantly, it also potentially initiates a whole series of accommodating adjustments, as the integrating partners and countries in the rest of the world (RoW) adjust their policies to the new circumstances. We must consider multilateralism at the end of this process, not just at the beginning. Moreover, in some circumstances the final outcome will not be determinate; rather, regionalism might affect the probabilities with which different outcomes occur. Several of the models surveyed below examine whether regionalism makes it more or less likely that countries within and without the RIA can strike a deal to create or maintain world-wide free trade. Such models do not forecast particular outcomes, but nonetheless comment pertinently on the environment in which they might flourish.

The previous paragraph mentioned a 'process'. Multilateralism is sometimes referred to as a process whereby countries solve problems in an interactive and cooperative fashion (Yarbrough and Yarbrough, 1992). While such interactions could clearly be affected by regionalism, I do not use this definition here. It is a view far too closely associated with professional negotiators and international bureaucrats for my taste, and is far too vague on the question of what purpose a process serves if it is not to generate outcomes.

Other commentators might focus entirely on the final outcome – the pattern of international trade. If one could determine the perfectly multilateral volume and pattern of trade, one could then easily define the index of actual multilateralism by any of several distance measures between actual and 'perfect' trade. The problem is all too obvious, however: how do we determine perfectly multilateral trade? From a policy point of view I should also be uneasy about a definition that focused on outcomes rather than trade policy instruments, for such a

10   **L. Alan Winters**

definition might imply indifference between methods of achieving
particular trade patterns. I recognise, however, that such unease should
not influence us too much in the intellectual business of defining the
phenomenon.

 Finally, many economists explore the interactions between countries
and the effects of regionalism on them by focusing on country welfare
and, usually, world welfare. These contributions are not strictly about
regionalism vs. multilateralism, for we surely cannot define multilateralism in terms of increasing welfare – even if, slightly less indefensibly, we
sometimes equate them. Nonetheless, welfare is sufficiently basic to the
business of economics that I include this class of studies in this survey.

## 2.2   A classification

To try to organise the rapidly growing model-based literature on
'regionalism vs. multilateralism', I have classified contributions according
to four characteristics of their basic approach. These concern political
objectives and organisation rather than economics *per se* for, in fact,
most models adopt one of two main representations of the economy: the
simple competitive homogeneous good model or the monopolistically
competitive model. In each there is usually a one-to-one correspondence
between goods and geographical entities – each entity having comparative advantage in one good – but in the latter several entities (say,
provinces) accrete into one country. The four characteristics are:

(*A*) Is the objective function (1) national economic welfare or (2) some
      other criterion deriving from political considerations? Within the
      latter set, (2), does the analysis explicitly treat (i) one country, (ii)
      two (i.e. the partners) or (iii) three-plus (the partners and the RoW)?
(*B*) Is the model (1) symmetric or (2) asymmetric, the former entailing
      that the model deals only with circumstances in which all blocs are
      qualitatively identical? Within the latter set, I distinguish models
      which consider (i) only the integrating blocs, (ii) only the non-
      member countries (which are candidates for accession), or (iii) both.
(*C*) Is the interaction between countries (1) one-off or (2) repeated? The
      latter is operationalised (universally, I believe) in the form of trigger
      strategies.
(*D*) Is the aggregation of preferences or behaviour in the post-integration
      bloc (1) implicit – by far the more common assumption – or (2)
      explicit? While dimension ($A_2$) considers the roles of groups and
      interests as they affect each of the governments involved in the
      integration, this dimension ($D_2$) explicitly focuses on the interactions

between pressure groups and between governments within the bloc when it comes to making post-integration decisions.

It is not possible to find examples of work in each of the 64 boxes that this classification defines. Equally, many authors offer examples in several boxes, and in a survey of this length one cannot enumerate all of these explicitly. Rather I locate studies according to their principal insights or those of the stream of literature to which they belong. Section 3 is based loosely on the classification. It starts with the conceptually simple symmetric welfare-maximising models ($A_1$, $B_1$, $C_1$, $D_1$) and then moves on to asymmetric models ($A_1$, $B_2$, $C_1$, $D_1$). Subsection 3.3 deals with models of negotiated tariffs ($A_1$, $B_1$ or $B_2$, $C_2$, $D_1$) and 3.4 with models of political economy ($A_2$). Finally, I consider models of the institutional structure of policy-making within an integrated bloc ($D_2$).

## 3    Models of tariff regimes

### 3.1   Symmetric models

While the consistency of regional trading arrangements with the multi-lateral trading system had attracted some debate previously and had, indeed, been modelled formally, the subject took off with a seminal article by Paul Krugman (1991a).[2] This considers a simple model of integration and trade policy in which there are $N$ identical countries and $B$ identical blocs. Each country produces one product; these are differentiated symmetrically from all others and all consumers consume all goods (Dixit–Stiglitz differentiation); there are no transport costs, but each country levies a tariff on imports from all non-partner countries. When $B = N$ each country is a bloc, but as $B$ falls (with $N/B$ taking integer values) the countries within each bloc offer each other free market access and levy a common tariff on all non-partners. Within each country some products are available tariff-free – domestic and partner supplies – while all others face an identical tariff, $t$. Tariffs are set to maximise bloc welfare given the tariffs charged elsewhere in the world – a traditional Nash optimum tariff game.

Krugman shows that as the number of blocs in the world decreases (that is, as integration occurs) each bloc's share in the other blocs' consumption rises, conferring more market power on each and raising the optimum tariff. Integration creates trade diversion but in this model it is exacerbated by raising the external tariff. Krugman (1993) shows that the effect of the latter on economic welfare is relatively weak, however, and that even if it is suppressed his main conclusion continues

### 12   L. Alan Winters

to hold. The latter is that the pessimum number of blocs in terms of welfare is very small – three for most of his examples.

Krugman (1993) disaggregates the causes of the welfare losses from regionalism and finds that they owe far more to trade diversion than to increases in the optimum tariff. That is, the first-order impact of what countries do to themselves through regionalism matters more than the second-order interactions between countries. This is a useful lesson when considering any trade policy, but it is particularly salutary for our discussion, reminding us that multilateralism is not the only dimension of relevance. According to the imperfect index developed above, regionalism with a fixed external tariff may or may not harm multilateralism *ceteris paribus* (see figure 2A.1, p. 43) but the act of raising the external tariff certainly does.

Krugman's work stimulated a storm of criticism and extension. The most pressing theoretical criticism was that his production structure contained no element of comparative advantage, and that this led him to over-emphasise trade diversion. Srinivasan (1993) offers one counterexample and Deardorff and Stern (1994) another; the latter have equal numbers of two kinds of country in the world and show that blocs containing equal numbers of each type realise the full benefits of free trade regardless of their external trade policies. Thus the latter become irrelevant.

A more sophisticated alternative is to be found in Bond and Syropoulos (1996a), who introduce comparative advantage in an elegant way. Each country has an equal endowment of all goods plus a supplementary amount (positive and negative) of one of them; the relative size of the supplement and the regular endowment represents the degree of comparative advantage. Working with a lower elasticity of substitution than Krugman, Bond and Syropoulos find that optimum tariffs can fall as bloc size increases symmetrically. The world welfare-minimising number of blocs is two if comparative advantage comprises having more of one good than others, but may be three or even higher if it comprises having less of only one. Thus the Krugman result – and, indeed, the effect of regionalism on multilateralism – is obviously sensitive to issues of comparative advantage.

Sinclair and Vines (1995) reproduce Bond and Syropoulos' result about the possibility of a falling optimum tariff as the number of blocs decreases, but in slightly more general circumstances – CES preferences (as in Krugman) rather than Cobb–Douglas. They also relate it to another important qualification. Krugman and most of his successors in this literature consider the creation of customs unions (CUs), which can increase tariffs above pre-integration levels because, by coordinating several countries' policies, they can exert more market power than any individual country. If the integration takes the form of FTAs, however, countries retain control of their own tariffs on the RoW and these will fall as regionalism proceeds. As more and more partners receive tariff-free access to one country's market the smaller becomes the set of goods subject to the tariff and thus the more distortionary the effect of a given tariff. Thus the incentive arises to cut the tariff in order to achieve better balance in the composition of imports –through what Sinclair and Vines call the 'optimal import-sourcing condition'.

The optimal import-sourcing condition also helps to explain why the optimal tariff for a CU might fall as the union enlarges. If countries have rather similar endowments,[3] they trade rather small proportions of their output and income and hence have rather little monopsony power over each other. Thus the optimal import allocation condition which promotes equal tariffs across partners (equal to zero if some tariffs are constrained by regional arrangements) can overcome the increased monopsony power arising from larger bloc size which tends to raise the tariff on the RoW. Krugman has wholly different endowments across countries, and hence for him the monopsony effect always dominates.

An important extension of Krugman's model is to recognise the role of transport costs. Krugman was the first to do this, in Krugman (1991b), but the issue has been most thoroughly taken up by Frankel, Stein and Wei in a series of papers.[4] Krugman (1991b) subdivided the world into continents and observed that if inter-continental trading costs were infinite – thus precluding inter-continental trade – a series of regional blocs each covering one continent would produce a first-best outcome equivalent to global free trade.[5] Krugman inferred a notion of 'natural blocs' from this – blocs for which low trade costs made regionalism a natural and beneficial policy.

Frankel, Stein and Wei (1995, 1996) and Frankel (1997) fill in the middle ground between the two Krugman views by allowing transport costs to be finite but non-zero. As might be expected they find that, as inter-continental transportation and business costs increase relative to intra-continental ones, regionalism becomes a better policy in welfare terms. For a particular parameter constellation (three continents each with two countries, tariffs of 30 per cent, an elasticity of substitution between varieties of four, and zero intra-continental trading costs) they find that if inter-continental costs absorb above 15 per cent of the gross value of an export, intra-continental regionalism is welfare-improving. This result is interesting, but not very robust. Frankel, Stein and Wei themselves quote contrary results and Nitsch (1996a) shows that just raising intra-continental costs to 5 per cent in the case above means that regional blocs

14   **L. Alan Winters**

are welfare-improving for all values of inter-continental costs. Inter-continental regionalism (i.e. blocs between countries in different continents) is always harmful for Frankel Stein and Wei, although as inter-continental costs rise it becomes less so because it affects less and less trade. This result has also been challenged by Nitsch (1996b) who gives examples with relatively low inter-continental transport costs in which 'unnatural' integration dominates 'natural' integration!

Frankel, Stein and Wei also consider preferential trading areas which merely reduce rather than abolish tariffs between partners. Preferential areas can always be constructed to be welfare improving – essentially because they ensure that the optimal import-sourcing condition is not too badly violated. In this sense Frankel, Stein and Wei argue that bloc formation is a stepping stone towards multilateral free trade, but since there is no mechanism through which the benign path is ensured or even encouraged this does not seem a particularly powerful characterisation. Merely referring to the welfare benefits is not sufficient, for one could equally well refer to the (greater) benefits of jumping straight to free trade.[6] I shall not pursue this (GATT-proscribed) analysis of preferential trading blocs further. It seems to me seriously flawed on the political economy grounds that it could completely undermine the MFN clause (which could easily prevent multilateral progress towards liberalisation) and encourages too much trade activism.

A further wrinkle on the Frankel model is provided by Spilimbergo and Stein (1996) who introduce trade based on comparative advantage in addition to Krugman's and Frankel's basic intra-industry variety. If inter-continental trading costs are very low Spilimbergo and Stein replicate the results above – i.e. Krugman's (1991a) 'anti-bloc' result if variety effects are strong, and welfare-increasing with the size of blocs (and thus their fewness) if these effects are weak. With moderate inter-continental costs, on the other hand, Spilimbergo and Stein replicate Frankel, Stein and Wei. This model is the current encompassing model for CUs – all the above discussion is, at least loosely speaking, a special case of Spilimbergo and Stein.

For completeness I mention one final symmetric welfare-maximising model which suggests that regionalism can provide stepping stones to multilateralism within a somewhat unconventional framework. Collie (1997) considers countries each with a constant returns to scale (CRS) sector and one differentiated good sector. The latter compete in a third market and receive export subsidies as in the traditional strategic trade policy story. Integration between these countries allows – and encourages – better coordination of export subsidies and hence reduces distortions and raises welfare. This effect continues as bloc size grows until all the (producing) countries are integrated. This is not a particularly persuasive model, however, for the CRS sectors do not change their level of integration, export subsidies are not the instrument of concern in regionalism and there is, in this model, no incentive for any country to join a bloc. For these reasons, Collie's is not a convincing refutation of the concerns that regionalism undermines multilateralism.

## 3.2 Asymmetric models

A feature of all the results discussed so far is that regionalism is always symmetric in the sense that as bloc size increases countries recombine into groups of equal size. This is a useful simplification for asking what the effects are of having bloc size $B_1$ in the world economy and how such effects compare with those of having bloc size $B_2$ in an otherwise identical world. But there is no sense of evolution or expansion in such a static setup and this severely limits the light it can shed on the issue of whether regionalism might *lead to* multilateralism. I turn now, therefore, to models in which blocs grow endogenously and thus which at some stage are asymmetric.

Bond and Syropoulos (1996a) make a start in the required direction by allowing their blocs to expand asymmetrically. Starting from a symmetric equilibrium, they show that a bloc would gain by admitting new members drawn equally from each of the other blocs. The terms of trade benefits of boosting demand for the bloc's comparative advantage goods would outweigh the trade diversionary effects in this model, even if the enlarged bloc did not increase its tariff on other countries. Second, Bond and Syropoulos ask what bloc size maximises member countries' welfare given that other countries levy optimum tariffs. The answer is large but not the whole world, for the benefits depend on terms of trade gains which are obviously missing if the bloc contains all countries.

Frankel (1997) also sheds a little light on this issue. In a world of four continents the countries of which initially practice MFN trade policy, he shows that a sequential Nash game leads to regionalism and lower welfare for all. (This does, of course, depend on parameter values.) Specifically, one continent (any one, since all are identical) can improve its welfare by creating an FTA, assuming that the other three keep their MFN tariffs. These three lose because, even absent the bloc increasing its tariff, their terms of trade decline. From here a second continent benefits itself by integrating, assuming unchanged policies elsewhere, and thence the third and fourth continents. In the end all are worse off than under MFN policies, but none has the incentive to undo the regionalism. Whether the process then continues to create two inter-continental blocs,

16　L. Alan Winters

however, Frankel does not say, but at least for a variety of parameter values this does not seem likely since inter-continental blocs have previously been shown not to be desirable.

Very similar results were derived by Goto and Hamada (1994, 1997) using a Krugman (1993)-type model with four countries.[7] They, too, found a scenario in which one regional bloc begat another but in which the two 'superblocs' then had an incentive to combine in order to achieve global free trade. More sinister, however, they also showed that once $A$ and $B$ had combined into a bloc it would pay them to pre-empt $C$ and $D$'s combining similarly, by bringing one of the latter into their own bloc. Of course, this would impose high costs on the country that was left out, but unless the other three acquiesced this country could do nothing about achieving freer trade. In detail this result just reflects an overly powerful terminal condition to an $N$-country game – the last country is always powerless. In more realistic circumstances the superbloc excludes more than one country and these countries would then have an incentive to create their own bloc. The insight that integrators may veto indefinite bloc expansion is real enough, however.

Nordström (1995) discusses these issues in a slightly more general framework, although at the cost of having to simulate his model rather than solve it analytically. Nordström starts with a model very similar to that of Frankel and his collaborators – with product differentiation and finite transport costs. He starts by considering just one bloc – a CU. Its creation and expansion harm excluded countries even at constant external tariffs; but in mitigation, these countries can always raise their welfare above free trade levels by joining the bloc and 'exploiting' further the remaining outsiders. As suggested by Goto and Hamada and by Bond and Syropoulos, however, this process does not lead to the so-called 'global coalition' (all countries within the CU), because existing members will eventually lose from further growth as the set of outsiders to exploit declines. Nordström suggests that after about half the countries are inside the CU, further growth will be vetoed from the inside.

Nordström observes that if the CU chooses an optimum tariff rather than a constant one, it will increase its tariff as it grows, hitting outsiders harder than in the previous example. Then, in the absence of retaliation, the optimum size of the union is about 60 per cent of the world economy. But, of course, the excluded countries might retaliate against such aggression. If they alter their MFN tariffs so that they are punishing each other as well as the CU, there is little they can do, but if they maintain tariffs against each other and coordinate their punishment tariff against the CU they can exercise significant market power. Such retaliation could reduce the CU's welfare below what it could achieve at a constant external tariff (and no retaliation) if it is smaller than about 75 per cent of countries.[8] A CU of more than 75 per cent of countries would win the tariff war even in the face of coordinated opposition.

The implication of all this for 'regionalism vs. multilateralism' is ambiguous. The assumed form of retaliation effectively transforms the excluded countries into a second CU, albeit one with non-zero internal tariffs. This raises the possibility that the two blocs could gain jointly from cooperation. However, in this model there is no identified way out of their prisoner's dilemma: the issue is not addressed. The threat of retaliation if the union raises its tariffs does nothing to prevent the creation of the union, it just limits its behaviour once formed.

Nordström explores inter-bloc issues more formally by breaking his world into two 'continents' – *A* and *B* – and allowing blocs in each, very similar to the approach taken by Frankel, Stein and Wei. Nordström finds that a CU on continent *A* hurts all excluded countries, but impinges much more heavily on those in *A*, which are the CU's 'natural' trading partners, than on those in *B*. The incentives are for both sets of countries to seek integration; as previously, the CU in *A* may close its doors, but nothing can stop a CU forming in *B*. However, if there is the prospect that after the formation of blocs on both continents an inter-bloc negotiation will take place, the blocs seem likely to include all the countries on their continents in order to maximise their power in this second round. Then, provided the continents are not of very disparate sizes, the subsequent negotiation of inter-bloc free trade would be mutually advantageous.

If one couples the previous paragraph with an argument that countries operating independently would not be able to negotiate global free trade, and if one is lucky with the relative sizes, Nordström's results are very favourable to regionalism. Starting from MFN tariffs a local CU forms; it is matched elsewhere in the world; both CUs expand to increase their bargaining power and then ultimately they negotiate global free trade.

Clearly there are many points at which this rosy scenario could break down. One, noted almost *en passant* by Perroni and Whalley (1994), arises because one can interpret the anxiety of small countries to join large neighbouring blocs as seeking insurance – a desire not to be left isolated if global trade war breaks out. Small countries pay for the privilege of belonging to a bloc by offering up their markets preferentially.[9] Insurance premia are higher the more uncertain the world and the costs of errors are lower if one is insured: in other words, the large powers may gain from sabre-rattling while small countries are deciding whether to join them, and after they have joined, the small countries will

18   **L. Alan Winters**

be less concerned to preserve a global system than previously. Since sabre-rattling is effective only if there is some chance of violence, this makes the *possibility* of regionalism look quite hostile to multilateralism.

Finally, again for completeness, I note an interesting model of a quite different nature in which regionalism is benign and welfare increases monotonically with bloc size. No country has any special characteristics, but the model is asymmetric in allowing for the formation of any coalition to block global free trade. In Kowalczyk and Sjostrom (1994) countries have monopolies in their own export goods and exploit each other by charging monopoly prices. The only policy variables in use are import price ceilings, although equivalent results would arise if import subsidies were used. Integration entails agreeing to use ceilings to force firms to price exports at marginal cost in partners' markets – i.e. it entails moving from free trade to intervention (!). The details of preferences and cost functions ensure that excluded countries are quite unaffected by such integration. In this world, identical or nearly identical countries that behaved rationally would find their way to global integration. If countries differed strongly, however, coalitions could arise that block this evolution, because they would find it more advantageous to exploit certain other countries. In these cases, however, a system of side-payments could be devised to achieve the first-best optimum. While Kowalczyk and Sjostrom's model is very stylised, it does suggest that regionalism may not lead to multilateralism and that this may be because global institutional structure cannot support mechanisms for side-payments.

A significant criticism of the work surveyed so far is that tariffs and other forms of protection are determined not by optimal tariff considerations but rather by domestic political processes mitigated by international negotiation. This is true, but the simple models are still useful in illustrating the spillovers and interactions between countries and in identifying threat points for various negotiating games. Moreover, the apparently related criticism – that GATT's Article XXIV prevents integrating countries from raising their tariffs – is not particularly powerful. Article XXIV has been notable for its weak enforcement so far; many trade policies have been unbound under the GATT and hence free of constraint; there are several GATT-consistent policies of protection – e.g. anti-dumping; and in a world of trend liberalisation, merely going more slowly than you otherwise would is essentially a form of increased protection. For these reasons I am not unhappy with models that take seriously the threat that blocs could raise barriers. On the other hand, the implications of strictly optimal tariffs (e.g. indifference to changes in trade volumes) are uncomfortable and generalisations would be welcome. The rest of this part of the chapter therefore considers a broader set of models, starting by recognising the importance of negotiations.

## 3.3 Negotiated tariffs

An early and elegant step in the direction of incorporating trade agreements into the analysis of regionalism is Bond and Syropoulos (1996b). Using the same basic model as Bond and Syropoulos (1996a), they consider trigger strategies such that initially there is inter-bloc free trade supported by the threat of perpetual trade war if any party breaks the agreement. They then ask what rate of discount just leaves blocs indifferent between defecting and continuing to cooperate. (The discount rate is critical because the decision balances current benefits to defection against future costs.) If the actual discount rate is above this value, blocs defect from free trade; thus, if integration (moving from smaller to larger blocs) reduces the critical discount rate, it makes cooperation less likely to be maintained.

Two countervailing forces exist as we consider larger blocs: the incentive to deviate is greater the larger are the blocs, but so too is the welfare loss in the resulting trade war. Bond and Syropoulos find that the former effect dominates, making it more difficult to maintain free trade in a bloc-ridden world. They also find that for any given discount rate the minimum supportable cooperative tariff rises as bloc size increases, also suggesting that integration increases the pressures for protectionism. Bagwell and Staiger (1997a, 1997b) reach a similar conclusion in a somewhat similar fashion, although only in the context of a temporary transition phase.

The discount rate is crucial to the assessment of trigger strategies because it trades off the immediate benefits of defection against the eventual costs of trade war. This raises the question of the time scale over which these games are played. In terms of individual tariffs and tariff wars – e.g. the occasional EC–US spats such as the Chicken War and the tussle over public procurement in early 1993 – the period required for retaliation is so short that there are hardly any gains to defection. Thus discipline seems virtually complete and the model suggests that nothing much affects the cooperative outcome. (This may change if finite rather than infinite periods of punishment were permitted, whereupon the main question would become what determines the punishment period.) If, on the other hand, we view this as a game in regimes, so that the GATT rounds represent the natural periodicity, and policies such as Super 301, the zeal with which anti-dumping policies are applied and the use of

20   **L. Alan Winters**

health and technical regulations become the weapons, the periods
required to recognise defection and retaliate become much more meaningful. I find the latter interpretation more plausible: namely that the
important effect of integration is not on the 'tactics' of trade policy, but
on the 'strategy'; in some sense it tends to reduce the incentive to take a
world view. In this regard I find the European Community's concern
with the volume of intra-EC trade as an indicator of the success of
integration disturbing – see, for example, Jacquemin and Sapir (1988).

Campa and Sorenson (1996) apply the repeated game model of tariff
setting to something like Nordström's (1995) problem, and with similar
results. In part they consider a hegemon facing a competitive fringe of
small countries, and conclude that if the latter coordinate they might
offset the former's market power and move the world towards freer
trade. Of course, if the (ex-)fringe were too large it might become
hegemonic in which case it would dominate the original one. In a second,
symmetric, exercise they conclude that, as the number of blocs falls, the
probability of free trade falls (i.e. the critical discount rate falls), but that
equi-sized blocks are preferable (more likely to be liberal) than disparate-
sized ones.

In a specifically EU application Bond, Syropoulos and Winters (1996)
use the Bond and Syropoulos framework to consider explicitly the
deepening of an existing regional arrangement. They consider a world of
$N$ symmetric provinces split initially into one large country (the United
States) and two smaller ones (France and Germany); the latter have
already combined into a bloc (the European Union) with a CET that is
the result of a self-sustaining agreement between the European Union
and the United States. They then allow the latter pair to integrate more
deeply by reducing trade frictions between them and ask whether tariff
cuts within the union affect the incentive-compatibility of agreements
with the outside country. It turns out that the Kemp–Wan tariff
reduction – the reduction in the union's external tariff that just leaves the
outside country indifferent to the internal tariff reduction – is a useful
benchmark for this.

For the outside country, the reduction in the union's internal tariffs
reduces the attractiveness of an initial trade agreement because its trade
with the union is reduced. The Kemp–Wan reduction in the union's
external tariff, however, will just restore incentive compatibility for the
outside country because it restores to their initial levels both its welfare
under the agreement and its incentive to violate it. For the union, a
Kemp–Wan adjustment generates two conflicting forces. First, the initial
trade agreement becomes more attractive to union members because the
expanded volume of intra-union trade raises the welfare of member

countries at the initial level of the external tariff. This suggests that the union could 'live with' a lower tariff on the outside country. On the other hand, deviating from the agreement also becomes more attractive because the payoff to cheating also rises. This suggests that the external tariff needs to rise in order to keep the union in the agreement. (A higher tariff makes sticking to the agreement more attractive.) The first effect almost always dominates the second, so that incentive-compatibility is consistent with a fall in the union's external tariff.

To be more precise, the two forces on the union exactly offset each other if the share of union expenditure on union goods is invariant with respect to the external tariff. In that case, since the Kemp–Wan tariff reduction is incentive-compatible for both the union and the outside country, internal liberalisation plus a Kemp–Wan reduction will generate a new sustainable agreement. Of course, many other agreements will also be sustainable, so there is no guarantee that the Kemp–Wan reduction in the external tariff will actually be chosen, but at least for one simple representation of the negotiating process Bond, Syropoulos and Winters show that it will be.

If the share of union expenditure on union goods rises as the external tariff rises (heuristically, if demand is elastic) the Kemp–Wan tariff reduction is not incentive-compatible for the union: that is, if the original agreement was just sustainable, internal liberalisation plus a Kemp–Wan reduction will leave the union preferring to defect than to cooperate. As a result, the union, while likely to reduce its external tariff somewhat, will not be prepared to go as far as the Kemp–Wan reduction. Since the latter is necessary to keep the outside country at its initial level of welfare, the presumption is that, under these circumstances, the outside country will suffer from the union's internal liberalisation. This illustrates the dilemma of defining multilateralism starkly. By reducing all tariffs in the model we have presumably enhanced multilateralism, and yet the RoW – the intended beneficiary of multilateralism – suffers a decline in welfare.

Somewhat similarly to Bond, Syropoulos and Winters, Bagwell and Staiger (1996b) analyse a three-country model in a repeated game context. They assume two countries are patient (*A* and *B*) – and hence are happy with low tariff equilibria – while the third (*C*) is very impatient. Under MFN rules *A* and *B* offer *C* lower tariffs than it reciprocates with because they wish to have low tariffs on their mutual trade. How is this affected if they sign an FTA? Under such an eventuality the import-sourcing condition suggests further reducing *A*'s and *B*'s tariffs on *C*, but, pushing in the opposite direction, the same condition suggests that *A* and *B* are likely to impose less harsh punishment on *C* if it defects, and *A*'s and *B*'s mutual tariffs are no longer dependent on their tariff on *C*.

22   **L. Alan Winters**

The net effect is ambiguous, but Bagwell and Staiger show that if $C$ is very impatient and $A$ and $B$ very patient it could entail higher tariffs on $C$. This is more likely if $A$ and $B$ form a CU rather than an FTA because, being larger, a CU is less interested in freer trade.

Bagwell and Staiger's model is quite special because it assumes that, out of three goods, each country imports one from both partners while exporting both others, one to each partner. Its real significance, however, is to highlight the sensible proposition that if we ask 'how useful is regionalism?', part of the answer must be 'that depends on how well the MFN rule was doing initially'.

Bond and Syropoulos introduce regional blocs exogenously – e.g. for political reasons – and ask how they disturb an existing equilibrium. Ludema (1996) asks a more sophisticated question: how does the *possibility* of creating a regional bloc affect the conduct of multilateral negotiations aimed at achieving free trade? He uses welfare-maximisation as his objective function and considers a three-country multi-round two-step negotiation. In each negotiating round the first step is a multilateral offer, and if this is rejected a bilateral one may be made. If this is rejected, a new round is initiated. A very strong assumption is that international transfers of utility are feasible. This guarantees that negotiations will always eventually end up with global free trade – the only efficient solution – and because in these games (a) time is money (the discount rate is positive) and (b) information is complete, they actually get there straight away. Thus negotiation is *only* about distribution – every offer is 'global free trade plus some vector of transfers'.

In this context, Ludema does not help us much on 'regionalism vs. multilateralism', except to the extent that his results may condition attitudes towards whether to rewrite Article XXIV to ban regional arrangements. Ludema considers two questions. First, how would a pre-existing regional bloc affect a multilateral negotiation? If it is an FTA, not very much, because an FTA does not constrain the partners' negotiations with outside countries. If it is a CU, however, the effect is stronger because a CU precludes independent negotiation. However, this effect is weakened if the partners are asymmetric because the partners' ideal policies *vis-à-vis* outsiders would differ. Ludema's second question is: how does the possibility of regionalism affects negotiations? If only FTAs are possible the multilateral outcome resembles that of three separate bilateral negotiations, whereas if only CUs are permitted the first-mover advantage for the country that can first propose a CU allows it a disproportionate share of world income. In Ludema's model, this is randomly decided.

A model of negotiated tariffs in which the repeated game is only implicit is Bagwell and Staiger's chapter 3 in this volume. This starts from the position that countries gear trade policy to their own ends – be they political, economic, or whatever – and that trade agreements (and the GATT) exist to internalise the effects that $A$'s policy has on $B$ – specifically to internalise terms of trade effects. If MFN trade rules allow complete internalisation, then countries can reach the efficiency frontier (defined over their own objectives, not the economics community's) and regional arrangements have nothing to add. If, on the other hand, MFN tariffs cannot yield efficiency or, say, they pose enforcement problems, regional arrangements may have a role to play. In these cases regionalism is (potentially) optimal; there is no question of 'building blocs' or 'stumbling blocs' unless we wish to challenge governments' objectives. This brings us neatly to the next group of models, which recognise that governments are not always economic welfare-maximisers.

### 3.4 Pressure groups and voters

I now move on to what might loosely be called political economy models of integration – those in which governments are driven by economic considerations but not merely the (unweighted) maximisation of welfare/ utility. In this section we take governments' objective functions as given and assume they are efficiently pursued. In the next we ask how the decision process itself – the institutions which determine government behaviour – affects the outcome. Many of the political economy models have a lot in common with the models I have already surveyed, but I collect them into one section because their focus on political economy is their main distinguishing characteristic.

Much of the political economy modelling derives from Grossman and Helpman (1994, 1995).[10] They argued persuasively that lobbying influences governments less in terms of determining which of the two polar policy stances wins an election than in terms of what policies an incumbent or newly elected government will pursue – the market for influence. In general, consumers find it hard to organise a lobby and so lobbying is dominated by producers, who organise along sectoral lines. This effectively gives profits additional weight in the government's objective function; they enter once in the traditional calculus of surpluses (consumer, producer and government revenue), and again as the source of lobbying funds which the government values in their own right. Thus moving into the realms of political economy effectively biases integration outcomes towards what producers desire.

Grossman and Helpman (1995) consider a negotiation between two governments that have suddenly been offered the chance of concluding an FTA. That is, they compare *staying* with MFN trade policy with creating mutual preferences. In certain circumstances they find that the latter is politically feasible (i.e. that it raises government 'welfare', which depends on consumer and producer surpluses but with unequal weights). The FTA is feasible either if it enhances consumer welfare while producers are unable to lobby against it, or if it enhances the profits of well organised producers who pass some of the benefit on to the government via lobbies. The latter possibility is malign, for it makes likely precisely those FTAs which generate most trade diversion. Trade creation is a mixed blessing for a negotiating government: it generates surpluses for consumers at home and for exporters in the partner country, but reduces them for domestic import-competing producers; trade diversion, on the other hand, generates no such reduction in profits, and although it correspondingly generates no (or fewer) consumer gains, that matters less to governments. If two such governments can swap trade-diverting concessions, trade diversion is good politics even if it is bad economics. Grossman and Helpman do not consider whether their process continues to create superblocs, although if it were driven by diversion alone it would have to stop before it achieved the global coalition, because the last step in that direction would generate only trade creation.

Krishna (1994) has an elegant stripped-down three-country version of Grossman and Helpman in which policy is determined solely by its effects on profits. He assumes imperfectly competitive markets that are segmented from each other. He replicates the Grossman–Helpman result that, considering two of the countries, the more trade-diverting an FTA between them, the stronger its backing and hence the more likely it is to come about. He then shows that the backing for further multilateral liberalisation with the third country is reduced. Included in this is the possibility that multilateral liberalisation that was feasible before the FTA would cease to be so afterwards – i.e. that, if the world attempted to achieve the multilateral free trade it desired via regionalism, progress would stop at the intermediate stage.

Very simply, let a sector's profits be $\pi_1$ under MFN tariffs, $\pi_2$ under the FTA and $\pi_3$ under global free trade. The gains from FTA ($\pi_2 - \pi_1$) may be sufficient to allow successful lobbying for the FTA; similarly, if it were the only option, the gains from global liberalisation ($\pi_3 - \pi_1$) might also permit successful lobbying; the gains from moving from an FTA to free trade ($\pi_3 - \pi_2$), however, might be insufficient to encourage lobbying for that step: they would certainly be smaller than ($\pi_3 - \pi_1$) because $\pi_2 > \pi_1$ if the FTA was formed, and they might actually be negative. Moreover, this 'suspended liberalisation' outcome is more likely the more trade-diverting was the initial FTA. Krishna shows that it may not even be possible for producers in the outside country to bribe those in the partner countries to adopt global free trade. This is because much of the benefit of the latter is 'wasted' on consumers.

Krishna's is a *very* simple model – which is one of its attractions – and clearly requires some generalisation. However, it is rather convincing that regionalism may hinder multilateralism – 'the good' preventing 'the best'!

The second extension of Grossman and Helpman is Baldwin (1995). This model of 'domino' regionalism has many countries each with a CRS (numeraire) sector and a differentiated product sector with capitalists who receive the rent. Government objectives are a convex combination of worker and capitalist welfare, the latter being enhanced by their ability to lobby. Baldwin assumes that a bloc already exists and that this situation is an equilibrium in the sense that countries on the outside wish to remain so because the economic benefits of joining do not outweigh the non-economic costs. He then shocks this world by deepening integration within the bloc – '1992' – or by allowing one country's desire for integration to increase – the United States in the 1980s. Each shock would increase the incentives for new members to join – starting with those that were previously just on the margin of joining – and as they do so the costs to others of remaining outside grow. This in turn attracts others, and so on.

Baldwin notes that the process of enlargement could stop as soon as all remaining non-members had high enough objections to joining. It could also, of course, do so when existing members shut the door. Baldwin deals, in fact, only with the demand for membership. As a parable for the absorption of the EFTA countries into the EC following '1992' – its intended purpose – Baldwin's explanation is admirable; however, its generalisation to other accessions looks less secure – think, for example, of Poland, Cyprus and Turkey. Given that deepening integration is bad for excluded countries (see above), Baldwin does not actually need political economy to generate his results, but it does help to explain some of the facts of political activity that surrounded the EFTA accession. Overall, however, the implications of all this for multilateralism are quite unclear.

An early contribution to the theory of endogenous protection and integration is Richardson (1993, 1995). Like Baldwin, Richardson's basic insight does not require a political economy dimension – welfare-maximisation would suffice. Suppose one country creates an FTA with a large partner (with a horizontal supply curve) and suppose that for certain imported goods the FTA is trade-diverting because $p_P < p_W$

26   **L. Alan Winters**

$(1 + t)$ where $p_P$ is the partner's price, $p_W$ is the world price and $t$ the MFN tariff. Domestic firms and consumers now face $p_P$ instead of $p_W$ $(1 + t)$, but the government loses tariff revenue. A rational government would now reduce its MFN tariff to just below $t'$, where $p_W (1 + t') = p_P$. This would leave domestic residents unaffected relative to the FTA but generate tariff revenue. The main constraint on this behaviour is the reaction of the partner country which loses the rents it expected under the FTA. But if it is large and has other objectives in the integration, it might acquiesce. A reservation to this elegant model is the extent to which tariff revenues really motivate trade policy – the prevalence of VERs casts some doubt on this.

Political economy considerations support the rational outcome in Richardson's model. The initial reduction in the domestic price would probably reduce the size of the lobby for tariffs on the goods concerned,[11] and, besides, no one in the lobby has any interest in whether they are hurt by partner imports rather than non-partner imports. Richardson's results seem to require that partner and non-partner imports are perfect substitutes with fixed prices. If import supply curves slope upwards and/or the imports (and the home good) are imperfect substitutes in demand, then free access for the partner could well increase the demand for protection against non-members and this may outweigh the government's revenue concerns. The necessary condition for this to occur seems to be that imports are drawn from both sources after integration.

Two contributions offer significant generalisations of Richardson's work. Cadot, de Melo and Olarreaga (1996) have a three-country model with Grossman–Helpman lobbying for influence by the fixed factors in each of the three industries. They ask what $A/B$ integration does to protection against $C$'s exports and focus carefully on different types of integration. They find that if $A$ and $B$ create an FTA without rules of origin, protection is likely to fall, essentially for the reasons identified by Richardson. If there are rules of origin, however, the protective effects of the FTA are more complex and it is possible that either $A$ or $B$ will increase protection above either of the pair's pre-integration tariffs. Similar outcomes are also possible under a CU. The reason is that in this model tariffs on different goods are substitutes: if one is reduced (by FTA membership), others rise (on $C$). This is because the unprotected sector contracts, increasing the sizes and reducing the lobbying costs of the other sectors.[12] Cadot, de Melo and Olarreaga do not consider how $C$ reacts to integration – it always offers free trade – but the propensity of the bloc members to raise their tariffs is likely to move us away from multilateralism.

The second generalisation of Richardson is Levy (1996b) who considers many countries in a model that also includes lobbying for influence and negotiated tariffs. He focuses on two major countries negotiating with each other and asks how this negotiation is affected if each acquires (exogenously) a fringe of FTA partners. Each country has effective lobbying in one import-competing ('sensitive') sector; export interests aim to reduce the other country's tariff in its 'sensitive' sector by inducing reductions in their own country's. The existence of the fringe affects the extent to which trade policy changes translate into increases in profits in the major powers. For example, suppose $A$'s fringe can supply $A$'s export good along a fairly elastic supply curve. $A$ now has less interest in inducing $B$ to reduce its tariff on these goods because part of the benefit spills over onto $A$'s fringe's suppliers so that $A$'s own producers get a smaller increase in price.[13] Levy shows that considering both countries' fringes, these effects could go in any direction, so that giving major negotiating powers FTA fringes could either increase or reduce tariffs on their mutual trade. Thus if it is the major powers that determine the progress of multinational negotiations (e.g. the United States and European Union in the Uruguay Round), Levy's model suggests we cannot necessarily be sanguine about the EU Association Agreements, APEC and NAFTA.

I turn now to models with slightly different pressure group technologies. Richardson and Desruelle (1997) use an analysis with features of both Krishna's and Baldwin's model to explain the height of EC countries' tariffs before and after integration: they have three countries and an economic specification like Baldwin's except that they explicitly consider the distribution of tariff revenues. In addition, they allow both workers and capitalists (now a single group) to lobby. Richardson and Desruelle compare Nash tariffs before and after the creation of a CU, assuming that the partners of the latter are identical.[14] Integration does not affect the relative weights of workers and capitalists in the formation of trade policy. The partners export the differentiated good both to each other and to the excluded country, while the latter exports the CRS good.

It turns out that integration could push the external tariff (on imports of the CRS good) either way in Richardson and Desruelle's model. Generally it will raise it: before integration each partner moderates its desire to tax the CRS good because doing so will increase its costs in the differentiated sector with a resultant loss of sales and rents to the other partner. A CU internalises this spillover, and hence allows a higher price. The counter-example occurs when workers determine the tariff but receive little of the revenue. Before integration they drive the tariff very high because they have no interest in the rents of the differentiated sector but do benefit from the Stolper–Samuelson effect on real wages. But this spills over to the other partners in terms of higher costs and prices of differentiated goods. Under the CU this spillover is recognised, and the tariff on the CRS good falls to the revenue-maximising level. Overall, Richardson and Desruelle's results seem to suggest that RIAs increase trade restriction, for the starting point of their counter-case – very high tariffs on the CRS good – does not accord very closely with reality.

Levy (1997) continues (implicitly) with labour and capital and explores the stepping-stones argument with a median voter model. He reaches similar conclusions to Krishna. The median voter's response to the offer of a trade policy change depends on his labour–capital ratio and the labour–capital ratio of the trading blocs to which he belongs before and after the change. An important restriction is that voters first consider autarky vs. a bilateral deal and then whatever they choose first vs. multilateralism. This allows Levy to show that in a simple Heckscher–Ohlin model one does not get stuck at the bilateral stage.

Suppose $A$ and $B$ consider forming a bloc and that $k^A < k^{AB} < k^B$ where $k^i$ is the capital-labour ratio of country $i$ and $k^{AB}$ that of $A$ and $B$ combined. The median voter in $A$ will agree to the FTA if increasing his economy's $k$ is beneficial *to him* and the median voter in $B$ will approve if he gains from a decrease. Suppose both approve and that we then pose the second question which would produce a world economy with ratio $k^w$. If $k^w > k^{AB}$ voter $A$ will favour multilateralism. Voter $B$ might also if $k^w$ far exceeds $k^{AB}$, but more likely he will reject it, leaving the world stuck in bilateral mode. But voter $A$ can foresee this and will therefore veto bilateralism at the first stage relying on the second ballot – which will then become autarky vs. multilateralism – to achieve his goals. Essentially no two countries that favoured multilateralism initially can create an FTA, so the world is safe!

Now Levy adds variety effects so that the median voter receives utility not just from his real income but also from increased variety. This can cause a breakdown at the intermediate stage. Suppose the median voter is only just in favour of multilateralism, balancing increased variety against disadvantageous price–wage effects. If the FTA offers disproportionate gains it could push the voter's utility above the multilateral level. For example, if $A$ and $B$ have identical capital–labour ratios $k^A = k^{AB} = k^B$ there are no price–wage effects but there are variety effects. These could leave the median voter better off and resisting the move to multilateralism, even though the latter would have been chosen relative to autarky. It is FTAs between similar countries that pose the greatest threats to multilateralism, those between dissimilar ones that pose the least. This suggests that the current rash of North–South arrangements, such as NAFTA and the EU Association Agreements, are not likely to be very harmful. However, subsequent work – Levy (1996b), see above – rebuts this presumption.

Frankel and Wei (1996) offer a counter-example to Levy's argument that bilateralism can never increase support for multilateralism. They do so in a Ricardian world with costs of adjustment for workers changing sectors. There are three countries (*A, B* and *C*) each with comparative advantage in one of three goods (*a, b* and *c*, respectively); in each of two potential partner countries (*A* and *B*) workers are spread over the three sectors such that none has a majority. If workers focus on the costs of adjustment a majority in *A* will oppose multilateral liberalisation (those in *b* and *c*), but favour bilateral liberalisation (those in *a* and *c*, who will benefit from the falling price of *b*). If the bilateral bloc is formed workers will have to move – perhaps all *b* workers move to *a*. Now there will be a majority in favour of opening up with *C* as well.

Frankel and Wei's argument relies either on workers not realising that the multilateral vote will follow the bilateral one (otherwise *c* workers would oppose bilateralism) or on voters believing that the following voting structure will be used regardless of outcomes: vote first on an *A/B* bloc and then, whatever the outcome, vote on opening up to *C*. In the latter case *c* workers cannot avoid liberalisation and so would go along with the *A/B* bloc. The latter seems implausible to me, but not the former given the uncertainties and glacial pace of trade diplomacy. It also seems fairly plausible that voters do focus on adjustment costs. Almost any discussion of trade liberalisation with policy-makers takes about ten minutes to get around to unemployment. Thus contrary to Levy's (1996a) comments on Frankel and Wei's paper, it seems to me a plausible counter-example, albeit one which is far from categorical, for the voting weights could easily generate alternative outcomes.

General conclusions from the political economy literature are elusive. One such conclusion is that the dominance of sector-based lobbies over economy-wide ones (factor-based or consumer) makes trade diversion more attractive to policy-makers, for trade diversion shifts rents and/or activity towards producers. While one cannot be categorical, this tendency seems likely to gravitate away from multilateralism, for trade diversion is possible *only* from preferential arrangements. The tendency is manifest first in the notion that integration beyond a trade-deflecting FTA may induce higher tariffs on the rest of the world and, second, in the more interesting observation that one might get stopped on a regional stepping stone before achieving free trade. While there are counter-examples, I find the broad thrust of this argument convincing.

30   **L. Alan Winters**

### 3.5   *Institutional arrangements for regional blocs*

The discussion in subsection 3.4 presupposed that all the features of a regional bloc are fully determined at its onset – implicitly in the negotiation phase during which national governments, pressure groups and voter interests are identifiable and distinct. For FTAs this seems a reasonable assumption for, other than maintaining mutual free trade, governments are quite unconstrained by an FTA. Even for an FTA, however, it would be worth asking – rather along the lines of Levy (1996b) – how the existence of an FTA conditions governments' reactions to exogenous shocks. For example, if the price of a major exportable falls, will governments be more likely to resort to protection with or without an FTA? Bhagwati and Panagariya (1996) have suggested that being in NAFTA made the Mexican government's response to the 1994–5 crisis *less* liberal than if it had been unencumbered: the previous mid-1980s' crisis eventually led to thorough-going liberalisation whereas the mid-1990s' crisis produced tariff increases on some non-NAFTA imports. Most other commentators have argued that since the response in the mid-1980s was initially very protectionist, NAFTA appears to have constrained behaviour to be moderately liberal. While the literature surveyed so far sheds some light on these issues by asking whether an FTA increases propensities to protectionism, it does not address it directly because it does not really consider how FTA members take decisions.

If consideration of this issue is desirable for FTAs it is indispensable for CUs and deeper forms of integration. One might determine the initial CET in the negotiation phase, but thereafter one needs mechanisms for deciding how to change it either in multilateral negotiations or ad hoc via anti-dumping actions, etc. How one does this – how one aggregates preferences across members – is likely to be very important in determining the outcomes. This problem does not arise in models of welfare-maximising governments where members are symmetric, for one maximises the representative country's welfare. Thus it is essentially a problem of asymmetry and politics.

One interesting aspect of joint decision-making concerns how formerly national lobbies interact to bring pressure to bear on the CU authorities. The only formal analyses of this question all suggest that interest group pressure is diluted by the CU. The essential point is that it costs more to lobby for a 1 per cent increase in your tariff in a CU than in a constituent member country with the right to set its own tariffs: there is more opposition to overcome (Panagariya and Findlay, 1994; de Melo, Panagariya and Rodrik, 1993) or more representatives to influence

(Richardson, 1994). Given the lower returns, less lobbying occurs and the sum of the members' lobbying activity falls as a result of integration. This can equivalently be viewed as a public good problem, for a CET is a public good: the lobby from *A* does not wish to devote resources to lobbying for protection for producers in country *B*. Whether the resulting tariff is lower than that which would rule in *all* member countries in the absence of integration is unclear, however, and so one might be trading less protection in some members for more in others. Whether this enhances multilateralism clearly depends on precisely how you trade off breadth against depth in the external tariff.

All these models presuppose that lobbies in different member countries will oppose each other, but it is also possible that some of them have their power enhanced through integration (Winters, 1993). For example, anti-protectionist forces might also be diluted by the free-riding problem. Alternatively each member state might initially start with a lobbying game in which industry and agriculture more or less cancel each other out, but if integration lets the agriculture lobbies cooperate (because they produce the same things) while the industry lobbies compete (because they produce different things), the union may end up with high agricultural protection. Overall, therefore, while dilution effects will undoubtedly be present, it is not proven that they will always predominate.

I turn now to the organisation of government. Gatsios and Karp (1991, 1995) show that it might matter which member state 'leads' negotiations with the rest of the world on a particular issue. In their model, if a more aggressive member determines the union's position, the union is able to extract a more favourable deal from RoW than if the 'average' member does so. This is because the former is more credible in its threats to retaliate (with the whole of the union's resources). In this model, 'passive' members could benefit from delegating power for certain policies to aggressive ones because, although for any given RoW policy they would prefer a less aggressive union stance, the RoW is so much more accommodating under the delegation that they are better off overall. What about multilateralism? That depends on whether a more aggressive union can achieve a more liberal outcome with the RoW by virtue of its readiness to retaliate, or whether it actually needs to use its muscle. Gatsios and Karp's model deals with this essentially only by assumption.

The formal delegation of the power to settle negotiating positions is of limited relevance in real CUs, but informal and partial delegation clearly exists. It has commonly been observed (e.g. Winters, 1993) that the European Union allows countries disproportionate influence over policy in areas in which they claim vital interests, allowing them, *in extremis*, veto power. Given that for all the reasons noted above a country's 'interest' in a sector is commonly correlated with that sector's share of its GDP, it is easy to imagine this feature enhancing further the interests of producers. What effect this has on the union's trade policy depends on whether a sector's having a high share of a member's GDP reflects its comparative advantage or past policy distortions. If the former, one might expect relatively liberal stances,[15] whereas if the latter, protection will be more strongly favoured. One encouraging aspect of this is that since integration will tend to relocate union production in a sector towards relatively more efficient countries, over time this argument could lead to reduction in protectionist pressure.

Winters (1994, 1995) considers the institutional basis of decision-making more closely and, in an EU context, observes several features that could lead to protectionist biases in the aggregation of preferences. If the union is essentially inter-governmental, rather than democratic in its own right, policy will be made by groups of bureaucrats and, eventually, ministers representing their own governments. This can be protectionist, first because, as Messerlin (1983) notes, the incentives for bureaucrats tend towards protectionism and, second, because as Scharpf (1988) notes, adding layers of inter-governmental decision-making tends to swing influence away from voters and towards official preferences for administrative convenience and a quiet life. The secrecy that surrounds EU deliberations reinforces these tendencies because it confuses public perceptions of where the responsibility for trade policy outcomes actually lies.

Within the European Union, trade policy is essentially made by committee – the so-called '113 Committee' – the members of which represent particular constituencies (countries) and none of whom is publicly accountable for the final outcome. This gives rise to at least two (related) failures of aggregation. First, the 'restaurant bill' problem: suppose the benefits of a policy on product $j$ to a country $i$ are proportionate to the latter's share of union output ($x_{ij}$) and the costs to its share of GDP ($g_i$), and suppose that each country has a veto, or at least that consensus is valued very highly. If representatives sit down to decide a package of policies on $j = 1 \ldots N$ products, each will press for inclusion of any good for which $x_{ij} > a\, g_i$, where $a > 1$ reflects the inefficiency of the conversion of costs into benefits. Since each is highly likely to have some $j$ for which this is true and, provided the *perceived a* is not too large, the easiest package to construct will cover nearly all products even if, overall, each country would prefer no change to the final outcome.

The second failure is similar but operates in probability space – see

Table 2.1. *The universalist argument: costs and benefits for a single country if the measure passes*

| | | |
|---|---|---|
| Total number of countries voting 'for/in' | 2 | 3 |
| Cost | $-2(c+d)/3$ | $-(c+d)$ |
| This country votes 'in' | | |
| Benefit | $c$ | $c$ |
| Probability of measure passing | 0.5 | 0.25 |
| This country votes 'out' | | |
| Probability of measure passing | 0.25 | 0 |

Shepsle and Weingast (1981), who christened the phenomenon 'universalism', Schattschneider (1935) on the Smoot–Hawley tariff, and Winters (1994) on the European Union. Imagine that protecting footwear is being discussed and that each of three member states is a producer of one type. If any one type is protected, the government in whose country it is produced perceives benefits of $c$ (surplus to producers, political convenience, etc.) and each member bears cost of $-(c+d)/3$, where $d$ (>0) is the deadweight cost of transferring $c$ through protection. Net costs are zero if the measure is rejected. The issue is to be decided by simple majority, and each member must decide how to vote; each accepts that if it votes against the measure, its type of footwear will not be protected.

Table 2.1 reports the costs and benefits of the proposal passing according to whether a member votes 'for/in' or 'no/out'. It also reports the probability of the proposal passing, assuming that the other countries vote randomly with probability one-half each way. The expected value of voting 'for/in' is $0.5*[c-2(c+d)/3]+0.25*[c-(c+d)]$ ($\geqslant 0$), while that of voting 'no/out' is $-0.25*2(c+d)/3$ (<0). Thus a government will vote 'for/in' if $4c>5d$ – i.e. if its 'benefits' from the protection exceed the deadweight loss by 25 per cent or more – and even if it expects negative returns to doing so!

A more sophisticated view of voting for trade policy in the European Union is offered by Widgrén (1995a, 1995b) drawing on Hamilton (1991). Widgrén notes that small countries have disproportionate numbers of votes; he considers voting coalitions and calculates countries' voting power in terms of the frequency with which they might command a pivotal position in the European Union's qualified majority voting system. He argues that if we contrast liberals (the Netherlands, Luxembourg, Germany, Denmark, Belgium and the United Kingdom) with protectionists (Spain, Portugal, Italy and France) with Ireland and Greece as uncertain, no group has power in a deterministic sense (each

34   **L. Alan Winters**

has a blocking minority). The EFTA enlargement does not change this, and so changes to the status quo look unlikely. However, allowing for probabilistic voting, with the probabilities being the same for each member of each group but varying by group, change is possible most probably in a protectionist direction: the power of the two groups is roughly balanced over proposals covering the whole range of restrictiveness (as measured by the probability of receiving support from the liberals), but in the more protective range the protectionists appear to muster rather greater power and thus are more likely to get their way. Widgrén's work clearly depends on particular constitutional structure, but it illustrates how voting patterns may generate aggregation biases. Given that in the post-war period liberalism has required positive action, the EU system favouring the status quo is not particularly multilateral.

## 4   What the evidence suggests

This section briefly surveys the evidence on 'regionalism vs. multilateralism'. Regrettably it seems to be as ambiguous as the theory, at least so far as issues of current policy are concerned. As noted above, among current RIAs only the European Union is large enough and long-lived enough to have had identifiable consequences on the world trading system itself, and it is more or less impossible to sort out what is generic and what specific among the lessons it teaches. Perhaps the only unambiguous lesson is that the creation of one regional bloc does not necessarily lead to the immediate breakdown of the trading system.

Several fundamental problems confront the scholar in this area. Foremost is creating an *anti-monde* – how can we know what member countries' trade policy would have been in the absence of the RIA? Second, systems evolve over long periods of time; it is not inconceivable that while post-war RIAs have been liberal so far, they are sowing the seeds of destruction, for example by reducing the number of independent middle-sized states which have an interest in maintaining the world system. Third, as noted above, trade policy responds to shocks from other areas: RIAs may be benign under one set of circumstances, but not another. How, then, do we allocate responsibility over causes? Fourth, how do we define and measure multilateralism? Fifth, the rhetoric required to achieve a political objective does not necessarily reflect actual causes. Even if policy-makers say they are responding to an instance of regional integration – e.g. in raising a tariff or seeking a multilateral negotiation – how do we know this is the real cause?

One solution to these difficulties is to dispense with looking at the evidence altogether, on the grounds that nothing concrete can emerge. I prefer an alternative view: as long as we are frank about the degree of confidence we can have in various conclusions, it is better to consider actual cases than to ignore them.

### 4.1   Members' own trade policies

The evidence on whether the European Union has led to higher or lower tariffs and non-tariff barriers (NTBs) for member states' non-partner trade continues to defy simple conclusions. Hufbauer (1990) argues that it created the conditions for France and Italy to contemplate liberalisation and that Germany would not have proceeded without its continental partners. Messerlin (1992) agrees that the EEC aided French liberalisation indirectly by creating the appropriate macroeconomic environment. *Prima facie* these views of France do seem plausible, for she has always appeared a reluctant liberalizer. On the other hand, crises and sudden perceptions that one is getting left behind can have dramatic effects: France's switch in the early 1980s from Keynesian expansionism to fiscal orthodoxy arose precisely because the former failed to work. A similar 'road to Damascus' could also have affected a highly protectionist France in a more liberal continent – consider Mexico in the mid-1980s, for example. Hufbauer, it seems to me, may well be wrong about Germany: in each of the two years prior to the creation of the EEC, Germany undertook tariff cuts of 25 per cent (Irwin, 1995). Thus not only did the tariff averaging attending the creation of the EEC raise German tariffs, it also possibly curtailed a liberalising momentum.

No one, I suspect, would argue that the EU has set external tariffs above the levels that would otherwise have ruled in at least one of its member countries, but this is quite different from arguing that it has not raised protection in some countries and sectors – e.g. footwear in Germany, agriculture in the United Kingdom and textiles and clothing in Sweden. The trade-off between the breadth and depth of protection is not well defined and so we cannot satisfactorily rule on whether these examples constitute increases or decreases in multilateralism.

Other recent evidence on countries' own trade is equally mixed. Following NAFTA, Canada reduced tariffs on 1,500 tariff items (mostly inputs) to help her industry compete with the United States where tariffs were lower (WTO, 1995). This looks similar to Richardson's tariff competition. On the other hand Mexico increased tariffs on 500 items – see above. In Mercosur, Argentina's tariffs on capital goods' imports will be raised to Brazilian levels.

Going back further in time, the 1960s' RIAs in Latin America were inward-looking and frequently maintained and even raised barriers against the RoW. The Central American Common Market, for example, generated huge growth in intra-trade behind such barriers (Nogues and Quintanilla, 1993). In all probability the import-substitution policy would have been less broad and/or foundered sooner if it had been restricted to small countries operating on an MFN basis. Even further back, in the 1930s, one also finds high external tariffs and burgeoning regionalism, but here the evidence is probably more favourable to regionalism (Oye, 1992; Irwin, 1993). Trade barriers were going up anyway and regional arrangements probably served to reduce the coverage of the increases by exempting some flows.

## 4.2   *Other countries' policies*

When one thinks of the effects of regionalism on the multilateral system one is obliged to deal with interactions between countries. How does an RIA cause other countries to respond? WTO (1995) suggests three classes of response: to seek to join an existing group; to create a new group; and to seek multilateral liberalisation.

The observation that regional arrangements have recently attracted new members is commonplace; one need not even list examples. However, whether this is good or bad for multilateralism is moot, for we are clearly far away from achieving a global coalition. Moreover, accretion is not inevitable and irreversible. Countries do leave groups – e.g. Chile and Peru effectively left the Andean Pact, although admittedly after it had become rather rigid. In both cases, multilateralism benefited from the defections.

The second option, of creating new RIAs, also looks popular according to the evidence. Regionalism has proceeded in waves – the 1960s and the later 1980s and 1990s – and policy-makers variously refer to demonstration effects, to the need to create their own market areas in case other blocs turn inwards, and the desire to create bargaining power. Examples include the establishment of EFTA, and recent discussions surrounding AFTA (the Asean Free Trade Area) and the CBI (the Cross-Border Initiative in Africa). Again, of course, it is moot whether this enhances or undermines multilateralism.

Finally, most directly relevant and most contentious, many commentators argue that excluded countries will seek multilateral liberalisations in response to RIAs. This occurs mainly in the realms of superpower trade diplomacy, because only superpowers can manipulate the multilateral system but even smaller powers may warm towards multilateral talks if they perceive a fragmenting world economy. Arguments of this sort have been made about each of the last four GATT Rounds, as well as in certain earlier instances.

Many commentators have argued that the creation of the EEC led directly to the Dillon and Kennedy Rounds as the United States sought to mitigate the former's trade-diversionary consequences – see, for example, Lawrence (1991), Sapir (1993) and WTO (1995). I have expressed some reservations about this linkage – Winters (1993, 1994). I do not deny some connection between these events, but I am still concerned that we have not established a necessary link between them, that any such link was benign, or that it is generalisable to other instances of integration.

First, it seems implausible to argue that multilateral progress would have stopped had the EEC not been created. After all, the benefits of liberalisation are not much affected by other countries' regionalism, it is just that, following the creation of an RIA, multilateral liberalisation may be necessary to avoid actual harm to excluded countries. The United States still had considerable hegemonic power in the late 1950s and early 1960s and so could probably have generated enough support for a Round whenever it wanted. It is not generally maintained that the EEC made the Europeans more willing to negotiate. Thus overall, I suspect that, at most, we are talking about the timing not the existence of the next Round.

Second, the Administration played the EEC card hard in public and in Congress. But whether they actually believed they *had to* respond to its creation and whether that creation was the major factor behind the push for talks is less clear. Recent debate in the United States about trade issues has sometimes demonstrated a disconnection between rhetoric and economic reality and so the EEC could just have been a convenient handle with which to manoeuvre US domestic interests and the EC nations into talks.

Third, since agriculture played such an important and delicate role in its formation, it is not surprising that the EEC resisted that sector's inclusion in the negotiations. But the fact that it got away with this (because the United States refused the '*montant de soutien*' offer) reinforced agricultural protectionism throughout the world and made it doubly difficult to negotiate in future rounds. Future agricultural disarmament may have been easier in the absence of the EEC.

Fourth, suppose it were true that the creation of the EEC forced the US Congress into trade talks. That would be tantamount to the aggressive unilateralism that many currently deplore in US trade policy. 'The Six' would have done something to harm their partners, at least in the partners' eyes, and then mitigated it in return for concessions. This is a dangerous game, even if a successful one, and might be playable only a few times. Indeed, if it were the case, it could explain why US policy has become more belligerent towards the latest enlargement and towards '1992'. However, in fact, the United States was generally sympathetic towards EC integration and actually encouraged it by allowing the Administration to offer deeper tariff cuts to a European CU than to the separate European nations (see Jackson, 1991).[16]

It has also been argued – although less frequently – that regionalism was behind the Tokyo Round. Winham (1986) reports both the first EEC enlargement (including free trade with EFTA) and the restrictiveness of the CAP as factors in the US view. The former observation seems no more compelling than those surrounding the creation of the EEC, while the latter is distinctly two-edged from our perspective: it requires, first, that the CAP induced negotiations and, second, that regionalism induced the CAP – i.e. that regionalism increased trade restrictions. Again, for this to be advantageous in its net effect on multilateralism requires a negotiating model in which might and countervailing power are the critical elements of liberalisation, quite contrary to the hegemonic views of, say, Keohane (1984). It has also been suggested to me that enlargement finally achieved a US goal by bringing the four biggest economies of Europe into one bloc and that this required a commensurate foreign policy response. Maybe, but why this response took the form of initiating a trade negotiation in the face of European opposition is unclear.

Finally, consider the Uruguay Round. Its initiation has not been related to regionalism, but its completion has. WTO (1995) says 'there is little doubt that ... the spread of regionalism [was a] major factor in eliciting the concessions needed to conclude' the Round. Bergsten's (1977) reports senior European policy-makers stating that the 1993 APEC meeting in Seattle was a major jolt to the European Union and the key which prompted it to reach settlement in the Round. On the WTO's general assertion there was a perception that the failure of the Round would lead to regional fragmentation, and this certainly encouraged the spread of defensive regionalism. How much pressure this put on the two major negotiating parties is not clear, however, for they would not have been the principal casualties of fragmentation. Bergsten's interlocutor seems to me (albeit from the outside) likely to have been confusing rhetoric and substance. The European Union had set up the conditions for settlement in the MacSharry farm reforms in 1991–2 and some insiders (e.g. Hathaway and Ingco, 1996) report that as early as 1990 EU negotiators recognised that they would complete the Round as soon as they had built an appropriate domestic coalition on agriculture.

A common theme runs through all these accounts of regionalism and GATT multilateral rounds: the threat of (or, worse, actual) violence and response. All the accounts report countries running back to the multi-lateral system to counter the damage that other countries' RIAs may do them. This may be an effective way forward but it clearly relies on rather fine judgement by both (all) protagonists that folding is better than fighting. Perhaps if regionalism has raised the average *de facto* level of multilateralism it has done so at the expense of increasing the chances of catastrophe.

Earlier evidence on regionalism is somewhat more positive, but in different circumstances. Irwin (1993) reports how the Cobden–Chavalier Treaty spawned a rash of MFN trade treaties and so created an era of significant liberalism (if not formal multilateralism). After about 1880, however, this began slowly to erode, not in a regional fashion but with MFN rates being increased. Nonetheless, the last quarter of the nine-teenth century remained a reasonably liberal period. In the inter-war period the multilateral trading system fell apart very rapidly following the imposition of the (MFN) Smoot–Hawley tariff. Both Oye (1992) and Irwin (1993) argue that whereas multilateral attempts to halt and reverse the collapse failed, regional attempts induced a measure of liberalism. Britain, France and Germany sought to protect their export markets by preferential arrangements, and in so doing did violence to US exports. This in turn induced the United States to turn to bilateral approaches in the Reciprocal Trade Agreements Act of 1934.

I draw two lessons from these historical analyses. First, regionalism–bilateralism, which entails much more obvious payoffs for exporters (internalisation) than multilateralism, can help to break down restrictive regimes. Whether it can lead all the way to multilateral liberalism is not proven, but it clearly has the ability to start the process off. This is consistent with the observation that difficult issues such as public procurement, standards and services feature more strongly in regional than in multilateral arrangements. The challenge for the policy-makers is to establish a means of switching to the multilateral horse once the race has started.

Second, building on Oye's analysis of 'shiftable externalities', poten-tially regionalised systems are likely to break down much more quickly than purely multilateral ones – cf. the late 1800s and the 1930s. 'Shiftable externalities' are externalities which an action creates but whose incidence can be moved between other agents according to their actions. Suppose I import equally from five partners and want to cut my total imports by 20 per cent. An MFN tariff increase might cut those from *A*, *B*, *C*, *D* and *E* each by 20 per cent. But suppose *A* offers me a concession to exempt itself from the cut. The others now have to bear a 25 per cent cut if I am to make the same target. Now suppose *B* wants to negotiate.

40   **L. Alan Winters**

It has to offer a bigger concession because it has to claw back a bigger cut in exports. And so on. There is a clear incentive for any supplier to strike an exclusionary deal and as quickly as possible. The possibility of regionalism increases the speed of decay.

Perhaps the crucial question is 'where is the world economy now?' Fairly closed, so that regionalism is necessary (efficient) to crack open widespread barriers, or fairly open, so that the danger is that regionalism could precipitate a collapse if someone made a wrong call? Perhaps the answer differs by sector, so that while regional arrangements are important in new issues, they are a potential danger in areas such as goods trade.

## 5     Finale

This section collects together the principal lessons from this survey in terms both of conclusions and of directions for future research. Before doing so, however, it reports one final contribution to the literature that I have been unable to fit into the schema above.

### 5.1     Investment not trade

Many commentators argue that the recent crop of North–South RIAs – e.g. NAFTA and the Europe Agreements – have been aimed at locking in the southern partner's economic reforms and stimulating inflows of foreign direct investment (FDI). Ethier (1996) offers a brilliant formalisation of these ideas. Briefly, developing countries start in autarchy, and as the world grows and liberalises they start to think about opening up themselves. If they reform successfully and attract an inflow of FDI, they gain a step increase in productivity. Their problem is that if several of them reform simultaneously, none can guarantee that it will get the FDI – maybe the inflow will go to their rivals. Regionalism, by which an industrial country offers a particular developing country small preferences on its exports, overcomes this problem by ensuring that the industrial country will invest in its partner developing country rather than any other. (Since all industrial countries are assumed to be identical, as are all developing countries, the smallest preference on return exports stemming from an FDI flow is sufficient to create this link.) Thus regionalism ensures the success of reform, not only increasing the proportion of reforming developing countries that succeed, but also encouraging more to try. This is regionalism as coordination – it removes a source of uncertainty and thus encourages reform and openness.

Ethier's paper is original and important, but its model is very special. In particular, there are no conceivable costs to regionalism to the partners and, because countries are identical within their type-class, no dangers of inefficient regional arrangements growing up within the classes. Thus coordination comes essentially risk-free. Additionally, small changes to the model would allow the same coordination to be achieved multi-laterally. For example, if each developing country considers coming out of the closet of autarchy at a unique time (because they all differ slightly from one another in dimensions that affect the timing of their reform decision), or if the supply of FDI for the industrial world is sufficiently large or the movements of factor prices in developing countries sufficiently strong, every developing country can be sure of getting some FDI if it opens up. Nonetheless the focus on FDI rather than trade is a powerful attraction of this approach, given the structure of and rhetoric surrounding current North–South regional arrangements.

## 5.2    Conclusions and future research

The issue of 'regionalism vs. multilateralism' is new analytically and deficient of empirical evidence. It is hardly surprising, therefore that this survey should conclude with more statements about research strategy than about the world we live in. Indeed, as I noted above, the only categorical statement that can be made in the last class is that one incident of regionalism is not sufficient to undermine a relatively multilateral system immediately.

  My main conclusions from working on this fascinating literature include:

- Since we value 'multilateralism', we had better work out what it means and, if it means different things to different people, ensure that we identify the sense in which we are using the term when we do so.
- The symmetric models looking at the welfare effects of regionalism have served their purpose, and probably offer rather little return to future research. Their structure is not plausible and their results seems very fragile with respect to assumed parameter values. If completely new ways of thinking about regionalism emerge, it may be worth exploring them in a symmetric framework as a way of elucidating their properties, but this is not going to resolve the positive 'stepping-stones' question.
- Asymmetric models are more plausible, but it is important to model both the demand for and supply of bloc membership.
- Models of negotiated trade policy also take a significant step towards realism. However, it would be nice, in future, to try to move beyond the repeated game trigger strategies approach to model a richer set of objectives and disciplines. This, of course, is a challenge not only to

researchers on regionalism, but also to those working on the trading system in general.

- Sector-specific lobbies are a danger if regionalism is permitted. Trade diversion is good politics even if it is bad economics. I find the view that multilateral liberalism could stall because producers get most of what they seek from regional arrangements quite convincing.
- The direct effect of regionalism on multilateralism is important, but possibly more so is the indirect effect it has by changing the ways in which (groups of) countries interact and respond to shocks in the world economy. The way in which the existence of fringes of small partners affects relations between large players seems to be a fruitful avenue, as does the structure of post-integration institutions.
- It would be useful to embed the 'regionalism vs. multilateralism' question in a framework of general economic reform and/or economic growth to generate richer menus of potential benefits and chains of causation.
- Regionalism, by allowing stronger internalisation of the gains from trade liberalisation, seems likely to be able to facilitate freer trade in highly restrictive circumstances or sectors.
- The possibility of regionalism probably increases the risks of catastrophe in the trade system. The incentives established by the insurance motive for joining regional arrangements and Oye's (1992) analysis of 'shiftable externalities' both lead to such a conclusion. So, too, does the view that regionalism is a means to bring trade partners to the multilateral negotiating table, because it is essentially coercive. The latter may have been an effective strategy, but it is risky.

## APPENDIX : AN INDEX OF MULTILATERALISM?

A country's multilateralism index is a positive function of:

(a) the absence of discrimination in its trade policy
(b) the closeness its trade regime is overall to free trade.

Assume that only one commodity is traded in the world and that our country imports it from every other country in an $(N+1)$ country world. Assume also that initially all partners face the same (MFN) tariff at level $t$ and that no other distortions exist. Suppose now that the country signs an FTA with some $(n)$ partners. How do $t$ and $n$ enter the index of multilateralism $(M)$?

Figure 2A.1 plots contours of equal $M$ in the space of the MFN tariff

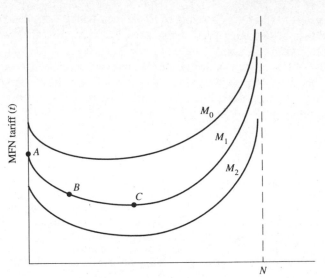

**Figure 2A.1   Iso-multilateralism loci**

($t$) and the number of FTA partners ($n$). Starting at, say, $A$, with a positive $t$, assume we sign an FTA with one partner. This increases discrimination and so would require a decrease in $t$ to keep $M$ constant; similarly if another partner entered the FTA, $t$ would need to fall further. Thus the iso-$M$ curve would include a point like $B$. Eventually, however, say, at $C$, enough countries would be in the FTA that increasing $n$ would, *ceteris paribus*, increase measured multilateralism, allowing an increase in $t$ along the iso-$M$ curve. Now imagine the far end of the curve. When the final country gets into the FTA, our country offers everyone free trade and the MFN tariff can be infinity.

For any $n$, $n$ countries pay a tariff of zero, while ($N-n$) pay $t$. Since freer trade entails higher multilateralism, if, say, $m$ countries are 'exceptional ($m < N/2$)', $M$ will be higher if the majority ($N-m$) pay zero than if the minority ($m$) does. Looked at alternatively, for many values of the tariff ($t$), a given level of multilateralism ($\overline{M}$) could arise with two different values of $n$, say $n_1$ and $n_2$, $n_1 < n_2$. We require that $n_1 < (N-n_2)$, as in figure 2A.1. Figure 2A.1 presents three such iso-multilateralism loci, with the degree of multilateralism increasing the closer the locus is to the $x$-axis. In the limit the locus for perfect multilateralism runs along the $x$-axis and up the vertical from $N$.

Clearly this index is quite complex and will become even more so once we recognise that more than two trade regimes might exist (in this

44   **L. Alan Winters**

example partners pay either $t$ or 0) and that regimes will actually vary across commodities. It becomes even worse once we recognise that we need to aggregate across countries.

The conclusions of this appendix are twofold. First, we actually need to think what we mean by 'multilateralism' if we think we are worried about it. Second, in the meantime our conclusions about 'regionalism vs. multilateralism' will remain a little fuzzy.

## NOTES

I am grateful to Anju Kapur for research assistance, to conference participants and to Richard Baldwin, Will Martin, Pier Carlo Padoan and André Sapir for comments on an earlier draft, and to Audrey Kitson-Walters for logistical support. The views expressed here are the author's alone. They do not necessarily represent those of the World Bank or any of its member governments.

1  The appendix (p. 42) offers a little more detail on such an index.
2  Earlier contributions include Riezman (1985) and Kennan and Riezman (1990).
3  Sinclair and Vines model the similarity somewhat differently from Bond and Syropoulos.
4  They refer to their discussion as 'Krugman vs. Krugman', my nomination for title of the year.
5  Deardorff and Stern (1994) effectively use the same approach but pairing countries by complementary comparative advantage rather than transportation costs. Arguably, however, their results gravitate away from continental blocs rather than towards them if comparative advantage varies more across continents than within them.
6  Similar arguments surround the Kemp and Wan (1976) result that a CU can always find a common external tariff (CET) that renders it welfare-improving and thus that unions can beneficially expand and combine until they arrive at global free trade. 'Can', but there is no analysis of 'do'. This is not to criticise Kemp and Wan: their focus was not on stepping stones.
7  That is, blocs do not raise their optimum tariffs as a result of integration.
8  An alternative strategy would be for the union to *reduce* its tariff to keep non-member welfare constant – a so-called 'Kemp–Wan reduction'. The union would prefer this to trade war if it had below about 40 per cent of countries.
9  As Perroni and Whalley observe, in strict trade policy terms Eastern Europe, the Mediterranean countries and Mexico gain little from their associations with larger blocs relative to unilateral MFN liberalisation.
10  See also Helpman (1997) for a summary.
11  This point is also made by McCulloch and Petri (1994).
12  Similar causal channels are found in Panagariya and Findlay (1994).
13  The analysis revolves around the elasticities with which the fringe demands and supplies sensitive products, not its excess supply *per se*. Presumably the latter would enter the decision to create the FTA in the first place. The link with Richardson (1993) is best seen on the import analogue of the argument in the text. If the fringe supply curve of the sensitive import is perfectly elastic, the lobbies in $A$ lose all interest in maintaining a higher post-tariff price on $B$.

14 They still gain from integration because of the differentiated goods.
15 Such a sector may prefer high EU protection, so that it can reap high rents on EU sales, but at least it could survive with lower protection.
16 Maybe this reflected US fears of the EEC – i.e. that it felt obliged to offer and to seek bigger tariff reductions if the EEC completed its integration – but publishing the fact seems a clumsy negotiating ploy if that were the case.

## REFERENCES

Bagwell, K. and Staiger, R. W., 1996a. 'Preferential Agreements and the Multilateral Trading System', mimeo
  1996b. 'Regionalism and Multilateralism Tariff Cooperation', paper prepared for the International Economics Association Round-Table Conference, International Trade Policy and the Pacific Rim (15–17 July)
  1997a. 'Multilateral Tariff Cooperation During the Formation of Regional Free Trade Areas', *International Economic Review*, **38**, 291–319
  1997b. 'Multilateral Tariff Cooperation During the Formation of Customs Unions', *Journal of International Economics*, **42**, 91–123
Baldwin, R.E., 1995. 'A Domino Theory of Regionalism', chapter 2 in Baldwin, Haaparanta and Kiander (eds.), 25–48
Baldwin, R.E., Haaparanta, P. and Kiander, J., 1995. *Expanding Membership in the European Union* (Cambridge: Cambridge University Press for the CEPR)
Bergsten, F., 1997. 'Open regionalism', *The World Economy*, **20**, 545–66
Bhagwati, J.N., 1991. *The World Trading System at Risk* (Princeton: Princeton University Press)
Bhagwati, J. N. and Panagariya, A., 1996. 'Preferential Trading Areas and Multilateralism: Strangers, Friends or Foes?', in J.N. Bhagwati and A. Panagariya (eds.), *Free Trade Areas or Free Trade? The Economics of Preferential Trading Agreements* (Washington, DC: AEI Press)
Bond, E.W. and Syropoulos, C., 1996a. 'The Size of Trading Blocs: Market Power and World Welfare Effects', *Journal of International Economics*, **40**, 411–37
  1996b. 'Trading Blocs and the Sustainability of Inter-regional Cooperation', in M. Canzoneri, W. Ethier and V. Grilli (eds.), *The New Transatlantic Economy* (Cambridge: Cambridge University Press)
Bond, E.W., Syropoulos, C. and Winters, L.A., 1996. 'Deepening of Regional Integration and External Trade Relations', *CEPR Discussion Paper*, **1317**
Cadot, O., De Melo, J. and Olarreaga, J., 1996. 'Regional Integration and Lobbying for Tariffs Against Non-Members', University of Geneva, mimeo
Campa, J.M. and Sorenson, T.L., 1996. 'Are Trade Blocs Condusive to Free Trade?', *Scandinavian Journal of Economics*, **98**, 263–73
Collie, D., 1997. 'Bilateralism is Good: Trade Blocs and Strategic Export Subsidies', *Oxford Economic Papers*, **49**, 504–20
Deardorff, A.W. and Stern, R.M., 1994. 'Multilateral Trade Negotiations and Preferential Trading Arrangements', in A.V. Deardorff and R.M. Stern, *Analytical and Negotiating Issues in the Global Trading System* (Ann Arbor: University of Michigan Press)

### 46   L. Alan Winters

De Melo, J. and Panagariya, A. (eds.) 1993. *New Dimensions in Regional Integration* (Cambridge: Cambridge University Press for the CEPR)

De Melo, J. Panagariya, A. and Rodrik, D. (1993) 'The New Regionalism: A Country Perspective', in J. De Melo and A. Panagariya (eds.), *New Dimensions in Regional Integration* (Cambridge: Cambridge University Press for the CEPR)

Eichengreen B. (ed.), 1995. *Europe's Post-War Recovery* (Cambridge: Cambridge University Press)

Ethier, W.J., 1996. 'Regionalism in a Multilateral World', mimeo

Frankel, J.A., 1997. *Regional Trading Blocs* (Washington, DC: Institute for International Economics)

Frankel, J.A. and Wei, S.J., 1996. 'Regionalization of World Trade and Currencies: Economics and Politics', chapter 7 in J.A. Frankel (ed.), *The Regionalization of the World Economy* (Chicago: Chicago University Press)

Frankel, J.A., Stein, E. and Wei, S. J., 1995. 'Trading Blocs and the Americas: The Natural, the Unnatural, and the Super-Natural', *Journal of Development Economics,* **47**, 61–95.

     1996. 'Continental Trade Blocs: Are They Natural and Super-Natural?', chapter 4 in J.A. Frankel (ed.), *The Regionalization of the World Economy* (Chicago: Chicago University Press)

Gatsios, K. and Karp, L., 1991. 'Delegation Games in Customs Unions', *Review of Economic Studies,* **58**, 391–97

     1995. 'Delegation in a General Equilibrium Model of Customs Unions', *European Economic Review,* **39**, 319–33

Goto, J. and Hamada, K., 1994. 'Economic Integration and the Welfare of Those Who are Left Behind: An Asian Perspective', RIEB Kobe University, *Discussion Paper,* **47**

     1997. 'EU, NAFTA and Asian Responses: A Perspective from the Calculus of Participation', chapter 4 in T. Ito and A.O. Krueger (eds.), *Regionalism vs. Multilateral Trade Agreements* (Chicago: Chacago University Press), 91–110

Grossman, G. and Helpman, E., 1994. 'Protection for Sale', *American Economic Review,* **85**, 667–90

     1995. 'The Politics of Free-Trade Agreements', *American Economic Review,* **84**, 833–50

Hamilton, C.B., 1991. 'The Nordic EFTA Countries' Options: Community Membership or a Permanent EEA Accord', chapter 7 in *EFTA Countries in a Changing Europe* (Geneva: EFTA), 97–128

Hathaway, D.E. and Ingco, M.D., 1996. 'Agricultural Liberalization and the Uruguay Round', chapter 2 in W. Martin and L.A. Winters (eds.), *The Uruguay Round and the Developing Countries* (Cambridge: Cambridge University Press)

Helpman, E., 1997. 'Politics and Trade Policy', chapter 2 in D.M. Kreps and K.F. Wallis (eds.), *Advances in Economics and Econometrics: Theory and Application, vol. I* (Cambridge: Cambridge University Press)

Hufbauer, G.C., 1990. *Europe 1992: An American Perspective* (Washington, DC: Brookings)

Irwin, D.A., 1993. 'Multilateral and Bilateral Trade Policies in the World Trading System: A Historical Perspective', chapter 4 in De Melo and Panagariya (eds.), 90–119

——— 1995. 'The GATT's Contribution to Economic Recovery in Post-war Western Europe', chapter 5 in Eichengreen (ed.), 127–50

Jackson, J.H., 1991. 'The European Community and World Trade: The Commercial Policy Dimension', Institute for Public Policy Studies, University of Michigan, Ann Arbor, *Discussion Paper*, **298**

Jacquemin, A. and Sapir, A., 1988. 'European Integration or World Integration?', *WeltwirtschaftlichesArchiv*, **124**, 127–39

Kemp, M.C. and Wan, H., Jr., 1976. 'An Elementary Proposition Concerning the Formation of Customs Unions', *Journal of International Economics*, **6**, 95–7

Kennan, J. and Riezman, R., 1990. 'Optimal Tariff Equilibria with Customs Unions', *Canadian Journal of Economics*, **23**, 70–83

Keohane, R.O., 1984. *After Hegemony: Cooperation and Discord in the World Political Economy* (Princeton: Princeton University Press)

Kowalczyk, C, and Sjostrom, T., 1992. 'Bringing GATT into the Core', *Economica*, **61**, 301–17

Krishna, P., 1994. 'Regionalism and Multilateralism: A Political Economy Approach', *Quarterly Journal of Economics*, forthcoming

Krugman P., 1991a. 'Is Bilateralism Bad?', in E. Helpman and A. Razin (eds.), *International Trade and Trade Policy* (Cambridge, MA: MIT Press)

——— 1991b. 'The Move Towards Free Trade Zones', in 'Policy Implications of Trade and Currency Zones', a symposium sponsored by the Federal Reserve Bank of Kansas City, Jackson Hole, Wyoming (22–24 August)

——— 1993. 'Regionalism versus Multilateralism: Analytical Notes', in J.De Melo and A.Panagariya (eds.), 58–78

Lawrence, R.Z., 1991. 'Emerging Regional Arrangements: Building Blocs or Stumbling Blocks?', in R. O'Brien (ed.), *Finance and the International Economy 5*, The AMEX Bank Review Prize Essays (New York: Oxford University Press), 23–35

Levy, P.I., 1997. 'A Political-economic Analysis of Free Trade Agreements', *American Economic Review*, **87**, 506–19

——— 1996a. 'Lobbying and International Cooperation in Tariff Setting', Yale University, mimeo

——— 1996b. 'Comment on "Regionalization of World Trade and Currencies: Economics and Politics" ', chapter 7 in J.A. Frankel (ed.), *The Regionalization of the World Economy* (Chicago: Chicago University Press)

Ludema, R., 1996. 'On the Value of Preferential Trade Agreements in Multilateral Negotiations', Georgetown University, *Working Paper*, **97–22**

McCulloch, R. and Petri, P., 1994. 'Alternative Paths toward Global Markets', paper presented at a conference in honour of Robert Stern, University of Michigan (20 November)

48   **L. Alan Winters**

Messerlin, P.A., 1983. 'Bureaucracies and the Political Economy of Protection: Reflections of a Continental European', *WeltwirtschaftlichesArchiv*, **117**, 468–96

    1992. 'Trade Policies in France', in D. Salvatore (ed.), *National Trade Policies. Handbook of Comparative Economic Policies*. vol. 2 (Westport, CN and London: Greenwood Press)

Nitsch, V., 1996. 'Natural Trading Blocs: A Closer Look', paper prepared for the European Economic Association Meeting, Istanbul (August)

    1996 'Do Three Trade Blocs Minimize World Welfare?', *Review of International Economics*, **4**, 355–63

Nogues, J. and Quintanilla, R., 1993. 'Latin America's Integration and the Multilateral Trading System', in De Melo and Panagariya (eds.), 278–313

Nordström. H., 1995. 'Customs Unions, Regional Trading Blocs and Welfare', chapter 3 in Baldwin, Haaparanta and Kiander (eds.), 54–78

Oye, K., 1992. *Economic Discrimination and Political Exchange: World Political Economy in the 1930s and 1980s* (Princeton: Princeton University Press)

Panagariya, A. and Findlay, R., 1994. 'A Political Economy Analysis of Free Trade Areas and Customs Unions', *Policy Research Working Paper*, **1261** (Washington, DC: World Bank)

Perroni, C. and Whalley, J., 1994. 'The New Regionalism: Trade Liberalization or Insurance?', *NBER Working Paper*, **4626**

Richardson, M., 1993. 'Endogenous Protection and Trade Diversion', *Journal of International Economics*, **34**, 309–24

    1994. 'Why a Free Trade Area? The Tariff Also Rises', *Economics and Politics*, **6**, 79–96

    1995. 'Tariff Revenue Competition in a Free Trade Area', *European Economic Review*, **39**, 1429–37

Richardson, M. and Desruelle, D., 1997. 'Fortress Europe: Jericho or Château d'If?', *Review of International Economics*, **5**, 32–46

Riezman, R., 1985. 'Customs Unions and the Core', *Journal of International Economics*, **19**, 355–65

Sapir, A., 1993. 'Discussion of chapter 7', in De Melo and Panagariya (eds.), 230–3

Scharpf, F., 1998. 'Joint Decision Trap: Lessons from German Federalism and European Integration', *Public Administration*, **66**, 239–78

Schattschneider, E.E., 1935. *Politics, Pressures and the Tariff* (New York: Prentice-Hall)

Shepsle, K.A. and Weingast, B.R., 1981. 'Political Preferences for the Pork Barrel: A Generalisation', *American Journal of Political Science*, **25**, 96–111

Sinclair, P. and Vines, D., 1995. 'Bigger Trade Blocs Need not Entail More Protection', University of Birmingham, mimeo

Spilimbergo, A. and Stein, E., 1996. 'The Welfare Implications of Trading Blocs among Countries with Different Endowments', chapter 5 in J.A. Frankel (ed.), *The Regionalization of the World Economy* (Chicago: Chicago University Press)

Srinivasan, T.N., 1993. 'Regionalism vs. Multilateralism: Analytical Notes: Discussion', in De Melo and Panagariya (eds.), 84–9

Summers, L., 1991. 'Regionalism and the World Trading System', in 'Policy Implications of Trade and Currency Zones', a symposium sponsored by the Federal Reserve Bank of Kansas City, Jackson Hole, Wyoming, 295–302

Widgrén, M., 1995a. 'Voting Power and Control in the EU: The Impact of EFTA Entrants', chapter 5 in Baldwin, Haaparanta and Kiander (eds.), 113–42

  1995b. 'Probabilistic Voting Power in the EU Council: The Cases of Trade Policy and Social Regulation', *Scandinavian Journal of Economics*, **97**, 345–56

Winham, G.R., 1986. *International Trade and the Tokyo Round Negotiation* (Princeton: Princeton University Press)

Winters, L.A., 1993. 'The European Community: A Case of Successful Integration', *CEPR Discussion Paper*, **755**

  1994. 'The EC and Protection: The Political Economy', *European Economic Review*, **38**, 596–603

  1995. 'Who Should Run Eastern European Trade Policy and How', chapter 2 in L.A. Winters (ed.), *Foundations of an Open Economy: Trade Laws and Institutions for Eastern Europe* (London: Cambridge University for the CEPR), 19–39

World Trade Organization (WTO), 1995. *Regionalism and the World Trading System* (Geneva: WTO) (April)

Yarbrough, B.V. and Yarbrough, R.M., 1992. *Cooperation and Governance in International Trade: The Strategic Organizational Approach* (Princeton: Princeton University Press)

*Journal of Economic Literature*
*Vol. XXXVIII (June 2000) pp. 287–331*

# Preferential Trade Liberalization: The Traditional Theory and New Developments

## ARVIND PANAGARIYA[1]

## 1. *Introduction*

THE CURRENT wave of preferential trade arrangements, like the first wave in the 1950s and 1960s, has given rise to a lively debate between the free trade economists who view the arrangements as harmful and others who see them as beneficial. To the old concerns relating to welfare effects, captured in Jacob Viner's (1950) influential "static" concepts of trade creation and trade diversion, the current debate has added what Jagdish Bhagwati (1993) calls the "dynamic" time-path issue.

The effective regional arrangements during the first wave did not spread beyond Western Europe.[2] Consistent with this reality, the debate at the time, and the literature it spawned, remained largely confined to the question whether regional arrangements resulted in higher or lower welfare for their members. Today, with "trade blocs" being vigorously sought by virtually all countries in the

world, economists and policy analysts are also focusing on the implications of such blocs for the global trading system. In terms of Bhagwati's (1991) memorable phrase, they are asking whether trade blocs serve as "building blocks" or "stumbling blocks" for worldwide freeing of trade.

The purpose of this essay is to bring together the key theoretical contributions addressing both the old and new themes. Two features distinguish this essay from others that have appeared in recent years.[3] First, its emphasis is almost exclusively on theory. In spite of a number of recent books and survey articles, we lack a single source synthesizing the large body of theoretical literature on the subject. Second, rather than simply report the results derived in various contributions, the essay offers a deeper treatment of them. A special effort is made to provide an intuitive but

---

[1] University of Maryland. I am indebted to Jagdish Bhagwati, John McMillan, and three anonymous referees for numerous helpful comments. Thanks are also due to Kyle Bagwell, Rupa Duttagupta, David Evans, Pravin Krishna, Philip Levy, and Robert Staiger for useful suggestions.

[2] Throughout this essay, the term "regional arrangements" refers to preferential trade arrangements, defined more precisely below.

[3] Survey articles include Richard Baldwin and Anthony Venables (1995), Bhagwati and Panagariya (1996a,b), Alan Winters (1996), Bhagwati, David Greenaway, and Panagariya (1998), Raquel Fernandez and Jonathan Portes (1998), and Panagariya (1999a). Recent book-length treatments are Kym Anderson and Richard Blackhurst (1993), Jaime de Melo and Panagariya (1993), Jeffrey Frankel (1997, 1998) and Panagariya (1999b). Many of the contributions reviewed in this paper can be readily found in Bhagwati, Pravin Krishna, and Panagariya (1999).

rigorous explanation of the mechanism underlying many of the contributions reviewed.

My concern in the essay is solely with the literature on *preferential* liberalization of tariffs on goods. Thus, I do not review many of the recent contributions on "trade agreements" in which trade preferences play no explicit role. Also excluded from consideration are issues such as preferential trade in services, the role of investment in regional arrangements, and harmonization of domestic policies. Though these issues figure in the current policy debate, they have not been seriously addressed in the theoretical literature.[4]

Three terms are used frequently in the essay: preferential trade area (PTA), free trade area (FTA) and customs union (CU). Throughout, a PTA refers to a union between two or more countries in which lower tariffs are imposed on goods produced in the member countries than on goods produced outside. An FTA is a PTA with tariffs eliminated entirely on goods produced in member countries. A customs union (CU) is an FTA with all members imposing a common external tariff on a given good. The term PTA being wider, it is used to include the arrangements with limited tariff preferences, FTAs, and CUs.

In Section 2, I discuss briefly the multilateral trade policy framework within which PTAs are formed. In Section 3, I develop the traditional welfare analysis, adding several new twists to it. In Section 4, I discuss the Kemp-Wan-Vanek-Ohyama theorem on CUs (and its recent extension to FTAs by Pana-

gariya and Pravin Krishna 1997) that cuts through the ambiguities of trade creation and trade diversion and offers a clear approach to identifying welfare-enhancing FTAs. In Section 5, I turn to the more recent literature that focuses on the welfare effects of a simultaneous, exogenous division of the world into several blocs. The emphasis of this literature is on the relationship between the number of blocs and welfare. In Section 6, I turn to the literature on endogenous policy. Two sets of questions are discussed. First, if the decision to form an FTA is endogenous, under what circumstances is the latter likely to be accepted and under what conditions is it likely to be rejected? Second, what is the impact of FTAs and CUs on the outside tariff? In Section 7, I turn to the models addressing directly the relationship between regionalism and multilateralism. In Section 8, I briefly examine some theoretical issues underlying the empirical approaches to resolving the ambiguity in welfare outcomes. In Section 9, I conclude the paper.

## 2. *The Multilateral Trade Policy Framework*

International trade in goods is governed by the General Agreement on Tariffs and Trade (GATT). Signed in 1947, this agreement was incorporated into the 1994 Marrakesh Agreement establishing the World Trade Organization (WTO). The centerpiece of GATT is the Most Favored Nation (MFN) principle enunciated in its Article I. Accordingly, in matters of trade policy, each WTO member is to grant to all members the same advantage, privilege, favor, or immunity that it grants to any other country. A key implication of this provision is that member countries are not to discriminate in their tariff policy across other members.

PTAs are thus in conflict with Article

---

[4] Even within this narrow definition of regional arrangements, space constraints preclude full coverage. For instance, the analysis of the effects of a policy change (e.g., a reduction in the common external tariff) on individual union members within an existing common market with internal factor mobility, pioneered by Richard Brecher and Bhagwati (1981), is not considered.

I of GATT, and had to be accommodated through a variety of additional provisions. As it stands currently, there exist three alternative provisions for trade preferences within the GATT/WTO system. First, developed countries can give developing countries *one-way* trade preferences. This provision is the basis of the Generalized System of Preferences, designed to promote exports from developing to developed countries. Second, under the Enabling Clause, developing countries can exchange virtually any trade preferences to which they agree. This provision is intended to promote trade among developing countries themselves. Under the Enabling Clause, preferences need not lead to a full free trade area; partial preferences across a subset of goods are permitted. All PTAs among developing countries, including the prominent ones such as the Southern Cone Common Market, popularly known by its Spanish acronym MERCO-SUR, and the ASEAN Free Trade Area (AFTA), were formed under this provision.[5] Finally, under Article XXIV of GATT, any two or more members of the WTO can form an FTA or CU. The European Economic Community (EEC) and its various association agreements and the North American Free Trade Agreement (NAFTA) were concluded under Article XXIV.

Article XXIV offers the only avenue to PTAs in which developed countries are *recipients* of trade preferences. Given the large share of developed countries in both world trade and world GDP, this fact gives Article XXIV a central role in any discussion of PTAs. A key requirement of Article XXIV is that the exchange of preferences not be partial. Instead, it should result in the formation of an FTA or CU with duties

and other restrictive regulations of commerce eliminated with respect to "substantially all the trade" in products originating in union members. In the case of FTAs, external tariffs of member countries must not be raised. In the case of CUs, the incidence of the common external tariff on outside countries' trade is not to exceed that of individual tariffs of union members prior to the formation of the union.

To date, GATT and the WTO have not actively enforced the provisions of GATT Article XXIV. For one thing, the definition of "substantially all trade" has never been clarified satisfactorily. Thus, even though trade in agriculture was not freed within the EEC, GATT never censured that arrangement. The EEC's association agreements with its neighbors also have frequently carried exceptions with respect to product coverage, but these have not been questioned either. In effect, matters have been left to the member countries themselves.

This is not to suggest, however, that Article XXIV has not influenced the design of PTAs in which developed countries are participants. Despite aberrations and exceptions, the EEC and NAFTA are closer to free trade among union members than any of the PTAs concluded under the Enabling Clause. Article XXIV has also kept in check the temptation to exchange partial trade preferences when member countries have no intention to form an FTA or CU. Thus, in the absence of Article XXIV, it is conceivable that some developed-country members of the Asia Pacific Economic Cooperation (APEC) forum would have opted for an exchange of partial trade preferences but were restrained by this provision.

## 3. *The Traditional Welfare Analysis*

Though the current wave of regionalism has given rise to new concerns, the

---

[5] ASEAN stands for the Association of Southeast Asian Nations.

290          Journal of Economic Literature, Vol. XXXVIII (June 2000)

old concerns have remained alive. Therefore, it is appropriate to begin our review with the traditional, static welfare
analysis pioneered by Viner (1950) in his
classic work, *The Customs Union Issue*. I
first spell out the broad structure of the
model to be used throughout this section.
Within this framework, I then employ a
set of partial-equilibrium models to identify the key factors which determine the
welfare outcome. The modifications implied by general equilibrium considerations are brought into the picture only
at the last stage of the analysis.

. Assume three countries, A, B and C,
which trade a product, steel, with each
other. Countries A and B are potential
union partners and C represents the
rest of the world. Between the union
members, A is the importer of steel and
B the exporter.[6] If an FTA is formed,
each member sets the external tariff at
its pre-union level. If a CU is formed,
the common external tariff is set equal
to the pre-union tariff of A, the importing member of the union.[7] Other details
relating to demand, supply, trade, and
tariffs are spelled out in the context of
specific models.

### 3.1 Trade Creation and Trade Diversion

Any discussion of the welfare effects
of PTAs must inevitably begin with the
influential concepts of trade creation
and trade diversion, introduced by
Viner (1950). As James Meade (1955,

---

[6] Based on the analysis to be presented, the
reader can analyze the remaining, less interesting,
cases in which A and B are both importers or exporters of steel.

[7] In the case of a CU, it will be assumed that B
keeps a non-negative tariff on the books even
though it is nonbinding in the initial equilibrium.
As long as this tariff is no lower than A's, equating
the common external tariff to the latter is consistent with GATT Article XXIV. But in other cases,
this traditional assumption made implicitly or explicitly by all analysts employing the partial-equilibrium framework is inconsistent with GATT Article XXIV.

ch. 2) noted in his seminal contribution, *The Theory of Customs Unions*,
these concepts are best introduced
within a model exhibiting infinite supply elasticities and zero demand elasticities. This model avoids some of the
ambiguities that arise in more general
models.

Let us then begin by representing
country A's demand for steel by the vertical line $D_A D_A$ in Figure 1a. Firms in
A, B, and C supply at constant prices
shown by $P_A$, $P_B$ and $P_C$, respectively.
Under perfect competition, these prices
also represent the constant average and
marginal costs of production in the
three countries. By assumption, A is the
least efficient supplier of steel and C
the most efficient one. Thus, we have
$P_A > P_B > P_C$.

We assume that countries B and C do
not trade with each other. This will be
true, for example, if B applies a per-
unit tariff higher than $P_B - P_C$ on imports. Initially, country A imposes a
nondiscriminatory tariff at rate $t$ *per
unit* on steel.[8] The tariff rate is chosen
such that $P_A > P_C + t > P_B$. The entire
quantity demanded, $OQ_0$, is imported
from C. The price paid by consumers is
$P_C + t$, with area $e + f$ collected in tariff
revenue by A's government.

Suppose now that country A eliminates
the tariff on B but retains it on C. Given
$P_C + t > P_B$, A now purchases its imports
from B rather than C at price $P_B$. Because the change creates no new trade
and merely substitutes the less efficient
B for the more efficient C, in Viner's
terminology, the union is "trade diverting." Country A loses the tariff revenue
$e + f$, with $e$ used up to pay for the
higher production cost in B and $f$ becoming a part of A's consumers' surplus.

---

[8] A per-unit tariff rate is employed mainly to simplify the figures. Unless otherwise noted, replacing
this rate by an ad valorem rate will not change any
of the conclusions.

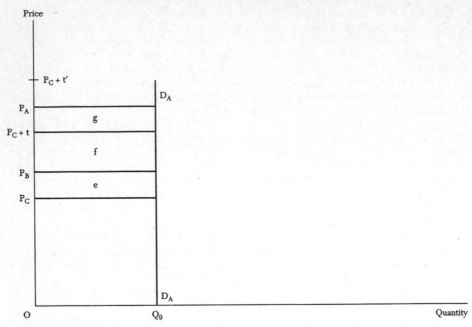

*Figure* 1a. Trade Creation and Trade Diversion

The net loss to A and the world from the union is area $e$.

Next, suppose the initial nondiscriminatory tariff in A is $t'$, where $t'$ is sufficiently high to result in $P_A < P_C + t' < P_B + t'$. Thus, the high tariff prices out both B and C from A's market. The entire demand for steel, $OQ_0$, is satisfied by A's own firms at price $P_A$. Once again, let A remove the tariff on B but not C. This change leads to a switch in the source of supply from A to B. The price of steel paid by A's buyers drops from $P_A$ to $P_B$, yielding a gain in consumers' surplus equal to $f + g$. Because the union creates new trade between A and B and is associated with a switch from higher-cost suppliers in A to lower-cost suppliers in B, in Viner's terminology, the union is "trade creating."[9] Welfare

[9] Observe that even though the lowest-cost source of supply is C, this union is trade creating

of A and the world rises by $f + g$, while that of B and C is unchanged.

Within the confines of the model under consideration, trade diversion is associated with a welfare loss, and trade creation with a welfare gain. Viner argued that since a union is trade creating in some products and trade diverting in others, in general, we cannot say whether it increases or decreases welfare. The answer depends on the relative magnitudes of trade creation and trade diversion.

But as Meade (1955, ch. 2) has rightly pointed out, even the relative

since the switch is to a lower-cost source. Viner (1950, p. 43) was quite explicit about this possibility: "This shift in the locus of production as between the two countries is a shift from a high-cost to a lower-cost point, a shift which the free-trader can properly approve, as at least a step in the right direction, even if universal free trade would divert production to a source with still lower costs."

292 *Journal of Economic Literature, Vol. XXXVIII (June 2000)*

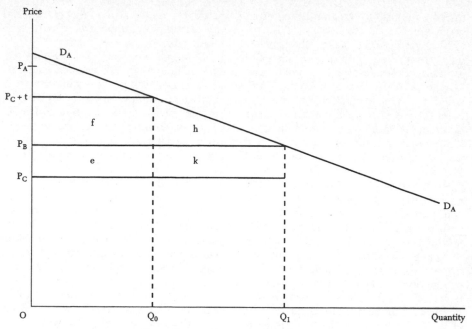

*Figure* 1b. A Welfare Gain under Trade Diversion

magnitudes of trade creation and trade diversion alone are insufficient to determine the welfare effect of the union for two reasons. First, benefits of preferential liberalization depend on not only the extent of trade creation, but also the magnitude by which costs are reduced on each unit of newly created trade. Similarly, losses are determined not just by the amount of trade diversion but also the magnitude of the increase in costs due to trade diversion. In terms of Figure 1a, the benefit from trade creation, area $f + g$, equals $OQ_0.P_AP_B$ while the loss due to trade diversion, area $e$, equals $OQ_0.P_BP_C$. We cannot infer the gain or loss from $OQ_0$ alone.

The second problem, formalized subsequently by Franz Gehrels (1956–57) and Richard Lipsey (1957) within a one-factor, general-equilibrium model, is that once we drop the unrealistic assumption of zero elasticity of demand in A, even a wholly trade-diverting union may lead to a net increase in welfare. This can be demonstrated by replacing the vertical demand curve in Figure 1a by a downward-sloped demand curve. Thus, in Figure 1b, let the demand curve in A, $D_AD_A$, be negatively sloped. The initial nondiscriminatory tariff is set at $t$ with country A importing $OQ_0$ from C. A removal of the tariff on B but not C prices out the latter, the least-cost producer of steel, but allows an expansion of imports from $OQ_0$ to $OQ_1$. The result is a loss of area $e$ on the original imports but a gain of area $h$ on new imports. Area $f$ is a redistribution of tariff revenue to consumers in A (ignore area $k$ for now). In principle, area $h$ can be larger than area $e$, establishing the possibility that a wholly trade-diverting union can lead to an improvement in welfare.[10]

Bhagwati (1971) makes the further point that even with a zero demand elasticity, a trade-diverting union can lead to an improvement in welfare provided the supply elasticity of steel in country A is positive but finite. To see this, revert to Figure 1a and imagine that country A's supply curve is upward sloped, starting below $P_B$ and meeting $D_A D_A$ above $P_C + t$. Under a nondiscriminatory tariff, the price in A is $P_C + t$ with steel supplied partially by C and partially by A. A free trade area with B leads to a replacement of C by B as the foreign supplier, which is trade diverting. Nevertheless, the internal price falls so that inefficient domestic production is partially replaced by imports. The net effect on welfare depends on the magnitude of this gain in efficiency relative to the loss from replacing higher-cost source B for the original quantity of imports from C. As Bhagwati (1971) correctly concludes, to eliminate the possibility of a trade-diverting union leading to welfare gains, we must assume the elasticity of demand for *imports* in A to be zero and the elasticity of supply from B and C to be infinity.

To Meade's caveats, we may add one further limitation. When union members are themselves large, even leaving aside the two considerations noted by Meade, we can rely on trade creation and trade diversion to infer the welfare effects of preferential trade liberalization only if we are interested in world welfare. If the focus of the analysis is the welfare of the union instead, trade diversion is likely to be beneficial due to the improvement in the terms of trade it brings. Likewise, trade creation, which enhances the union's income at constant world prices, could generate a harmful second-round effect through deterioration in the terms of trade. Meade himself did not have to confront this problem since he analyzed PTAs exclusively from the viewpoint of global welfare.

Despite these limitations, trade creation and trade diversion have remained central to policy debates on PTAs.[11] This is presumably because economists have found these terms to be highly effective tools for focusing policy makers' attention on the ambiguous welfare effects of PTAs.

### 3.2 *The Revenue-Transfer Effect in a Customs Union*

Even after we allow for downward-sloped demand and upward-sloped supply in A, the model just considered remains unrealistic in one key respect: it necessarily implies that all of A's imports come from either B or C but not both. To capture the realistic case, in which imports come from the union partner as well as the outside country, we must introduce a finite elasticity of supply in at least one of B and C.

---

[10] Because quantity $Q_0 Q_1$ is new trade rather than a replacement of old trade by the partner, it is not entirely clear whether Viner would have called it trade diversion. There is at least one statement in Viner (1950, p. 44) that contradicts the Meade-Gehrels-Lipsey interpretation: "It will be noted that for the free-trader the benefit from a customs union to the customs union area as a whole derives from that portion of the new trade between the member countries which is wholly new trade, whereas each particular portion of the new trade between the member countries which is a substitute for trade with third countries he must regard as a consequence of the customs union which is injurious for the importing country, for the external world, and for the world as a whole, and is beneficial only to the supplying member." Given the references to the gains and losses to the partner and the outside country, this statement also undermines the interpretation that Viner thought purely in terms of a constant-costs model. The difficulty, however, is that nonconstant costs do not sit well with the bulk of the analysis in the book.

[11] Carsten Kowalczyk (1990) has argued in favor of replacing these terms by volume-of-trade and terms-of-trade effects but without impact.

294          *Journal of Economic Literature, Vol. XXXVIII (June 2000)*

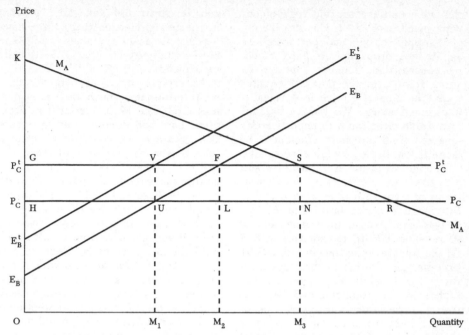

*Figure 2.* CU: A Preferential Removal of a Tariff by A Leads to a Loss of GFLH to Itself, a Gain of GFUH to Partner B, and a Net Loss of FLU to the Union as a Whole

As shown originally in Panagariya (1996) and elaborated further in Bhagwati and Panagariya (1996a), the introduction of a finite supply elasticity on the part of one or both of B and C leads to a fundamental change in the effects of preferential trade liberalization on welfare. Thus, continuing to assume that A is the potential importer of steel, subtract its supply from demand and obtain its import-demand curve. Similarly, assuming that B is an exporter of steel, subtract its demand from supply and obtain its export-supply curve. In Figure 2, represent these curves by $M_A M_A$ and $E_B E_B$, respectively, and C's infinitely elastic supply by $P_C P_C$.

Initially, A imposes a per-unit tariff at rate $t$ on both B and C. As viewed by buyers and sellers in A, this tariff shifts export-supply curves of B and C to $E_B^t E_B^t$

and $P_C^t P_C^t$, respectively. The internal price in country A comes to a rest at $P_C^t$ with imports from B and C equaling $OM_1$ and $M_1 M_3$, respectively. A's gains from trade (relative to autarky, of course) are represented by triangle *KGS* plus rectangle *GSNH*. The triangle is the net change in the consumers' and producers' surplus while the rectangle represents tariff revenue. Since B exports steel, the internal price there equals $P_C$ even if the country happens to have a positive tariff on the books.

Precisely how a preferential freeing of trade by A with respect to B changes the equilibrium depends on the level of the external tariff on steel imports in B in the post-union equilibrium. Initially, consider the simpler, CU case in which B's external tariff on steel coincides with A's. Freeing up of trade between the two countries leads to a single union-wide price, $P_C^t = P_C + t$. Country B's export-supply curve, as perceived by agents in A, drops down to $E_B E_B$. Since, by construction, imports continue to come from C in the post-CU equilibrium, the domestic price in A remains unchanged at $P_C^t$. We have a case of pure trade diversion with imports $M_1 M_2$ diverted from the more efficient C to less efficient B. No new trade is created.

Though extra-union terms of trade are fixed by assumption, *intra-union* terms of trade shift in favor of B by the full amount of the tariff. For A, this shift is manifested in the transfer of tariff revenue, GFLH, to exporters in B.[12] Of the total revenue transferred, GFUH becomes an addition to the gains from trade for B while FLU pays for the higher cost of production of $M_1 M_2$ in B over C. The latter constitutes a deadweight loss. On a net basis, A loses GFLH, B gains GFUH and the union as a whole and the world lose FLU.

## 3.3 *Extension to Free Trade Areas*

Traditionally, the analysts focusing on FTAs have assumed that the price facing consumers and producers in each member country is the world price plus its own external tariff.[13] If we were to make this assumption, the extension of the above analysis to FTAs would be straightforward. But, as Martin Richardson (1994) pointed out, this is problematic, since producers are free to sell their output anywhere within the union. If the price is higher in country A, producers in B will sell all their output in that country and let the demand in B be satisfied entirely by imports. Gene Grossman and Elhanan Helpman (1995)

and Bhagwati and Panagariya (1996a) further elaborated on this point, showing that it makes the analysis of FTAs more cumbersome than traditionally recognized.

To explain, begin as before with a nondiscriminatory tariff in A at a per-unit rate of $t_A$. Make the tariff in B explicit now and denote it by $t_B$, where $t_B < t_A$. Since we continue to assume that B is a net exporter of steel, the pre-FTA price of steel in that country continues to coincide with the world price. In Figure 3, $E_B^t E_B^t$ is B's export supply curve, inclusive of $t_A$ along the vertical axis. Imports come partially from B and partially from C, with each paid the net price of $P_C$. Suppose now that A and B form an FTA with A setting its external tariff at $t_A$ and B at $t_B$. Three cases may be distinguished, based on the total supply of steel by A and B in relation to the demand in A in the post-FTA equilibrium.[14]

*Case 1: The Total Supply by A and B is Less than the Demand in A.* Let us first consider the simpler case when $t_B = 0$. Since country B is an exporter of steel,

---

[12] This revenue-transfer effect is also present in the general-equilibrium analyses of Eitan Berglas (1979) and Raymond Riezman (1979).

[13] For example, see Peter Lloyd (1982) and John McMillan and Ewen McCann (1981).

[14] The following analysis assumes that FTAs are supported by rules of origin that ensure that a lower-tariff member does not import goods from outside to re-export them to a higher-tariff member. If such trade deflection was permitted, ignoring internal transport costs, all imports into the union would be routed through the member with the lowest tariff and the FTA would be turned into a CU. In practice, when goods cross the common border between two FTA members, they qualify for a tariff-free entry only upon presentation of documents proving a within-union origin. Because a product is rarely produced in its entirety in a single country, the rules defining within-union origin can be manipulated to effectively deny a union partner's good the tariff preference. Though the rules of origin have been criticized for their protectionist effects, especially by Anne Krueger (1999), in principle, they can lead to an improvement in efficiency by reversing the trade-diverting effect of a tariff preference on the final good. Rod Falvey and Goeff Reed (1997), Jiandong Ju and Kala Krishna (1998), Panagariya (1999a), and Rupa Duttagupta (2000) offer further discussion of the analytic aspects of the rules of origin.

296          Journal of Economic Literature, Vol. XXXVIII (June 2000)

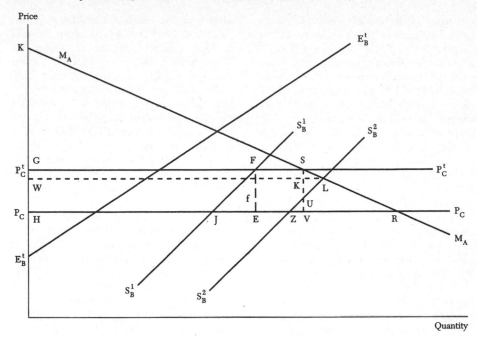

*Figure* 3. The Effect of Preferential Removal of Tariff by A under FTA

this is a plausible assumption. The combined supply of steel in A and B being insufficient to satisfy the demand in A, the latter must necessarily import the product from C. This, in turn, implies that the price in A must settle at $P_C + t_A$. With imports into B being free of duty, the price there is $P_C < P_C + t_A$. As a result, producers in B divert their entire supply of steel to A. In terms of Figure 3, the FTA leads to a replacement of $E_B^t E_B^t$ by B's *total* supply curve, $S_B^1 S_B^1$.

As in the CU case, we have a revenue-transfer effect from A to B that now equals rectangle $EFGH$, with no new trade created. Country A necessarily loses. Country B gains rectangle $EFGH$ minus the triangle marked $f$. It is readily verified that the net gain to B is strictly positive. The loss to the union as a whole is strictly positive and is represented by triangle $f$.

The conclusion that the FTA hurts A which gives the tariff preference, benefits B which receives the preference and hurts the union as a whole remains valid even if we allow $t_B$ to be strictly positive. Recall that since B exports steel, this tariff is initially redundant. The pre-FTA price in B continues to be $P_C$. The formation of the FTA has effects identical to those just discussed for the case when $t_B = 0$ plus a triangular welfare loss to B and the union as a whole. The additional loss arises because the redundant tariff in B becomes effective in the post-FTA equilibrium. With all of B's supplies diverted to A, its own demand is satisfied by imports from C. But given $t_B > 0$, the domestic price rises above $P_C$ to $P_C + t_B$, leading to the triangular welfare loss just mentioned. The reader may verify that even after we take this loss into account, on a net basis, B necessarily gains from the tariff preferences received from A.

*Case 2: The Total Supply by A and B Equals the Demand in A.* Let us revert back to the assumption $t_B = 0$. If B's supply curve lies sufficiently far to the right to cross $M_AM_A$ below point $S$, as shown by $S_B^2S_B^2$ in Figure 3, the FTA eliminates C as a source of imports to A. This delinks the steel price in A from $P_C^t$. Instead, it is determined by the intersection of A's import-demand curve and B's supply curve.

The net effect of the tariff preference by A is now ambiguous on itself and the union as a whole and, as before, non-negative on B. With the decline in the internal price, new trade in the amount $KL$ is created, which is associated with a rise in the union's welfare equal to triangle $SLU$. At the same time, since A's protection is extended to B's firms, there is harmful trade diversion: the cost of production of units $ZV$ (previously imported from C) in B exceeds that in C by area $UVZ$. The union as a whole gains or loses as area $SLU$ is larger or smaller than area $UVZ$. The farther to the right does $S_B^2S_B^2$ lie, the larger is $SLU$ and smaller $UVZ$. In the limit, if $S_B^2S_B^2$ crosses $P_CP_C$ at or to the right of $V$, area $UVZ$ disappears altogether and the union as a whole necessarily benefits.

Turning to A, it gains area $SKL$ from trade creation, but loses area $WKVH$ due to tariff-revenue transfer to B's exporters. The remaining part of tariff revenue, $GSKW$, becomes a part of A's own consumers' and producers' surplus. The farther to the right B's supply curve lies, the closer is A's internal price to $P_C$ and more likely that it will be a net gainer. In the limit, if the internal price drops to $P_C$, no revenue transfer to B takes place, and there is benefit from trade creation, implying a net gain.

Finally, the effect on B's welfare is

non-negative. As drawn in Figure 3, the price received by its exporters, as well as the quantity of exports, rises. It benefits on both counts, receiving a net gain of $WLZH$. In the limiting case when B's supply is sufficiently large that the price in A drops to $P_C$, it makes no gain, but it also does not lose.

This analysis is modified if $t_B$ is positive. As long as $P_C + t_B$ is less than the height of point $L$ in Figure 3, the modification is minor. We continue to obtain the effects just discussed but, in addition, have a triangular welfare loss in B. As in Case 1, this results from the initially redundant tariff becoming effective. If $P_C + t_B$ exceeds the height of point $L$, the modification is more substantive. The reason is that the price in B's market in this case exceeds the height of point $L$. Therefore, no producer within the union will sell at the price indicated by point $L$. In effect, the price in A cannot fall below $P_B + t_B$. With the union-wide price settling at $P_B + t_B$, the combined supply of A and B exceeds the demand in A, bringing us to Case 3.

*Case 3: The Total Supply by A and B Exceeds the Demand in A.* If B's supply curve intersects $M_AM_A$ at a price below $P_C + t_B$, the union-wide price settles at $P_C + t_B$. The key difference with the previous case is that producers in B are now indifferent between markets in A and B. But welfare effects are unchanged qualitatively: B benefits, while A and the union as a whole may or may not benefit. The lower is $t_B$, the more likely that the union as a whole and A benefit. In the limit, as $t_B$ approaches zero (and B's supply curve, therefore, crosses $M_AM_A$ below point $R$), the FTA degenerates into the free-trade equilibrium, with the price in both A and B dropping to $P_C$. In this limiting case, A and the union benefit, while B neither gains nor loses.

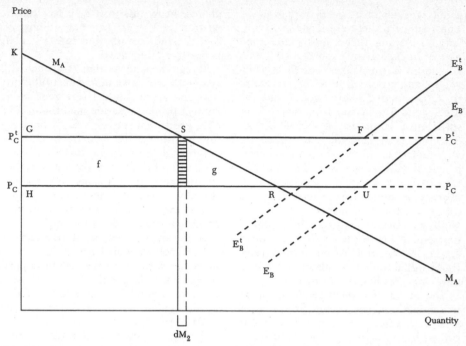

*Figure* 4. FTA: No Imports Come from Country C. Preferential Liberalization Coincides with Non-Discriminatory Liberalization

### 3.4 *The Meade-Lipsey General-Equilibrium Model*

The above analysis suggests that if we are seeking unambiguous gains from a CU or FTA, we must look for sectors in which the partner country is the sole source of imports even at the initial equilibrium. In such sectors, there is no outside trade to be diverted in the first place. Maintaining the small-union assumption, the point is illustrated in Figure 4. Given $P_C$ as the price in the rest of the world, the export-supply curve of B facing country A is $HUE_B$. Under a nondiscriminatory tariff, the supply curve, as perceived by consumers and producers in A, is $GFE_B^t$. Country A imports $GS$ from B and collects rectangle $f$ in tariff revenue. Country B exports $GS$

to A and $SF$ to C. There is no trade between A and C. As A lowers the tariff on B, $GFE_B^t$ shifts down with the internal price in A declining by the full amount of tariff reduction. Country A's trade with B expands and welfare in A rises every step of the way. With country C essentially out of the picture—though not entirely, since it is needed to fix the external price at $P_C$—the possibility of trade diversion as well as revenue-transfer effect is ruled out.

By itself, this case is uninteresting since it avoids trade diversion by assumption and leads to an FTA that is effectively equivalent to free trade. The case can be made to yield something more interesting, however, if it is embedded in a general-equilibrium model. This was demonstrated by Lipsey (1958), using Meade's three-good framework.[15] Thus, suppose there are three goods, 1, 2 and 3. Assume that A specializes completely in good 1 and exports it to B and C, while B specializes completely in good 2 and exports it to A and C. Country C produces all three goods and exports good 3 to A and B. Country C is sufficiently large that A and B act as price takers in its market. By appropriate choice of units, we can set the prices of all three goods in C at unity.

Consider now country A. Suppose it initially imposes tariffs at rates $t_2$ and $t_3$ on goods 2 and 3, respectively, where $t_2 = t_3 \equiv \bar{t}$. Given all prices in C equal unity, prices in A for goods 1, 2, and 3 are 1, $1 + t_2$, and $1 + t_3$, respectively. Preferential trade liberalization involves lowering $t_2$ without lowering $t_3$.

The effect of a small reduction in $t_2$ in sector 2 can be gleaned from Figure 4. Preferential liberalization lowers the price of good 2 in A and leads to trade creation in this sector. Denoting the rise in the imports of good 2 by $dM_2$, the associated welfare gain is represented by $t_2 dM_2 > 0$ as shown by the shaded strip in Figure 4.

But this is not the end of the story. Assuming the demand for good 2 exhibits substitutability with goods 1 and 3, the reduction in the price of the former leads to a reduction in the demands for the latter. Imports of good 3 fall and exports of good 1 rise. Since good 3 is imported from C, the decline in its imports can be characterized as trade diversion. Moreover, since good 3 is subject to a tariff, the diversion is associated with a welfare loss. For a small change in $t_2$, this welfare effect can be written $t_3 dM_3 < 0$. The net welfare effect depends on whether $t_2 dM_2 + t_3 dM_3$ is positive or negative.

It can be shown that, starting with $t_2 = t_3 = \bar{t}$ and assuming substitutability between goods 2 and 1 (the good being subject to liberalization, and the exportable good, respectively), for a small reduction in $t_2$, the benefit from trade creation dominates the loss from trade diversion. Recall that the tariff reduction lowers the demand for good 1 thereby releasing goods for export. Since exports rise, the trade-balance condition implies that total imports, valued at world prices, must rise as well. Given that all world prices have been normalized to unity, the rise in imports of good 2 is larger than the decline in imports of good 3. That is to say, $dM_2 > -dM_3$, which, given $t_2 = t_3 = \bar{t}$, implies $t_2 dM_2 + t_3 dM_3 > 0$.

Though a small preferential reduction in the tariff is, thus, beneficial, pushing preferential liberalization all the way to free trade may be harmful. After the initial reduction in $t_2$, we have $t_2 < t_3 = \bar{t}$ so that $dM_2 > -dM_3$ no longer necessarily implies $t_2 dM_2 + t_3 dM_3 > 0$. Indeed, as $t_2$ approaches 0, the weight of the positive term in this expression also approaches zero. The likely pattern of welfare as $t_2$ moves from $t_2 = t_3 = \bar{t}$ towards $t_2 = 0$ is shown in Figure 5. There is no guarantee that welfare at $t_2 = 0$ will be higher than at $t_2 = t_3$. That is to say, the FTA may lower or raise welfare.[16]

---

[15] The three-good model to be outlined below originated in Meade (1955). But whereas Meade focused on the effects of preferential trading in this model on the world welfare, Lipsey (1958) analyzed the effects on the member countries assuming the small-union context. The small-union model has been explored further by McMillan and McCann (1981) and Lloyd (1982).

[16] Indeed, in general, we cannot even be sure that the initial tariff preference is welfare improving. If good 2 exhibits complementarity with good 1, exported by A, the tariff preference increases the demand for good 1 in A and, thus, lowers its exports. Via trade balance condition, this change leads to a greater decline in the imports of good 3 than the increase in the imports of good 1 and makes $t_2 dM_2 + t_3 dM_3 < 0$ even at $t_2 = t_3 = \bar{t}$.

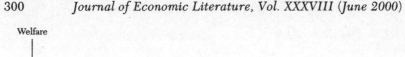

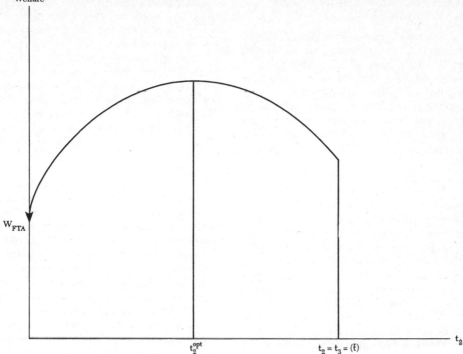

*Figure* 5. Meade-Lipsey Model: The Change in Welfare as the Tariff on the Partner ($t_2$) is reduced from $\bar{t}$ to 0

Though the Meade-Lipsey model has been influential in the literature on preferential trading, it suffers from four key limitations. First, in this model, the member countries have no incentive whatsoever to coordinate their liberalization through an FTA. The liberalization by one member has no effect whatsoever on the economy of the other member and vice versa. The formation of the FTA is identical to a unilateral trade reform.[17] Second, the model as-

sumes a very specific structure of trade flows. Recall that our partial-equilibrium analysis in Sections 3.2 and 3.3 emphasized the importance of the case in which the good imported from the partner is also imported from the rest of the world. The Meade-Lipsey model rules out this case entirely by assumption. Third, as traditionally analyzed, it rules out the arbitrage in producer prices within the union by imposing the assumption that the price in each union member equals the world price plus its own tariff. Finally, the analysis is conducted in terms of infinitesimally small changes in tariffs. As such, it does not offer clear conditions for an improvement in welfare following a move to complete FTA.

[17] Not surprisingly, the result just discussed is identical to the concertina theorem of piecemeal trade reform, according to which a reduction in the highest tariff to the next highest one by a small country is beneficial provided the good with the highest tariff exhibits substitutability with respect to the exportable.

### 3.5 *A More General Analysis of the Small-Union Case*

In a recent paper, Panagariya (1999c) offers a more general analysis of the small-union case, which is able to overcome all these limitations. He allows for all possible patterns of trade by incorporating goods that are exported by both partners, those that are imported by both partners, and those that are exported by one partner and imported by the other. He also considers large changes in tariffs and compares pre- and post-FTA equilibria directly. All goods may be produced in all countries with producer prices fully arbitraged across the union in the post-FTA equilibrium. Finally, on the demand side, the only restriction imposed is that all goods are normal in consumption. Even this restriction is a sufficient rather than necessary condition for the results to hold. In production, as usual, constant returns to scale are assumed.

This level of generality is achieved at the cost of two key restrictive assumptions, however. First, there are no redundant tariffs in the initial equilibrium. For example, if a good is exported in the pre-FTA equilibrium, no tariff is imposed on it. This assumption is commonly made in general-equilibrium analyses of PTAs but is not entirely innocent, as we saw in Section 3.3.[18] Second, the union member with the higher tariff on a good continues to import that good after the formation of the FTA. This ensures that post-FTA prices remain linked to world prices via the relevant tariff rates. Once again, this assumption is commonly made in general-equilibrium analyses but rules out cases 2 and 3 discussed above.

[18] In defense of the assumption, it may be noted that if a political-economy process such as that in Grossman and Helpman (1994) generates initial tariffs, no redundant tariffs are obtained.

Panagariya (1999c) demonstrates that an FTA between two countries increases or reduces the union's joint welfare as it increases or reduces the value of the union-wide output at world prices. If the production of the numeraire good (exported by both member countries) requires only labor and the production of all other goods requires a specific factor and labor, the FTA necessarily lowers the value of the union's output at world prices and hence its joint welfare.

Next, revert back to the general production structure and suppose a small country removes partially or wholly its tariffs on another small country, retaining them at their original levels against the rest of the world. Assume as before that, after the preferential liberalization, the country continues to import from the rest of the world each good that it initially imports from the latter. Then the country's welfare necessarily declines, with the loss in real income equaling the lost tariff revenue on the imports from the union partner. The more the country imports from the partner and the greater the magnitude of tariff preference, the more it loses. If we further assume that the numeraire good uses only labor, and other goods use a specific factor and labor, the partner country necessarily benefits from the tariff preference. And the more it exports to the union member giving the tariff preference and the higher the margin of preference, the more it gains. These results imply that if two small countries with approximately balanced bilateral trade form an FTA, the member with higher tariffs is likely to lose.

These results contradict the so-called "natural-trading-partners" hypothesis, enunciated by Paul Wonnacott and Mark Lutz (1989) and espoused by Lawrence Summers (1991) and Paul Krugman (1993). According to this hypothesis, the more two countries trade with each other relative to the outside world, the less likely that a union between them will be harmful. The results relating to the joint welfare of the union are independent of the volume of trade. Instead, they depend on the value of output at world prices. In the specific-factors case, the decline in the union's welfare is independent of the volume of trade as well. From the viewpoint of an individual union member, the volume of trade can work against it. Ceteris paribus, the more it imports from the partner, the larger its losses or the smaller its gains.[19]

These results are modified if we abandon the assumption that the goods initially imported from the outside world continue to be imported from it into the member with higher tariffs after the FTA is formed. Allowing the partner to become the sole supplier of one or more products takes us into the realm of cases 2 and 3 discussed above. The internal price in the country which gives the tariff preference is no longer tied to the world price through its tariff. Instead, it declines, permitting new trade to be created, which contributes positively to welfare. Trade diversion is also smaller due to a smaller difference between the union's and C's price. The larger the price decline, the larger the positive effect or the smaller the negative effect on the union.

### 3.6 *The Large-Union Case*

Some of the strong conclusions in the previous section are also modified if the outside country's export supplies are less than perfectly elastic. As noted in Section 3.1, in this large-union case, trade diversion is beneficial to the union: the diversion of demand away from C as a consequence of preferential liberaliza-

tion is likely to improve the union's terms of trade relative to the outside country.

Interestingly, however, even in this case, the effects on the welfare of the preference-granting and preference-receiving country remain asymmetric along the lines indicated in Section 3.5. To see this, let us return briefly to the Meade-Lipsey model, which, despite the limitations noted earlier, remains suitable for analyzing the implications of preferential trade liberalization for the terms of trade. Suppose country A gives a one-way tariff preference to country B. At constant border prices, the change increases A's demand for good 2 and reduces it for goods 1 and 3. The border price of good 2 increases relative to goods 1 and 3, which implies that B's terms of trade improve with respect to both trading partners. The effect on the relative price between goods 1 and 3 is ambiguous. Therefore, A's intra-union terms of trade deteriorate while its extra-union terms of trade may improve or worsen. Thus, the conflict between the interests of the country offering tariff preference and the one receiving it, central to the discussion in Sections 3.3 and 3.5, is resurrected even in the model in which the good imported from the partner is not imported from the rest of the world.

In a neglected but important paper, Robert Mundell (1964) formally studied the Lipsey-Meade model with flexible terms of trade. Assuming import demands for all goods exhibit gross substitutability and that initial tariffs are low, he reached the following conclusions:

"(1) A discriminatory tariff reduction by a member country improves the terms of trade of the partner country with respect to both the tariff reducing country and the rest of the world, but the terms of trade of the tariff-reducing country might rise or fall with respect to third countries.
(2) The degree of improvement in the terms of trade of the partner country is likely to be

---

[19] A systematic critique of the natural trading partners' hypothesis can be found in Bhagwati and Panagariya (1996a).

larger the greater is the member's tariff reduction; this establishes the presumption that a member's gain from a free-trade area will be larger the higher are initial tariffs of partner countries." Mundell (1964), p. 8

Interestingly, the revenue-transfer effect emphasized in Sections 3.2 and 3.3 comes back to dominate the outcome. Intra-union terms of trade move against a country and in favor of the partner when the country offers a tariff preference.[20]

### 3.7 *A Differentiated Products Model*

So far, we have assumed that goods are homogeneous. It is sometimes asserted that the results derived from homogeneous-goods models are dramatically altered once we allow for differentiated goods.[21] At least for the problem at hand, this is an incorrect assertion. The main complication in the presence of differentiated goods is that we can no longer use the simplifying, small-union assumption. Each country has monopoly power over its products and can influence its terms of trade. For example, as Daniel Gros (1987) demonstrated, in this setting, the optimum tariff for a country, no matter how small, is strictly positive and finite.

It is easy to see that Mundell's analysis, quoted above, can be brought to bear on the differentiated-products case. Assume, as in Krugman (1980), that there is a single good in the economy with a large number of potential

varieties. The consumer preferences are symmetric and CES over these varieties. Furthermore, there is a single factor of production, labor, and the cost function of a representative variety is characterized by a fixed cost and a constant marginal cost. Free entry drives all profits to zero. We know from Krugman (1980) that, in this model, the equilibrium output of each variety is fixed and, for a given labor force, the equilibrium number of varieties is also fixed.

Remembering that the CES form of the utility function implies substitutability in demand, this model reduces to a special case (in terms of the generality of the utility function) of Mundell's model discussed in Section 3.4. The only cosmetic difference is that each country produces several varieties. But since each country's varieties are symmetric in all respects, they can be aggregated into a single product and Mundell's analysis invoked.[22]

### 3.8 *Transport Costs*

Perhaps guided by the observation that, *in practice*, PTAs often form among countries that are geographically proximate, some analysts have gone on to argue that low transport costs make them more likely to be beneficial.[23] This is a new development. For example, in his comprehensive work, Viner (1950) noted the presence of departures from the Most Favored Nation (MFN) principle in commercial pacts between countries within Europe going as far back as the nineteenth century. But

[20] Panagariya (1997a) recently extended Mundell's (1964) analysis by decomposing the total welfare effect into a pure efficiency effect, an intra-union terms-of-trade effect, and an extra-union terms-of-trade effect.

[21] The implications of differentiated goods should be distinguished from those of economies of scale. Though both are present in the Krugman (1980) monopolistic competition model on which this sub-section is based, economies of scale do not play a substantive role in it. The implications of economies of scale are discussed below separately. They also figure in some of the contributions discussed in Section 7 (e.g., Philip Levy 1997, and Wilfred Ethier 1998).

[22] Product differentiation and its implications for trade creation and trade diversion will appear more explicitly later in Section 5 when we consider Krugman's analysis of a simultaneous division of the world into two or more blocs. Also see Section 3.9 below.

[23] In particular, see Wonnacott and Lutz (1989), Krugman (1991b, 1993), Summers (1991), and Frankel, Ernesto Stein, and Shang-Jin Wei (1995).

rather than link these departures to low transport costs within Europe, he attributed them to "close ties of sentiment and interest arising out of ethnological, or cultural, or historical political affiliations."

There is little basis for giving transport costs a special treatment in evaluating PTAs.[24] Leaving aside the possibility that sufficiently high transport costs can eliminate the scope for mutually beneficial trade between countries, the principle of comparative advantage and the proposition on the optimality of nondiscriminatory free trade (from the global standpoint) are valid with and without these costs. Lower transport costs may give a proximate trading partner a cost advantage over a distant one, but this may be outweighed by lower production costs in the latter. This is certainly demonstrated by the ability of distant countries in East Asia to compete effectively with Latin American countries in the U.S. market.

Indeed, even a ceteris paribus proposition that PTAs among proximate partners are superior to distant ones is not valid in general. Thus, Bhagwati and Panagariya (1996a) provide an example in which, between two otherwise identical potential partners, a country achieves a superior outcome by giving the trade preference to the distant one. The reason is that, with an initial nondiscriminatory tariff, the country imports less from the distant partner. A preference to that partner leads to a smaller transfer of tariff revenue than to the proximate one.

---

[24] For detailed critiques, see Bhagwati and Panagariya (1996a) and Panagariya (1998). Paul Wonnacott and Ronald Wonnacott (1981) give a special role to transport costs but, as shown by Berglas (1983) and further discussed in Panagariya (1998), their examples require transport costs to be sufficiently high to rule out the distant partner as a trading partner either entirely or in the pre-union equilibrium.

## 3.9 *Economies of Scale and Imperfect Competition*

Let us now turn to a discussion of the implications of economies of scale and imperfect competition for the theory of preferential trading. The first point to note is that even though many models incorporate economies of scale and imperfect competition simultaneously into the analysis, they can be treated separately. Indeed, the discussion in this section begins with a simple model of economies of scale in which the assumption of perfect competition is maintained. Likewise, several contributions discussed later in the essay incorporate imperfectly competitive market structure without recourse to economies of scale.

Consider then a partial-equilibrium model with economies of scale where the good in question, steel, is homogeneous.[25] To maintain the assumption of perfect competition, assume that scale economies are external to the firm. Make the further simplification that scale economies derive from the industry-wide output of steel. These assumptions allow us to represent the industry-wide average cost of production by a downward sloping curve such as $AA'$ in Figure 6. The precise form of the scale economy is such that the cost curve first declines, reaches a minimum, and becomes horizontal thereafter.

To bring out the implications of scale economies most sharply, it is best to focus on the case in which countries A

---

[25] Corden (1972) first analyzed the implications of economies of scale for preferential trading in a homogeneous goods model. The following discussion is heavily influenced by his contribution but differs from it in details. Corden assumes a single producer of the product in each country with price determined by the world price plus external tariff. He also allows for transport costs, which introduce a wedge between the prices at which steel can be imported from and exported to the outside country. By contrast, I assume external economies and average-cost pricing and do not allow for transport costs.

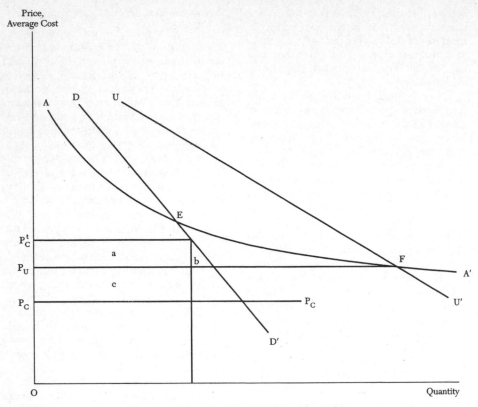

*Figure 6.* Economies of Scale and Preferential Trading

and B are identical in all respects. Thus, let $AA'$ represent the average cost of steel production in both countries. Similarly, let $DD'$ be the demand in each country. $UU'$, the horizontal sum of the two demand curves, represents the combined demand for steel by union members in the absence of trade barriers between them. Initially, the two countries levy a nondiscriminatory tariff at the same rate.

The first point to note is that the outcome in this setting depends critically on the price prevailing in C, $P_C$. If this price is above the minimum average cost along $AA'$, trade barriers in A and B are redundant. Producers in each

country produce the maximum quantity of steel they can, satisfy the domestic demand at $P_C$, and export the remainder of steel. The formation of an FTA, which happens to be equivalent to a CU given the same external tariff in the two countries, leaves the equilibrium entirely undisturbed.

If $P_C$ is below the minimum cost of production in A and B as shown by $P_C P_C$ in Figure 6, however, the outcome is different. Consider first the case in which C's tariff inclusive price, $P_C^t$, is between points $E$ and $F$. In the initial equilibrium, both countries import steel from C. In each country, the area under $DD'$ up to price $P_C^t$ represents the consumers' surplus while area $a + c$ represents tariff revenue. The formation of an FTA permits one of the two union members to enter production by exploiting the larger union-wide market. Though trade is diverted from C, declining costs lead to a decline in the union's internal price. The former effect is harmful and is accompanied by the usual revenue loss, but the latter is beneficial. Each country loses area $c$ due to trade diversion while gaining area $b$. The net effect on welfare is ambiguous.

Outcomes more favorable to PTAs can arise under higher initial tariffs, however. Thus, suppose $P_C^t$ lies above point $E$. Then, in the initial equilibrium, domestic production is viable and both countries produce and consume their own steel. If they now form an FTA, setting the external tariff at its original level, one of the two countries ceases to produce steel. The union-wide price declines to $P_U$ and each member gains a trapezium-shaped area. With no trade with C initially, there is no scope for trade diversion, and the CU is unambiguously welfare improving. Due to the decline in the average cost, made possible by economies of scale, the gain is larger than the traditional welfare triangles.

A key difference between this model and those considered before is that we now have a stronger tendency towards the elimination of country C as a source of imports in the post-FTA equilibrium. As is common with scale-economy models, we get all-or-nothing outcomes with respect to imports: either all steel comes from the outside country or none does. Such outcomes are also accompanied by a delinking of the internal price with the outside country's price (precisely as in cases 2 and 3 above) and generate gains that counteract revenue losses from trade diversion.

An alternative approach to analyzing the implications of economies of scale is to combine them with imperfect competition and, often, product differentiation. Some of the key applications of this category of models have been developed in the context of the more recent issues, such as the welfare implications of a simultaneous division of the world into several trade blocs and the expansion of a bloc through addition of new members. These applications will be discussed later in the context of the relevant questions. The survey by Baldwin and Venables (1995), on the other hand, discusses the implications of imperfect competition and scale economies in the three-country framework employed in the present section. While these authors carefully discuss the scale and cost effects of FTAs, identifying the relevant channels, they do not explicitly derive the welfare effects. It is presumably this complexity which has led some researchers in this strand of the literature to resort to numerical simulations.[26]

## 4. Welfare-Increasing CUs and FTAs

The preceding analysis fixes the pre-union external tariffs and allows external trade flows to adjust endogenously as intra-union trade barriers are removed. The welfare effects on the union in this setting turn out to be either negative or ambiguous but never unambiguously positive. Remarkably, if we take the opposite approach, fixing the initial extra-union trade flows and letting the external tariffs adjust endogenously, the outcome is essentially the opposite. Regardless of whether potential members are small or large, neither the union as a whole nor the rest of the world can lose from a CU or FTA, and the union is likely to benefit.

[26] Thus, see Alasdair Smith and Venables (1988), and Diego Puga and Venables (1995).

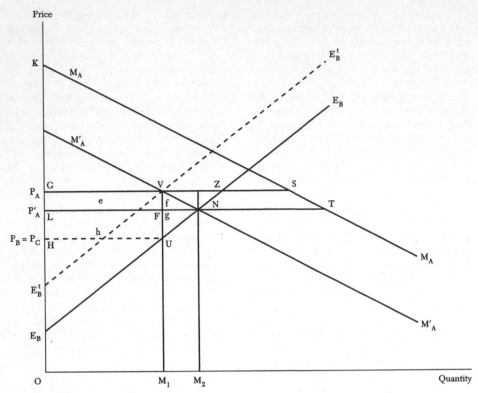

Figure 7. The Kemp-Wan-Vanek-Ohyama Customs Union

## 4.1 Customs Unions

This result was first stated for a CU by Murray Kemp (1964) and Vanek (1965) independently, and proved by Ohyama (1972) and Kemp and Henry Wan (1976), and will be called the Kemp-Wan-Vanek-Ohyama theorem in this paper.[27] The logic behind the theorem is simple. Freezing the net trade vector of A and B with the rest of the world ensures that the rest of the world can be made neither better off nor worse off by the union. Then, taking the external trade vector as a constraint, the joint welfare of A and B is maximized

by equating the marginal rate of transformation (MRT) and marginal rate of substitution (MRS) for each pair of goods across all agents in the union. This is, of course, accomplished by eliminating all intra-union trade barriers and setting the common external tariff (CET) vector at a level just right to hold the extra-union trade vector at the pre-union level.

To get an idea of the CET and welfare effects on member countries, let us consider a diagrammatic illustration of the Kemp-Wan-Vanek-Ohyama theorem.[28] In Figure 7, various curves have

[27] In their survey, Baldwin and Venables (1995) attribute the result to Meade (1955). In Panagariya (1997b), I argue that this is an error.

[28] Srinivasan (1997) derives the external tariff in the Kemp-Wan-Vanek-Ohyama CU within a two-sector general-equilibrium model. Also see the comment on this paper by Davis (1997).

the same interpretation as in Figure 2 except that we do not show the export supply of C, which may or may not be horizontal. Let $P_A$ be the pre-CU domestic price in country A, with quantity $GV$ imported from B and $VS$ from C. Since $UV$ is per-unit tariff initially, the price in B and C is given by the height of point $U$.

As a part of the CU, A and B eliminate all trade barriers between themselves and set the CET at a level that freezes their joint quantity of imports from C at $VS$. To derive the resulting equilibrium, at every price, subtract $VS$ from $M_AM_A$ and obtain $M'_AM'_A$ as the import demand to be satisfied by B. Since no tariffs apply to B now, its export supplies are given along $E_BE_B$. The market-clearing price, in turn, is $P'_A$. Country A imports $LN$ ($>GV$) from B and $NT$ ($=VS$) from C. Since the imports from C are unchanged, the price in that country is still given by the height of point $U$, yielding $UF$ ($<UV$) as the CET per unit. The expansion of intra-union trade leads to a net gain for the union equal to area $f + g$. The reader can verify that, holding imports from C fixed at $VS$, this is the best the union can do.

Observe that the external tariff falls due to the fact that, at constant tariff rate, trade would be diverted from C, causing imports from the latter to decline. To maintain the imports from C at their original level, the external tariff must fall.

It can be seen that, in the spirit of Sections 3.2 and 3.3, country B necessarily gains, while country A may or may not gain despite total absence of trade diversion. With outside imports held fixed, the internal price declines by the full amount of the decline in the external tariff. The revenue lost on the imports from C (due to the reduction in the external tariff) is redistributed to

A's consumers. But, to the extent of the tariff preference, the revenue lost on imports from B is redistributed to the latter's exporting firms. The loss to A on this account is area $h$ which must be compared against the gain $f$ on the new trade created with B. The gain to B is $h + g$ with $h$ being the redistribution from A and $g$ the gain on new intra-union trade. This analysis suggests that in a multi-commodity setting, if trade is approximately balanced between the partners, the member with high initial tariffs will lose and the member with low initial tariffs will benefit from the Kemp-Wan-Vanek-Ohyama CU.

### 4.2 *Free Trade Areas*

Proving an analogous result for FTAs is tricky. If we freeze member countries' *individual* trade vectors with the rest of the world, the resulting external tariff vectors will, in general, be different for different member countries. This means the condition $MRT = MRS$ for each pair of countries across all agents in the union cannot be satisfied in general.

Panagariya and Krishna (1997) overcame this difficulty, however. Fully in the spirit of the Kemp-Wan-Vanek-Ohyama theorem, they show that if two or more countries form an FTA, freezing their initial, *individual* trade vectors via country-specific tariff vectors, welfare of neither the union nor the rest of the world falls and that of the former is likely to rise.

The key to explaining this result lies in the analysis in Section 1.3. For the products for which within-union supply is sufficiently large that the union-wide price coincides with the price in the lower-tariff country (i.e., when B's supply curve in Figure 3 crosses $M_AM_A$ below point $W$), we effectively obtain a CU with the $MRT = MRS$ condition satisfied unionwide. For products for which the unionwide supply is smaller, the domestic price is lower in the lower-tariff country. But in this case, the entire unionwide output is sold in the high-tariff country, so that the marginal rates of transformation are equalized across the union members. Furthermore, the marginal rate of substitution in the high-tariff country is also equalized to this marginal rate of transformation. Only the marginal rate of transformation in the lower-tariff country is lower. But given the requirement that *individual* import vectors be frozen, this is also the best that can be done. Any move from FTA necessarily lowers the union's joint welfare.

### 4.3 *Customs Unions with Noneconomic Objectives*

Recently, Krishna and Bhagwati (1997) showed that if two or more countries are pursuing certain noneconomic objectives, they can still form a CU between themselves and be jointly better off. The result relates to an old issue discussed in the development literature: given any level of import substitution vis-a-vis the developed countries, can the developing countries open up trade preferentially among themselves and reduce the cost of their individual import substitution? At the time, an affirmative answer was given by authors but one relying on the presence of economies of scale. Krishna and Bhagwati (1997), by contrast, show that scale economies are not essential to the argument. The solution involves a Kemp-Wan-Vanek-Ohyama CU complemented by tax-cum-subsidies to achieve the noneconomic objectives of member states as indicated by the theory of optimal intervention in the presence of noneconomic objectives.

### 5. *Exogenous Division of the World into Blocs*

The massive wave of regional arrangements that started in the 1980s

raises the question of how the welfare of the world, individual blocs, and individual countries will change if the world is divided simultaneously into several blocs. We may also ask how the welfare of these entities changes with the number and size of blocs.

We have already seen that the analysis of preferential liberalization turns out to be complex even when we consider the formation of a single bloc in isolation and impose the small-union assumption. Therefore, it should come as no surprise that when several blocs are allowed to form simultaneously, with inter-bloc terms of trade allowed to change, strong assumptions must be made.

### 5.1 *Symmetric Blocs*

The simplest approach to the problem is to imagine that all countries are identical, and then consider their division into two or more identical blocs. This simplification makes the problem tractable, since it implies that the welfare of each country and bloc must move in the same direction. It also allows us to relate the number of blocs to welfare in a straightforward manner. Thus, following Krugman (1991a), let us postulate a world consisting of a large number of small, identical units, called "provinces." Each province specializes in the production of a distinct good. Products of all provinces enter symmetrically into the utility function with an identical, constant elasticity of substitution between each pair of products.

Assume that the world is divided into B identical blocs where B is exogenous. There are no barriers on within-bloc trade and a common external tariff on extra-bloc trade. Given complete symmetry, the external tariff of each bloc is the same. Though each bloc acts as a Nash player and chooses the external tariff optimally, since this endogeneity

310        *Journal of Economic Literature, Vol. XXXVIII (June 2000)*

is not crucial to the results (Krugman 1993), it is best not to introduce it at this stage. A key point to bear in mind is that, given complete symmetry, a change in the number of blocs and hence the size of each bloc generates no terms-of-trade effects. Welfare outcomes are driven entirely by the effect of bloc expansion on efficiency. This is a very special feature of a model with endogenous terms of trade.

Begin with a single bloc initially so that we have worldwide free trade. Given no distortions, this naturally maximizes the welfare of each province and the world. Suppose that we divide this bloc into two equal-sized blocs. This division leads to trade diversion: each province trades more with the provinces in the same bloc at the expense of the provinces in the other bloc. With no trade creation to offset this effect, welfare necessarily declines.

Suppose next that we take one-third of the provinces of each existing bloc and create a third bloc. We now have trade creation as well as trade diversion. Seen from the viewpoint of the provinces within an existing bloc, trade diversion results from the decline in trade with the provinces that have just been moved outside to create the new bloc. Trade creation results from an expansion of trade with provinces that were already outside and subject to the external tariff. The net effect on welfare is ambiguous. Given the symmetry of blocs, what applies to provinces within an existing bloc also applies to provinces in the newly created bloc. We need not analyze the latter separately.

It can be shown that as the number of blocs grows, the trade creation effect must come to dominate the trade diversion effect. Given a large number of blocs, the representative bloc is small, and most of its trade is with outside provinces. Therefore, when another

bloc is created, the expansion of trade with these outside provinces dominates the contraction of trade with the provinces that are moved out to create the new bloc. Welfare must rise.

This basic story is reinforced when external tariffs are chosen endogenously, with each bloc acting noncooperatively. As the number of blocs rises, each bloc becomes smaller and its optimum tariff declines. The trade creation effect is reinforced.

Remembering that the initial division of the world into two blocs necessarily lowers welfare, this discussion implies that welfare exhibits a U-shaped pattern as a function of the number of blocs. Krugman (1993) simulates the model for an elasticity of substitution of four and finds the number of blocs at minimum-welfare point to be two for a tariff rate of 10 percent and three for tariff rates of 20 and 30 percent. In view of the fact that the world may be dividing into precisely two or three blocs, this is a provocative result.

### 5.2 Asymmetric Blocs

Given the special, highly symmetric structure of the model just considered, its results turn out to be fragile. Thus, Alan Deardorff and Robert Stern (1994) provide a simple example in which a small number of blocs lead to the maximization of world welfare. They assume that all goods are homogeneous so that trade is of interindustry type. Economies of scale are ruled out. Assuming further that there are $n/2$ types of different countries where $n$ is the total number of countries, we can divide the world into two identical blocs such that each of them consists of exactly one country of each type. This allows each bloc to exploit all the gains from trade without any trade whatsoever with the other bloc. Alternative examples in which welfare bears no relationship to the number of blocs can also be constructed. T. N. Srinivasan (1993) does this within a Ricardian, constant costs model.

### 5.3 *"Natural" and "Unnatural" Blocs*

Following the suggestion in Krugman (1991b) that proximity between member countries minimizes trade diversion, Frankel, Stein, and Wei (1995) went on to extend the Krugman (1993) model to incorporate transport costs. Like Krugman (1993), these authors assume a highly symmetric world: identical continents with identical and equal number of countries that follow identical trade policies before as well as after the formation of CUs. The only difference with Krugman is that there are (identical) positive transport costs of moving goods between countries on different continents but not those on the same continent. By analogy with the melting of an iceberg, transport costs take the form of a fraction of each unit of a good being lost in transit.

Frankel, Stein, and Wei consider two types of blocs: (i) continental blocs such that each bloc consists of all countries on the same continent but no others; and (ii) across-continent blocs such that each bloc consists of exactly one country from each continent. The authors call the former "natural" and the latter "unnatural" blocs. In either case, each bloc has the same common external tariff that equals the initial tariff.

This model works entirely like the Meade-Lipsey model discussed in Section 3.4. Because of the symmetry, bloc formation has no effect whatsoever on the terms of trade. Therefore, bloc formation is like the formation of a CU between two small countries. Moreover, products imported from the partner are not imported from the rest of the world and vice versa, just as in the Meade-Lipsey model. Finally, the substitutabil-

ity between own and partner-country products also obtains since preferences are symmetric. Applying the logic outlined in Section 3.4, welfare follows an inverted-U path as in Figure 5. In general, welfare of a member country when all within-bloc tariffs have been eliminated may be higher or lower than at the initial equilibrium.

This result applies to both "natural" and "unnatural" blocs and is confirmed by the simulations done by Frankel, Stein, and Wei. Assuming three continents, two countries per continent, and an external tariff of 30 percent, they find that if transport costs (between continents) result in the "melting away" of 15 percent or less of the product in transit, bloc formation reduces welfare whether blocs are natural or unnatural. Unnatural blocs do consistently worse than natural ones in these simulations, however. Moreover, as transport costs rise above 15 percent of the product, natural blocs become welfare superior to the initial equilibrium. As expected, when transport costs rise to 100 percent of the product, thereby precluding trade between continents, natural blocs lead to the same outcome as global free trade. Unnatural blocs always remain inferior to the status quo, though the harm done by them is less and less as transport costs rise.

From Figure 5, we can deduce that a partial tariff preference up to the point where welfare is maximized $(t_2 = t_2^{opt})$ will yield a superior outcome in the Frankel, Stein, and Wei model than either the initial nondiscriminatory tariff or a full CU. This is confirmed by various simulations that the authors undertake. Based on this result, Frankel, Stein, and Wei conclude that "some degree of preferences along natural continental lines . . . would be a good thing, . . ."

This is a questionable conclusion.

What the authors have done is to provide an *example* (with highly unrealistic assumptions, I might add) in which sufficiently high transport costs make blocs among neighbors welfare superior to the status quo. But it is equally possible to construct examples showing the opposite result, as done in Panagariya (1998). Thus, consider a two-good Ricardian world. Assume there are two continents, each consisting of two countries. Transport costs are zero within each continent but positive, *albeit* non-prohibitive, across continents. The opportunity costs of production are identical between countries on the same continent but different between countries on different continents. If blocs are now formed between countries on the same continent, there is no change in welfare. But if they are formed between countries located on different continents, welfare improves and is the same as under global free trade. The point here is that benefits from trade in general, and preferential trade in particular, depend on differences in costs between trading partners irrespective of the sources of these differences. As argued in Section 3.8, transport costs are not special.

## 6. *Endogeneity of Policy*

So far, we have assumed that the decision to form a trade bloc as well as the choice of the external tariff is exogenous.[29] In view of the developments on endogenous choice of policy, it is natural to ask under what circumstances countries are likely to exercise the option to form an FTA and, alternatively, how the decision to form an FTA is likely to affect the choice of the external tariff. These questions take us

into the realm of political-economy theoretic analysis.

### 6.1 *The Decision To Form an FTA*

Let us revert to the three-country setup of Section 3 but make the decision to form an FTA endogenous. The central question we now ask is whether an FTA is more likely to form when it is largely trade creating and hence welfare improving or when it is trade diverting and therefore welfare reducing. We also ask whether the exclusion of certain sectors from preferential liberalization and the rules of origin make an otherwise infeasible FTA feasible.

*A Perfect Competition, Small-Union Model.* The natural starting point for the analysis of these questions is the small-union model we discussed in Sections 3.3 and 3.5. What we need to do is to embed that essential model into a general equilibrium model and construct a political-economy model around it that allows trade policy to be determined endogenously. This is the approach taken by Grossman and Helpman (1995). To outline their model, consider two potential union members, which are both small relative to the outside country. Each of them produces $n$ non-numeraire goods that use a sector-specific factor and labor, and a numeraire good that uses only labor. This structure of factor use makes all non-numeraire goods independent of each other in production (i.e., neither substitutes nor complements). Assume further that preferences are additively separable and the numeraire good enters into them linearly. This makes the demands for non-numeraire goods independent of each other as well. The net result is that each non-numeraire good behaves exactly like steel in the partial-equilibrium model discussed in Section 3.3.

By assumption, neither country imposes a tariff on the numeraire good.

---

[29] Two exceptions were Kemp-Wan-Vanek-Ohyama CU and Krugman (1991a). But even in these cases, the endogeneity is based on welfare maximization rather than an explicit political-economy model.

The political-economy model developed in Grossman and Helpman (1994) determines the initial tariffs on nonnumeraire goods. The objective function each government pursues in this model is a weighted sum of campaign contributions from the lobbies and overall welfare of voters. Each lobby represents the owners of a sector-specific factor and maximizes their welfare. The campaign contribution is made in return for the lobby's desired action by the government on tariffs. In the game, the lobbies move first and the government second. In equilibrium, the contribution is made only if the government takes this desired action. This model generates zero tariffs on exportables (export subsidies are ruled out by assumption) and non-negative tariffs on import-competing goods. The precise structure of tariffs depends on the parameters of the model including the relative weight placed by the government on campaign contributions.

Taking an initial set of tariffs determined by this process as given, let us introduce the possibility of an FTA. The FTA involves the removal of tariffs by A and B on goods produced within the union but leaves the external tariffs at their initial levels. The only decision facing the (incumbent) governments in the two countries is whether to accept the FTA agreement or reject it.

The solution to the problem is complex, but it is possible to give some flavor of the results with the help of the analysis associated with Figures 3 and 4 in Section 3. Thus, letting $n$ be an even number, suppose $n/2$ of the nonnumeraire products are imported by A and exported by B while the reverse holds for the remaining $n/2$ products. Assume complete symmetry so that we can speak in terms of representative imports of A and B. Let the import demands for the representative imports of

A be $M_A M_A$ in Figure 3 or 4, and imagine an identical curve for the representative import of B. The import good of A is subject to a tariff $t_A$ by itself and zero by B. Analogously, the import good of B is subject to a tariff $t_B = t_A$ by itself and zero by A. Consider two extreme cases shown in Figures 3 and 4, respectively, based on the exporting country's supply curve.

First, suppose the supply curve of the exporting country is as shown by $S_B^1 S_B^1$ in Figure 3. We know that, in this case, exporting firms benefit and import-competing firms are unaffected by the FTA. Given that each country exports $n/2$ products, exporting firms in each member benefit while import-competing firms are unaffected. Welfare of the union as a whole declines, which, given the symmetry, implies that welfare of each union member also declines. It follows that the governments of the two countries will accept the FTA agreement provided the lobbying contributions from exporters who stand to gain outweigh the political cost of the decline in welfare. In the initial game of free trade versus protection, if firms prevailed and got high tariffs, it is likely that they will also prevail in the FTA versus status quo game. Thus, high initial tariffs in this case coincide with the acceptance of the FTA. Ex post acceptance of the FTA is associated with large increases in exporters' profits and large trade diversion.

Second, suppose the export supply curve of the exporting country crosses $M_A M_A$ below point $R$ as in Figure 4. In this case, the FTA hurts the import-competing firms and does not benefit the exporting firms. But welfare rises in each member country. The FTA can be rejected in this case provided lobbying contributions by import-competing firms, who stand to lose from the FTA, more than outweigh the political benefit to the government from the gain in welfare. Once again, if, in the initial game for free trade versus protection, firms prevailed and got high tariffs, they are also likely to prevail in the FTA versus status quo game so that the FTA will be rejected. Ex post, a trade-creating FTA is rejected.

These are, of course, highly simplified examples. But they are sufficient to suggest some of the problems that will be faced in asymmetric cases. For example, taking the basic setting in the first example, if one of the countries happens to be the exporter of many more than half the products, the government of the other country will likely refuse to accept the FTA proposal. For in that case, exporting firms are unlikely to make campaign contributions in equilibrium, and the FTA lowers welfare. Reflecting this underlying logic, Grossman and Helpman reach the following important conclusion: "A free-trade agreement requires the assent of both governments. We have found that this outcome is most likely when there is relative balance in the potential trade between the partner countries and when the agreement affords enhanced protection rather than reduced protection to most sectors." Enhanced protection here refers to trade diversion (as in Figure 3) whereas reduced protection refers to trade creation (as in Figure 4).[30]

Grossman and Helpman (1994) further show that the allowance for the exclusion of certain sectors from an FTA agreement can make a previously infeasible FTA feasible. More recently, Duttagupta (2000) has introduced an intermediate input into the Grossman-Helpman model and addressed frontally the role of rules of origin in a general

equilibrium model. She assumes that one partner exports the input to the other and imports from it the final good using the input. Thus, the union members are necessarily asymmetric. She shows that the introduction of a rule of origin in this setting can make acceptable an FTA that is otherwise rejected, though, under some circumstances, the reverse may also happen. The former possibility arises because the country that exports the input and votes against the FTA in the absence of the rules of origin switches its vote in the presence of such rules. As regards the welfare of the union, there are two notable possibilities. First, an FTA that lowered the joint welfare of the union and was rejected in the absence of the rules of origin becomes feasible upon the inclusion of such rules. Second, an FTA that improved joint welfare of the union but was nevertheless rejected in the absence of the rules of origin becomes feasible, but the rules of origin can be so distortionary that the FTA becomes welfare inferior relative to the status quo.

*A Cournot Oligopoly Model.* So far, our analysis of the decision to form an FTA has been conducted in the context of a perfect competition model. In view of the growing popularity of imperfectly competitive models, we may ask whether the key results just derived remain valid in the presence of imperfect competition. Pravin Krishna (1998) performs this task using a Cournot oligopoly model in which firms belonging to three countries compete in one another's market. Asymmetries across countries are admitted both in terms of the market size and number of firms in a given country. Producers are given the decisive role in determining the policy outcome via the assumption that governments base their policy decisions on the home firms' profits. Initially, each country imposes a nondiscriminatory tariff

[30] In Figure 3, the FTA extends A's higher tariff to producers in B, thereby "enhancing" overall protection. In Figure 4, the FTA extends B's free trade price to A's market, "reducing" overall protection.

on imports from all sources. The tariff is the same across all countries. Two countries, A and B, must decide whether or not to form an FTA which, given equal initial tariffs, is equivalent to a customs union. For the FTA to be accepted by both governments, profits of home firms must rise in each potential member.

Like Grossman and Helpman (1995), Krishna (1998) finds that the greater the degree of trade diversion, the more likely that the FTA will be accepted. The intuition behind the result is straightforward. When an FTA is formed, each member benefits (in terms of profits of its firms) from obtaining preferential access to the partner's market, but loses from giving a similar access to the partner in its own market. In the absence of trade diversion, this is more or less a zero-sum game. But if the members can capture a part of the outside country's share in the union's market (trade diversion) without a corresponding loss of their share in the outside market, they can generate positive net benefits. The FTA is more likely to be accepted.

Krishna's analysis is based on what is essentially a one-sector, partial equilibrium model. Therefore, he is unable to address the role of sectoral exclusions in making FTAs more or less acceptable. Likewise, intermediate inputs being absent as well, the role of the rules of origin is not considered.

## 6.2 *The Extra-Union Tariff*

Le us now turn to the second question raised at the beginning of this section: how does the decision to form a PTA by a country impact its choice of external tariff in a choice-theoretic model? In raising the question initially, Bhagwati (1993) expressed the concern that such a decision may result in a rise in the extra-union trade barriers either via an increase in tariff or more vigorous implementation of anti-dumping

measures against outside countries.[31] This may turn even an initially trade-creating union into a trade-diverting union. He argued that within the traditional three-country framework, increased imports from the PTA partner that threaten a member country's firms will lead the latter to seek higher tariffs on imports from the outside country.[32] The issue can be analyzed from a variety of viewpoints, however.

*Lobbying and the External Tariff in Small-Union Models.* One way to address this issue is to begin with a model in which industry-specific lobbies play a decisive role in the determination of tariffs, and an FTA is introduced as an exogenous institutional change. Panagariya and Ronald Findlay (1996) take this approach. Following them, consider a three-good, Meade-Lipsey model in which the country under consideration imports two goods and exports the remaining one. Each good is produced using a sector-specific factor and labor. One of the imports comes from the partner and the other from the outside country. The tariff in each sector is determined by the amount of labor employed by that sector's lobby. The lobby, in turn, represents the interests of the factor specific to the sector.

The grant of a tariff preference is modeled as an institutional change that lowers the effectiveness of lobbying in gaining protection against imports from the partner country. The change reduces the level of lobbying in the sector competing with the partner country's good and releases labor into the economy.

[31] For developed countries, GATT bindings do not permit an increase in tariff so that increased barriers must take the form of safeguard measures such as anti-dumping or voluntary export restraints. For virtually all developing countries, tariff bindings have water so that they can raise tariffs.

[32] A formal presentation of this point can be found in Bhagwati and Panagariya (1996a).

This, in turn, puts downward pressure on the wage rate and makes lobbying in the sector competing against the outside country's good less costly. The magnitude of lobbying in the latter sector rises, as does the external tariff. The impact of the tariff preference on welfare, which may have been positive at constant external tariff, is now ambiguous.[33]

Cadot, de Melo, and Olarreaga (1999) also use the Meade-Lipsey, three-good model in which tariffs are determined endogenously via the Grossman-Helpman (1995) political-economy process. They find that in FTA arrangements without rules of origin whereby goods destined to a high-tariff member can be imported through the low-tariff member, competition for tariff revenue may lead to competitive reductions in external tariffs until they are removed completely. In a CU setting, by contrast, lobbies may cooperate on a union-wide basis and win increased external protection.

*Turning Trade Diversion into Tariff Revenue.* As hinted by the tariff-revenue-competition result just mentioned, under some circumstances, FTAs may actually lead to a reduction in the external tariff. Richardson (1993) shows this in an elegant paper. His argument can be illustrated with the help of Figure 1b where country A's import demand is downward-sloped and export-supplies of B and C are horizontal. In the initial equilibrium, A has an FTA with B, which is the less efficient supplier of the product in comparison with C.

In this setting, if A reduces the tariff on C to $P_BP_C\text{-}\varepsilon$ where $\varepsilon$ is infinitesi-

mally small, it can switch all its imports from the less efficient B to more efficient C and collect areas $e$ and $k$ in tariff revenue. If the government maximizes a political support function to which tariff revenues contribute positively, it will, in fact, take that course. Richardson shows that this basic argument is valid in a general equilibrium setting.

A key limitation of this argument, however, is its reliance on a model in which imports come from either B or C but not both. As already discussed in Section 3, this specialization in the source of imports results from the assumption that supply curves of both B and C are infinitely elastic. A moment's reflection shows that the results break down as soon as we allow for imports from both B and C by assuming B's supply curve to be upward sloped. As is easily verified with the help of Figure 3, lowering the tariff on C just enough to allow it to sell in A at a price slightly below $P_C$ yields no more than the conventional gains from unilateral liberalization. At the margin, B is able to compete with C at a slightly lower level of output and cannot be eliminated as a source of supply.

*Increased Monopoly Power of Trade Blocs.* The simplest model in which the formation of a CU can lead to a rise in the external tariff is the one in which the external tariff is chosen to maximize the union's welfare. This is, indeed, the outcome in Krugman's (1991a) model: as the world is consolidated into fewer and fewer symmetric blocs, the external tariff rises monotonically. As each bloc gets larger, the proportion of income spent by the rest of the world on its exports rises, giving it a greater market power.

But this outcome is not inevitable. Eric Bond and Constantinos Syropoulos (1996) modify Krugman's model slightly

---

[33] A referee has argued that labor employed in lobbying constitutes such a small fraction of total labor force that any changes in it are unlikely to have significant labor-market effects. The analysis can be resurrected, however, by introducing a lobbying-specific factor, lawyers. A shift in lobbying function that alters the return to this specific factor—a reasonable outcome—will yield results similar to those discussed in the text.

and are able to generate an ambiguous effect of larger blocs on the outside tariff. In the Krugman model, each province is endowed with a fixed amount of one product that it exports and none of any other product. Bond and Syropoulos (1996) modify this assumption and postulate that each province is endowed with some of each product plus a little more of the one it exports. Formally, province $i$ is endowed with $x + z$ of good $i$ and $x$ of all other products ($x$, $z > 0$). The Krugman model is, thus, a special case in which $x = 0$. The authors show that, in this model, the relationship between bloc size and the external tariff is ambiguous due to two opposing effects at work. As the representative bloc grows larger, as in Krugman, the share of outside blocs' income spent on the goods exported by the bloc increases and gives it more market power. But the increase in bloc size also increases the representative bloc's share in the total world endowments of the goods it exports which reduces its market power.[34]

### 6.3 *Evidence*

Are FTAs and CUs largely trade diverting as political-economy-driven models suggest? And do these arrangements make member countries more, or less protectionist with respect to the rest of the world? Since I devote the entire Section 6 to the first question, let me confine myself to the second one here.

Though evidence is subject to alternative interpretations, the fact is that unilateral trade liberalization has come to a virtual standstill in Latin America where the forces of regionalism are most strongly at work. The advocates of regional arrangements argue that this

[34] In a Cournot oligopoly model, Sang-Seung Yi (1996) also finds that the external tariff may rise or fall as an existing bloc expands.

suspension of liberalization has little to do with regionalism. When tariffs are high, trade liberalization is simply easier politically. But once they reach the 10–20 percent range, political costs of further liberalization become prohibitive.

Multilateralists, on the other hand, argue that the slowdown is the result of expectations of securing preferential access to other countries' markets in exchange for giving similar access to one's own market. If countries eliminated their barriers unilaterally, there would be no preferences left to be given.

Quite apart from the suspension of unilateral trade liberalization, there is evidence that countries raise their external trade barriers following the conclusion of regional arrangements. As documented in Panagariya (1999a), Mexico, Israel, and MERCOSUR have raised their external tariffs since entering into regional arrangements. There is even evidence that the European Union has reacted to internal liberalization by implementing anti-dumping more vigorously against outside countries (Brian Hindley and Patrik Messerlin 1993).

### 7. *Regionalism and Multilateralism*

Indirectly, we have already begun to explore the relationship between regionalism and multilateralism by asking in the previous section whether PTAs lead to a rise or decline in the external tariff. But this approach is at best incomplete since it does not consider explicitly the role of the multilateral process itself in the determination of the outcome.

Following Bhagwati (1993) and Bhagwati and Panagariya (1996a), the implications of regionalism for multilateralism can be addressed along two separate lines. First, assuming regional and multilateral processes do not interact, i.e., they are strangers, will one or more trade blocs continue to expand until they encompass the entire world? Second, if these processes interact, will the option to form regional blocs make the success of the multilateral process more, or less likely, i.e., will the two processes act as friends or foes? To these, the recent literature has added a third question: what is the impact of multilateralism on regionalism? We take these questions in turn.

### 7.1 *Strangers: Bloc Expansion*

Bloc expansion depends on the willingness of the existing members to offer entry and the incentives facing outsiders to seek entry. Baldwin (1995) analyzes formally the incentive of outsiders to seek entry. He assumes that potential entrants face "non-economic" costs of acceding to a bloc. The entrants can be indexed along the real line such that a rising value of the index is associated with a country with higher noneconomic cost of entry. This means that successive countries require larger and larger economic incentive to seek entry.

Baldwin takes a variant of the Helpman-Krugman (1985, ch. 10) model of economic geography and combines it with the Grossman-Helpman (1994) political-economy model. Trade barriers in this model take the form of transport costs, and entry into an existing bloc is modeled as a reduction in the transport cost. At the initial equilibrium, the economic benefit of membership to the last member in the bloc equals its noneconomic cost. Baldwin disturbs this equilibrium by introducing an exogenous shock, which he calls an idiosyncratic event, and likens it to the European Single Market initiative. The shock increases relative profitability within the bloc, thereby encouraging the firms in the outside country at the margin to lobby their government harder for en-

try.[35] As this country accedes to the bloc, the potential economic benefits of entry for the next country on the outside margin rise and may offset the higher noneconomic costs of entry it faces. Thus, bloc expansion generates a "domino" effect. Unless noneconomic costs rise faster than the benefits of entry, given Baldwin's assumption of open entry, the bloc can come to encompass the entire world and, hence, global free trade.[36]

There are two key limitations of Baldwin's otherwise elegant analysis. First, as already noted, working in the tradition of economic-geography models, he formalizes trade barriers as transport costs. As such, accession to the PTA becomes equivalent to a reduction in transport costs. The revenue aspect of trade barriers, central to traditional models, is completely absent in his analysis. It is not clear whether his result will remain valid once transport costs are replaced by tariffs and, hence, the revenue-transfer effect of entry into the bloc is taken into account. Second, even if we ignore this problem, Baldwin (1995) assumes that "insiders" have no incentive to block entry. It may be conjectured that even within his own model, once the bloc reaches a certain size, insiders will have an incentive to block further entry.

This is indeed the message of a recent paper by Soamiley Andriamananjara (1999) that explicitly models the incentives facing outsiders to seek entry and willingness of insiders to give entry. He uses a Cournot oligopoly model of identical countries in which the outside tariff is fixed by assumption, and decisions

[35] From the viewpoint of the firms in an outside country, the protected market within the bloc becomes larger while the outside market becomes smaller.

[36] Baldwin does assume that noneconomic costs of entry rise faster so that the process comes to an end before global free trade is achieved.

to seek and offer entry are driven by profits. He shows that in this model as the CU expands, profits of insiders first rise, reach a maximum, and then decline. Moreover, the maximum-profit point is reached before the CU comes to encompass all countries. Profits of outsiders, on the other hand, decline monotonically as the CU expands. Thus, while outsiders have an increasing incentive to seek entry, insiders stop short of taking all of them into the club. The CU fails to expand into a global bloc.

Bond and Syropoulos (1996) ask this same question, albeit in a slightly circuitous manner, using the model discussed in Section 6. They hypothesize a world that is initially divided into several identical blocs. They then allow one of these blocs to expand by drawing one country at a time from each of the remaining blocs, with Nash-optimum tariffs applied at all times by all blocs. With the help of simulations, they show that as this bloc expands, the welfare of its members peaks before it absorbs all members of other blocs.[37]

### 7.2 *Impact of Regionalism on Multilateralism: Friends or Foes?*

Next, let us turn to the issue of whether regionalism serves as a building block or stumbling block for multilateralism. A number of different approaches can be distinguished.

*Stumbling Blocks: A Median Voter Model.* There are two key questions we may ask: (i) Can the option to form a trade bloc make a previously infeasible multilateral liberalization feasible; and (ii) Can this additional option render a previously feasible multilateral liberalization infeasible? Levy (1997) addresses this question in a median voter model.

[37] Yi (1996) also considers the issue of bloc expansion in a Cournot oligopoly model.

The answer to the first question is a straightforward "no." The initial infeasibility of multilateral liberalization implies that the median voter enjoys higher utility under autarky than under free trade. The option to form a bloc is exercised only if it increases the voter's utility further. But this raises his reservation utility and must make him even less willing to accept multilateral liberalization.

The second question requires deeper analysis and necessitates spelling out the model explicitly. Levy (1997) addresses it within two popular models: a two-sector, two-factor, multi-country, Heckscher-Ohlin model and a variant of it in which one of the sectors produces a differentiated, monopolistically competitive good. He shows that in the first model, the option of a trade bloc cannot block a previously feasible multilateral accord but, in the second one, it can.

The analysis requires some strong assumptions. It is assumed that when blocs are formed, they adopt total free trade with each other but maintain complete autarky vis-a-vis the rest of the world. Furthermore, endowments of the countries in the world are sufficiently similar to permit factor price equalization when trade is free between two or more countries. These assumptions permit factor prices to be determined by the overall endowment ratio of the region within which trade is free.

Focusing on the Heckscher-Ohlin setting first, consider three countries, A, B, and C. Letting $k_0^A$ be the capital-labor-endowment ratio of the median voter in country A, his utility exhibits the pattern shown by curve $U^A U^A$ in Figure 8a (ignore $U^B U^B$ for now) with respect to the capital-labor ratio of the economy in which he operates. Under autarky, the relevant endowment ratio coincides with the endowment ratio of country A, under FTA, with that of A and B combined, and under global free

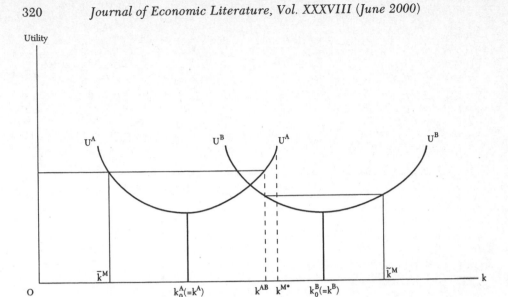

*Figure* 8a.  In the Heckscher-Ohlin Model, Trade Bloc Neither Helps nor Hurts the Multilateral Accord

trade, with that of the world. The key point is that when the median voter's endowment ratio coincides with that of the economy in which he operates, his utility is minimized. When it differs from the latter, utility is higher because he can benefit from "trading" with the rest of the economy.

Introduce country B now. For ease of exposition, consider the highly special case in which the endowment ratio of the median voter in each of A and B coincides with the country's endowment ratio. Let $k^A$ and $k^B$ denote the endowment ratios of A and B so that $k_0^A = k^A$ and $k_0^B = k^B$. Since the case $k^A = k^B$ is uninteresting, without loss of generality, assume $k_0^A = k^A < k^B = k_0^B$. The utility curves of median voters in A and B are then as shown by $U^AU^A$ and $U^BU^B$, respectively, in Figure 8a. The trade bloc's endowment ratio must lie somewhere between $k^A$ and $k^B$ and is shown by $k^{AB}$. By assumption, autarky minimizes each median voter's utility. Therefore, the bloc necessarily in-

creases their utility. From this, it would seem that an agreement to form the bloc will succeed. But the story is more complicated, requiring the introduction of the precise voting sequence between regionalism and multilateralism.

It is assumed that, in the first period, voters in both A and B decide whether they want to form a bloc. In the second period, they vote on multilateral free trade. Voters are fully informed and the two periods are sufficiently close to each other that the utility level of the second period guides the voters' decisions. What this means is that even if a bloc increases utility of a median voter, he will vote against it if multilateralism increases utility even more and he realizes that, after the bloc is formed, the other median voter will block the multilateral accord.

Recall that we assume that the multilateral accord is feasible in the absence of the option to form a bloc. In the specific case we have chosen for simplicity, since autarky minimizes the utility of

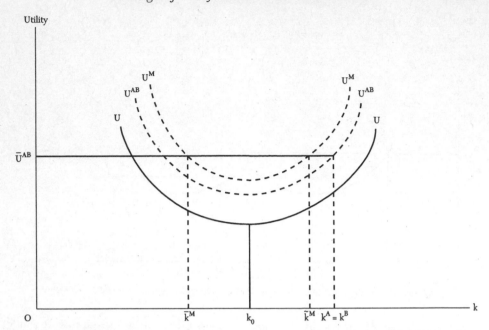

*Figure* 8b. With Product Differentiation Added to the Model, a Trade Bloc Can Block the Multilateral Accord

the median voter, multilateral accord cannot reduce their utility and, hence, is necessarily feasible in the absence of the option to form a trade bloc. To analyze the outcome when the option of a bloc is offered, we need to specify explicitly the multilateral capital-labor endowment ratio, $k^M$. If $k^M$ is no more than $\bar{k}^M$ or no less than $\tilde{k}^M$ in Figure 8a, the multilateral accord is at least as good as or better than a trade bloc for both $A$ and $B$. In this case, both countries approve the bloc in the first period and the multilateral accord in the second period. The trade bloc forms but it neither helps nor hinders multilateral accord.

Interestingly, even if $k^M$ lies anywhere between $\bar{k}^M$ and $\tilde{k}^M$, the multilateral accord survives due to the fact that one of the countries will defeat the trade bloc in period one. To see this, consider $k^M = k^{M*}$ in Figure 8a. In this

case, the median voter in A prefers a multilateral accord to a trade bloc while the opposite is true for the median voter in B. Knowing that B will block the multilateral accord in period two if the bloc is already in place, A blocks the trade bloc in period one in the first place.

Thus, in the standard Heckscher-Ohlin framework, regionalism neither helps nor hinders multilateralism. If one of the goods is differentiated, however, the trade bloc can become a stumbling block for multilateralism. The main difference now is that benefits from trade also arise from an increase in the variety of the differentiated product. The utility curves depend on not just the relative factor endowment of the economy in which the individual operates but also product variety.

To make the point most simply, consider Figure 8b where A and B are identical in all respects, including absolute

322     *Journal of Economic Literature, Vol. XXXVIII (June 2000)*

size and relative endowments. Let $k^A = k^B$ be the country-wide endowment ratio and $k_0$ the median voter's endowment ratio (which is different now from the country's endowment ratio). Each median voter's utility curve is given by *UU* under autarky. The initial level of the voter's utility is given by the height of *UU* at $k^A = k^B$. A trade bloc does not change the economy's endowment ratio (since $k^A = k^B$) but increases the available variety of the differentiated product. In the presence of the bloc, the utility curve is given by the dotted curve $U^{AB}U^{AB}$ and the level of utility by $\bar{U}^{AB}$.

Since multilateral free trade offers an even larger variety than the bloc, it shifts the utility curve further up to, say, $U^M U^M$. But if the multilateral accord also alters the economy's endowment ratio to anywhere between $\bar{k}^M$ and $\tilde{k}^M$, it yields a lower utility to both median voters than the trade bloc. Thus, even though both median voters would have accepted the multilateral accord in the absence of the trade bloc, they will reject it in its presence.

*Stumbling Blocks: A Cournot Oligopoly Model.* An alternative approach to the "friends versus foes" issue is in terms of an oligopoly model in which the decisions are driven by producer profits. This is the setting of the Pravin Krishna (1998) model discussed earlier in the context of the decision to form an FTA. Using that model, we can ask the same question asked by Levy: Does an initially feasible multilateral liberalization remain necessarily feasible after two of the three countries have formed an FTA? Krishna addresses this question and answers it in the negative. He finds, in particular, that the more the FTA benefits (in terms of the firms' profits) from trade diversion, the more likely it will turn into a stumbling bloc. Through a multilateral liberalization,

union members obtain tariff free access to the third country's market in return for offering it access to their own market on equal terms. But if the FTA was heavily trade diverting to begin with, the benefit in terms of the government's objective function from the former change is less than the loss due to the latter change.

*Insidious Regionalism.* An entirely different approach to the question at hand is taken by McLaren (1998) who models regionalism as a coordination failure in a world with sector-specific sunk costs and "friction" in trade negotiations. Based on the expectation that a regional bloc is likely to form, private agents make investments that make potential bloc members more specialized toward each other but, together, less specialized relative to nonmembers. These investments, assumed to be irreversible, reduce the demand for multilateral free trade *ex post*. Thus, the expected supply of regionalism generates its own demand, creating a Pareto-inferior equilibrium.

*Stumbling Blocks in Transition but Building Blocks in the Long Run: FTAs.* Kyle Bagwell and Robert Staiger (1997a,b) investigate how multilateral tariff cooperation is impacted by the formation of FTAs and CUs during the *transition* period. A distinguishing feature of their approach is the assumption that countries cannot make binding commitments to enforce the international bargaining outcomes.[38] They are, therefore, limited to self-enforcing multilateral arrangements that balance short-term gains from deviation against the cost of an ensuing trade war.

The setup chosen by Bagwell and Staiger (1997a) is different from the

[38] For earlier contributions in this tradition, see Jensen and Thursby (1984), Avinash Dixit (1987), Bagwell and Staiger (1990), and Rodney Ludema (1992).

traditional three-country setup. They assume two countries, called Home and Foreign, which cooperate on reciprocal tariffs subject to the above-mentioned incentive constraint. The objective is to maximize welfare as represented by the sum of consumers' and producers' surplus and tariff revenue.

Trade relations between the two countries have three phases. In phase 1, they trade with each other with tariffs set cooperatively via a dynamic tariff game. Phase 2 corresponds to a transition phase, in which trade between Home and Foreign continues but each country has begun discussions about future free trade agreements with other (unmodeled) countries that are assumed to exist in the background. In phase 3, the free-trade agreements are fully implemented. Home and Foreign countries now trade less with one another since they divert some trade to their respective FTA partners and reset the cooperative tariffs. The new trade patterns and tariffs are stationary into the infinite future.

The authors focus on the impact of the negotiations for the FTA on tariff cooperation during phase 2. Their key result is that the emergence of FTAs is associated with temporarily heightened multilateral trade tensions between Home and Foreign. The tension arises because the current trade flows between the two countries have not changed (since FTAs are implemented in phase 3) but expected future flows have declined due to trade diversion. The former fact implies that the short-term gains from deviation have not changed but the latter one implies that the cost of a future trade war between them has declined. This leads to a temporary rise in the multilateral tariff. In phase 3, as the agreement is implemented fully, cooperation resumes and the tariff declines below the phase 1 tariff partially because of the reduced volume of trade between Home and Foreign.

*Building Blocks in Transition but Stumbling Blocks in the Long Run: CUs.* In Bagwell and Staiger (1997b), the authors consider a variation of this model and focus on the impact of customs unions on tariff cooperation during transition. Home and Foreign are now interpreted as regions with each of them consisting of several customs unions. There are two goods, with one exported by Home CUs and the other by Foreign CUs. Acting as independent units, Home CUs negotiate tariffs with Foreign CUs. Starting with phase 1 cooperative tariffs, the possibility of consolidating each of Home CUs and Foreign CUs into larger CUs is then introduced in phase 2. Once again, the agreement is actually implemented in phase 3.

In addition to the trade-diversion effect (which the authors choose not to highlight), there is now a market-power effect. The agreement to consolidate each of Foreign and Home into larger CUs implies that the market power of participants in phase 3 has gone up. In phase 2, this means that the cost of a future trade war has gone up. This leads to a reduction in the multilateral tariff in phase 2. In phase 3, reflecting increased market power, the multilateral tariff rises above the phase 1 tariff.

## 7.3 *The Impact of Multilateralism on Regionalism*

So far, the focus of the analysis in this section has been on how the option to form FTAs impacts decisions regarding multilateral liberalization. Let us now turn to the opposite question: How does multilateral liberalization impact the decision of countries to exercise the regionalism option? There are two principal contributions addressing this reverse relationship.

*Multilateral Liberalization Making PTAs More Sustainable.* The current wave of regionalism has been launched in the wake of a more liberal trading environment than the first wave during the 1950s and 1960s. This wave also promises to be more sustainable, as was predicted by Bhagwati (1993). We may, therefore, ask whether greater openness may imply greater sustainability of PTAs. Caroline Freund (1998) uses a symmetric, three-country, repeated games Cournot oligopoly model to analyze this issue. Initially, each country levies the same multilateral tariff on the other two countries. She shows that, in this setting, the welfare gain from joining a PTA is greater than the gain from a move to free trade when the multilateral tariff is low while the reverse is true when it is high. She goes on to show that this feature makes PTAs more sustainable when multilateral tariffs are low. Hence, PTAs may proliferate and be sustained as a result of multilateral freeing of trade.

The logic behind Freund's result can be best understood by considering the case when the initial multilateral tariff is near autarky. In this case, when two countries form an FTA, there is no room for exploiting the third country via better terms of trade: at near zero trade with the latter, the gain from improved terms of trade is also near zero. Thus, under the PTA, the benefits are limited to those arising from mutual liberalization by partners. But under multilateral liberalization, benefits also accrue from the liberalization of the third country.

When the multilateral tariff is initially low, however, the partner countries can benefit from mutual liberalization as well as the improvement in the terms of trade with respect to the third country that accompanies preferential liberalization. Under multilateral liberalization, by contrast, no terms-of-trade benefits accrue: the benefits are limited to the conventional efficiency triangles. These factors increase the attractiveness of preferential liberalization over multilateral liberalization at low tariffs.

*Liberalization in North Leading to North–South PTAs.* Some of the recent PTAs including NAFTA and the association agreements of the European Union with some of the North African countries have formed along North-South lines. As already stated, these agreements have also been concluded in the wake of considerable liberalization among the countries in North. Inspired by these observations, Ethier (1998) constructs a model in which preferential liberalization by South is the result of multilateral liberalization by North and has a happy coexistence with it.

A highly simplified account of Ethier's basic story can be given as follows. The world is divided into two regions to be called here North and South. Each region consists of several countries. Northern countries are all symmetric. Each Northern country produces one non-traded good, which uses skilled and unskilled labor, and one variety of a traded, differentiated good, which uses human capital and an intermediate good. Only North has human capital so that the differentiated good can be produced only in that region. The intermediate good uses skilled labor and can be produced anywhere. A key feature, which drives many of the results, is the presence of an (international) external economy in the production of the intermediate input.[39]

Southern countries have skilled labor

[39] Ethier defines the production of the input in another country as direct foreign investment, though no investment, technology flows or repatriation of earnings are associated with the shift in location. For simplicity I will call the location of production of intermediate input in South as "production" rather than foreign investment.

and could produce the intermediate input, trading it for the differentiated good with North. But they face resistance to openness. Initially, this resistance is sufficiently strong that even the country with least resistance is in autarky. Each Southern country produces and consumes a rudimentary good, which is a (poor) substitute for North's differentiated good. Northern countries trade initially but impose the Nash optimum tariff on the imports of the differentiated good from other countries. Because the countries are symmetric, the tariff is the same for all of them.

Suppose now that multilateral cooperation leads to a reduction in Northern tariffs. This leads to an expansion of the intermediate input and differentiated goods sectors in each Northern country. The international externality lowers the production cost of intermediate input and allows some Southern countries to overcome resistance to openness. The production of the intermediate input moves partially to the reforming Southern countries. This opening up itself creates opportunities for North-South regional arrangements. Some Northern countries give a tariff preference to the intermediate input produced in the Southern partner in return for exclusive access to the Southern partner's market for the differentiated good.[40]

## 8. Theoretical Considerations in Empirical Assessments of PTAs

Let us now return to the welfare issue, focusing this time on whether, *in practice*, FTAs and CUs lead to increased or reduced welfare. Broadly speaking, empiricists have taken two approaches to sort out this issue. First, they have conducted counterfactual analyses, based on partial- or general-

[40] By assumption, Southern partners are unable to distinguish between different varieties of the differentiated good.

equilibrium models. The idea here is to assume a certain model structure, with specific functional forms and parameter values, to represent the economies in a base year prior to the formation of the union. The model is then shocked by a preferential removal of tariffs and the welfare (and other) effects calculated. Second, empiricists have carried out *ex post* studies of the arrangements to measure the extent of trade creation and trade diversion. The typical approach here has been to estimate econometrically the so-called "gravity" equation which represents bilateral trade flows as a function of incomes and populations of trading partners, distance between them and membership in a common regional arrangement. Summaries of these studies can be found in Adela de la Torre and Morgan Kelly (1982), Srinivasan, John Whalley and Ian Wooton (1993) and Frankel (1997).

Unfortunately, paralleling the theoretical predictions, these studies generate ambiguous answers. After reviewing a large number of studies, Srinivasan, Whalley and Wooton (1993) conclude, "We, therefore, see these studies as shedding somewhat incomplete and at times conflicting light on the effects of post-war RIAs [Regional Integration Agreements] on trade and welfare, to say nothing of what might be the likely effects of prospective RIAs. There seems to be near unanimity that trade creation occurred in Europe, but its size and the precise contribution of the RIAs relative to other factors is unclear. Nor is it clear that significant trade creation from RIAs has occurred elsewhere."

There are sufficiently serious problems with both empirical approaches that the results based on them are unlikely to change the minds on either side of the regionalism debate. Consider first the simulation approach. It is relatively easy to manipulate the structure of the model, functional forms and parameter values in these models to obtain one's desired results.[41] Let me note just two factors.

First, most modelers rely on the so-called Armington assumption according to which goods are assumed differentiated by the country of origin. They then proceed to combine this assumption with the small-union assumption. But there is an inherent contradiction between these two assumptions: being the sole producer of its product, each country has some monopoly power in the world market. Again, the assumption plays a key role in determining the outcome. With the Armington assumption ruling out the import from the outside country of the goods imported from the partner and the small-union assumption ruling out the terms-of-trade effects, as in Figure 4, each country benefits solely from its own liberalization. Not surprisingly, so many studies of NAFTA predict high-tariff Mexico gaining much more relative to its GDP than the United States. If, instead, the theoretically correct, large-union assumption is employed, we find the low-tariff member (United States) benefiting from preferential liberalization by the high-tariff member (Mexico), as predicted by Mundell's (1964) analysis (see Section 3.4 above).

Second, even accepting the co-existence of the Armington structure and the small-union model for the sake of argument, the functional forms and parameter values can be exploited to obtain particular results and rule out others. For example, it is not uncommon to use Stone-Geary utility function or the linear expenditure system to represent demand.[42] This greatly limits the possibilities of substitution. For instance, it

can be shown that if the partner's product shows a high degree of substitutability with that of the outside country but low substitutability with the product of the home country (as is likely, for example, for Mexico in the NAFTA context), an FTA is likely to be harmful (Panagariya 1997a, pp. 482–83). Even the widely used, standard CES utility function rules out this possibility by assumption.

Turning next to the *ex post* approach, a key problem here is that investigators have tried to calculate simply *total* quantities of trade creation and trade diversion. As Meade demonstrated as far back as 1955 (see Section 3.1 above), however, aggregate trade creation and trade diversion are insufficient to infer the welfare effects of PTAs. We need to know trade creation and trade diversion by sector and, in each case, use the information on the decline in the prices of imports to evaluate the benefit from trade creation and the height of trade barriers to measure the damage from trade diversion.[43] The information requirements of such calculations are far too demanding for them to be carried out in practice.

McMillan (1993) tried to cut through this Gordian knot by suggesting that at least from the viewpoint of the GATT rules, the criterion for evaluating the regional arrangements should be the welfare of nonmember countries: "Trade theorists have usually evaluated RIAs either from the point of view of the world as a whole (asking whether the trade creation outweighs the trade diversion) or from the point of view of the members (asking how to maximize the gains from trade creation). I suggest that, for the rules of international trade, the

---

[41] The critique of CGEs in this section is based on Panagariya and Duttagupta (1999), which also provides numerical examples to illustrate the points discussed here.

[42] The wide use, rather than econometric evidence, has often been also cited as evidence that the assumption is "reasonable".

[43] Even this is valid only if the changes in question are small. Otherwise, the knowledge of the entire structure of the model will be necessary.

size of any trade creation among member countries is irrelevant. In practice, it is possible that some member countries will not benefit from an RIA. But it seems reasonable to have a hierarchy of concerns: to put preventing harm to third countries ahead of preventing members from hurting themselves." (McMillan 1993, p. 295)

Taking the welfare of nonmembers as the sole criterion, McMillan goes on to argue, by appeal to the Kemp-Wan-Vanek-Ohyama theorem, that outside countries will be protected from being harmed provided the union's total imports from them do not decline after the formation of the union. If correct, this criterion can serve as a simple basis for distinguishing desirable unions from undesirable ones, at least *ex post*.

It can be shown, however, that the McMillan test is insufficient to guarantee nonmembers their pre-union welfare. Thus, for instance, imagine a substantial deterioration in the terms of trade of nonmembers following the formation of an FTA or CU. Assuming no distortions in nonmembers, this change will lower their welfare. Yet, it is entirely possible that they now export more to the newly formed union in exchange for the same or smaller basket of imports than before. Though the McMillan test is met, the formation of the union hurts nonmembers.

Assuming that trade imbalance is exogenous, utility depends on the current consumption and there are no domestic distortions or tariffs in nonmembers, a sufficiency condition for them not to suffer a welfare loss is

$$\mathbf{p}^1\mathbf{e}^0 \geq \mathbf{p}^1\mathbf{e}^1 \qquad (1)$$

Here $\mathbf{p}$ denotes the price vector, $\mathbf{e}$ the net exports vector, and superscripts 0 and 1 identify pre- and post-union equilibria. The elements in $\mathbf{e}^0$ and $\mathbf{e}^1$ are positive in the case of exportables and negative in the case of importables. According to (1), welfare of nonmembers improves provided their pre-union net exports vector generates a larger trade surplus than their post-union net exports vector at post-union prices. The Kemp-Wan-Vanek-Ohyama theorem freezes the trade vector of nonmembers at its pre-union level. This, in turn, freezes the price vector and condition (1) is automatically satisfied as equality.

Inequality (1) admits the possibility of trade deficit or surplus in both pre- and post-union equilibria. If we impose the trade-balance condition in the post-union equilibrium, however, the inequality requires that nonmembers be able to buy their pre-union import bundle with their pre-union export bundle at post-union prices. This condition can be viewed as saying that the union should not lead to a deterioration of the terms of trade of outside countries.[44]

The relationship of (1) to the terms of trade becomes more explicit if we impose the trade-balance condition in both pre- and post-union equilibria. Trade balance in the pre-union equilibrium yields $\mathbf{p}^0\mathbf{e}^0 = 0$. Subtracting this equality from (1) and recognizing that trade balance in the post-union equilibrium implies $\mathbf{p}^1\mathbf{e}^1 = 0$, the condition for no loss of welfare reduces to

$$(\mathbf{p}^1 - \mathbf{p}^0)\mathbf{e}^0 \geq 0. \qquad (2)$$

This inequality is the traditional definition of an improvement in the terms of trade in the multi-good model.

[44] In his critique of McMillan, Winters (1997) also mentions the role of the terms of trade in ensuring that nonmembers do not suffer a loss in welfare. But, relying on the two-good model, he winds up arguing in favor of increased exports by the union as the criterion for welfare improvement. But making the plausible assumption that the import-demand elasticity in outside countries is no less than unity, in the two-goods model, increased exports are necessarily accompanied by increased imports. Thus, the test favored by Winters coincides with that suggested by McMillan.

In principle, (1) or (2) can serve as the simple test sought by McMillan to sort out desirable FTAs and CUs from undesirable ones. But, in practice, both of these conditions suffer from two key limitations. First, their ability to guarantee no harm to nonmembers is based on the assumption of no distortions in nonmembers. Second, and more importantly, they assume that all changes in post-union prices are due to the formation of the union. In practice, observed prices will reflect the impact of many other changes that are likely to take place independently of the union.

But the prospects for the McMillan criterion (that nonmembers not be harmed) need not be so bleak. Under one set of empirically relevant conditions, theory gives us a strong indication of the impact of the formation of a union on outside countries' terms of trade. If import demands exhibit gross substitutability and initial tariffs are low, the terms of trade of outside countries are highly likely to deteriorate if within-union barriers are lowered, holding the extra-union barriers at their original levels. Since gross substitutability is not an especially strong assumption in the present context and most FTAs (as opposed to CUs) leave their external barriers at pre-union level, the McMillan criterion will reject all FTAs involving large countries. It will also accept all small unions since these neither harm nor help nonmembers.

## 9. *Concluding Remarks*

As this review demonstrates, trade theorists have responded quickly to the challenges thrown by the current wave of regionalism. Within less than a decade, a solid body of scientific work, shedding light on the political economy of regional arrangements and their impact on external tariffs and multilateral freeing of trade has been created.

While there remain sharp divisions among economists and policy makers on the merits of PTAs, a consensus appears to be emerging on one issue of great policy relevance. Proliferation of FTAs is leading to the creation of what Bhagwati (1995) has called a "spaghetti bowl" of tariffs whereby a country subjects the same product to different tariff rates depending on its ostensible origin. There are two sources of this discrimination in tariff rates. First, with each country participating in multiple FTA agreements, the tariff during transition to full internal free trade depends on the FTA member from which the product is imported. Second, in the long run, even after FTAs have been fully implemented, varying degrees of discrimination across products and countries will remain due to differences in the rules of origin across FTA agreements.[45] Thus, ironically, free-trade intentions threaten to reproduce the chaos in the tariff regime that was created in the 1930s by protectionism and the absence of the MFN principle in trade policy. There is now a general agreement among free trade economists that the best solution to this problem is to speed up MFN liberalization. Once external tariffs drop to zero, tariff preferences and the spaghetti bowl created by them will automatically disappear.

In the meantime, on the theoretical front, at least two major gaps remain with respect to the theory of preferential trading. Theory remains almost nonexistent on the relationship among regional, multilateral and unilateral liberalization in trade in services. Formal

[45] Sapir (1998) notes that the European Union currently applies its MFN tariff to barely six countries (Australia, Canada, Japan, New Zealand, Taiwan, and the United States) which account for approximately one-third of its total imports. On other trading partners, it imposes a variety of different rates depending on its relationship with them.

models of PTAs deal almost exclusively with border barriers, which do not capture the reality of much of the trade in services. Yet, regional arrangements have now begun to focus on trade in services.

Equally, in the policy debate, direct foreign investment is frequently cited as a key reason for signing FTAs and CUs. Yet there is little theoretical work drawing the link between these two phenomena. Issues such as why a regional arrangement might be a better instrument of bringing foreign investment than multilateral liberalization have yet to be addressed.

REFERENCES

Anderson, Kym and Richard Blackhurst, eds. 1993. *Regional Integration and the Global Trading System*. NY: St. Martin's Press.

Andriamananjara, Soamiley. 1999. "On the Size and Number of Regional Integration Arrangements: A Political Economy Model," U. Maryland, mimeo.

Bagwell, Kyle and Robert W. Staiger. 1990. "A Theory of Managed Trade," *Amer. Econ. Rev.* 80:4, pp. 779–85.

———. 1997a. "Multilateral Tariff Cooperation During the Formation of Free Trade Areas," *Int. Econ. Rev.* 38:2, May, pp. 291–319.

———. 1997b. "Multilateral Tariff Cooperation During the Formation of Customs Unions," *J. Int. Econ.* 42:1–2, pp. 91–123.

Baldwin, Richard. 1995. "A Domino Theory of Regionalism," in *Expanding Membership of the European Union*. Richard Baldwin, P. Haaparnata, and J. Kiander, eds. Cambridge, UK: Cambridge U. Press, pp. 25–53.

Baldwin, Richard and Anthony Venables. 1995. "Regional Economic Integration," in *Handbook of International Economics, Volume III*. Gene Grossman and Ken Rogoff, eds. Amsterdam: North Holland, pp. 1597–644.

Berglas, Eitan. 1979. "Preferential Trading: The n Commodity Case," *J. Polit. Econ.* 87: 21, pp. 315–31.

———. 1983. "The Case for Unilateral Tariff Reductions: Foreign Tariffs Rediscovered," *Amer. Econ. Rev.* 73:5, pp. 1142–43.

Bhagwati, Jagdish. 1971. "Trade-Diverting Customs Unions and Welfare Improvement: A Clarification," *Econ. J.* 81:323, pp. 580–87.

———. 1991. *The World Trading System at Risk*. Princeton, NJ: Princeton U. Press.

———. 1993. "Regionalism and Multilateralism: An Overview," in *New Dimensions in Regional Integration*. Jaime de Melo and Arvind Panagariya, eds. Cambridge: Cambridge U. Press, pp. 22–51.

———. 1995. "U.S. Trade Policy: The Infatuation with Free Trade Areas," in *The Dangerous Drift to Preferential Trade Agreements*. Jagdish Bhagwati and Anne O. Krueger, eds. Washington, DC: American Enterprise Institute for Public Policy Research.

Bhagwati, Jagdish; David Greenaway, and Arvind Panagariya. 1998. "Trading Preferentially: Theory and Policy," *Econ. J.* 108:449, pp. 1128–48.

Bhagwati, Jagdish; Pravin Krishna, and Arvind Panagariya, eds. 1999. *Trading Blocs: Alternative Approaches to Analyzing Preferential Trade Agreements*. Cambridge, MA: MIT Press.

Bhagwati, Jagdish and Arvind Panagariya. 1996a. "Preferential Trading Areas and Multilateralism: Strangers, Friends or Foes?" in *The Economics of Preferential Trade Agreements*. Jagdish Bhagwati and Arvind Panagariya, eds. Washington, DC: AEI Press, pp. 1–78.

———. 1996b. "The Theory of Preferential Trade Agreements: Historical Evolution and Current Trends." *Amer. Econ. Rev.* 86:2, pp. 82–87.

Bond, Eric W. and Constantinos Syropoulos. 1996. "The Size of Trading Blocs, Market Power and World Welfare Effects," *J. Int. Econ.* 40:3–4, pp. 411–37.

Brecher, Richard and Jagdish Bhagwati. 1981. "Foreign Ownership and the Theory of Trade and Welfare." *J. Polit. Econ.* 89:3, pp. 497–511.

Cadot, Olivier; Jaime de Melo, and Marcelo Olarreaga. 1999. "Regional Integration and Lobbying for Tariffs Against Non-Members," *Int. Econ. Rev.* 40:3, pp. 635–57.

Corden, W. Max. 1972. "Economies of Scale and Customs Union Theory," *J. Polit. Econ.* 80:3, pp. 465–75.

Davis, Donald. 1997. "Comments on 'A Common External Tariff of Customs Unions: Alternative Approaches'," *Japan World Econ.* 9:4, pp. 467–70.

Deardorff, Alan and Robert Stern. 1994. "Multilateral Trade Negotiations and Preferential Trading Arrangements," in *Analytical and Negotiating Issues in the Global Trading System*. Alan Deardorff and Robert Stern, eds. Ann Arbor: U. Michigan Press, pp. 53–85.

De la Torre, Augusto and Margaret R. Kelly. 1992. "The Regional Trading Arrangements," Occasional Paper No. 93, IMF, Washington, DC.

Dixit, Avinash. 1987. "Strategic Aspects of Trade Policy," in *Advances in Economic Theory: Fifth World Congress*. T. F. Bewley, ed. NY: Cambridge U. Press, 329–62.

Duttagupta, Rupa. 2000. "Intermediate Inputs and Rules of Origin: Implications for Welfare and Viability of Free Trade Agreements," U. Maryland Ph.D. thesis.

Ethier, Wilfred J. 1998. "Regionalism in a Multilateral World, *J. Polit. Econ.* 106:6, pp. 1214–45.

Ethier, Wilfred J. and Henrik Horn. 1984. "A New Look at Economic Integration," in *Monopolistic Competition and International Trade*. Henryk

Kierzkowski, ed. Oxford: Clarendon Press, pp. 207–29.

Falvey, Rod and Geoff V. Reed. 1997. "Rules of Origin as Commercial Policy Instruments," U. Nottingham, mimeo.

Frankel, Jeffrey A. 1997. *Regional Trading Blocs in the World Trading System.* Washington, DC: Institute for International Econ.

——, ed. 1998. *The Regionalization of the World Economy.* Chicago: U. Chicago Press.

Frankel, Jeffrey A.; Ernesto Stein, and Shang-Jin Wei. 1995. "Trading Blocs and the Americas: The Natural, the Unnatural and the Supernatural," *J. Devel. Econ.* 47:1, pp. 61–96.

Fernandez, Raquel and Jonathan Portes. 1998. "Returns to Regionalism: An Analysis of Non-traditional Gains from Regional Trade Agreements," *World Bank Econ. Rev.* 12:2, pp. 197–220.

Freund, Caroline. 1998. "Multilateralism and the Endogenous Formation of PTAs," Board of Governors Fed. Reserve System, International Finance Discussion Paper 614, Washington, DC. Forthcoming in *J. Int. Econ.*

Gehrels, Franz. 1956–57. "Customs Union from a Single-Country Viewpoint," *Rev. Econ. Studies,* 24:6, pp. 61–64.

Gros, Daniel. 1987. "A Note on the Optimal Tariff, Retaliation and the Welfare Loss from Tariff Wars in a Framework with Intra-Industry Trade," *J. Int. Econ.* 23:3–4, pp. 357–367.

Grossman, Gene and Elhanan Helpman. 1994. "Protection for Sale," *Amer. Econ. Rev.* 84:4, pp. 835–50.

——. 1995. "The Politics of Free Trade Agreements," *Amer. Econ. Rev.,* 85:4, pp. 667–90.

Helpman, Elhanan. and Paul R. Krugman. 1985. *Market Structure and Foreign Trade: Increasing Returns, Imperfect Competition, and the International Economy.* Cambridge, MA: MIT Press.

Hindley, Brian and Patrik Messerlin. 1993. "Guarantees of Market Access and Regionalism," in *Regional Integration and the Global Trading System.* K. Anderson and R. Blackhurst, eds. London: Harvester Wheatsheaf.

Jensen, R. and M. Thursby. 1984. "Free Trade: Two Noncooperative Approaches," working paper, Ohio State U.

Ju, Jiandong and Kala Krishna. 1998. "Firm Behavior and Market Access in a Free Trade Area with Rules of Origin," NBER Working Paper 6857.

Kemp, Murray C. 1964. *The Pure Theory of International Trade.* Englewood Cliffs, NJ: Prentice-Hall, pp. 176–77.

Kemp, Murray and Henry Wan, Jr. 1976. "An Elementary Proposition Concerning the Formation of Customs Unions," *J. Int. Econ.* 6:1, pp. 95–97.

Kowalczyk, Carsten. 1990. "Welfare and Customs Unions," NBER Working Paper 3476.

Krishna, Pravin. 1998. "Regionalism and Multilateralism: A Political Economy Approach," *Quart. J. Econ.* 113:1, pp. 227–51.

Krishna, Pravin and Jagdish Bhagwati. 1997. "Necessarily Welfare-Enhancing Customs Unions with Industrialization Constraints," *Japan World Econ.* 9:4, pp. 441–46.

Krueger, Anne O. 1999. "Free Trade Agreements as Protectionist Devices: Rules of Origin," in *Trade Theory and Econometrics: Essays in Honor of John S. Chipman.* James Melvin, James Moore, and Raymond Riezman, eds. NY: Routledge.

Krugman, Paul. 1980. "Scale Economies, Product Differentiation, and the Pattern of Trade," *Amer. Econ. Rev.,* 70:5, pp. 950–59.

——. 1991a. "Is Bilateralism Bad?" in *International Trade and Trade Policy.* E. Helpman and A. Razin, eds. Cambridge, MA: MIT Press, pp. 9–23.

——. 1991b. "The Move to Free Trade Zones," in *Policy Implications of Trade and Currency Zones.* Symposium sponsored by Fed. Reserve Bank Kansas City, pp. 7–41.

——. 1993. "Regionalism versus Multilateralism: Analytical Notes," in *New Dimensions in Regional Integration.* Jaime de Melo and Arvind Panagariya, eds. Cambridge, UK: Cambridge U. Press, pp. 58–84.

Levy, Philip. 1997. "A Political-Economic Analysis of Free-Trade Agreements," *Amer. Econ. Rev.* 87:4, pp. 506–19.

Lipsey, Richard. 1957. "The Theory of Customs Unions: Trade Diversion and Welfare," *Economica,* 24:93, pp. 40–46.

Lloyd, Peter J. 1982. "3x3 Theory of Customs Unions," *J. Int. Econ.* 12:1–2, pp. 41–63.

Ludema, Rodney. 1992. "On the Value of Preferential Trade Agreements in Multilateral Negotiations," unpublished manuscript.

McLaren, John. 1998. "A Theory of Insidious Regionalism," Econ. Dept. mimeo, Columbia U.

McMillan, John. 1993. "Does Regional Integration Foster Open Trade? Economic Theory and GATT's Article XXIV," in *Regional Integration and the Global Trading System.* K. Anderson and R. Blackhurst, eds. NY: St. Martin's Press, pp. 292–310.

McMillan, John and Ewen McCann. 1981. "Welfare Effects in Customs Unions," *Econ. J.,* 91:363, pp. 697–703.

Meade, James E. 1955. *The Theory of Customs Unions.* Amsterdam: North-Holland.

Melo, Jaime de and Arvind Panagariya, eds. 1993. *New Dimensions in Regional Integration.* Cambridge, UK: Cambridge U. Press.

Mundell, Robert A. 1964. "Tariff Preferences and the Terms of Trade," *Manchester School Econ. Social Studies,* pp. 1–13.

Ohyama, Michihiro. 1972. "Trade and Welfare in General Equilibrium," *Keio Econ. Studies,* 9, pp. 37–73.

Panagariya, Arvind. 1996. "The Free Trade Area of the Americas: Good for Latin America?" *World Econ.* 19:5, pp. 485–515.

——. 1997a. "Preferential Trading and the Myth of Natural Trading Partners," *Japan World Econ.* 9:4, pp. 471–89.

———. 1997b. "The Meade Model of Preferential Trading: History, Analytics and Policy Implications," in *International Trade and Finance: New Frontiers for Research. Essays in Honor of Peter B. Kenen.* B. J. Cohen, ed. NY: Cambridge U. Press, pp. 57–88.

———. 1998. "Do Transport Costs Justify Regional Preferential Trade Arrangements? No," *Weltwirtschaftliches Archiv,* 134:2, pp. 280–301.

———. 1999a. "The Regionalism Debate: An Overview," *World Econ.* 22:4, pp. 477–511.

———. 1999b. *Regionalism in Trade Policy: Essays on Preferential Trading.* Singapore: World Scientific Press Co.

———. 1999c. "Preferential Trading and Welfare: The Small-Union Case Revisited," mimeo, U. Maryland.

Panagariya, Arvind and Rupa Duttagupta. 1999. "The 'Gains' from Preferential Trade Liberalization in the CGEs: Where from Do They Come?" U. Maryland, mimeo. Forthcoming in *Regionalism and Globalization: Theory and Practice.* Sajal Lahiri, ed. London: Routledge.

Panagariya, Arvind and Ronald Findlay. 1996. "A Political Economy Analysis of Free Trade Areas and Customs Unions," in *The Political Economy of Trade Reform: Essays in Honor of Jagdish Bhagwati.* Robert Feenstra, Douglas Irwin, and Gene Grossman, eds. Cambridge, MA: MIT Press, pp. 265–87.

Panagariya, Arvind and Pravin Krishna. 1997. "On the Existence of Necessarily Welfare-Enhancing Free Trade Areas," Working Paper 32, Center for Int. Econ., U. Maryland.

Puga, Diego and Anthony J. Venables. 1995. "Preferential Trading Arrangements and Industrial Location," CEPR Discussion Paper 1309.

Richardson, Martin. 1993. "Endogenous Protection and Trade Diversion," *"J. Int. Econ.* 34:3–4, pp. 309–24.

Richardson, Martin. 1994. "Why a Free Trade Area? The Tariff Also Rises," *Econ. Pol.* 6:1, pp. 79–95.

Riezman, Raymond. 1979. "A 3x3 Model of Customs Unions," *J. Int. Econ.* 9:4, pp. 341–54.

Sapir, Andre. 1998. "The Political Economy of EC Regionalism," *Europ. Econ. Rev.* 42:3–5, pp. 717–32.

Smith, Alasdair and Anthony J. Venables. 1988.

"Completing the Internal Market in the European Community: Some Industry Simulations," *Europ. Econ. Rev.* 32:7, pp. 1501–25.

Srinivasan, T. N. 1993. "Regionalism versus Multilateralism: Analytical Notes. Comment," in *New Dimensions in Regional Integration.* Jaime de Melo and Arvind Panagariya, eds. Cambridge, UK: Cambridge U. Press, pp. 84–89.

Srinivasan, T. N. 1997. "Common External Tariffs of a Customs Unions: Alternative Approaches," *Japan World Econ.* 9:4, pp. 447–70.

Srinivasan, T. N., John Whalley, and Ian Wooton. 1993. "Measuring the Effects of Regionalism on Trade and Welfare," in *Regional Integration and the Global Trading System.* Kym Anderson and Richard Blackhurst, eds. NY: St. Martin's Press, pp. 52–79.

Summers, Lawrence. 1991. "Regionalism and the World Trading System," in *Policy Implications of Trade and Currency Zones.* Symposium sponsored by Federal Reserve Bank Kansas City, pp. 295–301.

Vanek, Jaroslav. 1965. *General Equilibrium of International Discrimination. The Case of Customs Unions.* Cambridge, MA: Harvard U. Press.

Viner, Jacob. 1950. *The Customs Union Issue.* NY: Carnegie Endowment for International Peace.

Winters, L. Alan. 1996. "Regionalism versus Multilateralism," Policy Research Working Paper 1687, Washington, DC: World Bank.

———. 1997. "Regionalism and the Rest of the World: The Irrelevance of the Kemp-Wan Theorem," *Oxford Econ. Papers,* 49:2, pp. 228–34.

Wonnacott, Paul and Mark Lutz. 1989. "Is There a Case for Free Trade Areas?" in *Free Trade Areas and U.S. Trade Policy.* Jeffrey Schott, ed. Washington, DC: Institute for International Econ., pp. 59–84.

Wonnacott, Paul and Ronald J. Wonnacott. 1981. "Is Unilateral Tariff Reduction Preferable to a Customs Union? The Curious Case of the Missing Foreign Tariff," *Amer. Econ. Rev.* 71:4, pp. 704–14.

Yi, Sang-Seung. 1996. "Endogenous Formation of Customs Unions under Imperfect Competition: Open Regionalism is Good," *J. Int. Econ.* 41:1–2, pp. 153–77.

# Part V
# Political Economy and Time Inconsistency

# [18]

## Regionalism in a Multilateral World

Wilfred J. Ethier

*University of Pennsylvania*

Recent regional initiatives have been addressed from a Vinerian perspective of trade creation and trade diversion. This is true of both policy-oriented economists, who tend to be critical of the initiatives, and theorists, who have added dynamic and game-theoretic elements to the Vinerian structure. This paper describes the stylized facts of much recent regional integration and develops an alternative model. The analysis suggests that regional integration, far from threatening multilateral liberalism, may in fact be a direct consequence of the success of past multilateralism and an added guarantee for its survival.

## I. Introduction

Regionalism rules. This was not true until recently: With the notable exception of Western Europe, the numerous regional initiatives of the 1950s and 1960s eventually amounted to virtually nothing. But the late 1980s attempt of the European Community to complete its internal market by the end of 1992 has induced (or preceded) a new global wave of regional integration: most notably (1) the U.S.-Canada Free Trade Agreement and the subsequent incorporation of Mexico into the North American Free Trade Agreement (NAFTA); (2) the entrance of Austria, Finland, and Sweden into the European Union; (3) the Europe Agreements between the Euro-

I thank L. Alan Winters and an anonymous referee for useful comments and suggestions. This paper was originally prepared during an enjoyable stay as Tinbergen Professor at the Tinbergen Institute, Rotterdam. It has profited from comments and suggestions received at seminars, workshops, and conferences—too numerous to mention—in all quarters of our shrinking world. I disclaim the usual disclaimer.

[*Journal of Political Economy*, 1998, vol. 106, no. 6]

pean Union and former communist states of central Europe; and (4) the Mercosur customs union between Brazil, Argentina, Paraguay, and Uruguay. These are prominent examples. But dozens of other initiatives—whether negotiation, sincere intention, or vague aspiration—have appeared in most parts of the world. More than 100 regional arrangements, accounting for well over half of world trade, now exist.

Trade theorists have not been slow to respond. Responses have centered on two questions: (i) Will the division of the world into regional trading blocs raise or lower welfare? So far, answers have been mixed (see Krugman 1991; Bhagwati and Panagariya 1996). (ii) Will regionalism help or hinder multilateral trade liberalization? Answers have basically been negative, though with some qualifications (see Bond and Syropoulos 1996; Bagwell and Staiger 1997$a$, 1997$b$). Common to these responses has been the treatment of regional integration as exogenous.[1] Also common has been a Vinerian perspective on regional integration as a combination of trade creation and trade diversion.[2]

By contrast, economists concerned with trade policy have been much less ambiguous. The dominant view is now strongly negative: The increase in regional arrangements reflects frustration with the process of multilateral liberalization (e.g., the prolonged pains of the Uruguay Round negotiations) and poses a serious threat to the continued existence of the present liberal trade order.[3]

The Vinerian perspective was a response to the "old regionalism" after World War II. But the international environment greeting the "new regionalism" that has emerged since the late 1980s differs from that experienced by the old regionalism in critical ways: (1) Multilateral liberalization (at least of trade in manufactures among the industrial countries) is much more complete now, and (2) scores of economically less advanced countries have abandoned basically autarkic, antimarket, policies and are now actively trying to join the multilateral trading system. So one can also make a *qualitative* distinction between the old regionalism and the new. For example, the Vinerian paradigm of trade creation versus trade diversion drove analysis of the former, but it is by no means clear that it should drive

---

[1] Some recent contributions do endogenize regional integration: See Yi (1996), Baldwin (1997), and Freund (1997) and, for surveys of some recent developments, Ethier (1998$a$, 1998$b$).

[2] For other developments in the Vinerian tradition, see Ethier and Horn (1984), Anderson and Blackhurst (1993), and de Melo and Panagariya (1993).

[3] I have the impression that, in North America at least, the general public believes professional economists to be much more in favor of regional arrangements than they in fact are. Perhaps the reason is that the highly visible debate over NAFTA degenerated into (or was elevated into) a debate over the merits of liberal trade.

analysis of the latter. Yet it *has*. This is central to the ambiguity noted above. This paper attempts to develop an idea of what the *qualitative* new regionalism should be.[4]

Section II describes the salient characteristics of the new regionalism and how they differ from those of the old regionalism motivating the Vinerian perspective. Section III then presents an elementary model of trade and trade policy incorporating these characteristics—or capable of doing so—and Section IV contributes a rudimentary theory of multilateralism. Section V then investigates the potential role of regional arrangements in such a framework.

The analysis suggests a radically different interpretation of regionalism: a theoretical structure far removed from the Vinerian perspective and a policy implication at odds with the common negative view. In particular, three possibilities emerge: (i) Regionalism is an endogenous response to the development of the multilateral trading system, and treating it as exogenous is misleading. (ii) The primary purpose of regionalism is to adapt to multilateral developments. Thus the paper suggests a presumption that regional integration facilitates multilateral liberalization.[5] (iii) Regionalism promotes the successful entry of reforming countries into the multilateral trading system in a way that multilateralism by itself cannot do.

## II. What the New Regionalism Is

The following characteristics do not apply to all current regional initiatives, which are quite diverse, but do apply in varying degree to most of the more important ones.

1. Contemporary regionalism typically features one or more small countries linking up with a big country. In the examples above, Mexico and Canada are each small, economically, relative to the United States; the new members of the European Union are tiny compared to the European Union itself; so are the central European adherents to the Europe Agreements; and Brazil dominates Mercosur.

2. Very often the small countries have recently made, or are trying to make, significant unilateral reforms. This is most dramatically true of the central European countries (which had abandoned commu-

---

[4] One cannot expect the temporal and qualitative distinctions to correspond exactly to each other. Presumably some characteristics of the (qualitatively) new regionalism are relevant to earlier regional initiatives, and—more important, for present purposes—features of the (qualitatively) old regionalism remain relevant today. But I am interested in the nature of the new (qualitatively) regionalism.

[5] Chichilnisky (1994) also argues that, in the presence of economies of scale, regional integration may foster multilateral liberalization. But her argument is quite different from what follows.

nism), of Mercosur, and of Mexico. But it also characterizes, to a lesser degree, the small industrial country participants in the examples above. Canada had turned away from Trudeau-style economic nationalism, and the Scandinavian applicants to the European Union (except Norway, which significantly declined to join) had made notable reforms in some sectors (e.g., agriculture and banking). In Mercosur, in contrast to the other examples, the large country, Brazil, is also attempting unilateral reform.

3. Regional agreements seldom address only trade barriers: They usually involve what is known as "deep" integration. This is another reflection of the fact that the new regionalism is taking place in a context of wide economic reform.

4. A dramatic move to free trade between members is *not* what it is all about: The degree of liberalization is typically modest. Thus the Vinerian paradigm is not a natural starting point. The trade relations of Austria, Finland, and Sweden with the European Union are virtually identical to what they would have been had they decided not to join the Union! NAFTA provides only modest liberalization: U.S. tariffs were already low, and NAFTA hedges sensitive sectors. Canada and Mexico have done more, but the most significant measures (largely Mexican) were unilateral. The Europe Agreements provide for little in the way of concrete liberalization. Mercosur is admittedly more ambitious, but even here the liberalization is small relative to the members' unilateral liberalizations.

5. The liberalization that is achieved is due primarily to concessions by the small countries: The agreements are one-sided. The moderate liberalization in NAFTA is due much more to "concessions" by Mexico and Canada than by the United States (Ross Perot notwithstanding). In negotiations over enlargement, the European Union has been flexible on financial responsibilities and periods of adjustment but has always maintained a take-it-or-leave-it attitude regarding the nature and structure of the European Union itself. The Europe Agreements involve virtually no "concessions" by the European Union: Indeed the European Union instituted antidumping measures against some new partners even as the initial agreements were coming into effect! Mercosur does not display this asymmetry (perhaps because its big country is also a reformer?).

More typically the small countries get only small tariff advantages, often because the large countries have small tariffs to begin with. More important to the small countries is exemption from future acts of contingent protection—antidumping law, safeguards, and so forth. But usually they do not get much here either: The Europe Agreements were mentioned above; NAFTA does not give Canada and Mexico exemption from U.S.-administered protection; and as members of the European Area, Austria, Finland, and Sweden would not have been subject to E.U.-administered protection in any case.

In summary, *with regional integration, reform-minded small countries "purchase," with moderate trade concessions, deep links with large countries that confer relatively minor trade advantages.* So, why do the small countries do it?[6]

## III. The Model

My first building block is a simple trade model in which to embed the stylized facts described above. I use a modified version of the familiar, many-country, specific-factors model.

Suppose, first, $N$ (almost) identical industrial countries, each endowed with $H$ units of human capital, $L$ skilled labor, and $U$ unskilled labor. Second, assume $M$ (almost) identical less developed countries.

### Developed Countries

Each developed country $i$ can produce one output, $x_i$ (which I call a *good*), using human capital and skilled labor, and another output, $z_i$ (which I call a *commodity*), requiring skilled labor and unskilled labor. The respective goods are imperfect substitutes. Goods are tradable but commodities are nontraded.

### Production

Production of each good is a two-stage process, with one stage, using only human capital, necessarily performed at home. The other stage, using only skilled labor, can be performed anywhere; that is, the home firm can employ labor located in any country (foreign direct investment) to perform this stage. If this is done abroad, the resulting unfinished goods must be exported from the foreign subsidiary. If $a_i$ and $b_i$ denote the levels of operations of the respective stages, final output is

$$x_i = f(a_i, b_i), \tag{1}$$

where $f$ is a conventional neoclassical production function. Stage operations are

---

[6] Perroni and Whalley (1994) provide an answer very different from what follows to a related question.

$$a_i = H,\qquad(2)$$

and

$$b_i = kL_{bi},\qquad(3)$$

where $H_i$ denotes the stock of human capital, $L_{bi}$ the skilled labor allocated to stage $b_i$, and $k = k(\sum_{i=1}^{N} L_{bi})$, with $k' > 0$. Operation of each $b_i$ stage thus entails increasing returns to scale that depend on the size of global second-stage activity for all $N$ goods. I assume that these returns are external to the individual firm and that goods are produced in perfectly competitive markets. Furthermore, these scale economies are international in origin; that is, they depend on the *global* size of the labor employed in producing all $b_i$, not the labor employed in a single country. For international economies of scale, see Ethier (1979, 1982). As argued there, such economies will require trade in intermediate goods: trade in inputs to the various $b_i$ themselves. But introducing this trade would complicate the model to no purpose, so I abstract from it.[7]

The nontraded commodity, $z$, is produced by competitive firms operating under constant returns to scale:

$$z = g(U, L_z).\qquad(4)$$

Here $g$ is also a standard neoclassical production function, $U$ denotes the stock of unskilled labor, and $L_z$ the amount of skilled labor allocated to commodity production. Thus

$$L = L_b + L_z.\qquad(5)$$

Consumption

Each country behaves as though it has the utility function

$$u = N^{-\epsilon} \sum_{i=1}^{N} \frac{\epsilon}{\epsilon - 1} y_i^{(\epsilon-1)/\epsilon} + z,\qquad(6)$$

where $y_i$ denotes consumption of the good produced by country $i$ and $z$ consumption of the local commodity. This function will be used to measure the social welfare of developed countries. The implied demand for good $i$ in each country is

$$y_i = \frac{1}{N} p_i^{-\epsilon},\qquad(7)$$

---

[7] Henceforth I dispense with the commodity/country subscript $i$ whenever this generates no confusion.

where $p_i$ denotes the relative price of $y_i$ in terms of $z$. All other income is spent on $z$.

## Free-Trade Equilibrium for the Developed Countries

To fix ideas, consider a symmetric free-trade equilibrium between the developed countries in which all goods are produced equally, sell for the same price, and are consumed equally by all countries. Each country performs $b$-stage production equal to the total production of precisely one good, and the allocation of $b$-stage activity among countries is indeterminate (so cross-penetration of direct investment may take place) but inconsequential. So assume that each $x_i$ is produced by integrated firms located entirely in country $i$.

From (1), (2), and (3), the integrated production function for each country's good is

$$x = f(H, kL_b). \tag{8}$$

Designate $z$ as numeraire, and let $\omega$ denote the wage of skilled labor. Since skilled labor is paid the value of its marginal product in each use,

$$\begin{aligned} \omega &= p f_L(H, kL_b)k, \\ \omega &= g_L(U, L_z), \end{aligned} \tag{9}$$

where subscripts denote partial differentiation.[8] Thus

$$p f_L(H, kL_b)k - g_L(U, L_z) = 0. \tag{10}$$

Equations (5), (8), and (10) determine the supply function for each good:

$$x = x(p, L; L_b(N - 1)), \tag{11}$$

where $L_b(N - 1)$ denotes the total labor allocated to $b$-stage production by the other $N - 1$ countries. I make the following assumption.

ASSUMPTION 1. The response of the integrated production function to the second-stage input is sufficiently curved, relative to the degree of economies of scale in the $b$ stage, that

$$\sigma_f > \frac{\sigma_k/N}{1 + (\sigma_k/N)},$$

---

[8] The term $k$ is treated as a parameter by $b$ producers since the economies of scale are external to the firm.

where

$$-\frac{kL_bf_{LL}}{f_L} \equiv \sigma_f, \quad \frac{NL_bk'}{k} \equiv \sigma_k.$$

This will ensure that $x_p > 0$.

International equilibrium is determined by the requirement that the world supply $x$ of each good equal the world demand implied by (7):

$$y = p^{-\epsilon}. \tag{12}$$

Note that

$$\frac{L}{p}\frac{\partial p}{\partial L}\bigg|_x = -\frac{L}{p}\frac{x_L}{x_p} = -L\frac{g_{LL}}{-pf_Lk} = -\frac{\sigma_g}{\lambda_z} < 0, \tag{13}$$

where

$$\sigma_g = -\frac{L_z g_{LL}}{g_L}, \quad \lambda_z = \frac{L_z}{L}.$$

Thus an increase in the available supply of skilled labor shifts the supply curve to the left, raising equilibrium $x$ and lowering $p$. This change in output in one country will generate international spillovers, and consequent changes in foreign production will in turn generate repercussions in the original country.


## Protection in the Industrial World

I assume that each developed country levies an ad valorem tariff, $t$, on the imports of each foreign good (and its own $b$-stage output, if that stage is performed abroad). I assume that all developed countries are identical, and I shall confine attention to symmetric equilibria, so $t$ will be the same for all countries and all goods. The tariff revenue is distributed to the public in lump-sum fashion (and so is spent on $z$).

I assume that the commercial policy of each industrial country is the outcome of a political process in which unskilled labor attempts to secure rents. This will not be modeled explicitly. Instead I simply assume that the political process operates as though the country were maximizing a social welfare function that trades off labor's wage against aggregate welfare:

$$V = rw + (1 - r)u, \tag{14}$$

where $w = g_U(U, L_z)$. The parameter $r$ thus reflects the influence unskilled labor has over the political process. Detail concerning the constraints under which $V$ is maximized will be supplied below, when I consider explicit international commercial systems.

## Less Developed Countries

Each less developed country implements a commercial policy that is the outcome of a political process in which special interests attempt to secure rents. As with the industrial countries, this process will not be modeled explicitly. I am concerned not with marginal changes in protection, but with the possibility of fundamental economic reform. For this reason, I assume that the government of each less developed country must choose one of just two possible policies: autarky or reform. With autarky, the special interests secure their rents. But if the social welfare benefit $R$ of reform is expected to be sufficiently great, the government will attempt reform; let $r^*$ denote the minimum the expected value of $R$ must attain for the government to be tempted to forsake autarky for reform. The parameter $r^*$ thus reflects the influence special interests have over the political process.

The only aspect of the less developed countries that I need to model explicitly for what follows is the potentially open sector, where $R$ is generated. This potentially open sector contains an initial stock $L_A^*$ of skilled labor, which, in autarky, can be used to produce, for local consumption, a rudimentary good:

$$x^* = k(L_A^*) L_A^*. \tag{15}$$

The function $k(\cdot)$ is the same as that pertinent to the developed countries but is evaluated as a function of local input alone, since the less developed country is in autarky and is not part of the multilateral trading system. Finally, local goods are rudimentary because their production is undertaken without benefit of the sophisticated $a$ stage.

If the less developed country reforms successfully, firms from the developed countries will establish subsidiaries there that employ some quantity, $F$, of skilled labor for their own $b$-stage production. This production will then be exported for final assembly, and some portion of that will be paid to $F$ as wages. Because final output has not been customized for the less developed countries, assume that they regard the finished goods of the various developed countries as perfect substitutes for each other; because their own rudimentary goods are indeed rudimentary, assume that they regard one unit of their own goods as a perfect substitute for $\alpha$ units of any developed-country good ($\alpha < 1$). The direct investment involves the transfer of global technology, so the subsidiaries' output will be $b^* = kF$, where $k$ depends on the total amount of labor allocated to $b$-stage production by developed-country firms, including that of their subsidiaries in the less developed countries. In addition, with the less developed country now part of the multilateral trading system, global technology spills over to the production of rudimentary goods (valued in terms of finished goods): $y^* = \alpha(L^* - F)k$, with $k$ given by its international value and $L^*$ the stock of skilled labor in the open sector in the event of successful reform.

If $\omega^*$ denotes the wage, in terms of finished goods, paid by the foreign subsidiaries, the value $R$ of successful reform, also in terms of finished goods, is $y^* + \omega^*F - \alpha x^*$. If the labor market is competitive, $\omega^* = \alpha k$, and suppose that $L^*$ is a nondecreasing function of $\omega^*$. Thus $R$ is determined by

$$R(k) = \alpha[L^*(\alpha k)k - x^*]. \tag{16}$$

The less developed country will be tempted to undertake reform if and only if the global economy is sufficiently productive that $\rho R(k) \geq r^*$, where $\rho$ equals the probability that reform will succeed ($\rho$ will be endogenized in a subsequent section). Reform is successful if and only if the country succeeds in attracting foreign direct investment.

I assume that the less developed countries differ from each other in only one way: the propensity $r^*$ to favor special interests. There are distinct classes of less developed countries, and I denote the value of $r^*$ pertinent to class $j$ by $r_j^*$, number the classes from zero to one, and rank them so that $r_j^*$ rises as $j$ rises. Let $M(j)$ denote the number of (identical) less developed countries in class $j$, that is, the number of countries for which $r^* = r_j^*$. I shall simplify the following analysis by assuming a continuum of classes: the more relevant case of a finite number of classes is straightforward but tedious.

Let $M_R^*(\rho, k)$ denote the number of less developed countries that, given $\rho$ and $k$, would attempt reform. Then

$$M_R^*(\rho, k) = \int_0^i M(j), \tag{17}$$

where $r_i^* = \rho R(k)$. Clearly $M_R^*(\rho, k)$ is increasing in each of its arguments.

## IV. Multilateralism

This section develops a simple theory of multilateralism, the second basic building block of this paper.

*Unilateralism*

First I describe an international equilibrium in which $r$ and $r^*$ are sufficiently large that $F = 0$ in each less developed country and in which each developed country sets some arbitrary (but equal) $t$. Then I proceed to the symmetric Nash equilibrium in which the choice of $t$ is optimal, given that every other developed country chooses the same $t$ and that the less developed countries all choose autarky. This characterizes unilateralism.

## A Symmetric Protectionist Equilibrium

Suppose that each developed country levies a common ad valorem tariff $t$ on imports of each of the $N - 1$ foreign goods. Then equilibrium for each good is given by

$$f(H, k(NL_b)L_b) = \frac{p^{-\epsilon}}{N} + \frac{N-1}{N} [p(1 + t)]^{-\epsilon}$$

$$= \frac{p^{-\epsilon}}{N} [1 + (N - 1)(1 + t)^{-\epsilon}]. \tag{18}$$

An increase in $t$ shifts the demand curve down, moving equilibrium along the supply curve, with $x$ and $p$ both falling. But the supply curve itself will also shift because of changes in $b$-stage production by the remaining $N - 1$ countries. Differentiate (18) and (10) to obtain the final effects:

$$\hat{L}_b = -\epsilon X \frac{\lambda_z}{\Delta} \frac{dt}{1 + t}, \tag{19}$$

$$\hat{p} = -\epsilon X \frac{\lambda_b \sigma_g + \lambda_z(1 + \sigma_k)\{\sigma_f - [\sigma_k/(1 + \sigma_k)]\}}{\Delta} \frac{dt}{1 + t},$$

where

$$\Delta \equiv \epsilon \lambda_b \sigma_g + \lambda_z(1 + \sigma_k)\left[\theta_{Lx} + \epsilon\left(\sigma_f - \frac{\sigma_k}{1 + \sigma_k}\right)\right],$$

$$\theta_{Lx} \equiv \frac{wL_b}{px}, \quad X \equiv \frac{x - (p^{-\epsilon}/N)}{x}.$$

I make the following assumption.

ASSUMPTION 2. Suppose that the following condition is met: $\sigma_f > \sigma_k/(1 + \sigma_k)$. Then an increase in the tariff does lower both $p$ and $L_b$.

Note that assumption 1 does not imply assumption 2, so that, with assumption 1 alone, global protection could conceivably raise $L_b$ and influence $p$ in either direction. But, with assumption 2, which does imply assumption 1, $p$ falls proportionately less than the tariff itself: The domestic price of imported goods rises. In a symmetric equilibrium there are no terms-of-trade effects, and the reduction in $L_b$ worsens the distortion because of the presence of an externality, so the welfare of each country is reduced, relative to free trade.

## A Nash Equilibrium in Policy: Unilateralism

Consider next the conduct of trade policy in a single developed country, given the policies of the remaining $N - 1$ countries. I assume that $N$ is sufficiently large that the single country behaves as though its actions have no effect on the world prices of traded goods or on the global size of $b$-stage production.[9] Then the equilibrium of such a country corresponding to a choice of $t$ is described by

$$f(H, kL_b) = \frac{p^{-\epsilon}}{N} + \frac{P}{p}\frac{N-1}{N}[P(1 + t)]^{-\epsilon},$$

$$pf_L(H, kL_b)k - g_L(U, L - L_b) = 0. \tag{20}$$

Production of the national good equals domestic demand plus the exports required, at world prices, to pay for imports. The term $P$ denotes the relative price, in terms of home commodities, of each of the $N - 1$ foreign goods. The small-country assumption is that the home government proceeds as though $k$ and $P/p$ are exogenous. Then (20) gives

$$\hat{L}_b = \epsilon X \frac{\lambda_z}{\Delta'}\frac{dt}{1 + t},$$

$$\hat{P} = \hat{p} = -\epsilon X \frac{\lambda_z \sigma_f + \lambda_b \sigma_g}{\Delta'}\frac{dt}{1 + t}, \tag{21}$$

where $\Delta' \equiv \lambda_z \theta_{Lx} + \epsilon(\lambda_z \sigma_f + \lambda_b \sigma_g)$. Thus an increase in $t$ lowers both $p$ and $L_b$. The reductions in $p$ and $P$ constitute a rise in the price of nontraded commodities relative to traded goods. Protection deflects

[9] Each country conducts trade policy by separately choosing $N - 1$ import constraints, symmetry assuring that the $N - 1$ choices are all the same; no deliberate export policy is chosen. This is important: While the small-country assumption can be appealed to as justification for each country's perceiving no influence in each of its import markets or on global economies of scale, the country is nonetheless the sole supplier of its own good.

spending from imported goods to commodities, raising their price and drawing skilled labor away from the production of goods. This in turn raises the reward of unskilled labor:

$$\hat{w} = \epsilon X \frac{\lambda_b \sigma_{gx}}{\Delta'} \frac{dt}{1+t},$$ (22)

where $\sigma_{gx} \equiv L_z(g_{UL}/g_L)$. With terms-of-trade effects and external scale effects both absent, the effect of a tariff change on utility, measured in terms of the numeraire, is simply the change in import volume multiplied by $tp$, the excess of the social value of a marginal import over its social cost:

$$\frac{du}{dt} = tp \frac{d\left\{\frac{N-1}{N}[(1+t)p]^{-\epsilon}\right\}}{dt}.$$ (23)

The effect on the government's objective is

$$\frac{dV}{dt} = r\frac{dw}{dt} + (1-r)\frac{du}{dt}.$$

Note that $dV/dt > 0$ if $t = 0$: The government will always wish to institute some protection because, with $t$ initially zero, protection will produce a first-order increase in the wage of unskilled labor with no first-order effect on utility. From (22) and (23), $dV/dt = 0$ when

$$t^2 + \Lambda t - \frac{r}{1-rL_z}\frac{x}{} = 0,$$ (24)

with $\Lambda \equiv X\Delta' + \Delta' - X$. The positive solution to this quadratic equation defines the optimum (unilateral) tariff:

$$t^U = \frac{\left(\Lambda^2 + 4\frac{r}{1-rL_z}\frac{x}{}\right)^{1/2} - \Lambda}{2}.$$ (25)

The symmetric noncooperative equilibrium is given by (10), (18), and (25), which simultaneously determine $L_b$, $p$, and $t$.

*Multilateralism*

I now consider the possibility of multilateral trade liberalization by the developed countries. In such a multilateral equilibrium, each developed country adopts the policy that is optimal, if all other developed countries adopt the *same* policy, given the policies adopted by the less developed countries. That is, the developed countries jointly choose a common $t$. The less developed countries do not participate in the multilateral process, and I continue to assume that each has chosen a policy of autarky.

## Multilateral Equilibrium

Let $t^M$ denote the optimal multilateral tariff, and let $t^\circ$ denote what this tariff would be if the developed countries ignored all terms-of-trade effects and scale effects of a tariff reduction, but otherwise took account of the fact that equations (19), rather than (21), indicate the effects on $L_b$ and $p$ when a tariff reduction is multilateral rather than unilateral. Because of the symmetry there will, in fact, be no terms-of-trade effects. If assumption 2 is met, however, a reduction in $t$ will raise the common $L_b$, producing a positive scale effect. Since a small reduction of $t$ below $t^\circ$ will have a zero first-order effect on each government's objective function other than the positive scale effect, it must be that $t^M < t^\circ$ as long as assumption 2 holds.

Next, $t^\circ$ is, by definition, given by formula (25), with $\Delta'$ replaced by $\Delta$. Thus $t^\circ < t^U$ if $\Delta > \Delta'$, and, given assumption 2, a sufficient condition for this is the following assumption.

ASSUMPTION 3. $\theta_{Lx} > 1/(1 + \sigma_k)$.

Thus assumptions 2 and 3 provide sufficient (but by no means necessary) conditions that multilateralism produce a common tariff lower than that resulting from unilateral tariff setting.

## Multilateralism: Summary

Proposition 1 summarizes the results of this section.

PROPOSITION 1. *Multilateralism.*—Suppose that assumptions 2 and 3 hold and that each less developed country chooses a policy of autarky. Then if a symmetric unilateral equilibrium among the developed countries is replaced by a symmetric multilateral equilibrium, (1) the common tariff falls; (2) *b*-stage production of each good rises, enhancing scale effects; and (3) the welfare of each developed country increases.

*Remarks.*—This section has developed, as a basic building block, a rudimentary theory of multilateralism. To be useful for the model, the theory must mimic, in a stylized and transparent way, the essentials of post–World War II experience. I now try to indicate the distinctive features of this theory.

*First*, in this model no country attempts to manipulate the terms of trade to its advantage. I ensure this by abstracting from export policy and by imposing a small-country assumption, but it really reflects a belief that such attempts have just not been important in practice.[10] For this reason I want to make it clear that I do not *require* terms-of-trade manipulation; introducing such manipulation would strengthen further the incentive for multilateral cooperation and so would complicate the model to no purpose.[11] The absence of terms-of-trade manipulation does imply a critical role for special interests: Countries would otherwise adopt free trade unilaterally.

*Second*, national concern for social welfare also plays a key role. Countries would have no incentive to enter into multilateral arrangements otherwise.

*Third*, the purpose of multilateralism in this model is to internalize an externality: The development of a multilateral trading system confers benefits of technological spillovers, external economies of scale, and so forth on all participants. Jointly setting their commercial policies allows countries collectively to address this. This model expresses these beneficial effects in terms of the single technology parameter $k$. Consequently, it is tempting to index the benefits as $B = k^M - k^U$, where $k^U$ and $k^M$ denote, respectively, the value of $k$ in the unilateral equilibrium and in the multilateral equilibrium.

*Fourth*, the theory assumes, in contrast to much recent literature,[12] that individual countries can in fact credibly commit themselves to the multilateral policy even though, ex post, each government will not be doing the best it can—according to its own objective function—given the policies of the other governments. In practice, this has simply not been a significant problem with respect to the General Agreement on Tariffs and Trade (GATT)–sponsored rounds of multilateral tariff reductions by the industrial countries.[13] When these countries have retreated from liberal trade, they have done so not by repudiating in violation of the GATT the tariff bindings they have undertaken, but by utilizing other, internationally accepted tools (safeguards, antidumping duties, etc.) or by stepping outside the GATT structure (voluntary export constraints). Consideration of these latter possibilities is not needed for the purposes of this paper, and I want to keep the model of multilateralism as simple as possible.[14] Also, I would stray too far from my purpose were I to

---

[10] For an alternative view, see Bagwell and Staiger (1996).

[11] See Yi (1996) for a very different model in which endogenous integration is driven by the presence of terms-of-trade manipulation.

[12] For example, Bond and Syropoulos (1996) distinguish multilateralism from regionalism by assuming that, in the former, countries cannot precommit.

[13] It has sometimes been a problem in other contexts, such as China and the protection of intellectual property.

[14] An earlier version of this paper did in fact contain administered protection not determined multilaterally, but I deleted it because it had no fundamental effect on the theory of regionalism developed below. Instead, I address it in Ethier (1998c).

introduce features (e.g., trigger strategies in a repeated-game frame-work) to furnish explicit support for the multilateral equilibrium. So I simply assume that credible commitment to the multilateral policy is provided by something exogenous to the model. Presumably a higher value of the benefits index $B$ would, other things equal, render such commitment easier, but consideration of such issues is beyond the scope of this paper.

## V.  Regionalism

The previous section assumed both that $r_1^*$ was sufficiently large that $R(k) < r_1^*$ for the $k$ determined in the unilateral equilibrium and that the less developed countries did not participate in the multilateral process. These assumptions in effect excluded the less developed countries from the model. Now I bring them back in. I assume the following sequence of moves. Initially, the developed countries are in a unilateral equilibrium and the less developed countries have each chosen autarky. Then the developed countries, without participation by the less developed countries, negotiate the multilateral equilibrium and implement it. Next, the less developed countries observe $t^M$ and the multilateral equilibrium value of $k$ and *individually* decide whether to reform or not, taking $t^M$ and $k$ as given. Finally, the reform efforts are made, they succeed or fail, and a new international equilibrium emerges, with $t$ still fixed at $t^M$ but $k$ determined endogenously.

### *Multilateralism and the Less Developed Countries*

### Implications of Multilateralism for the Less Developed Countries

With assumptions 2 and 3, multilateralism will produce a lower tariff, and this could affect the less developed countries' unilateral choices of policy. From (19), the lower tariff will increase $L_b$, causing $k$ to rise. The value of $R(k)$, increasing in $k$, also increases: Multilateralism increases the motivation for the less developed countries to reform. Interest centers on the case in which $R$ rises enough so that some countries do indeed embark on reform. So I make the following assumption.

ASSUMPTION 4. $R(k^U) < r_1^* < R(k^M)$.

Assumption 4 ensures that all less developed countries choose autarky in the unilateral equilibrium and that some will attempt reform in the multilateral equilibrium if the probability of success $\rho$ is sufficiently high.

An attempted reform in a less developed country will succeed if and only if some firms from the developed countries undertake direct investment there, so I turn to this question next. Direct investment will introduce trade in *b*-stage products, so developed-country barriers to such trade must now be considered. Suppose that imports of *b* into the developed countries are subject to protection at the (possibly negative) rate $t_b$. I postpone discussion of how $t_b$ is determined.

If there is no direct investment, the cost, in terms of *b*, of obtaining a marginal unit of *b* by production in the home developed country is $\omega/pk = f_L(H, kL_b)$, and the cost of obtaining it by establishing a foreign subsidiary in some less developed country is $\omega^*(1 + t_b)/k = \alpha(1 + t_b)$. Thus direct investment will be undertaken—and a reform attempt by some less developed country will be successful—if, in the multilateral equilibrium with no direct investment, $f_L(H, kL_b) > \alpha(1 + t_b)$.

PROPOSITION 2. Suppose that assumptions 2, 3, and 4 hold. Then if the developed countries shift from a unilateral equilibrium to a multilateral equilibrium, some less developed countries will attempt reform if the probability of success is high enough. Such an attempt would be successful in some countries if, in the multilateral equilibrium, $f_L(H, kL_b) > \alpha(1 + t_b)$.

## International Equilibrium

Next, consider a symmetric equilibrium in which the developed countries undertake direct investment in a set of reformed less developed countries. Let *m* denote the total employment of skilled labor by the foreign subsidiaries of each developed country. Assume an interior solution in which the developed countries transfer some, but not all, *b*-stage employment of skilled labor abroad, and not all of the skilled labor of the reformed less developed countries is employed by foreign subsidiaries. Equilibrium for each good is described as follows:

$$f(H, k(N(L_b + m))(L_b + m)) = \frac{p^{-\epsilon}}{N}[1 + (N - 1)(1 + t)^{-\epsilon}]$$

$$+ \alpha k(N(L_b + m))m,$$

$$f_L(H, k(N(L_b + m))(L_b + m)) = \alpha(1 + t_b),$$

$$pf_L(H, k(N(L_b + m))(L_b + m)) = g_L(U, L - L_b).$$

(26)

The first equation of (26) requires that the supply of each good equal the total of demand at home, demand from other developed countries, and demand from less developed countries; the second that direct investment proceed until the cost of skilled labor to the firm is the same abroad as at home; and the third that the value of the marginal product of skilled labor be equated across alternative uses at home.

If, instead of an interior solution, each developed country shifts all $b$-stage production abroad, $L_b = 0$ and the third equation of (26) is dropped. If, on the other hand, all the skilled labor of each reformed less developed country is employed by foreign firms, $m = M_R L^*/N$, where $M_R$ denotes the number of countries undertaking successful reform and $L^*$ attains its maximal value, and the first equation of (26) is dropped.

Equations (26) determine $p$, $m$, and $L_b$, given $N$, $t$, $t_b$, and the endowment of each developed country. Note that (26) is independent of the number of less developed countries that undertake ($M_R^*$) or successfully implement ($M_R$) reform and that (26) does not determine how the total direct investment $Nm$ is distributed among the reformers. A symmetric equilibrium would allocate $Nm$ among all $M_R^*$ in equal amounts $F = Nm/M_R^*$, thus ensuring that $M_R = M_R^*$. But there is no reason to expect this outcome because, from the viewpoint of the investing firms, all less developed countries are identical. So I assume that, when all potential hosts are equivalent, investing firms decide where to invest, among all potential hosts, by some random process.

If $Nm > (M_R^* - 1)L^*$, at least some investment must go to each potential host, so $\rho = 1$ and $M_R = M_R^*$. But otherwise distributions of $Nm$ that leave some potential hosts without foreign subsidiaries do exist. With the location of direct investment determined at random,

$$\rho(M_R^*, m) = \phi\left[\frac{Nm}{(M_R^* - 1)L^*}\right],\qquad(27)$$

where $\phi$ reflects the random process by which investment is allocated. Assume that $\phi = 0$ if $m = 0$, $\phi = 1$ if $Nm > (M_R^* - 1)L^*$, and $\phi' > 0$ otherwise. Clearly $\rho$ is decreasing in $M_R^*$ and increasing in $m$ whenever its argument is less than unity.

Equations (26) determine $k$ and $m$, and (17) and (27) then simultaneously determine $\rho$ and $M_R^*$, and thus $M_R = \rho M_R^*$ as well. Since $\rho$ and $M_R^*$ are positively related in (17) and negatively related in (27), the solution is unique. Thus a switch from unilateralism to multilateralism induces some ($M_R$) less developed countries to reform successfully, some ($M_R - M_R^*$) to attempt reform and fail, and some ($\int_i^{i'} M(j)$, where $r_i^* = \rho R(k)$ and $r_i^* = R(k)$) to wish to reform but to refrain from trying because of the fear of failure. The condition for this is the following assumption.

ASSUMPTION 5. With multilateralism and no investment, $f_L(H, kL_b) > \alpha(1 + t_b)$; with multilateralism and investment, $Nm < (M_R^* - 1)L^*$.

In summary, I present the following proposition.

PROPOSITION 3. *Unilateral reform.*—Suppose that assumptions 2–5 hold. Then if the developed countries shift from unilateralism to multilateralism, some less developed countries will attempt reform and succeed, some will attempt reform and fail, and some will wish to reform but not attempt it.

## Implications of Reform for the Multilateral System

Successful reform by some less developed countries will influence the international equilibrium and thereby affect the developed countries. To investigate, suppose that $m = 0$ initially and ask what effect an introduction of direct investment ($dm$) will have on $L_b$. This can be deduced by differentiating the first and third equations of (26), solving, and evaluating at $m = 0$:

$$dL_b = -\frac{\lambda_z\theta_{Lx}[\sigma_k + 1 - (w^*/w)] + \epsilon\lambda_z[\sigma_f(1 - \sigma_k) - \sigma_k]}{\lambda_z\theta_{Lx}(\sigma_k + 1) + \epsilon\lambda_z[\sigma_f(1 - \sigma_k) - \sigma_k] + \epsilon\lambda_b\sigma_g} dm. \quad (28)$$

It thus follows from assumption 1 (or from assumption 2) that $dL_b < 0$ but $dL_b + dm > 0$. Reform causes the developed countries to lose second-stage jobs for skilled workers, but it creates such jobs worldwide. As a consequence, $k$ rises, and, therefore, $B$ does also.

PROPOSITION 4. Suppose that assumptions 2–5 hold. Then if the developed countries shift from unilateralism to multilateralism, the successful reforms by some less developed countries that follow will lower developed-country employment in $b$-stage production and increase world employment.

There are two important implications. *First,* reform raises the social welfare of the developed countries and the income of unskilled workers: Both components of the government's objective function rise. *Second,* the implied increase in $k$ means that the benefit index $B$ of being part of the multilateral system increases. Presumably this would enhance the strength of the commitment to that system.[15]

Thus far I have treated $t_b$ as arbitrary, but in what follows it will prove convenient to know something of its magnitude. Also, the emergence of positive direct investment in this section suggests the possibility that the developed countries' objective function be modi-

---

[15] This statement is speculative since this paper does not model any commitment mechanism.

fied to reflect the fact that direct investment has long been a contentious policy issue.

The multilateral negotiations cannot have determined $t_b$ since any nonnegative value is consistent with the multilateral equilibrium with all less developed countries in autarky. Also, setting $t_b = t^M$ is not satisfactory: As will be clear below, this will in general give each developed country an incentive unilaterally to reduce $t_b$. Instead I proceed as follows.

First, add to each developed-country government's objective function a third component, nonpositively related to $m$.[16] Second, suppose that $t_b$ is at its symmetric Nash equilibrium value in the equilibrium described by (26). That is, $t_b$ maximizes each developed country's objective function, in (26), given the multilateral solution $t = t^M$ and given that every other developed country has implemented the same $t_b$.[17]

Since reform affects the international equilibrium, it will induce the developed countries to renegotiate the multilateral tariff, and this would in turn induce a reconsideration in some less developed countries of whether to reform, and so on. One could analyze the outcome of such a sequence of events or, equivalently, analyze the multilateral process on the assumption that all countries correctly forecast the equilibrium response of the less developed countries and take this into account. The world negotiates the full equilibrium initially and directly implements it.

But this exercise is left to the reader: My interest is the direct implication of multilateral liberalization by the developed countries for policy reform in the less developed countries. There are two reasons. First, consideration of the full equilibrium promises to add nothing of interest. If the developed countries accurately forecast the equilibrium response of the less developed countries, they will negotiate a multilateral tariff, $t^F$, no higher than if they do not: $t^F \leq t^M$. The reason is that they anticipate (correctly) that a given reduction in $t$ will produce a larger increase in $k$ when less developed countries are induced to reform than when they are not. Propositions 1–4 (as well as propositions 5 and 6 to come) continue to hold, with $t^F$ replacing $t^M$, so that the message of this paper would be unchanged. Working back to write down the equations determining $t^F$ is a purely technical exercise. Second, the limited sequence described in this

---

[16] Note that this is consistent with a zero weight, i.e., with continuing to use (14).

[17] This does not require that $t_b > 0$. This can be assured by giving significant negative weight to $m$ in the government's objective function or by adding other components to that function reflecting the welfare of human capital or of skilled labor. I do not assume this, however.

paper appears to parallel history better than an initial negotiation of the final outcome would.

### Regionalism

I next introduce the possibility of regional arrangements between developed countries and less developed countries. Assume that such arrangements can be initiated after the developed countries switch from the unilateral equilibrium to the multilateral one, and while the less developed countries are considering whether to reform or not. I define such an arrangement as follows.

DEFINITION. *Regionalism.*—A regional arrangement is an agreement between one developed country and one less developed country in which (*a*) the less developed country agrees to attempt reform and to levy a tariff of $t^L$ on imports of goods from all developed countries other than those of its partner, whose goods will not be subject to duty; and (*b*) the developed country agrees to make a marginal reduction, $dt_b < 0$, in the duty applicable to *b*-stage output imported from its partner country.

Note that this definition is motivated directly by the stylized facts described in Section II. Writing the reform attempt into the agreement reflects deep integration, making the developed-country tariff reduction marginal reflects asymmetric liberalization, and so forth.

A less developed country that attempts reform without entering into a regional initiative is assumed to set $t^L = 0$ without discrimination. Thus a less developed country is now allowed to choose either of two roads to reform: unilateral, nondiscriminatory free trade or bilateral preferential trade.[18] Assuming that $t^L > 0$ only with regionalism avoids stacking the deck in the latter's favor.

### A Regional Initiative

The first task is to inquire whether any such regional arrangements will be negotiated. Suppose, then, that the developed countries have moved from a unilateral to a multilateral equilibrium and that assumptions 4 and 5 hold. Then some less developed countries will want to attempt reform, but $\rho < 1$. Consider how a regional arrangement would affect such a country.

---

[18] It is easy to see that a nondiscriminatory $t^L > 0$ will not in general be consistent with a Nash equilibrium for the less developed countries. Thus consideration of a nondiscriminatory protective policy would require that the model be given more structure.

The arrangement would commit the country to undertaking reform. This is a big commitment, but the country wants to do it anyway. The trade preference implies that all imports will come from the partner country, so that $t^L$ will be prohibitive, regardless of its positive level. This might cause the country's trade pattern to differ greatly from what it would be without a regional arrangement, but, again, this is of no consequence since the less developed country regards all goods as perfect substitutes. But the preferential reduction in $t_b$, though only marginal, is much more significant. From the point of view of firms considering direct investment to produce $b$-stage output for the partner country's good, all less developed countries choosing reform are completely equivalent, except for this marginal preference. Thus it serves to attract all such investment.[19] This ensures that the reform effort will succeed: In effect $\rho$ becomes equal to unity when the country signs the regional arrangement because of the "investment diversion" that the arrangement implies.

There will also be "investment creation." Distinguish variables pertaining to the developed country entering the regional arrangement by a degree symbol. Then equilibrium is described by

$$f(H, k((N-1)(L_b + m) + L_b^\circ + m^\circ)(L_b^\circ + m^\circ))$$

$$= \frac{(p^\circ)^{-\epsilon}}{N}[1 + (N-1)(1+t)^{-\epsilon}]$$

$$+ \alpha k((N-1)(L_b + m) + L_b^\circ + m^\circ)m^\circ, \qquad (29)$$

$$f_L(H, k((N-1)(L_b + m) + L_b^\circ + m^\circ)(L_b^\circ + m^\circ)) = \alpha(1 + t_b^\circ),$$

$$p^\circ f_L(H, k((N-1)(L_b + m) + L_b^\circ + m^\circ)(L_b^\circ + m^\circ)) = g_L(U, L - L_b^\circ)$$

and

$$f(H, k((N-1)(L_b + m) + L_b^\circ + m^\circ)(L_b + m))$$

$$= \frac{p^{-\epsilon}}{N}[1 + (N-1)(1+t)^{-\epsilon}]$$

$$+ \alpha k((N-1)(L_b + m) + L_b^\circ + m^\circ)m, \qquad (30)$$

$$f_L(H, k((N-1)(L_b + m) + L_b^\circ + m^\circ)(L_b + m)) = \alpha(1 + t_b),$$

$$pf_L(H, k((N-1)(L_b + m) + L_b^\circ + m^\circ)(L_b + m)) = g_L(U, L - L_b).$$

Equations (29) describe equilibrium for the developed country that is entering into a regional arrangement, and equations (30) describe the equilibrium of each of the remaining $N - 1$ developed

[19] Provided, of course, that $L^*$ is large enough to accommodate all such investment. Boundary solutions will be left to the reader.

countries. To see the effect of a regional initiative, suppose that (29) and (30) are initially identical and differentiate them, with $dt_b^o < 0 = dt_b$. From the second equation of (29) and the second equation of (30),

$$\frac{d(L_b^o + m^o)}{L_b^o + m^o} = - \frac{N + (N-1)\sigma_k}{\sigma_f N(1 + \sigma_k)} \frac{dt_b^o}{1 + t_b} > 0,$$

$$\frac{d(L_b + m)}{L_b + m} = - \frac{\sigma_k}{\sigma_f N(1 + \sigma_k)} \frac{dt_b^o}{1 + t_b} < 0, \quad (31)$$

$$\frac{N-1}{N} \frac{d(L_b + m)}{L_b + m} + \frac{1}{N} \frac{d(L_b^o + m^o)}{L_b^o + m^o} = - \frac{1}{\sigma_f N(1 + \sigma_k)} \frac{dt_b^o}{1 + t_b} > 0.$$

Thus the total labor allocated, worldwide, to production of the good of the partner developed country increases and the labor devoted to production of all other developed countries' goods falls; but the former effect dominates, so that $k$ increases, with the international spillovers this implies. The first and third equations of (29) imply that this will come about via an increase in $m^o$ and a smaller fall in $L_b^o$. These effects will not be large—I am talking about marginal changes here—but the direction is unambiguous.

Now consider the effect of a regional arrangement from the point of view of a potential developed-country partner. Such a country obtains a secure less-developed-country market for its good as a result of the preference it receives. But this may be of no real consequence: In equilibrium its export of goods to all less developed countries must equal the wage bill paid by its foreign subsidiaries, whether there is a regional arrangement or not. The developed country benefits from the agreement because of the investment creation it generates. This will produce a favorable effect on *social* welfare, but the marginal change in $t_b$ will have a zero first-order effect on the *government's* objective function since $t_b$ has been assumed to have been optimally set. The principal gain to the government is merely the assurance that it will not find itself facing a tariff of $t^L$—and thus higher production costs for its good—in the event that all reforming less developed countries conclude regional arrangements with other developed countries. Thus the government of a developed country may see little to gain from a regional arrangement. But it has nothing at all to lose, and its potential partner has much to gain. Thus it is reasonable to expect that, if necessary, a side payment by the potential partner would produce such an agreement. For this reason I assume that developed countries would agree to enter into regional arrangements. Furthermore, other developed countries should not

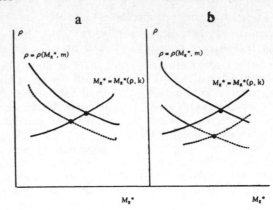

FIG. 1.—Reform destruction. *a*, No reform creation; *b*, reform creation

object to the regional arrangement because the only effect on them will be the favorable rise in $k$.

But the regional arrangement will not be uniformly benign. Other less developed countries wishing to reform will be harmed. Suppose that one less developed country enters into a regional arrangement, and suppose that this is a country that would undertake reform even in the absence of such an arrangement. Then the direct investment producing *b*-stage output for that country's partner will all be diverted there. Thus the numerator of the argument of $\phi$ in equation (27) falls by $m$; the denominator is unaffected since the less developed country with the regional arrangement still remains a potential host for other direct investment. Therefore, each value of $M_R^*$ now corresponds to a lower value of $\rho$ in equation (27) than before: The function shifts down (see fig. 1*a*). Equation (17) is unaffected. Accordingly, (17) and (27) now jointly determine lower values of both $\rho$ and $M_R^*$ than without the arrangement. Regionalism produces "reform destruction" by causing fewer countries to attempt reform and lowering the proportion of those that succeed.

Suppose now that the less developed country is one that, in the absence of the regional arrangement, would not have attempted reform at all. This can be termed "reform creation." Then the numerator of the argument of $\phi$ in equation (27) still falls by $m$, but the denominator now also rises by $L^*$ since the number of potential hosts increases by one. Thus (27) shifts down even more than before, tending to reduce both $\rho$ and $M_R^*$ more than before. But, in addition, (17) now shifts to the right by one, again because the number of potential hosts increases by one. This tends to nullify the fall in $M_R^*$ but further accentuate that in $\rho$ (see fig. 1*b*). Thus the probability of success falls even more than before, but the number of countries attempting reform may either rise or fall, depending on the balance between reform creation and reform destruction.

PROPOSITION 5. *Regionalism.*—Suppose that assumptions 2–5 hold. Then if the developed countries shift from unilateralism to multilateralism, both the developed countries and the less developed countries would each wish to enter into regional arrangements. If one such arrangement takes place, (*a*) the less developed participant will successfully implement its reform by attracting all direct investment intended to supply *b*-stage output to its partner (investment diversion); (*b*) the opportunity to enter into the arrangement may induce a less developed country to reform that would otherwise not have attempted to do so (reform creation); (*c*) the arrangement will induce the developed-country partner to invest more abroad (investment creation); (*d*) equilibrium *k* will rise, conferring spillover benefits on all developed countries and on all less developed countries that successfully reform, and increasing the benefit *B* of multilateral liberalization; and (*e*) the number of less developed countries—other than the participant—that attempt reform will fall, as will their probability of success (reform destruction).

## Regional Equilibrium

Proposition 5 describes the consequences of a single regional arrangement. But all developed countries would be willing to participate in such an arrangement, and all less developed countries that attempt reform will wish to do so. Furthermore, the reduction in $\rho$ brought about by one initiative would, if anything, strengthen the resolve of the other less developed countries to do the same thing, and individual developed countries would also become more tempted as more less developed countries link up with other developed countries. So consider the international equilibrium that would emerge if all countries are allowed freely to enter into such arrangements. The fact that regional arrangements have become so widespread suggests that analysis of such a regional equilibrium is more important than that of a single arrangement.

I have defined a regional arrangement as one between a single developed country and a single less developed country. But I do not mean to exclude the possibility that one country might enter into several arrangements with different partners, thus, in effect, allowing larger groupings. Then, regardless of the relative number of developed and less developed countries, all can potentially participate in some arrangement. But there are some possible constraints.

The first is that, if many less developed countries enter into arrangements with a single developed country, these arrangements may not guarantee the success of their reform efforts. The reason is that, although the arrangements will divert investment from non-participants to participants, there is nothing to guarantee that it will be distributed among all participants. Suppose that $M_{RR}$ less developed countries establish regional arrangements with one developed country. The condition $m > (M_{RR} - 1)L^*$ guarantees the success of each country's reform effort. A less developed country will never enter into a regional agreement that violates this condition if an agreement with some other developed country would not violate it. Thus regional groupings would emerge in such a way as to satisfy the requirement, if that is possible. The number of less developed countries that would wish to undertake reform if they could be certain of its success is $M_R^*(1, k)$. Then the condition that guarantees that it is possible to accommodate all less developed countries that wish with regional arrangements that guarantee the success of their reforms is the following.

ASSUMPTION 6. $N[(m/L^*) + 1] > M_R^*(1, k)$.

The second possible constraint concerns whether a country that has already entered into one regional arrangement would be willing to enter into another arrangement as well. Consider first the decision of a developed country. If its partner is not large enough to supply fully its need for $b$-stage goods from abroad, this country will have every reason to take on another partner. But with an interior solution, the developed country has nothing to gain from a second arrangement. It has nothing to lose either, and its potential partner has much to gain. Thus it is again reasonable to expect that a side payment by the potential partner would produce such an agreement, and I accordingly assume that developed countries would agree to enter into multiple arrangements.

Now consider whether a less developed country would be willing to undertake additional arrangements. They would attract more investment, but, with the success of its reform effort already guaranteed by one arrangement, there is no benefit to this. The less developed country has nothing to gain from additional arrangements, but nothing to lose either. The developed country, on the other hand, now has much to gain. With all less developed countries linked to developed countries through regional arrangements, the developed country without such a link will find its exports of goods required to pay for the labor employed in its foreign subsidiaries subject to the tariff of $t^L$, even though it must pay the same wage as everyone else. Since one party has much to gain and the other nothing to lose, I again assume that such an arrangement would be negotiated.

The nature of the regional equilibrium should now be apparent. With assumption 6, all developed countries, and all less developed countries that wish to reform if $\rho = 1$, will be involved in regional arrangements that guarantee the success of all the reform efforts. Reform destruction will not take place, but reform creation will.

PROPOSITION 6. *Regional equilibrium.*–Suppose that assumptions 2–5 hold. Then if the developed countries shift from unilateralism to multilateralism and assumption 6 also holds, and if regional arrangements are freely allowed, a regional equilibrium with the following characteristics will emerge: (*a*) The *N* developed countries will establish regional arrangements with $M_R^*(1, k)$ less developed countries. (*b*) Relative to the equilibrium without regionalism, more less developed countries undertake reform and more (i.e., all) of them succeed (reform creation). (*c*) Relative to the equilibrium without regionalism, more foreign direct investment takes place (investment creation), *k* is greater, and so is the benefit *B* of multilateral liberalization. (*d*) Relative to the equilibrium without regionalism, both social welfare and the value of each developed country's objective function are higher. (*e*) Exports of goods from the developed countries to the less developed countries are free of duty.

*Remarks.*—Several distinct features of this approach to regionalism should be noted. *First,* the major role of regionalism in this model is to facilitate reform in the less developed countries. A secondary role (because it is done marginally) is to stimulate investment.

*Second,* the relation between multilateralism and regionalism in this model is benign. Regionalism is the consequence of multilateral success, not failure, and it in turn strengthens rather than undermines the basis for a commitment to the multilateral order.

*Third,* I have used the terms "investment creation" and "investment diversion" to acknowledge one way in which the present theory does parallel the Vinerian paradigm. But in fact the analogy is much more apparent than real. For example, trade diversion is the major negative influence in the Vinerian world, but investment diversion is strongly positive here, as the force behind the major benefit of regionalism.

*Fourth,* in this model regional arrangements are ways in which reforming countries compete among themselves for direct investment. In reality they of course can compete in other ways as well, such as with subsidies, tax holidays, and the like. If these methods are used *in addition to* regionalism, the concerns of this paper remain relevant. Not so if they are used *instead*. There are two reasons to expect that this will not be so. Regionalism is a costless way to compete. But this could be only an artifact of my special assumptions, so the second reason is more important. Regardless of whether other incentives are present, direct investment will be sensitive to the credibility of the announced reform effort. Analysis of this would require additional modeling, but one suspects that such an analysis would complement and reinforce the present one. A regional arrangement establishes an external commitment to reform that (weakly, perhaps) binds future governments, thereby making the future preservation of reform (slightly, perhaps) more credible. This in turn makes the country more attractive for direct investment, relative to similar countries without such external commitments. The role of deep integration in this model is to write a commitment to reform into an arrangement with a big country that is a natural enforcer and, as a result of the investment induced by the arrangement, has an interest in enforcing it. Only regionalism has this property, so it can be expected to be employed even if other tools are used as well.

*Fifth,* in this model the global interest is served if reform is as widespread as possible, that is, if direct investment flows to all those countries that want to reform. But no agent has an interest in ensuring this: There is another externality here. The regional equilibrium serves as an invisible hand inducing competition among reforming countries in a form that effectively disperses direct investment.

*Sixth,* the discussion following proposition 4 pointed out that a full equilibrium had not been described, and suggested that multilateral liberalization could be stronger if it were performed by countries correctly anticipating the equilibrium responses of reformers who also correctly anticipated the nature of the final equilibrium. The same discussion applies now. Furthermore, the full equilibrium multilateral tariff when a regional equilibrium is correctly anticipated, $t^{FR}$, could well differ from the full equilibrium when it is correctly anticipated that regionalism will not be allowed, $t^F$ again. The regional equilibrium maximizes the extent of successful reform. Then a given reduction in $t$ can be expected to cause $k$ to rise by no less if a regional equilibrium is correctly anticipated than it would if the world were constrained away from that equilibrium. Thus I expect $t^{FR} \leq t^F \leq t^M$. An equilibrium with a lower $t$ is characterized by a larger $k$, a larger $B$, and a larger $M_R^*(1, k)$, yet another sense in which multilateralism and regionalism are mutually beneficial.

## VI.  Concluding Remarks

This paper described the stylized facts of the new regionalism and then constructed a simple formal model suggested by those facts. Analysis of that model generated a theory of regionalism, quite different from the standard Vinerian perspective, with strong conclusions about the nature and implications of regional integration.

The argument that is suggested consists of several components that give crucial roles to the success of postwar multilateralism, the role of direct investment, and policy reform in many countries. (1) The small-country participants in regional arrangements have embarked on programs of policy reform intended, at least in part, to enhance the role of international trade. (2) Direct investment has been surging since the late 1980s. (3) Reforming countries anxious to join the multilateral trading system as soon as possible see the attraction of foreign direct investment as a key step. (4) Attracting foreign direct investment requires making the country attractive relative to other, similar potential hosts, not relative to source countries.[20] (5) Regional arrangements can give a small country a marginal advantage—over other, similar, small countries—in attracting direct investment because they obtain marginally more favorable access to a large market than other nonparticipating small countries. (6) The regional arrangements, by in effect internalizing a critical externality, help spread the benefits of the multilateral trading system around the globe and enhance its value to all participants, thereby reinforcing, rather than undermining, support for multilateralism.

This paper developed a very special model and then imposed specific assumptions on its parameters, so I should offer some comments on robustness. *First*, assumptions 2–6 are sufficient conditions for my results, not necessary conditions. Furthermore, possible consequences of their failure can be examined in a straightforward way and do not threaten the validity of the basic approach of this paper.

*Second*, my results are obviously sensitive to the very special structure of my model. But that structure was chosen neither at random nor with a view to obtaining the present results. Instead it is intended to reflect—accurately but in sharp relief—just those features that I argued do in fact define the new regionalism. Indeed, relaxing some of the assumptions would likely strengthen the conclusions: Allowing countries to manipulate directly their terms of trade just increases the motivation for multilateralism; allowing other subsidiaries themselves to experience some of the externalities conferred on host countries by direct investment would cause that investment to cluster in fewer locations, thereby accentuating the basis for com-

[20] See Brainard and Riker (1997) and Riker and Brainard (1997) for relevant evidence that workers in foreign affiliates of multinational firms compete for jobs primarily with workers in other affiliates located in countries with similar characteristics, rather than with workers in dissimilar source countries.

petition between reforming countries for direct investment. But I want to emphasize two features of the model that I believe are of special importance for the relevance of the paper's conclusions. These are the assumptions that the less developed countries regard all goods as perfect substitutes and that the developed countries regard all the less developed countries as perfect substitutes for the location of $b$-stage production. The consequences of these assumptions are that harmful trade diversion does not emerge and that investment diversion is not harmful in the regional equilibrium. Harmful trade diversion is not absent from my model because countries, in Kemp-Wan (1976) fashion, choose to avoid it; it is absent because I do not let it in. So relaxation of these assumptions has the potential to introduce a downside to regionalism that is at present not in the model. My prime reason for making these assumptions is to abstract from Vinerian concerns and to focus sharply on what is new here. But a consequence of the dramatic change in the world trading environment between the 1950s and the 1990s is that trade diversion is much less important. There may be a huge volume of such diversion—indeed it may well be at an all-time high—but the welfare significance does not have the same order of magnitude as it would have 40 years ago.

*Third,* the formal model described the small-country participants as less developed and modeled them differently than the "large" industrial countries, but only some of the small countries in the examples that motivated this paper can be described as less developed. I suspect that the present analysis applies, in whole or in part, to the other cases as well. For example, the former communist countries of central Europe are eager to attract direct investment, the ultimate success of their reform efforts remains both in doubt and dependent on their ability to attract such investment, and the Europe Agreements have given them a small advantage over other, similar, countries: not by trade preferences, but by a higher implicit likelihood of future integration into the European Union. For small industrialized nations joining the European Union, the problem is not so much to attract new direct investment as to remain attractive sites, in an increasingly integrated world, for activities currently conducted there. The small advantage they obtain is not additional preference, but future participation in E.U. decision making.[21]

*Fourth,* the structure of the model I developed was motivated very strongly by the five stylized facts I described. So the relevance of the model is limited by the relevance of the stylizations. I think this relevance compelling, but I acknowledge that my list of stylized facts

---

[21] For more on this, see Baldwin and Flam (1994).

is neither universal nor exhaustive. There is a lot of diversity out there.

This paper suggests the following relation of regionalism to multilateralism. (1) The new regionalism is a direct result of the success of multilateral liberalization. (2) Regionalism is the means by which new countries enter the multilateral system and a means by which small countries already in it exploit its success. (3) Regionalism is creating new industrial groups with an interest in preserving the liberal trade order.

Of course, any changes—regional initiatives are no exceptions—offer protectionists new scope for their efforts. An argument that regional initiatives reflect causes much more benign than a desire to divide the globe into several highly protected blocs does not establish that this will not in fact be the ultimate result.

### References

Anderson, Kym, and Blackhurst, Richard, eds. *Regional Integration and the Global Trading System.* New York: St. Martin's, 1993.
Bagwell, Kyle, and Staiger, Robert W. "Reciprocal Trade Liberalization." Working Paper no. 5488. Cambridge, Mass.: NBER, March 1996.
———. "Multilateral Tariff Cooperation during the Formation of Customs Unions." *J. Internat. Econ.* 42 (February 1997): 91–123. (*a*)
———. "Multilateral Tariff Cooperation during the Formation of Free Trade Areas." *Internat. Econ. Rev.* 38 (May 1997): 291–319. (*b*)
Baldwin, Richard E. "The Causes of Regionalism." *World Economy* 20 (November 1997): 865–88.
Baldwin, Richard E., and Flam, Harry. "Enlargement of the European Union: The Economic Consequences for the Scandinavian Countries." Occasional Paper no. 16. London: Centre Econ. Policy Res., September 1994.
Bhagwati, Jagdish N., and Panagariya, Arvind. "Preferential Trading Areas and Multilateralism: Strangers, Friends or Foes?" Working Paper no. 22. College Park: Univ. Maryland, Center Internat. Econ., 1996.
Bond, Eric W., and Syropoulos, Constantinos. "Trading Blocs and the Sustainability of Interregional Cooperation." In *The New Transatlantic Economy,* edited by Matthew B. Canzoneri, Wilfred J. Ethier, and Vittorio Grilli. Cambridge: Cambridge Univ. Press, 1996.
Brainard, S. Lael, and Riker, David A. "Are U.S. Multinationals Exporting U.S. Jobs?" Working Paper no. 5958. Cambridge, Mass.: NBER, March 1997.
Chichilnisky, Graciela. "Trading Blocks with Endogenous Technology and Increasing Returns." Manuscript. New York: Columbia Univ., 1994.
de Melo, Jaime, and Panagariya, Arvind, eds. *New Dimensions in Regional Integration.* Cambridge: Cambridge Univ. Press, 1993.
Ethier, Wilfred J. "Internationally Decreasing Costs and World Trade." *J. Internat. Econ.* 9 (February 1979): 1–24.
———. "National and International Returns to Scale in the Modern Theory of International Trade." *A.E.R.* 72 (June 1982): 389–405.

REGIONALISM                                                    1245

————. "Multilateral Roads to Regionalism." In *International Trade Policy and the Pacific Rim*, edited by John Piggott and A. Woodland. London: Macmillan, 1998 (in press). (*a*)

————. "The New Regionalism." *Econ. J.* 108 (July 1998). (*b*)

————. "Unilateralism in a Multilateral World." Manuscript. Philadelphia: Univ. Pennsylvania, Dept. Econ., 1998. (*c*)

Ethier, Wilfred J., and Horn, Henrik. "A New Look at Economic Integration." In *Monopolistic Competition and International Trade,* edited by Henryk Kierzkowski. Oxford: Oxford Univ. Press, 1984.

Freund, Carolyn. "Multilateralism and the Endogenous Formation of PTAs." Manuscript. Washington: Board Governors, Fed. Reserve System, 1997.

Kemp, Murray C., and Wan, Henry Y., Jr. "An Elementary Proposition Concerning the Formation of Customs Unions." *J. Internat. Econ.* 6 (February 1976): 95–97.

Krugman, Paul. "Is Bilateralism Bad?" In *International Trade and Trade Policy*, edited by Elhanan Helpman and Assaf Razin. Cambridge, Mass.: MIT Press, 1991.

Perroni, Carlo, and Whalley, John. "The New Regionalism: Trade Liberalization or Insurance?" Working Paper no. 4626. Cambridge, Mass.: NBER, January 1994.

Riker, David A., and Brainard, S. Lael. "U.S. Multinationals and Competition from Low Wage Countries." Working Paper no. 5959. Cambridge, Mass.: NBER, March 1997.

Yi, Sang-Seung. "Endogenous Formation of Customs Unions under Imperfect Competition: Open Regionalism Is Good." *J. Internat. Econ.* 41 (August 1996): 153–77.

# [19]

# A Political-Economic Analysis of Free-Trade Agreements

*By* Philip I. Levy *

*This paper demonstrates that bilateral free-trade agreements can undermine po-
litical support for further multilateral trade liberalization. If a bilateral trade
agreement offers disproportionately large gains to key agents in a country, then
their reservation utility is raised above the multilateral free-trade level, and a
multilateral agreement would be blocked. Bilateral agreements between countries
with similar factor endowments are most likely to have this effect. It also follows
that bilateral free-trade agreements can never increase political support for multilateral free trade. (JEL F15)*

The recent pursuit of bilateral and regional trade agreements, marked most notably by the conclusion of the North American Free Trade Agreement (NAFTA) and the further lowering of trade barriers in Europe, raises questions about the wisdom of this approach to trade liberalization. Governments have asserted that bilateral free-trade negotiations are compatible with the goal of multilateral trade liberalization,[1] but others (e.g., Jagdish Bhagwati, 1992) have questioned whether bilateral arrangements will eventually lead to broader liberalization.[2]

If trade liberalization is to proceed in stages, a formal approach to the process should consider the decision to liberalize at each stage and explore how the decision to liberalize multilaterally is affected by bilateral liberalization. This paper uses a median-voter setting to show a mechanism by which bilateral arrangements may undermine political support for a multilateral arrangement but can never enhance political support for broader free trade.

In the burgeoning literature on preferential trading arrangements and their effects, a number of studies address the impact of bilateral or regional free-trade agreements on trade relations with nonmembers. Unlike this paper, most use the tariff on nonbloc members' goods as a measure of the agreement's effects.

Paul Krugman (1991) constructs a model in which the trading world divides symmetrically into blocs. Each bloc—a customs union rather than a free-trade agreement—sets tariffs non-cooperatively to take advantage of its market power and move terms of trade in its favor. The larger the individual blocs, the greater is their market power and the higher their tariffs.

Several works address the issues of free-trade agreements (FTAs). Kyle Bagwell and Robert Staiger (1993) focus on the transition period during which an FTA is being formed and posit that the effect of an FTA will be to reduce the volume of trade between the home country and nonparticipants once it is fully implemented. They find that the anticipation of a future drop in multilateral trade volumes interferes with the enforcement of low multilateral tariffs early in the FTA formation process, leading to temporarily higher multilateral tariffs. However, they find that, once an FTA is completed, tariff levels between

* Economic Growth Center, Department of Economics, Yale University, P.O. Box 208269, New Haven, CT 06520 (e-mail: levy@econ.yale.edu). I would like to acknowledge the financial support of the Center for Economic Policy Research at Stanford. I also thank the participants in the Stanford Workshop on International Trade, Anne Krueger, Alice Enders, and anonymous referees for their comments. I am especially grateful to Bob Staiger for his guidance. All remaining errors are my own.

[1] A recent report of the Council of Economic Advisors (1995 pp. 217–19) considers several arguments for free-trade agreements as "building blocks" or "stumbling blocks" and concludes that they will further multilateral liberalization.

[2] Bhagwati (1992) does not formally answer that question but does conclude that many of the arguments in favor of preferential arrangements are of dubious merit. For further general work on regionalism and multilateralism, see the collections edited by Jaime De Melo and Arvind Panagariya (1993) and Kym Anderson and Richard Blackhurst (1993).

the home country and nonparticipants will be no higher.

Martin Richardson (1993) considers the effect of an FTA in a different setting, in which governments maximize a political-support function which gives added weight to export- and import-competing producers' interests. In his model, the small home country has two trading partners supplying a good: the non-FTA partner, with perfectly elastic supply at a low price, and the FTA partner, with perfectly elastic supply at a high price. If an FTA were to make the FTA partners's price less than the tariff-ridden price of the nonpartner, Richardson argues that the home country would lower the tariff against the nonpartner. If it lowered the tariff to the point where the nonpartners's tariff-ridden price was equal to (or just below) the tariff-free price of the partner, the home country would gain tariff revenue on the good and would not harm consumers or import-competing producers (since the domestic post-FTA price would not change).

Panagariya and Ronald Findlay (1994) demonstrate one mechanism by which an FTA could lead to greater protection between blocs. In their model, an exogenously imposed function translates lobbying inputs (labor) into protection. When an FTA is enacted, the labor that was formerly employed lobbying for protection against the FTA partner countries will be released into the labor pool. The wage will be driven down, and thus more labor will be employed lobbying for protection against the rest of the world. Tariffs between blocs should rise.

In Levy (1996), I describe a different mechanism whereby exogenous introduction of a free-trade agreement could induce higher or lower tariffs between trading blocs. It is shown that, in a lobbying framework of the sort originated by Gene Grossman and Elhanan Helpman (1994), FTAs alter pressures for and against trade liberalization by shifting the payoffs to export industries and import-competing industries associated with any given level of protection. The net effect can be to raise or lower barriers between blocs, depending on the characteristics of FTA partners.

The present paper takes a very different approach by portraying national decisions on trade relations as binary choices; countries choose whether to join a free-trade agreement and then choose whether to participate in a broader multilateral agreement.[3] In such a setting, there are two readily apparent ways in which bilateral trade agreements could undermine multilateral liberalization: countries could abandon multilateralism in anticipation of future bilateral agreements; or countries could sign bilateral agreements before a multilateral accord is concluded and then lose the desire to pursue multilateralism further. The latter possibility is the topic of this paper.

This possibility is addressed using a political-economy approach similar to that of Wolfgang Mayer (1984), in which a simple majority of voters is required to pass a proposal. Agents are presented first with a potential bilateral free-trade agreement and then with a multilateral free-trade agreement. Each potential agreement offers agents new equilibrium prices and product varieties in a trade model of the sort discussed by Helpman and Krugman (1985). A majority of voters must support a trade agreement for passage.

The sequence of votes is important, in that voters have perfect foresight. They will approve a bilateral agreement only if it is preferable to a multilateral arrangement or if the bilateral agreement will not prevent the adoption of a preferred multilateral agreement.

Agents have different holdings of capital and labor and thus react differently to any given proposal. In the rich version of the model, every trade agreement offers agents an increased number of product varieties, which uniformly enhances the welfare of agents. The shifts in goods and factor prices may be beneficial or detrimental depending on an agent's capital–labor ratio. In this approach the voter with the median capital–labor ratio is of primary importance, since that voter will always be in the majority on any vote.

The primacy of the median voter ensures that no proposal that diminishes the median

---

[3] An example would be the United States's choice to participate in NAFTA and then its choice of whether to pursue free trade with the fuller membership of the World Trade Organization. In each case, liberalization proceeds through agreements which are adopted or rejected.

voter's utility can ever pass. This means, for instance, that if a multilateral free-trade proposal is not politically feasible under autarky— because the median voter and thus at least half the populace oppose it—then that same multilateral proposal cannot be rendered feasible by any bilateral free-trade agreement. If a bilateral free-trade agreement is politically feasible, it will only raise the reservation utility level of the median voter to which the multilateral proposal will be compared.

For this reason, the paper focuses on cases in which multilateral free trade is politically feasible in autarky. The most interesting cases are those in which the median agent is roughly indifferent between multilateral free trade and the status quo. For the median agent to be indifferent, multilateral free trade must offer a balance of additional product variety (a gain) and adverse price shifts (a loss).

A bilateral free-trade agreement can undermine support for multilateral free trade by offering the median agent disproportionately large gains with relatively small losses. If such a combination raises the utility of the median voter above the level offered by a multilateral free-trade agreement, then the multilateral agreement will no longer be politically viable. This undermining is more likely to occur in bilateral agreements involving countries with similar capital–labor ratios and roughly indifferent median voters. In the extreme case, a bilateral agreement with an identical partner country would bring variety gains without any price shifts. The remaining variety gains offered by a move from the bilateral agreement to multilateral free trade could be insufficient to compensate the median agent for the factor-price losses, in which case the multilateral accord would be blocked.

The kinds of bilateral agreements that would do the least damage to the political feasibility of multilateral free trade would be those that leave the median voter's utility unchanged by combining price shifts with variety gains. This combination could be found in partner countries with capital–labor ratios different from that of the home country. Such agreements would also necessarily engender the most political opposition of any feasible bilateral agreement, since they do the least to enhance the welfare of swing voters.

To develop the point about undermining, this paper begins with a two-good Heckscher-Ohlin model. In this model there are no variety gains to trade, and it is shown that in this setting voters will never forsake multilateral free trade in favor of a bilateral free-trade agreement. If a majority of voters in one country prefers a bilateral trade agreement with a given partner to multilateral free trade, the majority of voters in the partner country will prefer multilateral free trade to the bilateral accord. This result follows from the strict quasi-convexity of indirect utility as a function of the relative price; if a shift in relative prices increases an agent's utility, a further shift in the same direction will increase utility even more. Bilateral free trade can preclude multilateral free trade only in the trivial case when multilateral free trade would result in the same relative price as bilateral free trade, in which case there would be no incentive to trade on a multilateral basis once the bilateral agreement had been struck.

This result is reversed in the second half of the paper with a specific trade model incorporating increasing returns to scale and product varieties. The introduction of product varieties allows agreements that would not be politically feasible in their absence. Specifically, these are agreements in which the median voter in one partner country would suffer from adverse price shifts but is compensated by increased variety gain. The introduction of product varieties into the welfare analysis also allows agreements between identical countries to raise the reservation utility levels in each. Thus, undermining is possible in the latter model, whereas in the former it was not.

An unusual feature of the analysis is the assumption that tariffs are either zero or prohibitive. While this has the virtue of simplicity, the paper's reasoning would carry through with some different fixed level of tariff protection as the alternative to complete liberalization. The lack of tariffs allows a focus on the choice of trading regime and avoids the difficult question of how external tariffs might be determined simultaneously.

Although specific models are used, the lesson of the paper is more general. When agents are roughly indifferent between an initial situation and multilateral free trade and that indifference results from a balance of gains (increased variety) and losses (adverse price shifts), then any intermediate agreement offering disproportionately large gains will undermine support for multilateral free trade. To the extent that the opinion of the broader public (or a subset thereof) plays an important role in determining trade policy, this paper illustrates a potentially harmful effect of pursuing regional trade agreements.[4]

The next section will present the Heckscher-Ohlin model along with the voting procedure. The assertion that bilateral agreements cannot preclude multilateral agreements in such a setting will then be proved. In Section II, a specific example of a model with differentiated products and intraindustry trade will be presented, along with a proof that in this setting, bilateral agreements can undermine multilateral agreements. Conclusions and implications will be presented in Section III.

## I. Bilateral Agreements in a Heckscher-Ohlin Model

This section will consider bilateral agreements in a standard two-good, two-factor[5] Heckscher-Ohlin trade model. Let there be many countries, distinguishable only by their fixed endowments of the two factors of production, capital ($K$) and labor ($L$). These factors are used in the constant-returns-to-scale production of goods $X$ and $Y$. The internationally identical technologies will be assumed to be such that $K$ is used relatively intensively in $X$ (and $L$ in $Y$) with no factor-intensity reversals. Perfect competition will ensure that profits are zero.

Agents in these economies own shares of their country's capital and labor stocks. If the return to a unit of labor is denoted as $w$ and the return to a unit of capital as $r$, the income of an agent $i$ is:

$$(1) \qquad I_i = wL_i + rK_i,$$

where $K_i$ and $L_i$ are the number of units owned by agent $i$. Agents are assumed to have identical and homothetic preferences. Income is fully spent on goods $X$ and $Y$. Arbitrarily, let $Y$ be the numeraire good and $p$ the relative price of $X$ in terms of $Y$.

It will be assumed throughout this paper that countries' relative endowments are sufficiently similar that when they join together in a free-trade area, bilateral or multilateral, there is factor-price equalization.[6] Within the trading area, the integrated economy that would result from factor mobility will be achieved instead through trade flows. It is also assumed that tariffs are either zero or prohibitive, so a country only trades with its free-trade partners.[7]

In this setting, when two countries with different capital–labor ratios form a free-trade area, the resulting relative price will lie between the autarky prices in the two countries and the capital-abundant country will export $X$ and import $Y$ (the Heckscher-Ohlin theorem).

When two or more countries join to form free-trade areas, the resulting capital–labor

---

[4] Public opinion is likely to be one important mechanism among several in the actual formation of trade policy. Intuitions about other mechanisms, such as interest-group lobbying, are addressed elsewhere in the literature, as described above. For a general standard reference on public choice, see Dennis C. Mueller (1989). For a recent survey of the political economy of trade, see Dani Rodrik (1994).

[5] The assumption that there are only two factors of production is important for the median-voter analysis that follows, in that it permits identification of a median voter (the holder of the median capital–labor ratio). With $n$ factors of production ($n > 2$), it might be impossible to array voters along a single dimension, which would preclude the identification of a median voter. However, even in a more general case, if one were able to identify a key voter (who determined whether or not an agreement would be adopted) the rest of the paper's analysis would pertain.

[6] A sufficient condition for this to hold is that the endowments of all countries lie in the intersection of the cones of diversification of the country with the highest, and the country with the lowest, capital–labor ratio.

[7] This assumption is restrictive; participants in free-trade agreements do trade with nonparticipants. If there were some fixed tariff level that applied against all nonparticipants, then the magnitudes of effects would be altered, but the basic arguments of the present paper would not. If, however, trade barriers against nonparticipants were endogenous, this might or might not affect the basic arguments of the paper, depending on the nature of the endogeneity. Such a case is beyond the scope of this paper, but models of endogenous tariff determination and free-trade agreements can be found in Richardson (1993), Panagariya and Findlay (1994), and Levy (1996).

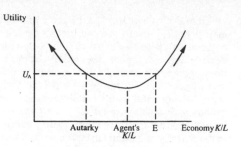

FIGURE 1. THE STRICTLY QUASI-CONVEX UTILITY OF AN AGENT WITH A GIVEN CAPITAL–LABOR RATIO AS A FUNCTION OF THE ECONOMY'S CAPITAL–LABOR RATIO (i.e., THE CAPITAL–LABOR RATIO OF THE ENTIRE TRADING REGION)

*Notes:* If this represented the median voter in a country, she would reject trade agreements which resulted in economy capital–labor ratios in the range (Autarky, E). Outside of that range, utility increases as the distance from Autarky increases.

ratio of the integrated economy is likely to differ from any of the countries' autarky ratios (unless they originally had identical capital–labor ratios). The effects of these shifts on agents' utility can be characterized as follows:

PROPOSITION 1: *The utility of an agent i, with an endowment $(L_i, K_i)$, can be depicted as a function of $K/L$, the integrated economy's capital–labor ratio. This function is strictly quasi-convex in $K/L$ and has a unique minimum when the agent's capital–labor ratio is equal to that of the economy.*

PROOF:

Let $H(p, K_j, L_j)$ represent the indirect utility of a country $j$ where it will initially be assumed that there is a single agent. A. D. Woodland (1980) proves that

$$\frac{\partial H}{\partial p} = V_I(p, K_j, L_j)e^j_x(p, K_j, L_j),$$

where $V_I$ is the marginal utility of income, which will always be positive, and $e_X(p, K_j, L_j)$ is defined as the excess supply of good $X$ (production minus consumption). In autarky equilibrium, $e_X(p^A, K_j, L_j) = 0$ by definition. The law of comparative advantage requires that when $p > p^A$ country $j$ exports good $X$

and imports $Y$, so $e_X > 0$. Similarly, when $p < p^A$ it follows that $e_X < 0$. Thus,

$$\frac{\partial H}{\partial p} < 0 \qquad \text{for } p < p^A$$

$$\frac{\partial H}{\partial p} > 0 \qquad \text{for } p > p^A$$

$$\frac{\partial H}{\partial p} = 0 \qquad \text{for } p = p^A.$$

In a Heckscher-Ohlin model without factor-intensity reversals, $p = p(K/L)$ and $p' < 0$, since $p$ is the price of the capital-intensive good, $X$. Thus one can replace $p$ in $H$ with $K/L$, the capital–labor ratio of the broader integrated economy. It follows that $H$ is strictly quasi-convex in $K/L$ with a unique minimum at $K/L = K_j/L_j$, the autarky capital–labor ratio.

Finally, it can be seen that the parallel between a country in an integrated economy and an individual in a broader economy is exact. In both cases, an economic entity with some fraction of the total capital and labor stock uses those endowments to maximize utility, either through international or interpersonal trade. Therefore, there is an indirect utility function $U(K/L, L_i, K_i)$ for any agent $i$ which is strictly quasi-convex in $K/L$ with a minimum at $K/L = L_i/K_i$.

To illustrate the proposition given above, suppose an agent has a capital–labor ratio slightly higher than that of her country. For purposes of the agent's welfare, one can index all possible free-trade agreements by the continuum of possible capital–labor ratios that would result.[8] As depicted in Figure 1, any trade agreements with countries less capital-abundant than the agent's country will increase this agent's welfare by increasing the

---

[8] It should be noted that, as in the proof of Proposition 1, the relative price $p$ decreases monotonically with increases in the capital–labor ratio. I omit descriptions of most price changes in the paper because of this immediate correspondence.

return to capital and raising the price of good $X$, which would then be the export good. Such agreements would lie to the left of the point labeled "Autarky" in Figure 1. Trade agreements that increase the integrated economy's capital–labor ratio will first hurt the agent. Then, as the capital–labor ratio rises above the agent's own, the agent's utility will increase. To the right of point E in Figure 1, this agent's utility rises above its autarky level.

Next, I use this result to consider whether voters might ever opt for a bilateral trade agreement instead of multilateral free trade. The following voting structure will be assumed. Voters will be asked in a first period whether they would prefer a bilateral trade pact to autarky. Then, in a second period, voters are offered the choice between the existing trade regime (either autarky or bilateral free trade) and multilateral free trade.[9]

It is assumed that voters are fully informed about all aspects of endowments, economies, and voting. It is also assumed that the periods are close enough together in time or discount rates are sufficiently low that discounting may be ignored. Thus, agents all vote to maximize their expected utility under the final integrated trading economy.[10] Any proposal that garners the support of a majority of voters will be enacted.

Once a free-trade agreement has been approved, the participating countries retain their rights to veto an extension of the agreement to include a new country or countries. Thus free-trade agreements are distinct from political unions.[11]

While each voter has a single vote and the majority will prevail, one can predict the outcome of any vote by considering the behavior of the voter with the median capital–labor ratio. Suppose, for example, that a trade agreement under consideration would lead to a capital–labor ratio in the resulting integrated economy that was lower than the alternative economywide capital–labor ratio (either under autarky or a bilateral agreement). If this increases the utility of the voter with the median capital–labor ratio, one can deduce from Proposition 1 that all voters with higher capital–labor ratios than this median voter would also gain. Together, these agents must constitute a majority, by the definition of median. The same reasoning applies if an agreement would reduce the median voter's utility. Therefore, agreements will be approved if, and only if, they enhance the welfare of all participating countries' median voters. I will call such agreements politically feasible.

Now the major result of this section can be stated:

PROPOSITION 2: *In a Heckscher-Ohlin setting, there can be no politically feasible bilateral agreements that would supplant a politically feasible multilateral trade agreement.*

PROOF:

It is useful at this stage to enhance the notation. I will use $k$ as generic notation for a capital–labor ratio. Next, let $k_0^c$ represent the capital–labor ratio of the median agent in country $c$. Finally, I will distinguish between countries and integrated economies; the latter can consist of a single country (autarky) or two or more countries (free-trade areas). The ratio of all the capital to all the labor in an integrated economy $e$ will be written as $k^e$. Now let the function

$$U_c(k_0^c, k^e)$$

denote the maximum attainable utility of the median agent in country $c$, given the capital–labor ratio in economy $e$, as in Proposition 1.

---

[9] This is not the only possible vote ordering, of course. There are permutations in which a multilateral pact could be voted on before a bilateral offer or in which voting sequences are repeated. These permutations can affect some of the results of this paper, and I hope to explore them in later work. For this paper, though, the voting structure is assumed to be the one described above.

[10] I assume that agents vote their utility whether or not they believe their vote will decide the election, perhaps as a civic duty. This avoids the issue of agents' expectations about other agents' voting behavior. While that issue may be of theoretical interest, empirically one observes elections in which the winner wins by a substantial margin.

[11] As an empirical basis for this assumption, it should be noted that the EC has moved the furthest toward political union of any existing regional trade group, yet for

admission of new members even the EC has relied upon the unanimous approval of its members.

Although the levels of capital and labor endowments determine utility, the ratios are sufficient to explore the welfare effects of policy changes, and thus the levels are omitted.

Consider two countries, A and B, which might pair to create a free-trade area. In the first stage of voting, voters in both countries decide whether to continue functioning in autarky or whether to join to form a free-trade area (AB). In the second stage, voters will determine whether to maintain the outcome of the first stage or join in a multilateral free-trade area (M) including the other countries. Since the proposition is only concerned with politically feasible multilateral free-trade agreements, assume

$$U_j(k_0^j, k^M) > U_j(k_0^j, k^j)$$

for each country $j$ (i.e., all median agents prefer multilateral free trade to autarky).

Returning to the potential free-trade agreement, AB, one can see that if $k^A = k^B$ then there is no basis for trade between the two countries. Therefore, I will arbitrarily say that $k^A > k^{AB} > k^B$. For agreement AB to pass, both countries must approve it. This requires that

$$(2) \qquad U_A(k_0^A, k^{AB}) > U_A(k_0^A, k^A)$$

$$U_B(k_0^B, k^{AB}) > U_B(k_0^B, k^B).$$

Because of the strict quasi-convexity of utility functions, if condition (2) holds, this implies that the median voter in A must gain from decreases in the economy's capital–labor ratio at $k^{AB}$, while the median voter in B must gain from increases (see Figure 1).

Next consider the second stage of voting. The aim here is to show that there are no sets of capital–labor ratios (for the two countries A and B and the rest of the world) such that both A and B prefer the bilateral free-trade agreement to multilateral free trade. In relation to free-trade area AB, multilateral free trade can have one of three effects:

(i) Multilateral free trade could leave the integrated economy's capital–labor ratio unchanged ($k^M = k^{AB}$). In this case,

there is no basis for trade, so both A and B would be indifferent.

(ii) Multilateral free trade could increase the integrated economy's capital–labor ratio ($k^M > k^{AB}$). In this case,

$$U_B(k_0^B, k^M) > U_B(k_0^B, k^{AB})$$

$$> U_B(k_0^B, k^B)$$

so B would approve of the change. It is possible that

$$U_A(k_0^A, k^M) > U_A(k_0^A, k^{AB})$$

only if $k^M$ is sufficiently greater than $k^A$, in which case both countries would approve the change. If

$$U_A(k_0^A, k^M) < U_A(k_0^A, k^{AB}),$$

which will occur if A is capital-abundant relative to the world, then A would want to block multilateral free trade. However, country B would foresee the result and vote against the bilateral free-trade agreement in period 1.

(iii) Multilateral free trade could decrease the integrated economy's capital–labor ratio ($k^M < k^{AB}$). This case is simply the reverse of case 2. Country A would approve of the change. If B would want to block multilateral free trade, A would foresee the result and vote against the bilateral free-trade agreement in period 1.

Thus, the strict quasi-convexity of utility functions guarantees that no two countries that originally wanted multilateral free trade can establish a bilateral free-trade area that both prefer.

While the proof given above was tailored for a two-country free-trade agreement, the reasoning can be readily extended to regional trade agreements with two or more countries.

COROLLARY 1: *In a Heckscher-Ohlin setting, there can be no politically feasible regional agreement that would supplant a politically feasible multilateral trade agreement.*

VOL. 87 NO. 4                    *LEVY: FREE-TRADE AGREEMENTS*                                        513

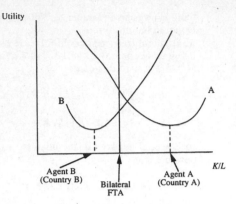

FIGURE 2. THE IMPOSSIBILITY OF UNDERMINING IN THE HECKSCHER-OHLIN SETTING

*Notes:* For the special case depicted, utility curves are shown for two agents, A and B, each of whom is assumed, for simplicity, to have the same capital–labor ratio as his country. Also shown is the capital–labor ratio that would result in a free-trade area involving the two countries.

PROOF:

Define a regional agreement (R) as a free-trade agreement among any proper subset of the countries in a multilateral agreement. Denote the capital–labor ratio of the combined countries in the regional agreement as $k^R$. Let country A be any country that is capital-abundant relative to the combined countries in R. Let country B be any country that is relatively labor-abundant. Thus, $k^A > k^R > k^B$. For agreement R to pass, all member countries must approve it. One can now repeat the proof of Proposition 2 with $k^R$ in place of $k^{AB}$.

The bilateral argument is demonstrated in Figure 2. A special case is depicted in which the median voters in countries A and B have the same capital–labor ratios as their countries. These capital–labor ratios are the minima of the two utility curves. The capital–labor ratio of a bilateral free-trade area between A and B must lie between these two points. The three cases in the proof given above correspond to situations when multilateral free trade would result in a capital–labor ratio the same as, to the right of, or to the left of the bilateral FTA point. In either of the latter two cases, at least

one country would strictly prefer multilateral free trade to the bilateral agreement.

Of course, if the discount rate were sufficiently high or the periods sufficiently far apart, then it would be possible for a bilateral agreement to undermine multilateral free trade. This is a caveat applicable to almost any sequential result. The point remains that, in a Heckscher-Ohlin setting in which voters are asked to consider both a bilateral and a multilateral trade agreement, there cannot be coalitions of countries that would prefer the bilateral agreement to multilateral free trade.[12]

It is worth noting that bilateral agreements are feasible in this model if, and only if, the capital–labor ratios of both participating countries lie on the same side of the multilateral integrated economy's capital–labor ratio. To see how this might happen, return to the example in which $k^A > k^B$. If both ratios were greater than that of the integrated economy under multilateral free trade, it is possible that country B would gain by both an initial increase in the broader economy's capital–labor ratio and a subsequent decrease sufficiently large that B became relatively capital-abundant. In Figure 2, this situation would involve a multilateral free-trade capital–labor ratio well to the left of country B's. The same argument could be made if both countries were labor-abundant relative to the multilateral economy. As shown in Proposition 2, though, these politically feasible bilateral agreements could not preclude multilateral free trade.

One can also readily see that a politically feasible bilateral agreement can never increase the political feasibility of multilateral free trade. If multilateral free trade is not politically feasible initially in a country $j$, $U_j(k_0^j, k^M) < U_j(k_0^j, k^j)$. If a bilateral free-trade agreement ($ij$) is politically feasible, then $U_j(k_0^j, k^{ij}) > U_j(k_0^j, k^j)$. By transitivity, then, $U_j(k_0^j, k^{ij}) > U_j(k_0^j, k^M)$, so there would not be political

---

[12] If countries were able to dissolve a bilateral agreement, then one could see bilateral agreements formed in cases in which one country preferred the multilateral outcome to the bilateral outcome. There would be no incentive to form such an agreement unless sufficient time passed between voting stages. Of course, in such a setting, it would still be the case that a bilateral agreement could not undermine a multilateral agreement.

support for an expansion from a bilateral trade agreement to a multilateral trade agreement.

Finally, note that the logic of this section would also apply to political unions. A political union between two countries would imply that majority support from the *pooled* populations would be necessary for expanding the union. Under such an arrangement, there would likely be a new median voter. However, if the voters in the two partner countries are fully informed, they would block the bilateral political union unless they concurred with the predictable ensuing choice on multilateral union.

## II. A Differentiated-Product Model

In this section it will be shown that, in a richer model, the result of the previous section can be overturned; there may be bilateral trade coalitions that can supplant multilateral free trade. To demonstrate this, a standard differentiated-product model will be introduced. This model will retain the important features of the Heckscher-Ohlin model but will add another dimension to agents' utility: the number of varieties of the differentiated product that are available. It is this new dimension that allows bilateral agreements to undermine multilateral agreements.

This section will begin by extending the model of the previous section and deriving the effect of trade agreements on agents' welfare. It will be shown that the median voter is still the agent with the median capital-labor ratio. Finally, it will be shown that trade agreements between similar countries can win voter approval and undermine support for multilateral free trade.

The only differences between countries will be their endowments of the two factors of production—capital ($K$) and labor ($L$)—and the distribution of factor ownership. I now add the simplifying assumption that each agent $i$ will be assumed to own one unit of labor and some amount of capital, $k_i$, where

$$(3) \qquad \sum_{i=1}^{L} k_i = K.$$

Since labor ownership is assumed not to vary, $k_i$ also measures an agent's relative wealth.

The two factors receive returns per unit of $w$ for labor and per unit of $r$ for capital. Thus, agent $i$ enjoys an income of

$$(4) \qquad I_i = rk_i + w.$$

I turn now to the two sectors of production and adopt a specific functional form. $Y$ will denote the economy's output of the homogeneous product. The constant-returns production process uses factors in the following way:

$$(5) \qquad Y = \gamma_Y K_Y^\mu L_Y^{1-\mu},$$

where all parameters are assumed to be positive and $\mu \in (0, 1)$. $Y$ will be assumed to be the numeraire good.

The goods in the $X$ sector are now differentiated products produced under increasing returns to scale. For an individual variety $x$, the production function is

$$(6) \qquad x = \gamma_x K_x^{\xi\eta} L_x^{\xi(1-\eta)},$$

where parameters again are positive, $\eta \in (0, 1)$, and the returns to scale are reflected by $\xi > 1$. In equilibrium, $n$ will denote the number of varieties in production, and $X$ will denote the sum of output over all $n$ varieties in an economy.[13]

Agents are assumed to have identical utility functions of the following form:

$$(7) \qquad U = U_X^\alpha Y^{1-\alpha},$$

$$(8) \qquad U_X = \left( \sum_{i=1}^{n} D_i^\beta \right)^{1/\beta}$$

$$\beta = \left( 1 - \frac{1}{\sigma} \right) \qquad \sigma > 1,$$

where $D$ represents the consumption of an individual variety $x$ and $i$ indexes the varieties. The homotheticity of (7) ensures that expenditure patterns will not vary as income is

---

[13] The results do not depend on the Cobb-Douglas form of the production functions. They do depend, however, on the assumption of homotheticity in production.

redistributed or augmented. The parameter $\alpha$ lies in the range $(0, 1)$. The Spence-Dixit-Stiglitz (SDS) subutility function implies that individuals prefer variety and have a constant cross-price elasticity of substitution ($\sigma$) between varieties.[14]

In this framework, each firm in sector $X$ produces at an identical optimal level of output, denoted by $x$, where

$$x = \frac{\sigma}{\xi(\sigma - 1)}$$

and sells at an identical equilibrium price, $p$. For a large number of firms, $\sigma$ approximates the elasticity of demand facing each firm.[15] The number of firms, $n$, is thus determined by

$$(9) \qquad\qquad X = nx.$$

Returning to the utility of agents, by substituting equilibrium values into the utility function described by (7) and (8), I derive an indirect utility function for an agent $i$:

$$(10) \quad U_i = I_i(1 - \alpha)^{1-\alpha}\alpha^{\alpha}n^{\alpha/\sigma-1}p^{-\alpha}.$$

Next, I use this result to explore the effect of any free-trade agreement on agents' utility.

From equation (10) the change in agent $i$'s utility due to a trade agreement can be described as

$$(11) \quad \frac{U_i^{FT}}{U_i^{AUT}} = \left(\frac{I_i^{FT}}{I_i^{AUT}}\right)\left(\frac{p^{FT}}{p^{AUT}}\right)^{-\alpha}$$

$$\times \left(\frac{n^{FT}}{n^{AUT}}\right)^{\alpha/(\sigma-1)},$$

where FT denotes values after a free-trade agreement and AUT denotes values in autarky. Define $\lambda_K$ as the percentage increase from an economy's capital stock to the capital stock of the integrated economy resulting from a free-trade agreement (and $\lambda_L$ as the percentage increase in the labor stock). The final term of (11) can be shown to equal

$$(12) \quad \left(\frac{n^{FT}}{n^{AUT}}\right)^{\alpha/(\sigma-1)}$$

$$= [(1 + \lambda_K)^{\eta}(1 + \lambda_L)^{1-\eta}]^{\alpha/(\sigma-1)}.$$

Since $\lambda_K$ and $\lambda_L$ are always greater than zero, this "variety" effect always exceeds one (i.e., it has a positive effect on utility). Note that, if an agreement offered only this variety effect, it would raise the welfare of all agents and win unanimous support.

I call the remaining effect on utility the "comparative advantage" effect.[16] This is the effect that would remain if $\sigma$ went to $\infty$ and the differentiated product became homogeneous. It is a specific example of the utility arguments underlying Section I. To sign to this effect, first parameterize the shift in the economy's capital–labor ratio by the variable $\varphi$, where $\varphi$ is implicitly defined by

$$(13) \quad \frac{K^{FT}}{L^{FT}} = \frac{(1 + \lambda_K)K^{AUT}}{(1 + \lambda_L)L^{AUT}} = \varphi\,\frac{K^{AUT}}{L^{AUT}}.$$

Note that the free-trade capital–labor ratio is that obtained by pooling the endowments of the partner countries. I assume, as before, that

---

[14] An alternative assumption described by Helpman and Krugman (1985) is that subutility preferences are of the Lancaster variety. In this case, consumers have an ideal variety and prefer products which are closer to the ideal. Lancaster preferences would not fundamentally alter the results of this paper but would make the analysis more complicated.

Avinash Dixit and Joseph Stiglitz (1977) interpret the SDS subutility function as a Samuelsonian social utility function rather than that of an individual, and caution is necessary in extending its use to describe the preferences of individuals. While the functional form is used here mostly for its convenience, it is quite appropriate for a large number of commodities, although certainly not all. It is reasonable to assume that, at least within a certain range, individuals benefit from the availability of greater product variety. As real-world examples of commodities for which increased product variety typically raises an individual's utility, one may think of apparel products, toys, food, and beverages.

[15] For a fuller discussion of the demand structure, see Helpman and Krugman (1985 Ch. 6). Note also that the fixed level of firm production is a by-product of the Spence-Dixit-Stiglitz approach. Under Lancaster's approach, $x$ would vary.

[16] Alternatively, one could refer to this as the Stolper-Samuelson effect, since this effect of liberalization on real returns to factors is that identified by W. Stolper and Paul Samuelson (1941).

endowments are such that the integrated equilibrium can be replicated through trade. Therefore, $\varphi$ will be greater than 1 if a country's counterpart is relatively capital-abundant and less than 1 if the counterpart is relatively labor-abundant.

One can also parameterize agent $i$'s capital holdings by $\rho_i$, where $\rho_i$ is implicitly defined by

$$(14) \qquad \left(\frac{K}{L}\right)_i = k_i = \rho_i \left(\frac{K^{\text{AUT}}}{L^{\text{AUT}}}\right).$$

Therefore, $\rho_i > 1$ if agent $i$ is relatively capital-abundant, $\rho_i < 1$ if agent $i$ is relatively labor-abundant, and $\rho_i = 1$ if agent $i$ has the same capital–labor ratio as the country.

With these parameterizations, the comparative-advantage effect is

$$(15) \qquad \left(\frac{I_i^{\text{FT}}}{I_i^{\text{AUT}}}\right)\left(\frac{p^{\text{FT}}}{p^{\text{AUT}}}\right)^{-\alpha}$$

$$= \varphi^{1/1+\theta}\left(\frac{\dfrac{\rho_i}{\varphi}+\theta}{\rho_i+\theta}\right)$$

where [17]

$$\theta \equiv \frac{1}{\mu(1-\alpha)+\eta\alpha} - 1.$$

Thus, the comparative-advantage effect of an agent's utility change can be seen to depend on the capital abundance of the agent and the capital–labor ratio of the partner country. It will prove useful to work with the natural logarithm of equation (15). Define

$$(16) \quad f(\varphi, \rho, \theta)$$

$$= \frac{1}{1+\theta}\ln\varphi + \ln\left(\frac{\rho}{\varphi}+\theta\right)$$

$$- \ln(\rho+\theta)$$

[17] To interpret $\theta$, note that the denominator of the fraction term can be seen as a weighted average of the capital-intensity parameters in the two sectors. Recall also that $\alpha$ denotes the utility weight on the capital-intensive differentiated product sector.

so that $f > 0$ implies an increase in utility and $f < 0$ implies a decrease in utility due to a free-trade agreement. Then,

$$(17) \qquad \frac{\partial f}{\partial \varphi} = \frac{\theta(\varphi - \rho)}{\varphi^2(1+\theta)\left(\dfrac{\rho}{\varphi}+\theta\right)},$$

which describes the change in desirability of an agreement as the factor abundance of a partner country changes.

It is now possible to establish the identity of the median voter in this new framework.

PROPOSITION 3: *The median voter for a country will be the agent with the median capital–labor ratio in that country.*

PROOF:

Consider a given free-trade agreement characterized by $\varphi$. Consider the agent with the median capital–labor ratio, whom we can identify as $\rho_{\text{median}}$. From the log of the utility ratio, $f(\varphi, \rho_{\text{median}}, \theta)$, one can derive

$$(18) \qquad \frac{\partial f}{\partial \rho} = \frac{\theta(1-\varphi)}{(\rho+\varphi\theta)(\rho+\theta)}.$$

The sign of this expression depends only on whether the partner country is relatively capital-abundant ($\varphi > 1$) or labor-abundant ($\varphi < 1$). One can thus say, in terms of the comparative-advantage effect, that, if the partner country is relatively capital-abundant, then all agents with $\rho > \rho_{\text{median}}$ are worse off than the median agent and all agents with $\rho < \rho_{\text{median}}$ are strictly better off. Since variety gains affect all voters equally, this demonstrates that the agent with the median capital–labor ratio is the median voter.

If a median voter gains from both the comparative-advantage effect and the variety effect, the arguments from Section I against a bilateral agreement undermining a multilateral agreement will still apply. The interesting counterexample will occur when the median voter is abundant in the same factor as the partner country. Equation (17) indicates that as $\varphi$ moves from 1 toward $\rho_{\text{median}}$, the corresponding comparative-advantage effect on the median voter's utility will be negative and declining.

Balanced against this comparative-advantage loss is a gain from the variety effect. In terms of Figure 1, it is now possible for trade agreements to occur in the region between Autarky and E if, and only if, variety gains compensate for the adverse shifts in goods and factor prices.

I now return to the sequential consideration of a free-trade agreement among a subset of countries and a multilateral free-trade agreement involving the entire set and state the following results:

PROPOSITION 4: *No agreement involving a proper subset of countries can render politically feasible an otherwise infeasible agreement involving the full set of countries.*

PROOF:

Return to the notation of Proposition 2, in which $k_0^c$ represents the capital–labor ratio of the median agent in country $c$ and the ratio of all the capital to all the labor in an integrated economy $e$ will be written as $k^e$. Let the possible values of $e$ be: MFT for multilateral free trade, $c$ for autarky in country $c$, and FTA for a free-trade agreement involving a subset of the countries. The utility notation must now also include $n^e$ to represent the number of varieties in economy $e$. Now the utility function for an agent in country $c$ can be written as

$$U_c(k_0^c, k^e, n^e).$$

Suppose that

$$U_c(k_0^c, k^{\text{MFT}}, n^{\text{MFT}}) < U_c(k_0^c, k^c, n^c).$$

This implies that multilateral free trade is politically infeasible. An agreement involving a proper subset of countries is politically feasible if, and only if,

$$U_c(k_0^c, k^{\text{FTA}}, n^{\text{FTA}}) \geq U_c(k_0^c, k^c, n^c).$$

But that implies

$$U_c(k_0^c, k^{\text{FTA}}, n^{\text{FTA}}) > U_c(k_0^c, k^{\text{MFT}}, n^{\text{MFT}}).$$

Therefore multilateral free trade must remain infeasible.

PROPOSITION 5: *An agreement involving a proper subset of countries can render politically infeasible an otherwise feasible agreement involving the full set of countries.*

PROOF:

Using the same notation, suppose that

$$U_c(k_0^c, k^{\text{MFT}}, n^{\text{MFT}}) > U_c(k_0^c, k^c, n^c)$$

so that multilateral free trade is initially politically feasible. If

$$U_c(k_0^c, k^{\text{FTA}}, n^{\text{FTA}}) > U_c(k_0^c, k^{\text{MFT}}, n^{\text{MFT}})$$

then the subset agreement will have rendered an otherwise politically feasible multilateral agreement infeasible. For an agreement that does this, consider an FTA between country $c$ and a country that is identical to country $c$ in every respect. Such an agreement would leave goods and factor prices unchanged.[18] Thus, the income of any agent $i$, with capital $k_i$, remains unchanged by the opening of trade. By equation (10), utility increases with $n$. All agents in each economy benefit from the liberalization, so under any distribution of capital, agents would choose the free-trade agreement over autarky.[19] If $k_0^c$ is such that

$$U_c(k_0^c, k^{\text{MFT}}, n^{\text{MFT}}) - U_c(k_0^c, k^c, n^c)$$

is sufficiently small (i.e., the variety gain just outweighs the comparative-advantage loss for the median voter), then the variety gains offered by the FTA would render the move to multilateral free trade undesirable (since the comparative-advantage loss would be

---

[18] The result that prices remain unchanged requires homotheticity in production. The fixed-optimal-output result, as stated above, is particular to the Spence-Dixit-Stiglitz subutility assumption. With increasing returns, if the optimal output level increased, it is possible that the relative price of the differentiated product would fall while factor returns remained constant. This could further enhance welfare.

[19] This proposition readily extends to an agreement involving $n$ identical countries, where $n > 2$, since a larger group simply implies a larger number of varieties. Thus, the results apply to regional agreements as well as to bilateral agreements.

unaffected). This would necessarily hold for the identical partner country as well.

This result can be generalized beyond the case of countries with equal capital–labor ratios. For any pair of countries, the closer their capital–labor ratios are, the more variety gains they offer in proportion to comparative-advantage effects, the more popular the agreements are likely to be, and the more potentially damaging they are to multilateral free trade.

It is of some interest to explore how a country could avoid undermining support for multilateral liberalization in this setting. One answer, of course, is to pursue only a policy of multilateral liberalization from the start. If bilateral free-trade agreements are to be sought, though, the answer would be to pursue agreements with countries or groups of countries with different factor endowments. A capital-abundant country needs partner countries with less capital and more labor. A free-trade agreement will preserve the feasibility of multilateral free trade so long as it balances variety gains and comparative-advantage effects in such a way as to leave the median voter in each country preferring multilateral free trade to the subset free-trade agreement.

### III. Conclusion

This paper has shown that in a Heckscher-Ohlin setting it is politically impossible for a bilateral trade agreement to supplant multilateral free trade. In contrast, it was shown that, in a model with differentiated products and variety gains, bilateral free trade can undermine support for multilateral free trade. Conditions were described under which this could happen. To explain the difference, it is important to understand that the differentiated-product setting permits trade agreements that would have been politically impossible in the setting of Section I by allowing gains through variety gains as well as price shifts. In the Heckscher-Ohlin setting, a voter's utility depended solely on the capital–labor ratio. For undermining to occur in the differentiated-product setting, the median voter would have to experience lower utility under free trade in the absence of variety gains and higher or equal utility once variety gains are taken into account.

Throughout, the distribution of factors was shown to be crucial. The task of maintaining political support for multilateral free trade when countries negotiate side agreements in a differentiated-product setting was shown to require a clear understanding of the political situation (i.e., factor distribution) in all participating countries as well as a careful selection of those participating countries. The general principle emerged that the more politically popular a bilateral agreement is, the more likely it is to undermine political support for further multilateral liberalization.

The applicability of these results to more intricate models merits further research. Still, the general lesson should remain: intermediate accords can upset the balance of gains and losses offered by multilateralism and can therefore undermine political support. Only when such balances are impossible (as in the Heckscher-Ohlin setting) do these concerns subside.

As stated above, all such difficulties are readily avoidable if countries are restricted to pursuing multilateral liberalization. This is not necessarily an argument against more lenient World Trade Organization rules of the sort endorsed by Alan Deardorff and Robert Stern (1991). The World Trade Organization must accommodate the strong desires of its most powerful members if it is to survive as an institution. Were it to veto major policy initiatives put forward by the United States or the European Community countries, it would be more likely to come apart at the seams than to prevail. Instead, this paper suggests that those powerful member countries might wish to return their attentions to the task of multilateral liberalization.

### REFERENCES

Anderson, Kym and Blackhurst, Richard, eds. *Regional integration and the global trading system*. New York: St. Martin's Press, 1993.

Bagwell, Kyle and Staiger, Robert. ''Multilateral Tariff Cooperation During the Formation of Regional Free Trade Areas.'' National Bureau of Economic Research (Cambridge, MA) Working Paper No. 4364, May 1993.

Bhagwati, Jagdish. ''Regionalism and Multilateralism: An Overview.'' Columbia University Discussion Paper Series No. 603, April 1992.

Council of Economic Advisers. *Economic report of the President*. Washington, DC: U.S. Government Printing Office, 1995.

De Melo, Jaime and Panagariya, Arvind, eds. *New dimensions in regional integration*. Cambridge: Cambridge University Press, 1993.

Deardorff, Alan and Stern, Robert. "Multilateral Trade Negotiations and Preferential Trading Arrangements." Unpublished manuscript presented at the Conference on Analytical and Negotiating Issues in the Global Trading System, Ann Arbor, Michigan, October 31–November 1, 1991.

Dixit, Avinash and Stiglitz, Joseph. "Monopolistic Competition and Optimum Product Diversity." *American Economic Review*, June 1977, *67*(2), pp. 297–308.

Grossman, Gene and Helpman, Elhanan. "Protection for Sale." *American Economic Review*, September 1994, *84*(4), pp. 833–50.

Helpman, Elhanan and Krugman, Paul. *Market structure and foreign trade*. Cambridge, MA: MIT Press, 1985.

Krugman, Paul. "Is Bilateralism Bad?" in Elhanan Helpman and Assaf Razin, eds., *International trade and trade policy*. Cambridge, MA: MIT Press, 1991, pp. 9–23.

Levy, Philip I. "Free Trade Agreements and Inter-Bloc Tariffs." Mimeo, Yale University, 1996.

Mayer, Wolfgang. "Endogenous Tariff Formation." *American Economic Review*, December 1984, *74*(5), pp. 970–85.

Mueller, Dennis C. *Public choice II*. Cambridge: Cambridge University Press, 1989.

Panagariya, Arvind and Findlay, Ronald. "A Political-Economy Analysis of Free Trade Areas and Customs Unions." World Bank Policy Research Working Paper No. 1261, March 1994.

Richardson, Martin. "Endogenous Protection and Trade Diversion." *Journal of International Economics*, May 1993, *34*(3–4), pp. 309–24.

Rodrik, Dani. "What Does the Political Economy Literature on Trade Policy (Not) Tell Us That We Ought to Know?" National Bureau of Economic Research (Cambridge, MA) Working Paper No. 4870, 1994.

Stolper, W. and Samuelson, Paul. "Protection and Real Wages." *Review of Economic Studies*, November 1941, *9*(1), pp. 58–73.

Woodland, A. D. "Direct and Indirect Trade Utility Functions." *Review of Economic Studies*, October 1980, *47*(5), pp. 907–26.

# [20]

ELSEVIER        Journal of International Economics 42 (1997) 91–123

Journal of
INTERNATIONAL
ECONOMICS

# Multilateral tariff cooperation during the formation of customs unions

Kyle Bagwell[a,b], Robert W. Staiger[c,d]

[a]*Department of Economics, Northwestern University, Evanston, IL 60208, USA*
[b]*Department of Economics, Columbia University, New York, NY 10027, USA*
[c]*Department of Economics, The University of Wisconsin, Madison, WI 53706, USA*
[d]*National Bureau of Economic Research, Cambridge, MA 02138, USA*

Received 19 July 1995; revised 18 January 1996; accepted 14 March 1996

## Abstract

We study the implications of customs-union formation for multilateral tariff cooperation. We model cooperation in multilateral trade policy as self-enforcing, in that it involves balancing the current gains from deviating unilaterally from an agreed-upon trade policy against the future losses from forfeiting the benefits of multilateral cooperation that such a unilateral defection would imply. The early stages of the process of customs-union formation are shown to alter this dynamic incentive constraint in a way that leads to a temporary "honeymoon" for liberal multilateral trade policies. We find, however, that the harmony between customs unions and multilateral liberalization is temporary: eventually, as the full impact of the emerging customs union becomes felt, a less favorable balance between current and future conditions re-emerges, and the liberal multilateral policies of the honeymoon phase cannot be sustained. ©1997 Elsevier Science B.V. All rights reserved.

*Key words:* Customs unions; Preferential agreements; The Multilateral Trading System

*JEL classification:* F13; F15

## 1. Introduction

Recently, there has been renewed interest in regional trade agreements as countries turn with increasing frequency to regional options regarding trade policy. The continued integration of the European Community (EC) embodied in EC92,

92        *K. Bagwell, R.W. Staiger / Journal of International Economics 42 (1997) 91–123*

and the integration of North America beginning with the US–Canada Free Trade Agreement and continuing with the addition of Mexico under the North American Free Trade Agreement (NAFTA), are but the most prominent examples of regional approaches to trade liberalization that have come about over the last decade. Much of the interest in the effects of such agreements reflects a growing concern that their recent proliferation, with the United States in particular now actively engaged in the pursuit of regional trade agreements, could serve to undermine multilateral cooperation under the General Agreement on Tariffs and Trade (GATT) and its successor, the World Trade Organization (WTO).

The view that regionalism might be antithetical to multilateral cooperation is new and somewhat ironic, as the previous experience with the formation and extension of the EC seems to suggest just the opposite interpretation. For example, the EC was formed among its six original members in 1957 and phased in over the ensuing decade, and the prospect of an integrated EC market appears to have been a major stimulus to the successful Kennedy Round of multilateral negotiations under GATT initiated in 1964. Impetus for the Tokyo Round of multilateral GATT negotiations initiated in 1973 can be similarly linked in part to the EC enlargement to include the United Kingdom and other countries. Indeed, Bhagwati (1991) has observed that the perception surrounding these experiences was of general compatibility between regional agreements and multilateral cooperation through GATT negotiations.[1]

Given the recent spate of regional agreements, and the evolving views regarding their implications for multilateral cooperation, it is important to set out formal models that explore the impact of regional agreements for multilateral cooperation. We present such a model here in the context of regional customs unions, and offer the prediction that the relationship between customs-union formation and multilateral tariff cooperation is non-stationary. In particular, we argue that the early experience with the formation of customs unions and their effects on multilateral tariff cooperation may be a poor guide to the impact that their formation has on sustainable multilateral tariff cooperation in the long run. On the contrary, our model suggests that the early phases of customs-union formation will be associated with a temporary "honeymoon" for multilateral trade policies that cannot be sustained.

We adopt the view, as in Dam (1970) and Bagwell and Staiger (1990), that (i) enforcement issues are central to an understanding of the dynamic behavior of trade intervention in a world where countries attempt to maintain cooperative trade policies, and (ii) in practice, the enforcement of agreed-upon behavior under

---

[1]On the link between the formation of the EC and the Kennedy Round, see for instance the remarks made by former Secretary of State Christian Herter (1961) before the Joint Economic Committee. For a broader review of the historical links between multilateral liberalization and the formation of the EC and its subsequent enlargement, and for a reassertion of the complementary relationship between regional integration and multilateral liberalization, see WTO (1995, pp. 53–56).

GATT is limited by the severity of retaliation that can be credibly threatened against an offender by its trading partners. Specifically, we view cooperation in multilateral trade policy as involving a delicate balance between, on the one hand, gains from deviating unilaterally from an agreed-upon trade policy, and on the other, the discounted expected future benefits of maintaining multilateral cooperation, with the understanding that the latter would be forfeited in the trade war which followed a unilateral defection in pursuit of the former. In such a setting, changes in current conditions or in expected future conditions can upset this balance, requiring changes in existing trade policy that will bring incentives back into line. We explore here the sense in which the formation of regional trade agreements upsets the balance between current and future conditions, and trace through the dynamic ramifications of these effects for multilateral cooperation.

A crucial focus of our analysis is the period of *transition*, during which the regional agreement is being implemented. Both because regional trade agreements involve a lengthy staging period (typically a decade or longer) during which tariff changes are implemented, and because trade patterns take time to reflect changes in trade barriers in any event, there will inevitably be a substantial lag between the signing of a regional trade agreement and the changes in trading relationships that it eventually brings about. This lag creates a period of transition within which, at least initially, the important changes are with regard to expected future trading relationships rather than current conditions. It is this basic observation that is central to our results.

To understand our main findings, it is helpful first to categorize two of the principal effects of a regional agreement. A first consequence of such an agreement is the *trade diversion effect*, whereby the removal of internal tariffs between member countries acts to enlarge intra-member trade volume and reduce the volume of trade between member and non-member countries. A second effect is the *market power effect*. While the trade diversion effect arises for both free trade agreements and customs unions, the market power effect is particular to the formation of customs unions: under a customs union, the member countries adopt a common external tariff on imports, and this in turn enables them credibly to impose a higher import tariff on their multilateral trading partners than if their external tariff were not harmonized, should such a punitive tariff be desired.

In a separate paper (Bagwell and Staiger, 1997), we argue that the trade diverting effect of free trade agreements leads to higher multilateral tariffs during the transition period over which such agreements are negotiated and implemented. Intuitively, during the period of transition, trade volume between member and non-member countries is still large, as internal tariffs between member countries have not yet been eliminated. Yet, member and non-member countries recognize that they will trade less with one another in the future, once the agreements are implemented. Thus, during the transition phase, the incentive to deviate unilaterally is large as compared with the now smaller discounted future value of maintaining a cooperative relationship. To ensure some measure of cooperation

94      *K. Bagwell, R.W. Staiger / Journal of International Economics 42 (1997) 91–123*

between member and non-member countries it is then necessary to raise the transition-period tariffs between the two sets of countries, reducing the volume of their trade and the associated incentive to defect.

In the present paper, we consider the formation of customs unions. While generally both trade diversion and market power effects will be associated with customs-union formation, we provide a model in which the market power effect is isolated. In this setting, we show that the emergence of customs unions will be associated with temporarily reduced multilateral trade tensions between member and non-member countries, and consequently, with a temporary honeymoon for liberal multilateral trade policies. This easing of tensions arises during the period of transition, when the current degree of market power possessed by each member country (and hence the current incentive to deviate unilaterally) is more or less unchanged at the same time that the expected future degree of market power possessed by each member country (and hence the value to non-member countries of maintaining future multilateral cooperation) has increased. Intuitively, under such conditions, non-member countries are less apt to take a confrontational stance in trade disputes with member countries of the emerging customs union, as the risk of a possible trade war with such countries now poses a greater deterrent to confrontation than it once did. Our results suggest, however, that the harmony between customs unions and multilateral liberalization is temporary: eventually, as the impact of the emerging customs union on the degree of market power becomes felt, a less favorable balance between current and expected future conditions re-emerges, and liberal multilateral trade policies cannot be sustained.

While the economic and political determinants of regional agreements and multilateral cooperation certainly extend beyond the reach of any one model, our model does provide a novel perspective on the EC experience. Specifically, the original EC customs-union formation and its subsequent enlargement may have contributed to a honeymoon period for GATT negotiations, over which the market power effect associated with customs-union development made possible further multilateral tariff liberalization. Viewed in this light, recent concerns regarding the compatibility of multilateral tariff cooperation and regional agreements may in part reflect the passing of this honeymoon period and the consequent heightening of multilateral trade tensions.

Our work relates to a broad literature. The economics of customs unions has formed a central arm of the study of international commercial policy since Viner (1950)'s classic treatment of the subject. Viner stressed the trade-creating and trade-diverting consequences of customs-union formation, concluding that world welfare need not rise when customs unions are formed. The welfare consequences of customs unions have since been further explored by Bond and Syropoulos (1996a), Deardorff and Stern (1994), Kemp and Wan (1976) and Krugman (1991), among others. A second set of work shares the focus of this paper and examines the impact on multilateral tariff cooperation of regional agreements. Papers in this category include Kowalczyk (1990), Kowalczyk and Sjostrom (1994), Kowalczyk

*K. Bagwell, R.W. Staiger / Journal of International Economics 42 (1997) 91–123*     95

and Wonnacott (1991) and Ludema (1992), who explore how multilateral bargains can be altered by the opportunity to make regional deals, as well as Levy (1997), who examines the sense in which regional options undermine political support for multilateral liberalization.[2] These papers point to interesting issues, but they also assume that binding commitments can be made to enforce the international bargaining outcome. By contrast, our theory is driven by the tradeoffs associated with the construction of self-enforcing agreements. The focus on self-enforcing agreements seems particularly appropriate for international agreements, such as GATT, since it is not clear how binding commitments could be enforced.[3]

The paper is organized as follows. The next section sets out the basic model within which we will study the formation of customs unions, and establishes several properties in a stationary setting that will be useful in the dynamic non-stationary analysis to follow. Section 3 then characterizes the dynamic behavior of equilibrium multilateral tariffs in the non-stationary environment of emerging customs unions. Section 4 derives various comparative statics results. Finally, Section 5 concludes and discusses the implications of our results for the design of GATT Article XXIV, which specifies the conditions under which customs unions may be formed.

## 2. Multilateral tariff determination in stationary environments

In this section we develop and explore the properties of a stationary model of multilateral tariff formation in the presence of customs unions. In the next section we will describe the non-stationarities that arise when the process of customs-union formation is explicitly considered.

### 2.1. A static customs-union model

To direct attention to the main effects, we analyze a simple, partial-equilibrium exchange economy. There are two types of countries, "foreign" countries denoted by a "*", of which there are a total of $K$, and "domestic" countries denoted by the absence of a "*", of which there are also $K$. The $K$ foreign countries are

---

[2] Arndt (1969) was apparently the first to attempt to formalize the effect of customs-union formation on the tariffs of non-member countries, concluding that: "An interesting by-product of the foregoing analysis is the suggestion that optimum tariff strategy may dictate that some countries remaining outside the union reduce their prevailing tariffs. Much depends upon the extent of tariff warfare prior to formation of the union, and upon the dynamics of tariff competition about which very little is known. It is nevertheless intriguing to speculate about the extent to which the existence of the European Economic Community facilitated the Kennedy Round" (p. 117).

[3] A paper written independently of ours which shares our focus on self-enforcing agreements is Bond and Syropoulos (1996b). They consider a stationary environment, and compare cooperative multilateral tariffs across equilibria with blocs of different sizes.

96        *K. Bagwell, R.W. Staiger / Journal of International Economics 42 (1997) 91–123*

grouped symmetrically into $R$ foreign customs unions or *foreign regions*, while the $K$ domestic countries are similarly grouped symmetrically into $R$ *domestic regions*.[4] Thus, $k \equiv K/R$ gives the number of member countries per region. With this framework, we can investigate the consequences of customs unions for multilateral tariffs by varying the number of regions, $R$, while holding fixed the total number of countries, $K$.

There are only two goods, referred to as the domestic and the foreign export goods, respectively, and there exist two units of each good in total in the world. Each domestic country is endowed with $2/K$ units of the domestic export good and none of the foreign export good, while each foreign country is endowed with $2/K$ units of the foreign export good and none of the domestic export good. On the demand side, we suppose that each country $j$ has linear demand for good $i$ of

$$C(P_j^i) = \frac{1}{K}[\alpha - \beta P_j^i]; \; C(P_j^i*) = \frac{1}{K}[\alpha - \beta P_j^i*] \tag{1}$$

where $P_j^i$ is the price of good $i$ in domestic country $j$, and $P_j^i*$ is the price of good $i$ in foreign country $j$.

We note that our assumptions on endowments and demands imply that domestic countries do not trade with each other, and likewise that foreign countries do not trade with each other. Thus, customs-union formation among domestic countries and among foreign countries entails no trade diversion, but occurs rather among competing suppliers of a common export good, and competing demanders of a common import product. This property of the model allows us to abstract from trade diversion/trade creation issues that are common to both free trade areas and customs unions so that we may highlight the market power effect associated with the harmonization of external tariffs that is unique to customs-union formation.[5]

We now proceed to characterize static equilibrium import tariff choices. Recalling that a common import tariff is selected by all members of a customs union or region, we may let $\tau_r$ represent the (specific) import tariff levied by domestic region $r$, and $\tau_r^*$ represent the import tariff levied by foreign region $r$, where $r = 1,...,R$. Given the endowment structure described above, we also may simplify the notation and define prices as follows: $P_{xr}$ ($P_{xr}^*$) is the price in domestic

---

[4] We discuss the generalization of our results to asymmetric cases in our working paper (Bagwell and Staiger, 1993).

[5] Our partial equilibrium model can be closed with the addition of a traded numeraire good $z$ under the assumption that utility of the representative agent is given by $U = C_z + \sum_{i=1}^{2} [(\alpha/\beta)C_i - (1/2\beta)(C_i)^2]$ with $C_z$ denoting consumption of the numeraire good $z$ and $C_i$ denoting consumption of good $i = 1,2$. Provided that $z$ is sufficiently abundant in each country so that it is always consumed in positive amounts by each agent, the marginal utility of income will be fixed at one and partial equilibrium analysis of the non-numeraire sectors is appropriate. Trade in the numeraire good will then be determined by the requirement of overall trade balance.

(foreign) region $r$ of the good that $r$ exports, and $P_{mr}$ ($P^*_{mr}$) is the price in domestic (foreign) region $r$ of the good that $r$ imports. Since import taxes are assumed not to discriminate across sources, the domestic export good will face the same constellation of import tariffs regardless of the good's region of origin, and similarly for the foreign export good. Thus, since regions are otherwise symmetric, each export good will have a single price in all exporting regions, and so we may remove the $r$ subscript and let $P_x$ ($P^*_x$) denote the domestic (foreign) export good's price in any export region. Of course, import prices may differ across regions, as different regions may select different import tariffs.

Now, for any domestic region $r$, we have $P_{mr} = P^*_x + \tau_r$, provided $\tau_r$ is non-prohibitive. This, together with the world market clearing condition for the foreign export good, $2 = \alpha - \beta P^*_x + \sum_{r=1}^{R}(1/R)(\alpha - \beta P_{mr})$, gives the equilibrium prices, $\hat{P}^*_x(R,\bar{\tau})$ and $\hat{P}_{mr}(R,\bar{\tau})$, and per-region import quantities, $\hat{M}_r(R,\bar{\tau}) \equiv kC(\hat{P}_{mr}) = (1/R)(\alpha - \beta \hat{P}_{mr})$, for the foreign export good, when it faces the vector of domestic import tariffs $\bar{\tau} \equiv (\tau_1,...,\tau_R)$. These solutions are:

$$\hat{P}^*_x(R,\bar{\tau}) = \frac{\alpha - 1}{\beta} - \frac{1}{2R}\sum_{\ell=1}^{R}\tau_\ell; \quad \hat{P}_{mr}(R,\bar{\tau}) = \frac{\alpha - 1}{\beta} - \frac{1}{2R}\sum_{\ell=1}^{R}\tau_\ell + \tau_r \quad (2)$$

$$\hat{M}_r(R,\bar{\tau}) = \frac{1}{R} - \frac{\beta}{R}\left[\tau_r - \frac{1}{2R}\sum_{\ell=1}^{R}\tau_\ell\right]. \quad (3)$$

The symmetric structure of the model assures that equilibrium prices and per-region import quantities for the domestic export good are given by expressions exactly analogous to Eq. (2) and Eq. (3) with the vector of foreign import tariffs $\bar{\tau}^* \equiv (\tau^*_1,...,\tau^*_R)$ replacing $\bar{\tau}$.

With Eq. (2) and Eq. (3) in place, we can define regional welfare per member country. Specifically, a domestic country's welfare when domestic and foreign regions respectively select import tariffs $\bar{\tau} \equiv (\tau_1,...,\tau_R)$ and $\bar{\tau}^* \equiv (\tau^*_1,...,\tau^*_R)$ is given by

$$W(R,\bar{\tau},\bar{\tau}^*) = \int_{\hat{P}_{mr}(R,\bar{\tau})}^{\alpha/\beta} C(P)dP + \int_{\hat{P}_x(R,\bar{\tau}^*)}^{\alpha/\beta} C(P)dP + \int_0^{\hat{P}_x(R,\bar{\tau})} (2/K)dP$$

$$+ \tau_r[R/K]\hat{M}_r(R,\bar{\tau}) \quad (4)$$

which corresponds to the consumer surplus received on the foreign export good, the consumer surplus received on the domestic export good, the producer surplus received on the domestic export good, and the tariff revenue received on the foreign export good, respectively, when $r$ is the domestic region to which the country belongs. Welfare is defined symmetrically for any foreign country.[6]

The main features of $W$ are summarized as follows. First, $W$ is maximized at the regional tariff choice

$$\tau_r^D\left(R, \sum_{\substack{\ell=1 \\ \ell \neq r}}^{R} \tau_\ell\right) = \frac{2R}{\beta(4R^2 - 1)} + \frac{1}{(4R^2 - 1)} \sum_{\substack{\ell=1 \\ \ell \neq r}}^{R} \tau_\ell \tag{5}$$

which is the best "defect" tariff for a country in domestic region $r$ – and equivalently for the domestic region $r$ to which the country belongs – when other domestic regions select import tariffs $\tau_\ell$, where $\ell \neq r$. Thus, the optimal tariff is positive, and it is also independent of the tariff levels selected by trading partners (namely *foreign* regions). The latter property is a consequence of our assumptions that demands are independent across goods and that export taxes are not possible.

Second, notice from Eq. (5) that the optimal tariff for the domestic region $r$ is increasing in the tariffs selected by other *domestic* regions. Intuitively, this is because the respective domestic regions "compete" for imports: when other domestic regions raise their import tariffs, additional import volume is released for domestic region $r$, and this increases the incentive for region $r$ to raise its own tariff and receive even greater tariff revenue.

Third, an interesting pattern of externalities is apparent. Examination of Eq. (4) reveals that an increase in a foreign-region tariff reduces the welfare of any domestic country, as the domestic country then receives lower producer surplus. On the other hand, there is a *positive* externality between similarly-endowed countries: as a domestic region raises its tariff, more import volume is directed to other domestic regions, and the countries in these regions experience a welfare gain. When domestic and foreign regions all select the same tariff, however, the former effect dominates, in that each country's welfare increases as the symmetric tariff is reduced.

Finally, let us now define the *static tariff game* to be the game in which each region simultaneously selects an (external) import tariff in order to maximize its

---

[6]The essential feature of our static model is its prisoners' dilemma property. It is important to emphasize that this property is robust to inclusion of domestic political economy influences. Following Baldwin (1987), political influences can be represented with a parameter that attaches additional weight to producer surplus in the government welfare function. As this parameter affects government preferences as to the distribution of surplus within the domestic economy, the efficient trade policy is also affected by domestic political economy pressures. It remains true, however, that countries face a prisoners' dilemma problem in their dealings with one another: the efficient trade policy that maximizes joint welfare is not a Nash equilibrium, since each country does even better when it unilaterally exploits the terms-of-trade consequences of its policy choices and thereby redistributes surplus from its trading partner to itself. The inclusion of a political economy parameter therefore amounts to a renormalization of the traditional framework, changing only the level of the efficient tariff to which countries aspire and not the basic terms-of-trade incentives that frustrate the pursuit of this objective. See Bagwell and Staiger (1996) for further elaboration on these points.

K. Bagwell, R.W. Staiger / Journal of International Economics 42 (1997) 91–123 99

welfare per member country. Calculations reveal that the symmetric Nash equilibrium for the static tariff game occurs when all regions select the positive import tariff:

$$\hat{\tau}^N(R) = \frac{2}{\beta(4R - 1)}. \tag{6}$$

This expression exposes the "market power effect" of customs-union formation: when customs unions expand in the sense of being fewer in number and larger in size (i.e. as $R$ decreases), the newly-joined similarly-endowed countries internalize their joint incentive for higher import-tariffs, and consequently the Nash tariff rises.[7]

### 2.2. A stationary dynamic customs-union model

We now explore the possibility that the $R$ domestic and $R$ foreign regions can achieve greater efficiency through a multilateral trade agreement that calls for reciprocal trade liberalization below the Nash tariff level and that is self-enforcing. To this end, we consider a *stationary dynamic tariff game*, which is defined by the infinite repetition of the static tariff game described above. In each period the regions observe all previous import tariff selections and simultaneously choose import tariffs. For the reasons given above, we continue to assume that each region applies the same tariff to imported goods from all sources in any given period. The game is stationary in the sense that none of the model's parameters changes through time. Let $\delta \in (0,1)$ denote the discount factor between periods.

In order to express our ideas in a simple manner, we focus on a particular class of subgame perfect equilibria for the stationary dynamic tariff game. Specifically, we consider equilibria in which (i) symmetric stationary non-negative import tariffs are selected along the equilibrium path, meaning that in equilibrium all regions select the same import tariff in each period, and (ii) if a deviation from this common tariff occurs, then in the next period and forever thereafter the regions revert to the Nash equilibrium tariffs of the static tariff game. We then refer to the *most-cooperative equilibrium* of the stationary dynamic tariff game as the subgame perfect equilibrium which yields the lowest possible equilibrium tariff

---

[7]The finding that static Nash tariffs increase with customs-union formation is a robust implication of the market power effect of customs-union formation that we have isolated in this model, but it can be overturned in certain circumstances with the introduction of sufficient trade diversion. (See Krugman (1991) for a model of customs-union formation with both market power and trade diverting effects, in which customs-union formation leads to higher static Nash tariffs, and Bond and Syropoulos (1996a) for an example of how trade diverting effects can overturn this result.) We return in the concluding section to discuss more broadly the sensitivity of our results to the relative strengths of the market power and trade diversion effects associated with the formation of customs unions.

100      K. Bagwell, R.W. Staiger / Journal of International Economics 42 (1997) 91–123

while satisfying restrictions (i) and (ii). The corresponding import tariff is then termed the *most-cooperative tariff* for the stationary dynamic tariff game.[8]

In a dynamic model, regions have the possibility of supporting a cooperative tariff, $\tau^c$ with $\tau^c < \hat{\tau}^N(R)$, since any attempt to raise the current-period tariff will be greeted with retaliatory (Nash) tariffs from other regions in future periods. Intuitively, a cooperative tariff $\tau^c$ can then be supported in an equilibrium for the stationary dynamic tariff game if the one-time incentive to cheat is sufficiently small relative to the future value of maintaining a cooperative relationship among trading regions.

To formalize this intuition, let us first examine the incentive a region has to cheat. For a fixed cooperative tariff $\tau^c < \hat{\tau}^N(R)$, and given the class of subgame perfect equilibria upon which we focus, if a region is to deviate and select a tariff other than $\tau^c$, then it will deviate to its best-response tariff, as defined in Eq. (5). We now simplify the notation slightly and use $\tau^D(R,\tau^c)$ to represent the best-response tariff for a given region when all other same-type regions are selecting the cooperative tariff, $\tau^c$. The per-member-country gain when the associated region cheats is then given by:

$$\Omega(R,\tau^c) \equiv W(R,(\tau^D,\bar{\tau}^c);\bar{\tau}^c) - W(R,\bar{\tau}^c,\bar{\tau}^c), \tag{7}$$

where $\tau^c$ is a scalar and $\bar{\tau}^c$ is a vector in which the scalar $\tau^c$ is present in each component.[9] Intuitively, $\Omega$ is the difference between (i) the per-member-country welfare when the region to which the country belongs selects the best-defect tariff while all other regions – domestic and foreign – continue to select the cooperative tariff $\tau^c$, and (ii) the per-member-country welfare when the country's region cooperates in choosing the same cooperative tariff as do all other regions.

When a region cheats, however, it also causes future welfare to drop, and we now examine this cost of cheating. Define the one-period value to cooperation per member country to be:

$$\omega(R,\tau^c) \equiv W(R,\bar{\tau}^c;\bar{\tau}^c) - W(R,\bar{\hat{\tau}}^N(R);\bar{\hat{\tau}}^N(R)). \tag{8}$$

where $\bar{\hat{\tau}}^N(R)$ is an $R$-dimensional vector in which the scalar $\hat{\tau}^N(R)$ as defined in

---

[8]We could consider other forms of symmetric punishment, some of which would allow for greater levels of cooperation than the infinite Nash reversion considered here. However, the qualitative nature of our dynamic results concerning the behavior of cooperative tariffs is unlikely to be affected. Moreover, infinite reversion is not an entirely implausible representation of actual tariff wars: the high US tariffs on imports of light-duty trucks imposed as a result of the "chicken war" with the EC in 1963, for example, are still in place 30 years later. Our restriction to *symmetric* punishments, however, could be more substantive as we discuss in our discussion paper (Bagwell and Staiger, 1993).

[9]The notation in Eq. (7) is slightly awkward: $\bar{\tau}^c$ is an $R$-dimensional vector in each appearance, except for when $(\tau^D,\bar{\tau}^c)$ is written, in which case $\bar{\tau}^c$ is an $R-1$-dimensional vector. This latter case is meant to symbolize that the domestic region of interest defects to $\tau^D$ while all other domestic regions continue to each select the tariff $\tau^c$.

Eq. (6) is present in each component. Then the cost to cheating is $\delta/(1-\delta) \cdot \omega(R,\tau^c)$, since once a region defects and selects a high import tariff, cooperative tariffs are thereafter replaced by the higher Nash tariffs.

Using Eq. (7) and Eq. (8), the fundamental "no-defect" condition is that the benefit of cheating be less than the discounted future value of cooperation, or:

$$\Omega(R,\tau^c) \leq \frac{\delta}{1-\delta} \omega(R,\tau^c). \tag{9}$$

Any cooperative tariff $\tau^c$ that satisfies Eq. (9) can be supported in a subgame perfect equilibrium of the stationary dynamic tariff game.

Our interest lies in the most-cooperative tariff $\hat{\tau}^c$, which is the smallest non-negative tariff that satisfies Eq. (9). To characterize this tariff, we first investigate the properties of $\Omega(R,\tau^c)$ and $(\delta/(1-\delta))\omega(R,\tau^c)$. Calculations reveal that:

$$\Omega(R,\tau^c) = \frac{\beta(4R-1)^2}{8K(4R^2-1)}[\hat{\tau}^N(R) - \tau^c]^2. \tag{10}$$

Using Eq. (10), it follows that:

$$\frac{\partial \Omega(R,\tau^c)}{\partial R} < 0 \text{ if } \tau^c < \hat{\tau}^N(R) \tag{11}$$

$$\frac{\partial \Omega(R,\tau^c)}{\partial \tau^c} < 0 \text{ and } \frac{\partial^2 \Omega(R,\tau^c)}{\partial \tau^{c^2}} > 0 \text{ if } \tau^c < \hat{\tau}^N(R). \tag{12}$$

Thus, a decrease in $R$, which corresponds to more concentrated customs-union formation, acts to raise the benefit from defection, since a given customs union has greater power to affect world prices with its tariff increase. Notice also that lower cooperative tariffs heighten the incentive to cheat, because a deviation then represents a more significant tariff increase.

Calculations also reveal that:

$$\frac{\delta}{1-\delta}\omega(R,\tau^c) = \frac{\delta}{1-\delta}\frac{\beta}{4K}[(\hat{\tau}^N(R))^2 - (\tau^c)^2] > 0 \text{ if } \tau^c < \hat{\tau}^N(R). \tag{13}$$

Using Eq. (13), it follows that:

$$\frac{\partial}{\partial R}\left(\frac{\delta}{1-\delta}\omega(R,\tau^c)\right) < 0 \text{ if } \tau^c < \hat{\tau}^N(R) \tag{14}$$

$$\frac{\partial}{\partial \tau^c}\left(\frac{\delta}{1-\delta}\omega(R,\tau^c)\right) < 0 \text{ and } \frac{\partial^2}{\partial \tau^{c^2}}\left(\frac{\delta}{1-\delta}\omega(R,\tau^c)\right) < 0 \text{ if } \tau^c > 0. \tag{15}$$

Thus, as $R$ falls and customs unions become fewer in number and larger in size, the non-cooperative Nash tariff rises and so the cost of a trade war grows.

102      *K. Bagwell, R.W. Staiger / Journal of International Economics 42 (1997) 91–123*

However, higher cooperative tariffs lower the discounted value of future cooperation.

The determination of the most-cooperative tariff is now easily illustrated by Fig. 1. Observe in Fig. 1 that the no-defect condition (Eq. (9)) is satisfied for all $\tau^c \in [\hat{\tau}_s^c(R), \hat{\tau}^N(R)]$. These are the tariffs that are supportable as subgame perfect equilibrium tariffs for our stationary dynamic tariff game, given the class of equilibria upon which we focus. Solving Eq. (9) for the tariff that gives equality yields the most-cooperative tariff, which is given by:

$$\hat{\tau}_s^c(R) = \hat{\tau}^N(R)\left\{\frac{(4R-1)^2(1-\delta) - 2\delta(4R^2-1)}{(4R-1)^2(1-\delta) + 2\delta(4R^2-1)}\right\}. \tag{16}$$

Two observations can be made about the equilibrium most-cooperative tariff in the stationary dynamic game. First, note that $\hat{\tau}_s^c(R)$ is decreasing in $\delta$, with $\hat{\tau}_s^c = 0$ at

$$\delta = \frac{(4R-1)^2}{2(4R^2-1) + (4R-1)^2} \equiv \delta^*(R).$$

This decreasing relationship is intuitive: as $\delta$ increases, the discounted value of future cooperation is enhanced, and so a lower tariff can be supported (despite the

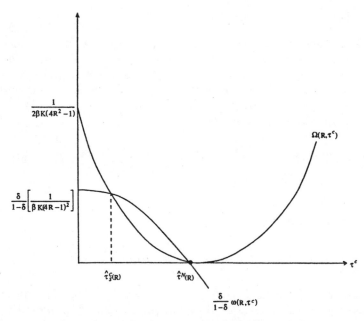

Fig. 1. Determining the most-cooperative stationary tariff.

K. Bagwell, R.W. Staiger / Journal of International Economics 42 (1997) 91–123    103

consequent greater incentive to cheat). To avoid cases in which the most-cooperative tariff corresponds to either of the extreme polar outcomes of free trade or the non-cooperative tariff $\hat{\tau}^N(R)$, we assume in what follows that $\delta \in (0, \delta^*(R))$ for all $R$ that we consider.

Second, whether or not the existence of smaller numbers of larger customs unions is good or bad for multilateral tariff cooperation between regions in the stationary dynamic game depends on the discount factor $\delta$. This makes sense, since the market power effect associated with customs-union formation (a falling $R$) makes higher tariffs more attractive and thus increases both the onetime benefit from cheating ($\Omega(R, \tau^c)$ – see Eq. (11)) and the cost of a tariff war (($\delta/(1 - \delta))\omega(R, \tau^c)$ – see Eq. (14)). If countries do not weigh the future too heavily, then the effect of customs-union formation on the one-time benefit from cheating dominates its effect on the cost of a tariff war, and the most-cooperative stationary tariff must be raised to keep the incentive constraint in check. In the limit, when $\delta = 0$, the most-cooperative tariff is simply $\hat{\tau}^N(R)$, which by Eq. (6) is declining in $R$. On the other hand, for $\delta$ sufficiently high, customs-union formation may be good for multilateral tariff cooperation in the stationary dynamic game, as the effects of customs-union formation on the added benefits from cheating become overwhelmed by the added cost of a tariff war. In the limit, as $\delta$ approaches $\delta(R)$, customs-union formation must be good for multilateral cooperation, since $\delta(R)$ in increasing in $R$; i.e. customs-union formation lowers the discount factor at which free trade is sustainable.

The dependence of the most-cooperative stationary tariff on the discount factor is illustrated in Fig. 2, where customs-union expansion corresponds to a reduction in the number of customs unions from $R_0$ to $R_1$, where $R_0 > R_1$. As the figure indicates, when countries do not weigh the future heavily, customs-union expansion results in a higher most-cooperative stationary tariff; but, when the discount factor is large, customs-union expansion is reflected in a lower most-cooperative stationary tariff. It follows that a critical discount factor, $\tilde{\delta}(R_0, R_1)$, must exist at which the most-cooperative stationary tariff is neutral with respect to customs-union expansion, and below which customs-union expansion results in a higher most-cooperative stationary tariff.[10]

In what follows we assume $\delta < \tilde{\delta}(R_0, R_1)$ so that customs-union formation is bad for multilateral cooperation in the stationary dynamic game. We choose to do this for several reasons. First, for simple cases of customs-union formation, this captures most of the relevant range of discount factors.[11] For example, in the case

---

[10] Fig. 2 has been drawn to illustrate the case in which there is a unique $\delta$ under which the most-cooperative stationary tariff is neutral with respect to customs-union expansion. If more than one such $\delta$ exists over the relevant range – and there could be at most two – then we define $\tilde{\delta}(R_0, R_1)$ as the smallest such $\delta$.

[11] In a related context to our stationary dynamic environment, Bond and Syropoulos (1996b) argue that this is the relevant case as well.

104    *K. Bagwell, R.W. Staiger / Journal of International Economics 42 (1997) 91–123*

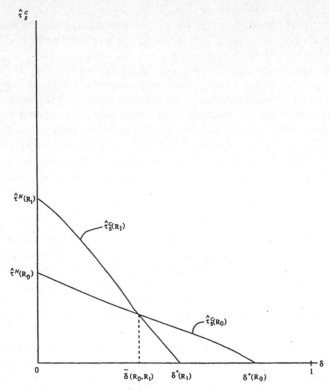

Fig. 2. Customs-union expansion and the most-cooperative stationary tariff for different discount factors.

where customs-union formation takes $R$ from $R_0 = 2$ to $R_1 = 1$, we require that $\delta < \delta(R_1) = 0.60$ to ensure that free trade cannot be sustained when $R = 1$. If $\delta < \tilde{\delta}(R_0, R_1) = 0.58$ also, the customs-union formation represented by the move from $R_0 = 2$ to $R_1 = 1$ will be bad for multilateral cooperation in the stationary dynamic game. Second, as we will show below, even adopting this "pessimistic" view of the stationary effect of customs unions on multilateral cooperation, there will nevertheless be a honeymoon phase during which multilateral tariffs first fall before they later rise.

## 2.3. Summary

We summarize the results of this section with the following proposition:

K. Bagwell, R.W. Staiger / Journal of International Economics 42 (1997) 91–123    105

*Proposition 1.*

(i) *The Nash equilibrium of the static tariff game occurs when each region sets an external import tariff of* $\hat{\tau}^N(R) = 2/(\beta(4R - 1))$.

(ii) *The most-cooperative equilibrium of the stationary dynamic game occurs when each region sets an external tariff of*

$$\hat{\tau}^c_s(R) = \hat{\tau}^N(R)\left\{\frac{(4R - 1)^2(1 - \delta) - 2\delta(4R^2 - 1)}{(4R - 1)^2(1 - \delta) + 2\delta(4R^2 - 1)}\right\}$$

*provided that* $\delta \in (0, \delta(R))$.

## 3. The formation of customs unions

We turn now to a dynamic model in which, at some point in time, customs-union expansion occurs, in that the number of domestic regions and also the number of foreign regions decreases. While understanding the timing of customs-union formation is important in its own right, it is a problem that has many dimensions, and a proper treatment is well beyond the scope of this paper. Instead, we assume that the process of customs-union expansion occurs randomly and for exogenous, political reasons. The possibility that the number of regions may change through time introduces a non-stationarity into the dynamic interaction between countries, and our focus here is on how customs-union expansion affects the ability of domestic and foreign regions to continue to cooperate multilaterally in the setting of low tariffs.

### 3.1. The customs-union model

We envision a multilateral trading relationship that passes through three phases. Countries seek to maintain low multilateral trade barriers in each phase. In phase 1, there are $R_0$ domestic regions and also $R_0$ foreign regions. The domestic and foreign regions trade with one another just as above. The countries are aware, however, that a time may come at which it becomes politically feasible for customs-union expansion to occur, both among domestic countries and among foreign countries. Phase 2 corresponds to a transition phase, in which there are still $R_0$ regions of each type, but in which customs-union-expansion discussions have already commenced. Finally, in phase 3, the customs-union-expansion talks are completed, the new regions are fully implemented, and there are now $R_1$ regions of each type, where $R_1 < R_0$. This final set of trading patterns then persists into the infinite future.

Equilibria of repeated games with non-stationarities are often difficult to characterize. For tractability, therefore, we impose two assumptions. First, we assume that the transition process obeys a constant-hazard-rate (i.e. stationary-

106     *K. Bagwell, R.W. Staiger / Journal of International Economics 42 (1997) 91–123*

Markov) property. Namely, if the countries are in phase 1 at any date $t$, then $\rho \in (0,1)$ is the constant probability that they will be in phase 2 at date $t + 1$. Similarly, $\lambda \in (0,1)$ is the fixed conditional probability of transition from phase 2 to phase 3. Note that $\rho$ and $\lambda$ are assumed independent of the tariff history between countries. As will become clear, while the constant-hazard-rate assumption is not completely general, it does make possible some very precise predictions. Second, we assume that the domestic and foreign countries pass through their respective phases at the same dates. This enables us to exploit symmetry between the two country types, and thereby simplifies the analysis.

The *customs-union game* is now defined as the infinite-period game, in which countries pass through the described three phases, and regions select tariffs in each period with the goal of maximizing the welfare of their respective current-member countries, where at any given date all regions are perfectly informed as to past tariffs and the current phase of the game. For this game, we examine a class of subgame perfect equilibria, for which (i) along the equilibrium path, in any given phase of the game, the domestic and foreign regions select a common import tariff for all dates within that phase; and (ii) if at any point in the game a deviation from the equilibrium tariff for the corresponding phase occurs, then in the next period and forever thereafter all regions select the Nash equilibrium tariffs of the relevant static tariff game.[12]

For such equilibria, there will be three cooperative tariff levels, with each corresponding to a different phase. Let $\tau_1^c$, $\tau_2^c$ and $\tau_3^c$ refer to the cooperative tariff levels in phases 1, 2 and 3 respectively. Once again, we look for a most-cooperative equilibrium, and we solve for the associated most-cooperative tariffs, $\hat{\tau}_1^c$, $\hat{\tau}_2^c$ and $\hat{\tau}_3^c$. The most-cooperative tariffs may be found using a recursive solution approach. Specifically, we first identify the no-defect condition for phase 3 and find the lowest tariff that can be supported in this phase in an equilibrium of the desired class. With $\hat{\tau}_3^c$ thus determined, we next turn to phase 2, represent the relevant no-defect condition for this phase, and then solve for the phase-2 most-cooperative tariff, $\hat{\tau}_2^c$. Finally, having solved for the most-cooperative tariffs in phases 2 and 3, we characterize next the no-defect condition for phase 1 and solve for the lowest tariff in this phase that does not invite cheating. The resulting tariff is the most-cooperative phase-1 tariff, $\hat{\tau}_1^c$. This recursive method does indeed identify the most-cooperative tariffs for the overall game, since the discounted value of cooperation as viewed from any given phase rises as future cooperative tariffs drop. Thus, by selecting the lowest possible cooperative phase-3 tariff, we raise the cost to countries of defecting and igniting a trade war in phases 2 and 1, and we thereby make possible lower tariffs in these phases as well. Similarly, a lower phase-2 tariff makes it possible to support lower cooperative tariffs in phase 1.

---

[12]Note that the constant hazard rate assumption enables us to look for a single tariff for all dates within a phase. Observe also that the level of the static Nash tariff will depend upon the phase, since as shown above the Nash tariff is sensitive to the number of existing regions.

K. Bagwell, R.W. Staiger / Journal of International Economics 42 (1997) 91–123     107

We are now ready to formally represent the no-defect conditions for each of the three phases. Let us begin with phase 3. At any date within this phase, there are $R_1$ regions of each kind, the future is known to be stationary, and the no-defect condition is:

$$\Omega(R_1,\tau_3^c) \le \frac{\delta}{1-\delta}\omega(R_1,\tau_3^c). \tag{17}$$

This has the same form as Eq. (9), the no-defect condition in our stationary model, except that the number of regions is now $R_1$. Thus, it follows that $\hat{\tau}_3^c = \hat{\tau}_s^c(R_1)$; in other words, the phase-3 most-cooperative tariff is the most-cooperative stationary tariff for a world in which there are $R_1$ domestic and foreign customs unions, respectively.

Consider now phase 2. The no-defect condition for this phase is:

$$\Omega(R_0,\tau_2^c) \le \delta\sum_{n=1}^{\infty} \lambda(1-\lambda)^{n-1}\left[\sum_{q=1}^{n-1}\delta^{q-1}\omega(R_0,\tau_2^c) + \sum_{k=n}^{\infty}\delta^{k-1}\omega(R_1,\hat{\tau}_3^c)\right] \tag{18a}$$

where $n$ indexes the period at which phase 3 begins, with $n = 1$ meaning that phase 3 begins in the next period, and where $q$ and $k$ correspond to periods within phases 2 and 3, respectively.[13] Observe in phase 2 that there are $R_0$ domestic and foreign regions, respectively, and this is reflected in the left-hand side of Eq. (18a). With some further simplification, the phase-2 no-defect condition may be written as:

$$\Omega(R_0,\tau_2^c) \le \frac{(1-\lambda)\delta}{[1-(1-\lambda)\delta]}\omega(R_0,\tau_2^c) + \frac{\lambda\delta/(1-\delta)}{[1-(1-\lambda)\delta]}\omega(R_1,\hat{\tau}_3^c)$$

$$\equiv V_2(\tau_2^c;\lambda,\delta,R_0,R_1) \tag{18b}$$

*where* $V_2$ is defined to be the expected discounted value to future cooperation, as viewed in phase 2. Intuitively, $V_2$ is a weighted average of $\omega(R_0,\tau_2^c)$ and $\omega(R_1,\hat{\tau}_3^c)$, since a defection in phase 2 induces a trade war, thus sacrificing the cooperative welfare that could have been received in the remainder of phase 2 (at the tariff level $\tau_2^c$) as well as the cooperative welfare that would have been forthcoming once phase 3 was entered (at the tariff level $\hat{\tau}_3^c$). The lowest tariff satisfying Eq. (18b) defines $\hat{\tau}_2^c$.

Finally, we come to the phase-1 no-defect condition:

$$\Omega(R_0,\tau_1^c) \le \delta\sum_{s=1}^{\infty}\rho(1-\rho)^{s-1}\left[\sum_{t=1}^{s-1}\delta^{t-1}\omega(R_0,\tau_1^c)\right.$$

$$\left. + \delta^{s-1}(\omega(R_0,\hat{\tau}_2^c) + V_2(\hat{\tau}_2^c;\lambda,\delta,R_0,R_1))\right] \tag{19a}$$

---

[13] $\sum_{q=1}^{0}\delta^{q-1}\omega \equiv 0$ is understood here.

108 *K. Bagwell, R.W. Staiger / Journal of International Economics 42 (1997) 91–123*

where $s$ indexes the period at which phase 2 begins, with $s = 1$ meaning that phase 2 begins in the next period, and where $t$ represents periods within phase 1. Using Eq. (18b), Eq. (19a) becomes:

$$\Omega(R_0, \tau_1^c) \leq \frac{(1 - \rho)\delta}{[1 - (1 - \rho)\delta]} \omega(R_0, \tau_1^c)$$

$$+ \frac{\rho\delta}{[1 - (1 - \rho)\delta]} \frac{\{\omega(R_0, \hat{\tau}_2^c) + [\lambda\delta/(1 - \delta)]\omega(R_1, \hat{\tau}_3^c)\}}{[1 - (1 - \lambda)\delta]}$$

$$\equiv V_1(\tau_1^c; \rho, \lambda, \delta, R_0, R_1) \tag{19b}$$

*where $V_1$* gives the expected discounted value to future cooperation as viewed from phase 1. Note now that $V_1$ is a weighted average of $\omega(R_0, \tau_1^c)$, $\omega(R_0, \hat{\tau}_2^c)$ and $\omega(R_1, \hat{\tau}_3^c)$, reflecting the fact that a deviation in phase 1 sacrifices the ability to cooperate in the remainder of phase 1 as well as throughout phases 2 and 3. The smallest tariff satisfying Eq. (19b) is then defined to be $\hat{\tau}_1^c$.

## 3.2. Characterization of the most-cooperative tariffs

We are prepared now to characterize the three most-cooperative tariff levels, so that their relative magnitudes may be determined. In this way, we will be able to assess the consequences of customs-union expansion for multilateral tariff cooperation.

The tariffs are characterized in a recursive fashion, beginning with the phase-3 most-cooperative tariff. As discussed above, this tariff is simply the most-cooperative stationary tariff for a world in which there are $R_1$ customs unions of each country type:

*Lemma 1.*

$$0 < \hat{\tau}_3^c = \hat{\tau}_s^c(R_1) < \hat{\tau}^N(R_1).$$

Thus, over the range of discount factors on which we focus, the phase-3 most-cooperative tariff lies between free trade and the Nash tariff (for $R_1$ regions).

Consider now the phase-2 most-cooperative tariff. To characterize this tariff, we first record the following:

*Lemma 2.*

$$\omega(R_1, \hat{\tau}_s^c(R_1)) > \omega(R_0, \hat{\tau}_s^c(R_0)).$$

Lemma 2 states that the per-period value of cooperation at the most-cooperative *stationary* tariff is highest when there are fewer regions. Intuitively, two forces are at work in the proof of this lemma. First, for any fixed cooperative tariff, a smaller number of regions results in a greater value of cooperation, as Eq. (14)

*K. Bagwell, R.W. Staiger / Journal of International Economics 42 (1997) 91–123*     109

demonstrates, since under the market power effect a trade war is more damaging when regions are larger in size and fewer in number. Second, over the range for $\delta$ on which we focus, the most-cooperative stationary tariff is higher when there are fewer regions, and, as Eq. (15) indicates, this higher cooperative tariff acts to diminish the gain from cooperation. Lemma 2 establishes that the direct effect of a smaller number of regions outweighs the indirect effect of a higher cooperative tariff, and so the per-period value of cooperation at the most-cooperative stationary tariff is higher when there are fewer regions. A proof of this lemma is found in Appendix A.

With Lemma 2 in place, we can record some properties of the $V_2$ function:

$$\frac{\partial V_2(\tau_2^c; \lambda, \delta, R_0, R_1)}{\partial \tau_2^c} < 0 \tag{20}$$

$$V_2(\hat{\tau}_s^c(R_0); \lambda, \delta, R_0, R_1) > \frac{\delta}{1 - \delta} \omega(R_0, \hat{\tau}_s^c(R_0)). \tag{21}$$

Intuitively, the discounted value of future cooperation as viewed from phase 2 is lower when the cooperative tariff in phase 2 is higher, since in this case cooperation in phase 2 is already modest, and so a trade war instigated in this phase would result in less welfare loss during any remaining periods of phase 2. More formally, Eq. (20) follows directly from Eq. (18b) and Eq. (15). As for Eq. (21), observe from Lemma 1 and Eq. (18b) that $V_2(\hat{\tau}_s^c(R_0); \cdot)$ is a weighted average of $\omega(R_0, \hat{\tau}_s^c(R_0))$ and $\omega(R_1, \hat{\tau}_s^c(R_1))$, the per-period values of cooperation at the most-cooperative stationary tariffs when there are $R_0$ and $R_1$ regions, respectively. Now, Lemma 2 tells us that the per-period value of cooperation at the most-cooperative stationary tariff is greatest when the number of regions is small, and it thus must be that the discounted value of future cooperation as viewed from phase 2 exceeds that obtained in a stationary setting with a large number of regions.[14] Fig. 3 illustrates the implications of Eq. (20) and Eq. (21) by depicting $V_2(\tau_2^c = \tau^c; \cdot)$ as declining in $\tau^c$ and lying strictly above $(\delta/(1 - \delta))\omega(R_0, \tau^c)$ at $\tau^c = \hat{\tau}_s^c(R_0)$.

It is convenient to ensure that free trade is never supportable, and that the no-defect condition therefore always binds with equality. To guarantee this, we further require that:

$$\Omega(R_0, 0) > \frac{\delta}{1 - \delta} \omega(R_1, 0) \tag{22}$$

which in turn implies that $\Omega(R_0, 0) > V_2(0; \cdot)$, indicating that free trade is not

---

[14]Formally, Lemmas 1 and 2 imply
$$V_2(\hat{\tau}_s^c(R_0); \cdot) \equiv \{(1 - \lambda)\delta / [1 - (1 - \lambda)\delta]\}\omega(R_0, \hat{\tau}_s^c(R_0)) + \{[\lambda\delta/(1 - \delta)]/[1 - (1 - \lambda)\delta]\}\omega(R_1, \hat{\tau}_s^c)$$
$$> \{(1 - \lambda)\delta / [1 - (1 - \lambda)\delta]\}\omega(R_0, \hat{\tau}_s^c(R_0)) + \{[\lambda\delta/(1 - \delta)]/[1 - (1 - \lambda)\delta]\}\omega(R_0, \hat{\tau}_s^c(R_0))$$
$$= [\delta/(1 - \delta)]\omega(R_0, \hat{\tau}_s^c(R_0)).$$

110     *K. Bagwell, R.W. Staiger / Journal of International Economics 42 (1997) 91–123*

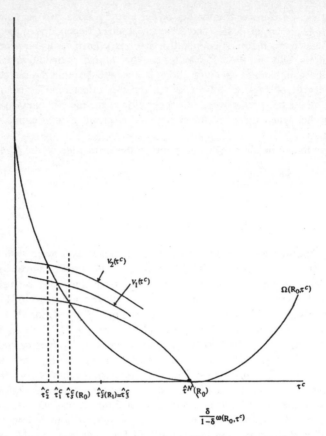

Fig. 3. Determining the most-cooperative tariffs in the customs-union game.

supportable in phase 2.[15] Observe that Eq. (22) will clearly hold under our existing assumptions if $R_0 - R_1$ is small, since in that event Eq. (22) basically requires again that free trade not be supportable in stationary environments. More generally, Eq. (22) is satisfied if $\delta$ is restricted to lie below some critical level, $\delta^\dagger(R_0,R_1)$.[16] Thus, Eq. (22) may be understood as a further strengthening of our small $-\delta$ orientation.

[15]To see this, observe that

$$V_2(0;\cdot) \equiv \{[(1-\lambda)\delta]/[1-(1-\lambda)\delta]\}\omega(R_0,0) + \{[\lambda\delta/(1-\delta)]/[1-(1-\lambda)\delta]\}\omega(R_1,\hat{\tau}_3^c)$$
$$< \{[(1-\lambda)\delta]/[1-(1-\lambda)\delta]\}\omega(R_0,0) + \{[\lambda\delta/(1-\delta)]/[1-(1-\lambda)\delta]\}\omega(R_1,0)$$
$$< [\delta/(1-\delta)]\omega(R_1,0),$$

which uses Eq. (14) and Eq. (15).

[16]Specifically, Eq. (22) holds if $\delta < \delta^\dagger(R_0,R_1) \equiv [R_1(4R_1 - 1)^2]/[R_1(4R_1 - 1)^2 + 2R_0(4R_0^2 - 1)]$.

K. Bagwell, R.W. Staiger / Journal of International Economics 42 (1997) 91–123     111

We are now prepared to characterize $\hat{\tau}_2^c$, which is the lowest tariff for which $\Omega(R_0,\tau_2^c) \leq V_2(\tau_2^c:\lambda,\delta,R_0,R_1)$. As Fig. 3 illustrates, given Eq. (20), Eq. (21) and Eq. (22), $\hat{\tau}_2^c$ must lie strictly between 0 and $\hat{\tau}_3^c$:

*Lemma 3.*

$$0 < \hat{\tau}_2^c < \hat{\tau}_3^c.$$

Thus, a honeymoon phase occurs during the transition to a fully implemented customs union, as multilateral tariffs are low throughout this process. Once the customs-union expansion is fully implemented, however, multilateral tariff cooperation must deteriorate and higher multilateral tariffs prevail.

Lemma 3 may be understood in the following intuitive terms. If the number of regions were stationary through time, with $R_0$ regions of each type of country, then the regions could support a tariff level of $\hat{\tau}_s^c(R_0)$, as this is the tariff that just balances a region's immediate incentive to cheat against the long-term consequences of a trade war. This situation now may be contrasted with that which arises in the transition phase of the customs-union game. At this point, the various countries are still aligned with $R_0$ regions of each country type, and so the incentive to cheat is the same as in the associated dynamic stationary game, but the countries are also aware that customs-union expansion – and the greater punishment that this makes possible – will soon occur. Thus, as compared with the stationary environment that supports $\hat{\tau}_s^c(R_0)$, in the transition phase of the customs-union game, the countries perceive the expected discounted value of future cooperation now to be higher (as Eq. (21) states). It follows, therefore, that the most-cooperative stationary tariff, $\hat{\tau}_s^c(R_0)$, is easily supported in the transition phase of the customs-union game. In fact, the balance between the incentive to cheat and the expected discounted value of future cooperation is not restored until a lower phase-2 cooperative tariff is selected and the incentive to cheat is correspondingly raised to a level commensurate with the expected discounted value of future cooperation. Hence, it must be that $\hat{\tau}_2^c < \hat{\tau}_s^c(R_0)$. The final step now is to recall that $\hat{\tau}_s^c(R_0) < \hat{\tau}_s^c(R_1) = \hat{\tau}_3^c$, and so the phase-3 most-cooperative tariff must exceed the phase-2 most-cooperative tariff.

More generally, the honeymoon prediction may be understood as a reflection of the evolution of market power throughout the customs-union game. While customs unions are being negotiated and phased in, countries recognize that once these larger regions are in place, the world will have better enforcers, because under the market power effect larger regions can credibly impose higher Nash tariffs, should such punitive tariffs be called for. The prospect that a trade war initiated today might reach such proportions in the future then makes countries reluctant to pursue unilateral objectives in the present, and so the recognition of eventual customs-union expansion gives rise to a honeymoon period in which low multilateral tariffs can be supported. This honeymoon eventually gives way, however, since once the customs-unions are actually expanded, each country realizes that its region's enhanced market power also makes possible a large welfare gain from defection to a higher import tariff. Thus, after the customs-union expansion is finalized, multilateral tariffs must rise to diminish the incentive to cheat and restore balance.

We turn next to the initial-phase tariff, $\hat{\tau}_1^c$, which is the lowest tariff such that $\Omega(R_0,\tau_1^c) \le V_1(\tau_1^c;\rho,\lambda,\delta,R_0,R_1)$. To characterize this tariff, we first show that:

**Lemma 4.**

$$\omega(R_1,\hat{\tau}_s^c(R_1)) > \omega(R_0,\hat{\tau}_2^c).$$

Recalling that $\hat{\tau}_s^c(R_1) = \hat{\tau}_3^c$, we see that Lemma 4 states that the per-period equilibrium value of cooperation rises from phase 2 to phase 3. Once again, there are two effects, as phase 3 involves a smaller number of regions, which act to raise the per-period value of cooperation, and yet phase 3 also entails a higher most-cooperative tariff (by Lemma 3), which works to reduce the per-period value of cooperation in phase 3. As above, however, the direct effect of a smaller number of regions dominates, and thus the per-period equilibrium value of cooperation is higher in phase 3. This lemma is proved in Appendix A.

Three key properties of the $V_1$ function may now be reported:

$$\frac{\partial V_1(\tau_1^c;\rho,\lambda,\delta,R_0,R_1)}{\partial \tau_1^c} < 0 \tag{23}$$

$$V_1(\hat{\tau}_2^c;\rho,\lambda,\delta,R_0,R_1) < V_2(\hat{\tau}_2^c;\lambda,\delta,R_0,R_1) \tag{24}$$

$$V_1(\hat{\tau}_s^c(R_0);\rho,\lambda,\delta,R_0,R_1) > \frac{\delta}{1-\delta}\omega(R_0,\hat{\tau}_s^c(R_0)). \tag{25}$$

As before, a higher cooperative tariff reduces the fear of a trade war, at least during the associated phase, and therefore reduces the overall expected discounted value of future cooperation. More formally, Eq. (23) is direct from Eq. (19b) and Eq. (15). To understand Eq. (24), observe that, under Lemma 4, the per-period equilibrium value of cooperation is higher in phase 3 than in phase 2; consequently, the expected discounted value of future cooperation is higher in phase 2 than in phase 1 (at the relevant tariff), because the transition to phase 3 is more imminent when countries begin in phase 2.[17] Finally, to gain some insight into Eq. (25), recall that $V_1(\hat{\tau}_s^c(R_0);\cdot)$ is a weighted average of the associated per-period values of cooperation across the three phases, namely, $\omega(R_0,\hat{\tau}_s^c(R_0))$, $\omega(R_0,\hat{\tau}_2^c)$ and $\omega(R_1,\hat{\tau}_s^c(R_1))$; however, the per-period value of cooperation in the third phase exceeds that in the first by Lemma 2, and the per-period value of cooperation in the second phase also exceeds that in the first, since the most-cooperative

---

[17]Formally, using Lemma 4, calculations reveal that:
$$V_2(\hat{\tau}_2^c;\lambda,\delta,R_0,R_1) - V_1(\hat{\tau}_2^c;\rho,\lambda,\delta,R_0,R_1) = \{\lambda\delta/\{[1-(1-\lambda)\delta][1-(1-\rho)\delta]\}\}[\omega(R_1,\hat{\tau}_s^c(R_1))$$
$$- \omega(R_0,\hat{\tau}_2^c)] > 0.$$

K. Bagwell, R.W. Staiger / Journal of International Economics 42 (1997) 91–123    113

second-phase tariff is lower than the most-cooperative stationary tariff that is specified in Eq. (25) for the first phase. Thus, Eq. (25) clearly must hold.[18]

The implications of Eq. (23), Eq. (24) and Eq. (25) are illustrated in Fig. 3, which depicts $V_1(\tau_1^c = \tau^c; \cdot)$ as declining in $\tau^c$, lying strictly below $V_2(\tau_2^c = \tau^c; \cdot)$ at $\tau^c = \hat{\tau}_2^c$, and lying strictly above $(\delta/(1-\delta))\omega(R_0, \tau^c)$ at $\tau^c = \hat{\tau}_s^c(R_0)$. We may thus conclude, as Fig. 3 illustrates, that:

*Lemma 5.*

$$\hat{\tau}_2^c < \hat{\tau}_1^c < \hat{\tau}_3^c.$$

Thus the initial-phase tariff is lower than the final-phase tariff, but it is not as low as the tariff that occurs during the transition phase.

The intuition underlying Lemma 5 is easily related. Consider first why tariffs are lower in the initial phase than in the final phase. When the countries are in phase 1, there are $R_0$ regions, and each of these small regions has some incentive to cheat. Balancing against this defection incentive is the cost of a future trade war, and if the world were stationary with $R_0$ regions of each country type for ever, then the incentive to cheat would be just balanced against the cost of a trade war at the most-cooperative stationary tariff, $\hat{\tau}_s^c(R_0)$. In phase 1 of the customs-union game, however, the countries recognize that (i) the very cooperative honeymoon phase will arrive soon, and (ii) eventually customs-union expansion will occur and there will be only $R_1$ regions of each country type. For both of these reasons, the expected discounted value of future cooperation (i.e. the expected cost of a trade war) is quite high as viewed from phase 1 (as Eq. (25) indicates), and so the most-cooperative stationary tariff with $R_0$ regions is easily supported in phase 1 of the customs-union game. In fact, an even lower cooperative tariff (with the concomitant larger defection incentive) can be supported at this phase, and it therefore follows that $\hat{\tau}_1^c < \hat{\tau}_s^c(R_0) < \hat{\tau}_s^c(R_1) = \hat{\tau}_3^c$.

At a more general level, before countries begin negotiations on customs-union expansion, each region has little market power, since each region is comprised of only a few countries. Given this, there is little benefit to the countries in a region from cheating and selecting a high tariff. On the other hand, the countries correctly perceive that larger regions with great market power are on the horizon; thus, a trade war begun today would sacrifice the very cooperative tariffs that would otherwise be enjoyed while the customs-union expansion was being negotiated and phased in, and it would also culminate in a very costly tariff war once the large regions were actually in place. This imbalance between a low current gain from

---

[18]Formally, Lemmas 1 and 2 and also $\hat{\tau}_2^c < \hat{\tau}_s^c(R_0)$ and Eq. (15) imply that
$$V_1(\hat{\tau}_s^c(R_0);\cdot) \equiv \{(1-\rho)\delta/[1-(1-\rho)\delta]\}\omega(R_0,\hat{\tau}_s^c(R_0)) + \{\rho\delta/[1-(1-\rho)\delta]\}\{\omega(R_0,\hat{\tau}_2^c) + [\lambda\delta/(1-\delta)]\omega(R_1,\hat{\tau}_3^c)\}/[1-(1-\lambda)\delta]$$
$$> \{(1-\rho)\delta/[1-(1-\rho)\delta]\}\omega(R_0,\hat{\tau}_s^c(R_0)) + \{\rho\delta/[1-(1-\rho)\delta]\}\{\omega(R_0,\hat{\tau}_s^c(R_0)) + [\lambda\delta/(1-\delta)]\omega(R_0,\hat{\tau}_s^c(R_0))\}/[1-(1-\lambda)\delta]$$
$$= [\delta/(1-\delta)]\omega(R_0,\hat{\tau}_s^c(R_0)).$$

114     *K. Bagwell, R.W. Staiger / Journal of International Economics 42 (1997) 91–123*

cheating and a large future cost to a trade war enables the countries to support a very low cooperative tariff in the period of time that precedes customs-union negotiations. Once the customs unions are fully implemented, however, the natural balance between the incentive to cheat and the expected discounted value of future cooperation is restored, since each region then has substantial market power in the present, with the corresponding greater incentive to cheat. Thus, once customs unions are fully implemented (in phase 3), the cooperative tariff must rise above that found prior to customs-union negotiations (in phase 1).

Finally, consider why the phase-2 most-cooperative tariff is lower than the phase-1 most-cooperative tariff. In both phases, the incentive to cheat is small, since a region has little market power, being comprised of only $R_0$ countries. The essential difference between the initial and transition phases is that actual customs-union expansion can be expected to occur sooner when countries are already in the negotiation or transition phase. As Eq. (24) indicates, this in turn means the expected discounted value to future cooperation is higher in phase 2, since a trade war initiated in that phase will be exacerbated more quickly by the higher Nash tariffs that large regions are prone to select. Hence, a lower cooperative tariff can be supported in phase 2.

Our main results may now be summarized in the following proposition:

*Proposition 2. For the customs-union game, in the most-cooperative equilibrium, the domestic and foreign regions set the most-cooperative import tariffs, $\hat{\tau}_1^c$, $\hat{\tau}_2^c$ and $\hat{\tau}_3^c$ in phases 1, 2 and 3, respectively, and these tariffs may be ranked as follows: $0 < \hat{\tau}_2^c < \hat{\tau}_1^c < \hat{\tau}_3^c$.*

These rankings are captured in Fig. 4, which depicts the most-cooperative tariffs in the three phases of the customs-union game. As the figure illustrates, the prospect of a future customs-union expansion serves to lower current cooperative tariffs, and particularly so as the expansion becomes more imminent. Once the customs-union expansion is fully implemented, however, multilateral tariffs must rise to maintain cooperation.

## 4. Comparative statics

The customs-union model developed above has a variety of parameters, and it is important to assess the sensitivity of the most-cooperative tariffs to these parameters. In addition, some of these parameters may be loosely associated with aspects of GATT policy toward customs unions as embodied in Article XXIV. Thus, in this section, we present comparative-statics results, and in the concluding section we discuss their implications with regard to the design of Article XXIV. Examining the respective no-defect conditions presented above, it is apparent that

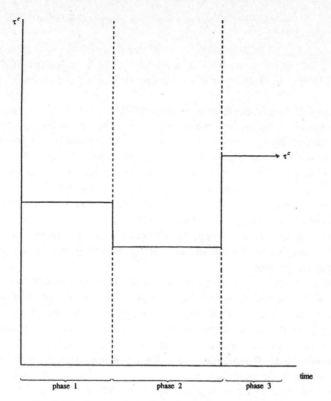

Fig. 4. The 'honeymoon' effect of customs-union formation.

the most-cooperative tariffs have the following functional dependencies: $\hat{\tau}_3^c = \hat{\tau}_3^c(\delta,R_1)$, $\hat{\tau}_2^c = \hat{\tau}_2^c(\lambda,\delta,R_0,R_1)$ and $\hat{\tau}_1^c = \hat{\tau}_1^c(\rho,\lambda,\delta,R_0,R_1)$.

Before proceeding, it is important to record the following corollary:

*Corollary 1.*

$$\omega(R_1,\hat{\tau}_3^c) > \omega(R_0,\hat{\tau}_2^c) > \omega(R_0,\hat{\tau}_1^c).$$

Corollary 1 indicates that the per-period equilibrium value of cooperation increases through time. The proof is direct, as the first inequality is simply a restatement of Lemma 4 (recall that $\hat{\tau}_3^c = \hat{\tau}_s^c(R_1)$), while the second inequality follows from Proposition 2 and Eq. (15). This corollary will be important for the proofs of the comparative-statics results derived below.

Our central set of results is contained in the following proposition:

116    *K. Bagwell, R.W. Staiger / Journal of International Economics 42 (1997) 91–123*

*Proposition 3. For the customs-union game, the most-cooperative tariffs satisfy the following relationships:*

*(i)$\hat{\tau}_1^c(\rho,\lambda,\delta,R_0,R_1)$ is decreasing in $\rho$, $\lambda$ and $\delta$, and it is increasing in $R_1$.*

*(ii)$\hat{\tau}_2^c(\lambda,\delta,R_0,R_1)$ is decreasing in $\lambda$ and $\delta$, and it is increasing in $R_1$.*

*(iii)$\hat{\tau}_3^c(\delta,R_1)$ is decreasing in $\delta$, and decreasing in $R_1$ if $\delta$ is sufficiently small.*

The proof of this proposition is in Appendix A.

To gain some intuition, let us start with the effect of an increase in $\rho$ on the phase-1 most-cooperative tariff. As $\rho$ rises, countries that are currently in phase 1 recognize that the transition to phase 2 and, ultimately, the transition to phase 3 will occur sooner. This in turn raises the expected discounted value to cooperation (i.e. $V_1$) as viewed from phase 1, since Corollary 1 establishes that the per-period equilibrium value of cooperation is larger in later phases. With the perceived cost of a trade war thereby increased, lower phase-1 tariffs (with the associated higher incentive to cheat) can be supported. Hence, an increase in the likelihood that customs unions will be formed in the near future will give a temporary boost to multilateral cooperation.

The consequences of a larger value for $\lambda$ are similar, although the argument is slightly more involved. Consider first the phase-2 most-cooperative tariff. As $\lambda$ rises, the transition to the final phase is expedited, and, using Corollary 1 once more, it follows that the expected discounted value of future cooperation (i.e. $V_2$) as viewed from phase 2 rises. Thus, a higher value for $\lambda$ acts to lower the phase-2 most-cooperative tariff. In phase 1, a higher $\lambda$ also results in a lower most-cooperative tariff, though now for two reasons. First, as before, when $\lambda$ is increased, the final phase is reached more quickly, and using Corollary 1 this enables a lower phase-1 most-cooperative tariff. Second, an increase in $\lambda$ lowers the phase-2 most-cooperative tariff, as argued just above, and the anticipation of this more-cooperative phase-2 behavior in turn acts to raise the expected discounted value of future cooperation as viewed from phase 1, thereby making possible a lower phase-1 most-cooperative tariff. Thus, for both direct and indirect reasons, a higher value for $\lambda$ results in a lower phase-1 most-cooperative tariff.

An increase in $\delta$ has the anticipated effect on the most-cooperative tariffs, as all such tariffs then decline. Intuitively, the direct effect of an increase in $\delta$ is that the future is valued more, and so countries are more reluctant to sacrifice cooperation and enter into a trade war. Thus, a higher value for $\delta$ serves to raise the expected discounted value to future cooperation, and thereby makes possible the support of lower most-cooperative tariffs in all phases. Second, for phases 1 and 2, an increase in $\delta$ also has beneficial indirect effects. For example, in phase 2, when $\delta$ increases, countries recognize that the phase-3 most-cooperative tariff will be lower as a result, and so the cost of a future trade war is raised for this reason as well. Similar indirect effects arise in phase 1.

Finally, we may view $R_0$ as an initial condition and investigate the consequences of greater customs-union expansion by allowing $R_1$ to be smaller. For sufficiently small $\delta$, a decrease in $R_1$ raises the phase-3 most-cooperative tariff. Intuitively, as Lemma 1 indicates, the phase-3 most-cooperative tariff is simply the most-cooperative stationary tariff for a world with $R_1$ regions of each country type. Further, as we argued in Section 2, in stationary environments a reduction in the number of regions enhances each region's market power, and this results in a higher most-cooperative stationary tariff if countries discount the future sufficiently. Thus, given our small-$\delta$ orientation, it must be that the phase-3 most-cooperative tariff rises as customs-union expansion becomes more significant.[19]

The effect of greater customs-union expansion generates a rather different consequence for the phase-1 and phase-2 most-cooperative tariffs. As we show in Appendix A while proving Lemma 2, a key feature of our model is that $\omega(R,\hat{\tau}_s^c(R)) \equiv f(R)$ is declining in $R$, so that the per-period value of cooperation at the most-cooperative stationary tariff is always higher when there are fewer regions. In other words, the direct positive effect that a reduction in the number of regions has for the per-period value of cooperation always outweighs any possible negative indirect effect from a consequent increase in the most-cooperative stationary tariff.[20] Using Lemma 1, it follows immediately that a reduction in $R_1$ acts to raise the per-period equilibrium value of cooperation in phase 3, and this in turn implies that a lower phase-2 most-cooperative tariff can be supported when greater customs-union expansion is anticipated. Given that greater customs-union expansion has the direct effect of raising the per-period equilibrium value of cooperation in phase 3 and the indirect effect of lowering the phase-2 most cooperative tariff, it follows that the expected discounted value of future cooperation (i.e. $V_1$) as viewed from phase 1 rises for two reasons, and a lower phase-1 most-cooperative tariff can be supported as a result.

Thus, in general, customs-union expansion has a beneficial effect on multilateral tariff cooperation before the expansion is fully implemented. Further, any parameter change that speeds up the transitional process that leads to customs-union expansion, or which increases the extent of the eventual expansion, will

---

[19]Heretofore, we have assumed that $\delta$ is sufficiently small that a customs-union expansion in which the number of regions of each country type changed from $R_0$ to $R_1$ would result in a higher most-cooperative stationary tariff. This defines a range of $\delta$, which we stated as $\delta \leq \bar{\delta}(R_0,R_1)$, and we argued in Section 2 that this range seemed to rule out few $\delta$, other than those which we had already ruled out in assuming that free trade is not viable. The comparative static investigated here is slightly different, since $R_0$ is held fixed and we examine what happens to the most-cooperative stationary tariff as $R_1$ declines. Thus, if $\delta \leq \bar{\delta}(R_1,R_1 - \varepsilon)$, then the most-cooperative stationary tariff will rise as $R_1$ declines. This additional small-$\delta$ restriction appears to rule out few if any additional values for $\delta$; for example, when $R_1 = 2$, $\bar{\delta}(2,2 - \varepsilon) = 0.59$. Recall that $\bar{\delta}(2,1) = 0.58$. Nevertheless, because $\delta \leq \bar{\delta}(R_1,R_1 - \varepsilon)$ is not a maintained assumption on $\delta$, as it is employed only in deriving the comparative static for the phase-3 most-cooperative tariff as a function of $R_1$, we have included in the statement of Proposition 3 that this comparative static need hold only for sufficiently small $\delta$.

[20]This result does not require any additional assumption on the range of permissible $\delta$ (for example, $\delta \leq \bar{\delta}(R_1,R_1 - \varepsilon)$), and so parts (i) and (ii) of Proposition 3 are stated without additional restrictions on $\delta$.

result in even greater multilateral tariff cooperation prior to the full implementation of the regional agreements. On the down side, however, if countries are sufficiently impatient, greater regional expansion can have negative consequences for multilateral tariff cooperation once the expansion is fully implemented. In this sense, our results imply that the formation of customs unions will enhance multilateral cooperation in the early stages of the regional integration process, but that multilateral cooperation is likely to suffer once this formation process is complete.

## 5. Conclusion

We have presented a model of customs unions which predicts that the early stages of the process of customs-union formation will lead to a temporary honeymoon for liberal multilateral trade policies which ultimately must be reversed as the customs union becomes fully implemented. Intuitively, during the period of transition toward customs-union formation, non-member countries recognize that member countries will soon experience an enhancement of market power and find higher tariffs more attractive; thus, a trade war initiated in this period could have especially dire implications in the near future, and so low multilateral tariffs become feasible during the transition period. Once the customs union complete, however, the market power consequences become real, and the customs union faces a greater incentive to defect to a higher tariff. A self-enforcing agreement can then be maintained only if multilateral tariffs rise, quelling the incentive to deviate.

We have highlighted the special effects of customs-union formation as distinct from the formation of free trade areas by constructing a model that isolates the market power effect which comes with customs-union formation, and abstracts from the trade diversion effect which is common to both customs unions and free trade agreements. Since a comparison of our results here with those of Bagwell and Staiger (1997), which considers free trade agreements and the associated trade diversion effect, establishes that trade diversion effects of regional agreements run opposite to market power effects in terms of their implications for multilateral tariff cooperation, we can only claim to have captured the implications of customs-union formation for multilateral tariff cooperation when the market power effect dominates the trade diversion effect.[21] Nevertheless, the two papers together underscore the two distinct forces that determine the impacts of regional integration on multilateral tariff cooperation, with free trade agreements reflecting primarily the trade diversion effects and customs unions in general reflecting some combination of both trade diversion and market power effects.

---

[21] As discussed in footnote 7, sufficient trade diversion could also overturn our results through the possible effect on the relationship between static Nash tariffs and customs-union formation.

While a thorough understanding of the implications of the formation of the EC for multilateral tariff cooperation under GATT would require consideration of a variety of economic and political influences, our model does supply a novel perspective that is broadly consistent with facts. Provided that the market power effects of EC formation were sufficiently important relative to trade diversion effects, our model predicts that multilateral tariff liberalization would be initially stimulated by the formation and subsequent extension of the EC customs union, but that this complementarity would ultimately give way to a more dissonant relationship and multilateral tariff cooperation would suffer as a result.[22]

Finally, we comment briefly on the institutional implications of our analysis with regard to the design of GATT Article XXIV. This article permits customs-union formation, provided that member countries achieve free trade on substantially all goods they trade and that the union is formed in a timely manner.[23] In terms of our model, these restrictions may be understood as an attempt to reduce the frequency with which such unions occur (related to the parameter $\rho$) and the length of the transition period to the fully implemented agreement (related to the parameter $\lambda$) from what these parameters would look like in an unrestricted world. The comparative statics results reported here suggest that Article XXIV could have important consequences for multilateral tariff cooperation. In particular, efforts to reduce the frequency with which customs-union agreements are negotiated will tend to diminish multilateral cooperation as long as those efforts are successful and customs-union formation is deterred, and will delay the start of the harmonious transition phase associated with the early stages of customs-union implementation, but will also postpone the post-customs-union high-tariff world. At the same time, efforts to shorten the transition period over which a customs-union agreement is implemented will tend to boost multilateral cooperation up until the final implementation is achieved, but such efforts will also hasten the arrival of the post-customs-union high-tariff world.

## Acknowledgments

We have benefited from helpful discussions with Don Davis, John Kennan, Carsten Kowalczyk, Karl Scholz, from the comments of Bill Ethier as our discussant at NBER's 1993 Conference on Trade Rules and Institutions, and from the comments of seminar participants at Harvard, the NBER 1993 Summer Institute, CEPR's 1993 Workshop on the Political Economy of Trade Negotiations, IGIER, and an anonymous referee. Staiger gratefully acknowledges financial

---

[22] Our model differs from the EC experience, in that we consider symmetric formation of customs unions. As we show in our earlier discussion paper (Bagwell and Staiger, 1993), however, our central results extend to the case of asymmetric customs-union formation.

[23] As Dam (1970, chapter 16) argues, these restrictions are not always enforced.

support from Stanford's Center for Economic Policy Research, and as an Alfred P. Sloan Research Fellow.

## Appendix A

### Proof of Lemma 2

Observe that

$$\frac{d\omega(R,\hat{\tau}_s^c(R))}{dR} = \frac{\partial\omega(R,\hat{\tau}_s^c(R))}{\partial R} + \frac{\partial\omega(R,\hat{\tau}_s^c(R))}{\partial\tau^c}\frac{\partial\hat{\tau}_s^c(R)}{\partial R}. \tag{A.1}$$

To sign this expression, we first calculate that

$$\omega(R,\hat{\tau}_s^c(R)) = \frac{8\delta(1-\delta)(4R^2-1)}{K\beta[(4R-1)^2(1-\delta)+2\delta(4R^2-1)]^2}. \tag{A.2}$$

Further calculations then yield that

$$\frac{d\omega(R,\hat{\tau}_s^c(R))}{dR} = \frac{64\delta(1-\delta)\{(8R^3-7R+2)\delta-(16R^3-9R+2)\}}{K\beta[(4R-1)^2(1-\delta)+2\delta(4R^2-1)]^3}$$

$$<0 \tag{A.3}$$

where the inequality follows since the bracketed expression in the numerator is negative for all $\delta \in (0,1)$ and $R \geq 1$. $\square$

### Proof of Lemma 4

Define $D(\tau_2^c) \equiv \omega(R_1,\hat{\tau}_s^c(R_1)) - \omega(R_0,\tau_2^c)$. Observe that $D(\tau_2^c)$ is increasing for $\tau_2^c > 0$; thus, since $\hat{\tau}_2^c > 0$, Lemma 4 is sure to hold if $D(0) \geq 0$. Assume then that $D(0) < 0$. In this event, using Lemma 2, there exists a unique $\tau^* \in (0,\hat{\tau}_s^c(R_0))$ at which $D(\tau^*) = 0$. The lemma is thus proved if $\hat{\tau}_2^c > \tau^*$.

Let $\hat{\tau}_2^c(\lambda = 1)$ denote the most-cooperative phase-2 tariff when $\lambda = 1$. Since under Eq. (22) the no-defect condition (Eq. (18b)) must hold with equality, we use $D(\tau^*) \equiv \omega(R_1,\hat{\tau}_s^c(R_1)) - \omega(R_0,\tau^*) = 0$ and Lemma 1 to conclude that

$$\Omega(R_0,\hat{\tau}_2^c(\lambda = 1)) = \frac{\delta}{1-\delta}\omega(R_0,\tau^*). \tag{A.4}$$

But $\tau^* \in (0,\hat{\tau}_2^c(R_0))$ then implies that $\hat{\tau}_2^c(\lambda = 1) \in (\tau^*,\hat{\tau}_s^c(R_0))$ (see Fig. 1). Thus, the lemma holds for $\lambda = 1$ and $D(\hat{\tau}_2^c(\lambda = 1)) > 0$.

Examining Eq. (18b) and Eq. (9), it is apparent that $\hat{\tau}_2^c(\lambda = 0) = \hat{\tau}_s^c(R_0) > \tau^*$. Thus, $D(\hat{\tau}_2^c(\lambda = 0)) > 0$ is also true, and the lemma holds when $\lambda = 0$.

We next compute $\partial\hat{\tau}_2^c/\partial\lambda$. Since Eq. (18b) holds with equality, this is given by

$$\frac{\partial \hat{\tau}_2^c}{\partial \lambda} = \frac{\partial V_2(\hat{\tau}_2^c; \lambda, \delta, R_0, R_1)/\partial \lambda}{\partial \Omega(R_0, \hat{\tau}_2^c)/\partial \tau_2^c - \partial V_2(\hat{\tau}_2^c; \lambda, \delta, R_0, R_1)/\partial \tau_2^c}. \tag{A.5}$$

The denominator of Eq. (A.5) is negative, since $V_2$ cuts $\Omega$ from below at $\hat{\tau}_2^c$, as Fig. 3 illustrates. It follows that

$$\text{sign} \frac{\partial \hat{\tau}_2^c}{\partial \lambda} = - \text{sign} \frac{\partial V_2(\hat{\tau}_2^c; \lambda, \delta, R_0, R_1)}{\partial \lambda}. \tag{A.6}$$

Using Eq. (18b) and Lemma 1, we find that

$$\frac{\partial V_2(\hat{\tau}_2^c; \lambda, \delta, R_0, R_1)}{\partial \lambda} = \frac{\delta}{(1 - (1 - \lambda)\delta)^2}[\omega(R_1, \hat{\tau}_s^c(R_1)) - \omega(R_0, \hat{\tau}_2^c)], \tag{A.7}$$

from which it follows that

$$\text{sign} \frac{\partial \hat{\tau}_2^c}{\partial \lambda} = - \text{sign} D(\hat{\tau}_2^c). \tag{A.8}$$

Now suppose that $\lambda^\dagger \in (0,1)$ exists for which $D(\hat{\tau}_2^c(\lambda^\dagger)) = 0$. From Eq. (A.8), it follows that $\hat{\tau}_2^c(\lambda) = \tau^*$ for all $\lambda \geq \lambda^\dagger$. But this contradicts $\hat{\tau}_2^c(\lambda = 1) > \tau^*$. It thus must be that $D(\hat{\tau}_2^c(\lambda)) > 0$ for all $\lambda \in [0,1]$, which proves Lemma 4. Note also from Eq. (A.8) that $\hat{\tau}_2^c$ decreases in $\lambda$. $\square$

*Proof of Proposition 3*

Begin with part (iii). Using Lemma 1 and Eq. (16), straightforward calculations reveal that $\hat{\tau}_3^c$ has sign which decreases in $\delta$ for $\delta \in (0, \delta^*(R_1))$. Further, $\partial \hat{\tau}_3^c/\partial R_1$ is quadratic in $\delta$ and is (i) zero at $\tilde{\delta}(R_1, R_1 - \varepsilon)$ for some small $\varepsilon > 0$, (ii) negative at $\delta = 0$, and (iii) positive at $\delta = 1$. It follows that $\hat{\tau}_3^c$ decreases in $R_1$ for $\delta \in (0, \tilde{\delta}(R_1, R_1 - \varepsilon))$.

Consider next part (ii). The proof of Lemma 4 establishes that $\hat{\tau}_2^c$ decreases in $\lambda$. Arguing as in that proof, it is apparent that $\hat{\tau}_2^c$ decreases in $\delta$, if $V_2$ increases in $\delta$ when $\tau_2^c$ is fixed at $\hat{\tau}_2^c$. Calculations reveal that

$$\frac{\partial V_2(\hat{\tau}_2^c; \lambda, \delta, R_0, R_1)}{\partial \delta} = \frac{\lambda \delta/(1 - \delta)}{1 - (1 - \lambda)\delta} \frac{\partial \omega(R_1, \hat{\tau}_3^c)}{\partial \tau_3^c} \frac{\partial \hat{\tau}_3^c}{\partial \delta}$$

$$+ \frac{\lambda[1 - \delta^2(1 - \lambda)]}{(1 - \delta)^2(1 - (1 - \lambda)\delta)^2}\omega(R_1, \hat{\tau}_3^c)$$

$$+ \frac{(1 - \lambda)}{(1 - (1 - \lambda)\delta)^2}\omega(R_0, \hat{\tau}_2^c) > 0.$$

Thus, $\hat{\tau}_2^c$ declines in $\delta$. Similarly, $\hat{\tau}_2^c$ is increasing in $R_1$, since using Lemma 1 and Eq. (A.3),

$$\frac{\partial V_2(\hat{\tau}_2^c;\lambda,\delta,R_0,R_1)}{\partial R_1} = \frac{\lambda\delta/(1-\delta)}{1-(1-\lambda)\delta}\frac{d\omega(R_1,\hat{\tau}_s^c(R_1))}{dR_1} < 0.$$

Consider finally part (i). Using Corollary 1,

$$\frac{\partial V_1(\hat{\tau}_1^c;\rho,\lambda,\delta,R_0,R_1)}{\partial\rho} = \frac{\delta}{(1-(1-\rho)\delta)^2}\left\{\frac{1-\delta}{1-(1-\lambda)\delta}\left[\omega(R_0,\hat{\tau}_2^c) + \frac{\lambda\delta}{1-\delta}\omega(R_1,\hat{\tau}_3^c)\right] - \omega(R_0,\hat{\tau}_1^c)\right\}$$

$$> \frac{\delta}{(1-(1-\rho)\delta)^2}\left\{\frac{1-\delta}{1-(1-\lambda)\delta}\left[\omega(R_0,\hat{\tau}_1^c) + \frac{\lambda\delta}{1-\delta}\omega(R_0,\hat{\tau}_1^c)\right] - \omega(R_0,\hat{\tau}_1^c)\right\}$$

$$= 0,$$

and so $\hat{\tau}_1^c$ is decreasing in $\rho$. Next, using Corollary 1 again,

$$\frac{\partial V_1(\hat{\tau}_1^c;\rho,\lambda,\delta,R_0,R_1)}{\partial\lambda} = \frac{\rho\delta}{(1-(1-\rho)\delta)(1-(1-\lambda)\delta)^2}$$

$$\left\{(1-(1-\lambda)\delta)\frac{\partial\omega(R_0,\hat{\tau}_2^c)}{\partial\tau_2^c}\frac{\partial\hat{\tau}_2^c}{\partial\lambda}\right.$$

$$\left. + \delta(\omega(R_1,\hat{\tau}_3^c) - \omega(R_0,\hat{\tau}_2^c))\right\} > 0,$$

and so $\hat{\tau}_1^c$ *decreases in* $\lambda$.
    *To evaluate the dependence of* $\hat{\tau}_1^c$ *on* $\delta$, *re-write* $V_1$ *as*

$$V_1(\tau_1^c;\rho,\lambda,\delta,R_0,R_1) = \left[\frac{\rho\delta}{(1-(1-\rho)\delta)(1-(1-\lambda)\delta)}\right]\left[\omega(R_0,\hat{\tau}_2^c)\right.$$

$$\left. + \frac{\lambda\delta}{1-\delta}\omega(R_1,\hat{\tau}_3^c)\right] + \left[\frac{(1-\rho)\delta}{1-(1-\rho)\delta}\right]\omega(R_0,\tau_1^c).$$

*Calculations reveal that each bracketed term increases with* $\delta$, *so that* $V_1$ *increases with* $\delta$. *Thus,* $\hat{\tau}_1^c$ *declines as* $\delta$ *increases. Finally, using Lemma 1 and Eq. (A.3) we have that*

$$\frac{\partial V_1(\hat{\tau}_1^c;\rho,\lambda,\delta,R_0,R_1)}{\partial R_1}$$

$$= \frac{\rho\delta}{1-(1-\rho)\delta}\left[\frac{\dfrac{\partial\omega(R_0,\hat{\tau}_2^c)}{\partial\tau_2^c}\dfrac{\partial\hat{\tau}_2^c}{\partial R_1} + \dfrac{\lambda\delta}{1-\delta}\dfrac{d\omega(R_1,\hat{\tau}_s^c(R_1))}{dR_1}}{1-(1-\lambda)\delta}\right] < 0,$$

*It thus must be that* $\hat{\tau}_1^c$ *increases in* $R_1$. □

*K. Bagwell, R.W. Staiger / Journal of International Economics 42 (1997) 91–123* 123

# References

Arndt, S.W., 1969, Customs union and the theory of tariffs, American Economic Review 59, 108–118.

Bagwell, K. and R.W. Staiger, 1990, A theory of managed trade, American Economic Review 80, 779–795.

Bagwell, K. and R.W. Staiger, 1993, Multilateral cooperation during the formation of customs unions, NBER Working Paper No. 4543.

Bagwell, K. and R.W. Staiger, 1997, Multilateral cooperation during the formation of free trade areas, International Economic Review, forthcoming.

Bagwell, K. and R.W. Staiger, 1996, Reciprocal trade liberalization, NBER working paper No. 5488 (National Bureau of Economic Research, Cambridge, MA).

Baldwin, R., 1987, Politically realistic objective functions and trade policy, Economics Letters 24, 287–290.

Bhagwati, J., 1991, The world trading system at risk (Princeton University Press, Princeton, NJ).

Bond, E.W. and C. Syropoulos, 1996a, The size of trading blocs: Market power and world welfare effects, Journal of International Economics 40, 411–437.

Bond, E.W. and C. Syropoulos, 1996b, Trading blocs and the sustainability of inter-regional cooperation, in: M.B. Canzoneri, W.J. Ethier and V. Grilli, eds., The new transatlantic economy (Cambridge University Press, Cambridge).

Dam K.W, 1970, The GATT: Law and international economic organization, (The University of Chicago Press, Chicago, IL).

Deardorff, A. and R. Stern, 1994, Multilateral trade negotiations and preferential trading arrangements, in: A. Deardorff and R. Stern, eds., Analytical and negotiating issues in the global trading system (University of Michigan Press, Ann Arbor, MI).

Herter, C., 1961, Statement before the Joint Economic Committee of the Congress of the United States, December 4–14, pp. 8–13.

Kemp, M.C., and H. Wan Jnr, 1976, An elementary proposition concerning the formation of customs unions, Journal of International Economics 6, 95–97.

Kowalczyk, C., 1990, Welfare and customs unions, NBER working paper No. 3476 (National Bureau of Economic Research, Cambridge, MA).

Kowalczyk, C. and T. Sjostrom, 1994, Bringing GATT into the core, Economica 61, 301–317.

Kowalczyk, C. and R. Wonnacott, 1991, Substitute and complement trading clubs, Working Paper No. 91–16, Department of Economics, Dartmouth College, UK.

Krugman, P.R., 1991, Is bilateralism bad?, in: E. Helpman and A. Razin, eds., International trade and trade policy (MIT Press, Cambridge, MA) 9–23.

Levy, P.I., 1997, A political-economic analysis of free trade agreements, American Economic Review, forthcoming.

Ludema, R., 1992, On the value of preferential trade agreements in multilateral negotiations, Unpublished Manuscript.

Viner, J., 1950, The customs union issue (Carnegie Endowment for International Peace, New York).

WTO (World Trade Organization), 1995, Regionalism and the world trading system, Geneva.

# Part VI
# The Optimal Number of Blocs
# and Optimal Size of Nations

# A
## Optimal Number of Blocs

# [21]

### Is Bilateralism Bad?

**Paul R. Krugman**

In the 1980s the process of trade liberalization through multilateral negotiations within the GATT framework seems to have run ground. Major
areas where conventional trade restrictions remain legion, such as agriculture and services, appear resistant to major progress. Meanwhile the
"new protectionism" of voluntary restraint agreements, antidumping actions, and so on, has eroded the effectiveness of the GATT in dealing
with trade in manufactures. The result has been increasing disillusionment
with the multilateral process, and an increasing focus on alternative trade
strategies.

Perhaps the most important of these strategies has been the turn to
bilateral or regional arrangements for trade. The most important agreements on trade in the past decade have been the "completion of the internal
market" that the European Community has agreed to achieve by 1992 and
the free trade agreement between the United States and Canada. Regionalism is also apparent in the enlargement of the European Community to
include several semi-industrialized countries on Europe's rim. Japan, while
not explicitly engaging in regional trading pacts, has recently sharply
increased its manufactures imports from East Asian NICs; it is widely
argued that the de facto protectionism that results from Japan's cartelized
distribution system is being selectively dismantled for nearby countries in
which Japanese direct foreign investment is increasingly significant. With
growing discussion of further enlargement of the Economic Community
and of the possibilities for special trading arrangements between the United
States and Mexico, many economists and business managers have begun
to raise the possibility that the multilateral GATT trading system is giving
way to a world of three main trading blocs.

One might expect that experts in trade negotiation would be at least
fairly positive about the bilateral and regional trade liberalization that has
taken place in recent years. Worldwide liberalization might be better still,
but isn't half a loaf better than none? In fact, however, there are widespread
misgivings. While it is difficult to get a very explicit statement of the
concern, in general what trade policy experts seem to be worried about is
the possibility that countries that join trading blocs will be more protectionist toward countries outside the blocs than they were before, so
world trade as a whole will be hurt more than helped by moves that at first
sight seem to be liberalizing in intent. The clearest example of this concern

10                                                   Paul R. Krugman

is the widespread discussion of the possibility that 1992 will lead to the creation of "Fortress Europe," an increasingly closed market to the rest of the world.

A full analysis of the costs and benefits of bilateral trading arrangements would require a healthy dose of political science and a careful analysis of the process of bargaining in trade negotiations. It would also require some realism in modeling the actual participants in the game. As a first step, however, it may be useful to have a minimal model in which the concerns about formation of trading blocs can be expressed in order to give us some more foundation for our intuition about the subject. That is the purpose of this chapter. I offer a simple approach to modeling trade liberalization and trade conflict in which the tension between the benefits of special trading arrangements and their negative effect on the world trading system can be clearly seen. In answer to the question posed by the title of this chapter, whether bilateralism is bad or good depends; but as we will see, in the context of a simple model we can get a pretty good idea of what it depends on.

This chapter is in four sections. The first reviews some of the existing theory on preferential trading arrangements and sets out the basic logic of this analysis in an informal way. The second section sets out a simple economic model that can be used to offer a more precise treatment of the issue, in which we can show how the outcome of trade policy at a world level varies with the number of trading blocs into which the world is organized. The third section examines the welfare implications of changes in the number of trading blocs. Finally, the chapter concludes with a brief discussion of an extended model in which there are "natural" trading blocs defined by transportation costs, and asks how the presence of such natural blocs alters the results.

## 1.1 Preferential Trading Arrangements: General Considerations

A naive view would be that since free trade is better than protection, any movement toward freer trade must be a good thing; that preferential trading arrangements are at any rate a step in the right direction. It is a familiar and indeed famous result, however, that this is not always true— half a loaf may be worse than none. In the celebrated analysis of Viner (1950), it was shown that a customs union may cause losses because it leads to "trade diversion" instead of "trade creation"—that is, instead of specializing more and increasing efficiency, countries that form a trading bloc may substitute each others' more expensive goods for goods from outside the bloc, leading to a loss of efficiency. Thus at one level we could argue that bilateral or regional trading arrangements could be destructive if they lead to trade diversion instead of trade creation.

As a general source of concern, however, the risk of trade diversion seems a weak point. It shows that under certain circumstances a customs union could be a mistake—but this is true of many economic policies, and policy concern based on the possibility of widespread stupidity by governments may be realistic though not very interesting. Also, while a customs union with a *given* external tariff may be harmful to the members, a customs union that adjusts its tariff optimally is always beneficial; while optimal adjustment may be unlikely in practice, again this seems to reduce the concern over bilateralism to a fear that governments will make mistakes.

The point that a customs union is always potentially beneficial to its members has been made formally by Kemp and Wan (1976). It may be useful to state the point informally. Suppose that two countries that happen to have the same tariff rate form a customs union. If they did not alter their external tariff rate, the increased trade within the union would represent a mixture of trade creation and trade diversion. Since the trade diversion would be harmful while the trade creation would be beneficial, the overall welfare effect would be ambiguous. (There may also be a terms of trade effect, to which we return below). The Kamp-Wan point, however, is that by adjusting the external tariff, the members of a customs union can always ensure a gain. Specifically, by reducing the tariff to the point at which external trade remains at its preunion level, the countries can ensure that there is no trade diversion. Also, since at this reduced tariff rate the offer to the rest of the world would be unchanged, the terms of trade of the customs union would also remain the same. So the welfare effect of a customs union that lowers its external tariff enough to prevent trade diversion is unambiguously positive. Now, in general, the customs union may choose to have a different tariff level than this; but if it does so, it is because this other tariff level yields still higher welfare. Thus a customs union is always potentially beneficial.

So far as good. But the last point—that a customs union may choose a tariff rate that is different from the one that leaves external trade at its preunion level—raises a potential negative possibility. The reason is that almost surely the optimal tariff rate for the customs union will be higher than this constant-trade level because the customs union will want to take advantage of its size to improve its terms of trade. Indeed, we may expect as a general presumption that a customs union, being a larger unit with more market power than any of its constituent members, will have an optimal external tariff that is higher than the preunion tariff rates of the member nations. Thus while our proof of potential gains relies on the hypothetical case of a customs union that does not lead to any trade diversion, in fact a customs union ordinarily will choose policies that *do* lead to trade diversion.

But this means that the formation of a customs union, while necessarily beneficial to the members, will certainly be harmful to the rest of the world and may reduce the welfare of the world as a whole (if such a measure can be defined).

Now let us return to the concern over bilateral and regional trading arrangements. One way to rationalize the concern of the trade negotiation professionals is the following: They fear that there may be a Prisoner's Dilemma at work in the formation of trading blocs. Imagine a world consisting of four countries, *A*, *B*, *C*, and *D*. Let *A* and *B* form a customs union; then other things equal they will be better off. However, they will have an incentive to improve their terms of trade by maintaining an external tariff that induces trade diversion—indeed, probably an external tariff that is higher than either of them would have on their own—and which therefore leaves *C* and *D* worse off. Similarly, *C* and *D* will be better off, other things equal, if they form a customs union, but their optimal external tariff will similarly induce trade diversion in the effor to achieve improved terms of trade. What could happen is that the resulting tariff war will induce enough trade diversion to leave everyone worse off than if they had not formed the customs unions.

This story is, of course, a caricature of the actual process of tariff-setting. I have described a world in which trade policy of nations is set to maximize national welfare and in which trading blocs behave noncooperatively. This makes internal politics look better and external relations worse than they are in fact. In reality nations set trade policy in a fashion that reflects internal conflicts of interest more than promotion of national interest vis-à-vis foreigners, and international trade policy reflects a fair degree of bargaining. However, this story does capture the basic idea that formation of trading blocs, while advantageous in itself, may have an adverse effect on the multilateral system and in the end be harmful. Thus, although we will eventually need a more realistic story, this seems like a useful starting point.

The story also points us toward an interesting question: How does world welfare vary with the number of trading blocs into which the world is organized? Absent any market imperfections, the *optimal* number of trading blocs is, of course, one: free trade. One might at first suppose that this implies that the fewer trading blocs, the better. However, in the general second-best logic that prevails here, that is far from clear. If a world consisting of many small trading blocs, each of which is very open to external trade, consolidates into a somewhat smaller number of blocs, each of which is still very open to external trade, most of the expansion of intrabloc trade may come from trade diversion rather than trade creation. Thus when the number of blocs is reduced from a very large number to a still fairly large number, it would not be surprising to find that world welfare falls. Conversely, when there are only a few trading blocs, doing only limited trade with each other, most of the expansion of intrabloc trade when they consolidate into a still smaller number of blocs will represent trade expansion, and welfare will probably rise. Thus the number of trading blocs at which world welfare is minimized—henceforth referred to as the *pessimal* number—will probably be some moderate number of blocs. A world that is either more or less fragmented will have higher welfare.

This is about as far as informal argumentation can take us. To firm up the intuition and to provide further insight, we now turn to a formal model.

## 1.2   Trading Blocs and Tariff-Setting: A Formal Model

In order to make the analysis of the problem of bilateralism tractable, I consider a very special model. In this model all nations and trading blocs appear symmetrically so that we can meaningfully describe the world in terms of the representative nation or trading bloc. Also it turns out to be helpful to assume particular functional forms. Thus this model is illustrative rather than conclusive. However, it does, as we will see, yield some striking insights.

Consider, then, a world whose basic elements are geographic units which I will refer to as "provinces." There are a large number $N$ of such provinces in the world. A country, in general, consists of a number of provinces. For the analysis here, however, I will basically ignore the country level of analysis, focusing instead on "trading blocs" that contain a number of countries (perhaps only one), and thus a larger number of provinces. Specifically, there are $B < N$ trading blocs in the world. These trading blocs will be assumed to be symmetric so that each contains $N/B$ provinces; the integer constraint is ignored. A main purpose of the analysis will be to find how world welfare depends on $B$.

Each province is specialized in the production of a single good that is an imperfect substitute for the products of other provinces. All provinces will be assumed to be the same economic size, so without loss of generality I will choose units so that each produces one unit of its good. All provinces have the same tastes, into which the products of all provinces enter symmetrically, with the specific functional form

$$U = \left[ \sum_{i=1}^{N} c_i^{\theta} \right]^{1/\theta}, \qquad 0 < \theta < 1, \tag{1}$$

where $c_i$ is the province's consumption of the good of province $i$. This is of course a CES utility function, where the elasticity of substitution between any two products is

$$\sigma = \frac{1}{1 - \theta}. \tag{2}$$

The resemblance between this setup and standard monopolistic competition models of trade is obvious and not coincidental; indeed this formulation was suggested by an analysis of optimal tariffs in a monopolistically competitive world by Gros (1987). If you like, you may regard a "province" as an area with fixed resources that specializes in a limited number of differentiated products because of increasing returns. However, this interpretation is not necessary, and the model may also be viewed as arising from a perfectly competitive environment.

A trading bloc is a group of provinces with internal free trade and a common external ad valorem tariff. The external tariff rate is chosen so as to maximize welfare, taking the policies of other trading blocs are given (because of the symmetry among provinces there are no internal income distribution effects). This is a standard problem in international economics: The optimal tariff for a bloc is

Is Bilateralism Bad?                                                    15

$$t^* = \frac{1}{\varepsilon - 1}, \tag{3}$$

where $\varepsilon$ is the elasticity of demand for the bloc's exports.

To determine $\varepsilon$, consider the imports of the rest of the world from a representative trading bloc. The "rest of the world" consists of the $N(1 - B^{-1})$ provinces that are not part of the bloc; given the symmetry of the model, the price of the goods produced by all these provinces will be the same. Let $y^W$ equal the volume of output of the rest of the world, equal to

$$y^W = N(1 - B^{-1}). \tag{4}$$

Also let $d^W$ be the volume of rest-of-world consumption of rest-of-world products, and $m^W$ be rest-of-world imports from our trading bloc. Then we must have

$$d^W + pm^W = y^W, \tag{5}$$

where $p$ is the price of our bloc's output relative to rest-of-world output on world (not internal) markets.

Now consider the effects of a change in $p$, holding the ad valorem tariff rates constant. Placing a "hat" over a variable to represent a proportional change, we have

$$(1 - s)\hat{d}^W + s(\hat{p} + \hat{m}^W) = \hat{y}^W = 0 \tag{6}$$

where $s = pm^W/y^W$ is the share of imports from our bloc in income at world prices. Also with ad valorem tariffs internal prices will change in the same proportion as external; therefore given the constant elasticity of substitution, we have

$$(\hat{d}^W - \hat{m}^W) = \sigma\hat{p}. \tag{7}$$

Combining (6) and (7), and rearranging, we have

$$\hat{m}^W = -[s + (1 - s)\sigma]\hat{p}, \tag{8}$$

which implies that our bloc faces an elasticity of demand for exports

$$\varepsilon = s + (1 - s)\sigma \tag{9}$$

and therefore that the optimal tariff rate is

$$t^* = \frac{1}{(1 - s)(\sigma - 1)}. \tag{10}$$

There are two interesting things to notice about this expression. First is that the optimal tariff is increasing in $s$; that is, the larger the share of a trading bloc's exports in rest-of-world expenditure, the higher the tariff it will charge. On the other hand, no matter how small the share, the optimal tariff does not go to zero; as $s$ goes to zero, $t^*$ goes down only to $1/(\sigma - 1)$. This is because there are no "small countries" in the sense of price-takers in this model: Even an individual province produces a differentiated good and therefore has a positive optimal tariff. As Gros (1987) has pointed out, this is normally the case in monopolistically competitive models, where the optimal tariff for a small country equals the markup of price over marginal cost.

The share variable $s$ is of course endogenous, depending for a given number of trading blocs on the tariff rate. Thus we turn next to the determination of $s$.

Let $y$ be the volume of output of a representative trading bloc; we know that

$$y = \frac{N}{B}. \tag{11}$$

Let $m$ be the volume of this trading bloc's imports and $d$ the volume of consumption of its own goods. In a symmetric equilibrium, in which all blocs have the same tariff rate, the goods of all regions will sell at equal prices on world markets. Thus the budget constraint for a representative bloc is

$$m + d = y. \tag{12}$$

Next consider the relative demand for goods produced inside and outside of the bloc. There are $N/B$ goods produced by provinces inside a representative trading bloc, implying $N(B - 1)/B$ goods produced outside. If consumers faced the world prices of these goods, which are equal, then given the symmetrical way in which the goods enter into demand we would have $m/d = B - 1$. Since consumers must pay a tariff rate of $t$ on extrabloc goods, however, and since the elasticity of substitution is $\sigma$, we have

$$\frac{m}{d} = (1 + t)^{-\sigma}(B - 1). \tag{13}$$

Is Bilateralism Bad? 17

From (11)–(13) we find that

$$m = \frac{y}{(1 + t)^{\sigma}/(B - 1) + 1} = \frac{N/B}{(1 + t)^{\sigma}/(B - 1) + 1}. \tag{14}$$

This determines the imports of a representative bloc. Because trade must be balanced, however, imports equal exports (i.e., $m = m^{W}$). Thus the share of bloc exports in nonbloc income is

$$s = \frac{m}{y^{W}}$$

$$= \frac{m}{N(1 - B^{-1})}. \tag{15}$$

Substituting and rearranging, we have

$$s = [(1 + t)^{\sigma} + B - 1]^{-1} \tag{16}$$

so that the share of bloc exports in nonbloc income is decreasing in both the tariff rate and the number of blocs.

Figure 1.1 shows how equations (10) and (16) simultaneously determine the tariff rate and the export share for a given number of blocs $B$. The downward-sloping curve $SS$ represents (16); it shows that the higher the

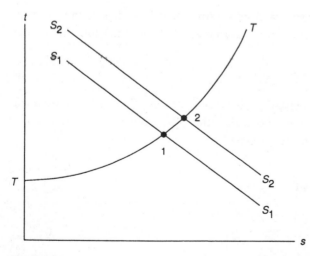

Figure 1.1

tariff rate of a representative bloc, the lower is the share of each bloc in rest-of-world income. The curve $TT$ represents (10); it shows that the tariff rate levied by blocs is higher, the larger their export share. Equilibrium is at point $E$, where each bloc is levying the unilaterally optimal tariff.

Now consider the effect of a change in the number of blocs. Suppose, for example, that there are a series of negotiations between pairs of blocs that reduces the number of blocs from some initial number $B_0$ to $B_0/2$. It is immediately apparent what the result will be. For any given tariff rate, the effect of the reduction in $B$ is to shift $SS$ up; at a given $t$ each bloc will have a higher $S$. Thus in figure 1.1 $S_1 S_1$ shifts up to $S_2 S_2$. As a result the tariff rate rises as equilibrium shifts from 1 to 2.

It is clear that this process will reduce the volume of trade between any two countries that are in different blocs. Even at an unchanged tariff, the removal of trade barriers between members of the expanded bloc would divert some trade that would otherwise have taken place between blocs. This trade diversion will be reinforced by the rise in the tariff rate.

Thus this model suggests that there is something to the concern of trade specialists that bilateral trade pacts may impair multilateral trade. The obvious next question, however, is whether this is actually bad for welfare.

## 1.3   The Number of Trading Blocs and World Welfare

The effect of the tariffs levied by trading blocs is to distort the consumer choice between intrabloc and external goods. The utility function (1) may be written as

$$U = [N(1 - B^{-1})(c^{W})^{\theta} + NB^{-1}(c^{D})^{\theta}]^{1/\theta}, \tag{17}$$

where $c^{W}$ and $c^{D}$ represent a province's consumption of a representative good produced outside and inside the bloc, respectively. After a little manipulation we can show that

$$c^{W} = \frac{B/N}{(1 + t)^{\sigma} + B - 1} \tag{18}$$

and that

$$c^{D} = \frac{[B(1 + t)^{\sigma}/N]}{(1 + t)^{\sigma} + B - 1}. \tag{19}$$

For evaluating how welfare changes when the number of trading blocs changes, the number of regions $N$ is unimportant; so it is harmless to simplify by normalizing $N$ to equal 1. Under this assumption welfare equals

$$U = \left[\frac{B}{(1+t)^{\sigma} + B - 1}\right][(1 - B^{-1}) + B^{-1}(1+t)^{\sigma\theta}]^{1/\theta}. \tag{20}$$

If trade were free, we would always have $U = 1$. Since the tariff rate is also a function of $B$, (20) together with (10) and (16) allows us to determine how welfare varies with the number of trading blocs.

Rather than attempting to prove general results here, since the model is so special in any case, it makes more sense to adopt a numerical approach. This is especially true because the model has only one parameter: $\sigma$, the elasticity of substitution in world trade. Thus we can plot welfare as a function of $B$ for a number of plausible values of $\sigma$. In what follows I use three values of $\sigma$: 2, a rather low estimate; 4, a somewhat high estimate; and 10, which is much higher than any empirical estimates.

As an initial step, figure 1.2 plots equilibrium tariff rates as a function of

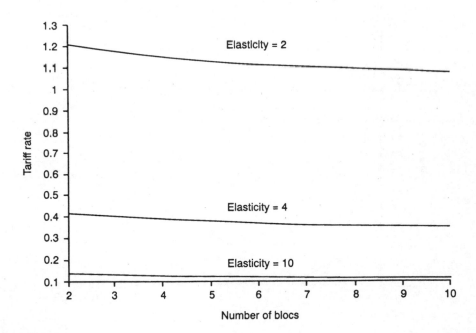

**Figure 1.2**

*B.* We note that the tariff declines as B is increased, but not to zero as already pointed out. Two other points are worth noting. First, the actual relationship between *B* na *t* is rather flat. This is because when there are fewer blocs, trade diversion tends to reduce interbloc trade, and thus leads to less of a rise in *s* than one might expect. Second, except in the case of a very high *σ*, the tariff rates are much higher than the actual rates of protection on trade among advanced nations. This is a useful caution on taking this model too seriously; actual relations among trading blocs are clearly far more cooperative than envisaged here.

We now turn to the level of welfare as a function of the number of trading blocs, shown in figure 1.3. In each case world welfare is maximized with free trade (i.e., with *B* = 1). The costs from lack of free trade are larger, the lower the elasticity of substitution. As suggested informally in section 1.1, the relationship between welfare and the number of blocs is U-shaped, with the pessimum at a moderate number of blocs. The surprise is that the pessimal number is the same for all plausible elasticities of substitution. Three trading blocs is the number that minimizes world welfare.

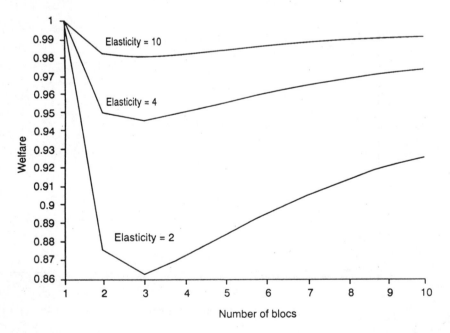

**Figure 1.3**

This is an interesting result, since many observers suggest that the world is in fact evolving precisely into a three-bloc economy. Before we put too much weight on the result, however, we should examine why we get it and whether it is really plausible.

The basic explanation of the result is the following: In the model as stated so far, there are no natural trading blocs. That is, except for the effect of tariffs, each province tends to consume the products of all provinces equally. Even with tariffs, as long as there are more than a few trading blocs most of each province's consumption comes from provinces outside its own bloc. The result is that as long as there are more than a few blocs, the trade diversion that results from consolidation outweighs the trade creation. Notice that if there were no tariffs, consumption from outside the bloc would exceed intrabloc consumption as soon as the number of blocs exceeds two. The presence of tariffs alters this, but it is not surprising that the number of blocs at which trade diversion begins to outweigh trade creation is small—though it is still fairly remarkable that the number always turns out to be three.

It is apparent from this intuitive story, however, that the result that a three-bloc world represents a pessimum is crucially dependent on the assumption that there are no natural trading blocs. The final argument of this chapter will be that this result does not hold up if transportation costs give rise to the existence of natural regions.

## 1.4   Natural Trading Blocs

To get a fix on the issue of natural trading blocs, let us now imagine a world in which there is a structure of transportation costs. Specifically, we now assume that the $N$ provinces in the world are located on three "continents": $X$, $Y$, and $Z$. Each continent contains $N/3$ provinces.

The structure of production and preferences will be assumed exactly the same as before. Also we continue to assume that there are zero transportation costs within each continent. However, we now suppose that there are transportation costs between continents. These take Samuelson's "iceberg" form: Of a unit of a good shipped from one continent to another, only a fraction $1 - \gamma$ arrives. Thus the continents in effect form natural trading regions, with the extent of natural regionalism determined by the transport cost $\gamma$.

Suppose next that each continent is initially divided into two equal-sized trading blocs. What will happen to world welfare if each bloc reaches an agreement with its neighbor, consolidating each continent into a single trading bloc?

We can immediately see that the result depends on intercontinental transportation costs. Consider first the case where $\gamma = 0$ so that there are no transportation costs. In this case we are back to the symmetric case studied before, where three trading blocs represents the pessimal trading structure for all plausible parameter values. So in this case the bilateral deals end up reducing world welfare. On the other hand, consider the case where $\gamma$ is close to one, so that transport costs are nearly prohibitive. In this case intercontinental trade is unimportant. Thus in effect each continent is a world unto itself, which moves from two blocs to one—which we know is welfare improving.

The result then is that the assessment of regional trading arrangements depends on whether there is enough inherent regionalism in the structure of transportation costs. If trading arrangements follow the lines of natural trading regions, they will have a much better chance of improving welfare than trade arragements between "unnatural" partners.

## 1.5   Conclusions

Is bilateralism (or more accurately, regionalism) in trading arrangements bad? This chapter has shown that in the context of a highly stylized model, it might be. Although a world that consolidates into trading blocs could simultaneously reduce tariffs so as to avoid trade diversion, the optimal noncooperative behavior of the blocs is actually to increase external tariffs. Thus a reduction in interbloc trade is the normal outcome of the formation of regional trading blocs.

In the simplest version of the model presented here it is also highly likely that the net effect of regionalization will be to reduce world welfare. This is a fragile result. The result might be softened considerably by either a realistic appreciation of the role of transport costs (as shown here) or a recognition that real-world trade policies are set through negotiation, not through wholly noncooperative actions. Nevertheless, the analysis given here suggests at least some grounds for the widespread concern over the apparent trend toward regionalization of international trading arrangements.

Is Bilateralism Bad?                                           23

## References

Gros, D. 1987. A note on the optimal tariff, retaliation, and the welfare loss from tariff wars in a model with intra-industry trade. *Journal on International Economics* 23: 357–367.

Kemp, M., and Wan, H. 1976. Elementary proposition concerning the formation of custom unions. *International Economic Review* 6: 95–97.

Viner, J. 1950. *The Customs Union Issue*. New York: Carnegie Endowment for International Peace.

# [22]
## Regionalism and the World Trading System

*Lawrence H. Summers*

Increasing economic integration has been one of the major forces driving the world economy's impressive growth over the last forty-five years. Today, however, more than at any time since World War II, the future of the world trading system is in doubt. Ironically, just as the Soviet Union, Eastern Europe, and many developing countries rush to join the General Agreement on Tariffs and Trade (GATT), many in the developed world have become disillusioned with the GATT process. The nearing completion of Europe's 1991 process, the North American Free Trade Agreement (NAFTA) apparently on the way, and even the dissolution of Comecon has forced the question of regional trading blocs increasingly to the fore. It is useful at the outset to consider how the world trading system is now faring. World trade grew 3 percent a year faster than GNP in the 1960s, 2 percent a year faster in the 1970s, and 1 percent a year faster in the 1980s. The good news is that integration has continued; the bad news is that it has increased ever more slowly.

Why did integration increase less rapidly in the 1980s? I think there are two important reasons. First, the technological push toward integration has slowed. Transportation and communication costs fell less quickly in the 1980s than in previous decades. Air transport, for example, is usually thought of as a dynamic industry. Yet the last major innovation was the jumbo jet, introduced nearly a generation ago. Moreover, as the total share of transportation and communication costs declines, incremental reductions have ever smaller effects;

a reduction from $5 a minute to $2.50 a minute will have a greater impact on communication than a fall from 50 cents a minute to 25 cents a minute. Progress in this sense reduces the potential for future progress.

Second, the momentum of trade liberalization has slowed as well. While sixty developing nations significantly reduced barriers to imports over the last decade, twenty of twenty-four Organization for Economic Cooperation and Development (OECD) countries, including the United States, raised such barriers. The United States, which on some measures has trebled the protectionist impact of its policies, has a particularly ignominious record.

In the long run, however, it is those sixty liberalizing developing countries and those that emulate them that are ultimately of greatest importance for the future development of the world trading system. Ninety-five percent of the growth in the world's labor force over the next twenty-five years will occur in what are now developing nations. Even assuming only modest productivity performance, these demographic trends imply that these nations will be the most rapidly growing markets in the world over the next two decades. And this is a moment of historic opportunity in the developing world. There is abundant evidence—most obviously in Eastern Europe, but also in large parts of Latin America, in China, where industrial production has grown at a 30 percent annual rate over the last six years, in India, where a new finance minister has pledged radical change, and even in Africa, where twenty nations are undertaking adjustment programs—that the desirability of market systems has become apparent. Our top priority must be to reinforce these trends.

Trade policy not only needs to proceed on all fronts to lock in the gains that have occurred but also to provide examples that will lead to new trade gains, and even to insure viable investment opportunities for OECD companies—GATT yes, but regional arrangements as well. I therefore assert and will defend the following principle: economists should maintain a strong, but rebuttable, presumption in favor of all lateral reductions in trade barriers, whether they be multi, uni, bi, tri, plurilateral. Global liberalization may be best, but regional liberalization is very likely to be good.

This position is based on four propositions: (1) given the existing structure of trade, plausible regional arrangements are likely to have trade creating effects that exceed their trade diverting effects; (2) there is a very good chance that even trade diverting regional arrangements will increase welfare; (3) apart from their impact on trade, regional trading arrangements are likely to have other beneficial effects; (4) reasonable regional arrangements are as likely to accelerate the general liberalization process as to slow it down.

Are trading blocs likely to divert large amounts of trade? In answering this question, the issue of natural trading blocs is crucial because to the extent that blocs are created between countries that already trade disproportionately, the risk of large amounts of trade diversion is reduced. Table 1 sheds some light on the importance of natural trading blocs. It compares the ratio of observed trade for various entities to the trade one would expect if it were equiproportional to GNP. For example, the number in the upper lefthand corner indicates that the United States and Canada engaged in six times as much trade as they would if U.S. trade with Canada were proportional to Canada's share of world, non-U.S., GDP. Looking at the table, I draw three conclusions:

(1) Existing and many contemplated regional arrangements link nations that are already natural trading partners. Note the disproportionate share of U.S. trade with Canada, of trade within the developing Asian countries, and of trade within industrialized Europe. If I included Mexico in the table it would have a ratio of about 7 with the United States, Korea would have a ratio of nearly 4, and even Israel would have a ratio well in excess of unity.

(2) There is very little sense in which the United States and Canada have a natural affinity with the rest of the Western Hemisphere. American, and to an even greater extent Canadian, trade is disproportionately low, with Europe about equivalent between developing Asia and Latin America. This suggests that America should not be content with an Americas-based approach to trade reduction.

(3) What is striking about the numbers in Table 1 is the isolation of industrial Europe, which trades disproportionately with itself.

This is not an artifact of the fact that Europe is broken up into many countries; this rationalization would fail to explain why it occupies so small a fraction of both Asian and Western Hemisphere trade.

### Table 1
### Trading Neighbors: Ratio of Share of Trade to Partner's Share of World Output, 1989

**Trader**         **with:**

| | U.S. | Canada | Other Americas | Japan | Developing Asia | EC |
|---|---|---|---|---|---|---|
| United States | — | 6.06 | 2.38 | 0.87 | 2.34 | 0.61 |
| Canada | 2.63 | — | 0.66 | 0.47 | 0.97 | 0.39 |
| Other Americas | 1.13 | 0.63 | 3.16 | 0.31 | 0.57 | 0.67 |
| Japan | 0.95 | 1.15 | 0.75 | — | 4.33 | 0.53 |
| Developing Asia | 0.73 | 0.62 | 0.43 | 1.26 | 4.83 | 0.54 |
| EC | 0.22 | 0.30 | 0.42 | 0.17 | 0.63 | 1.75 |

I conclude from this exercise that most seriously contemplated efforts at regional integration involving industrialized countries cement what are already large and disproportionately strong trading relationships. To this extent they are likely to be trade creating rather than trade diverting. The one idea that looks bad from this perspective is that of a North Atlantic trading bloc which would be building on

### Table 2
### Trading Neighbors: Ratio of Share of Trade to Partner's Share of World Output, 1975

**Trader**         **with:**

| | U.S. | Canada | Other Americas | Japan | Developing Asia | EC |
|---|---|---|---|---|---|---|
| United States | — | 6.42 | 2.68 | 0.60 | 1.56 | 0.51 |
| Canada | 2.32 | — | 0.90 | 0.37 | 0.58 | 0.36 |
| Other Americas | 1.19 | 0.74 | 2.81 | 0.55 | 0.23 | 0.72 |
| Japan | 0.65 | 1.17 | 1.12 | — | 4.70 | 0.26 |
| Developing Asia | 0.71 | 0.65 | 0.19 | 1.53 | 3.68 | 0.56 |
| EC | 0.18 | 0.37 | 0.46 | 0.09 | 0.44 | 1.25 |

a weak trading relationship. Amongst regional groups of smaller developing countries, even trade disproportionate to GDP may constitute a small fraction of total trade and hence the argument carries less force.

It is sometimes suggested that whatever may have been true in the past, today's market is worldwide and regional arrangements are therefore more likely to be damaging than would once have been the case. Table 2 provides a fragment of evidence on this issue by redoing the exercise reported in Table 1 for 1975. It is striking how similar the pattern of trade is. Perhaps this should not be too surprising; it is well known that intra-European trade has risen much faster than Europe's external trade.

Let me come now to my second point: trade diverting regional arrangements may be desirable despite their trade diverting effects. I find it surprising that this issue is taken so seriously—in most other situations, economists laugh off second best considerations and focus on direct impacts. Further, it is a consequential error to think that just because a regional trading agreement's trade diverting effects exceed trade creating effects it is undesirable. Suppose that Korea and Taiwan were identical—a free trade area between the United States and Korea would divert Taiwanese trade to Korea but would have no welfare costs. Only where trade diversion involves replacing efficient producers with inefficient producers is it a problem.

I think this point has considerable force. We too often forget that more than half of U.S. imports are either from U.S. firms operating abroad or to foreign firms operating within the United States. And the fraction is rising rapidly. Under these circumstances, trade and investment decisions are inseparable. With many similar sites for investment by U.S. firms producing for the U.S. market, it is far from clear that trade diversion would have important welfare impacts.

While trade diversion is unlikely to involve large efficiency costs, trade creation is much more likely to involve real efficiency gains. First, it will help realize economies of scale which can be gained through creation, but are unlikely to be lost due to trade diversion. Second, especially where agreements link developed and developing countries, or developing countries that are heavily specialized, the trade they create is likely to be substantially welfare enhancing.

My third reason for eclectically favoring integration schemes is a reading of where the real benefits are. To the chagrin of economists, the real gains from trade policies of any kind cannot, with the possible exception of agriculture, lie in the triangles and welfare measures we are so good at calculating. Instead, they can be found in the salutary effects of competition and openness on domestic policy more generally. Pedro Aspe in his speech yesterday clearly thought more of NAFTA as a device for locking in good domestic policies and attracting investment than as a mechanism for gaining market access. To the extent that the benefits of trade integration lie in these areas, it may not be important how geographically general it is, or whether it is trade diverting. Take the case of Enterprise for the Americas. If the rest of Latin America desires to follow in Mexico's footsteps, a standstill on future U.S. protection for reassurance, and the political and symbolic benefit that it can bring in promoting domestic reform, it seems almost absurd to resist them on the grounds that some trade might be diverted from some part of Asia that would produce a little more efficiently.

It is instructive to consider the breadth of the European Community (EC) 1992 and GATT agendas. No small part of what is good about 1992 is the downward pressure on regulation created by mutual recognition policies. Similarly, competition for investment within the EC will have salutary effects on tax and regulatory policies. But there are diminishing returns to increasing numbers of policy competitors. A significant part of the benefits of trade liberalization in improving domestic policy may be realizable within small groups of countries.

The fourth and final part of the case for supporting regional arrangements is their impact on the multilateral system. I do not share the view held by some that GATT is to trade policy what the League of Nations became to security policy. I believe that a successful completion of the Uruguay Round and its successors would be highly beneficial to the world economy and that the developed nations especially must work to bring one about.

But I am far from persuaded that over time regional arrangements make multilateral trade reduction impossible. The essential reason for concern is that large blocs will have more monopoly power than small ones—and will then use it. The argument is that the resulting reduced cross bloc trade would do more harm than increased within bloc trade would do good. This is a legitimate concern. But it is also true that three parties with a lot to gain from a successful negotiation are more likely to complete it than are seventy-one parties, each with only a small amount to gain. It may be well that a smaller number of trade blocs are more likely to be able to reach agreement than a larger number of separate countries.

This is not just a theoretical proposition. I doubt that the existence of the EC has complicated the process of reaching multilateral trade agreements. Instead, I suspect that the ability of Europe to speak with a more common voice would have helped, not hurt, over time.

Furthermore, there is the beneficial effect of successful arrangements in attracting imitation and in providing a vehicle for keeping up the momentum of liberalization. Those concerned that the U.S.-Mexico or possible follow-on agreements will divert attention from the Uruguay Round ought to consider whether they will also divert Congress' attention from the Super 301 process, or that of the business community from negotiating further import restrictions.

Even strong presumptions remain rebuttable. Obviously some past and current proposals for regional integration would fail to satisfy the conditions. Agreements within groups of small, highly distorted, and protectionist countries that diminish momentum for greater overall liberality are clear candidates for welfare worsening regional agreements.

But the crux of the argument is this: regional arrangements will necessarily speed up the GATT, and moving the GATT along is important if it is possible. But, holding the degree of multilateral progress constant, the world will be better off with more regional liberalization. And the case that regional integration will slow multilateral progress is highly speculative at best. The Uruguay Round may well be the best hope for the world trading system, but it is surely not the last best hope.

# B
# Optimal Size of Nations

# [23]

# Economic Integration and Political Disintegration

By Alberto Alesina, Enrico Spolaore, and Romain Wacziarg*

*In a world of trade restrictions, large countries enjoy economic benefits, because political boundaries determine the size of the market. Under free trade and global markets even relatively small cultural, linguistic or ethnic groups can benefit from forming small, homogeneous political jurisdictions. This paper provides a formal model of the relationship between openness and the equilibrium number and size of countries, and successfully tests two implications of the model. Firstly, the economic benefits of country size are mediated by the degree of openness to trade. Secondly, the history of nation-state creations and secessions is influenced by the trade regime. (JEL F02, O57)*

In a regime of Free Trade and free economic intercourse it would be of little consequence that iron lay on one side of a political frontier, and labor, coal, and blast furnaces on the other. But as it is, men have devised ways to impoverish themselves and one another; and prefer collective animosities to individual happiness. John Maynard Keynes, *The Economic Consequences of the Peace*, 1920 p. 99.

The number of countries in the world increased from 74 in 1946 to 192 in 1995. In 1995, 87 countries had less than 5 million inhabitants, 58 less than 2.5 million, and 35 less than 500,000. More than half of the world's countries are smaller (in population) than the State of Massachusetts.[1] In the same half century, the volume of imports plus exports as a share of world GDP, in a sample of 61 countries, has increased by roughly 40 percent.

Figure 1 displays a strong positive correlation, from 1870 to today, between the number of countries in the world and a measure of trade openness, the average ratio of imports plus exports to GDP in a group of nine countries.[2] Similarly, Figure 2 shows an inverse relationship between average tariff rates on manufactured products and the number of countries, in a selected group of countries for which tariff data were available. Tariff rates were slowly increasing between 1870 and the 1920's, while the number of countries was stable or slowly decreasing. After the Second World War tariff rates fell dramatically and the number of countries increased rapidly.[3] Figures 3 and 4 present scatterplots of the detrended number of countries against the detrended trade to GDP ratio,

* Alesina: Department of Economics, Harvard University, Cambridge, MA 02138, National Bureau of Economic Research, and Centre for Economic Policy Research (e-mail: aalesina@kuznets.fas.harvard.edu); Spolaore: Department of Economics, Brown University, Box B, Providence, RI 02912 (e-mail: Enrico_Spolaore@brown.edu); Wacziarg: Graduate School of Business, Stanford University, 518 Memorial Way, Stanford CA 94305 (e-mail: wacziarg@gsb.stanford.edu). We thank Francesco Caselli, William Easterly, Jeffrey Frieden, Casper Kowalczyk, David Laibson, Ronald Rogowski, Fabio Schiantarelli, Jeffrey Williamson, two anonymous referees, and seminar participants at Brown University, Georgetown University, Harvard University, the Massachusetts Institute of Technology, Pennsylvania State University, Tulane University, the University of Maryland, the London School of Economics, the IMF, the University of Bologna, and the Catholic University of Milan for useful suggestions, and Teng Chamchumrus for excellent research assistance. This research was supported by a National Science Foundation grant to the NBER. Alesina also acknowledges financial support from the Weatherhead Center for International Affairs at Harvard University.

[1] In 1990 Massachusetts had a population of 6,016,425. Ninety-eight countries have smaller populations.

[2] These countries are France, Britain, Denmark, Italy, Norway, Portugal, Australia, Brazil, and Sweden—the only countries for which reliable trade data were available continuously since 1870. These countries are representative of trends that affected world trade volumes, however, as the correlation between their average trade to GDP ratio since 1950 and that of a much wider sample of 61 countries since 1950 is 0.93.

[3] These relationships are statistically significant, even when controlling for a time trend. Time-series regression results are available upon request.

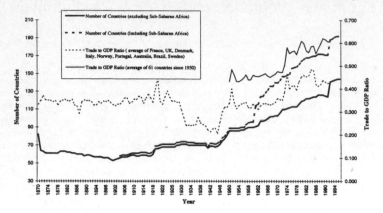

FIGURE 1. TRADE OPENNESS AND THE NUMBER OF COUNTRIES

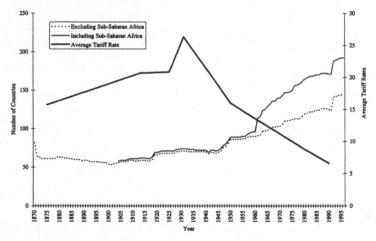

FIGURE 2. AVERAGE TARIFF RATE AND THE NUMBER OF COUNTRIES
(UNWEIGHTED COUNTRY AVERAGE OF AVERAGE TARIFF RATE FOR AUSTRIA, BELGIUM, FRANCE, GERMANY, SWEDEN, UNITED STATES)

showing again a strong positive correlation between the degree of openness of the world trade regime and the number of countries.

This paper argues that trade openness and political separatism go hand in hand: economic integration leads to political "disintegration."

We build upon a simple idea. Consider a model where the size of the market influences productivity. In a world of trade restrictions, the political boundaries of a country influence the size of the country's market, and therefore its productivity level. On the contrary, with free trade the size of countries is irrelevant for the size of markets, so the *size* of a country is unrelated to its productivity.[4] It follows that the equilibrium number of countries and the extent of economic integration are interdependent.

---

[4] These ideas are discussed informally by historians of nation-building, such as Eric Hobsbawm (1990), are tested by Alberto Ades and Edward Glaeser (1999), and are modeled in a stylized fashion by Spolaore (1995), Kashif S. Mansori (1996), and Alesina and Spolaore (1997). Donald Wittman (1991) also mentions this point.

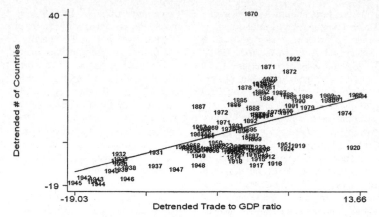

FIGURE 3. SCATTERPLOT OF DETRENDED NUMBER OF COUNTRIES PLOTTED AGAINST DETRENDED TRADE TO GDP RATIO
(WITHOUT SUB-SAHARAN AFRICA—1870–1992)

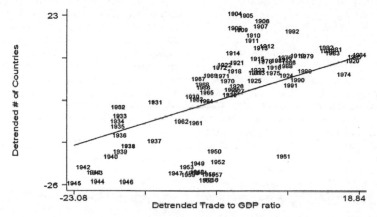

FIGURE 4. SCATTERPLOT OF DETRENDED NUMBER OF COUNTRIES PLOTTED AGAINST DETRENDED TRADE TO GDP RATIO
(WITH SUB-SAHARAN AFRICA—1903–1992)

More specifically, this paper pursues two goals: Firstly, we develop an explicit model of geography and trade which endogenously derives the equilibrium number and size of countries as a function of the trade regime. Secondly, we provide empirical evidence for two critical implications of the model: (i) the effect of country size on economic growth is mediated by the degree of openness; (ii) the long-term history of country formation and separation has been influenced by the pattern of trade openness and economic integration and vice versa. In particular, we emphasize a trade-off between the economic benefits of size, which are a function of

the trade regime, and the costs of heterogeneity resulting from large and diverse populations.

On the theory side, this paper links the literature on geography and trade with a recent formal literature on country formation and, in particular, a paper by Alesina and Spolaore (1997).[5] It also relates to the analysis of economic integration and preferential trade agreements, but unlike the traditional analysis of trade blocs, we focus on the endogenous forma-

---

[5] For a recent survey of this literature, see Patrick Bolton et al. (1996).

tion of sovereign jurisdictions.[6] Empirically, our paper is related to the recent literature on the effects of openness on economic growth, such as Jeffrey Sachs and Andrew Warner (1995), Wacziarg (1998), and Ades and Glaeser (1999), and the effects of openness on public policy, such as Alesina and Wacziarg (1998) and Dani Rodrik (1998).

The organization of this paper is as follows: Section I presents the model linking country size to productivity and derives endogenously the equilibrium number of countries as a function, among other things, of the trade regime. Section II provides cross-country evidence on how the interaction between country size and the degree of trade liberalization influences economic growth. The last section concludes by discussing the relationship between country formation and trade regimes in history and in modern times.

## I. The Model

### A. Production, Trade, and Growth

The world is composed of $W$ "economic units" (in short "units"), which are the basic entities carrying out economic activities. These units are not geographically mobile. They can be interpreted as homogeneous regions, themselves composed of one or more identical and geographically immobile individuals. A "country" $k$ is made of $S_k$ units, where $1 \leq S_k \leq W$.

A unique final good, $Y$, is produced at time $t$ in each unit $i$, using the following production function:

$$(1) \qquad Y_{it} = A_i \left( \sum_{j=1}^{n} X_{ijt}^{\alpha} \right) L_{it}^{1-\alpha}$$

with $0 < \alpha < 1$. $X_{ijt}$ denotes the amount of intermediate input $j$ used in region $i$ at time $t$, and $L_{it}$ is unit $i$'s labor at time $t$, which is supplied inelastically. There is no labor mobility across regions. The markets for the final good and for labor are perfectly competitive.

Each region produces one and only one in-

termediate input ($X_{it}$ for region $i$) using an immobile, region-specific stock of capital $K_{it}$.[7] Each unit of region $i$'s specific capital yields one unit of the intermediate input $i$.

We assume that $n = W$, which implies that every region can use the intermediate inputs produced by all other regions in order to produce the final good. Intermediate goods are sold in a competitive market within the region. They can also be sold to other regions, in which case costs associated with trade are incurred. We model these costs with the following standard "iceberg" assumption.

*Barriers to trade:* When $Z$ units of an intermediate good are shipped from region $i'$ to region $i'' \neq i'$, only $q(i', i'')$ arrive, with $0 \leq q(i', i'') \leq 1$.

$q(\cdot)$ is a function of all the obstacles which make interregional trade costly. These obstacles can be geographical, technological, and political. In particular, costs associated with exchange across political borders arise because trade takes place between different political and legal systems.[8] A simple and useful specification of $q(i', i'')$ is the following:

$$(2) \qquad q(i', i'') = (1 - \beta_{i'i''})(1 - \delta_{i'i''})$$

where $0 \leq \beta_{i'i''} \leq 1$ and $0 \leq \delta_{i'i''} \leq 1$. The parameter $\beta_{i'i''}$ measures political trade barriers between $i'$ and $i''$, while $\delta_{i'i''}$ measures physical barriers.[9]

In order to obtain a closed-form solution for the model, we make the following simplifying assumptions.

ASSUMPTION 1: $A_i = A$; $L_{it} = 1$ for $i = 1, 2, \dots, W$ at every $t$.

ASSUMPTION 2: $\delta_{i'i''} = 0$ for every $i', i''$.

---

[6] The classical reference is Jacob Viner (1950). More recent contributions to this large literature include Paul Krugman (1991a, b) and the papers in the volumes edited by Jaime de Melo and Arvind Panagariya (1993) and Jacob Frenkel (1997).

[7] As usual, region-specific capital can be interpreted as a broad aggregate which includes human capital.

[8] John McCallum (1995) and John Helliwell (1998) document that, in fact, national borders create barriers to trade that go beyond the existence of explicit, policy-induced trade restrictions.

[9] Some political barriers to trade, such as tariffs, may generate fiscal revenues. We are assuming that these revenues do not influence the levels of consumption and/or production. This would not be the case, for instance, in a model where productive public goods were used in production.

ASSUMPTION 3: *Political barriers are zero for regions belonging to the same country and constant for international trade. More formally:*

$$\beta_{i'i''} = 0$$

*if i' and i" belong to the same country*

$\beta_{i'i''} = \beta$ *otherwise.*

The first two assumptions impose symmetry in the model. Although they considerably simplify the algebra, they should not affect the qualitative nature of our results.[10] Assumption 3 is, in a sense, the definition of a country in our model: unlike exchange within countries, trade across borders entails some costs.[11]

We can now proceed to derive the equilibrium input prices and the levels of international trade at each time $t$:

Suppose that $D_{it}$ units of input $i$ are used domestically (i.e., either within region $i$ or within another region which belongs to the same country as region $i$). By contrast, when $F_{it}$ units of input $i$ are shipped to a *foreign* region (i.e., a region that does *not* belong to the same country as region $i$), only $(1 - \beta)F_{it}$ units will be used for production. In equilibrium, as markets are perfectly competitive, each unit of input $i$ will be sold at a price equal to its marginal product both domestically and internationally. Therefore:

$$(3) \quad P_{it} = A\alpha D_{it}^{\alpha-1} = A\alpha(1-\beta)^{\alpha}F_{it}^{\alpha-1}$$

where $P_{it}$ is the market price of input $i$ at time $t$.

At each time $t$, the resource constraint for each input $i$ is:

$$(4) \quad S_i D_{it} + (W - S_i)F_{it} = K_{it}$$

where $S_i$ is the size (i.e., the number of regions) of the country to which region $i$ belongs.[12]

Define:

$$(5) \quad \theta \equiv (1 - \beta)^{\alpha/(1-\alpha)}$$

The parameter $\theta$ can be interpreted as a measure of "international openness": the lower are the barriers to international trade, the higher is $\theta$.

Equations (3)–(4) and definition (5) imply that, at each time $t$:

(i) The amount of intermediate input $i$ that region $i$ ships to any other region belonging to the same country is:

$$(6) \quad D_{it} = \frac{K_{it}}{(1 - \theta)S_i + \theta W}.$$

(ii) The amount of intermediate input $i$ that region $i$ ships to any other region *not* belonging to the same country is:

$$(7) \quad F_{it} = \frac{\theta K_{it}}{(1 - \theta)S_i + \theta W}.$$

*A Simple One-Period Example.*—Consider the simple case in which, at time 0, each region is endowed with a given amount of capital $K_0$ (equal across regions for simplicity). Suppose that individuals in each region $i$ only care about their own consumption in period 0 (denoted by $C_{i0}$), and that countries have all equal size $S$. In this highly simplified setting, it is easy to show that both income $Y$ and consumption $C$, in equilibrium, are equal across regions and are given by:

$$(8) \quad Y = C = AK_0^{\alpha}[(1 - \theta)S + \theta W]^{1-\alpha}.$$

Note that in equation (8) output and consumption are:

(a) increasing in openness $\theta$ (for a given country size $S$);
(b) increasing in country size $S$ (for a given level of openness $\theta$), and
(c) decreasing in size of countries multiplied by openness $S\theta$.

As we will see next, these results generalize to a dynamic model, in which different regions can start with different levels of initial capital, and capital is accumulated over time.

---

[10] A relaxation of Assumption 2 is examined in a previous version of this paper (Alesina et al., 1997) with no interesting changes in the results.

[11] We are not pursuing here a distinction between a country and a customs union. For results on this point, see Spolaore (1998).

[12] For the moment, we are taking country sizes as given. We will endogenize the number and size of countries in the following subsection.

*The Dynamic Case.*—We now consider the case in which, while at each time $t$ the level of capital in each region $i$ is given, households can increase the stock of capital by saving. We assume that, in continuous time, the intertemporal utility function in each region $i$ is given by:

$$(9) \qquad U_i = \int_0^\infty \ln C_{it} e^{-\rho t}\, dt$$

where $C_{it}$ denotes consumption at time $t$ by the representative household living in region $i$, and $\rho > 0$. We select log-utility for notational simplicity. All of the results generalize to any standard constant relative risk aversion (CRRA) utility function $(C_{it}^{1-\sigma} - 1)/(1 - \sigma)$ with $\sigma > 0$. Household net assets in region $i$ are identical to the stock of region-specific capital $K_{it}$. Each household will maximize its intertemporal utility given its initial level of capital $K_{i0}$ and the following dynamic constraint:

$$(10) \qquad \frac{dK_{it}}{dt} = r_{it} K_{it} + w_{it} - C_{it}.$$

From standard intertemporal optimization:

$$(11) \qquad \frac{dC_{it}}{dt} \frac{1}{C_{it}} = (r_{it} - \rho).$$

As each unit of capital yields one unit of intermediate input $i$, the net return to capital $r_{it}$ is equal to the market price of intermediate input $P_{it}$ (for simplicity, we assume no depreciation). Using equations (3) and (6), we have that:

$$(12) \qquad r_{it} = P_{it} = \alpha A D_{it}^{\alpha - 1}$$

$$= \alpha A [(1 - \theta) S_i + \theta W]^{1 - \alpha} K_i^{\alpha - 1}.$$

The steady-state level of capital is the same in each region of a country of size $S_i$,[13] and is given by:

$$(13) \qquad K_i^{ss} = \left[\frac{\alpha A}{\rho}\right]^{\alpha/(1-\alpha)} [(1 - \theta) S_i + \theta W].$$

[13] In other words, within each country, all regions will converge to the same level of steady-state capital, independently of their initial level of unit-specific capital.

The steady-state level of output in each unit of a country of size $S_i$ is given by:

$$(14) \qquad Y_i^{ss} = A^{1/(1-\alpha)} \left[\frac{\alpha}{\rho}\right]^{\alpha/(1-\alpha)} \left(S_i + \theta \sum_{j \neq i} S_j\right).$$

Therefore, the difference between the steady-state levels of income of two units $i$ and $j$, belonging to different countries of size $S_i$ and $S_j$ respectively, can be written as:

$$(15) \qquad Y_i^{ss} - Y_j^{ss} = A^{1/(1-\alpha)} \left[\frac{\alpha}{\rho}\right]^{\alpha/(1-\alpha)}$$

$$\times (1 - \theta)(S_i - S_j).$$

Equation (15) implies that:

(a) When $\theta = 1$ (i.e., $\beta = 0$ : complete openness), each region in the world reaches the same steady-state level of output independently of the size of its country: $Y_i^{ss} = Y_j^{ss}$. In this case, country size imposes no constraint on the steady-state level of output within each country.

(b) When $\theta < 1$ (i.e., $\beta > 0$ : there exist barriers to international trade, larger countries have greater incomes in steady state. Note that the difference $|Y_i^{ss} - Y_j^{ss}|$ associated with a given difference $|S_i - S_j|$, is decreasing in $\theta$. This means that, at higher levels of openness, country size imposes less of a constraint on income. Equivalently, larger countries experience lower gains from increased openness than smaller countries.

In order to illustrate these results more clearly, we now examine the case of countries of equal size. When all countries have equal size $S$, the steady-state level of output can be written as:

$$(16) \qquad Y^{ss} = A^{1/(1-\alpha)} \left[\frac{\alpha}{\rho}\right]^{\alpha/(1-\alpha)} [(1 - \theta) S + \theta W].$$

As we have assumed away depreciation, output and consumption are equal in steady state: $C^{ss} = Y^{ss}$. In equation (16) the steady-state level of output is increasing in openness $\theta$ (for a given country size $S$), increasing in country size (for a given level of openness), and decreasing in size of countries multiplied by openness $S\theta$.

Around the steady-state the growth rate of output can be approximated by:

$$(17) \quad \frac{dY}{dt}\frac{1}{Y} = \xi e^{-\xi}(\ln Y^{ss} - \ln Y(0))$$

where $\xi \equiv \dfrac{\rho}{2}\left[\left(1 + \dfrac{4(1-\alpha)}{\alpha}\right)^{1/2} - 1\right]$ and $Y(0)$ is initial income.

Equations (11)–(12) and (16)–(17) immediately imply the following important results.

PROPOSITION 1: *The growth rate of income (in the neighborhood of the steady state) and the growth rate of consumption are increasing in size $S$, increasing in trade openness $\theta$, and decreasing in size $S$ multiplied by openness $\theta$.*

Furthermore, as we showed above, from equation (15) we derive the following.

PROPOSITION 1': *The steady-state level of income and the steady-state level of consumption are increasing in size $S$, increasing in trade openness $\theta$, and decreasing in size $S$ multiplied by openness $\theta$.*

These results are explored empirically in Section II.

### B. *The Number and Size of Countries*

We now turn to the relationship between trade openness and the equilibrium number and size of countries. Consider the simple one-period example [equation (8)]. In this case, everyone's income and consumption would be maximized if the entire world belonged to the same country, so that $S = W$. Analogously, in the dynamic model, growth and steady-state income would be maximized when $S = W$.[14]

This is an extreme and implausible case,

since it ignores the costs associated with the excessive size of countries and the heterogeneity of their populations. Indeed, substantial costs may be involved if the British and Irish, Israeli and Arabs, Turks and Greeks, Tutsi and Hutu were to belong to the same country, with the same governments, laws, and public goods. We model this feature by assuming that each individual bears some *heterogeneity costs* $h(S)$ which are a function of the size of the country:

$$(18) \qquad h(S) \geq 0$$

$$(19) \qquad h'(S) > 0 \quad ; \quad h''(S) \geq 0.$$

While it is a priori reasonable to assume that heterogeneity is not decreasing in the size of a country, there are obvious exceptions. Relatively small countries can be very heterogeneous (for example, Rwanda) while larger countries, in terms of population, can be more homogeneous (for example, Japan). Equations (18)–(19) are a rough reduced form for a model capturing the costs of heterogeneity. For instance, Alesina and Spolaore (1997) provide a model where, as in equation (18)–(19), *average heterogeneity* in each country is increasing in size. In that model, a group of heterogeneous individuals forming a country have to agree on a common set of public policies. Individuals are uniformly distributed on an ideological segment, so that the larger the country, the larger the average distance between the common policy adopted and each individual's preferred policy. Equation (19) also assumes that the cost function is weakly convex.

*The One-Period Example.*—Again, we start with the simple case in which individuals only care about one period, and each region is endowed with $K_0$ units of capital.

The most general formulation for the utility function, defined over consumption and heterogeneity costs, is $U(C, h)$. Without loss of generality, we assume that the utility function is separable in $C$ and $h$. In particular, we

---

[14] Only in the case $\theta = 1$, namely complete openness, would the size of each country be uninfluential. Needless to say, if $S = W$, the trade regime, i.e., the value of $\theta$, is irrelevant.

assume that the utility of an individual living in country $i$ is given by:[15]

$$(20) \quad U(C_i, h(S_i)) = \ln C_i - h(S_i).$$

We focus on the case of equal country sizes. Given the symmetry of the model, and given the results in Alesina and Spolaore (1997), the case of equal sizes is clearly the natural one to focus upon. However, we do not explore the possibility that other equilibria may exist, with countries of different sizes. We begin by considering the optimal number of countries (thus, the size $S*$), which maximizes the sum of individual utility, as if $S*$ were chosen by a worldwide benevolent social planner. This optimal number of countries chosen by the social planner is also the number of countries that would be selected unanimously by referendum, if the world population were asked to vote on the number of equally sized countries in the world.[16]

The equilibrium country size $S*$, defined as the size $S$ that maximizes $U(C, h) = \ln C - h(S)$ given (8), is implicitly identified by the first-order condition, as the unique solution to:[17]

$$(21) \quad (1 - \alpha)(1 - \theta)[(1 - \theta)S* + \theta W]^{-1}$$
$$= h'(S*)$$

which implies:

$$(22) \quad \frac{dS*}{d\theta}$$
$$= -\frac{(W - S)h'(S) + (1 - \alpha)}{(1 - \theta)h'(S) + (1 - \theta)Sh''(S)}$$
$$< 0.$$

As the equilibrium number of countries is given by $N* = W/S*$, we can state the following.[18]

PROPOSITION 2: *For any (weakly) convex* $h(S)$, *the equilibrium number of countries is increasing in the degree of openness* $\theta$.

A closed-form solution can be easily obtained in the case of linear heterogeneity costs, namely:

$$(23) \quad h(S) = hS$$

where the parameter $h$ captures the magnitude of heterogeneity costs.

Using equation (23) we obtain:

$$(24) \quad S* = \frac{1 - \alpha}{h} - \frac{\theta}{1 - \theta} W$$

which clearly illustrate Proposition 2: *for given heterogeneity costs, the number of countries should increase with trade liberalization*, an implication which we explore empirically in Section III.

*The Dynamic Case.*—A complete study of the equilibrium number and size of countries in a dynamic framework could quickly become intractable, especially as it should involve an explicit modeling of adjustment costs and potentially complex transitional dynamics. However, the analysis remains relatively simple if we focus on the "steady-state" number and size of countries.

Define the equilibrium country size $S^{ss}$ as the size that maximizes everyone's utility in steady state. From the previous subsection, we know that, when all countries have equal size and the economy is in steady state, $C^{ss}$ and $Y^{ss}$ are equal and given by equation (16). Hence, the

---

[15] Note that in this paper, for simplicity, we assume that heterogeneity costs are identical for everyone regardless of their location within countries.

[16] One can show that under mild, sufficient conditions, the social planner maximizing the sum of individual utilities would *choose* to create countries of equal size. The treatment of voting, however, with the assumption of equal country sizes, raises difficult technical problems, as discussed in Alesina and Spolaore (1997).

[17] Clearly, equilibrium size and equilibrium number of nations are positive integers. For simplicity, we will abstract from those integer constraints.

[18] Note that this proposition holds for any $U = u(C) - h(S)$, where $u'(C) > 0$, $u''(C) < 0$, $h'(S) > 0$, $h'' \geq 0$. By using $Y(S, \theta) = AK^{\alpha}[(1 - \theta)S + W]^{\alpha}$ it is easy to verify that

$$\frac{dS*}{d\theta} = -\frac{u''\left(\frac{\partial Y}{\partial S}\right)^2 + u'\frac{\partial^2 Y}{\partial S^2} - h''}{u''\frac{\partial Y}{\partial S}\frac{\partial Y}{\partial \theta} + u'\frac{\partial Y}{\partial S \partial \theta}} < 0.$$

equilibrium size $S^{ss}$ is implicitly defined by the following first-order condition:

$$(25) \quad (1 - \theta)[(1 - \theta)S^{ss} + \theta W]^{-1} = h'(S^{ss})$$

which implies that higher openness is associated with smaller countries in steady state.[19] That is, Proposition 2 extends to this dynamic setting.

### C. *Unilateral Secessions*

The equilibrium size $S^*$ derived above may or may not be robust to unilateral secessions. The latter can take two forms:

1. A subset of "units" or individuals from one given country forms a new country, keeping the size of all of the other countries and the degree of openness of the world economy as given.
2. A subset of "units" or individuals from two or more different countries separate from their original countries and form a new entity, keeping the size of all of the other countries and the degree of openness constant.

An important point is that the degree of openness is assumed to be given when regions are contemplating secessions. To the extent that "openness" captures the features of the world trade regime as a whole, this assumption is appropriate. The same assumption implies that any new country would adopt the *same* trade regime as the rest of the world, including the trade regime of the country or countries from which it seceded.

Straightforward, although tedious calculations permit to check the conditions under which $S^*$ is secession free.[20] In general, one needs to impose restrictions on the parameters of the model ($W$, $h$ and $\theta$) in order to guarantee this property of the unanimous equilibrium derived above. These restrictions ensure that $S^*$ is not too large, otherwise unilateral secessions

become profitable. In order to ensure the existence of a stable equilibrium, we assume that these restrictions on parameter values hold.[21]

The incentives for unilateral secessions will also depend on whether regions more prone to breaking away are receiving transfers from the remaining regions. The issue of interregional transfers is, however, not our focus here.[22]

### D. *Endogeneity of Trade Barriers*

Thus far, we have assumed that the degree of openness $\theta$ is exogenous, and taken as given by countries contemplating secessions or mergers. While this is appropriate from the point of view of an individual country, in the aggregate the number and size of countries would influence the choice of a world trade regime. Ceteris paribus, small countries have an incentive to maintain low trade barriers and to advocate an open world trading system. Consider, for instance, an exogenous increase in heterogeneity costs $h$. This would lead to a reduction in the equilibrium size of countries. In turn, smaller countries would benefit more from trade openness, providing support for a more open trade regime.[23]

However, barriers to trade across countries are not only induced by trade policy. Differences in languages, culture, business practices, legal systems, etc., make trade within a country easier than trade across borders. Therefore, even in a world of no tariffs and no other formal trade restrictions, national borders would still matter. Convincing evidence which is consistent with this point is provided by McCallum (1995) who studies trade flows between Canadian regions, and across the border with the United States. In other words, even leaving aside other reasons

---

[19] Since: $\dfrac{dS^{ss}}{d\theta} = -\dfrac{(W - S)h'(S) + 1}{(1 - \theta)h'(S) + (1 - \theta)Sh''(S)} < 0.$

[20] See the working paper version (Alesina et al., 1997) of this article for precise details on the derivation.

[21] Similarly, Alesina and Spolaore (1997), in a different but related model, show that the optimal number of countries may or may not be self-enforcing and secession free. In the present paper, the set of parameter values for which $S^*$ is secession free is large, and in no way "knife-edged." More details are available upon request.

[22] In order to address this point, one would need a model with heterogeneity amongst regions and individuals. See Alesina and Spolaore (1997) and Bolton and Gerard Roland (1997).

[23] For an analytical treatment of this point, see the working paper version (Alesina et al., 1997) of this article and, also, Spolaore (1995, 1997).

for why excessively small countries would be unfeasible, a "zero tariff" regime does not imply that the optimal size of countries is infinitesimal. In fact, being part of a political unit may facilitate trade, even in a world without tariffs. Hence, while an exogenous reduction in the size of countries may lead to the adoption of a more open trade regime which, in turn, would bring about a further reduction in equilibrium country size, the existence of cross-country trade barriers which are beyond the reach of policy implies that the resulting equilibrium cannot be characterized by infinitesimally small countries.

It is worth noting that we have always, until now, maintained the assumption that, while heterogeneity costs influence the choice of country size, they do not influence the benefits of trade. Suppose, instead, that heterogeneity costs across units also affect the propensity or benefits of trade. For instance, people may have a preference for trading with people who are similar to them. In this case, a reduction in the costs of heterogeneity would bring about, simultaneously, larger countries and easier trade. Thus, a direct effect of increased "tolerance" would run against, and partly counterbalance, the relationship between country size and trade emphasized in this paper. Furthermore, to the extent that formal or informal barriers to trade emerge endogenously from the heterogeneity of individuals, even domestic trade is not unrelated to country size. For instance, domestic (or within-country) trade barriers may be higher in larger, more heterogeneous countries, than in smaller, more homogeneous ones.

Finally, in our model, the number and size of countries adjust smoothly to underlying changes in the parameters; in practice, border changes and secessions or unifications are costly and lengthy processes. This implies that we may observe border changes only when the underlying parameters have suffered a sufficiently large change. Also, to the extent that border changes are less costly when many borders are changing, the process of country formation and destruction may be lumpy rather than continuous. The end of major wars provides a good example of this fact. In Section III, we show that, in fact, the process of country formation and secession was "lumpy" and occurred in geographical clusters.

## II. Size, Openness, and Growth

In this section, we test Propositions 1 and 1' of Section I, which suggests that both the steady-state level of per capita income and its growth rate in the neighborhood of the steady state are:

1. Positively related to trade openness.
2. Positively related to country size.
3. Negatively related to country size multiplied by openness.

In other words, smaller countries benefit more from being open to trade than large countries, or, to put this in another way, more open countries benefit less from size than countries that are more closed to trade.[24] Throughout, we measure openness to trade using the ratio of imports plus exports to GDP. This variable has the advantage of capturing a broad definition of openness, such as we have adopted in the theory. Namely, trade ratios incorporate both a policy component and a gravity component, as well as determinants of the degree of trade openness that do not enter the traditional definition of policy openness (differences between legal and political systems, language barriers, etc.). Furthermore, measures of trade volume are available for more countries than policy measures.[25] Lastly, trade volume measures are more widely used than policy measures in cross-country studies of trade and growth, allowing comparability of our results with previous findings.[26] We measure country size using

[24] Previous research has provided some support for this hypothesis: Ades and Glaeser (1999), with a sample restricted to the poorest countries, show that the interaction between openness and country size bears a significant negative estimated coefficient. However, they use per capita income as a measure of market size, whereas we use total income or population. Wacziarg (1998) extended the Ades and Glaeser result to a wider sample of countries. Finally, Athanasios Vamvakidis (1997) presents similar regressions, but uses policy measures for openness, rather than trade volumes, and also obtains a significantly negative estimate on the interaction between openness and market size.

[25] For a discussion of the measurement issues involved in assessing the effects of trade openness on growth, see Wacziarg (1998).

[26] See for instance Sebastian Edwards (1993), Vamvakidis (1997), Wacziarg (1998), Ades and Glaeser (1999), and Jeffrey A. Frankel and David Romer (1999).

two different variables. Firstly, the log of total GDP reflects the overall purchasing power of the economy, i.e., its *economic size*. Secondly, we also employ the log of total population, which reflects perhaps more closely the *political size* of a country. The former is closer to the spirit of our theory, since it approximates more closely the size of the market.

### A. *Summary Statistics and Conditional Correlations*

Tables 1 and 2 present summary statistics for the main variables used in this section, averaged over the 1960–1989 time period. Table 1 provides orders of magnitudes, while Table 2 provides simple correlations between openness, country size, and growth. Openness is positively correlated with growth, but negatively correlated with both of our measures of country size, which is consistent with our discussion of the relationship between a country's size and its own degree of openness to trade (Section I, subsection D).

Table 3 presents a set of *conditional correlations*. Firstly, the correlation between openness and the growth of per capita income is equal to 0.641 for small countries (where "small" is defined by restricting the sample to countries with the log of population below the full sample median), while it is only 0.150 for large countries (large countries are the complement of the group of "small" countries). The same pattern holds when conditioning on different levels of total GDP. Secondly, the correlation between the log of population and growth is 0.454 conditional on openness being below the full sample median, while it is slightly negative ($-0.116$) for open countries. Again, the same holds when considering the correlation of the log of GDP with growth. These simple conditional correlations provide strong suggestive evidence consistent with our first hypothesis: namely, country size correlates much less with growth for countries that are more open to trade. Similarly, openness and growth are more tightly linked for small countries than for larger ones.

### B. *Least-Squares Results*

In Table 4, we present simple least-squares regressions for averaged variables over the pe-

riod 1960 to 1989. For each measure of country size, we show three sets of results. Firstly, we present regressions of growth on a constant, openness, country size, and their interaction. These regressions are meant to capture the specification derived from Proposition 1', namely the independent variables are viewed as determinants of growth in the neighborhood of the steady state. Secondly, we added the log of per capita income, measured in 1960, to the regression. According to the modified neoclassical model of growth presented is Section I, the interpretation of the other conditioning variables in this regression is now that they represent the determinants of the *steady-state level* of per capita income.[27] In other words, this specification is meant to test Proposition 1. Lastly, in order to investigate whether our results are due to the omission of other determinants of growth, not accounted for by our theory, we included other common determinants of growth in our regression. These included the ratio of government consumption to GDP, the fertility rate, male and female human capital, and the investment rate. To select these variables, we followed closely the specification in Robert Barro (1991), a benchmark in cross-country growth studies. Throughout, the size of the sample was determined solely by the availability of data. That is, the sample size decreases as more variables are included in the regressions, as some newly included variables are available for fewer countries.

The results from these simple regressions are encouraging for our theory. The signs of the estimated coefficients are as predicted by the Propositions 1 and 1': the interaction term bears a negative coefficient, while both country size and openness bear positive coefficients. While

---

[27] See N. Gregory Mankiw et al. (1992) for the formal derivation of the standard cross-country growth specification from "augmented" versions of the Solow model. The relationship between "levels" and "growth" is well known: If $y_{it}$ is GDP per capita at time $t$ in country $i$, we can write:

$$\log y_{it} - \log y_{it-1} = \alpha + \beta \log y_{it-1} + \text{other controls.}$$

This is the standard growth regression which allows for conditional convergence. One can rewrite this regression in levels:

$$\log y_{it} = \alpha + (\beta + 1)\log y_{it-1} + \text{other controls.}$$

TABLE 1—SUMMARY STATISTICS FOR THE MAIN VARIABLES OF INTEREST

|  | Mean | Median | Maximum | Minimum | Standard deviation | Number of observations |
|---|---|---|---|---|---|---|
| Average annual growth | 2.156 | 2.161 | 6.730 | −1.817 | 1.739 | 120 |
| Openness ratio | 62.214 | 52.559 | 306.901 | 12.589 | 39.287 | 120 |
| Log per capita GDP 1960 | 7.325 | 7.138 | 9.200 | 5.549 | 0.888 | 119 |
| Log total GDP | 16.361 | 16.049 | 21.737 | 11.545 | 1.993 | 119 |
| Log population | 8.653 | 8.629 | 13.649 | 3.992 | 1.702 | 127 |
| Fertility rate | 5.076 | 5.724 | 7.988 | 1.855 | 1.817 | 126 |
| Female human capital | 0.815 | 0.507 | 4.695 | 0.003 | 0.883 | 106 |
| Male human capital | 1.150 | 0.897 | 4.844 | 0.037 | 0.963 | 106 |
| Investment rate (percent GDP) | 16.028 | 15.913 | 34.843 | 1.370 | 8.178 | 120 |
| Government consumption (percent GDP) | 18.473 | 16.772 | 39.445 | 6.097 | 7.036 | 120 |

*Note:* All variables except log income per capita 1960 are averaged over the 1960–1989 period.

TABLE 2—SIMPLE CORRELATIONS FOR GROWTH, PER CAPITA INCOME, OPENNESS AND COUNTRY SIZE

|  | Growth | Log GDP | Log per capita GDP 1960 | Log population | Openness |
|---|---|---|---|---|---|
| Average annual growth | 1.000 |  |  |  |  |
| Log total GDP | 0.228 | 1.000 |  |  |  |
| Log per capita GDP 1960 | 0.197 | 0.521 | 1.000 |  |  |
| Log population | 0.042 | 0.872 | 0.053 | 1.000 |  |
| Openness ratio | 0.368 | −0.418 | 0.111 | −0.602 | 1.000 |

*Notes:* All variables except log income per capita 1960 are averaged over the 1960–1989 period.
Number of observations: 119.

TABLE 3—CONDITIONAL CORRELATIONS

| Variable | Conditioning statement[a] | Correlation with growth[b] | Number of observations |
|---|---|---|---|
| Openness | Log population > median = 8.629 | 0.150 | 58 |
| Openness | Log population ≤ median = 8.629 | 0.641 | 61 |
| Openness | Log GDP > median = 16.049 | 0.353 | 59 |
| Openness | Log GDP ≤ median = 16.049 | 0.637 | 60 |
| Log population | Openness > median = 52.559 | −0.116 | 59 |
| Log population | Openness ≤ median = 52.559 | 0.454 | 60 |
| Log GDP | Openness > median = 52.559 | 0.089 | 59 |
| Log GDP | Openness ≤ median = 52.559 | 0.547 | 60 |

[a] Medians are computed from individual samples, while correlations are common sample correlations.
[b] Average annual growth rate of per capita GDP, 1960–1989.

the estimated coefficients on the latter are also consistently significant, the coefficient on interaction term is, at worst, only significant at the 13-percent level. In three of the six regressions, however, it is statistically significant at the 5-percent level. Numerically, the results suggest that a hypothetically infinitesimal country (that is, with a log of total GDP equal to zero), the effect of a 10-percentage-point increase in openness on annual growth is contained between 0.60 and 0.95 percentage points, depending on the specification. This effect falls in the range 0.12 to 0.30 when the log of total GDP falls to the sample median (equal to 16.049). Similarly, the effect of a standard-deviation increase in the log of total GDP (equal to 1.99) on annual growth rates, for a hypothetical closed country (zero openness), varies between 0.61

TABLE 4—DETERMINANTS OF GROWTH RATES: OLS ESTIMATES

| Dependent variable: Growth of per capita GDP 1960–1989 | Size = log of GDP | | | Size = log of population | | |
|---|---|---|---|---|---|---|
| | (1) | (2) | (3) | (4) | (5) | (6) |
| Intercept | −9.956 | −9.247 | 6.299 | −4.900 | −6.330 | 7.884 |
| | (2.231) | (2.260) | (2.828) | (1.375) | (1.773) | (2.495) |
| Size*openness | −0.004 | −0.004 | −0.003 | −0.004 | −0.004 | −0.004 |
| | (0.002) | (0.002) | (0.002) | (0.0025) | (0.0026) | (0.002) |
| Country size | 0.646 | 0.742 | 0.306 | 0.624 | 0.606 | 0.278 |
| | (0.133) | (0.139) | (0.102) | (0.143) | (0.142) | (0.1187) |
| Openness | 0.094 | 0.095 | 0.060 | 0.057 | 0.057 | 0.044 |
| | (0.035) | (0.035) | (0.030) | (0.020) | (0.021) | (0.017) |
| Log of per capita income 1960 | — | −0.339 | −1.277 | — | 0.229 | −1.144 |
| | | (0.189) | (0.216) | | (0.137) | (0.198) |
| Fertility rate | — | — | −0.322 | — | — | −0.306 |
| | | | (0.126) | | | (0.127) |
| Male human capital | — | — | 1.684 | — | — | 1.817 |
| | | | (0.440) | | | (0.454) |
| Female human capital | — | — | −1.465 | — | — | −1.587 |
| | | | (0.441) | | | (0.448) |
| Government consumption (percent GDP) | — | — | −0.043 | — | — | −0.044 |
| | | | (0.020) | | | (0.020) |
| Investment rate (percent GDP) | — | — | 0.076 | — | — | 0.084 |
| | | | (0.024) | | | (0.024) |
| Adjusted $R^2$ | 0.321 | 0.333 | 0.652 | 0.244 | 0.249 | 0.647 |
| Regression standard error | 1.437 | 1.4238 | 1.0129 | 1.5123 | 1.5112 | 1.0196 |
| Number of observations | 119 | 119 | 97 | 120 | 119 | 97 |

*Notes:* All variables are averaged over the 1960–1989 period, except initial income in 1960. Heteroskedastic-consistent (White-robust) standard errors are in parentheses.

and 1.48. At the median of openness (equal to 52.56), the effect falls between 0.30 and 1.06. The same pattern holds when size is measured by the log of population. These orders of magnitude suggest that the estimated effects are large economically, and their signs are consistent with our theory.

## C. *Endogeneity Issues*

Several authors have suggested that the estimated effect of trade openness on economic growth is biased due to the endogeneity of openness. To address this issue, Frankel and Romer (1999) construct an instrument for openness using exogenous gravity variables, and show that the estimated coefficient on the trade to GDP ratio in a cross-country income-level regression is actually *increased* when endogeneity issues are properly accounted for. The endogeneity of openness is a concern in the present paper as well, as discussed in Section I, subsection D. Furthermore, this problem potentially extends to the endogeneity of the interac-

tion term between openness and country size. We follow Frankel and Romer (1999) in selecting gravity variables as potential instruments for openness and for the interaction term between openness and country size. These variables are likely to be strongly associated with the degree of openness, and unlikely a priori to be affected by reverse causation. We provide instrumental variables evidence largely to evaluate the robustness of our basic results. In any case, previous results by Frankel and Romer (1999) show that the endogeneity of openness is unlikely to be a major problem.

We focus upon the following set of purely geographic variables: dummy variables for whether a country is an island, a small island, a small country, and a landlocked country.[28] These are mostly "gravity" variables that are widely used as instruments in the cross-country

[28] All of these variables are more precisely defined in the Appendix. We thank an anonymous referee for suggesting this set of variables.

openness and growth literature. In addition, we added the interaction between each of these variables and the log of population to the list of instruments, in order to explicitly account for the potential endogeneity of the interaction term between openness and country size. Since they are pure geography variables, these instruments are unlikely to be affected by reverse causation with respect to post-1960 economic growth. To check this fact, we can perform Hausman tests for overidentification, since we have eight instruments and two endogenous variables.

Tables 5A and 5B presents Hausman $\chi^2$ statistics pertaining to the null hypothesis that the set of instruments other than the small country dummy and its interaction with country size are valid instruments. The results are not sensitive to which instruments are tested for. Specifically, the choice of other pairs of instruments as "benchmark" instruments in the Hausman procedure does not change the result: in all cases we cannot reject the null hypothesis that the coefficients obtained from an (inefficient) IV model using only the small country dummy and its interaction with size as instruments are the same as those obtained using the full set of instruments. Indeed, the $p$-values for this hypothesis are always greater than 68 percent.

Next, we checked whether the instruments are closely related to openness and the interaction term between openness and country size, another requirement for valid instruments: these are likely to provide little identifying information unless they are strongly jointly correlated with the corresponding endogenous variables. To investigate this, we regressed the three endogenous variables on the instruments plus the included exogenous variables in each specification of Table 5A. We then performed $F$-tests for the joint significance of the instruments in these regressions. As shown in Table 5B, for all specifications our instruments are indeed significantly associated with openness, the interaction between openness and the log of population, and the interaction between openness and the log of total GDP. This again suggests that the instruments do indeed provide identifying information.

The results from the instrumental variables procedure, in Tables 5A and B, are in line with the previous OLS results, which come out reinforced in terms of statistical significance. The

pattern of signs, as predicted by the theory, is maintained. The magnitude of the coefficients on openness is raised somewhat, in line with results in Frankel and Romer (1999). This suggests that the endogeneity issue applied to openness and the interaction term is unlikely to be an important source of fragility for our results. Furthermore, the use of instruments has increased the significance of some of the coefficients, particularly on the interaction term between openness and country size.

### D. *Levels Approach*

To further establish the robustness of our results, we ran regressions using the level of per capita income in 1989 as a dependent variable (without including lagged per capita income on the right-hand side).[29] Although our theory delivers predictions for the growth rate of income [or, in neoclassical growth theoretic terms, for the steady-state level of income, see equation (15) and Barro and Xavier Sala-i-Martin (1995)], levels regressions constitute useful complements to empirical tests of Proposition 1, and may lead to reducing measurement error inherent in the dependent variable of growth regressions. As stressed in Robert Hall and Charles I. Jones (1999), levels regressions require a broader set of controls than growth regressions, since the source of variation previously captured by initial income now has to be accounted for otherwise. We address this issue by controlling for a wide set of covariates. Another important issue that arises with level regressions is endogeneity with respect to trade and the interaction term between trade and country size. We address this issue by using end-of-period income as a dependent variable and by instrumenting for the trade and the interaction between trade and size using the aforementioned instruments.

In spite of the difficulties associated with levels regressions, Table 6 further establishes the robustness of our main findings. Namely, the signs of the relevant coefficients are in line with the theory, although their significance has fallen relative to growth regressions. In the regressions without any controls, the coefficient on the interaction term between size and

---

[29] In doing so we follow the recommendations of an anonymous referee.

TABLE 5A—DETERMINANTS OF GROWTH RATES: INSTRUMENTAL VARIABLES ESTIMATES

| Dependent variable: Growth of per capita GDP 1960–1989 | Size = log of GDP | | | Size = log of population | | |
|---|---|---|---|---|---|---|
| | (1) | (2) | (3) | (4) | (5) | (6) |
| Intercept | −13.793 | −14.299 | −1.271 | −9.955 | −10.365 | 3.083 |
| | (3.869) | (3.825) | (3.713) | (3.233) | (3.293) | (3.032) |
| Size*openness | −0.006 | −0.0075 | −0.007 | −0.007 | −0.007 | −0.007 |
| | (0.004) | (0.0037) | (0.002) | (0.005) | (0.005) | (0.003) |
| Country size | 0.833 | 1.133 | 0.701 | 1.066 | 1.035 | 0.603 |
| | (0.226) | (0.255) | (0.201) | (0.307) | (0.315) | (0.204) |
| Openness | 0.131 | 0.163 | 0.136 | 0.102 | 0.101 | 0.077 |
| | (0.061) | (0.058) | (0.038) | (0.039) | (0.039) | (0.023) |
| Log of per capita income 1960 | — | −0.662 | −1.229 | — | 0.118 | −0.980 |
| | | (0.329) | (0.228) | | (0.179) | (0.200) |
| Fertility rate | — | — | −0.253 | — | — | −0.243 |
| | | | (0.132) | | | (0.133) |
| Male human capital | — | — | 1.501 | — | — | 1.561 |
| | | | (0.459) | | | (0.471) |
| Female human capital | — | — | −1.319 | — | — | −1.346 |
| | | | (0.477) | | | (0.472) |
| Government consumption (percent GDP) | — | — | −0.043 | — | — | −0.043 |
| | | | (0.023) | | | (0.022) |
| Investment rate (percent GDP) | — | — | 0.055 | — | — | 0.072 |
| | | | (0.029) | | | (0.027) |
| $R^2$ | 0.271 | 0.246 | 0.617 | 0.116 | 0.149 | 0.629 |
| Regression standard error | 1.508 | 1.541 | 1.115 | 1.656 | 1.636 | 1.099 |
| Number of observations | 119 | 119 | 97 | 120 | 119 | 97 |
| Hausman $\chi^2$ | 0.87 | 0.68 | 0.39 | 1.48 | 1.19 | 0.00 |
| $p$-value | 0.832 | 0.953 | ≈1.00 | 0.686 | 0.880 | ≈1.00 |

*Notes:* Instruments used—small country dummy, island dummy, small island dummy, landlocked country dummy, and the interaction of each of these variables with the log of population. Heteroskedastic-consistent (White-robust) standard errors are in parentheses.

TABLE 5B—FIRST-STAGE $F$-TESTS FOR THE INSTRUMENTS

| Endogenous variable: | Openness | Openness*log population | Openness*log total GDP |
|---|---|---|---|
| Specification 1—$F$-statistic | 6.12 | — | 5.31 |
| ($p$-value) | 0.000 | | 0.000 |
| Specification 2—$F$-statistic | 5.93 | — | 4.52 |
| ($p$-value) | 0.000 | | 0.0001 |
| Specification 3—$F$-statistic | 4.20 | — | 3.69 |
| ($p$-value) | 0.0003 | | 0.001 |
| Specification 4—$F$-statistic | 4.48 | 4.27 | — |
| ($p$-value) | 0.0001 | 0.0002 | |
| Specification 5—$F$-statistic | 4.56 | 4.04 | — |
| ($p$-value) | 0.0001 | 0.0003 | |
| Specification 6—$F$-statistic | 3.81 | 3.17 | — |
| ($p$-value) | 0.001 | 0.0035 | |

*Note:* $F$-tests on the instruments from a regression of the three endogenous variables on the list of instruments plus the exogenous regressors in each specification (8 degrees of freedom in the numerator).

openness is insignificant, although of the right sign. Focusing on the regressions which include the greatest set of controls [columns (3) and (6)], both the interaction term between openness and size and the openness term appear with significant coefficients, while the coefficient on size is now insignificant, although again of the desired sign. Therefore, we take these results as providing additional evidence in favor of Proposition 1.

TABLE 6—DETERMINANTS OF INCOME LEVELS: INSTRUMENTAL VARIABLES ESTIMATES

| Dependent variable: Log of per capita income 1989 | Size = log of GDP | | | Size = log of population | | |
|---|---|---|---|---|---|---|
| | (1) | (2) | (3) | (4) | (5) | (6) |
| Intercept | −4.736 | 0.906 | 8.010 | 1.725 | 6.444 | 8.820 |
| | (2.233) | (5.253) | (2.148) | (1.929) | (1.873) | (1.002) |
| Size*openness | −0.001 | −0.008 | −0.004 | −0.0002 | −0.010 | −0.006 |
| | (0.002) | (0.003) | (0.002) | (0.002) | (0.003) | (0.002) |
| Country size | 0.636 | 0.442 | 0.068 | 0.494 | 0.243 | 0.004 |
| | (0.131) | (0.314) | (0.143) | (0.184) | (0.206) | (0.121) |
| Openness | 0.049 | 0.141 | 0.063 | 0.032 | 0.079 | 0.040 |
| | (0.038) | (0.064) | (0.029) | (0.020) | (0.027) | (0.016) |
| Number of observations | 114 | 80 | 71 | 115 | 81 | 72 |
| Adjusted $R^2$ | 0.12 | 0.80 | 0.93 | 0.13 | 0.86 | 0.92 |
| Regression standard error | 1.052 | 0.566 | 0.361 | 1.1769 | 0.469 | 0.368 |

*Notes:* Included controls (output suppressed):

Columns (1) and (4): No controls.

Columns (2) and (5): Ethnolinguistic fractionalization, urbanization rate in 1970, distance from major trading partners, average number of revolutions and coups per year, and a set of dummies for whether there was a war between 1960 and 1985, whether the country was ever a colony (since 1776), postwar independence, oil exporting countries, Muslim majority, Catholic majority, Protestant majority, Confucian majority, Hindu majority, socialist country, Latin America, South East Asia, OECD, Sub-Saharan Africa.

Columns (3) and (6): Same as columns (3) and (6) plus fertility rate, male human capital, female human capital, government consumption as a share of GDP, investment rate.

Instruments used: Log of population, dummies for small country, small island, island, landlocked country, and each of the interactions of these dummies with the log of population.

Heteroskedastic-consistent (White-robust) standard errors are in parentheses.

## III. Discussion

### A. Historical Overview

In the working paper version (Alesina et al., 1997) of this paper, we analyzed, in a brief historical overview, the evolution of trade regimes and country formation since the early nineteenth century.[30] We made a few points which we will only mention here. Firstly, we argued that the process of nation-building in the first half of the nineteenth century can be interpreted as resulting from the trade-off between the benefits of market size and the costs of population heterogeneity.[31]

Secondly, at the end of the nineteenth century the emergence of colonial empires can be viewed, at least in part, as a response to stagnant trade

amongst European powers and to the need to expand markets in a period when protectionism was on the rise.[32] As a referee correctly pointed out, a colonial empire allowed the European powers to have large markets without having to bear too much of the cost of heterogeneity, since the colonies did not share the same institutions as the colonizers (and in particular were not generally granted the right to participate in the colonizers' political processes).

Thirdly, the pattern of trade regimes and country formation in the interwar and post-Second World War periods is consistent with the predictions of our model. In the interwar period, borders remained "frozen," namely virtually no new country obtained independence and, concurrently, international trade collapsed as a result of protectionist policies and the Great Depression. At the same time, colonial empires remained largely intact.

Figure 5 shows the number of countries

---

[30] The working paper version (Alesina et al., 1997) is available from the National Bureau of Economic Research as Working Paper No. 6163 and, for a more recent version, directly from the authors.

[31] In our reading of the historical records, we found a number of references pointing to precisely this trade-off in debates amongst the framers of the new nation-states in Europe.

[32] According to Eric Hobsbawm (1987 p. 67, the British prime minister in 1897 told the French ambassador that "if you were not such persistent protectionists, you would not find us so keen to annex territories."

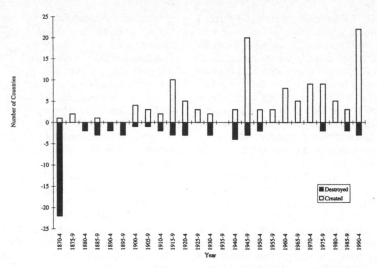

FIGURE 5. COUNTRIES CREATED AND DESTROYED
(FIVE-YEAR PERIODS, EXCLUDES SUB-SAHARAN AFRICA)

created and destroyed in five-year periods from 1870 until today. It excludes Sub-Saharan Africa, for which the identification of "countries" in the nineteenth century is somewhat problematic. The German unification, in which 18 previously independent entities disappeared, explains the dip at the beginning of Figure 5. This figure also shows that very few new countries were created from 1875 to the Treaty of Versailles, while some countries disappeared. As was argued above, this was also a period of growing trade restrictions.

The same figure identifies a peak, i.e., a large number of countries created with the Treaty of Versailles in 1919. International borders hardly changed at all in the interwar period, until the late thirties, with the unfolding of the Second World War. In fact, Figure 5 shows that in the interwar period very few new countries appeared in the world.[33]

On the contrary, after the Second World War, trade restrictions were gradually reduced and the number of countries rapidly increased (see, again, Figure 3). In the 50 years that followed the Second World War, the number of independent countries exploded. As shown in Figure 1, there were 64 independent countries in the world (outside Sub-Saharan Africa) in 1871, after the first German unification. This number declined slightly, to 59, until the First World War. In 1920, the world (including Sub-Saharan Africa) consisted of 69 countries. There were 89 in 1950 and 192 in 1995. As a consequence of this increase in the number of independent nations, the world now comprises a large number of relatively small countries: in 1995, 87 of the countries in the world had a population of less than 5 million, 58 had a population of less than 2.5 million, and 35 less than 500 thousand. At the same time, the share of international trade in world GDP increased dramatically.

We should stress that the increase in international trade in the last half-century, as documented by Figure 1, is not the simple result of an accounting illusion. In fact, if two countries

[33] Note that, among the very few new country creations, at least one, Egypt (independent in 1922) results from a classification problem: Egypt in 1922 was already largely independent from Britain, but its status switched from a protectorate to a semi-independent country. Leaving aside Vatican City, the only other countries created between 1920 and the Second World War were Ireland (1921), Mongolia (1921), Iraq (1932), and Saudi Arabia (1932) (although,

again, Saudi Arabia was de facto independent since the mid-1920's).

were to split, their resulting trade to GDP ratios would automatically increase, as former domestic trade is now counted as international trade. But Figure 1 only features the average trade to GDP ratio for a set of countries *whose borders did not change since 1870.*[34] Furthermore, Figure 2 employs average tariffs on foreign trade for a selection of countries with available data, a more direct reflection of trade policy, to display a similar historical pattern. Obviously, such policy measures are not subject to the accounting illusion either.

Finally, it is useful to discuss two recent or current cases of border changes. One is Québec's separatism, in the context of NAFTA. An important issue in the discussion of Québec's independence is how this region benefits, in terms of trade flows, from being part of Canada relative to being an independent country in NAFTA.[35] In studying precisely this point both McCallum (1995) and Helliwell (1998) conclude that, at least for Canada, national borders still matter, so that trade among Canadian provinces is ceteris paribus much easier than between Canadian provinces and U.S. states. This implies that there might be a cost for Québec in terms of trade flows if it were to become independent. Such arguments were made by the proponents of the "no" in the self-determination referendum of 1996.

The second case is that of the European Union. At first glance, the process leading toward European integration and monetary union could be seen as contrary to our argument, since several major countries are increasing their politico-economic ties in a period of worldwide trade liberalization. According to many observers, however, Europe will never be a federal state, in the usual sense. Instead, several countries in Europe will form a loose confederation of independent states, joined in a common currency area, coordinated macroeconomic policies to support this common currency, in addition to a free-trade area supplemented by a harmonization of regulations and standards.

In fact, while economic integration is progressing at the European level, regional separatism is more and more vocal in several member countries of the Union, such as Spain, Belgium, Italy, and even France.[36] So much so, that many an observer has argued that Europe will (and, perhaps should) become a collection of regions (Brittany, the Basque Region, Scotland, Catalonia, Wales, etc.) loosely connected within a European federation.[37] The motivation of these developments is consistent with our argument: linguistic, ethnic, and cultural minorities feel that they are economically "viable" in the context of a truly European common market, thus they can "safely" separate from the home country.[38] In other words, the nation-state in Europe is threatened from above because of the necessity of developing supranational juridical institutions, and from below because of rampant regional movements. These movements feel they do not really need Madrid, Rome, or Paris, when they can be loosely associated to the "Europe of Regions" politically, and be fully integrated in the Union economically. Newhouse (1997) puts it rather starkly: "[In Europe], the nation-state is too big to run everyday life and too small to manage international affairs."

An exhaustive discussion of the relationship between economic an political integration in Europe is beyond the scope of this paper.[39] However, to the extent that we can interpret Europe as an area of "deep economic integration" rather than as an area of political integration, recent developments in Western Europe do not contradict the main argument of this paper.

## B. *Concluding Comments*

We have argued that trade liberalization and average country size are inversely related. Thus,

---

[34] Trade with formerly colonized countries is counted as international trade, so that decolonization had no "artificial" effect on trade volumes.

[35] For an in-depth discussion of Québec's separatism and its economic consequences, see McCallum (1992).

[36] For a recent discussion of "rising regionalism" in Europe, see Joseph Newhouse (1997).

[37] See Jean Drèze (1993) on this point.

[38] Interestingly this argument is often mentioned in the press. For an example pertaining to Scotland, see the *Financial Times,* September 16, 1998: "(...) the existence of the European Union lowers the cost of independence for small countries by providing them with a free trade area (...) and by creating a common currency which will relieve the Scots of the need to create one for themselves (...)."

[39] See Alesina and Wacziarg (1999) for a more complete discussion.

the "globalization" of markets goes hand in hand with political separatism.

While this paper has emphasized the link from trade regime to country size, one may argue that the opposite channel may also be operative; namely a world of small countries has to adopt a relatively free-trade regime, because this is in the interest of small countries. The two channels are not mutually exclusive. Suppose that a certain region (say, Québec, Catalonia, Ukraine, etc.) considers demanding independence. Each of these regions takes the trade regime in the world, at the moment of their declaration of independence, as given. However, if the process of political separatism continues, and average country size declines, more and more "players" in the international arena have an interest in preserving free trade, thus reinforcing the movement toward trade liberalization that may have influenced their decision about secession in the first place.

An implication of this paper is that as the process of economic "globalization" will progress, political separatism will continue to be alive and well. The concept of relatively large and centralized nation-states is and will be more and more threatened by regional separatism from below, and the growth of supranational institutions from above, in a world of "global" markets.

### Appendix A: Number of Countries Data

#### Definitions

In most cases the determination of when a country appeared or disappeared is fairly uncontroversial. For example it is clear that the first German unification happened in 1871, that Algeria was born in 1962, and so on. In a number of cases, however, it may be unclear whether a country was independent or not. For instance, Afghanistan was under British "influence" for some time, but never became a crown colony. For such cases, we had to use decision rules to determine the number of countries in any single year. These rules are the following:

1. For most of the countries, the dates of colonization and independence are specified in Encyclopedia Britannica, so we used those dates. We also double-checked with Centen-

nia, a computerized map program, whenever the data in Centennia was available. If conflicts occurred, we consulted country-specific history books.

2. For a few countries, the process of colonization and gaining independence took a long time. We used the year in which a country lost control over its foreign policies as the starting point of colonization and the year that a country "fully" gained its independence as the year that it became independent. The word "fully" is usual terminology in the Encyclopedia Britannica and implies that the colonizer has left all powers to the local government.

3. If formal colonization did not occur for a given country, e.g., Bhutan, we used the criterion that its foreign policies was controlled by a foreign power as the starting point of colonization.

4. Countries that were under suzerainty of another country, e.g., Serbia and Romania under the Ottoman Empire, were classified as colonies.

5. A few countries, e.g., Afghanistan, were not colonized but were under the influence of foreign countries. They were classified as independent countries.

### Appendix B: Data Sources and Description

Variable name: Growth
Source: Summers-Heston v. 5.6. Unit: Percentage points
Definition: Growth rate of PPP adjusted gross domestic product

Variable name: Trade/GDP ratio
Source: Summers-Heston v. 5.6. Unit: Percentage points
Definition: Ratio of imports plus exports to GDP

Variable name: Initial income per capita
Source: Summers-Heston v. 5.6. Unit: Log of per capita GDP in dollars
Definition: Real gross domestic product per capita in a given year (PPP adjusted)

Variable name: Human capital (male and female)
Source: Barro-Lee. Unit: Years

Definition: Average years of secondary and higher education in the total population over age 25

Variable name: Investment rate
Source: Summers-Heston v. 5.6. Unit: Percentage points
Definition: Real investment share of GDP (1985 international prices)

Variable name: Fertility rate
Source: World Bank. Unit: Number of children per woman
Definition: Total fertility rate (children per woman)

Variable name: Public consumption
Source: Summers-Heston v. 5. Units: Percent
Definition: Share of government consumption of goods and services in GDP, excluding transfers and public investment

Variable name: Log population
Source: Barro-Lee. Unit: Logarithm of population
Definition: Country population

Variable name: Log of area
Source: Barro-Lee. Unit: Millions of square kilometers (log)
Definition: Log of country land area

Variable name: Landlocked dummy
Source: Authors. Unit: Dummy variables
Definition: Equals 1 if the country is landlocked

Variable name: Island dummy
Source: Authors. Unit: Dummy variables
Definition: Equals 1 if the country is an island

Variable name: Small country dummy
Source: Authors. Unit: Dummy variables
Definition: Equals 1 if the country's land area is smaller than 50 million square kilometers

Variable name: Small island dummy
Source: Authors. Unit: Dummy variables
Definition: Equals the island dummy multiplied by the small country dummy

## REFERENCES

**Ades, Alberto and Glaeser, Edward.** "Evidence on Growth, Increasing Returns, and the Extent of the Market." *Quarterly Journal of Economics*, August 1999, *114*(3), pp. 1025–45.

**Alesina, Alberto and Spolaore, Enrico.** "On the Number and Size of Nations." *Quarterly Journal of Economics*, November 1997, *112*(4), pp. 1027–56.

**Alesina, Alberto; Spolaore, Enrico and Wacziarg, Romain.** "Economic Integration and Political Disintegration." National Bureau of Economic Research (Cambridge, MA) Working Paper No. 6163, September 1997.

**Alesina, Alberto and Wacziarg, Romain.** "Openness, Country Size, and the Government." *Journal of Public Economics*, September 1998, *69*(3), pp. 305–21.

_____. "Is Europe Going Too Far?" *Carnegie-Rochester Conference Series on Public Policy*, December 1999, *51*(1), pp. 1–42.

**Barro, Robert.** "Economic Growth in a Cross-Section of Countries." *Quarterly Journal of Economics,* May 1991, *106*(2), pp. 407–43.

**Barro, Robert and Sala-i-Martin, Xavier.** *Economic growth.* New York: McGraw-Hill, 1995.

**Bolton, Patrick and Roland, Gerard.** "The Breakup of Nations: A Political Economy Analysis." *Quarterly Journal of Economics*, November 1997, *112*(4), pp. 1057–90.

**Bolton, Patrick; Roland, Gerard and Spolaore, Enrico.** "Economic Theories of the Break-Up and Integration of Nations." *European Economic Review*, April 1996, *40*(3–5), pp. 697–705.

**de Melo, Jaime and Panagariya, Arvind,** eds. *New dimensions in regional integration.* Cambridge: Cambridge University Press, 1993, pp. 3–21.

**Drèze, Jean.** "Regions of Europe: A Feasible Status, to Be Discussed." *Economic Policy*, October 1993, *8*(17), pp. 265–87.

**Edwards, Sebastian.** "Openness, Trade Liberalization, and Growth in Developing Countries." *Journal of Economic Literature*, September 1993, *31*(3), pp. 1358–93.

*Financial Times.* September 16, 1998.

**Frankel, Jeffrey A. and Romer, David.** "Does Trade Cause Growth?" *American Economic Review*, June 1999, *89*(3), pp. 379–99.

**Frenkel, Jacob,** ed. *The regionalization of the world economy.* Chicago: Chicago University Press, 1997.

**Hall, Robert and Jones, Charles I.** "Why Do Some Countries Produce So Much More

Output Per Worker Than Others?" *Quarterly Journal of Economics*, February 1999, *114*(1), pp. 83–116.

Helliwell, John. *How much do national borders matter?* Washington, DC: Brookings Institution Press, 1998.

Hobsbawm, Eric. *The age of empire.* New York: Vintage Books, 1987.

_____ . *Nations and nationalism since 1870.* Cambridge University Press, 1990.

Keynes, John Maynard. *The economic consequences of the peace.* New York: Harcourt, Brace and Howe, 1920.

Krugman, Paul. "Is Bilateralisme Bad?" in Elhanan Helpman and Assaf Razin, eds., *International trade and trade policy.* Cambridge, MA: MIT Press, 1991a, pp. 9–23.

_____ . "The Move to Free Trade Zones." *Federal Reserve Bank of Kansas City Review*, December 1991b.

Mankiw, N. Gregory; Romer, David and Weil, David N. "A Contribution to the Empirics of Economic Growth." *Quarterly Journal of Economics*, May 1992, *107*(2), pp. 407–37.

Mansori, Kashif S. "Interregional Trade: Effects on the Build-Up and Breakdown of Nations." Unpublished manuscript, Princeton University, November 1996.

McCallum, John. "On the Economic Consequences of Québec's Separation," in A. R. Riggs and Tom Velk, eds., *Federalism in peril: National unity, individualism, free markets, and the emerging global economy.* Vancouver: Fraser University Press, 1992, pp. 163–67.

_____ . "National Borders Matter: Canada–U.S. Regional Trade Patterns." *American Economic Review*, June 1995, *85*(3), pp. 615–23.

Newhouse, Joseph. "Europe's Rising Regionalism." *Foreign Affairs*, January/February 1997, pp. 67–84.

Rodrik, Dani. "Why Do More Open Economies Have Bigger Governments?" *Journal of Political Economy*, October 1998, *106*(5), pp. 997–1032.

Sachs, Jeffrey and Warner, Andrew. "Economic Reform and the Process of Global Integration." *Brookings Papers on Economic Activity*, 1995, (1), pp. 1–95.

Spolaore, Enrico. "Economic Integration, Political Borders, and Productivity." Prepared for the CEPR-Sapir conference on "Regional Integration and Economic Growth," Tel Aviv University, December 1995.

_____ . "Borders and Barriers." Mimeo, Ohio State University, 1997.

_____ . "Countries, Unions, and International Openness." Mimeo, Brown University, October 1998.

Vamvakidis, Athanasios. "How Important Is a Large Market for Economic Growth?" Mimeo, International Monetary Fund and Harvard University, 1997.

Viner, Jacob. *The customs union issue.* New York: Carnegie Endowment for International Peace, 1950.

Wacziarg, Romain. "Measuring the Dynamic Gains from Trade." World Bank Policy Research Working Paper No. 2001, November 1998.

Wittman, Donald. "Nations and States: Mergers and Acquisitions; Dissolution and Divorce." *American Economic Review*, May 1991 (*Papers and Proceedings*), *81*(2), pp. 126–29.

*Journal of Economic Perspectives—Volume 14, Number 1—Winter 2000—Pages 177–186*

# How Far Will International Economic Integration Go?

## Dani Rodrik

I n a famous passage from *The Economic Consequences of the Peace*, Keynes (1920) drew a vivid picture of an integrated world economy at the pinnacle of the gold standard. While sipping his morning tea in bed, Keynes reminisced nostalgically, the Englishmen of his time could order by telephone various commodities of the world, invest in far-off places, purchase unlimited amounts of foreign currency or precious metals, and arrange for international travel without even requiring a passport. Keynes, who was writing in the aftermath of a devastating world war and was anticipating a period of economic turbulence and protectionism—correctly, as it turned out—considered this a lost era of great magnificence.

What will a latter-day Keynes, writing a century from now, say about today's global economy with its unparalleled prosperity and integration (illustrated by Figure 1)? Will she bemoan, as the original Keynes did, its collapse into disarray and autarky yet again? Or will she look back at the tail end of the 20th century as the era that launched a new process of internationalization? Since economists rank second only to astrologers in their predictive abilities, the correct answer is that we have no idea. The best that one can do is speculate wildly, which is what I am about to do.

In these speculations, I will use the term "international economic integration" rather than "globalization," for two reasons. First, while not as trendy, my preferred term has a distinct meaning that will be self-evident to economists. Globalization, by contrast, is a term that is used in different ways by different analysts. Second, the term "international economic integration" does not come with the value judge-

■ *Dani Rodrik is Professor of International Political Economy, John F. Kennedy School of Government, Harvard University, and Research Associate, National Bureau of Economic Research, both in Cambridge, Massachusetts. His e-mail address is ⟨dani_rodrik@harvard.edu⟩.*

*178    Journal of Economic Perspectives*

**Figure 1**
**World Exports/GDP** (*in 1990 constant dollars, percent*)

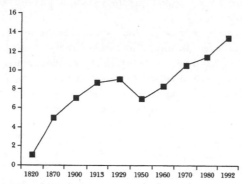

*Source:* Maddison (1995), Tables G-2, I-4.

ments—positive or negative—that the term "globalization" seems to trigger in knee-jerk fashion.

## How Much More Integration Could There Be?

The natural benchmark for thinking about international economic integration is to consider a world in which markets for goods, services, and factors of production are perfectly integrated. How far are we presently from such a world?

The answer is that we are quite far. Contrary to conventional wisdom and much punditry, international economic integration remains remarkably limited. This robust finding comes across in a wide range of studies, too numerous to cite here.[1] National borders, such as the U.S.-Canadian one, seem to have a significantly depressing effect on commerce, even in the absence of serious formal tariff or nontariff barriers, linguistic or cultural differences, exchange rate uncertainty, and other economic obstacles. International price arbitrage in tradable commodities tends to occur very slowly. Investment portfolios in the advanced industrial countries typically exhibit large amounts of "home bias;" that is, people invest a higher proportion of assets in their own countries than the principles of asset diversification would seem to suggest. National investment rates remain highly correlated with and dependent on national saving rates. Even in periods of exuberance, capital flows between rich and poor nations fall considerably short of what theoretical models would predict. Real interest rates are not driven to equality even among advanced countries with integrated financial markets. Severe restrictions on the international mobility of labor are the rule rather than the exception. Even the

[1] See in particular Feldstein and Horioka (1980) and Helliwell (1998).

Internet, the epitome of technology-driven internationalization, remains parochial in many ways; for example, Amazon.com feels compelled to maintain a distinct British site, Amazon.co.uk, with different recommendations and sales rankings than its American parent.

While formal barriers to trade and capital flows have been substantially re-duced over the last three decades, international markets for goods, services, and capital are not nearly as "thick" as they would be under complete integration. Why so much trade in goods and capital has gone missing is the subject of an active research agenda in international economics. The answers are not yet entirely clear.

But at some level there is no mystery. National borders demarcate political and legal jurisdictions. Such demarcations serve to segment markets in much the same way that transport costs or border taxes do. Exchanges that cross national jurisdictions are subject to a wide array of transaction costs introduced by discontinuities in political and legal systems.

These transaction costs arise from various sources, but perhaps the most obvious is the problem of contract enforcement. When one of the parties reneges on a written contract, local courts may be unwilling—and international courts unable—to enforce a contract signed between residents of two different countries. Thus, national sovereignty interferes with contract enforcement, leaving international transactions hostage to an increased risk of opportunistic behavior. This problem is most severe in the case of capital flows, and has the implication that national borrowing opportunities are limited by the *willingness* of countries to service their obligations rather than their *ability* to do so. But the problem exists generically for any commercial contract signed by entities belonging to two differing jurisdictions.[2]

When contracts are implicit rather than explicit, they require either repeated interaction or other side constraints to make them sustainable. Both of these are generally harder to achieve across national borders. In the domestic context, implicit contracts are often "embedded" in social networks, which provide sanctions against opportunistic behavior. One of the things that keeps businessmen honest is fear of social ostracism. The role played by ethnic networks in fostering trade linkages, as in the case of the Chinese in southeast Asia, is a clear indication of the importance of group ties in facilitating economic exchange.[3]

Ultimately, contracts are often neither explicit nor implicit; they simply remain incomplete. Laws, norms and customs are some of the ways in which the problem of incompleteness of contracts is alleviated in the domestic sphere. To borrow an example from Tirole (1989, pp. 113–114), what protects a consumer from the small likelihood that a soda-pop bottle might explode is not a contingent contract signed with the manufacturer, but that country's product liability laws. International law

---

[2] See Anderson and Marcouiller (1999) for empirical evidence which suggests that inadequate contract enforcement imposes severe costs on trade.

[3] Casella and Rauch (1997) were the first to emphasize the importance of group ties in international trade, using a model of differentiated products.

provides at best partial protection against incomplete contracts, and international norms and customs are hardly up to the task either.

This line of argument has important implications for the question of how far international economic integration will go. If the depth of markets is limited by the reach of jurisdictional boundaries, does it not follow that national sovereignty imposes serious constraints on international economic integration? Can markets become international while politics remains local? Or, to ask a different but related question, what would politics look like in a world in which international markets had nothing to fear from the narrower scope of political jurisdictions? The rest of the paper will advance some answers to these questions, and in so doing lay out a framework for thinking about the future of the world economy.

## Caught in an International Trilemma

A familiar result of open-economy macroeconomics is that countries cannot simultaneously maintain independent monetary policies, fixed exchange rates, and an open capital account. This result is fondly known to the cognoscenti as the "impossible trinity," or in Obstfeld and Taylor's (1998) terms, as the "open-economy trilemma." The trilemma is represented schematically in the top panel of Figure 2. If a government chooses fixed exchange rates and capital mobility, it has to give up monetary autonomy. If it wants monetary autonomy and capital mobility, it has to go with floating exchange rates. If it wants to combine fixed exchange rates with monetary autonomy (at least in the short run), it had better restrict capital mobility.

The bottom panel of Figure 2 suggests, by analogy, a different kind of trilemma, one that we might call the political trilemma of the world economy. The three nodes of the extended trilemma are international economic integration, the nation-state, and mass politics. I use the term "nation-state" to refer to territorial-jurisdictional entities with independent powers of making and administering the law. I use the term "mass politics" to refer to political systems where: a) the franchise is unrestricted; b) there is a high degree of political mobilization; and c) political institutions are responsive to mobilized groups.

The implied claim, as in the standard trilemma, is that we can have at most two of these three things. If we want true international economic integration, we have to go either with the nation-state, in which case the domain of national politics will have to be significantly restricted, or else with mass politics, in which case we will have to give up the nation-state in favor of global federalism. If we want highly participatory political regimes, we have to choose between the nation-state and international economic integration. If we want to keep the nation-state, we have to choose between mass politics and international economic integration.

None of this is immediately obvious. But to see that there may be some logic

*Figure 2*
**Pick Two, Any Two**

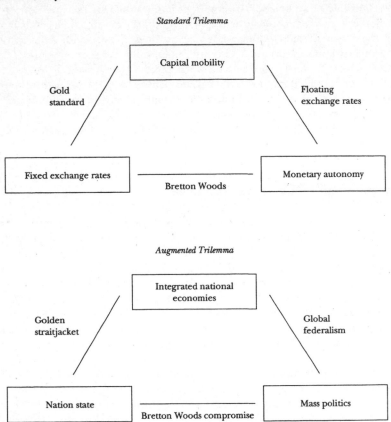

*Standard Trilemma*

*Augmented Trilemma*

in it, consider our hypothetical perfectly integrated world economy. This would be a world economy in which national jurisdictions do not interfere with arbitrage in markets for goods, services or capital. Transaction costs and tax differentials would be minor; convergence in commodity prices and factor returns would be almost complete. The most obvious way we can reach such a world is by instituting federalism on a global scale. Global federalism would align jurisdictions with the market, and remove the "border" effects. In the United States, for example, despite the continuing existence of differences in regulatory and taxation practices among states, the presence of a national constitution, national government, and a federal judiciary ensures that markets are truly national.[4] The European Union, while very far from a federal system at present, seems to be headed in the same direction. Under a model of global federalism, the entire world—or at least the parts that matter economically— would be organized along the lines of the U.S. system. National governments would not necessarily disappear, but their powers would be severely circum- scribed by supranational legislative, executive, and judicial authorities. A world government would take care of a world market.

But global federalism is not the only way to achieve complete international economic integration. An alternative is to maintain the nation-state system largely as is, but to ensure that national jurisdictions—and the differences among them—do not get in the way of economic transactions. The overarching goal of nation-states in this world would be to appear attractive to international markets. National jurisdictions, far from acting as an obstacle, would be geared towards facilitating international commerce and capital mobility. Domestic regulations and tax policies would be either harmonized according to international standards, or structured such that they pose the least amount of hindrance to international economic integration. The only local public goods provided would be those that are compatible with integrated markets.

It is possible to envisage a world of this sort; in fact, many commentators seem to believe we are already there. Governments today actively compete with each other by pursuing policies that they believe will earn them market confidence and attract trade and capital inflows: tight money, small government, low taxes, flexible labor legislation, deregulation, privatization, and openness all around. These are the policies that comprise what Thomas Friedman (1999) has aptly termed the Golden Straitjacket.

The price of maintaining national jurisdictional sovereignty while markets become international is that politics have to be exercised over a much narrower domain. Friedman notes (1999, p. 87):

> As your country puts on the Golden Straitjacket, two things tend to happen: your economy grows and your politics shrinks. . . . [The] Golden Straitjacket narrows the political and economic policy choices of those in power to relatively tight parameters. That is why it is increasingly difficult these days to find any real differences between ruling and opposition parties in those countries that have put on the Golden Straitjacket. Once your country puts on the Golden Straitjacket, its political choices get reduced to Pepsi or Coke—to slight nuances of tastes, slight nuances of policy, slight alterations in design to account for local traditions, some loosening here or there, but never any major deviation from the core golden rules.

Whether this description accurately characterizes our present world is debat-

---

[4] However, Wolf (1997) finds that state borders within the United States have some deterrent effect on trade as well.

able. But Friedman is on to something. His argument carries considerable force in a world where national markets are fully integrated. In such a world, the shrinkage of politics would get reflected in the insulation of economic policy-making bodies (central banks, fiscal authorities, and so on) from political participation and debate, the disappearance (or privatization) of social insurance, and the replacement of developmental goals with the need to maintain market confidence. The essential point is this: once the rules of the game are set by the requirements of the global economy, the ability of mobilized popular groups to access and influence national economic policy-making has to be restricted. The experience with the gold standard, and its eventual demise, provides an apt illustration of the incompatibility: by the interwar period, as the franchise was fully extended and labor became organized, national governments found that they could no longer pursue gold standard economic orthodoxy.

Note the contrast with global federalism. Under global federalism, politics need not, and would not, shrink: it would relocate to the global level. The United States provides a useful way of thinking about this: the most contentious political battles in the United States are fought not at the state level, but at the federal level.

Figure 2 shows a third option, which becomes available if we sacrifice the objective of complete international economic integration. I have termed this the Bretton Woods compromise. The essence of the Bretton Woods-GATT regime was that countries were free to dance to their own tune as long as they removed a number of border restrictions on trade and generally did not discriminate among their trade partners.[5] In the area of international finance, countries were allowed (indeed encouraged) to maintain restrictions on capital flows. In the area of trade, the rules frowned upon quantitative restrictions but not import tariffs. Even though an impressive amount of trade liberalization was undertaken during successive rounds of GATT negotiations, there were also gaping exceptions. Agriculture and textiles were effectively left out of the negotiations. Various clauses in the GATT (on anti-dumping and safeguards, in particular) permitted countries to erect trade barriers when their industries came under severe competition from imports. Developing country trade policies were effectively left outside the scope of international discipline.[6]

Until roughly the 1980s, these loose rules left enough space for countries to follow their own, possibly divergent paths of development. Hence, western Europe chose to integrate within itself and to erect an extensive system of social insurance. Japan caught up with the developed economies using its own distinctive brand of capitalism, combining a dynamic export machine with large

---

[5] Ruggie (1994) has written insightfully on this, describing the system that emerged as "embedded liberalism."

[6] Lawrence (1996) has termed the model of integration followed under the Bretton Woods-GATT system as "shallow integration," to distinguish it from the "deep integration" that requires behind-the-border harmonization of regulatory policies.

doses of inefficiency in services and agriculture. China grew by leaps and bounds once it recognized the importance of private initiative, even though it flouted every other rule in the guidebook. Much of the rest of east Asia generated an economic miracle relying on industrial policies that have since been banned by the World Trade Organization. Scores of countries in Latin America, the Middle East, and Africa generated unprecedented economic growth rates until the late 1970s under import-substitution policies that insulated their economies from the world economy.

The Bretton Woods compromise was largely abandoned in the 1980s, for several reasons. Improvements in communication and transportation technologies undermined the old regime by making international economic integration easier. International trade agreements began to reach behind national borders; for example, policies on antitrust or health and safety, which had previously been left to domestic politics, now became issues in international trade discussions. Finally, there was a shift in attitudes in favor of openness, as many developing nations came to believe that they would be better served by a policy of openness. The upshot is that we are left somewhere in between the three nodes of the augmented trilemma of Figure 2. Which one shall we eventually give up?

## Where Next?

I have argued so far that we are presently nowhere near complete international economic integration, and that traveling the remaining distance will require either an expansion of our jurisdictions or a shrinkage of our politics. Now I have to stick my neck out farther and make a prediction.

I would place my bet on global federalism, as unlikely as that may seem at the moment. In the next 100 years or so, I see a world in which the reach of markets, jurisdictions, and politics are each truly and commensurately global as the most likely outcome.[7] I may also be biased, since that is the option that I personally like best.

The bet is based on the following reasoning. First, continuing technological progress will both foster international economic integration and remove some of the traditional obstacles (such as distance) to global government. Second, short of global wars or natural disasters of major proportions, it is hard to envisage that a substantial part of the world's population will want to give up the goodies that an increasingly integrated (hence efficient) world market can deliver. Third, hard-won

---

[7] I am purposefully vague about the specific form that global federalism might take, other than state that it will entail much greater political centralization than the current setup. See Frey (1996) on some intriguing ideas for the design of federal political systems. See Bergsten (1993) for an alternative scenario that combines political fragmentation—rather than centralization—with full international economic integration.

citizenship rights (of representation and self-government) are also unlikely to be given up easily, keeping pressure on politicians to remain accountable to the wishes of their electorate.

The most dicey projection is that we shall see an alliance of convenience in favor of global governance between those who perceive themselves to be the "losers" from economic integration, like labor groups and environmentalists, and those who perceive themselves as the "winners," like exporters, multinational enterprises, and financial interests. The alliance will be underpinned by the mutual realization that both sets of interests are best served by the *supranational* promulgation of rules, regulations, and standards. Labor advocates and environmentalists will get a shot at international labor and environmental rules. Multinational enterprises will be able to operate under global accounting standards. Investors will benefit from common disclosure, bankruptcy, and financial regulations. A global fiscal authority will provide public goods and a global lender-of-last resort will stabilize the financial system. Part of the bargain will be to make international policymakers accountable through democratic elections, with due regard to the preeminence of the economically more powerful countries. National bureaucrats and politicians, the only remaining beneficiaries of the nation-state, will either refashion themselves as global officials or they will be shouldered aside.

Global federalism does not mean that the United Nations will turn itself into a world government. What we are likely to get is a combination of traditional forms of governance (an elected global legislative body) with regulatory institutions spanning multiple jurisdictions and accountable to perhaps multiple types of representative bodies. In an age of rapid technological change, the form of governance itself can be expected to be subject to considerable innovation.

Many things can go wrong with this scenario. One alternative possibility is that an ongoing series of financial crises will leave national electorates sufficiently shell-shocked that they willingly, if unhappily, don the Golden Straitjacket for the long run. This scenario amounts to the Argentinization of national politics on a global scale. Another possibility is that governments will resort to protectionism to deal with the distributive and governance difficulties posed by economic integration. That would be the backlash scenario. If I were making a prediction for the next 20 years rather than 100, I would regard either one of these scenarios as more likely than global federalism. But a longer time horizon leaves room for greater optimism.

Now let me tell you about the Wars of Secession of 2120 . . .

■ *I thank Brad De Long, Alan Krueger and Timothy Taylor for very useful suggestions.*

## References

**Anderson, James E. and Douglas Marcouiller.** 1999. "Trade, Insecurity, and Home Bias: An Empirical Investigation." NBER Working Paper No. 7000, March.

**Bergsten, C. Fred.** 1993. "The Rationale for a Rosy View: What a Global Economy Will Look Like." *The Economist.* September 11.

**Casella, Alessandra and James Rauch.** 1997. "Anonymous Market and Group Ties in International Trade." NBER Working Paper No. W6186, September.

**Feldstein, Martin S. and Charles Horioka.** 1980. "Domestic Saving and International Capital Flows." *Economic Journal.* June, 90, pp. 314–29.

**Frey, Bruno.** 1996. "FOCJ: Competitive Governments for Europe." *International Review of Law and Economics.* 16, pp. 315–27.

**Friedman, Thomas L.** 1999. *The Lexus and the Olive Tree: Understanding Globalization.* New York: Farrar, Straus and Giroux.

**Helliwell, John F.** 1998. *How Much Do National Borders Matter?* Washington, DC: Brookings Institution.

**Keynes, John Maynard.** 1920. *The Economic Consequences of the Peace.* New York: Harcourt, Brace, and Howe.

**Lawrence, Robert Z.** 1996. *Regionalism, Multilateralism, and Deeper Integration.* Washington, DC: Brookings Institution.

**Maddison, Angus.** 1995. *Monitoring the World Economy 1820–1992.* Paris: OECD.

**Obstfeld, Maurice and Alan Taylor.** 1998. "The Great Depression as a Watershed: International Capital Mobility over the Long Run," in *The Defining Moment: The Great Depression and the American Economy in the Twentieth Century.* Bordo, Michael D., Claudia D. Goldin, and Eugene N. White, eds. Chicago: University of Chicago Press, pp. 353–402.

**Ruggie, John G.** 1994. "Trade, Protectionism and the Future of Welfare Capitalism." *Journal of International Affairs.* Summer, 48:1, pp. 1–11.

**Tirole, Jean.** 1989. *The Theory of Industrial Organization.* Cambridge, MA: MIT Press, 1989.

**Wolf, Holger C.** 1997. "Patterns of Intra- and Inter-State Trade." NBER Working Paper No. W5939, February.

# C
# Home Bias

# [25]

## National Borders Matter: Canada–U.S. Regional Trade Patterns

*By* JOHN MCCALLUM[*]

National borders around the world seem to be in a state of flux, with changes occurring in the physical location of borders and perhaps their economic significance as well. Though few economists would agree with Kenichi Ohmae's statement that borders have "effectively disappeared" (1990 p. 172), many have argued that regional trading blocs such as the North American Free Trade Agreement and the European Union are making national borders less important. This paper provides a case study of the impact of the Canada–U.S. border on regional trade patterns. Although the choice of this particular case was dictated by a data source that could be unique to Canada, the Canada–U.S. case may be particularly interesting because the two countries are so similar in terms of culture, language, and institutions. If, as will be seen to be the case, the border separating these two very similar countries exerts a decisive impact on continental trade patterns, then it seems likely, though not proven, that borders separating less similar countries will also have decisive effects on trade patterns.

The methodology of the paper is very simple and derives from a literature including studies by Jan Tinbergen (1962), Hans Linneman (1966), Jeffrey Frankel (1993), and others. These studies use gravity-type equations to examine the determinants of international trade patterns, including the impact of preferential trade blocs. Trade between any two countries is a function of each country's gross domestic product, the distance between them, and possibly other variables. The effect of a trade bloc on trade patterns is then estimated by appending to the equation a dummy variable set equal to 1 for cases of intrabloc trade and zero for all other cases. This paper makes use of a Statistics Canada data set that includes both interprovincial trade flows and flows between each Canadian province and each state of the United States (it would appear that data on interstate trade flows within the United States do not exist). Whereas the literature just cited uses international trade flows to estimate the impact of multinational trade blocs on trade patterns, this paper uses a combination of subnational and international trade flows to estimate the impact of the nation state on trade patterns.

The remainder of the paper is organized as follows. Section I presents the basic results using the simplest specification. Section II presents a sensitivity analysis that focuses on specification issues and econometric questions relating to heteroscedasticity and a possible simultaneity problem. The results of these first two sections provide a snapshot of a single year, 1988. Since this is the year in which the Canada–U.S. Free Trade Agreement (FTA) was signed, some might argue that results based on 1988 could change radically as the effects of the FTA, followed by the North American Free Trade Agreement (NAFTA), come into play. While only time will provide a definitive answer to this question, Section III addresses the issue with a brief overview of the evolution of trade patterns and tariff protection over the period 1950–1993.

### I. Basic Results

In his survey on the testing of trade theories, Alan Deardorff (1984) commented that despite their "somewhat dubious theoretical

[*]Royal Bank of Canada, 200 Bay Street, Toronto, Ontario, Canada, M5J 2J5, and (before June 1, 1994) Department of Economics, McGill University. My thanks to Stanley Hartt for helpful discussions at an early stage of this project, to John Galbraith for comments, Marc Gaudry for his collaboration in supplementary sensitivity tests, and Audrae Erickson and Zachary James for their excellent research assistance.

heritage, gravity models have been extremely successful empirically" (p. 503), and also useful as the basis for tests of other propositions. It is in this spirit that the results of this paper are presented. The simplest version of the estimated equation can be written as follows for any given time period:

$$x_{ij} = a + by_i + cy_j + d\,\mathrm{dist}_{ij}$$
$$+ e\,\mathrm{DUMMY}_{ij} + u_{ij}$$

where $x_{ij}$ is the logarithm of shipments of goods from region $i$ to region $j$, $y_i$ and $y_j$ are the logarithms of gross domestic product in regions $i$ and $j$, $\mathrm{dist}_{ij}$ is the logarithm of the distance from $i$ to $j$, $\mathrm{DUMMY}_{ij}$ is a dummy variable equal to 1 for interprovincial trade and 0 for province-to-state trade (it may be recalled that we have no data on interstate trade), and $u_{ij}$ is an error term.

In principle, the data set, described in greater detail in the Data Appendix, consists of imports and exports for each pair of provinces, as well as imports and exports between each of the 10 provinces and each of the 50 states. The data are for 1988, which, as noted above, is the latest year for which the numbers are available. To limit the scope of the operation, it was decided to include only 30 states, defined as the 20 states with the largest population, plus all border states. These 30 states[1] accounted for more than 90 percent of Canada–U.S. trade in 1988. In principle, then, there are 690 observations: $10 \times 9 = 90$ observations for interprovincial trade, as well as $10 \times 30 \times 2 = 600$ observations for province–state trade. In seven cases there was no recorded trade, leaving 683 nonzero observations.

The simplest versions of this equation are reported in the first two rows of Table 1. Row 1 is the Canada-only version of the

equation, with 90 observations and no dummy variable. Row 2 includes the U.S. observations and the dummy variable, for a total of 683 observations. It can be seen that this simple model has considerable explanatory power and that the elasticities of exports with respect to own GDP, importing-region GDP, and distance are respectively 1.3, 1.0, and $-1.5$ according to the first equation. These numbers are of similar magnitude in the second equation. The estimated coefficient on the distance variable is substantially larger than the estimated coefficients from the international studies referred to earlier, which tend to be less than 1 in absolute value. One possible explanation of this difference rests on the fact that water transport is much cheaper than other modes of transport and that, whereas most global trade is transported by water, most North American trade goes by air and land. More interestingly, the second regression implies that, other things equal, trade between two provinces is more than 20 times larger than trade between a province and a state [$\exp(3.09) = 22$]. The range of this estimate, plus or minus two standard errors, is 17–29.

Table 2 sets out both the actual regional pattern of trade flows and the pattern that the regression equations would predict for a borderless North America (minus Mexico). For Canada as a whole in 1988, shipments of goods by destination were as follows: own province, 44 percent; other provinces, 23 percent; United States, 24 percent; and rest of the world, 9 percent. East–west interprovincial shipments, then, were of very similar value to north–south exports to the United States. As just seen, the gravity-model equation predicts a radically different distribution of this trade in a borderless world. If, for purposes of illustration, one assumes that the sum of the east–west and north–south trade remains a constant 47 percent of total shipments, then the prediction for a borderless world is that interprovincial trade should account for 4 percent of shipments rather than 23 percent, while shipments to the United States should account for 43 percent of shipments rather than 24 percent. The table presents this

---

[1]The thirty states are Alabama, Arizona, California, Florida, Georgia, Idaho, Illinois, Indiana, Kentucky, Louisiana, Maine, Maryland, Massachusetts, Michigan, Minnesota, Missouri, Montana, New Hampshire, New Jersey, New York, North Carolina, North Dakota, Ohio, Pennsylvania, Tennessee, Texas, Vermont, Virginia, Washington, and Wisconsin.

TABLE 1—SENSITIVITY TESTS: ECONOMETRIC ISSUES

$$x_{ij} = a + by_i + cy_j + d\,\mathrm{dist}_{ij} + e\,\mathrm{DUMMY}_{ij}$$

| | Equation | | | | | | |
|---|---|---|---|---|---|---|---|
| Independent variable | 1 | 2 | 3 | 4 | 5 | 6 | 7 |
| $y_i$ | 1.30 | 1.21 | 1.15 | 1.20 | 1.24 | 1.20 | 1.36 |
| | (0.06) | (0.03) | (0.04) | (0.03) | (0.03) | (0.03) | (0.04) |
| $y_j$ | 0.96 | 1.06 | 1.03 | 1.07 | 1.09 | 1.05 | 1.19 |
| | (0.06) | (0.03) | (0.04) | (0.03) | (0.03) | (0.03) | (0.04) |
| $\mathrm{dist}_{ij}$ | −1.52 | −1.42 | −1.23 | −1.34 | −1.46 | −1.43 | −1.48 |
| | (0.10) | (0.06) | (0.07) | (0.06) | (0.06) | (0.06) | (0.07) |
| $\mathrm{DUMMY}_{ij}$ | | 3.09 | 3.11 | 3.09 | 3.16 | 3.08 | 3.07 |
| | | (0.13) | (0.16) | (0.13) | (0.13) | (0.13) | (0.14) |
| Estimation method: | OLS | OLS | OLS | OLS | OLS | IV | OLS |
| Number of observations: | 90 | 683 | 462 | 683 | 690 | 683 | 683 |
| Standard error: | 0.80 | 1.10 | 0.97 | 1.07 | 1.13 | 1.11 | 1.15 |
| Adjusted $R^2$: | 0.890 | 0.811 | 0.801 | 0.887 | 0.820 | 0.811 | 0.797 |

Notes: Standard errors are given in parentheses. Definitions of the equations are as follows:
  Equation 1: Basic equation, Canada only;
  Equation 2: Basic equation, Canada + United States;
  Equation 3: Sample includes only jurisdictions with GDP exceeding $10 billion;
  Equation 4: Regression weighted by $y_i + y_j$;
  Equation 5: Seven observations of zero trade set equal to minimum values;
  Equation 6: Logarithms of population, $\mathrm{pop}_i$ and $\mathrm{pop}_j$, used as instruments for $y_i$ and $y_j$;
  Equation 7: Regression estimated by ordinary least squares, but with population variables replacing income variables.

same information for each of Canada's five regions.[2]

Since experience suggests that people regard these numbers as unbelievably large, it might be useful to illustrate the findings with a map and two examples. Figure 1 provides what might be called an economic map of North America. Each black circle represents a province, and each white circle represents a state. The mid-point of each circle is the "central place" of the province or state (described in the Data Appendix), while the area of each circle is proportional to gross domestic product of the jurisdiction in question. The ten circles spread out across the northern part of the continent tend to be small and distant from each other in comparison with the larger, more numerous, and less distant circles that constitute the American states. Hence the gravity-model prediction that Canadian trade should be overwhelmingly north–south is not surprising.

Turning now to the examples, a borderless gravity model predicts that Ontario and Quebec should export about ten times as much to California as to British Columbia. The distances are inconsequentially different, and California's GDP is more than ten times that of British Columbia. In fact, in 1988 both Quebec and Ontario exported more than three times as much to British Columbia as to California. A second example: in 1988 British Columbia exported about nine times as much to Ontario ($1.4 billion) as to Texas ($155 million), but in a borderless world British Columbia's exports to Texas should be about 50-percent greater than her exports to Ontario. The distances are the same, and the gross domestic product of Texas is 50-percent greater than that of Ontario.

[2]These numbers are based on the Canada-only regression, but the results are virtually identical when based on the second reported regression, which includes U.S. variables.

TABLE 2—CANADIAN SHIPMENTS OF GOODS BY DESTINATION, 1988

| Origin | Shipments ($ billion) | Destination (percentage of total shipments) | | | |
|---|---|---|---|---|---|
| | | Own province | Other provinces | United States | Rest of world |
| Canada | 387 | 44 | 23 [4] | 24 [43] | 9 |
| Atlantic provinces | 18 | 37 | 29 [12] | 19 [36] | 15 |
| Quebec | 85 | 47 | 27 [6] | 19 [40] | 7 |
| Ontario | 179 | 45 | 21 [3] | 29 [47] | 5 |
| Prairie provinces | 67 | 41 | 28 [9] | 18 [37] | 13 |
| British Columbia | 37 | 43 | 13 [2] | 19 [30] | 25 |

*Note:* Figures in brackets are predictions based on the gravity model.
*Source:* Statistics Canada (1989a, b, 1992).

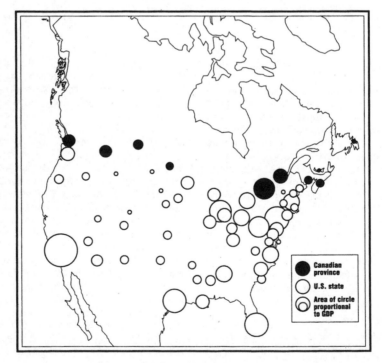

FIGURE 1. ECONOMIC MAP OF NORTH AMERICA

Before proceeding to the sensitivity tests, it is worth noting that my 22-to-1 result is much bigger than the corresponding numbers that Frankel (1993) obtains for the trade-generating impact of regional blocs. He runs regressions at five-year intervals from 1965 to 1990 and finds that the effects of the various regional groupings on total trade reach maximum levels as follows: Western Hemisphere, 2.8 to 1 in 1990; East Asia Economic Community, 5.8 to 1 in 1970; Pacific Rim countries, 6.4 to 1 in 1985; European Community, 3.1 to 1 in 1985.[3] My result is also in the spirit of Paul Krugman's (1991) comparison of the degree of economic integration of the states of the United States with that of the countries of the European Union. However, the differences reported in this paper are greater by several orders of magnitude than the differences reported by Krugman (1991).

## II. Sensitivity Tests

Tables 1 and 3 set out alternative regressions designed to deal with potential problems of econometrics and specification. In all there are 11 regressions reported in the two tables combined, and these are labeled equations 1–11. Equations 1 and 2 are the basic regressions that were reported in the text above. Equations 3–5 deal with the possibility of heteroscedasticity: equation 3 includes only the larger jurisdictions, defined as states or provinces with GDP exceeding \$10 billion; equation 4, following the example of Frankel and Shang-Jin Wei (1993), is a weighted regression, with weights defined as the logarithm of the product of the GDP's (i.e., the regression is weighted by $y_i + y_j$); and equation 5, following Linnemann (1966) and Zhen Kun Wang and L. Alan Winters (1992), substitutes minimal trade flow values for cases where recorded trade values are zero.[4]

A second possible econometric problem arises from the fact that the dependent variable (exports) is a component of one of the regressors (GDP). Hence, by an accounting identity, the included regressor is going to be correlated with the disturbance term. Accordingly, equation 6 uses the logarithms of the corresponding populations as instruments for the GDP variables, while equation 7 replaces the logarithms of GDP with the logarithms of population.[5] As can be seen from Table 1 all of the coefficients and standard errors of the seven equations are remarkably stable. In particular, the estimated coefficient on $DUMMY_{ij}$ lies in the range 3.07–3.16 with standard errors between 0.13 and 0.16.

The remaining four regressions, labeled equations 8–11 and reported in Table 3, test alternative, more complicated specifications. Equation 8 enters distance in logarithmic form as before, but also as a natural number (DIST) and the square of DIST. There is a modest increase in explanatory power but no significant effect on the coefficient on $DUMMY_{ij}$. Next, equation 9 tests for province-specific constant terms and province-specific coefficients on $DUMMY_{ij}$. The former are indicators of the overall volume of each province's exports (given GDP, distance, etc.), while the latter are indicators of the degree to which each province's trade is biased toward exports to other provinces. It can be seen that British Columbia and Alberta have significantly above-average constant terms (i.e., more trade), while British Columbia and Newfoundland have significantly below-average coefficients on $DUMMY_{ij}$ (i.e., proportionally less east–west trade as compared with other provinces). The other provinces did not diverge significantly from each other. Other things equal, province-to-province

---

[3] These numbers, which correspond to my 22-to-1 figure, are taken from Frankel's (1993) table 2. For example, he reports a coefficient of 1.04 on the Western Hemisphere dummy variable in 1990. The figure reported in the text is exp(1.04) = 2.8.

[4] This last adjustment is not likely to be very important in the present context, since only seven of the 690 trade flows were recorded as zero.

[5] A regression of the logarithms of the GDP's on the logarithm of the populations yields an $R^2$ of 0.99.

TABLE 3—SENSITIVITY TESTS: SPECIFICATION ISSUES

| Independent variable | Equation | | | |
|---|---|---|---|---|
| | 8 | 9 | 10 | 11 |
| Constant | −1.37 | −3.24 | −3.06 | −3.31 |
| | (1.82) | (0.70) | (0.72) | (1.80) |
| Constant (British Columbia) | | 1.08 | 1.16 | 1.21 |
| | | (0.21) | (0.20) | (0.21) |
| Constant (Alberta) | | 0.63 | 0.29 | 0.32 |
| | | (0.18) | (0.20) | (0.21) |
| $y_i$ | 1.21 | 1.18 | 1.18 | 1.22 |
| | (0.03) | (0.03) | (0.03) | (0.04) |
| $y_j$ | 1.06 | 1.03 | 1.03 | 1.05 |
| | (0.03) | (0.03) | (0.03) | (0.04) |
| $\text{dist}_{ij}$ | −2.00 | −1.48 | −1.54 | −1.63 |
| | (0.33) | (0.06) | (0.06) | (0.33) |
| $\text{DIST}_{ij}$ | 0.0016 | | | 0.0005 |
| | (0.0007) | | | (0.0007) |
| $\text{DIST}_{ij}^2$ | $-3.7\times10^{-7}$ | | | $-1.7\times10^{-7}$ |
| | $(1.4\times10^{-7})$ | | | $(1.4\times10^{-7})$ |
| $\text{DUMMY}_{ij}$ | 3.11 | 3.22 | 3.21 | 3.30 |
| | (0.13) | (0.14) | (0.14) | (0.15) |
| DUMMY (British Columbia) | | −1.39 | −1.38 | −1.35 |
| | | (0.43) | (0.43) | (0.44) |
| DUMMY (Newfoundland) | | −1.18 | −1.13 | −1.02 |
| | | (0.38) | (0.38) | (0.39) |
| $\text{PRIM}_{ij}$ | | | 2.87 | 2.60 |
| | | | (0.89) | (0.92) |
| $\text{MFG}_{ij}$ | | | 0.58 | 0.72 |
| | | | (0.75) | (0.80) |
| Estimation method: | OLS | OLS | OLS | IV |
| Number of observations: | 683 | 683 | 683 | 690 |
| Standard error: | 1.10 | 1.07 | 1.07 | 1.09 |
| Adjusted $R^2$: | 0.81 | 0.82 | 0.82 | 0.83 |

*Note:* Standard errors are given in parentheses.

trade is now six times greater than province-to-state trade for British Columbia, eight times greater for Newfoundland, and 25 times greater for the other eight provinces. It is perhaps natural that the east–west trade bias should be weakest for Newfoundland and British Columbia, the provinces on the two extremities of the country. Also, it is interesting to note that, in spite of linguistic differences, the estimates for Quebec were consistently close to the national average.

The next step was to incorporate variables reflecting differences in comparative advantage or resource endowments as reflected in different structures of production. The variable $\text{PRIM}_{ij}$ is defined as abs(prim$_i$ − prim$_j$), where "abs" denotes the absolute value and prim$_i$ is the ratio of primary-sector production (agriculture, mining, forestry, fishing) to GDP in jurisdiction $i$. Similarly, the variable $\text{MFG}_{ij}$ is defined as abs(mfg$_i$ − mfg$_j$), where mfg$_i$ is the ratio of manufacturing-sector production to GDP in jurisdiction $i$. The absolute values of these differences in sectoral shares of GDP are indicators of the degree to which the structure of production differs between any two jurisdictions. Standard trade theory would predict a positive relation between trade and the degree to which structures of production are different. Equation 9 indicates that this prediction is supported empirically, although the addition of these variables has little effect on the other parameter estimates and adds little to the overall explanatory power of the regression. Finally, equation 11 combines the various extensions by including all of the additional variables, estimating the regression with instrumental variables, and including the seven observations with zero reported trade. Again, one sees that the results remain robust.

Other estimated regressions (not reported) incorporated interaction terms between DUMMY$_{ij}$ and the other explanatory variables or the squares of $y_i$, $y_j$, and dist$_{ij}$. Also, two explanatory variables used by Frankel (1993) were included but found not to be statistically significant. These are a dummy variable that is set equal to 1 when two jurisdictions are adjacent and a per capita income variable. The latter is intended to capture a positive relation between the extent of trade and stage of development. However, differences in stage of development or per capita income across North American provinces and states are much less than differences across a global sample of countries.[6] In none of these cases was there any significant effect on the coefficient on DUMMY$_{ij}$. Finally, and with the help of my colleague Marc Gaudry, I ran a series of more sophisticated specification and heteroscedasticity tests. The technique is described in Gaudry (1993). The results are available to the interested reader upon request, but they yielded no significant difference in terms of the coefficient on DUMMY$_{ij}$.

---

[6] It should be observed that one cannot both use population as an instrument for GDP and test the hypothesis that trade is affected by both aggregate and per capita GDP. A partial consolation is that other researchers who have used instrumental variables in similar contexts have found that this correction makes no difference to their results (see David Hummels and James Levinsohn, 1993).

### III. Trade Patterns over Time: FTA and NAFTA

The analysis to this point has been a snapshot of the year 1988, which happens to be the year in which the Canada–U.S. Free Trade Agreement (FTA) was signed. It is conceivable, then, that the apparently decisive impact of the Canada–U.S. border on continental trade patterns in 1988 will diminish rapidly as the integrating effects of the FTA and NAFTA come into play. If this were the case, then the basic finding reported in this paper would quickly vanish. To investigate this issue, it may be useful to observe longer-run trends, including trends over the six years that have passed since the signing of the FTA. Since the detailed information on interprovincial and international trade is available only for the years 1984–1988, we consider a longer time series on international trade only.

Figure 2 plots Canada–U.S. trade (average of merchandise exports and imports) as a percentage of GDP over the period 1950–1993, as well as an admittedly crude indicator of the level of tariff protection (import duties as a percentage of the value of merchandise imports). In Canada, as in most other industrialized countries, protection has trended downward since the early 1960's, while international trade shares have trended upward beginning around the same time. Indeed, the simple correlation coefficient between our measures of tariff protection and trade shares over the period 1950–1993 is −0.91.

The evidence to date suggests that the effects of continental free trade could turn out to be relatively modest, or if not modest, at least gradual. On the one hand, to the extent that the rising trade share has been driven by reduced tariff protection, the impact of free trade will be quite modest, because tariff protection is already low and does not have a great deal further to fall before reaching zero. On the other hand, the post-1988 increase in the trade share is certainly no greater than would have been predicted on the basis of either earlier trends or the rate of tariff protection shown

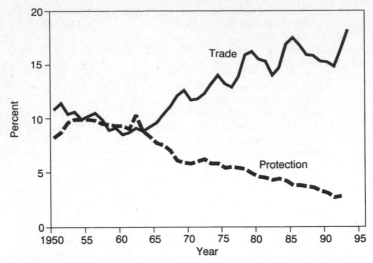

FIGURE 2. CANADA–U.S. TRADE AND CANADIAN TARIFF PROTECTION

*Notes:* Canada–U.S. trade is defined as the average of Canada's merchandise imports from and exports to the United States as a percentage of Canadian GDP. Protection is defined as Canadian custom import duties as a percentage of merchandise imports. Data for 1993 are for the first six months of the year.

*Source:* Canadian Socio-Economic Information Management System (CANISM).

in Figure 2.[7] Although this prognosis could turn out to be wrong for a number of possible reasons (e.g., diminished nontariff barriers associated with NAFTA, a role for countervailing short-term factors in the early 1990's, psychological effects of NAFTA), it is certainly not a foregone conclusion that NAFTA will lead to a radical shift in Canadian trade patterns over the next decade or so.

## IV. Conclusions

Whatever the reasons may be and whatever the future may hold, the fact that even

the relatively innocuous Canada–U.S. border continues to have a decisive effect on continental trade patterns suggests that national borders in general continue to matter. That is the basic message of this paper.

### DATA APPENDIX

The fundamental data source for this paper is the matrix of interprovincial trade produced by the Input–Output Division of Statistics Canada (*Interprovincial and International Trade Flows of Goods, 1984–1988*, Technical Series No. 49, June 1992). For each of the years 1984–1988 and for a variety of commodity groupings, this document provides estimates of shipments from each province to each other province, as well as shipments between each province and the rest of the world (imports and exports). To generate the dependent variable of the regressions, these data were combined with a second data source providing estimates of exports from each province to each state, as well as imports into each province from each state (Statistics Canada, *Merchandise Trade — Exports, 1988*, Catalogue No. 65-202 and *Merchandise Trade — Imports, 1988*, Catalogue No. 65-203). This second data source was used to determine the shares of each province's aggregate exports that went to the

[7]The trend increases in the trade share, in percentage points per decade, were as follows: 1963–1973, 4.1; 1973–1988, 2.3; 1988–1993, 0.4. Alternatively, if one regresses the trade-share variable on a constant, its own lagged value, the rate of tariff protection, and a dummy variable for the period 1989–1993, then the coefficient on the dummy variable is −0.07, with a standard error of 0.44.

United States and to each state, as well as the shares of each province's aggregate imports that came from the United States and from each state. These export and import shares were then applied to the aggregate export and import figures taken from the first source. As noted in the text, all reported regressions were based on a sample of 30 states.

Shipments are valued at producer prices or "factory-gate prices." In principle, to quote from the basic data source for this study, "the point of origin is where the good is produced or removed from inventories of produers, wholesalers and retailers. ...The point of final destination is where goods are purchased for final consumption or for use in the production of other commodities or added to inventories" (Statistics Canada, 1992 p. 3). However, as the document acknowledges, for want of precise information, the actual estimates do not always accord with the theoretical definitions.

Turning now to the data on provincial and state gross domestic product (GDP), both aggregate and sectoral provincial data are from the Statistics Canada publication *Provincial Economic Accounts* (1991, 13-213P). State data are from the U.S. Department of Commerce's *Survey of Current Business* (December 1991, pp. 47–50).

With regard to distances, in most cases distances were measured from the single, principal city of the province or state. Exceptionally, the central point of a jurisdiction was defined as an average (weighted by population) of the longitudes and latitudes of two or more cities (e.g., in California, San Francisco and Los Angeles).

### REFERENCES

**Deardorff, Alan V.** "Testing Trade Theories and Predicting Trade Flows," in R. Jones and P. Kenen, eds., *Handbook of international economics*, Vol. 1. Amsterdam: Elsevier, 1984, pp. 467–517.

**Frankel, Jeffrey.** "Trading Blocs: The Natural, the Unnatural, and the Super-natural." Mimeo, University of California-Berkeley, 1993.

**Frankel, Jeffrey and Wei Shang-Jin.** "Emerging Currency Blocs." Mimeo, University of California-Berkeley, 1993.

**Gaudry, Marc.** "Cur cum TRIO." Publicaton No. 901, Centre de Recherche sur les Transports, Université de Montréal, 1993.

**Hummels, David and Levinsohn, James.** "Product Differentiation as a Source of Comparative Advantage?" *American Economic Review*, May 1993 (*Papers and Proceedings*), *83*(2), pp. 445–49.

**Krugman, Paul.** *Geography and trade.* Gaston Eyskens Lecture Series, London: Leuven University Press, 1991.

**Linneman, Hans.** *An econometric study of international trade flows.* Amsterdam: North-Holland, 1966.

**Ohmae, Kenichi.** *The borderless world: Power and strategy in the interlinked economy.* New York: Harper Business, 1990.

**Statistics Canada.** *Merchandise trade—Exports, 1988.* Catalogue 65-202, Ottawa: Statistics Canada, 1989a.

_____. *Merchandise trade—Imports, 1988.* Catalogue 65-203, Ottawa: Statistics Canada, 1989b.

_____. *Interprovincial and international trade flows of goods, 1984–1988.* Input–output Division, Technical Series No. 49, Ottawa: Statistics Canada, 1992.

**Tinbergen, Jan.** *Shaping the world economy—Suggestions for an international economic policy.* New York: Twentieth Century Fund, 1962.

**Wang, Zhen Kun and Winters, L. Alan.** "The Trading Potential of Eastern Europe." Centre for Economic Policy Research (London) Discussion Paper No. 610, November 1991.

# [26]

# Do national borders matter for Quebec's trade?

JOHN F. HELLIWELL    University of British Columbia

*Abstract.* Using a gravity model of 1988–90 merchandise trade flows among Canadian provinces and between Canadian provinces and U.S. states, this paper, building on earlier work by McCallum, shows that Quebec trades twenty times more with other provinces than it does with U.S. states of similar size and distance. Comparison with survey evidence shows that these internal trade linkages are far stronger than previously was thought. The possible implications for Quebec separation, and for international economics, are considerable. If more broadly confirmed, the results imply that the fabric of national economies is far tighter than that of the global trading system, even for countries operating without substantial trade barriers.

*Est-ce que les frontières nationales ont de l'importance pour le commerce extérieur québécois?* A partir d'un modèle d'interaction spatiale des flux de commerce de marchandises de 1988–90 entre les provinces canadiennes et et entre les provinces canadiennes et les états américains, ce mémoire montre, en utilisant le travail de McCallum, que le Québec commerce vingt fois plus avec les autres provinces canadiennes qu'avec les états américains de même taille et à même distance. Des comparaisons avec les résultats des études sur le terrain montrent que les liens de commerce interne sont bien plus forts qu'on ne le croyait. Les implications de ces résultats sont importantes tant pour les analyses d'impact de la séparation du Québec que pour les travaux en économie internationale. Si ces résultats devaient être largement confirmés, on devrait conclure que la trame des économies nationales

I am very grateful for the research collaboration of John McCallum, the research assistance of Julie Chu and Ross McKitrick, and research support from the Social Sciences and Humanities Research Council of Canada. Philip Cross, Jim Nightingale, and Claude Simard of Statistics Canada have been helpful in providing access to and understanding of the latest provincial trade and output data. Earlier versions of this paper have been presented at the 1995 Annual Meetings of the Canadian Economics Association, at the NBER (and also as NBER Working Paper No. 5215), at the University of Western Ontario Political Economy Seminar, the Harvard International Economics Seminar, and as a Laurier Lecture at Wilfrid Laurier University. In revising the paper, I have been aided by helpful suggestions from many, including three anonymous referees, Bob Allen, Paul Beaudry, Don Davis, Mick Devereux, Erwin Diewert, Marc Duhamel, Marc Gaudry, Manfred Keil, Phil Neher, and Shang-Jin Wei.

Canadian Journal of Economics  Revue canadienne d'Economique, XXIX, No. 3
August août 1996. Printed in Canada  Imprimé au Canada

0008-4085 / 96 / 507–22 $1.50 © Canadian Economics Association

508   John F. Helliwell

est bien plus serrée que celle du système de commerce global, même pour des pays opérant dans un espace économique sans entraves importantes au commerce.

I. INTRODUCTION

Growing trade and capital mobility, and much talk of globalization, may have created the impression that national boundaries no longer matter much for trade and capital movements. John McCallum (1995) has compared trade flows among Canadian provinces with those between Canadian provinces and U.S. states, making use of a gravity model in which trade is determined primarily by the economic size of the trading partners and the distance between them, to calculate that Canadian provinces trade about twenty times as much with each other as they do with U.S. states of a similar size and distance. Thus the trade-generating powers of the Canadian federation are more than an order of magnitude larger than those of the European Union.[1]

These new results are important, since they challenge assumptions often made about the relative importance of international and interprovincial trade and about the ability of trade flows to arbitrage away international price differences. Survey results presented in this paper show that experts and non-experts alike think that trade among provinces and trade between provinces and states tend to be fairly similar in magnitude, after adjustment for the effects of distance and market size. The median respondent estimated that the factor of 20 quoted above was actually less than 1.0. Even those who thought interprovincial trade to be more active than trade from Canadian provinces to U.S. states usually guessed the extent to be between 1.0 and 1.4, more than an order of magnitude below the latest estimates presented in the next section. The gulf between perceived and measured trade linkages emphasizes the potential importance of the new results, if it is fair to treat the impact of an empirical finding as a product of how dramatically it differs from received opinion and the strength of the evidence on which it is based. If the McCallum results are confirmed, they also have important implications for the assessment of the economic effects of Quebec separation. If national boundaries are such an important determinant of trade, the ability to maintain the existing trade linkages with the rest of Canada after separation becomes both more important and more uncertain. Similarly, if interprovincial trade is so much more important than international trade, it is less easy to assume that expanded trade with the United States can be used to replace interprovincial trade now taking place.

---

1 Frankel and Wei (1993) estimate that trade flows among the countries of the European Union are 1.6 times larger than those between EU countries and non-EU countries, after using a gravity model to allow for the effects of size and distance. Using a differenced version of the gravity model, Bayoumi and Eichengreen (1995) estimate that from 1956 to 1973 trade among the six original members of the European Economic Community (EEC) grew 3.2 per cent per annum faster than would be predicted by the gravity model. Trade among the seven largest members of the European Free Trade Association (EFTA) grew 2.3 per cent faster over the same period. The estimated cumulative level effects amount to 88 per cent for the EEC and 58 per cent for EFTA.

In this paper an attempt is made to assess the importance of this new research for Quebec by first updating and extending McCallum's analysis to make use of revised and additional data and then examining the extent to which Quebec's interprovincial and U.S. trade patterns support the revised national results. The new results are then placed in the context of other studies of the differences between national and global markets. Finally, some attempt is made to assess the possible implications for trade theory and policy, as well as for the economic consequences of Quebec independence.

## II. REVISED AND EXTENDED NATIONAL RESULTS

The basic explanatory equation used by McCallum (1995) embodies the long-established gravity model of trade, wherein trade flows from an exporting region $i$ to an importing region $j$ are a loglinear function of real GDPs in the two regions and the distance between them:

$$\ln S_{ij} = \alpha_0 + \alpha_1 \ln \text{GDPX} + \alpha_2 \ln \text{GDPM} + \alpha_3 \ln (\text{dist}) + \epsilon_{ij} \tag{1}$$

where, in the present application, shipments ($S_{ij}$), and the GDPs of exporters (GDPX) and importers (GDPM) are measured in million Canadian dollars,[2] distance is measured in miles between the principal cities in the respective states and provinces,[3] and the error term $\epsilon_{ij}$ is assumed to be normally distributed. The gravity model of trade is an example of a long-established empirical regularity (Linneman 1966) that seemed to have no ready derivation from the standard Heckscher-Ohlin model of comparative advantage that dominated trade theory at the time. In the last fifteen years, however, there has been an outpouring of trade theory which includes one or more forms of product differentiation or market segmentation, often in the context of some type of increasing returns to scale. Helpman (1984) surveys some of the models and shows how differentiated products give rise to the gravity equation as the predictor for bilateral trade flows. More recently, Deardorff (1955) has shown that the gravity model is also consistent with a much wider variety of models, including the Heckscher-Ohlin model itself.

2 Purchasing power parties for GDP, taken from version 5.6 of the Penn World Table (Summers and Heston 1991) are used to convert U.S. state GDPs to Canadian dollars. In McCallum (1995) an exchange rate of 0.85 $US/$C was used to convert provincial GDPs to U.S. dollars, and the state GDPs were left in their original published form. Here we use PPPs, in terms of $C/$US, of 1.2090, 1.2087, and 1.2074 for 1988, 1989, and 1990.

3 The results for the border effect are very robust with respect to changes in the specification of the distance variable. For example, adding distance and the square of distance to supplement the ln (dist) variable already in equation 1 does not alter (to three significant figures) the coefficient on the border variable. The logarithmic distance variable is statistically preferred, by a very large margin, to the quadratic form. The loglinear distance variable could not plausibly be excluded from a general model that includes all three distance variables ($p < 0.00001$ using a Wald test for restricting the coefficient of ln (dist) = 0 with the linear and quadratic variables still in the equation), while both the linear and the quadratic terms could be removed from the general model, in any of the annual equations reported in table 1, with an insignificant drop ($p = 0.15$, based on a Wald test for restricting both coefficients to zero) in the explanatory power of the equation.

510    John F. Helliwell

TABLE 1
Revised estimates of the effects of the border on trade flows

| Equation | (i) | (ii) | (iii) | (iv) |
|---|---|---|---|---|
| Observations | 678 | 678 | 678 | 3 × 678 |
| Estimation method | OLS | OLS | OLS | SUR |
| Dependent variable | ln (ship) 1988 | ln (ship) 1989 | ln (ship) 1990 | ln (ship) 1988, 1989, 1990 |
| Constant | −4.36 (6.2) | −4.25 (5.9) | −5.70 (7.5) | −4.66, −4.75, −4.92 (7.0, 7.2, 7.4) |
| ln GDPX | 1.19 (38.0) | 1.19 (37.3) | 1.24 (36.5) | 1.20 (40.9) |
| ln GDPM | 1.05 (34.1) | 1.03 (32.7) | 1.05 (31.7) | 1.05 (36.1) |
| ln (dist) | −1.39 (22.5) | −1.41 (22.1) | −1.33 (19.7) | −1.38 (23.5) |
| Cdummy | 2.99 (23.3) | 2.93 (22.1) | 3.22 (23.0) | 3.05 (25.1) |
| $\bar{R}^2$ | 0.806 | 0.797 | 0.784 | 0.81, 0.80, 0.79 |
| S.E.E. | 1.09 | 1.12 | 1.19 | 1.09, 1.12, 1.18 P of restrict = 0.114 |
| Border effect | 19.9 | 18.7 | 25.0 | 21.1 |

NOTES
Absolute values of $t$-statistics are in parentheses. The dependent variable is the logarithm of total shipments of goods from province or state $i$ to province or state $j$, with ln GDPX the logarithm of $i$'s GDP and ln GDPM that of $j$'s GDP. The data include province-to-province trade for ten provinces plus trade between each province and each of the thirty largest states. Observations with zero shipments in any of the three years (twelve in total) are excluded. Cdummy take the value 1 for each observation recording trade from one province to another.

Table 1 reports the latest results, using data for 1988, 1989, and 1990 to estimate separate equations for each year and then to estimate a system of three equations using an iterative version of Zellner's SUR with the coefficients restricted to be the same in all years. The new equation for 1988 differs slightly from that of McCallum, mainly because of revisions to the shipments data for 1988 and to our current use of shipments of total good rather than the slightly smaller manufacturing-plus-primary aggregate used by McCallum. The latest 1988 estimate of interprovincial trade as a multiple of province-state trade is 19.9 (calculated as the antilog of 2.99), compared with McCallum's original estimate of 22. The estimated trade multiple for 1989 is 18.7, while that for 1990 is 25.0. When data for all three years are combined, the estimated border effect is 21.1. Although there have been no direct measures of interprovincial trade flows since 1990, some results will be reported in figure 1 that make use of the approximate measures of interprovincial trade published in the provincial accounts for 1991–4.

III. IS QUEBEC'S TRADE DIFFERENT?

Table 2 shows the effect of adding separate variables for covering first Quebec's trade with the thirty U.S. states (Quus) in the study, and then Quebec's interprovincial trade (Quc). If Quebec's trading relations with U.S. states are stronger than those between other provinces and the U.S. states, then Quus would take a positive sign. Similarly, if Quebec's trading links with other provinces are stronger than those among the anglophone provinces, then Quc will take a positive sign. The results show that Quebec's imports from and exports[4] to the thirty U.S. states are significantly below those of the other provinces. Quebec's interprovincial trade is slightly less than is true for the other provinces, although the latter differences are not statistically significant. If we add these Quebec effects to the national border effect, we can answer for Quebec the analogous question to that asked by McCallum for the country as a whole: How large is Quebec's trade with other provinces, compared with its trade with the U.S. states after adjustment for the effects of size and distance? When the data for 1988–90 are pooled, the answer for Quebec is 32.1 if we include only the significant U.S. effect (32.1 is exp (3.08 + 0.39)), or 26.8 if the coefficient on Quc is also included (26.8 = exp (3.08 + 0.39 − 0.18)). This suggests that Quebec's trading links with the rest of Canada, relative to those with the United States, are at least as strong as they are for other provinces.

A simpler and more conclusive way of estimating border effects for Quebec, if the data sample proves to be large enough, involves using data relating only to shipments to and from Quebec. This strategy would ensure that the Quebec results are not based on the particular situation of some other province. Since Quebec is also the second-largest trading province, the results will also help to reveal if the border effects already established are somehow due to the trade of the smaller provinces that may be unrepresentative of total national trade. Table 3 shows separate Quebec equations for each of the three years, 1988 to 1990, and then the results using data for the three years combined using the iterative Zellner technique. The layout of table 3 is thus the same as that of table 1, and comparison of the results reveals that the border effects follow a similar year-to-year variation for Quebec and for two of the three years are higher for Quebec than for the average of all provinces. Comparison of tables 2 and 3 shows that the Quebec effects are estimated to be larger when the full data set is used (as in table 2) than when the shipments data for Quebec itself are used, as in table 3. The table 3 results for Quebec are very close to those in table 1 for Canada as a whole, and for the three years taken together are exactly the same. In no case are the differences between Quebec and Canada statistically significant. Using the results from equation (iv) in each table, the pooled three-year border effect for Quebec is 21.1 (from table 3) or 26.8 (from table 2) compared with 21.1 (from table 1) for the typical province. Thus the evidence from all three years, treated separately or together, suggests that

---

4 The effects on imports and exports are identical, as is revealed by splitting Quus into separate variables for imports and exports and finding identical values for the two coefficients.

512    John F. Helliwell

TABLE 2
Effects of the border on Quebec trade flows

| Equation | (i) | (ii) | (iii) | (iv) |
|---|---|---|---|---|
| Observations | 678 | 678 | 678 | 3 × 678 |
| Estimation method | OLS | OLS | OLS | SUR |
| Dependent variable | ln (ship) 1988 | ln (ship) 1989 | ln (ship) 1990 | ln (ship) 1988, 1989, 1990 |
| Constant | −4.53 (6.4) | −4.44 (6.1) | −5.91 (7.7) | −4.84, −4.94, −5.11 (7.3, 7.4, 7.6) |
| ln GDPX | 1.21 (37.3) | 1.22 (36.7) | 1.26 (35.9) | 1.22 (40.2) |
| ln GDPM | 1.07 (33.5) | 1.05 (32.2) | 1.08 (31.3) | 1.07 (35.6) |
| ln (dist) | −1.42 (22.5) | −1.44 (22.2) | −1.37 (19.9) | −1.41 (23.6) |
| Cdummy | 3.00 (21.0) | 2.97 (20.1) | 3.25 (20.9) | 3.08 (22.8) |
| Quc | −0.12 (0.4) | −0.23 (0.8) | −0.24 (0.7) | −0.18 (0.6) |
| Quus | −0.37 (2.3) | −0.36 (2.2) | −0.42 (2.5) | −0.39 (2.6) |
| $\bar{R}^2$ | 0.807 | 0.798 | 0.786 | 0.808, 0.799, 0.787 |
| S.E.E. | 1.09 | 1.12 | 1.18 | 1.08, 1.11, 1.18 |
| Border effect | 25.8 | 22.2 | 30.9 | 26.8 P of restrict = 0.317 |

NOTES
Quus is 1 for trade between Quebec and a state, and Quc is 1 for Quebec's trade with another province. The border effect shown includes the effects of both Quus and Quc. For example, for equation (iv) the border effect is exp (3.08 + (−0.18) − (−0.39)).

national borders matter at least as much for Quebec as they do for the rest of Canada.

IV.  HOW SUPRISING ARE THESE RESULTS?

The bilateral trade flows between Canada and the United States are the largest in the world. The two countries share an enormous land mass divided by a border that is part easily navigable water and part an unmarked line that cuts the continental divide almost at right angles. Tariffs and other border limitations to trade and capital movements are and have long been lower than almost anywhere in the world, and Canada has the largest degree of foreign ownership among any of the industrial countries, with the United States' being by far the largest source country. If ever one would expect to find a national border that had relatively little effect on

TABLE 3
Border effects using Quebec data only

| Equation | (i) | (ii) | (iii) | (iv) |
|---|---|---|---|---|
| Observations | 78 | 78 | 78 | 3 × 78 |
| Estimation method | OLS | OLS | OLS | SUR |
| Dependent variable Quebec only | ln (ship) 1988 | ln (ship) 1989 | ln (ship) 1990 | ln (ship) 1988, 1989, 1990 |
| Constant | −5.26 (3.2) | −4.75 (3.0) | −6.70 (4.2) | −5.25, −5.35, −5.50 (3.7, 3.7, 3.8) |
| ln GDPX | 1.09 (12.7) | 1.06 (13.0) | 1.15 (13.9) | 1.09 (14.5) |
| ln GDPM | 0.95 (11.1) | 0.95 (11.7) | 1.06 (12.8) | 1.00 (13.3) |
| ln (dist) | −0.96 (9.8) | −1.00 (10.7) | −1.08 (11.4) | −1.04 (12.0) |
| Cdummy | 3.02 (14.3) | 2.85 (14.2) | 3.31 (16.2) | 3.05 (16.4) |
| $\bar{R}^2$ | 0.814 | 0.822 | 0.847 | 0.821, 0.829, 0.851. |
| S.E.E. | 0.67 | 0.64 | 0.65 | 0.66, 0.62, 0.64 P of restrict = 0.010 |
| Border effect | 20.5 | 17.3 | 27.4 | 21.1 |

NOTES
Same as for table 1, except that all data refer to shipments to and from Quebec. The border effect is antilog of the coefficient on Cdummy.

trade and capital movements, it would be the line between Canada and the United States. There are also interprovincial trade barriers of various sorts, which have been considered important enough to require an interprovincial trade agreement.

When this information is combined with the fact much of the fresh produce that Canadians eat, especially in the winter, is trucked in from California, it is perhaps understandable that surveys uniformly showed no premonition of the results shown in tables 1 to 3. When asked to estimate how much trade Canadian provinces do with each other, in comparison with how much they trade with U.S. states of similar economic size and at a similar distance, a group of faculty and graduating students in economics and political science produced a median answer of 0.8, with two-thirds of the seventy-one responses falling between 0.7 and 1.1. That is, some thought that trade linkages among the provinces are slightly tighter than are the trade linkages between the Canadian provinces and U.S. states, and some thought that they are slightly weaker, with the range of answers being fairly narrow.

But the current econometric estimate of the same effect is not 0.7 or 1.1, or anything even remotely close. Figure 1 juxtaposes the survey responses with the estimated distribution of the national effect based on equation (iv) in table 1. The

514   John F. Helliwell

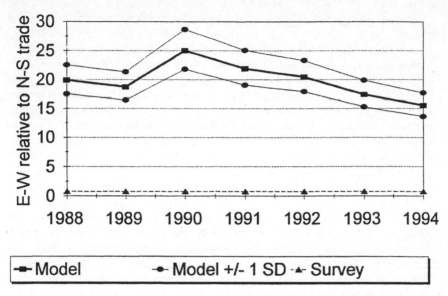

FIGURE 1   Internal versus external trade: survey versus model estimates 1988–94

survey responses are shown as unchanging from year to year, since the survey question was asked without reference to a specific year. Figure 1 also shows approximate estimates for the years 1991 through 1994, using procedures to be described later. If we ask whether the statistical results can come from the same realm as the survey results, the answer is surely not.[5] Unless there are some very large errors lurking in the measurement or modelling of interprovincial and international trade data, then previous impressions about the relative tightness of the economic union have been far off the mark.

Given the startling nature of the results, it is important to make confirming tests of these and related data to see if the results are due to some arbitrary or accidental feature of the data or the specification. Since the functional form of the distance relation might well be non-linear, we repeated McCallum's tests of alternative functional forms, including linear and squared distance terms, either separately or in addition to the log-linear term. The log-linear formulation was empirically superior, as described in a previous footnote.[6] More important, the coefficient on

5 More precisely, if we compare the distributions of the survey responses quoted above with the distribution of the antilogs of the estimated coefficient on the border variable for 1988, the z-value of the difference of the means is 57. This may be compared with a critical value, with a confidence limit of one-ten-millionth of 1 per cent, of 6. Thus there is much less than one chance in a billion that the two distributions have the same means.

6 Bayoumi and Eichengreen (1995) also find that changes in the functional form used for the distance variable had little impact on their estimates of the trade consequences of the EC and EFTA.

the border variable was unaffected by changing the functional form of the distance variable.

As in McCallum (1995), tests were done to make sure that the results did not change under instrumental variables estimation, or with weighted regression based on the geometric mean of trading partner GDPs. Additional tests have shown that trade flows are slightly better explained if the gravity model uses population and per capita GDP separately for importing states or provinces, but this does not change the border effects. Constraining the GDP coefficients to be unity would lower the Quebec border effect from 21.1 to 19.5 in the pooled equation of table 3, but these restrictions are sharply rejected by the data ($p < 0.00001$).

It has been suggested that there is a risk that some of the measured bilateral trade flows from provinces to border states are then directed to other states. This was tested for by first allowing for adjacency effects in general and then asking if there were additional trade flows from provinces to border states beyond those that could be explained by adjacency, GDP, and distance. We found both sorts of adjacency effects, of slight statistical significance, but they had no impact on the estimated border effect. We also considered whether being on the ocean might affect trade linkages in such a way as to compromise the estimated border effect. We hypothesized that being on the ocean might reduce a province's continental trade, whether with other provinces or with U.S. states, since relative transport costs to and from overseas markets are lower for the coastal provinces than for the others, who are therefore induced to trade more with each other and with the United States. If provinces and U.S. states are both on the ocean, however, their trade is likely to be greater than would otherwise be indicated by their distance, since shipping costs, especially for bulk cargoes, are less for ocean transport than for surface or air modes. The results show that both of these hypotheses are borne out. Simultaneously adding the adjacency and ocean effects to the table 1 system of equations for 1988 to 1990 improves the overall fit of the gravity model and increases rather than decreases the estimated border effects.[7]

To further investigate the possible sources and structure of the strong interprovincial trade linkages, we also considered the hypothesis that there are economies of scale in importation, with products from the United States being shipped to one province for subsequent distribution to the other provinces. Since location and corporate structure make Ontario the most obvious candidate to play such an entrepôt role, a variable was constructed taking the value of 1.0 for all trade flows from U.S. states to Ontario and equal to a higher value (to balance the estimated Ontario en-

---

7 The coefficient on dummy rises from 3.05 to 3.14 ($t = 26.3$), corresponding to an increase in the estimated border effect from 21.1 to 23.2. The GDP elasticities are unchanged, while the distance elasticity drops from $-1.38$ to $-1.23$, reflecting the trade-increasing effects of adjacency ($+0.31$, $t = 1.5$), the additional shipments to U.S. border states ($+0.78$, $t = 2.5$), the negative North American trade effects of being on an ocean ($-0.88$, $t = 8.6$), and the partially offsetting positive effects of both North American partners' being on the ocean ($+0.16$, $t = 1.8$). The standard errors of estimate are 1.04, 1.07, and 1.11 for 1988, 1989, and 1990, respectively, lower than those of the simpler model in table 1.

516   John F. Helliwell

trepôt trade) for observations covering shipments from Ontario to other provinces.[8] If this distribution channel is an important part of the story, we would expect to find a significant positive coefficient on the variable and a related drop in the estimated border effect. Although the coefficient is positive in two of the three years, it is small and insignificant and does not influence the estimated border effect. One reason why this effect does not show up in the equation may be that the raw data themselves may not fully track imports to their province of final use (just as was found for exports, which did not appear to be fully tracked to their state of final use). If so, then further work on the data could increase the relative importance of interprovincial compared with international trade. In any event, it would seem that the current estimates of high interprovincial trade densities are not due to an Ontario entrepôt effect.

Although weighted regression using the geometric mean of GDPs did not alter the results, weighted regression using shipments data themselves as the weights reduces the coefficients on the border variable sharply, from about 3.0 to about 2.2. This is what one might expect, since the largest trade flows are among the states and provinces heavily involved in the auto industry, which makes up a substantial part of total goods trade, and where a high level of industry integration has existed for many years. It is important to remember, however, that separate estimation using only data for Quebec, the second-largest trading province, gives very similar border effects to those estimated using the full data set. Thus the large estimated border effects cannot be due to some peculiarity of the data or trading patterns of one or more of the smaller provinces.

## V. FURTHER QUESTIONS

There are now several further lines of thought to follow. One is to ask what other evidence there may be that could support or weaken the finding that interprovincial trade linkages are much tighter than those between countries. A second is to ask why it can have been, if the result stands up to scrutiny, that prior beliefs were so out of line with the data. A third is to ask what downward trends are likely to occur in the estimated border effects when interprovincial trade data become available for the 1990s, and to assess the less complete data for trade in services.

Starting with the first question, the related literature in international economics should help to reveal from different perspectives the relative strength of interprovincial and international linkages. A useful starting point is provided by recent papers comparing price variability within and between countries. Since one of the incentives for and consequences of trade is to arbitrage spatial differences in prices, one would expect to find this arbitrage process faster and more complete where trade is more active. In particular, if trade within a nation is much denser than that among

---

8 Given the log-linear formulation of the equation, the dummy variables must adjust for differences in the size as well as the number of states and provinces. The values of the dummy variable are 1.0 for flows from states to Ontario and about 8 for the flows from Ontario to the provinces. In each year the number is calculated as $(30/10)*$(mean state GDP)/(mean provincial GDP).

nations, purchasing power parity should be much more quickly and completely evident within than between countries. This is exactly what recent comparisons of price differences for tradeable goods seem to show. Wei and Parsley (1995) find that half of international differences in the prices of tradeable goods are removed in four to five years,[9] while among U.S. cities Parsley and Wei (1995) estimate the comparable time to be four to five months, after adjustment for differences in distance. This is consistent with the results of Engel and Rogers (1994), who have studied the variability of prices among cities in the United States and Canada, with allowance for distance and a border effect. Comparing the border and distance effects, they found that the border reduced the covariability of prices by as much as would 2,000 or more miles of distance.

If domestic markets for goods are much tighter than international markets, then one would expect to find something similar for capital markets, despite the frequent assumption that global capital markets are completely integrated. In an important but controversial paper first presented more than fifteen years ago as a Mackintosh Lecture at Queen's University, Feldstein and Horioka (1980) showed that national savings and investment rates were highly correlated, which they took to imply that international capital markets were not anything like as tightly integrated as was commonly assumed. Other researchers argued that the Feldstein and Horioka results could be consistent with high capital mobility, although subsequent research has gradually led researchers to treat the Feldstein and Horioka results as being consistent with a number of other studies, using quite different methods, implying that international capital markets are much less integrated than are national ones.[10] If the Feldstein/Horioka interpretation of the cross-country results is correct, and if the new results about the tightness of the Canadian economic union are correct, then correlations of savings and investment rates across provinces should be far lower than those across countries. This seems to be the case, since private savings appear to flow sufficiently fluidly from one province to another to remove any-sectional correlation between savings rates and investment rates on a province-by-province basis.[11] Bayoumi and Klein (1995) also use the provincial trade balance data to test and compare interprovincial and international capital mobility, employing a somewhat different specification than Feldstein and Horioka do, and they conclude

9  This is similar to the four-year half life estimated for 150 countries and forty-five annual observations by Frankel and Rose (1995). As noted by Froot and Rogoff (1994), the use of panel data covering a large number of countries is required to get reliable estimates of PPP reversion times against the alternative random walk hypothesis.

10  For example, there is much evidence, recently surveyed by Engel (1995), of a negative correlation between the forward exchange premium and future movements of the spot rate. There is also strong evidence, surveyed by Lewis (1994), of a 'home bias' in equity investment. Both of these types of evidence imply that international capital markets are significantly less integrated than domestic markets.

11  This is based on recent work by Ross McKitrick. In addition, Brown (1992, especially figures B-1 and B-2) has compared the international and interprovincial correlations between savings and investment and has shown that the correlations apparent among countries do not appear among the provinces. There are similar results, using less complete data, for U.S. states (Sinn 1992) and for Japanese regions (Dekle 1995).

518   John F. Helliwell

that capital mobility is much higher among Canadian provinces than it is between Canada and other countries.

Thus there is some evidence of different types supporting the idea that the economic linkages within a nation are much tighter than those between nations. But why? The answers are simply not known at this stage, and in the meantime the result stands as a challenge to conventional views of trade that assume that international trade will be as dense as national trade in the absence of any special barriers or costs. The difference between domestic and international trade densities now appears to be much higher than could easily be explained by usual estimates of the effects of tariff barriers, exchange rate uncertainty, tax differences, and other costs that may apply differently to domestic and international shipments. The separate role of each of these factors needs to be assessed, but there is likely to remain a tendency for firms and individuals to trade more intensively with others in the same country. The reasons for this may lie in a mixture of educational, cultural, historical, political, associational, emotional, and geographical links based on migration and family ties and supported by networks of transportation, communication, and education. The relative importance of these and other possible explanations remains to be established.

Regarding the second question – how such an important fact, if it is that, could have avoided earlier discovery – the most likely reason is the lack of comparable data for trade flows within countries.[12] The Statistics Canada interprovincial trade data are probably unique, are relatively recent, and are available for only a few years. Only in a fairly decentralized federation are there likely to be serious efforts to put together accounts for the provincial economies, yet data collection needs to be either centralized or well coordinated if the data are to be collected on a sufficiently complete and thorough basis. In addition, only since 1988 have the Canadian international trade statistics been expanded to include exports and imports to and from each province and each U.S. state, permitting a geographically oriented model of province-state trade flows to be estimated with a reasonable sample size and sufficient geographic detail. When McCallum did his first estimates, there was only one year, 1988, for which both the interprovincial and international shipments data were available. Even now, there are only three years of data available, so the possibility for the research to be done is relatively recent. Only in late 1995 did funds become available to update the interprovincial shipments surveys and data into the 1990s, so that survey-based data for the 1990s are not likely to be available until 1997.

A second reason for perceptions to diverge from the new results is that there are trade data published showing international trade to be large and growing and showing international trade to be larger than interprovincial shipments for a number of provinces. Data drawn from the provincial accounts show international shipments of goods rising faster than interprovincial shipments from 1990 through

---

12 Another possibility, suggested by recent research by Wei (1996) using international trade among OECD countries and his own estimates of internal trade volumes and distances for each of the countries, is that the national border effect is larger for Canada than it is for other countries.

1994.[13] Since there are no post-1990 direct measures of interprovincial trade data, the subsequent interprovincial trade flows are based on the assumption that total interprovincial exports grow at the same rate as domestic final demand. These inter-provincial export figures are allocated among importing provinces, on a commodity-by-commodity basis for 300 commodities, according to the 1990 exports from each province to each other province. The directly measured data for foreign trade show sharp increases since 1990, while the method used to estimate interprovincial trade has it growing in line with domestic final demand, which was sluggish during the early 1990s. To derive the regression estimates for 1991 through 1994 shown in figure 1 the total interprovincial export estimates from the provincial accounts were allocated among importing provinces using the measured 1990 export shares, thus replicating in the aggregate the same assumptions used by Statistics Canada at a disaggregated level. Since the data thereby derived for each province's total interprovincial imports diverged from the numbers published in the interprovin-cial accounts, alternative estimates were also prepared, starting with the aggregate interprovincial import figures and allocating them among the exporting provinces using the 1990 import shares. The results were so similar that only the results of the first procedure are shown in figure 1.

What is likely to happen to estimates of the border effect when directly mea-sured interprovincial trade data are available for the 1990s? The sharp growth in international trade suggests that we might expect a downward trend to emerge during the 1990s. Our results for 1990, however, caution a wait-and-see attitude. We also need to consider whether the approximations used in the provincial ac-counts are likely to be confirmed by subsequent direct estimation. The current series for the 1990s are likely to be underestimates of directly measured flows if there are substantial interprovincial trade flows associated with international trade (exports were growing faster than domestic demand in the early 1990s) or if there are trend increases in interprovincial trade for some of the same reasons that international trade has grown relative to world GDP. The directly estimated numbers, when they become available, are likely to show interprovincial trade growing less fast than trade with U.S. states in the early 1990s. One reason for this is that foreign demand has risen faster than domestic demand for cyclical reasons, with Canada facing a larger recession than that in the United States. The cyclical increase in exports would be offset, in part or whole, by the cyclical reduction in imports, however, so the net foreign trade effect of the cyclical asymmetry is not certain. More important, there is ample evidence of post-NAFTA increases in trade with the United States. This may entail some facilitating expansions of interprovincial trade, although some of the new U.S. shipments may reflect diversion of what might otherwise have been interprovincial shipments. The net NAFTA effect is likely to be to increase province-state trade relative to province-to-province trade. Thus the downward trend shown for the 1990s in figure 1 is likely to be right, at least in

---

13 The ratio of interprovincial to international trade in services is always much higher than it is for goods, and it shows no downward trend in the 1990s. The ratios are shown separately for goods and services in Helliwell and McCallum (1995).

520   John F. Helliwell

direction. There seems to be little likelihood, however, that 1990s data, if and when they become available, will give mid-1990s estimates of the border effect that are much less than fifteen for merchandise trade and much more for services, for either Canada or Quebec.

VI. IMPLICATIONS

What are the implications of the new results for trade theory and policy and for the consequences of possible Quebec separation? Dealing first with trade theory and policy, the results pose a puzzle for previous estimates of the quantitative effects of trade liberalization. The implication of the new results is that international trade flows would remain much less dense than national trading ties even after all tariffs were removed. Why, and with what consequences for economic and social welfare? Does the relatively undeveloped state of international trade mean that there are many future gains from specialization and comparative advantage still to come? Are the border effects similar for different types of merchandise trade, or are they concentrated in particular industries? How much of the border effect is a currency effect?[14] Could there be multiple equilibria with very different trading patterns but fairly similar aggregate welfare effects, as might be the case if some of the additional variety provided by intra-industry trade leads to consumption bundles that differ more in brands than in basic characteristics? Could the information and other ties implicit in the political and information structure of most nation states provide lower transactions costs than would a more globally diversified set of trading links? If so, then the much greater relative density of national trade may be likely to persist even in the long run.

Another issue for theoretical and empirical work can be put in the form of three propositions and a resulting puzzle. If (i) much of the observed convergence is related to the transfer of technologies from the more to the less advanced countries or regions, (ii) the speed of convergence depends positively on a region's openness to trade, and (iii) trade is twenty times as dense within as between countries, then the puzzle is how to explain the apparent fact that interregional convergence within countries does not appear to be much faster than that between countries.

Finally, if it should be found, as suggested by the preliminary results of Wei (1996), that border effects are higher for Canada than for other OECD countries, there will arise the need to explain why such a decentralized federation should have such a high density of internal trade.

14 Attempts to estimate the trade level effects of exchange rate variability have shown mixed results. One of the higher estimates is by De Grauwe (1988), who estimated that 1986 trade among the large industrial countries was about 1.5 per cent lower than it would have been if exchange rate variability had not increased after 1973. This is very small compared with the twenty-fold border effects. Caporale and Doroodian (1994) find a significant effect of conditional real exchange rate variance on U.S. imports from Canada, but their functional form is such as to imply infinite imports if the real exchange rate were unchanging, so their equation cannot be used to estimate how much of the border effect might be explained by exchange rate variance. Frankel and Wei (1994), using data for sixty-three countries for 1980, 1985, and 1990, do not find systematic negative effects of exchange rate variability on bilateral trade flows.

Regarding the implications for Quebec, the current results show that Quebec is even more enmeshed in the fabric of Canada, relative to its ties to the United States, than are the anglophone provinces. One line of thinking about separation is based on the assumption that Quebec already has equally close trading ties with other provinces as it does with the United States, so that there could not be much at stake in converting the other provinces into another country. But since the assumption is wrong by a factor of more than 20, there is clearly more at stake than is commonly assumed. Since the welfare implications of high national trade densities have not been fully assessed, and since the ability of Quebec and Canada to maintain existing trade patterns after separation is not known, the trade-related costs of breaking up the political union cannot be fully assessed. The central point is that the fabric of the Canadian economic union is much tighter and more closely woven than anyone had previously believed. Since the discovery of the relative tightness of the economic union is relatively recent, a full understanding of what factors make the economic linkages among provinces so much stronger than those with the United States has not yet been developed. Thus it is not easy to tell which of these factors would be most likely to be put at risk if Quebec became an independent country. As shown by the gap between the survey results and the new evidence, there is a large gulf between perception and reality. This paper represents a small attempt to fill the gap.

REFERENCES

Bayoumi, T., and B. Eichengreen (1995) 'Is regionalism simply a diversion? Evidence from the evolution of the EC and EFTA.' NBER Working Paper No. 5283 (Cambridge, MA: National Bureau of Economic Research)
Bayoumi, T., and M.W. Klein (1995) 'A provincial view of capital mobility.' NBER Working Paper No. 5115 (Cambridge, MA: National Bureau of Economic Research)
Brown, D.M. (1992) 'Efficiency, capital mobility and the economic union.' In Free to Move: Strengthening the Economic Union, ed. D.M. Brown, F. Lazar, and D. Schwanen (Toronto: C.D. Howe Institute)
Caporale, Tony, and Khosrow Doroodian (1994) 'Exchange rate variability and the flow of international trade.' *Economics Letters* 46, 49–53
Deardorff, Alan V. (1995) 'Determinants of bilateral trade: does gravity work in a frictionless world?' NBER Working Paper No. 5377 (Cambridge, MA: National Bureau of Economic Research)
De Grauwe, Paul (1988) 'Exchange rate variability and the slowdown in growth of international trade.' IMF Staff Papers 35, 63–84
Dekle, R. (1995) 'Savings-investment associations and capital mobility: on the evidence from Japanese regional data.' International Finance Discussion Papers No. 496 (Washington: Board of Governors of the Federal Reserve System)
Engel, C. (1995) 'The forward discount anomaly and the risk premium: a survey of recent evidence.' NBER Working Paper No. 5312 (Cambridge, MA: National Bureau of Economic Research)
Engel, C., and J.H. Rogers (1994) 'How wide is the border?' NBER Working Paper No. 4829 (Cambridge, MA: National Bureau of Economic Research)
Feldstein, M., and C. Horioka (1980) 'Domestic saving and international capital flows.' *Economic Journal* 90, 314–29

Frankel, Jeffrey A., and Andrew K. Rose (1995) 'A panel project on purchasing power parity: mean reversion within and between countries.' NBER Working Paper No. 5006 (Cambridge, MA: National Bureau of Economic Research)

Frankel, J., and S.-J. Wei (1993) 'Trade blocs and currency blocs.' NBER Working Paper No. 4335 (Cambridge, MA: National Bureau of Economic Research)

— (1994) 'Yen bloc or dollar bloc? Exchange rate policies of the East-Asian economies.' In *Macroeconomic Linkage: Savings, Exchange Rates, and Capital Flows*, ed. Takatoshi Ito and Anne O. Kreuger (Chicago: University of Chicago Press)

Froot, Kenneth A., and Kenneth Rogoff (1994) 'Perspectives on PPP and long-run real exchange rates.' NBER Working Paper No. 4952 (Cambridge, MA: National Bureau of Economic Research)

Helliwell, John F., and John McCallum (1995) 'National borders still matter for trade.' *Policy Options / Options Politiques* 16 (July/August 1995): 44–8

Helpman, E (1984) 'Increasing returns, imperfect markets, and trade theory.' In *Handbook of International Economics*, vol. 1, ed. R. Jones and P. Kenen (Amsterdam: North-Holland)

Lewis, Karen (1994) 'Puzzles in international financial markets.' NBER Working Paper No. 4951 (Cambridge, MA: National Bureau of Economic Research)

Linneman, H. (1966) *An Econometric Study of International Trade Flows* (Amsterdam: North-Holland)

McCallum, John (1995) 'National borders matter: Canada-U.S. regional trade patterns.' *American Economic Review* 85, 615–23

Parsley, David C., and Shang-Jin Wei (1995) 'Convergence to the law of one price without trade barriers or currency fluctuations.' Working paper, Owen Graduate School of Management, Vanderbilt University, and Kennedy School of Government, Harvard University

Sinn, S. (1992) 'Savings-investment correlations and capital mobility: on the evidence from annual data.' *Economic Journal* 102, 1162–70

Summers, R., and A. Heston (1991) 'The Penn World Table (Mark 5): an expanded set of international comparisons, 1950–88.' *Quarterly Journal of Economics* 106, 327–68

Wei, Shang-Jin (1996) 'How stubborn are nations in global integration?' Paper presented at the Annual Meetings of the American Economic Association, San Francisco, January 1996

Wei, Shang-Jin, and David C. Parsley (1995) 'Purchasing power *dis*-parity during the floating rate period: exchange rate volatility, trade barriers and other culprits.' NBER Working Paper No. 5032 (Cambridge, MA: National Bureau of Economic Research)

# [27]

## How Wide Is the Border?

By CHARLES ENGEL AND JOHN H. ROGERS*

*We use CPI data for U.S. and Canadian cities for 14 categories of consumer prices to examine the nature of the deviations from the law of one price. The distance between cities explains a significant amount of the variation in the prices of similar goods in different cities. But the variation of the price is much higher for two cities located in different countries than for two equidistant cities in the same country. We explore some of the reasons for this finding. Sticky nominal prices appear to be one explanation but probably do not explain most of the border effect. (JEL F40, F41)*

The failure of the law of one price in international trade has been widely documented (see Peter Isard [1977] for an early example). It should be no surprise that similar goods sold in different locations have different prices. Indeed, Gerard Debreu (1959 pp. 29–30) in *Theory of Value* defines goods to be different if they are not sold in the same place: "Finally wheat available in Minneapolis and wheat available in Chicago play also entirely different economic roles for a flour mill which is to use them. Again, a good at a certain location and the same good at a different location are *different* economic objects, and the specification of the location at which it will be available is essential." Only when costs are borne to transport wheat from Chicago to Minneapolis will the miller in Minneapolis consider the

Chicago wheat equivalent to the Minneapolis wheat. But can the international failure of the law of one price be attributed entirely to this segmentation of markets by physical distance, or are there other factors, such as nominal price-stickiness, that help to explain the failure?

Recent evidence suggests that not only are failures of the law of one price significant, but they play a dominant role in the behavior of real exchange rates. Engel (1993, 1995) and Rogers and Michael Jenkins (1995) examine the time-series behavior of prices of goods across and within countries. They find that the movement of prices of similar goods across borders accounts for much of the motion in real exchange rates. The variation in these prices appears to be far more significant in explaining real exchange rates than are movements in relative prices of different goods within a country's borders (such as nontraded to traded goods prices.)

We examine the importance of distance between locations where goods are sold and the presence of national borders separating locations in determining the degree of the failure of the law of one price. We employ consumer price data disaggregated into 14 categories of goods. We make use of data available for nine Canadian cities and 14 cities in the United States. The basic hypothesis is that the volatility of the price of similar goods between cities should be positively related to the distance between those cities; but holding distance constant, volatility should be higher between two cities separated by the national border.

* Engel: Department of Economics, University of Washington, Seattle, WA 98195-3330, and National Bureau of Economic Research; Rogers: Division of International Finance, Board of Governors of the Federal Reserve System, Washington, DC, 20551. We thank the participants in the workshops at the Federal Reserve Board, the Federal Reserve Banks of Kansas City and New York, the NBER Summer Institute, Columbia University, Indiana University, Michigan State University, Penn State University, Princeton University, the University of California-Santa Cruz, UCLA, and the University of Washington for very helpful comments. Some of the work on this project was done while Engel was a Visiting Scholar at the Federal Reserve Bank of Kansas City. The views expressed in this paper are those of the authors and do not necessarily reflect those of the Board of Governors or the Federal Reserve System. The National Science Foundation provided support for this project under grant number SBR-932078.

Our basic empirical results show that both distance and the border are significant in explaining price dispersion across locations. We provide a measure of how important the border is relative to distance—the "width" of the border. While distance is an economically significant determinant of price dispersion, the effect of the border relative to distance is extremely large. We explore some of the possible reasons why the border is so important, such as nominal price stickiness, integration of labor markets and trade barriers. Nominal price stickiness appears to account for a large portion of the border effect, but most of the effect is left unexplained.

## I. Price Dispersion among Locations

The failure of prices of similar goods to equalize between sites is a sign that the markets are not completely integrated. There are several notions of market integration in the literature. It is helpful to enunciate a simple general framework that highlights the roles of distance and the border in determining price variation between locations.

Consider all final goods sold to consumers to be nontraded. (Kalyan K. Sanyal and Ronald W. Jones [1982] analyze a competitive model with this assumption.) Even the prices of goods that are normally classified as tradable, such as nonperishable commodities, must reflect costs of marketing and distribution, which are nontraded services. On the other hand, all goods contain a tradable intermediate component. If the final product is sold by a profit-maximizing monopolist in each location $j$, the price of good $i$ is determined by

$$(1) \qquad p_j^i = \beta_j^i \alpha_j^i (w_j^i)^{\gamma_i} (q_j^i)^{1-\gamma_i}.$$

With a Cobb-Douglas technology, $\gamma_i$ is the share of the nontraded service in final output. The price of the nontraded service, $w_j^i$, and the price of the traded intermediate input, $q_j^i$, are determined in competitive markets. The total productivity of the final-goods sector is measured by $\alpha_j^i$. The markup over costs, $\beta_j^i$, is inversely related to the elasticity of demand.[1]

Geographical separation of markets provides one reason that the price of similar goods might vary across locations. Recent work in international trade, spearheaded by Paul Krugman (1991) and including empirical work by Jeffrey Frankel et al. (1995) and John McCallum (1995),[2] suggests that much of the pattern of international trade can be explained by geographical considerations. Countries are more likely to trade with neighbors because transportation costs are lower. Transportation costs may also be an explanation for the failure of the law of one price (as in Bernard Dumas [1992]). In equation (1), $q_j^i$ may vary across locations if there are costs of transporting the tradable good. With the "iceberg" transportation costs of Krugman and others, price $q_j^i$ is not necessarily equalized with the price in location $k$, $q_k^i$. The relative price could fluctuate in a range, $1/d_i \le q_j^i/q_k^i \le d_i$. The transportation cost, $d_i$, should depend positively on the distance between locations, so that the range of variation in $q_j^i/q_k^i$ depends on that distance.[3]

It is also possible that places that are farther apart would have less similar cost structures, so that $w_j^i/w_k^i$ and $\alpha_j^i/\alpha_k^i$ might also vary more between more distant locations. From equation (1), these locations would have greater price dispersion.

However, we also entertain the possibility that price variation of similar goods over time might be higher if the cities lie across national borders, holding distance constant. The recent literature on pricing to market (e.g., Rudiger Dornbusch, 1987; Krugman, 1987; Avinash Dixit, 1989; Robert C. Feenstra, 1989; Kenneth A. Froot and Paul D. Klemperer, 1989; Michael N. Knetter, 1989, 1993; Kenneth Kasa, 1992) has examined markets that are segmented by borders.

There are a few reasons why the border might matter. Much of the pricing-to-market literature has emphasized that the markup, $\beta_j^i$, may be different across locations, and may

---

[1] If $\varepsilon$ is the elasticity, $\beta = \varepsilon/(\varepsilon - 1)$.

[2] The McCallum paper is complementary to this one, in that it uses data from the states in the United States and provinces in Canada to measure the effects on the volume of trade of distance and crossing the national border.

[3] In the iceberg model, a fraction $1 - (1/d_i)$ of the good melts.

TABLE 1—CATEGORIES OF GOODS IN DISAGGREGATED CONSUMER PRICE INDEXES AND CITIES USED

| Good | United States | Canada |
|------|---------------|--------|
| 1 | Food at home | Food purchased from stores |
| 2 | Food away from home | Food purchased—restaurants |
| 3 | Alcoholic beverages | Alcoholic beverages |
| 4 | Shelter | Shelter − 0.2135 (water, fuel, and electricity) |
| 5 | Fuel and other utilities | Water, fuel, and electricity |
| 6 | Household furnishings and operations | Housing excluding shelter |
| 7 | Men's and boy's apparel | 0.8058 (Men's wear) + 0.1942 (boy's wear) |
| 8 | Women's and girl's apparel | 0.8355 (Women's wear) + 0.1645 (girl's wear) |
| 9 | Footwear | Footwear |
| 10 | Private transportation | Private transportation |
| 11 | Public transportation | Public transportation |
| 12 | Medical care | Health care |
| 13 | Personal care | Personal care |
| 14 | Entertainment | 0.8567 (Recreation) + 0.1433 (reading material) |

*Note:* The cities included are: Baltimore, Boston, Chicago, Dallas, Detroit, Houston, Los Angeles, Miami, New York, Philadelphia, Pittsburgh, San Francisco, St. Louis, and Washington DC; Calgary, Edmonton, Montreal, Ottawa, Quebec, Regina, Toronto, Vancouver, and Winnipeg.

vary with exchange rate changes. Alternatively, the markets for the nontraded marketing service might be more highly integrated on a national basis, so that $w_j^i$ is more similar between two sites within a country than in two places separated by a border. These marketing services are likely to be highly labor-intensive. To the extent that the two national labor markets are more separated than are local labor markets within a country, there would be more variation in cross-border prices than in within-country prices. There might also be direct costs to crossing borders because of tariffs and other trade restrictions. In addition, there may be more homogeneity to the relative productivity shocks, $\alpha_j^i/\alpha_k^i$, for city pairs within the same country than for cross-border city pairs, so that, from equation (1), cross-border pairs have more price volatility.

An important reason why the border matters is unrelated to equation (1): the price of a consumer good might be sticky in terms of the currency of the country in which the good is sold. Goods sold in the United States might have sticky prices in U.S. dollar terms, and goods sold in Canada might have sticky prices in Canadian dollar terms. The nominal exchange rate is, in fact, highly variable. In this case, the cross-border prices would fluctuate along with the exchange rate, but the within-country prices would be fairly stable. Price

stickiness may be dependent upon market segmentation. It would be easier for a producer in one location to resist attempts to undercut his fixed nominal price if markets were separated.

The sticky-price explanation is a natural one that has been addressed in previous literature. Our test is in part inspired by Michael Mussa (1986), who noted that the variance of the real exchange rate based on all goods in the consumer price index is larger for Toronto versus Chicago, Vancouver versus Chicago, Toronto versus Los Angeles, and Vancouver versus Los Angeles than it is for Toronto versus Vancouver and Chicago versus Los Angeles when there are floating exchange rates between the United States and Canada. He attributes this pattern to sticky prices or, in his terms, nominal exchange-regime nonneutrality. Within the recent literature on pricing to market, Richard C. Marston (1990) and Alberto Giovannini (1988) specifically consider the role of nominal price stickiness.

## II. Distance and the Border

### A. *The Regressions*

We use consumer price data from 23 North American cities for 14 disaggregated consumer price indexes. The data cover the period from June 1978 to December 1994. Table 1 lists the goods and cities in our study. The Data Appendix provides more detail on the construction of the price data.

For our purposes, it is natural to choose the United States and Canada as the countries to study. First, the countries share a border. Were it not for the country borders, one would expect more trade to occur between Toronto and New York than between New York and Los Angeles. Indeed, there are no other examples of adjacent market economies that are as large in area (so that there can be significant distances between major cities within a country). Also, trade has been relatively free between the two countries. If the border matters, it is unlikely that it matters because of trade restrictions. The facts that both countries are mostly English-speaking and have similar cultural and political traditions suggest that there is likely to be more cross-border labor migration than between most countries.

We hypothesize that the volatility of the prices of similar goods sold in different locations is related to the distance between the locations and other explanatory variables, including a dummy variable for whether the cities are in different countries.

Let $P^i_{j,k}$ be the log of the price of good $i$ in location $j$ relative to the price of good $i$ in location $k$. (All prices are converted into U.S. dollars using a monthly average exchange rate before taking relative prices.) We take the difference in the log of the relative price between time $t$ and $t - 2$ as our measure of $P^i_{j,k}$. We take the two-month difference because, for some of our U.S. cities, the price data are only reported every other month. We calculate its volatility as the standard deviation.[4]

We also consider a filtered measure of $P^i_{j,k}$. We regress the log of the relative price on 12 seasonal dummies and six monthly lags.[5] We then take the two-month-ahead in-sample forecast error from this regression as our measure of $P^i_{j,k}$. The in-sample forecast errors cover the period from February 1979 to December 1994. Qualitatively, the results were very similar, irrespective of our measure of prices. We report regressions for the two-month difference of the logs because these numbers are easily reproducible.

For each good $i$, there are 228 city pairs for which we have observations.[6] For each city pair, we calculate our measure of volatility using the time series on relative prices. Then, we conduct our analysis based on the cross section of 228 volatility measures.

Table 2 reports selected summary statistics. For each of the 14 goods, we report the average standard deviation for pairs of cities that are (a) both in the United States, (b) both in Canada, and (c) one in each country. Table 2 also reports the average distance between those cities. The table reveals that the volatility of prices between U.S. city pairs is generally slightly higher than that between Canadian city pairs, but cross-border city pairs have much higher volatility. However, cross-border city pairs are farther apart, on average, as well.

These generalizations from Table 2 do not apply to goods 7, 8, and 9: men's and boys' apparel, women's and girls' apparel, and footwear. For these goods, the variance of prices across U.S. cities is substantial. In fact, on average, it is greater for the U.S. city pairs than for the cross-border city pairs, and far greater than for the Canadian city pairs. These are the only three goods that exhibit this pattern.

The apparel goods are different from the other goods in several respects: (i) This category of goods probably has some of the most product differentiation. (ii) The prices of these goods are very seasonal.[7] (iii) Compared to other goods, a large fraction of clothing is imported from outside of United States and Canada.

---

[4] We also performed all of our tests using the spread between the 10th and 90th percentiles as the measure of volatility. Our results were essentially identical to the results reported here.

[5] In the case of the data that are bimonthly, we regress the log of the relative price on three bimonthly lags and six seasonal dummies.

[6] We do not attempt to match the U.S. cities whose data is reported in odd-numbered months with the even-month cities.

[7] However, we note that the apparel commodities show the same pattern of volatility when we use the filtered data, which presumably take out seasonals.

TABLE 2—AVERAGE PRICE VOLATILITY

| Good | City pairs | | |
| --- | --- | --- | --- |
| | U.S.–U.S. | Canada–Canada | U.S.–Canada |
| 1 | 0.0139 | 0.0198 | 0.0247 |
| 2 | 0.0130 | 0.0100 | 0.0214 |
| 3 | 0.0185 | 0.0149 | 0.0271 |
| 4 | 0.0217 | 0.0085 | 0.0250 |
| 5 | 0.0486 | 0.0279 | 0.0498 |
| 6 | 0.0203 | 0.0097 | 0.0236 |
| 7 | 0.0483 | 0.0167 | 0.0461 |
| 8 | 0.0880 | 0.0178 | 0.0813 |
| 9 | 0.0618 | 0.0192 | 0.0505 |
| 10 | 0.0111 | 0.0186 | 0.0260 |
| 11 | 0.0443 | 0.0240 | 0.0628 |
| 12 | 0.0133 | 0.0190 | 0.0259 |
| 13 | 0.0258 | 0.0143 | 0.0271 |
| 14 | 0.0203 | 0.0083 | 0.0232 |
| 1–14 | 0.0321 | 0.0163 | 0.0367 |
| Distance (miles): | 1,024 (66 pairs) | 1,124 (36 pairs) | 1,346 (126 pairs) |

*Notes:* Entries give the mean value of price volatility across all intercity combinations within the United States, within Canada, and across the U.S.–Canadian border, respectively. The measure of volatility is the standard deviation of the relative price series. Prices are measured as two-month differences. The average distance between cities is given in the final row. The sample period is September 1978–December 1994.

Our regressions attempt to explain $V(P^i_{j,k})$, the volatility of $P^i_{j,k}$. We estimate

$$(2) \qquad V(P^i_{j,k}) = \beta^i_1 r_{j,k} + \beta^i_2 B_{j,k}$$

$$+ \sum_{m=1}^{n} \gamma^i_m D_m + u_{j,k}$$

where $r_{j,k}$ is the log of the distance between locations. As in the gravity model of trade, we posit a concave relationship between relative-price volatility and distance. $B_{j,k}$ is a dummy variable for whether locations $j$ and $k$ are in different countries. For reasons we have explained, we expect the coefficient on this variable to be positive. The regression error is denoted as $u_{j,k}$. Note this is a cross-section regression.

We also include a dummy variable in equation (2) for each city in our sample, $D_m$. That is, for city pair $(j, k)$ the dummy variables for city $j$ and city $k$ take on values of 1. There are a few reasons why we allow the level of the standard deviation to vary from city to city. First, there may be idiosyncratic measurement

error or seasonalities in some cities that make their prices more volatile on average. Second, for the cities that report prices only bimonthly, there may be additional volatility that is introduced by measurement error from the less frequent observation of prices. Third, as Table 2 indicates, there seems to be somewhat higher average volatility for U.S. cities than for Canadian cities. This may be because the United States is a more heterogeneous country. Either labor markets or goods markets may be less integrated, so there can be greater discrepancies in prices between locations. Alternatively, there may be differences in methodologies for recording prices that lead to greater discrepancies in prices between locations in one country compared to the other.[8]

Table 3 reports our regressions for each of the 14 goods. We find strong evidence that distance is helpful in explaining price dispersion

---

[8] We could impose the restriction that the coefficient on the dummy for all U.S. cities be equal, and that it be equal for all Canadian cities. In all of the regressions we report here, that restriction is strongly rejected.

TABLE 3—REGRESSIONS RELATING PRICE VOLATILITY
TO DISTANCE AND THE BORDER

| Good | Log distance | Border | Adjusted $R^2$ |
|------|--------------|--------|----------------|
| 1 | 4.95 | 7.50 | 0.94 |
|  | (2.32) | (0.18) |  |
| 2 | 1.84 | 9.71 | 0.97 |
|  | (0.89) | (0.11) |  |
| 3 | 3.50 | 9.98 | 0.93 |
|  | (2.80) | (0.22) |  |
| 4 | 8.37 | 9.42 | 0.93 |
|  | (1.78) | (0.21) |  |
| 5 | 35.7 | 10.5 | 0.81 |
|  | (6.88) | (0.74) |  |
| 6 | 1.11 | 8.26 | 0.97 |
|  | (0.97) | (0.12) |  |
| 7 | 10.5 | 12.9 | 0.96 |
|  | (2.79) | (0.34) |  |
| 8 | 28.1 | 26.4 | 0.93 |
|  | (7.34) | (0.89) |  |
| 9 | 7.74 | 9.20 | 0.97 |
|  | (3.23) | (0.36) |  |
| 10 | 9.80 | 10.8 | 0.95 |
|  | (2.19) | (0.20) |  |
| 11 | 32.9 | 27.3 | 0.87 |
|  | (7.70) | (0.95) |  |
| 12 | −1.25 | 9.66 | 0.97 |
|  | (2.23) | (0.23) |  |
| 13 | 0.02 | 6.70 | 0.94 |
|  | (1.67) | (0.18) |  |
| 14 | 5.08 | 8.58 | 0.97 |
|  | (1.13) | (0.14) |  |
| 1–14 | 10.6 | 11.9 | 0.77 |
|  | (3.25) | (0.42) |  |

*Notes:* All regressions contain as explanatory variables dummies for each of the 23 individual cities, in addition to the variables listed in the cell. Heteroscedasticity-consistent standard errors (Halbert White, 1980) are reported in parentheses. Coefficients and standard errors on log distance are multiplied by $10^4$, while those for "border" are multiplied by $10^3$. The dependent variable is the standard deviation of the two-month difference in the relative price. Standard deviations are computed over the sample period from September 1978 to December 1994. There are 228 observations in each regression.

across cities. The coefficient on the log of distance is positive for 13 of the 14 goods, and it is significant at the 5-percent level in ten of the regressions.[9] In the one case in which the sign

[9] We calculated bootstrapped distributions for the *t* statistics in the first line of Table 3. The inference from the bootstrapped distributions is approximately the same as from the *t* distribution. Details are in an econometric appendix available from the authors upon request.

is wrong, the coefficient is not significantly different from zero. In most of the cases, the *t* statistics are very large.

The coefficients on the dummy variable for the border are of the hypothesized sign and highly significant for all 14 of the goods. The interpretation of the coefficient on the border dummy in this regression is the difference between the average standard deviation of prices for city pairs that lie across the border less the average for pairs that lie within one of the two countries, taking into account the effect of distance.

We note that the model works well even for the apparel commodities. The excess volatility for U.S. apparel derives from a few cities, but with city dummy variables included, distance and the border still have significant explanatory power.

We test for the restrictions that the coefficients on distance are the same in all regressions and the coefficients on the border dummy are the same in all regressions. The test statistics (not reported) are large, and the restrictions are very strongly rejected. Nonetheless, we report the results for the regressions pooling the data across all goods. Because we allow a separate intercept term for each good and for all but one city, the coefficients reported for distance and the border dummy in the pooled regression are simply the average of the coefficients across the 14 goods. Thus, the pooled regression provides a useful summary of the relationship between price dispersion and the explanatory variables. The last row of Table 3 reports the pooled results for all goods. We find that the coefficients on distance and the border dummy are highly significant and of the hypothesized sign.

The results using the filtered measure for prices are recorded as specification 1 in Table 4 and are very similar to those for the two-month differences. Distance has a positive effect on price dispersion in all regressions and is significant for eight of the 14 goods. The coefficient on the border dummy is positive and significant in all cases. If we restrict our tests to just those cities for which we have monthly data, our results are virtually unchanged qualitatively. (These results are not reported.)

TABLE 4—ALTERNATIVE SPECIFICATIONS OF PRICE VOLATILITY REGRESSIONS

| | Specification 1 | | | Specification 2 | | | |
|---|---|---|---|---|---|---|---|
| Good | Log distance | Border | Adjusted $R^2$ | Distance | Distance squared | Border | Adjusted $R^2$ |
| 1 | 4.32 | 6.61 | 0.93 | 2.08 | −6.53 | 7.53 | 0.93 |
| | (1.92) | (0.17) | | (0.92) | (2.93) | (0.18) | |
| 2 | 2.26 | 9.81 | 0.97 | 1.00 | −3.57 | 9.72 | 0.97 |
| | (0.84) | (0.12) | | (0.42) | (1.69) | (0.11) | |
| 3 | 2.34 | 9.94 | 0.93 | 2.21 | −7.88 | 10.0 | 0.93 |
| | (2.79) | (0.21) | | (1.04) | (3.34) | (0.22) | |
| 4 | 7.00 | 9.96 | 0.95 | 3.56 | −11.1 | 9.45 | 0.94 |
| | (1.58) | (0.18) | | (0.76) | (2.78) | (0.20) | |
| 5 | 28.7 | 7.48 | 0.78 | 11.7 | −33.8 | 10.7 | 0.78 |
| | (5.29) | (0.59) | | (3.62) | (13.0) | (0.73) | |
| 6 | 1.21 | 8.90 | 0.97 | 0.48 | −1.54 | 8.27 | 0.97 |
| | (0.95) | (0.12) | | (0.43) | (1.60) | (0.12) | |
| 7 | 2.40 | 10.8 | 0.96 | 4.20 | −13.1 | 13.0 | 0.96 |
| | (2.40) | (0.32) | | (1.07) | (3.86) | (0.34) | |
| 8 | 12.2 | 17.0 | 0.97 | 8.76 | −24.5 | 26.6 | 0.93 |
| | (3.24) | (0.47) | | (2.95) | (10.6) | (0.88) | |
| 9 | 4.98 | 9.72 | 0.97 | 4.04 | −12.9 | 9.19 | 0.97 |
| | (3.04) | (0.33) | | (1.30) | (4.62) | (0.35) | |
| 10 | 9.04 | 11.0 | 0.96 | 4.17 | −13.4 | 10.9 | 0.95 |
| | (1.97) | (0.18) | | (0.82) | (2.71) | (0.20) | |
| 11 | 22.2 | 24.2 | 0.98 | 7.97 | −13.6 | 27.2 | 0.88 |
| | (4.91) | (0.65) | | (2.91) | (13.0) | (0.93) | |
| 12 | 0.25 | 8.51 | 0.98 | −0.42 | 0.75 | 9.68 | 0.97 |
| | (2.05) | (0.19) | | (0.98) | (3.25) | (0.23) | |
| 13 | 1.31 | 7.02 | 0.93 | 0.78 | −3.23 | 6.69 | 0.94 |
| | (1.77) | (0.19) | | (0.80) | (2.76) | (0.18) | |
| 14 | 3.13 | 9.75 | 0.98 | 2.43 | −7.69 | 8.58 | 0.97 |
| | (0.94) | (0.11) | | (0.39) | (1.34) | (0.13) | |
| 1–14 | 7.24 | 10.8 | 0.77 | 3.79 | −10.9 | 12.0 | 0.77 |
| | (2.73) | (0.35) | | (1.36) | (4.68) | (0.42) | |

*Notes:* All regressions contain as explanatory variables a dummy for each of the 23 individual cities, in addition to the variables listed in the cell. Heteroscedasticity-consistent standard errors (White, 1980) are reported in parentheses. Coefficients and standard errors on log distance, border, distance, and distance squared are multiplied by $10^4$, $10^3$, $10^6$, and $10^{10}$, respectively. In specification 1, the dependent variable is the standard deviation of the two-month-ahead forecast error from the filtered relative price. In specification 2, the dependent variable is the standard deviation of the two-month difference in the relative price. Standard deviations are computed over the sample period from September 1978 to December 1994. There are 228 observations in each regression.

Regression results when the distance function is quadratic, rather than logarithmic, are reported as specification 2 in Table 4. This specification is interesting because it allows a test for our assumption of a concave distance relationship. In fact, we find that distance has a positive effect on price variability in 13 of the 14 regressions and is significant at the 5-percent level in 11 of those regressions. Furthermore, in all 13 regressions where distance has a positive effect, the square of distance has a negative effect. It is significantly negative for the 11 goods that have a significantly positive

distance effect. This is what we would expect if the distance relationship were concave. Once again, in this specification, the border dummy is positive and significant in all cases.

Although we report White's (1980) heteroscedasticity-consistent standard errors, we also specifically allow for the possibility that the variance of the error term might be greater for more distant cities. The first specification in Table 5 reports results when the left- and right-hand-side variables are all deflated by the log of distance, so that the standard deviation of the regression error is modeled as being

TABLE 5—ASSESSING THE ROLE OF DISTANCE

| Good | Specification 1 | | | Specification 2 | | Specification 3 | |
| | Constant | Border Log distance | Adjusted $R^2$ | Log distance | Adjusted $R^2$ | Log distance | Adjusted $R^2$ |
|---|---|---|---|---|---|---|---|
| 1 | 2.84 | 0.96 | 0.79 | 0.26 | 0.83 | 1.99 | 0.61 |
| | (0.22) | (0.05) | | (0.12) | | (0.53) | |
| 2 | 1.79 | 1.30 | 0.88 | 0.30 | 0.93 | 0.36 | 0.89 |
| | (0.14) | (0.03) | | (0.11) | | (0.11) | |
| 3 | 2.95 | 1.31 | 0.77 | 0.39 | 0.91 | 1.67 | 0.20 |
| | (0.30) | (0.06) | | (0.21) | | (0.72) | |
| 4 | 3.06 | 1.27 | 0.86 | 1.50 | 0.67 | 0.96 | 0.49 |
| | (0.28) | (0.05) | | (0.36) | | (0.27) | |
| 5 | 5.04 | 1.39 | 0.77 | 6.06 | 0.76 | 4.04 | 0.80 |
| | (0.33) | (0.13) | | (1.00) | | (0.84) | |
| 6 | 5.66 | 1.03 | 0.81 | −0.05 | 0.87 | 50.2 | 0.58 |
| | (0.40) | (0.05) | | (0.18) | | (13.0) | |
| 7 | 10.2 | 1.59 | 0.87 | 0.38 | 0.85 | 1.91 | 0.55 |
| | (0.69) | (0.10) | | (0.40) | | (0.47) | |
| 8 | 19.1 | 3.41 | 0.89 | 2.29 | 0.85 | 1.57 | 0.90 |
| | (1.38) | (0.19) | | (0.74) | | (0.37) | |
| 9 | 10.2 | 0.95 | 0.87 | −0.31 | 0.88 | 1.85 | 0.70 |
| | (0.96) | (0.12) | | (0.72) | | (0.49) | |
| 10 | 1.50 | 1.52 | 0.89 | 1.45 | 0.79 | 2.25 | 0.81 |
| | (0.17) | (0.05) | | (0.24) | | (0.40) | |
| 11 | 7.11 | 3.74 | 0.82 | 1.08 | 0.74 | 5.49 | 0.89 |
| | (0.63) | (0.15) | | (0.51) | | (0.78) | |
| 12 | 2.32 | 1.22 | 0.89 | 0.14 | 0.79 | 0.31 | 0.99 |
| | (0.25) | (0.07) | | (0.16) | | (0.31) | |
| 13 | 4.42 | 0.76 | 0.73 | 0.36 | 0.85 | 0.18 | 0.89 |
| | (0.50) | (0.06) | | (0.26) | | (0.13) | |
| 14 | 4.14 | 1.13 | 0.85 | 0.33 | 0.88 | 1.70 | 0.92 |
| | (0.31) | (0.04) | | (0.17) | | (0.09) | |
| 1–14 | 19.8 | 12.3 | 0.77 | 1.01 | 0.91 | 1.77 | 0.61 |
| | (1.19) | (0.41) | | (0.32) | | (0.26) | |

*Notes:* Heteroscedasticity-consistent standard errors (White, 1980) are reported in parenthesis. Specification 1 is the same as the specification in Table 3, with all variables deflated by the log of distance. In specification 2, the standard deviation of the two-month difference in the relative price for within-U.S. pairs is regressed on the log of distance and 14 individual U.S. city dummies. In specification 3, the standard deviation of the two-month difference in the relative price for within-Canada pairs is regressed on the log of distance and nine individual Canadian city dummies. All coefficients and standard errors have been multiplied by 1,000. Standard deviations are computed over the sample period from September 1978 to December 1994. There are 228 observations in each regression.

proportional to the log of distance between cities. That is, we estimate

$$V(P_{j,k}^i)/r_{j,k} = \beta_1^i + \beta_2^i(B_{j,k}/r_{j,k})$$

$$+ \sum_{m=1}^{n} \gamma_m^i(D_m/r_{j,k}) + v_{j,k}.$$

The constant terms and the coefficients on the deflated border dummy are positive, as predicted, and highly significant in the regressions for each of the 14 goods.

We try several extensions to test the robustness of our results. In order to conserve space, we do not report these results. One variation is to alter the period covered by the data. We eliminate the early 1980's from our sample, using only data starting in September 1985. Over this later period the U.S. dollar experienced large swings in its value. There was virtually no change in the results in these regressions from the ones using the entire sample.

We also split the sample at January 1990, when the Canadian–U.S. Free Trade Agreement went into effect. If trade barriers are an important reason why the border variable is economically significant in explaining price dispersion, one would expect that the magnitude of this variable would decline after 1989. In fact, we found a slight tendency in the opposite direction: the estimated border coefficients were usually larger in the post-1989 period.

In general, there was very little difference in our full-sample estimates and our post-September 1985 and post-January 1990 results. Distance and the border dummy had positive coefficients for the same goods in all three samples. Not surprisingly, the $t$ statistics were smaller in the shorter samples.

One other convex specification of the distance variable we tried is one in which we hypothesize that, after a certain critical distance (arbitrarily chosen to be 1,700 miles), additional distance does not contribute at all to volatility. In this model, there is a linear relation between volatility and distance for distances up to 1,700 miles, and then after 1,700 miles the derivative of volatility with respect to distance is zero. This model performs almost identically to the log-distance function in terms of the number of correct signs on coefficient estimates, the degree of significance, the adjusted $R^2$, and the magnitude of the coefficients on the border dummy.[10]

### B. *How Important are Distance and the Border?*

We have seen that physical distance plays a significant role in explaining the failure in the law of one price between two locations. But physical distance alone does not explain the variability in prices of similar goods if the two locations are in different countries—the border matters.

We would like to get an idea of the economic significance of the border relative to distance in determining price dispersion. One way to do this is by examining the average coefficients on log distance and the border

dummy from the regression in Table 3, which equal the reported coefficients for the pooled regression. There, the coefficient on the border is $11.9 \times 10^{-3}$, and on the log of distance it is $10.6 \times 10^{-4}$. Thus, crossing the border adds $11.9 \times 10^{-3}$ to the average standard deviation of prices between pairs of cities. In order to generate that much volatility by distance, the cities would have to be 75,000 miles apart.[11] This calculation indicates that crossing the border adds substantially to volatility. Actually, this statistic may overstate the economic importance of the border, given that the natural log function is concave, and given the imprecision of the estimate of the coefficient on log distance. The 95-percent confidence interval for the distance coefficient is ($5.3 \times 10^{-4}$, $15.9 \times 10^{-4}$). If we were to use the upper end of the confidence interval as the measure of the impact of distance, then crossing the border is equivalent to 1,780 miles of distance between cities. The effect of distance may also be understated if the log-distance function is not the appropriate one.

This statistic may not be meaningful if distance does not contribute much to the dispersion of prices—but that is not the case. Consider the price dispersion for cross-border pairs of cities. From Table 2, the average standard deviation is 0.0367. The border, which adds 0.0119 to the standard deviation of cross-border pairs, accounts for 32.4 percent of this. The average log distance between cross-border pairs is 7.03, so on average distance adds 0.00745 to the standard deviation, which is 20.3 percent of the total.

Table 5 also reports the results of regressing the price dispersion on the log of distance (and city dummy variables) when we use only U.S. cities (second specification of Table 5) and only Canadian cities (third specification). We note that for U.S. cities distance has the hypothesized positive coefficient for 12 of the 14 cities and is significant at the 5-percent level for eight of the goods (and significant at the 6-percent level for two more). When all 14 goods are used jointly, the effect of distance is positive

---

[10] We also included a dummy variable for pairs of cities in the same province or state. Inclusion of this dummy did not appreciably alter our results.

[11] Calculated as $\exp[(11.9 \times 10^{-3})/(10.6 \times 10^{-4})]$ miles.

and highly significant. For the Canadian cities, distance has a positive effect for all 14 goods, and it is significant for 13 of those goods. Thus, if we do not consider the effect of the border at all, we find that distance has strong explanatory power for price dispersion.

## C. *Why Does the Border Matter So Much?*

Crossing the border adds significantly to price dispersion. In the Introduction, we proposed several reasons why the border would matter. Here we attempt to distinguish between a few of them.

We note that we have already tried a direct test for trade barriers and found that the size of the border coefficient was not diminished when the free-trade agreement between the United States and Canada went into effect. This, of course, does not rule out the possibility that informal trade barriers account for the price dispersion.

We suggested that labor markets might be more homogeneous within countries, so that $w_j^i/w_k^i$ is less variable for city pairs $(j, k)$ within a country than for cross-border pairs. We can investigate this hypothesis by seeing whether the explanatory power of the border dummy is affected by introducing relative wage volatility into the regression.

For each city, we construct a real wage as the average hourly wage for manufacturing employees (which is available for each city in the United States and by province in Canada) divided by the aggregate CPI for that city. We then calculate for each city pair the standard deviation of the two-month difference in the log of the relative real wages.

We add this wage-dispersion variable to our first regression, equation (2). These results are reported as the first specification in Table 6. As we expect, the wage dispersion coefficient is generally positive and significant. The coefficient is positive for 13 of the goods, and significant for ten.

However, the size of the border coefficient is not much affected by inclusion of the wage-dispersion variable. Apparently the border's importance does not arise because of the homogeneity of the labor markets within countries; but the distance coefficients are generally

smaller and less significant. As we discuss in the Introduction, one of the reasons distance matters for intercity price dispersion is that more distant cities have less-integrated labor markets. The results from this regression bear out that hypothesis.

We investigate whether the sticky-price explanation for the importance of the border has power. In all of the regressions we have reported, if $P_f$ is the U.S. dollar price of good $f$ in a U.S. city, and $P_f^*$ is the price in the Canadian city, the relative price is (the log of) $P_f/SP_f^*$, where $S$ is the exchange rate. If $P_f$ and $P_f^*$ are sticky, then $P_f/SP_f^*$ will fluctuate as $S$ fluctuates. The border will be significant because it picks up the effect of the fluctuating exchange rate.

However, if we calculate the relative prices of good $f$ between cities as relative real prices, then the nominal exchange rate will not appear in the calculation. That is, call $P_f/P$ the real price of good $f$ in the U.S. city, where $P$ is an aggregate price index for that city, and $P_f^*/P^*$ is the real price of good $f$ in the Canadian city. Then the relative intercity price is $(P_f/P)/(P_f^*/P^*)$. If nominal price stickiness were the reason the border matters when we use $P_f/SP_f^*$ as the measure of relative prices, then it should not be significant when we use $(P_f/P)/(P_f^*/P^*)$.

When the log of $(P_f/P)/(P_f^*/P^*)$ is taken to be the relative price, the filtered measure of prices is a better measure than the two-month difference. The log of $(P_f/P)/(P_f^*/P^*)$ appears to be stationary for all of our goods, so the two-month difference would be an over-differenced series.

The second specification reported in Table 6 is for the regressions when prices for the individual goods in each city are taken relative to the CPI for all goods in that city. The standard deviation of the filtered prices is regressed on the log of distance, the border dummy, and individual city dummies, so the explanatory variables are the same as in equation (2). We find that the coefficients on distance are all positive, and generally significant. The coefficients on the border dummy are all positive and highly significant. Thus, even without the nominal exchange rate in the calculation of cross-border prices, the border matters.

TABLE 6—ASSESSING WHY THE BORDER MATTERS

| Good | Specification 1 | | | Specification 2 | | Specification 3 | |
|---|---|---|---|---|---|---|---|
| | Log distance | Border | SD of real wage | Log distance | Border | Log distance | Border |
| 1 | 1.56 | 6.74 | 0.28 | 6.60 | 2.04 | 5.71 | 3.22 |
| | (1.15) | (0.23) | (0.08) | (1.87) | (0.14) | (2.08) | (0.16) |
| 2 | 0.62 | 9.44 | 0.10 | 2.95 | 1.98 | 1.74 | 4.32 |
| | (1.02) | (0.13) | (0.03) | (0.93) | (0.11) | (0.60) | (0.09) |
| 3 | −0.84 | 9.01 | 0.36 | 5.44 | 3.46 | 4.47 | 4.28 |
| | (1.56) | (0.27) | (0.09) | (2.69) | (0.17) | (2.70) | (0.19) |
| 4 | 5.72 | 8.83 | 0.22 | 4.99 | 2.66 | 6.69 | 6.15 |
| | (1.78) | (0.23) | (0.05) | (1.09) | (0.12) | (1.64) | (0.16) |
| 5 | 31.5 | 9.53 | 0.35 | 28.6 | 3.47 | 28.6 | 4.19 |
| | (7.16) | (0.94) | (0.19) | (5.15) | (0.59) | (5.59) | (0.63) |
| 6 | −0.76 | 7.84 | 0.16 | 2.66 | 1.66 | 1.75 | 3.79 |
| | (1.01) | (0.15) | (0.03) | (0.87) | (0.10) | (0.85) | (0.11) |
| 7 | 9.33 | 12.6 | 0.10 | 2.06 | 6.78 | 2.84 | 7.61 |
| | (2.97) | (0.46) | (0.11) | (2.42) | (0.32) | (2.38) | (0.31) |
| 8 | 34.5 | 27.9 | −0.54 | 11.0 | 13.0 | 13.2 | 13.7 |
| | (7.97) | (1.12) | (0.23) | (3.46) | (0.49) | (3.06) | (0.46) |
| 9 | 6.15 | 8.84 | 0.13 | 5.44 | 5.34 | 4.64 | 5.93 |
| | (3.14) | (0.45) | (0.11) | (2.86) | (0.31) | (3.02) | (0.32) |
| 10 | 7.03 | 10.2 | 0.23 | 8.34 | 3.15 | 9.82 | 4.66 |
| | (1.75) | (0.23) | (0.08) | (1.53) | (0.15) | (1.92) | (0.16) |
| 11 | 24.6 | 25.4 | 0.68 | 23.2 | 21.3 | 21.8 | 21.8 |
| | (6.82) | (1.11) | (0.22) | (4.98) | (0.66) | (5.18) | (0.67) |
| 12 | −4.60 | 8.91 | 0.28 | 3.17 | 1.99 | 1.36 | 3.89 |
| | (1.73) | (0.26) | (0.06) | (1.70) | (0.16) | (1.78) | (0.18) |
| 13 | −0.16 | 6.66 | 0.01 | 1.53 | 1.62 | 2.22 | 3.17 |
| | (1.80) | (0.23) | (0.06) | (1.39) | (0.16) | (1.48) | (0.17) |
| 14 | 3.21 | 8.16 | 0.15 | 4.98 | 2.11 | 3.70 | 3.99 |
| | (1.08) | (0.14) | (0.03) | (0.99) | (0.12) | (0.93) | (0.12) |
| 1–14 | 8.43 | 11.4 | 0.18 | 7.93 | 5.04 | 7.76 | 6.48 |
| | (3.22) | (0.52) | (0.11) | (2.68) | (0.35) | (2.76) | (0.36) |

*Notes:* All regressions contain a dummy for each of the 23 individual cities, in addition to the variables listed in the cell. Heteroscedasticity-consistent standard errors (White, 1980) are reported in parentheses. Coefficients and standard erorrs on log distance (border) are multiplied by 10,000 (1,000). Specification 1 is the same as the specification in Table 3 but adds the standard deviation of the two-month difference in the intercity real wage. Specifications 2 and 3 use a measure of the real price of each good: in specification 2, the individual goods prices are deflated by the city's overall CPI, while in specification 3 the deflator is the national PPI. The measure of volatility in each case is the standard deviation of the two-month-ahead forecast error from the filtered relative price, over the sample period from September 1978 to December 1994. There are 228 observations in each regression. The adjusted $R^2$ estimates, not reported in order to save space, were never less than 0.77

How much does the border matter in this regression as compared to the regressions in which relative prices are calculated as the log of $P_f/SP_f^*$? From the first specification reported in Table 4, the coefficient on the border dummy using the filtered measure of the log of $P_f/SP_f^*$ when all 14 goods are aggregated in a single regression is $10.8 \times 10^{-3}$.

(Recall that the coefficients reported for the pooled regressions are the averages of the coefficients for the regressions for each of the 14 goods.) The average standard deviation for all cross-border city pairs using the filtered measure is $32.4 \times 10^{-3}$, so the border accounts for 33.3 percent of that standard deviation. When the log of $(P_f/P)/(P_f^*/P^*)$ is used as the measure of the relative price, the coefficient on the border dummy for the regression using all goods is $5.04 \times 10^{-3}$ (last row of the second specification in Table 6). That compares to an average standard deviation of $26.6 \times 10^{-3}$ for cross-border city pairs. Thus, the border accounts for only 18.9 percent of that standard deviation. Hence, when we drop the nominal exchange rate from our calculation of intercity prices, the percentage of the cross-border standard deviation accounted for by the border drops from 33.3 percent to 18.9 percent. We might conclude that the sticky-price story accounts for this difference; but we note that the border still accounts for a fairly large portion of the cross-border dispersion even after taking into account the role of sticky prices.

We also consider calculating the individual goods prices in each city relative to the national-level producer price index. The third row of Table 5 reports regressions using these prices, again taking the filtered measure of the log of $(P_f/P)/(P_f^*/P^*)$. We note that the results are qualitatively similar to the previous regression. Here, in the regression that uses all 14 goods, the coefficient on the border dummy is $6.48 \times 10^{-3}$ (last row of the third specification in Table 6). The average standard deviation for cross-border city pairs with this measure of relative prices is $28.1 \times 10^{-3}$, so the border accounts for 23.1 percent of the total. This is still less than the 33.3 percent of the total when we use the log of $P_f/SP_f^*$ as the measure of relative prices, but only about 30-percent less. Therefore, we can tentatively conclude that our sticky-nominal-prices story can explain about 30 percent of the border size.

We have not been able to explain fully why the border matters so much for intercity price dispersion. We have cast some doubt on the notion that formal trade barriers can explain it, while leaving open the possibility that informal barriers are significant. The hypothesis that wage costs are more homogeneous within countries does not seem to explain the border's importance. Sticky nominal prices do seem to account for a significant portion of the magnitude of the border effect, but apparently less than half. Other possibilities that we have not explored include differences in demand elasticities in the United States and Canada (which has received attention in the pricing-to-market literature) and homogeneity of productivity shocks within countries in the nontraded sectors (so that $\alpha_j^i/\alpha_k^i$ from equation (1) has less dispersion within countries than between countries).

## III. Conclusions

The major message of our empirical results is not just that the border matters for relative price variability; it is that both distance and the border matter. The literature on pricing to market has emphasized that, when markets are segmented, price discrimination can occur. The finding that distance is important in explaining price differences between locations lends support to this literature and the associated work on geography and trade. But our findings seem to suggest that there is more than standard price-discrimination behavior involved in cross-border price movements.

To the extent that our results indicate sticky nominal prices, they also shed some light on the price-setting process. We have found that the distance between markets influences prices, suggesting that price-setters take into account prices of nearby competitors. It is probably not too far-fetched to infer that firms would respond more to changes in prices of near substitutes, whether the nearness is in geographical space or product space. A reasonable model of price stickiness must take into account how isolated the market is for the product of the price setter. There appears to be potential for a marriage of the new-Keynesian literature on menu costs and the new trade literature emphasizing the role of geography.

Nominal price stickiness cannot account for all of the price dispersion between markets, however. The results of this paper confirm McCallum's (1995) finding that, despite the relative openness of the U.S.–Canadian border, the markets are still segmented.

DATA APPENDIX

Our data for the United States was obtained from the Bureau of Labor Statistics. The 14 goods from the United States are listed on the left-hand side of Table 1. All of the price and wage data (for both countries) are seasonally unadjusted.

We use comparable price and wage data for Canada that were obtained from Statistics Canada. There is not always an exact match between the price indexes available in Canada and those available in the United States. However, we were able to construct indexes for the 14 categories of goods in Canada, in some cases by using even more disaggregated Canadian indexes. For example, the U.S. data contain a series on men's and boy's apparel. There is no comparable series in Canada. However, we can obtain from Canada individual series on men's wear and on boy's wear. We then construct a men's and boy's apparel series for Canada by taking a weighted average of the men's wear series and the boy's wear series.[12] This type of construction was needed to arrive at five of the 14 Canadian price series. Table 1 indicates how these series were derived.

These categories of goods are mutually exclusive. Together they comprise 94.6 percent of purchases (using the weights in the U.S. consumer price index).

Monthly price data were used for nine Canadian cities: Calgary, Edmonton, Montreal, Ottawa, Quebec, Regina, Toronto, Vancouver, and Winnipeg. Monthly price data for the United States are available for four "core" cities: New York, Philadelphia, Chicago, and Los Angeles. In addition, for five cities, data are released in even-numbered months: Dallas, Detroit, Houston, Pittsburgh, and San Francisco. For five other cities, there are data available in odd-numbered months: Baltimore, Boston, Miami, St. Louis, and Washington.[13]

Consumer price data are closer to being monthly average data than point-in-time data. Typically to get the price of a single product, several outlets are sampled during the month. The outlets are not all sampled on the same day. The change in the price of the product from the previous month is calculated as the average change across the various outlets. For the cities that report data every second month, the prices are for the second month of the interval (rather than an average across both months).

In order to nullify a potential bias, we use a monthly average (U.S. dollar)/(Canadian dollar) exchange rate from the Citibase tape. Averaging tends to reduce the volatility of the series. Thus, if we were to use an exchange rate at a specific point in time, but use price data which is

essentially averaged, we would introduce volatility into our measure of cross-border prices. That is compensated for by taking the monthly average exchange rate.

For each good, we calculated the intercity relative prices. Thus, when we are using only the Canadian cities and the core U.S. cities, for each good there are 78 intercity prices (13 cities × 12/2). Adding the five even-month U.S. cities adds another 75 prices, and adding the five odd-month U.S. cities adds another 75 prices.

We also use data on the distance between cities. We use two separate measures of distance, both obtained from the Automap (version 2) software. One measure is the great-circle distance, and the other is the quickest-driving-time distance. Our results were not affected by the choice of distance measure, so all results reported use the great-circle distance

REFERENCES

Debreu, Gerard. *Theory of value.* New Haven, CT: Yale University Press, 1959.

Dixit, Avinash. "Hysteresis, Import Penetration, and Exchange Rate Pass-Through." *Quarterly Journal of Economics,* May 1989, *104*(2), pp. 205–28.

Dornbusch, Rudiger. "Exchange Rates and Prices." *American Economic Review,* March 1987, *77*(1), pp. 93–106.

Dumas, Bernard. "Dynamic Equilibrium and the Real Exchange Rate in a Spatially Separated World." *Review of Financial Studies,* 1992, *5*(2), pp. 153–180.

Engel, Charles. "Real Exchange Rates and Relative Prices: An Empirical Investigation." *Journal of Monetary Economics,* August 1993, *32*(1), pp. 35–50.

_____. "Accounting for U.S. Real Exchange Rate Changes." National Bureau of Economic Research (Cambridge, MA) Working Paper No. 5394, December 1995.

Feenstra, Robert C. "Symmetric Pass-Through of Tariffs and Exchange Rates under Imperfect Competition: An Empirical Test." *Journal of International Economics,* August 1989, *27*(1/2), pp. 25–45.

Frankel, Jeffrey; Stein, Ernesto and Wei, Shang-Jin. "Trading Blocs and the Americas: The Natural, the Unnatural and the Super-natural." *Journal of Development Economics,* June 1995, *47*(1), pp. 61–96.

Froot, Kenneth A. and Klemperer, Paul D. "Exchange Rate Pass-Through when Market Share Matters." *American Economic Review,* September 1989, *79*(4), pp. 637–54.

[12] The weights come from the current weights used in the U.S. consumer price index, which we obtained from the Bureau of Labor Statistics.

[13] Data for Cleveland are available every other month. However, the data switched from being odd-month to even-month in the middle of our sample. Also, at the beginning of the sample, Detroit data were monthly, but switched to even-month, while the reverse is true for San Francisco. We make use only of the even-month data for these two cities.

**Giovannini, Alberto.** "Exchange Rates and Traded Goods Prices." *Journal of International Economics,* February 1988, *24*(1/2), pp. 45–68.

**Isard, Peter.** "How Far Can We Push the Law of One Price?" *American Economic Review,* December 1977, *67*(5), pp. 942–48.

**Kasa, Kenneth.** "Adjustment Costs and Pricing-to-Market: Theory and Evidence." *Journal of International Economics,* February 1992, *32*(1/2), pp. 1–30.

**Knetter, Michael N.** "Price Discrimination by U.S. and German Exporters." *American Economic Review,* March 1989, *79*(1), pp. 198–210.

_____. "International Comparisons of Pricing-to-Market Behavior." *American Economic Review,* June 1993, *83*(3), pp. 473–86.

**Krugman, Paul.** "Pricing to Market When the Exchange Rate Changes," in Sven W. Arndt and J. David Richardson, eds., *Real-financial linkages among open economies.* Cambridge, MA: MIT Press, 1987, pp. 49–70.

_____. "Increasing Returns and Economic Geography." *Journal of Political Economy,* June 1991, *99*(3), pp. 483–99.

**Marston, Richard C.** "Pricing to Market in Japanese Manufacturing." *Journal of International Economics,* November 1990, *29*(3/4), pp. 217–36.

**McCallum, John.** "National Borders Matter: Regional Trade Patterns in North America." *American Economic Review,* June 1995, *85*(3), pp. 615–23.

**Mussa, Michael.** "Nominal Exchange Rate Regimes and the Behavior of Real Exchange Rates: Evidence and Implications." *Carnegie-Rochester Conference Series on Public Policy,* Autumn 1986, *25*, pp. 117–214.

**Rogers, John H. and Jenkins, Michael.** "Haircuts or Hysteresis? Sources of Movements in Real Exchange Rates." *Journal of International Economics,* May 1995, *38*(3/4), pp. 339–60.

**Sanyal, Kalyan K. and Jones, Ronald W.** "The Theory of Trade in Middle Products." *American Economic Review,* March 1982, *72*(1), pp. 16–31.

**White, Halbert.** "A Heteroskedasticity-Consistent Covariance Matrix Estimator and a Direct Test for Heteroskedasticity." *Econometrica,* May 1980, *48*(4), pp. 817–38.

# D
# Regionalization and Sub-Regional Zones

Detlef Lorenz*

# Regionalisation versus Regionalism – Problems of Change in the World Economy

*The distinct trends towards regionalisation in the world economy that could be observed in recent years should not be interpreted merely as the formation of economic blocs or "fortresses". This would amount to adopting a biased, backward-looking approach that sees only the sombre experiences of the thirties and forties and does not take sufficient account of the different challenges of the post-war period.*

Since the mid-eighties we have seen a remarkable renaissance of regionalisation in the world economy, as evident in Europe, North America and East Asia. Initially, this development was discussed primarily in trade terms in parallel with the Uruguay Round of the GATT, which represents the established multilateral (and universal) world trade order. It gained wider coverage as a result of a conference held in 1988 by the Institute for International Economics in Washington under the title "More Free Trade Areas?" and the publication of the conference papers.[1] A number of other, more fundamental studies followed that dealt with far wider questions.[2] Finally, the Development Centre of the OECD recently began a wide-ranging programme of research on "Globalisation and Regionalisation".[3] It is therefore unlikely that the debate will degenerate into a superficial and dogmatic controversy about the formation of blocs and "fortresses". There is a good prospect that regionalisation will not be interpreted merely as bloc-forming region*alism* and the antithesis of multilateralism but as *open* regionalisation supplementing and modifying economic globalism because of development needs.[4] To equate regionalisation with the formation of economic blocs is to adopt a biased, backward-looking approach that sees only the sombre experiences of the thirties and forties and does not take sufficient account of the different challenges of the post-war period, and especially those of the eighties and nineties.

Political economy, and especially foreign trade theory, can unfortunately contribute little in this regard, for in both theory and policy it is concerned primarily with politically and historically determined states or with the world economy as a whole. In practice the two together become a global, universal system consisting of the *small* countries beloved of textbooks on international trade. The GATT, as guardian of the world trade order, also clings to this perception of the world trading system as a collection of a great many small countries. The coalescence of countries into regional trading communities, customs unions or free trade areas is sanctioned by Article 24 of the GATT, but it is often very quickly viewed askance by academics. For example, in the view of K.W. Dam this article is "one of the most troublesome provisions of GATT ..., a failure if not a fiasco".[5] When, finally, under a rule meant to define exceptions, the unforeseen emergence of the EC took place, this gave rise to the "spectre" of regionalism or, more recently, of "fortress Europe".

Although the available material is sparse – the analysis of *economic space* (regions) has generally taken second place to the examination of economic relations between national *states* – a few illuminating studies have been made on the regionalisation of international economic relations, such as the tripolarity and multipolarity approaches to economic development and the discrimination and integration approaches as an expression of economic policy objectives.

## Tripolarity

The first two approaches have many points in common with the foreign trade theory of Andreas Predöhl,[6] who in the past probably had the greatest success in both perceiving and empirically interpreting the world economy

---

* Free University Berlin, Germany.

[1] J. J. Schott (ed.): Free Trade Areas and U.S. Trade Policy, Washington 1989.

[2] Cf. D. Lorenz: Trends Towards Regionalism in the World Economy. A Contribution to a New International Order? in: INTERECONOMICS, Vol. 24, No. 2, 1989, pp. 64-70; L. Emmerij (ed.): One World or Several? Development Centre/OECD, Paris 1989; D. Lorenz: Regionale Entwicklungslinien in der Weltwirtschaft – Tendenzen zur Bildung von Wachstumszentren?, in: E. Kantzenbach and O. G.Mayer (eds.): Perspektiven der weltwirtschaftlichen Entwicklung und ihre Konsequenzen für die Bundesrepublik Deutschland. Hamburg 1990, pp. 11-31.

[3] Cf. C. Oman: Summary Note, Paris, September 1990.

[4] On open regionalisation, see D. Lorenz: Regionale Entwicklungslinien in der Weltwirtschaft, op. cit., pp. 27-28.

[5] K.W. Dam: The GATT, Law and International Organisation, Chicago 1970.

in terms of locational analysis. The premise of an increase in trilateralism has been discussed in greatest detail by Preeg and Minx and subjected to empirical criticism primarily by Sautter.[7] Broadly paralleling Predöhl's core regions or centres of gravity, trilateralism refers to the economic spaces of Western Europe, North America and Japan *as well as* taking account of certain groups of developing countries (the newly industrialising countries) in "proximity" to the industrial country regions. In his illuminating study, Sautter reaches three conclusions with regard to the long, but not unproblematic period from 1928 to 1976:[8]

❑ A clear trend towards increasing regionalisation during the period cannot be confirmed, but a number of developments in this direction can be discerned, such as a strengthening of trade ties within core regions and a decrease in the intensity of trade between cores.

❑ "The regionalisation of world trade is ... primarily the result of comparatively *durable* geographic, cultural and economic determinants and only to a lesser extent the result of more recent, regionally confined measures of integration policy" (the EC, for example).

❑ "The regionalisation of international trade will ... neither herald nor terminate the growth in world trade, but will be its enduring feature." He therefore regards the fear that "an increasing tendency towards worldwide regionalisation will lead to an erosion of multilateral world trade" as groundless.

## Multipolarity

Neither does a new approach to the analysis of regionalisation run counter to multilateralism, as the two go hand in hand. The most important substantiation of the multipolarity theory is the recognition that the extensive globalisation of many world markets has been accompanied by the formation of new regions that are remoulding the old North-North and North-South configuration into a multipolar world economy.[9] Remarkably, this manifestation of regionalisation in the form of multipolarity again takes account of groups of newly industrialising economies, the well-known generation of NIEs, and, furthermore, even adding to these

the potential "quasi-NIEs" by including the former Comecon countries and the continental states of India and China.

Extended in this way, the concept is bound to induce a significant inter-regional realignment on the basis of a global strategy of expansion: "One of the major questions facing the world community is how the trade and economic growth possibilities of the multipolar world structure can be utilised for the benefit of the world economy as a whole rather than primarily feed the dynamism of regional blocs".[10] This approach could, moreover, provide empirical support for the new concept of "open regionalism" via its world trade matrix. Nevertheless, besides the fact that the concept disregards "peripheral" regions, such as Latin America and Africa, the following point should be considered; although the important addition of the new economic areas of the NIEs to the trilateralists' three (the USA, the EC and Japan) should meet with approval, it is taken too far in this model, probably for operational reasons (world trade matrix). While the Comecon area will become more relevant in the world economic context in future, the inclusion of the former GDR, Czechoslovakia and the USSR as NIEs seems highly problematical. Moreover, the expansion of the group of NIEs by the inclusion of as many as three gigantic continental states – the USSR, India and China – seems equally questionable. Until recently only the People's Republic of China played any role as an NIE, and then only as regards the export zones in its coastal provinces and in increasing trade with Hong Kong and Taiwan. The more limited North-South regions used in another paper appear to be more realistic.[11]

## Discrimination and Integration

Trends towards regionalism have taken on particular relevance at the institutional and economic policy level as a result of the recent debate about a variety of views and US initiatives on free trade agreements.[12] In accordance with Pomfret,[13] this development can be classified under the broad heading of geographically discriminatory arrangements (GDAs). These include not only the new proposals for free trade areas but also the old and new arrangements in Western Europe (EEC, EC, EFTA, EES), various integration agreements between developing

---

[6] A. Predöhl: Außenwirtschaft, 2nd edition, Göttingen 1971.

[7] E. H. Preeg: Economic Blocs and U.S. Foreign Policy, Washington 1974; E. H. Preeg: The American Challenge in World Trade, Washington 1989; E. P. Minx: Von der Liberalisierungs- zur Wettbewerbspolitik, Berlin 1980; H. Sautter: Regionalisierung und komparative Vorteile im internationalen Handel, Tübingen 1983.

[8] Ibid., pp. 280 ff.

[9] See the contribution by C. I. Bradford Jr. in: L. Emmerij, op. cit., pp. 26 and 31-40, and C. I. Bradford Jr.: The World Economy in the Mid-1990s: Alternative Patterns of Trade and Growth, Strategic Planning and Review, Discussion Paper No. 2, The World Bank, November 1989.

[10] Ibid., p. 33.

[11] D. Lorenz: Trade in Manufactures, Newly Industrializing Economies (NIEs), and Regional Development in the World Economy – a European View, in: The Developing economies, Vol. 27, 1989, pp. 221-235.

[12] Cf. J. J. Schott, op. cit.

[13] R. Pomfret: Unequal Trade. The Economics of Discriminatory International Trade Policies, London 1988.

## INTERNATIONAL TRADE

countries, systems of preferences for developing countries and even bilateral voluntary restraint agreements. Pomfret's analysis concentrates on the violation of the central tenet of the GATT, namely the principle of non-discrimination, and on demonstrating how advanced the erosion of most-favoured-nation treatment in international trade has been for some time. If the GATT finds ever fewer convinced supporters and defenders (or rather innovators) and to some extent withers away, regionalism may take hold more easily by contagion. Pomfret is nevertheless not inclined to predict a proliferation of regional trading blocs. In his opinion, this danger was greater in the forties than in the eighties, for inter-regional trade is flourishing despite the spread of GDAs of various kinds.[14]

To regard the current trend towards regionalisation of the world economy in terms of discrimination, and especially in terms of trade discrimination only, is to adopt far too narrow a view. Regional developments and preferences should be seen as an economic policy phenomenon in a wider sense. That is quite clear in the case of the highest form of regional development, namely integration, which involves a combination of economic and political integration. There is apparently only one example of this in the world economy: the EC, and in some ways also the so-called European Economic Space (EES).

### Provision of Public Goods

If regional development is not linked with this non-universal final objective, it can only be interpreted as a better transitional method for achieving universal world economic objectives, a commendable means of resolving complex and difficult problems that must be tackled one step at a time. That this strategy was successful in the past is demonstrated by Western Europe's contribution to the liberalisation successfully carried out under the GATT during the long reintegration process of the world economy after 1945. However, the current debate shows that it no longer inspires confidence in different world economic conditions. Moreover, the regional approach now has to compete with the non-regionally based approach of so-called open clubs ("GATT Plus").

Matters can also be seen from a different standpoint, as expressed by Cooper.[15] Regionalisation need not be the final objective (integration/EC), nor need it merely be a means to an end (multilateralism/GATT); it may stem from responsibility for the "provision" of public goods. Returns to scale, external effects and stabilisation policies may call

for what Cooper terms optimal areas of jurisdiction, regions that are smaller than the world but larger than many states. The preferences of the population or politicians for collective goods and autonomy in the search for the "optimal" size of regions are also determinants. If two public goods that have recently been discussed intensively in the context of the management of the world economy are brought into the picture, namely deregulation and economic co-operation both within and between regions, there is much to be said for heeding regional, sub-global determinants, not least in the light of the experiences of the last two decades.[16] "Natural" regions are more realistic than the "abstract" regions represented by trade clubs, because the economic growth and efficiency of geographic regions can be greatly enhanced both by neighbourly co-operation of the "learning by doing" variety and by other social affinities.

### Parallel Tendencies

In addition to the approaches outlined above for explaining the phenomenon of regionalisation, another pragmatic approach also deserves to be considered, namely an examination of the three well-known regions that have drawn attention to themselves on account of their dynamism as regards regionalisation. As mentioned in the introduction to this article, these three regions, although different in many respects, began to display parallel tendencies towards regionalisation at approximately the same time in the mid-eighties. There seems to be little connection between these developments.

The programme for the creation of an internal market in the EC by 1992 partly represents "only" the belated completion of the Common Market or the continuation of this regional liberalisation policy using more appropriate and up-to-date means, and partly reflects the efforts to revitalise the Community in response to the diagnosis of "Euro-sclerosis". These two factors together give rise to justified hopes of an *open* integration policy, in which intra-regional and extra-regional growth support one another.

The international "market" integration in East Asia was activated and intensified by the appreciation of the yen in 1985 and other economic measures in response to the macro-economic imbalances within the region and in relation to the USA, in particular. The restructuring of intra-regional economic relations (trade plus direct investment) instigated by Japan also explicitly reflects the necessary switch from a strategy of exporting to countries outside the region to one of intra-regional development. Undoubtedly this change from an extra-regional to an intra-regional

---

[14] Ibid., pp. 182 ff.

[15] R. N. Cooper: Worldwide versus Regional Integration: Is there an Optimum Size of the Integration Area? in: F. Machlup (ed.): Economic Integration, London 1976, pp. 41-53.

[16] See D. Lorenz: Trends towards Regionalism in the World Economy, op. cit.

### INTERNATIONAL TRADE

orientation is due not only to protectionism and the limits on the absorption of imports by the USA and Europe but also to a strengthening of regional growth stimulated by development.[17]

Both developments, in Western Europe on the one hand and in East Asia on the other, can be interpreted as a specific manifestation of intra-regional integration, whether more on an institutional basis, as in the EC, or as de facto integration based on consensus. They are also influenced, but not dominated, by the state of the world trading system.

Things are different in the case of the USA. Here we are not dealing with an economic region that is still in the process of growing together and forming a single internal market. Even the inclusion of areas in the North (Canada) and South (the Caribbean and Mexico) can be compared only up to a point with the integration of industrial countries and NIEs in Europe and Asia. Accordingly, the above-mentioned trend towards trade regionalisation in the USA through the creation of free trade areas is much more superficial, being orientated more or less towards trade and not towards integration.

Of course, trends in the USA are connected most closely with the development of the GATT system and are a response to it. In the eighties the USA was hardest hit by the deficiencies of the multilateral order it had brought into being. The methods being used to restore the competitiveness of the US economy are by no means entirely consistent with the GATT, however. Strategies based on reciprocity, the creation of a "level playing field" and the emulation of EC regionalism are expressions of a two-tier trade policy. Interestingly, the USA resembles East Asia in that there are both intra-regional and extra-regional accents. However, whereas in East Asia there is a tendency to sell the extra-regional component short in favour of the intra-regional aspect, the USA appears to be pursuing a strategy facing in both directions at once (Canada/Mexico *plus* East Asia/Pacific).

However much the present tendencies towards regionalisation in each of the trilateralists clearly differ in intensity according to their known regional characteristics, the coincidence of these regional developments appears to be anything but pure chance. This is due not least to the fact that the era of "simple" multilateral GATT tariff rounds is over, although Hufbauer's assessment that "a multilateral approach almost certainly works best for tariff

reduction" is undoubtedly correct for the tasks that remain to be done in this field. However, for the real problems of international economic relations, and not only trade, it can be argued that "different (trade) issues should be addressed in different contexts and country groupings",[18] and this not only in relation to the problematic OECD club.

### Internationalisation of Production

As I have shown, there are many trends towards regionalisation, and undoubtedly more than those I have mentioned. Before examining other regional transformation problems, however, it is worth touching briefly on a factor that has provided some counterweight and which has increasingly characterised the globalisation of the world *market* economy of late.[19] This relates primarily to the consequences of the internationalisation of production through the mobility of production factors and the multinationals' various strategies of transferring and diversifying production as part of their worldwide cross-regional activities (strategic alliances, etc.). Indeed, one might ask whether regionalisation has not already been paralysed by a levelling process between the various regions. However, the existence and topicality of locational competition not only between national states but also between regions that are growing or integrating demonstrate that the opposite is true. Locational competition between such economic areas has become more important in the age of endogenous (man-made) and "arbitrary" (Cline) competitive advantages as well as of trilateral competition through innovation in the fields of high technology and services. It will become increasingly significant when the "growth competition between states" (Stegemann) — for example in the shape of the revitalisation policies of the USA and the EC and the concepts for strategic trade policies that depend on having larger economic spaces because of the dynamic scale and synergy effects — gain greater influence.[20] Since at the same time these neo-mercantilistic "players" are heavily dependent on one another at enterprise and regional level, specific problems of inter-regional specialisation will arise here in the context of *open* and *aggressive* regionalisation.

Apart from that, there is some merit in arguments for a continuation of trilateralism broadened out into a multicentric or multipolar world economy à la Predöhl and Bradford. The old core areas of industrial countries have clearly gained the upper hand, precisely in the context of intensified North-South competition. Not only have they

---

[17] Cf. D. Lorenz: Intra-Regional Trade and Pacific Cooperation: Problems and Prospects, in: W. Klenner (ed.): Trends of Economic Development in East Asia, Berlin 1989, pp. 65-74.

[18] G. Hufbauer: U.S. Trade Policy: Guideposts for the Bush Administration, Washington 1989.

[19] See the OECD project described in C. Oman, op. cit.

[20] Cf. K. Stegemann: Policy rivalry among industrial states: what can we learn from models of strategic trade policy? in: International Organisation, Vol. 43, 1989, pp. 73-100.

## INTERNATIONAL TRADE

asserted their supremacy, they have also proved to be centres of gravity for peripheral areas (NIEs). They may even be in the process of absorbing these regions. To that extent, there is therefore some evidence of an increase in regionalisation in the world economy, such as the increase in trade with near rather than distant trading partners, especially on the basis of intra-sectoral specialisation, as demonstrated empirically by the HWWA.[21]

One factor that continues to militate in favour of regional economic analysis is its relative independence from the indicators of empirical analysis. For example, we are no longer dependent on the iron and steel industry for the geographic concentration of world production. Its place has been taken by industrial technology complexes and so-called networks offering agglomeration advantages that are not confined to a single country and which create gravitational fields that draw in the NIEs. Admittedly, the dimension of *inter*-core trade as opposed to *intra*-core trade must be viewed somewhat differently today. Given the keener competition between approximately equal centres of gravity and the competition in terms of growth between innovating and imitating regions, *inter*-regional trade also increases on the basis of *intra*-industry two-way trade between the extended cores.

### Locomotives of Regional Growth

The linking of the regionalisation tendencies in the world economy with the concept of the *growth region* has recently led to a very superficial and sterile debate about the formation of blocs or "fortresses". This is entirely unterstandable against the background of the Uruguay Round of GATT negotiations, although there has been much international lobbying, too. I shall add nothing to these disputes here; it seems more appropriate to turn to other aspects that have received less attention.

For example, it would be worth examining what have been the locomotives of regional growth that have given the world economy significant demand stimulus since the Second World War, inasfar as the financing of regional deficits has permitted.[22] In highly simplified terms, three regional stimuli can be identified: first in the fifties and sixties the reconstruction and reintegration of Western Europe (or of the Atlantic region), then in the seventies the ambivalent effects of OPEC policy and recycling, and finally in the eighties the United States' appetite for imports. Recently it has not seemed impossible, in view of

the revolutionary changes occurring in the USSR and Eastern Europe, that the Western European, import-led "reconstruction spurt" of the past may now be repeated in Eastern Europe, if there is adequate scope for financial or other support. Leaving that aside, it is not inappropriate to point out the remarkable fact that the growth regions of East Asia played no active locomotive role in any of the three phases described above. Certainly, the first phase was limited mainly to the Atlantic economic space, but during the second and third phases the phenomenal export-led growth in Japan and the Asian NIEs depended on the fact that other "import poles" – first and foremost the USA – made this export offensive from the Far East possible. It is interesting that in more or less the same way as the terms of trade deficits created by OPEC's pricing policy were financed by recycling, the trade deficits caused by the East Asian export offensives have been financed to a large extent by Japanese capital exports to the USA and development aid to ASEAN.

### USA: Shift of Preferences?

A quite different, important aspect arises with regard to the growth region centred on the USA and encompassing North and South America. For some time now, the USA has been regarded increasingly as part of the Pacific economic region, which would obviously be far less attractive without the USA. However, if the USA shifts its preferences in favour of the Pacific, either voluntarily because of the area's dynamic growth or involuntarily because of the US deficits in relation to East Asia, this constitutes an *intercontinental* "arrangement", against which Wijkman has warned in the debate on free trade agreements: "... major trading nations such as the United States should not enter into intercontinental free trade agreements. An FTA to which the United States is one party is not just any FTA ... if it goes bilateral the effect on the international trading system will be profound".[23] An intercontinental arrangement in the Pacific transcends even regionalism and at the same time reduces multipolarity to a barren bipolarity: the Pacific versus Europe. Moreover, a US preference for the Pacific would almost automatically mean a weakening of the United States' commitment to South America and hence would reinforce the marginalisation of this sub-continent. However, the interregional initiatives by both the USA and Latin American countries appear to have intensified recently and to have gone beyond Mexico.[24] Up to now, North *and* Latin America together have been the most "unaligned"

[21] HWWA-Institut für Wirtschaftsforschung: Entwicklungslinien des internationalen Strukturwandels, Hamburg 1989.

[22] See also D. Lorenz: Regionale Entwicklungslinien in der Weltwirtschaft, op. cit., pp. 25-27, and H. P. Gray: The Mechanics of International Economic Locomotion, in: K. Fatemi (ed.): International Trade and Finance, 1989, pp. 24-34.

[23] P. M. Wijkman: The Effect of New Free Trade Areas on EFTA, in: J. J. Schott, op. cit., pp. 181-192.

[24] See the recent Bush initiatives and, for example, S. W. Sanderson and R. H. Hayes: Mexico – Opening Ahead of Eastern Europe, in: Harvard Business Review, September-October 1990, pp. 32-41.

region for a variety of reasons. On the other hand, regional cohesion is far greater in Europe and East Asia, despite all the "politico-economic" differences the two regions display.[25] Let us turn first to Europe.[26]

## European Economic Space

The European economic space suffered disintegration and reactive regionalism between the wars ("Großraumwirtschaft" of Nazi-Germany); after 1945 the political division of the continent forced it to develop in an economically irrational way. From the outset, this politically induced development was therefore under increasing geo-economic strain. The Eastern European Comecon countries (the little six) had been within the gravitational field of the Western European industrial countries. After 1945 they were "brought by political means into the Soviet orbit".[27] This went hand in hand with the export of the socialist (Soviet) model of industrial development via the establishment of heavy industry and led to double dependence and an atypical core-periphery relationship as a result of the rigorous dogma of specialisation within the Comecon: the little six were reliant on imported raw materials (petroleum) and depended on the Soviet Union to take their exports of industrial goods, which were urgently needed in the USSR whereas they could be sold in Western world markets only with difficulty and at a loss owing to the Eastern Europeans' increasingly poor competitiveness.

The Soviet Union could provide Eastern Europe with the blueprints of the development model, as well as with some additional knowhow, and thus become a centre of politico-economic gravity, but this "core" was increasingly unable to supply the peripheral countries with an adequate flow of goods. In particular, the conservative "complementary structure" was neither designed nor able to develop a modern system of intra-industry trade, partly for political reasons but mainly because of the many inefficiencies in the system of economic socialism. The replacement of the Soviet gravitational field by that of Western Europe therefore became ever more urgent and attractive. What applied to trade within Comecon also applied increasingly to East-West trade.[28] Once the political climate and the inefficiencies of the Comecon economic system had created the necessary conditions, it is not at all surprising

that Western Europe should revert to performing a core function. The hoped-for creation of a European Economic Space (EES) comprising not only the EC of the Twelve but also EFTA and Eastern Europe accords with this, at most causing a slight adjustment in the centre of the gravitational field. Only against the background of this return to some semblance of normality in Europe is it appropriate to discuss doubts about possible Euro-centric developments.

## Doubts about Euro-centric Developments

The first point relates to the both politically and economically delicate issue of the still relevant historical roots (recurrent "Anschluß") of the Comecon region, including the vast Soviet Union. As well as weighty political arguments against ignoring this historical burden, there are also economic reasons for not doing so. "In principle, revitalising economic relations within Eastern Europe, including the USSR, appears more promising than forcing these countries to orientate themselves towards the West."[29] In view of the dangerous momentum that the uncontrolled breakdown of economic relations within Comecon is now developing, such a revitalisation appears unavoidable, although it is far from clear how it should be achieved.

Secondly, the appropriate course of action will hardly be to stand Comecon's historical burden (orientation towards the Soviet Union) on its head, as a kind of shock therapy, particularly as the Eastern European countries will continue to have special relationships regarding raw materials supplies, despite the waning of the Soviet Union's gravitational pull.[30] However, the return to normality also demands a thorough modernisation of intra-regional economic relations; among the most important of these will undoubtedly be the transformation of the old geopolitical complementarity in the energy sector. Almost equally important will be efforts to make up the considerable lost ground as regards the *pan-European* division of labour in intra-industry and intra-firm trade within a largely deregulated EES. The question of whether and to what extent the Eastern European countries will soon be able to follow in the footsteps of the newly industrialising economies has been examined in detail elsewhere.[31]

Thirdly, proposals to reconfirm the European economic space at the institutional level are more problematic,

[25] P.M. W i j k m a n and E. S. L i n d s t r ö m : Pacific Basin Integration: A Step Towards free Trade, in: J. N i e u w e u h u y s e n (ed.): Towards Free Trade Between Nations, Melbourne 1989, pp. 144-162.

[26] For a more detailed discussion, see D. L o r e n z : West- und Osteuropa – Probleme des Zusammenwachsens in einer offenen Weltwirtschaft, in: Wirtschaftsdienst, Vol. 70, No. 12, 1990.

[27] Predöhl in the foreword to the illuminating study by E. W e b e r : Stadien der Außenhandelsverflechtung Ostmittel- und Südosteuropas, published by K. Schiller, Stuttgart 1971.

[28] See E. W e b e r, op. cit.

[29] H.W. M a u l l and A. v o n H e y n i t z : Osteuropa: Durchbruch in die Postmoderne? Umrisse einer Strategie des Westens, in: Europa-Archiv, Vol. 45, 1990, p. 446.

[30] See especially the Annual Report of the Centre for Economic Policy Research: Monitoring European Integration: The Impact of Eastern Europe, October 1990, chapter 1.

especially as regards substitutes for the collapsed Comecon integration, such as creating a Comecon European Payments Union or providing for other, possibly partial forms of East-East integration, for example between Poland, Czechoslovakia and Hungary. Here, using former associations would probably do more harm than good, quite apart from the possibility of damaging friction due to old and new animosity (nationalism) between former socialist brother countries.

These three Eastern European aspects should be complemented by *world economic* arguments. For example, the more efficiently the regional economic problems in Europe are solved against the background of an *imperfect* world economic order,[32] the greater the danger of a European diversion. If in addition Eastern Europe showed promising economic growth, the attraction of this centre of gravity in worldwide locational competition would increase. With the ever more effective globalisation of the world market economy, and especially of the capital and financial markets, worldwide allocative interdependence also steadily increases, so that regions compete more directly with one another for resources. The Pacific economic area, but also the USA during the Reagan era, have clearly profited from this situation. If profitability is raised in both the private and public sectors in Europe, the *deregulated* world markets will react in the proper way, without it being possible to criticise such a development as Euro-centric. This would only be justifiable if European multinationals acquired a "fascination" with the sales potential of the European market and treated the Pacific (East Asian) economic space with a kind of "benign neglect", something that should not be assumed of multinationals operating wordwide.

## Division of Labour in the Pacific

Finally, let us turn to the formidable growth region of the Pacific, which has already been touched upon in connection with the American region. The superficial and

long-winded debate about the shape of Pacific co-operation need not concern us here. The *functional* regionalisation of the East Asian region, in particular, appears to be a more decisive factor, quite apart from the region's great heterogeneity and the politico-economic Japanese "co-prosperity sphere" problem. As indicated above, the repercussions of the appreciation of the yen in 1985 gave considerable momentum to the changes that were already taking place in Japan's strategy of exporting to countries outside the region and in its increasing links with the East Asian NIEs. In recent years domestic factors have provided stronger stimulus to Japanese growth and there has been a stronger intra-regional element in intra-industry and intra-firm trade and in Japanese direct investment in East Asia.[33]

There is another aspect, however, that throws an inportant light on this process. The "flying geese" pattern of development that originated in Japan and East Asia seems to be a model for the emergence of new growth regions in the Pacific. This coalition of former and current NIEs, with Japan at their head followed by the "gang of four" and the ASEAN countries, is theoretically far more than just an Asian version of aggregated product cycles. The real essence of the model lies in the special nature of the coupling-together of economies at different stages of development but with the same foreign trade strategy and rapidly rising *parallel* competition. This dynamic intra-regional growth alliance was characterised in trade policy terms by Yamazawa and Watanabe as early as 1983 as a strategic combination of complementary and competing foreign trade flows. This has been demonstrated again on the basis of figures for 1986, with intra-industry trade also being rightly considered as complementary trade.[34]

Such dovetailing of foreign trade is significant on two counts. First, it is the regional manifestation of a general and extremely important process of structural change in the world economy, namely the switch from the old form of complementary *specialisation* typical of the colonial era to the new substitutive *division of labour* of the second half of

---

[31] D. Lorenz: Will the Industrialized Countries Also Face Export-Led Growth from Eastern Europe?, in: Journal of Asian Economics, Vol. 2, No. 1, to be published in the spring of 1991.

[32] See especially M. Schrenk: The CMEA System of Trade and Payments: Today and Tomorrow. Strategic Planning and Review, Discussion Paper No. 5, The World Bank, Washington, January 1990, p. 25, and D. Lorenz: Trends Towards Regionalism in the World Economy, op. cit.

[33] For a detailed discussion, see A.-R. Milton: Der asiatisch-pazifische Raum – ein neues Gravitationszentrum des Welthandels?, in: RWI-Mitteilungen, Vol. 41, 1990, pp. 231-264; P. M. Wijkman and E. S. Lindström, op. cit.; I. Yamazawa, A. Hirata and K. Yokota: Evolving Patterns of Comparative Advantage in the Pacific Countries, mimeo, Tokyo 1990. On the situation in the NIEs, see the illuminating study by D. Ernst and D. O'Connor: Technology and Global Competition. The Challenge for Newly Industrialising Economies, Development Centre Studies, OECD, Paris 1989.

[34] Op. cit., p. 17. The papers of Yamazawa and Watanabe are part of the special issue: Trends and Structural Changes in Pacific Asian Economies. Volume 21 (1983), No. 4, The Developing Economies.

[35] D. Lorenz: Explanatory Hypothesis on Trade Flows Between Industrial and Developing Countries, in: H. Giersch (ed.): The International Division of Labour. Problems and Prospects, Tübingen 1974, pp. 83-102.

[36] D. Lorenz: Deficiencies of Orthodox Foreign Trade Theory With Regard to Employment, in: INTERECONOMICS, Vol. 20, No. 3, 1985, pp. 122-129.

[37] S. Awanohara: Japan und Ostasien: Auf dem Weg zu einer pazifischen Arbeitsteilung, in: Europa-Archiv, No. 22, 1988, pp. 639-648, I. Yamazawa et al., op. cit., pp. 23-24, and D. Ernst and D. O'Connor, op. cit., pp.41-43.

[38] See P. M. Wijkman and E. S. Lindström, op. cit., p. 160.

the twentieth century via the intensive integration of newly industrialising countries via displacement competition.[35] Secondly, in view of the unavoidable problems of employment in the course of the re-allocation process (neo-protectionism), a satisfactory mix of substitutive and complementary industrial trade flows that can cushion the international structural changes and permit consensus in place of conflict is of great importance.[36] That this may be easier to achieve regionally rather than worldwide is a plausible hypothesis that is being discussed seriously in East Asia. Reservations about an undesired hierarchical division of labour, with Japan as the leading power and growth pole can be allayed partly by the argument that vertical relationships within this dynamic flying geese formation are not considered as rigid or permanent.[37] In broad terms, this means that the process of graduation must allow upward mobility so that all member states can climb the ladder in the international (regional)division of labour.

There is, however, one more weighty objection based on the limitations to regional policy and processes. This is whether the flying geese model can achieve equilibrium only if there is *extra*-regional interchange, in other words whether the regional engine must also have an external "vent for surplus".[38] What happens if, to maintain the goose metaphor, it is no longer sufficient for the head of the bird (Japan) to stretch forwards (to the USA) but must *also* be tucked into the bird's own plumage (East Asia)? Can worldwide imbalances resulting, for example, from East Asia's export-*surplus*-led growth strategy be *relieved by* an intensification and differentiation of intra-regional trade? This aspect is the only one that counts; there can be no question of choosing in principle between regionalism and multilateralism.

# [29]

# Sub-regional Economic Zones

*Richard Pomfret*

A distinctive feature of regionalism in East Asia has been the emergence in the 1980s and 1990s of sub-regional economic zones (SRZs). These are distinctive examples of regional integration because, although they cross national boundaries, not all parts of the nations involved are part of the zone. Moreover, while appropriate government policies may be necessary conditions for the emergence of an SRZ, governments have played little role in defining and establishing them. The Asian prototype is the area covering Singapore and parts of the Malaysian state of Johore and the Indonesian province of Riau. It has boomed since the second half of the 1980s, and it is clearly an integrated economic zone, even though official agreements between governments of the three countries have been minimal.

During the 1980s and 1990s the prime examples of SRZs have been in East Asia. The first section of this chapter discusses the concept of SRZs, and provides some historical examples from outside Asia. The next three sections deal with the three most readily identifiable Asian SRZs, and the fifth section discusses some other possible SRZs in East Asia. The final section offers some generalisations and conclusions.

## The Concept

An SRZ crosses national boundaries, and involves part, but not all, of at least one of the national economies concerned. The concept has two key ingredients, each of which raises a question about the location of economic activity and, since SRZs are areas of economic growth, about the determinants of international competitiveness. First, because an SRZ is not identified by national boundaries, its existence and size cannot be explained solely by national characteristics or national policies. What then is the relationship between national trade policies and the emergence of SRZs? Second, economic activities are not spread evenly in space. In the Asian examples of SRZs, the main economic activities are not based on natural resources; why do producers of manufactured goods and of services congregate?

National policies are important in providing the necessary conditions for a SRZ to emerge. If there are severe restrictions on international trade, on the movement of people across borders and on foreigners' right of establishment, then economic connections will remain largely domestic and will not spill over international boundaries. On the other hand, if such restrictions are minor, national policies will play a lesser role in determining the location of economic activity. Fairly liberal economic policies are a necessary, but not a sufficient, condition for the existence of a SRZ.

The salient SRZs in East Asia have a common pattern. They are centred on the newly industrialising economies (NIEs) of the 1970s, which began to encounter labour supply constraints in the 1980s. Rising wages reduced their comparative advantage in producing labour-intensive goods, even though their entrepreneurs had valuable skills in organising such production and marketing the goods overseas. Although NIE investors have scoured the world for low-cost production bases, nearby locations are favoured, other things being equal. Moreover, third-country investors, who may have previously gone to, say, Singapore in search of low-cost labour, shifted the operation to Johore or Batam so that they could continue to use established central services in Singapore. This spillover from dynamic urban centres first occurred from city-states with no hinterland within their own borders. It is also a feature of other NIEs, even if it took longer in Taiwan and South Korea, due to the larger domestic labour supply and political restrictions on economic integration with immediate neighbours.

In Asia, the phenomenon of SRZs is linked to the openness of the NIEs. While there is debate over the role of government policy in these successful economies, there is general agreement that openness was an ingredient of their success (Edwards, 1993; Pomfret, 1994). For a SRZ to emerge there must be at least two contiguous open economies; in all Asian SRZs, there was an NIE which provided one open economy, and formation of the SRZ waited upon liberalisation of trade and investment in neighbouring areas (such as Malaysia and Riau Province of Indonesia in relation to Singapore, or southern China in relation to Hong Kong). Where the neighbouring country did not open up its economy, spillover did not occur, as in the case of North Korea, despite its proximity to Seoul.

The SRZ phenomenon is, of course, not restricted to Asia. Before the rise of the nation-state, economic development was unevenly spread over space and did not match political boundaries, although rulers could exclude their territories from a growth region by bad policies. Many European examples of SRZs could be identified in the political patchwork of early modern Italy or Germany.

A more recent examples of an SRZ is the North American manufacturing belt, which emerged in the mid-nineteenth century and covered the industrial midwest of the USA and south-western Ontario. Another is the Western European industrial heartland, which covers parts of eastern France, western Germany, northern Italy and the Benelux countries. Economic historians have explained these two cases in terms of the location of natural resources, especially coal and iron ore, but many activities not dependent on these materials chose to locate in the manufacturing belts and the regions' pre-eminence in manufacturing continued even after coal and iron became less crucial. The importance of agglomeration effects, which are ignored in standard international trade theory, has been emphasised by Krugman (1991a), who used the North American industrial belt as his prime example.

One possible trigger for the creation of agglomeration economies is the need to use common services, such as banking and other financial and commercial services. The historical examples of SRZs, however, suggest that this is not a key reason. In North America, and in the earlier English industrial revolution, older financial and commercial centres physically outside the manufacturing belt (i.e. New York, Montreal and London) continued to dominate the provision of such services. In continental Europe, the financial centres of Germany and France were in the national capitals, rather than in the manufacturing regions of eastern France and western Germany, although in Italy this was not the case.[1] Agglomeration dictates that most countries have a single financial centre and that international financial transactions are heavily concentrated in London, Tokyo and New York, but there does not appear to be much pressure for these centres to be located where other economic activites are most concentrated.

Other triggers for the creation of agglomeration economies are the economies of scale external to the firm but internal to the industry, emphasised by Marshall (1961, IV.X.3).[2] Entrepreneurs can benefit from observing how other firms operate because it is impossible to conceal completely how profitable opportunities are being exploited. Porter (1990, pp. 117–22) has also emphasised the benefits of local rivalry in pushing entrepreneurs to do better, and hence creating competitive industries.[3] Such arguments can explain why entrepreneurs do not want to spend too long too far away from their home base, in case they miss a new twist found by their rivals. This chapter does not pretend to test explanations of the agglomeration effects, but by presenting case studies of the Asian SRZs, it does show that such effects are important, and that national policies are not the sole determinants of the location of economic activities.[4]

## The Singapore-Johore-Riau Growth Triangle[5]

Between the mid-1960s and mid-1980s, economic links between Singapore and its neighbours were not dynamic. After Singapore's separation from Malaysia, the Malaysian government actively sought to reduce the amount of trade flowing through Singapore. Links between Singapore and Indonesia were limited by the two countries' separate political histories, Indonesian restrictions on foreign investment, and the underdeveloped infrastructure in Riau Province.

The emergence of an SRZ involving Singapore, Johore and Batam in Indonesia first began to be noticed in the late 1980s. In 1989 land costs (in US dollars per square metre) were $4.3 in Singapore, $4.1 in Johore and $2.3 in Batam, while unskilled labour cost $350 per month in Singapore, $150 in Johore and $90 in Batam (Chia and Lee, 1993, p. 243).

In Johore, approved foreign investment grew rapidly during the second half of the 1980s (Table 14.1). Singaporean investors played a significant role in this boom, but Japanese investors were more important, and investors from Taiwan,

*Economic Analysis of Regional Trading Arrangements*

**Table 14.1**  Approved foreign investment in Johore, 1985–90 (million Malaysian ringgit)

|           | 1985 | 1986 | 1987 | 1988 | 1989 | 1990 |
|-----------|------|------|------|------|------|------|
| Total     | 51   | 102  | 200  | 558  | 686  | 1,618 |
| Singapore | 18   | 43   | 42   | 102  | 132  | 407  |
| Japan     | 3    | 29   | 44   | 50   | 283  | 508  |
| USA       | 0    | 1    | 11   | 124  | 16   | 145  |
| EU/EFTA   | 2    | 1    | 6    | 65   | 92   | 111  |

*Source:* Chia and Lee (1993, p. 247)

South Korea, Hong Kong, the USA and Western Europe also invested substantially in Johore. Proximity to Singapore does, however, seem critical, as Johore's share of foreign investment in Malaysia grew rapidly during this period. The role of governments in promoting links between Singapore and Johore was, however, negligible. The Malaysian central government has been lukewarm, although the Johore state government has advocated improved links with Singapore. The supporting physical infrastructure is overstrained, with heavy congestion on the causeway connecting Singapore with Johore. Discussions are under way for extending Singapore's rapid transit system to Johore and a second causeway linking Singapore to Johore is to be built, but infrastructure provision is obviously following demand rather than having contributed to the creation of the SRZ.

The Riau–Singapore link has been more influenced by government policy, but even in this case the formal agreements are minimal. In 1990 and 1991, bilateral agreements were signed on investment protection and on joint development of water resources in Riau. Ongoing efforts to harmonise regulations and procedures are taking place. The crucial policy step, however, was unilateral. Creation of the Batam duty-free zone in 1978 and subsequent liberalisation of foreign investment policy created a necessary condition for the upsurge of foreign investment. Actual growth in Batam accelerated in the second half of the 1980s, when exports increased from $21 million in 1986 to $210 million in 1991 and tourist arrivals (mainly from and through Singapore) grew from 60,000 in 1986 to over 600,000 in 1991.[6] Singapore accounts for more than half of approved foreign investment in Batam, both by number of projects and by value ($532 million out of $1055 million total by the end of 1991), followed by the USA, Japan and Hong Kong, with Malaysia accounting for a mere 0.3 per cent of the total value.

The nature of the boom in Johore and Batam is similar. It has been led by foreign investment, especially in labour-intensive and land-intensive activities. Singapore, which is physically connected to Johore and a 30–40-minute ferry journey from Batam, is the regional hub.

In part, the phenomenon has involved relocation of labour-intensive activities from Singapore as wage rates have risen in the city. A mail questionnaire survey (Yeoh et al., 1992) found that 48 per cent of the 310 respondents already had offshore production facilities, 46 per cent in Johore and 11 per cent in Batam. A January 1992 survey by the Singapore Manufacturers' Association, to which 270 members responded, showed that 40 per cent of respondents had moved or were planning to relocate activities to neighbouring areas, although less than 4 per cent said they would move their entire operations (Lee, 1993, p. 25). The picture is of a substantial shift of labour-intensive activities to neighbouring countries, with retention of some functions in Singapore.

Growth in incomes in Singapore has also fuelled rising demand for land-intensive activities, especially tourism but also housing. This also appears to be largely financed by Singaporean capital.

Non-Singaporean investors have, however, also played a major role, and the broader explanation of the boom in Johore and Riau must invoke more than a simple model of spillover from Singapore. Investors from Japan and the East Asian newly industrialising economies and from North America and Western Europe are relocating labour-intensive manufacturing activities to Johore and Batam.[7] The attraction of these locations lies primarily in low-cost labour and, perhaps, in low land costs in Batam, but many other locations share these advantages. Proximity to the urban services of Singapore tips the balance in favour of Johore and Batam.

The balance between the importance of low wages and of proximity is one that varies between activities. The situation is a dynamic one; as wages and rents rise in southern Johore and in Batam, some foreign investors are seeking locations further north in Malaysia and in other Riau islands, which are less convenient to Singapore but have cheaper land and labour.[8] The development of Bintan Island involves the Indonesian government, Singapore's Public Utilities Board and the state-owned Jurong Town Corporation, but most of the estimated $7 billion development cost is expected to come from private sources.[9] Elsewhere, the geographical expansion of the SRZ seems to be almost entirely driven by private entrepreneurs.

The concept of Growth Triangles caught the public imagination in Asia circa 1992.[10] The triangle image is, however, fundamentally misleading, because links between Riau and Johore are minimal. The popularity of the concept led to search for other triangles, such as the Northern Growth Triangle of southern Thailand, northern Malaysia and northern Sumatra, and other geometric shapes, such as the Golden Quadrilateral of northern Thailand, north-east Myanmar, north-west Laos, and Yunnan. None of these has any substance, because they lack the key component of the Singapore-Johore-Riau SRZ: this is not its triangular shape, but rather is in some way related to the central position of Singapore.

## The South China SRZ[11]

The South China SRZ began to take shape in the mid-1980s and has many similarities to that of Singapore-Johore-Riau. The core city is Hong Kong, which like

Singapore was experiencing increasing difficulty in remaining internationally competitive in the production of labour-intensive goods. An important prerequisite for establishing an SRZ was policy reform in the People's Republic of China, which made other parts of the zone suitable production bases for labour-intensive manufactures.

China's adoption of the open-door policy in 1979 was a critical necessary condition. The June 1979 Equity Joint Venture Law permitted foreign investment in China for the first time. Conditions for foreign investors still left much to be desired, but the operating environment gradually improved during the 1980s. Chinese authorities, joint venture partners and foreign investors gained increased understanding of the ingredients of successful joint ventures. Foreign trade conditions and currency restrictions were also gradually liberalised over the next fifteen years.

Despite China's dramatic policy shift in 1979, foreign investors did not flock to it over the next five years. By the end of 1983, only 190 equity joint ventures had been approved. Even fewer were in operation, and they tended to be small and concentrated in the Special Economic Zone of Shenzhen, adjacent to Hong Kong. In 1984–5, China experienced its first foreign investment boom. This was partly generated by improved legislation towards foreign investment and a booming domestic economy, which combined with a bandwagon mentality in the USA and Europe to attract many transnational corporations fearful of missing out. By number, however, the largest group of foreign investors was from Hong Kong.

In 1984–5 wage rates and property values were rising sharply in Hong Kong. The declining competitiveness of the labour-intensive manufactured exports, which had driven Hong Kong's growth for three decades, was exacerbated by the currency's tie to the appreciating US dollar. The response of the Hong Kong manufacturers was to shift labour-intensive activities across the border into China's Guangdong Province. By the end of the decade, Hong Kong firms were employing more workers in Guangdong than in Hong Kong.

The transfer of production activity went in waves. Initially it was concentrated in Shenzhen, with a smaller parallel shift from Macau to the adjacent Special Economic Zone of Zhuhai.[12] Then it moved further up the Pearl River Delta to country towns where wages and rents were lower than in Shenzhen, and where local authorities competed for part of the action. As transport and communication links became more extended, Hong Kong businesses moved into the provision of infrastructure; they financed highway projects, and in the 1990s moved to large integrated transport projects.

The initial stages of the establishment of an SRZ around Hong Kong are now well documented. By excluding Shenzhen, Zhuhai and Guangzhou (the provincial capital and established industrial centre), Table 14.2 emphasises the wave motion and the extent of the economic boom in the Pearl River Delta area, independent of the establishment of Special Economic Zones. During the first half of the 1980s, growth was fastest in the Inner Delta area, and especially in the counties closest to Hong Kong (Baoan and Dongguan) and to Macau (Zhongshan). In the mid-1980s the next ring of counties in the Outer Delta was booming. An

Table 14.2  Pearl River Delta, economic indicators, 1980–7

| | Economic growth (%) | | Ind. output per cap. 1987 (million RMB) | Share of PRD FDI (%) |
|---|---|---|---|---|
| | 1980–5 | 1980–7 | | |
| **Inner Delta** | | | | |
| Baoan | 312 | 651 | 32.4 | 6.3 |
| Dongguan | 215 | 411 | 23.9 | 11.5 |
| Panyu | 212 | 296 | 27.5 | 3.6 |
| Foshan City | 305 | 406 | 104.1 | 15.8 |
| Nanhai | 256 | 371 | 37.1 | 3.0 |
| Shunde | 278 | 379 | 39.0 | 12.5 |
| Zhongshan | 251 | 408 | 29.8 | 17.5 |
| **Outer Delta** | | | | |
| Doumen | 183 | 259 | 13.4 | 3.2 |
| Xinhui | 230 | 380 | 22.3 | 3.8 |
| Jiangmen City | 193 | 261 | 66.6 | 10.1 |
| Heshan | 210 | 357 | 13.0 | 1.1 |
| Taishan | 236 | 351 | 12.2 | 4.4 |
| Gaoming | 146 | 331 | 8.7 | 0.3 |
| Kaiping | 178 | 313 | 14.9 | 4.5 |
| Enping | 179 | 316 | 9.9 | 2.3 |
| Zengcheng | 162 | 239 | 5.7 | 0.2 |

*Notes:* Growth rates measure the increase in agricultural and industrial output at constant 1980 prices. FDI is the contracted value of equity and cooperative joint ventures, 1979-86.

The Inner Delta localities are listed in geographical order starting from the border with Shenzhen and moving north and west round a horseshoe to the Zhuhai border (i.e. from proximity to Hong Kong to proximity to Macau). The Outer Delta localities are more difficult to order, but the first five are closer to Macau, while the last four are the most remote from Hong Kong or Macau.

*Sources:* Vogel (1989, p. 193) for 1980-5; Thoburn et al. (1990, pp. 139, 143) for 1987 and FDI data.

established industrial base, dynamic political leadership and chance events played a part in determining variations in growth rates, but the geographical pattern is clear. By 1987 the Pearl River Delta jurisdictions listed in Table 14.2, with 16 per cent of Guangdong's population, produced 34 per cent of the province's industrial output. Other parts of the province, more remote from Hong Kong, have still to participate in Guangdong's rapid growth.[13]

The extent of economic integration between Hong Kong and neighbouring areas of Guangdong is obvious to any visitor, although it is difficult to document precisely. Hong Kong dollars circulate freely in Guangdong, and Hong Kong TV stations are received by Guangdong residents. The life styles are converging, as TV advertisements prepare the way for the establishment of Hong Kong-based fast food and retail chains in Guangdong. The magnitude is difficult to assess, because both the trade and foreign investment data are imperfect measures of ties within the SRZ. The trade data contain a large amount of entrepot trade coming from or going to other Chinese provinces. In the foreign investment data, 'Hong Kong' is a kind of catch-all for many categories.[14] Despite the weaknesses in the data, the huge numbers do include a large amount of genuinely regional trade and investment flows.

The Pearl River Delta has been less readily accepted as an SRZ than the Singapore-Johore-Riau triangle. First, there is a political and semantic issue in that Hong Kong is not a nation-state; it is a British colony, which the Chinese government considers an integral part of China. Second, it is viewed as a special case because of the cultural affinity of the Cantonese speakers of Hong Kong and Guangdong.[15] This undoubtedly facilitates economic intercourse, but equally certainly the integration would have been far more limited without economic stimuli (as was in fact the case before 1984). Third, it is difficult to establish the borders of the SRZ, which includes only part of Guangdong province. In my view, Hong Kong, Macau and the neighbouring region of Guangdong fulfil all the criteria of an SRZ, in that the zone involves separate customs areas. The definition of the SRZ's boundary is an operational matter rather than one of principle. Some observers, however, consider the Pearl River Delta too restrictive; they have identified a much larger area, including Taiwan and Fujian province, as the Greater South China SRZ (e.g. Chia and Lee, 1993).

The role of Taiwan is less clear than that of Hong Kong, because restrictions on trade and investment with the mainland have discouraged transparency on the part of Taiwanese participants. This situation has been changing: both trade and investment have boomed since 1989, and reporting has become more transparent. The reasons are essentially similar to those underlying Singaporean and Hong Kong outward investment. Taiwan was becoming uncompetitive in labour-intensive manufactured goods, but Taiwanese managers had valuable expertise in producing and exporting such goods. The answer was to move the manufacturing activity offshore, and apart from political restrictions the most convenient location was mainland China. By the 1990s, economic considerations had overcome political reservations.

Taiwanese investors have been especially noticeable in the city of Xiamen in Fujian Province, one of the closest ports to Taiwan. It is frequently maintained that Fujian is to Taiwan as Guangdong has been to Hong Kong. This would fit nicely with the idea of an SRZ, but the reality is that the most important destination for Taiwanese investment in China is Guangdong. Apparently, Guangdong's proximity to the commercial centre of Hong Kong is more important than any special cultural affinity between Fujian and Taiwan, or the physical proximity of Fujian.

The predominance of Guangdong in China's export-led growth since the early 1980s is striking, because the province was not previously an economic powerhouse. Before the revolution, China's industrial heartlands were the heavy industry centres of the north-east (Manchuria) and the more diversified region of Shanghai, southern Jiangsu and northern Zhejiang (Jiangnan, south of the Yangtze). As China's growth continued, the Jiangnan region participated strongly after the mid-1980s, while Manchuria continues to be passed by. The agricultural reforms which stimulated domestic production and demand after 1978–9 were also not especially favourable to Guangdong, which is not among China's most agriculturally productive areas. Guangdong had no natural advantage to justify its leading role in China's growth, apart from being far from the central government in Beijing and close to Hong Kong.[16]

## The Tumen River Project[17]

The Tumen River Area Development Project is a multilateral attempt to promote an SRZ in the area where the borders of China, North Korea and Russia meet. The project was floated by China at a conference in Changchun (capital of Jilin Province) in July 1990. At 1991 conferences in Pyongyang and Ulaanbaatar, the United Nations Development Program agreed to support the project, and in December it allocated an initial $3.5 million. (A mission report estimated that the total cost over twenty years would be in the order of $30 billion.)

The Tumen River Project involves the three riparian countries, as well as Mongolia and South Korea, with Japan as an observer. The broad goal is to promote trade within North-East Asia, including transit trade from and to Mongolia, Siberia and the Russian Far East, and the north-east provinces of China. The first two Program Management Committee meetings in 1992 achieved little. At the third, in May 1993, however, the three riparian countries agreed to establish a jointly owned corporation, which would lease land in the border area to create an international zone (the Tumen River Economic Zone). Russia (and to a lesser extent China) soon began to have reservations about leasing land to a supranational body, and all participants showed reluctance to put up money for the corporation. At a UN-sponsored meeting in New York these reservations were expressed, and the administrator of the project allowed the corporation and the economic zone to lapse, so that by early 1994 both were dead.[18]

As a forum the Tumen River project has value in a part of the world which could easily contain the flashpoint for a nuclear war.[19] It also could help coordinate some key infrastructure projects, such as the railway link between the Yanbian Prefecture of Jilin Province and Russia's Pacific ports. Such contributions to political stability and to infrastructure will help to promote regional trade and investment, but so far the direct impact of the project has been negligible.

Despite the slow process in creating a SRZ by international action, economic change is proceeding rapidly in some parts of the Tumen River area. All three riparian countries have created Special Economic Zones in the area. North Korea announced the creation of the Rajin–Sonbong free economic trade zone in December 1991, but so far it has had little impact. Russia established a free trade

*Economic Analysis of Regional Trading Arrangements*

**Table 14.3** Registered companies with foreign investment in Nakhodka Free Trade Economic Zone, 1 March 1994

| Type of investment | Number of companies |
| --- | --- |
| Joint ventures | 124 |
| Wholly foreign-owned subsidiaries | 166 |
| Affiliated representatives | 29 |
| Total | 319 |

*Source:* Primorski Krai government.

**Table 14.4** Registered companies with foreign investment in Nakhodka Free Trade Economic Zone by nationality, 1 March 1994

| Foreign partner | Number | Authorised foreign capital ($US000) |
| --- | --- | --- |
| China | 162 | 16,402 |
| Japan | 39 | 66,161 |
| Hong Kong | 27 | 2,614 |
| USA | 23 | 25,873 |
| South Korea | 11 | 5,793 |
| Taiwan | 6 | 100 |
| Singapore | 4 | 300 |
| Germany | 3 | 177 |
| Canada | 3 | 502 |
| North Korea | 3 | 11 |
| Switzerland | 3 | 37 |
| Norway | 2 | 4,395 |
| New Zealand | 2 | 100 |
| Other countries | 30 | 4,053 |
| Total | 318 | 126,518 |

*Source:* Primorski Krai government.

economic zone around Nakhodka, which began operation in August 1991, and a Greater Vladivostock Free Economic Zone in November 1991; since then the latter has been abandoned, and some of the privileges granted in Nakhodka have been rescinded by the central government. Despite the uncertain policy environment, both locally and nationally, some foreign investors have been attracted to

Primorski (the region of the Russian Far East between China and the Pacific Ocean).

Foreign investment in Primorski has grown rapidly since 1990. The number of registered enterprises with foreign investment increased from 24 in 1990 to 364 by June 1993, with foreign capital of $208 million. About three-quarters of the number, accounting for 60 per cent of the registered capital, were in Nakhodka, and information is best for these. By March 1994, more than 300 companies with foreign investment had been registered in the Nakhoda zone (see Table 14.3). In more than half, the foreign involvement is from China, although the average authorised capital of these is only $10,000. The largest investing nation in terms of capital is Japan ($66 million), followed by the USA ($26 million), China ($16 million) and South Korea ($6 million) (see Table 14.4). The enterprises range from manufacturing and raw-material processing to service and construction activities, with the largest category being 'commercial activity'. I have no data on how many of the registered enterprises are actually in operation, although from newspaper reports it is not negligible. There appear to be two dominant patterns: investment by Chinese individuals in small-scale activities (restaurants, shops, etc.); and more substantial investment based on local resources, especially seafood, which are export-oriented, often for South Korean or Japanese markets. In 1993–4, however, policy uncertainty developed, both at the macroeconomic level (i.e. whether hyperinflation would be contained) and at the microeconomic level (i.e. regarding tax and other benefits in the zone). The uncertainty dampened foreign investment. By one report, only $3 million was actually invested in the Nakhodka zone in 1993, which was a large decline from the two previous years.[20]

Economic expansion has been far more pronounced in Yanbian Prefecture during the 1990s. Although foreign direct investment (FDI) was first permitted in China under the June 1979 Equity Joint Venture Law, six and a half years later only three joint ventures had been approved in Yanbian. Yanbian was largely passed by during China's post-1986 FDI boom, and by the end of 1991 only 61 foreign-invested ventures had been approved. By March 1994, just over two years later, this number had increased to 480, of which some 150 were in operation.

Why did the local FDI boom occur? Before the 1990s Yanbian was in an obscure corner of China: it bordered two closed economies with whom China's trade was small and heavily regulated, and it had poor transport links to the world. With the disintegration of the USSR in December 1991 and the collapse of the CMEA came the prospects of new economic relations with Russia and North Korea, including improved access to ports on the Sea of Japan. At the same time, Chinese authorities began to allow sub-regions of Yanbian to offer preferential economic policies, and to encourage substantial infrastructure investment.

Even more critical was the normalisation of relations between China and South Korea in mid-1992, which was especially important for Yanbian as the centre of the Korean minority in China. Many traders and investors anticipated formal diplomatic recognition, but normalisation provided an added guarantee to

South Korean investors and was accompanied by improved transport and visa arrangements. The significance of South Korean FDI is that over one-third of the foreign-invested ventures approved in Yanbian by March 1994 had South Korean partners.

The location of the FDI has shifted markedly. Before 1993 about half of the foreign-invested ventures were in the prefectural capital, Yanji, and I have con-firmed information of only seven being in operation in the three border munici-palities (Hunchun, Tumen and Longjin) by January 1993. Since then, however, these three municipalities, and especially Hunchun which is the one nearest to the Tumen River mouth, have received a growing proportion of the approved for-eign-invested ventures; in the first two and a half months of 1994, one-third of all approvals were in Hunchun.

The impact on Yanbian's trade will not be felt for some time. Only 150 of the 480 approved foreign-invested ventures are operational. Many are export-oriented, but typically they start with domestic sales, while export arrangements take more time to be established. They are in light industries (e.g. socks, under-wear, electronic components, bags, plasticware, convenience noodles) where time-lags are not long, and there will soon be pressure for reliable transport con-nections for goods and people.

What is taking place in Yanbian, and to a lesser extent in Primorski, is the cre-ation of an SRZ. A key facilitating role is being played by South Korean busi-nesses, which are providing some of the infrastructure investment, buying Primorski's primary products and, most importantly, shifting their labour-inten-sive manufacturing operations to Yanbian. The overarching goal of the large South Korean corporations (and of the South Korean government) is to prepare the way for investment in North Korea, which will be a key source of low-wage labour and whose economy South Korea hopes to stimulate in order to reduce the difficulties of eventual reunification. Already, some Chinese joint ventures with South Korean involvement are operating within North Korea; since 1993, South Korean cargo ships have used Chongjin port in North Korea as a shipment point for Primorski and Yanbian.

## Other SRZs in East Asia

Reference is sometimes made to an emerging Baht Zone. In fact, Thailand's extraordinarily rapid growth since 1987 has been highly concentrated within the country. The population of greater Bangkok may have doubled from the five mil-lion of the mid-1980s, but it is still less than 20 per cent of the national total. Over half of Thailand's GDP is produced in Greater Bangkok, and average incomes there are as much as ten times higher than in rural areas, such as the north-east. The picture is a typical East Asian super-growth story, with labour being drawn into a sector producing labour-intensive manufactures for export. In Thailand's case the spatial dimension is extreme. Moreover, this pattern could conceivably continue for many years, as the supply of unskilled labour is far from exhausted.

Thus, Thai economic spillover into adjacent areas is not in search of low-wage labour, as was the case with the first generation of Asian super-exporters. Rather, Thai entrepreneurs with skills in other specific sectors, especially logging and precious stones, have transferred their skills to the (sometimes illegal) exploitation of logging and gemstones in Myanmar, Cambodia and Laos. It is, however, possible that Bangkok will emerge as the regional centre after two events in 1994; the lifting of the US embargo has removed a serious constraint on Vietnam's export-led growth, and the opening of the first bridge across the Mekong River has improved transport links with Laos.

One side-effect of Thailand's superlative economic growth performance has been a lack of interest in seeking artificial roads to success during the 1990s. Thailand's recipe has been a simple one of fiscally conservative macroeconomics (inflation has been low since the mid-1980s and the government ran a budget surplus during the early 1990s) and non-interventionist microeconomics. The Thai government sees little need to promote specific regions such as in the Northern Growth Triangle.[21] More recent pressure for government-promoted SRZs in ASEAN has come from Malaysia and the Philippines (as in the East Asian Growth Area).[22]

## Conclusions

International trade theory relies heavily on the nation-state as the unit of analysis, and as Krugman (1991a) has emphasised, much is lost by this bias. The phenomenon of SRZs is a case in point. The problem of spatial analysis is the frequent fuzziness of boundaries which are not defined physically or politically, and the Asian SRZs illustrate this point. The SRZ centred on Singapore does not cover all of Johore or Riau, although it does cover more than just Batam.[23] The South China SRZ is even more vaguely defined because Hong Kong entrepreneurs have by now reached into practically every corner of China to a greater or lesser extent—but the extent is far greater in the Pearl River Delta area, and far less in the inland provinces. The problem is exacerbated because the borders of SRZs are constantly moving.

What is the implication for the regionalism versus globalism debate? The Singapore-Johore-Riau SRZ is entirely in ASEAN, but a small part of ASEAN. Some national policy-makers in ASEAN have come to favour SRZs; during the 1990s they promoted the Northern Growth Triangle and the East Asian Growth Area as forces strengthening ASEAN integration, and complementary to national measures such as the preferential reduction of trade barriers (see Chapter 15). In fact, such policy-makers are trailing along behind the reality that the Singapore-Johore-Riau SRZ has promoted regional integration largely without government involvement and that a Bangkok-based SRZ is likely to overflow beyond ASEAN, while their own proposals may be too artificial to have any impact. Thus, SRZs are not a short-cut to promoting greater economic integration across ASEAN as a whole.

The broader lesson is that national trade policies are important only up to a point. Autarchic policies can, of course, choke off involvement in international trade, with neighbours or farther afield; North Korea and Myanmar are examples. Freer trade policies allow international trade and discriminatory trade policies may affect its direction, but other important factors in determining the direction of trade are the economic forces of complementarity and proximity. Hong Kong and Guangdong have no formal discriminatory trade policies favouring one another, and yet the SRZ has developed into one of the tightest bilateral links in all of world trade.

While the phenomenon of Asian SRZs occurred at a specific historic conjuncture and was exacerbated by the narrow geographical scope of Singapore and Hong Kong, there is a broader implication. Agglomeration effects create regional concentration of economic growth, which economists are ill equipped either to measure or to predict. In a world where national trade barriers have been substantially reduced, economic regions are increasingly unlikely to match the boundaries of nation-states; agglomeration effects, regional spillovers and other complementarities observed in the Asian SRZs will become relatively more important in determining location. National trade policies, and discriminatory trade policies in particular, will have less impact on the direction of trade flows.

# Notes

1   The Italian financial centre is in Milan rather than Rome. After the post-1945 division of Germany, the financial capital of the German Federal Republic moved from Berlin to Frankfurt, rather than to a location within the industrial heartland of the Ruhr, implying that proximity to the manufacturing centre was not an important consideration.

2   In Marshall's analysis, historical accidents may lie behind the original locational decision, but once the location has been chosen the industry 'is likely to stay there long' due to the external economies. A recent reformulation of Marshall's model concludes with a comment fitting Singapore and Hong Kong: 'the same forces that promote the agglomeration of footloose industries allow the details of seemingly transient and adventitious circumstance to exert an enduring influence upon the spatial distribution of economic activity and population' (David and Rosenbloom, 1990, p. 368).

3   Among Porter's arguments why local rivalry is beneficial, two are especially relevant to the Asian NIEs. With local rivals an entrepreneur cannot rely solely on the nation's favourable factor endowment, because all the rivals share that advantage. Thus, in the NIEs, businesspeople not only had to exploit the comparative advantage in labour-intensive activities, but if they were to do better than their rivals they had also to find novel ways of exploiting this opportunity. Secondly, losing ground to local rivals cannot be ascribed to 'unfair' competition or exogenous forces to do with culture, a foreign education system and so forth. Thus, the existence of successful local rivals

provided a model of what could be achieved and there was less temptation to absolve oneself of responsibility for failure to achieve similar success.

4   I address the relative importance of national policies and of other determinants of locational competitiveness in East Asia in Pomfret (1994).

5   This section relies heavily on Chia and Lee (1993).

6   Chia and Lee (1993, p. 248). By the early 1990s Batam had surpassed Bali as Indonesia's second tourist entry point, after Jakarta.

7   Some of this relocation is from Singapore, but I do not have data on the original location of activities shifted to Batam or on how much involves new activities.

8   Batam does not have abundant labour. Wages have been kept down only by substantial immigration from other parts of Indonesia, which increased the population from 7000 in the early 1970s to over 100,000 by the early 1990s.

9   The Public Utilities Board is involved in a $1 billion water development project. Water supply is a critical attraction for Singapore, which is currently dependent on Johore, but that should not obscure the enormous activity by private small-scale businesses.

10  The papers from a conference at the National University of Singapore in April 1992 on Regional Cooperation and Growth Triangles in ASEAN were widely reported on in the press. They were published in the following year (Toh and Low, 1993b).

11  Vogel (1989) describes the regional pattern of development in Guangdong Province. Thoburn et al. (1990) is a case study of the Pearl River Delta. On the geographical spread of foreign investment in China, see Pomfret (1991b, pp. 74-100).

12  The gross value of industrial and agricultural output in the Shenzhen zone increased from 77 million yuan in 1980 to 2368 million in 1985 (a 3075 per cent increase) and then doubled again between 1985 and 1987 (Crane, 1990, p. 57); much more rapid growth than any jurisdiction in Table 14.2, but from a low base.

13  In aggregate, Guangdong's growth performance has not differed so much from that of other dynamic coastal provinces such as Fujian, Jiangsu, Zhejiang and Shandong, but this is because the provincial performance is pulled down by the slow growth in areas away from the Pearl River Delta (with 63 million people, Guangdong is more populous than all but fourteen countries in the world). Informed guesses put average annual growth in per capita income in the Pearl River Delta area at 20–30 per cent since the start of the 1980s (Bell et al., 1993, p. 54).

14  Authorities in China are not careful in recording the nationality of foreign investment. The joint venture approval form (the basic raw data source) contains no explicit reference to nationality; officials infer this from the name of the foreign partner. Hong Kong partners include investment sourced through Hong Kong offices for convenience (in the case of some transnational corporations) or obfuscation (in the case of Taiwanese or South Korean investors before the early 1990s). Overseas Chinese investors are typically classified as 'Hong Kong' partners, although I have observed some of these which have no connection with Hong Kong.

15  The absence of cultural affinity appears to be why the Singapore-centred SRZ received more publicity as a generalisable phenomenon, although even in that case there is believed to have been a high involvement of Chinese businesspeople in Johore and Indonesia.

16  Initial growth was concentrated in Shenzhen Special Economic Zone, but this special status does not explain much. Other Special Economic Zones further from Hong Kong (especially Shantou) were backwaters, while the Pearl River Delta towns in

Table 14.2 quickly attracted Hong Kong capital irrespective of whether they had any special status.

17  The background to the Tumen River project is described in Valencia (1992) and von Kirchbach and Zhang (1993).

18  This outcome was not accepted by North Korea: it continued to insist on implementation of the 1993 decisions, but without Russian or Chinese support those decisions were meaningless. The situation was complicated because the North Korean delegation had not attended the New York meeting due to problems in obtaining visas for the USA.

19  The USSR and China fought a border war in 1969, which fortunately did not escalate. The situation is less tense since the signing of an agreement between China and the USSR on the Amur River border in 1990. Nevertheless, Chinese irredentism cannot be ruled out, given that the government continues to regard the treaty by which China lost its Sea of Japan coastline to Russia in 1860 as an 'unequal treaty' (and considers the name Vladivostock, 'ruler of the east', a provocation). Disputes over North Korea's nuclear capability hit the headlines in 1993–4, and could conceivably encourage South Korea and Japan to develop a nuclear capability should they feel threatened.

20  *Russian Far East Update* Vol. 4, No. 4, April 1994, p. 7.

21  The Thai government began promoting the southern seaboard area in 1989, with the aim of reducing the regional economy's dependence on tourism and creating a land-bridge from the Andaman Sea to the Gulf of Thailand. It met a roadblock when the major investor from Kuwait postponed participation after the Iraqi invasion of Kuwait. Thailand's attitude in the 1990s appears to be that it will participate in promoting the Northern Growth Triangle as long as it is consistent with the southern seaboard project. Indonesia is also lukewarm, because northern Sumatra has other options, including closer links with Riau and the southern triangle.

22  The East Asian Growth Area includes the southern Philippines, Sabah and Sarawak, Brunei, Sulawesi and the Moluccas. It was identified as an area for promotion in 1994, although what policies would support this decision remained unclear at the time of writing (just as the Northern Growth Triangle identified at least two years earlier still remains proposal rather than action).

23  It is revealing that we still use political or physical entities such as Johore or Batam, even when we know that they are not co-terminous with economic regions.

# Name Index

# The International Library of Critical Writings in Economics